1990

THE STATE
IN
CATHOLIC THOUGHT

A TREATISE
IN POLITICAL PHILOSOPHY

BY

HEINRICH A. ROMMEN, LL.D.

GREENWOOD PRESS, PUBLISHERS
NEW YORK

To

Monica, Irmgard, Margaret

Preface

IN wartime the people willingly concede extraordinary powers to their government. All-out war begets all-out governmental control of the lives of its citizens. Even in normal times the efficiency, or seeming efficiency, of totalitarianism may conceal the fundamental errors on which it is based. It is, therefore, fitting and timely that we re-examine the basic principles of civil government.

As the title of this book indicates, I am trying to present the principles and characteristics of the philosophy of the state as it has developed and found shape and substance in Catholic thought. For the sake of simplicity I have frequently used the term "Catholic political philosophy." The adjective "Catholic" here means, so to speak, the place where this philosophy grew and found its home. It does not imply that this political philosophy is based on theology or revelation. It is based on natural reason and on rational principles. Political philosophy is a branch of social philosophy and of moral philosophy, not of dogmatic theology or moral theology.

In the preparation of this volume I have received the generous help of my colleagues of the English Department at St. Joseph College, West Hartford, Connecticut: Sister M. Ancilla Sullivan, Ph.D., Sister M. Theodore Kelleher, M.A., and Mr. Edward L. Hirsh, Ph.D. The Reverend Newton Thompson, S.T.D., has patiently and thoroughly revised the manuscript. If the book is readable, credit must be given to this help, so unselfishly granted. For the contents and any defects in the work, I assume full responsibility.

To my wife's unceasing help and encouragement I owe much in this undertaking. To our children I dedicate this result of our common effort.

H. A. ROMMEN

Contents

vii

PART III

CHURCH AND STATE

PART IV

THE COMMUNITY OF NATIONS

Introduction

I. CHURCH AND WORLD

HUMAN culture is older than Christianity. Peoples had produced their states, powerful in organization and diversified in constitutional forms, had conquered and built empires and vanished from history before there was conceived a Christian political philosophy founded on the Gospels, on the principles and traditions of a *philosophia perennis,* and on the experiences and tribulations of the Church. The political philosophy of the Greeks and the civic wisdom and juristic prudence of the Romans were destined to be of significance to all subsequent political philosophies and doctrines. They had radiated their ideas through the ancient world before Christianity, the mother of Western civilization, emerged from the small decadent and despised nation-state of the Jewish people and began her world course through Orient and Occident. Working at first secretly, later freely and publicly, Christianity then became the great power, giving form and norm to the civilization of the West. Today she is still deeply influencing the life of the world, here working freely and publicly, there as it were in hiding, under oppression and derision, as she did in the catacombs at the beginning of the Christian era.

However, it would be superficial to consider history thus. Christ is not the beginner; He is the cornerstone, the finisher of the pre-Christian era, the beginner of the Christian era, the heir of all ages. Thus Christianity, too, is heir to all the intellectual wealth that Greece and Rome created in the times of the Advent. So at least thought the fathers of Church history. For them all history is the history of man's salvation; for them the human soul, by reason of its dignity as the image of God, naturally Christian, was active also in the philosophy of the Greeks and the Romans. So the Church Fathers conceived and elaborated the great idea of the City of God. This is the central idea of a philosophy of history which teaches that from the Fall of man nations wandered on through the night of Advent dimly enlightened by the glimmer of reason, waiting until the fullness of time for the

1

Savior who was to bring the City of God down to redeemed mankind. He was to found that kingdom unique in the possession of a divine promise of its endurance through the ever-changing forms in the political and cultural life of nations and peoples. He was to bring the Church that regenerates nature, sanctifies history, and blesses the world, though she herself never becomes mere nature, mere history, mere world.

This it is that gives to the Christian Church that quality of persevering through recurrent changes in the living forms of states and nations, an attribute which has aroused the astonishment of impartial historian and biased adversary. The Church has never been a mere ideological superstructure over the growing and withering socio-political forms of those nations that at different stages of cultural development were the leading and ruling nations. At times it may have seemed as if the Church universal were identifying herself with one or other of the leading nations, taking over its political forms, its culture and civilization, as the only true ones, and therefore accepting the political philosophy that created these forms or justified them. But again and again the collapse or decay of these historical forms failed to destroy the Church universal in its identity. These epochal changes affected only the temporal forms of adaptation, but the unchangeable substance, the lasting truth, remained.

So the Church outlasted the supreme longings of Greek philosophy and the mighty political structure of the Roman Empire in the West and in the East. Out of the tribulations of the barbarian invasions that annihilated the culture of North Africa, the home of St. Augustine, she alone remained with what her monks salvaged of the treasure of antiquity. She outlasted the colorful world of early medieval feudalism as she saw the political dreams of German imperial families wither away. She witnessed the glory of the medieval cities in Italy and in Germany, in France and in England, in Spain and in Flanders: their well-organized guilds and their flourishing economic life. The Church united all parts of the medieval world into the harmonious unity of a Christian culture; her learned doctors developed their great concordant systems of theology and philosophy embodying the legacy of Greece and Rome, amalgamating what was good in Arabian philosophy and comprising the elements of a Christian political philosophy.

When the Reformation began to dissolve the *orbis christianus,* the unity of Christendom was gradually submerged in the era of the wars of religion until a new and merely secular Western civilization arose. During that era the Church and the philosophy that found its home in her had to resist the reckless attempts of princely absolutism to compel her, under the yoke of Erastianism, to legitimize autocratic absolutism. Later, after the industrial revolution, capitalist interests tried to abuse her doctrine in order to defend the consolidation of vested property-interests against personal rights. In our time the Church has seen the collapse of states and realms under the impact of a violent collision between the selfish complacency of domineering capitalists and the hatred and longings of anticapitalist masses. Out of this conflict there grew the cataclysm of a second World War in one generation, a war that may be the final struggle for the fundamental principles of our now secularized Western civilization, that poor residue of our inheritance from our better and more pious Christian ancestors.

History demonstrates, then, that there exists a final independence, an ultimate separation between the Church of Christ and the diverse forms of the political, economic cultures and civilizations through which the Church lives in unchanged identity. Yet this separation constitutes a danger, a temptation. The Church has so far survived the various forms of political organization such as absolutism and democratic egalitarianism, the tyranny of the totalitarians and the cynical skepticism of anticlerical Liberalism. For this very reason there exists the danger of a quietist religious autarchy, the danger that churchmen, without a struggle, even without protest, may in an opportunist indifferentism tolerate all political forms and theories. It is a grave temptation of individual Christians: to exalt the Church too much over and beyond the world, to make her an idealistic realm, with the result that the average Christian is split into two personalities, one living for enthusiastic religious raptures in the private chamber, one living in the wicked world and accepting its standards of social conduct as an unavoidable consequence of sin. The true Church then becomes invisible, while the visible aspects of the Church's hierarchic constitution—the sacramental law, the visibility and the public life of the Church as the communion of saints, as a perfect society with her law and competencies, with her authority and dogma, with her code of moral and natural law—appear unimportant. These aspects may be regarded as merely external forms destined as modes of adaptation to the various stages of development of the world, forms that externally clothe the Christian's mysterious life of grace. The life of the Church, so far as it is socially and politically manifest, so far as it is public, is thus put under the dictatorship of secular civilization. Rudolf Sohm, the eminent jurist and Lutheran theologian, says: "Christendom does not produce a Christian order in this secular world. Christendom has not the task of creating a Christian civilization, for Christianization of the secular world means secularization of Christendom." [1] From such a point of view a Christian philosophy of the state is impossible; in practical politics what we call "Church" as a visible public institution then becomes necessarily, in an Erastian manner, a servant of the state, at least as long as the state does not turn openly anti-Christian. Man's inner religious life as a Christian and his public life as a citizen are then separated worlds. It is significant for the impossibility of this theory that Luther, who first adhered to such ideas, later had to abandon them, taught by practical life, and that he laid down the foundation of a Lutheran political philosophy which remained far weaker than the political philosophy which sprang from the moral activism of Calvin.

The Catholic Church could never fall into such spiritual quietism. In opposition to Luther's doctrine of grace, which asserted an intrinsic and essentially irreconcilable opposition between religion and grace on the one hand, and morality and secular life on the other, Catholic teaching always upheld the unity of religion and morality and the essential coordination of world and nature with grace and supernature. Catholic doctrine preserved itself from Luther's pessimistic belief in total depravity, as it kept itself free from that excessively optimistic concept of man held by nineteenth-century liberal theology, which had forgotten the gravity of sin, the fact that man's nature by original sin is *natura vulnerata*.

Consequently the Catholic Church cannot ignore the world in which the Christian has to live; she cannot permit that world to become a playground of diabolical powers. In the world the Christian, aided by grace, works for the salvation of his soul. This he does by

[1] This is the tenor of Rudolf Sohm's books on ecclesiastical law: *Kirchenrecht* (1892); *Das Decretum Gratiani*, etc. (1918); *Geistliches und weltliches Recht*. The author has discussed the influence of Sohm's ideas in *Die Kirche, ihr Recht und die neue Volksordnung* (1930).

fulfilling, *in* the family, *in* the state, and *in* his vocational or professional station or function, his natural but supernaturally exalted duties as a social and political being. The Christian is called to help perfect the order of creation. This City of men, the world, is therefore the station in which, by living according to the ordinances of God and the Church, man works for his salvation, thus participating in that universal *Benedicite* of all creatures to the greater glory of the Creator and Father of all. If thus world, nature, and the secular realm remain the substructure of the life of grace, the Catholic Church, the mediatrix of grace, cannot be indifferent to the shape and form of the world. The Church cannot be resigned in social quietism, it cannot give up a certain competence to assist, to admonish, and to teach those communities: the family, the state, and the other institutions of human social life in the secular sphere. It is true that this assistance brings dangers with it. "Too often the duty of the Church to teach the state has been allowed to seem the right of the clergy to control the laymen." [2] But such abuses do not change the fact that, according to Catholic doctrine, it is very much the task of the Christian and the Church to work for the Christianization of the world.

A profound understanding of the realities of human life makes us realize that, although grace in the absolute sense is independent of secular conditions, the social security and the peaceful order of secular life should be guaranteed if generally the Christian is to be able to fulfill his higher and sublimer tasks. Bishop von Ketteler, whom Leo XIII called his great predecessor, in dealing with the socio-economic problems of his time, said: "To the grace of the Church, as long as it is offered in the way of ordinary pastoral care, the proletarian masses of modern industry are inaccessible. Before we can think of their Christianization, we must initiate measures for the humanization of these masses that have run wild." [3] Similarily one of the greatest moral theologians of the nineteenth century, F. X. Linsenmann, warns of a wrong supernaturalist outlook which regards the higher supernatural life as the only thing that matters and hence neglects as a kind of necessary evil the material, sensual, and secular sphere of life.[4] St. Thomas never tires of pointing out that a sufficient amount

---

[2] Father P. Hughes in his review of Don Sturzo's *Church and State* in the *Tablet* (London), 1940, p. 352.

[3] *Gesammelte Schriften* (ed. Mumbauer, 1924), III, 148.

[4] F. X. Linsenmann, *Moraltheologie* (1878), pp. 17, 282, 298.

of earthly goods and a good order in the sphere of political and socio-economic life is necessary for a virtuous human life.[5] The famous encyclicals of Leo XIII and of Pius XI, particularly *Rerum novarum* of the former and *Quadragesimo anno* of the latter, rest on this conception of the Church as the helper and teacher of man in his social and political life. It is the idea of a Church that, rejecting the quietist attitude of the priest in the parable of the good Samaritan, turns her face and her charity to the secular part of human existence.

II. THE ORIGIN OF A POLITICAL PHILOSOPHY IN CATHOLICISM

This obligation of the Church to the world is the reason why a political philosophy could grow in the Catholic Church. Out of the task of the Church as an active community that cannot ignore the world, out of the presuppositions of the philosophy that found its home in the Church, and out of the problems presented for thousands of years before the Christian era, this great structure arose. The Gospel and reason are the foundation. Upon it the Fathers of the early Church began to build, incorporating the legacy of Greece and Rome. The great doctors of the Middle Ages and of Late Scholasticism continued the work. When, after the decay of medieval society, new forms of political life began to arise, the new problems were treated on the basis of the unchanging principles, with acumen and scholarly thoroughness. In fact, their discussion of the problems compares favorably with that by many great modern thinkers in their clash with the revived Leviathans of modern totalitarianism or in their profound understanding of the problems of modern democracy.

And the Catholic political philosophy which so developed cannot be evaluated in terms of such perpetually reiterated generalities as those employed by reviewers who know it only from the outside. For the connoisseur it is like a cathedral in an old city: the foundations have been laid by pious people that listened to the homilies of the early Fathers of the Church, who had amalgamated the treasures of the ancient world with the new spirit of the Gospels. Subsequent generations added their artistic products. The adepts of the Renaissance and the joyous dreamers of the baroque added testimonies of their arts, as today a modern artist adorns a niche or a new altar with his work.

[5] *On the Governance of Rulers*, Bk. I, chap. 15; *Summa theol.*, Ia IIae, q.114, a.10.

So the connoisseur views the work of that long line of political philosophers who found and still find their home in the Church. It is true that their philosophy circles round a center of perpetual problems and eternal principles. But whoever becomes familiar with its history will find that there is a colorful diversity of opinions and points of view and that sharp conflict is possible among schools, which nevertheless may all look to the same center. This unity in diversity explains the mystery of organic growth of this philosophy: "to augment the old by the new and perfect it." Or, as St. Thomas says: "It is natural to human reason that it progresses step by step from the imperfect to the perfect; therefore we see in philosophy that what the first philosophers handed down in an imperfect manner was by the later philosophers handed down in a more perfect manner." [6] There is thus room for true progress and perfection. Historical actuality is the most influential principle of selection in determining the particular problem to be discussed more profoundly; historical actuality may also lead to an overemphasis of one part of the whole doctrine; later that part may lose its importance and actuality and may need correction because of a change in historical development. At another time militant adversaries compel the philosophers to study more broadly and deeply a principle that has been carried through the books as self-evident, therefore not enough appreciated. Even the literary style of an era may clothe the identical doctrine in a form that later generations will have to remove, as open to grave misunderstandings. Thus industrious research, penetrating thought, and sympathetic insight into the changing problems and the unchanging principles have produced a Catholic political philosophy that in its architecture is a synthesis of inheritances of almost two thousand years of intellectual exertion.

Catholic Christianity, then, has always stood in opposition to the pure other-worldliness that Luther in his early years and most sects through the course of Christian history have so heavily stressed. They all declare that the world (the *saeculum*) is a matter of strict indifference to religion and supernature, because the world is essentially sin and has to remain unredeemed. Nor has Catholic Christianity ever gone so far in the other direction as to identify itself, the millennial, everlasting power, with an historically specific form of political life and its relative philosophy. These were, in fact, born out of the free-

---

[6] *Summa theol.*, Ia IIae, q.97, a.1.

dom of man to organize his state in comparative independence. Un-equivocally as the Catholic Church stresses her competence to help, to teach, and to admonish in the field of social and political life, yet she has always, though on certain occasions only at the last moment, avoided identifying herself with an historically existing, therefore transitory, political form or doctrine. Because of her eternal task the Church is ultimately independent of the world and its various forms of political and social organization. The Church always puts to history the question: *Quid hoc ad aeternitatem?* The ruling classes in politi-cal and economic life have always tried to identify their transitory interests with Christianity and thus to acquire perpetuity for them-selves. From the time of feudal lords to that of capitalist property, often there have likewise been attempts to use or rather abuse the Church and her political philosophy, not merely as a means of partici-pating in her dignity as the mother of the nations, but even more to inflict on political opponents the label of "anti-Christian."

An instance in point is the attempt of the Romantic antirevolution-ary movement to utilize the Church in her struggle against the Revo-lution. As daughter of the anti-Christian Enlightenment, the great Revolution of 1789 in France seemed to reject, in emotional appeal to the rights of man, any kind of authority, of legitimacy, of objective order. It tried to subject authority and order to the changing and arbitrary emotions of the volatile masses of the "citizens." Against these attempts—and they proved rather cruel and destructive under the rule of the Jacobins—the antirevolutionary political theory of Romanticism turned reactionary. It was not content to elaborate the ideas of authority, legitimacy, natural law, objective order, in a new historical situation; it tried to use these ideas to restore the authority and legitimacy of royal houses that by their incapacity, narrowness, and cynicism had helped to beget the Revolution. Romantic political philosophy appealed to tradition, to history, and to the providentially dispensed law in the history of nations to prove that the ancient regime (the monarchy) is historically and philosophically the best and only justified political form. The Romanticists tried to corroborate what they called tradition and the laws of history by connecting these ideas with revelation and with the Church and her political philosophy. Their model became Bossuet, who had attempted to prove that the royal absolutism of Louis XIV is the best polity and, on the basis of the Bible, the true political form.

The Romanticists appealed to "Catholicism," by which they meant preferably the monarchical organization of the papal Church and her hierarchical order and from which they drew the conclusion that monarchy is providentially the model form of government. Duration through history became for them the proof of legitimacy, while the principles of natural law as the foundation of legitimacy were neglected. According to this view it is the time-honored age of the monarchical constitution that proves its superiority over the new democratic form and, behold, the oldest organization in the West, the Church, is monarchically organized! Thus "Catholicism," in the sense of the hierarchical monarchy of the divinely instituted papacy, becomes the model and establishes monarchy as the only admissible form of government. The Romanticists were reproached with being too little aware of the Church in its sacramental life as the community of salvation of the believers, above the nations where there is neither Greek nor barbarian (Gal. 3:28). The reproach is fully justified. The Altar, so they thought, should restore the lost thrones and support the restored ones. So at all times the political philosophy that has found its home in the Church runs the same danger as the Church herself, that of becoming the servant of politics.

III. The Danger of "Sociological Pragmatism"

These attempts to use the Church for political ends and the blamable complaisance of churchmen to let the ecclesiastical organization be used for political interests as a price for secular advantages, may be called sociological pragmatism. Voltaire knew about it. However much he himself rejected its "childish superstitions," he was convinced that society and the state needed the Church for the control of the common people; the priest is a better and far cheaper policeman than the gendarme. Taine considered that the growing infidelity of the common people was worse for the nation than for the Church. Napoleon and many industrial Caesars repeated: "Religion must be preserved for the common people." All these had no belief in Christian doctrine. They said that they could afford to be unbelievers, but that the doctrine is useful for the protection of their interests. This sociological pragmatism reached its pinnacle in the writings of Charles Maurras, who confessed himself a "Catholique mais athée. Le catholicism c'est l'ordre." He distinguished sharply between the Christian and the Catholic element. The Christian element is the spirit of the Gospels, the love of the Sermon on the Mount, the individualism of Luther, who gave the Bible into the hands of the uneducated common people, educating them to revolt. The Catholic element is the concise order of the Roman dogma, the monarchic authoritarian power of the pope in the admirable order of the canon law. It is to Maurras the only protection against the revolting anarchism of the ideas of 1789 and of modern democracy.

At the basis of all this sociological pragmatism lies the following assumption. The Church fulfills her tasks, teaches her dogmas, dispenses the sacraments, consoles the unfortunate, admonishes the powerful, and helps political authority to establish good order: not that people may live and work for the salvation of their souls; no, all this she does for "culture." Culture is luxury beyond the unpleasant and debasing production of the necessities of life; culture is play, the play of a small ruling class of masters. It is the task of the Church and her doctrine in the interest of these masters to transfer into the other world the effects of the Christian doctrines, so dangerous to this aristocratic culture; she has to make them harmless to culture. Catholicism as the principle of order—that is the capsule enclosing the poison, the "Christian ideas," keeping it away from the common people—thus makes culture possible.

Like the Church herself, the political philosophy springing from her womb cannot be claimed by any of the historical forms of political life. Such a claim would contradict its fundamental issue, the idea of natural law that in some way represents the connection between world and Church. Natural law as the continuation of metaphysics is the fundamental norm of all moral and practical activity; consequently, of the political, too. It is the eternal law, emanating from God's being and will as do revelation and supernatural grace, that is recognized by human persons endowed with reason and free will, as natural law, as the norm of human acts and as their critical standard; therefore also as the norm and standard of political life. But natural law requires positive law, to be made concrete in every historical situation under perpetually changing circumstances. The natural order requires a positive concrete order between nations and in nations *hic et nunc*. Not all positive orders of political life together, nor any one of them in itself, is the natural order, however much the latter is the model of acting and the norm of judgment for any of the positive orders.

IV. The Principal Ideas of Catholic Political Philosophy

Catholic political philosophy, as its name shows, cannot disregard its origin. It lives encompassed by the theological and philosophical structure of Catholic doctrine. Only he who is conscious of this in studying its development can understand and grasp its true meaning. For instance, at first sight there may seem to exist, in its theory of popular sovereignty, interesting similarities and parallels to that of Rousseau so that the most outspoken authorities appear to be mere forerunners of Rousseau. Yet the Christian idea of popular sovereignty is profoundly different from that constructed on Rousseau's romantic and anarchical individualism. For the "new" political theory of Rousseauist observance proceeds from a different idea of man; it has no place for the freedom of the Church as a "perfect society" apart from the state. Whoever does not appreciate the fact that Catholic political philosophy lives in the cosmos—this in its true meaning—of Christian Catholic life, will easily come to strange conclusions, will find in it an uncritical eclecticism or an opportunist syncretism of unrelated parts, artificially put together and polished in accordance with the interests of the Church as a political instrument for the power of "popery" or of the clergy.

It has been said that this philosophy uncritically took over the Greek legacy. What it took over, however, was not the tribal Graecism but its universal human content. Heraclitus, the first Greek who used the word and coined the meaning of *philosophia,* distinguished the narrow tribal world around man as the *idios kosmos,* the private and privative order, and contrasted it with the *koinos kosmos,* the universal order, where man, fully awakened, grows to participate in the universal logos or reason above all narrowness, privacy, and limitations.[7] Man in some way is always the same, like the elements, the

---

[7] For this reason, says Justin Martyr, we might call Heraclitus a philosopher who was a Christian. *Apologia I pro Christianis;* Migne, *P.G.,* VI, 397.

earth, the sun, and the air that keep him alive. Under all tribal, national, and individual limitations there lives something that is universal, that is perpetually human. To the extent that political philosophy has to do with man, the universal man, and with Greeks and Romans, Germans and Frenchmen, Americans and Spaniards, not only so far as they are individual nationalities but also as they are historical exemplifications, individual forms of the perpetually identical human being, to that extent it is the idea of man that is the measure.

Catholic political philosophy remains a philosophy of man, not simply a philosophy for the believer. The state belongs to human culture and to the secular order. Its root is the social nature of man. Its nearest end is the order of secular felicity or happiness, the *ordo rerum humanarum*. Therefore the great doctors maintained at all times that the essential duties and rights of the citizens and of those in authority are independent of the state of grace. The fact that man is baptized exalts his rights, intensifies his duties. The ruler may be a Christian or not, may be in his private life a profligate or not. But as long as he fulfills his political function, the Christian owes obedience, even to the pagan ruler. (*"Non eripit mortalia qui regna dat coelestia."*) St. Justin could explain to the Roman Emperor in answer to the foolish attacks of Celsus that the better Christian a man was, the better citizen and subject he would be. That is the reason why in the recent centuries Catholic political philosophy used to call itself a political philosophy based on natural law. This philosophy does not make use of theological methods; it bases its principles not on theology, but on philosophy, and works out its conclusions through the medium of natural reason. Still we rightly speak of a Christian, of even a Catholic political philosophy, since by this is meant that body of principles that has always found its home in the Catholic Church.

By this is also meant an essential difference from the modern autonomous systems of philosophy that do not deserve the attribute Catholic, or even utterly decline it. Idealism, monism, utilitarianism, materialism, subjectivism, and experimental pragmatism, all these autonomous philosophical systems form as the substructure of their political philosophy systems of a quasi natural law. For all political philosophies of a reformatory, activistic, or revolutionary character and even those of a merely conservative character appeal to a natural order, that is, a "good" order, either against the existing bad order or for the defense of the existing good one. Even the "ascetics" of pure positivism who deny all metaphysics, which is the only admissible basis for a natural law, forget quickly about their dreary positivist frugality and often indulge in a hotspurred zeal for social improvement and political reform. Even the presumedly materialistic Karl Marx indulges again and again in appeals to justice and human dignity in spite of his presupposition that all ethics are only the empty ideological superstructure over the only real thing: the conditions of economic production. Thus we note the remarkable fact that the Marxist movement lives by moral indignation arising from a pathetic kind of proletarian natural law which in sober moments it utterly denies.

The attribute Catholic means that theology is recognized as influencing, even directing, the division of tasks between philosophy and theology. Philosophizing is done not altogether autonomously, but with continuous respect for theology. It means further that philosophy is aware of its limitations and avoids crossing the boundaries of theology and usurping what is preserved for faith and revelation. It accepts faith and revelation and knows that, whatever progress it may make, it cannot substitute for them. And finally in principle it accepts teaching and assistance from theology, does not seclude itself from it, and acknowledges that there is no twofold truth, so that what is philosophically true may be theologically false, and vice versa.[8] This *philosophia perennis* is older than the Church though the Church became and continues to be the homeland of this philosophy. It had as its ancestors Socrates and Aristotle, Plato and Heraclitus. Since it is philosophy, and not theology, it had as its adepts such men as Leibnitz and Trendelenborg, who did not belong to the Catholic Church. It is so broad that such modern ethnologists as W. Schmidt and his school are its followers; and it is so vital today that it inaugurates a revival in the New World. Pascal aptly says of this *philosophia perennis:* "Whilst all philosophers split up into various schools, there exist in a nook of the world people who belong to the oldest history of the

[8] Balduin Schwarz, *Ewige Philosophie* (1937), p. 75; cf. also J. Maritain, *Philosophie chrétienne* (1933).

world and declare that all are erring, that God has revealed the truth to them, and that this truth will forever be on this earth. Actually all schools pass away, but this school remains." [9]

Especially as practical philosophy, Catholic political philosophy cannot ignore the fact that state and Church live on the same globe. It must therefore elaborate their mutual natures, their mutual relations, their corresponding order. We should add that the state lives intrinsically by the socio-political virtues of its citizens and its rulers. As religion in its concrete form cannot be split off from morality without a drying up of political virtues, religion as revealed truth cannot be neglected by political philosophy. Furthermore, it is a concrete task for Catholic political philosophy, in considering the problem of the state and religion, not to content itself with general remarks of a negative character, but to represent the relation of this very concrete Catholic Church to the changing forms and ends of political life through the centuries. The position of the visible Church of Christ, herself a "perfect society," penetrating beyond the borderlines of the states, is truly singular. In Catholic political philosophy, therefore, are united theistic philosophy, developed in Christian traditions, and Catholic ideas originating in theology, governing especially the relations of state and Church.[10]

From this specific idea of man's nature and destiny, from the idea of the Christian person, and from the idea of God and of natural law, follows a fundamental structure of socio-political life. Furthermore, from the teleological point of view follow certain norms for the concrete formation of the socio-political institutions, norms that form at the same time the critical standards in judging existing concrete institutions and their right or wrong functioning. The basic lines of thought may be briefly characterized as follows: The Christian person has an intimate sphere of life that is intrinsically and fundamentally closed to state intervention. Similarly, the family possesses a sphere and a function that, as it existed before the state, must be preserved against the state; never can the state substitute itself for the family, without destroying the human values nursed by the family, however, the historical form and reach of the function and sphere of the family

---

[9] *Fragm.*, 6, 18.

[10] This should not be found strange. Proudhon regarded as amazing the fact that at the basis of every political theory is a theology; cf. N. Micklem, *Theology of Politics* (1941).

may change. As circumstances demand, the state may compress or enlarge this sphere of the family; there yet remains a basic social function that is essentially closed to the state. There exists further a sphere of socio-economic and cultural life, an organism of differentiated social functions for the attainment of which men organize themselves in at least an actual order, though not always in a juridical-institutional order.

To this social order, however, the state as the order of law may supply the legal standardized forms. Yet these groups owe their existence, not to the state, but to the initiative of individual persons and have a certain autonomy and the right of self-government. The state as sovereign power cannot transform either the individuals or their group formations, arising out of self-initiative and serving objective social ends, into mere instruments without rights, moved as passive tools by command and compulsion. Never must the greater community take over the ends and functions of the smaller communities. This principle is the reason for the deep abhorrence of any form of totalitarianism. The idea of a polar unity of tension between person and state, family and state, socio-economic and cultural groups and state, and lastly Church and state, springs from the conviction of a hierarchical economy of ends mirrored by that of social forms in which the social virtues and impulses, necessary for human happiness and the realization of man's destiny, are adequately nursed and fostered. In order that state, order, and "cosmos" ever be and ever be renewed, more is needed than the technical efficiency of a well-oiled administrative apparatus. *Virtus*, the whole organic body of social virtues, is the real and fertile principle of social life.

V. Misinterpretation of Catholic Political Philosophy

Catholic political philosophy as a system, as well as its particular doctrines, is in the same danger of misinterpretation as Catholic philosophy in general. The mind of one observer is thrilled by the magnificent unity of the theory and its principles, by the beautiful architecture of the whole, by the temperate preservation of the right balance between extreme opposites. Another observer, aware of the centuries of growth, stands amazed before the diversity of theories and statements, often seeming to contradict one another, in the polemic discussions of its schools. Hence this latter observer cannot conceive Catholic political philosophy as an internally coherent system, but only as an artificial conglomeration of doctrines and these held together only by dogmatic or authoritative decisions, as a *complexio oppositorum* arising out of the utilitarian considerations of theologians and out of the opportunism of ecclesiastic policy.[11]

Still another observer will see it as a confused product of elements that, in spite of all external accommodations, remain irreconcilable. To him it is a confused product of Greek city-state philosophy, of Stoic world-state philosophy, of the theological exegesis of the Scriptures, and of contradictory borowings from different philosophical and theological schools. He thinks that these elements were put together to meet the changing wants of practical work or even the ambitions of the papal Church which uses, or rather abuses, this political philosophy to afford the best legitimation now and here for its attempts at domination over the state and the world.[12]

Other more friendly observers prefer to see in Catholic political philosophy the idealized sociological system realized in the Christian culture of the Middle Ages: a system manifestly unfit for the solution of the pressing socio-political problems of today, despite the romantic and easily comprehensible longing of some among the Catholic laity and clergy for the restoration of that system in our times.[13]

All these views, no matter how wrong, are partly understandable. This mass of doctrine includes the early theories of the Church Fathers, the profound disputations of the Scholastics, the controversies of the sixteenth and seventeenth centuries, the authoritative documents of the Apostolic See, of the Councils, and of the Congregations, the compact treatises of Catholic philosophers in defense of their tradition against all the anarchists, liberalist doctrinaires, and Erastian quietists from the eighteenth century to our times. Every one who approaches the question from outside falls easily into one of the above-mentioned points of view. These points of view result from decisions of the heart made beforehand against the home of this philosophy, the

---

11 The authors of the document, "The City of Man," offer an interesting example.

12 The learned book of Ernst Tröltsch, *Sociallehren der christlichen Kirchen und Gruppen* (1912) is a good example of this view. English translation: *The Social Teaching of the Christian Churches* (New York, 1931).

13 From the era of Enlightenment on, especially through the nineteenth century until today, these views have been propounded in learned books, political pamphlets, and demagogic speeches in practically all modern states.

Catholic Church. Hence a just evaluation can be achieved only by an impartial attempt to understand this philosophy from within, from its principles and its internal history. Catholic political philosophy is not at variance with the *philosophia perennis*, of which it is a part and an application. There is a broad variance in the answers to those problems that are farthest from the general principles, a far-reaching unity in those conclusions nearest to the general and fundamental principles, and a complete unity in these principles themselves.

These differentiations do not, by the way, result in diametrically contradictory opinions but rather in parallel courses of reasoning on account of oscillations, because of the fact that these oscillations rest in the polar unity of the general principles themselves. Man, for instance, is intellect and will. But which faculty is superior? St. Thomas and the Thomists declare that the intellect is superior to the will. That decision gives an excellent and solid basis for the strict unchangeableness of the natural law. But it also produces a strong rationality, the stressing of the static elements and the general conclusions, and can lead to an undervaluation of the dynamism of history. Consequently the adherents of a more Augustinian school reproached the Thomists for intellectualism or rationalism and a lack of understanding of historical forces.

Against St. Thomas, the Scotist school and the school of the *via moderna* of nominalist origin stressed the superiority of the will, maintaining that the will is superior to the intellect. As the will refers to existence, individuality, and historic realization, this school showed a preference for the individual, for the singular historical events, and for the dynamism of historical evolution. Its adherents thus became the fathers of historical theology and the promoters of the natural sciences. Stressing the irrational will, the "heart," the mystical faculties of the soul, and the *amor* (*Nihil intelligitur quod non prius diligitur*), and consequently exalting the will as the primary attribute in God's omnipotence, they had not a little trouble in finding a well-established basis for the strict invariability of the principles of natural law. They were also inclined to disparage the importance and range of natural reason and consequently to show supernaturalist tendencies even in their political philosophy. The perpetual and primary question for the essence of law, alternating between the propositions, "law is reason" and "law is will," was then in opposition to St. Thomas answered by "law is predominantly will." If adherents of this school adopt Occam's blunt statement that law is will, then the essence of natural law vanishes. Ethics loses its basis of natural reason and becomes positivist. A rather futile and strange discussion may begin about the question, whether God, in order to be really omnipotent, must be able to will the hatred of Himself. If God's omnipotence was thus exalted the consequence had to be and has been a kind of nihilism in natural ethics, a transformation of the *fides rationalis* into an emotional faith of sentiment, the negation of natural theology and a one-sided supranaturalism. All too easily the world of politics and economics is then left to itself. This consequence tends to make the Church an obedient instrument of the state, which has the monopoly of nature, world, and power.

Similarly the tension between the individual and the community may give rise to a more individualist school that stresses freedom and self-initiative, as in the theological doctrine of grace the Molinists do, and another school that stresses *ordo*, authority, and is Thomistic in its doctrine of grace.[14] Whoever goes through the many volumes that discuss the problem of capitalism will find one school that may be called friendly to capitalism and another one that may be called hostile to capitalism. The basis of these positions is, on the one hand, a preference for the individual person, for self-initiative, and a more optimistic view of the individual's abilities, or, on the other hand, a more pessimistic view of man's weakness, a stronger emphasis on the role of authority and order, a conservative diffidence against "liberal" tendencies. We must content ourselves with these few remarks, but it should be stated that there is still much research to be done concerning the influence of theological schools and philosophical doctrines within the *philosophia perennis* upon the answers to many problems of social and political philosophy.

Even today we encounter such tensions accompanied by corresponding polemics of the schools; for instance, in the doctrine about the origin of the state. The general theory is that the state originates in the social nature of man. Man's nature is social because of the mind-and-body composition of man's essence; and man is free, rational substance, a person. Consequently two accentuations are possible and

---

14 Cf. Brauer, *Thomistic Principles;* chapter by Franz Mueller, "Person and Society according to St. Thomas," p. 186, notes 7 and 8.

admissible as long as the accentuation of the one element does not result in the disappearance of the other. One accentuation emphasizes the unconditional necessity of the state on the basis of the social nature of man as a mind-and-body compound and would give less stress to the free will of the individual person, and so to the role of freedom and consent in the doctrine of the origin of the state. Another accentuation prefers to lay weight rather upon the free will and upon consent as a conscious rational element; this is done by the so-called contract theories concerning the origin of the state.

Such accentuations may be conditioned by historical circumstances, as, for instance, at the time of the romantic Restoration after the French Revolution. In reaction to the Rousseauist type of social-contract theories, the scholastic theory of the social contract was pushed into the background by romantic writers. But these accentuations are frequently typical of the differences about the *philosophia perennis* that result from theological and philosophical schools within the Church. We may also find among the political writers of Romanticism a preference for the theory of a rather unconscious growth of the state out of human biological nature without much intervention of free will and conscious reasoning. The real cause of such a theory is the conviction that man, though a rational being, is far more influenced by his heart, by sentiment, by emotion, and by the forces of history than by reason. These sentiments and forces of history are revealed in the spirit, in the folklore, and in the individual history of a nation; it is the *Volksgeist* or *la tradition* that produces the state. The state is not so much the result of rational will and conscious decisions as it is an unconscious growth, a flowering of the seed of the social nature under the protecting hand of Providence, who prepares and fosters the garden of history. We may find that the eminent statesman and political philosopher, Donoso Cortes, is led to a bitter condemnation of Liberalism and egalitarian democracy by the pessimistic views of human nature that made him discuss with theologians the degree of corruption of human nature by original sin. He showed little trust in the human reason and the human will, which he thought almost destroyed. If that view is conceded, how can we leave order, authority, and the law at the mercy of the masses that are not masters of themselves, but the plaything of contradictory emotional strains and uncontrolled vices? The consequence is the demand for a strong authoritarian state and an antidemocratic accent. An interesting counterpoise to Donoso Cortes' views may be seen in some opinions of the great American Father Hecker, opinions known as "Americanism," some of which were censured by Leo XIII.[15] The root of some exaggerated views about democracy may be an excessive valuation of the natural virtues and of the active Christian virtues, of reason and of will.

Thus the diversity manifested in the history of Catholic political philosophy may be based on such accentuations or may be the consequence of historical situations wherever these form a kind of principle of selection; namely, what problems need a new or a profounder interpretation, or what accentuations become predominant. Nothing more. It is an accentuation of one pole, not a suppression of the other pole. It may happen that the tension ceases and that the thought is controlled exclusively by one pole, for instance, either the individual or the state in the relation between them. Then strict individualism or strict collectivism results. Both are impossible in Catholic political philosophy, which has shown a sensitive aversion to one-sided exaggerations.

VI. THE ALLEGED INFLUENCE OF HELLENISM

Often it is said, in hostile criticism, that Catholic political philosophy, especially since St. Thomas' acceptance of Aristotle's philosophy, has considered as generally valid and timeless the principles abstracted from the experiences and histories of Hellenistic culture and civilization. We are told that these principles were therefore valid only in the Hellenic city-state and its economic and cultural background. Furthermore, Catholic political philosophy is charged with having uncritically declared valid for general human existence those principles, forms of thinking, ethical rules, and political ideals of Hellenism. On account of this identification many uncongenial and even contradictory elements, it is contended, have been combined with specifically Christian principles into a political philosophy which is harmonious only superficially but is basically an artificial *complexio oppositorum*. And even more. In this "Christian camouflage" the ancient political ideas, it is said, have broken the medieval Christian

---

[15] Letter *Testem benevolentiae* to Card. Gibbons; Denzinger, 1967–76.

community ideas in favor of an individualist concept of the state.[16] By the infiltration of these individualist ideas the Christian idea of the universal *mundus christianus* has been decomposed.

A similar censure is made today, though in a glaring opposition to the one just mentioned. Frightened by the Aristotelian idea of the totalitarian character of the city-state and prompted by an understandable sensitiveness against all kinds of totalitarianism, some thinkers deplore the introduction of the Aristotelian philosophy and ethics by St. Thomas. They believe that the sooner and the more completely these Aristotelian ideas are eliminated, the better it will be for freedom and democracy.[17]

Two misinterpretations seem to lie at the bottom of these theories. One contends that Aristotle's ideas are so steeped in the specific Greek culture that they are of little avail today in a very different culture. But it was always the human, the general, the timeless, and the metaphysical element in Greek philosophy that attracted the Church Fathers and the Schoolmen—the idea of a *Koinos Kosmos,* as shown above. St. Thomas removed the arabesque covers in which Arabian philosophy had wrapped Aristotelian philosophy. Why could not that intellectual giant also free from its historical and sociological, and therefore transitory, coverings the generally human core, the metaphysical content, of Aristotelian philosophy? Why, we repeat, should we be compelled to accept the medieval historical exemplification of Christian political philosophy as the only genuine expression of it? Have not Leo XIII and Pius XI used this same philosophy as the basis for a profound and greatly admired criticism of modern political philosophy from Rousseau to the totalitarianism of today? It should not be forgotten that the incorporation of the Greek legacy was not an arbitrary, blind, and uncritical adoption, but a long-term process of continuous critical absorption of what is sound, and an even more toilsome process of the discovery and rejection of what is transitory, only Hellenistic, and therefore not suited for amalgamation.

The second misinterpretation is the individualist one, which assumes that socialistic pro-totalitarian ideas have been smuggled into Catholic political philosophy by the adoption of Aristotelianism.

[16] This is the reproach made by Otto von Gierke and his school, especially in *Deutsches Genossenschaftsrecht,* partly translated by Maitland under the title, *Medieval Political Theories.*
[17] Cf. C. Friedrich in *Review of Politics,* 1939.

About individualism and socialism as structural principles of political life, we must point out what we said above with regard to the polarism of the relation between individual and community. That medieval idea of community, so stressed as typically Christian by Gierke, is in reality accompanied by a searching and increasing introspection and a growing subjectivism of the emotional life and by a strong personalization of all community life. This fact is shown by the growth of mystical theology, the spirit of Franciscanism, and the development of historical theology and of natural sciences from Albertus Magnus to Roger Bacon. The school of Clemens Bäumker, with its scores of monographs on medieval philosophy, has proved that such a unity as is presupposed in the criticisms mentioned never actually existed beyond the fundamental principles. We should add that when Gierke regarded Suarez and Bellarmine as predecessors of Rousseau, he did not consider the fact that these great leaders tried again to do what St. Thomas had so successfully done. This was to work out an agreement of the Thomists and Scotists, of the "old way" and the "modern way," of the systematic method and the historical method.

Some critics forget that this is an everlasting process which is repeated again and again in all fields of intellectual life. Thus the new democratic and social ideas of the eighteenth and nineteenth centuries could be fully received only after a process of toilsome clearance in embittered discussions, as, for instance, in the controversies between Lacordaire, Montalembert, and the Catholic liberals in France, and the adherents of monarchy. These internal disputes do not destroy the unity of polar tension. No new philosophy is founded; only new problems are put before the *philosophia perennis,* that is by no means a static and brittle system. To be sure, Catholic political philosophy as a part of this *philosophia perennis* may be called conservative. It does not easily give up what has proved its value in long experience for alluring but unproved new ideas. But, on the other hand, it is not compelled to mummify theories and opinions in a stubborn conservatism that is closed to the perpetually changing life of God's creation. What may be called linear thinking goes straight out from one pole or from one idea of the cosmos of ideas, which every true philosophy is. This idea, cut off from its interrelations and interdependencies with the cosmos, it then fanatically thinks to a finish. Thus it becomes radical individualism or socialism or totalitarianism or anarchism. This linear thinking, so characteristic of the modern mind and its countless isms, is a stranger to Catholic political philosophy. For Catholic political philosophy is "spheric" thinking. Of the interdependencies and the mutual relations between ideas as united in a spheric cosmos and the concordance of these, spheric thinking must be always aware. This explains the unity in diversity, the conservative perseverance in principles and the flexible progressiveness, promoted by the disputes of the schools, in the application of the identical principles in a ceaselessly changing life.

VII. Ideas of Greek and Stoic Philosophy

It is the merit of Hellenism that it first grasped and systematically worked out a political philosophy. The Oriental nations living in the musty air of despotism, of a pagan theocracy, did not develop a political philosophy. State and political life, down to merely incidental forms and rules, were for them unimpeachable institutions established by the tribal gods, and were sacred beyond any human questioning. Not so for the Greeks. Living together in a restricted space, these agile people had to develop an increasing social and political integration. They quickly overcame the early stage of patriarchal authority and despotism and developed progressively democratic forms of government and constitutions that called for consent and free cooperation of the citizens in their small city-states. As the Greeks found more leisure, philosophy could freely develop apart from their traditional theology. Their colonial enterprises afforded a rich opportunity for experience and abundant material for observation and comparison, which are the basis of political philosophy. They made their city-state, its constitutions and laws, its political and social functions, and, on the basis of philosophy and ethics, the political virtues, an object of study and systematic research. This they did publicly in the market place and in the philosophical "clubs" of the various schools: in the noble Academy of Plato, in the individual Socratic way, in the soap-box oratory of the Sophists, in the dignified Aristotelian school of peripatetic observance.

Greek political philosophy reached its perfection in the teachings of Aristotle and, perhaps to a lesser degree, in those of Plato, whose antidemocratic and utopian aristocracy was not so well received by later generations. Thus it was chiefly the Aristotelian and the late Stoic political philosophy that attracted the early Fathers of Christianity. The Fathers themselves had no time for systematic endeavors. That time came when, after the settlement and Christianization of the barbarians, the medieval culture developed. In a rather revolutionary way St. Thomas incorporated the Aristotelian philosophy into the *Summa Christiana* after he had freed the former from what its Arabian and Jewish interpreters had added and after he himself, who had grown up in a tradition of Christian life, had critically eliminated all that was transitory, merely Hellenistic, or contradictory to the Augustinian legacy. It was in this critically refined and Christianized form that Aristotle's political philosophy was received, together with Roman jurisprudence, itself Christianized by the canon law. In continuous re-formulation it still influences the political thinking of Western civilization. Two ideas especially were adopted: first, that man is essentially a political being, that man's intrinsic nature and his desire for earthly happiness produce a social process attaining its completion in the state, as the sovereign order of the common good; secondly, that of the natural social forms—family, neighborhood, village, city-state—the city-state is a perfect, self-sufficient society of distinctive essence, while the others, though necessary and adequate stages of the social process, are imperfect societies.

Aristotle starts from experience and finds in man a natural urge for life in community. Language, the issue of reason, the sympathetic sentiments of love and of friendship, the urge to communicate to others what one thinks, feels, and wills, the love relations of a being that is bisexual: all these acts of man point intentionally to others and receive their intentional fulfillment only in community life. They are also natural properties, integral elements, of man's nature. Man is a social being as much as he is a rational being. All these "social acts" that are intentionally directed to others are not the consequence of utilitarian considerations, as some Sophists held, or vague sentiments without intentional aims, so that they could be satisfied by animals or the sentimental love of nature. On the contrary, often considerations of utility destroy the intentional nature of these acts, so natural are they, so essential in man's nature. Out of social acts in their different forms grow friendship in the strict sense, the family as a natural outcome of marital love and the bisexual nature of man, and associations formed for the common aim of worship, of economic cooperation, and of law where the collective aim is the intentional fulfillment of the social acts. But all these natural communities and freely produced associations point to one form of association where all collective aims coincide, where all conflicts between them can be settled: the city-state that embraces all social activities and all co-ordinated groups, thus establishing moral, social, and economic self-sufficiency and duration. This community is therefore "perfect." The social acts of man here reach their intentional aims in final perfection.

Aristotle reaches his concept of perfect society from his ethics. All human willing and desire is directed to something that is considered a good. There exists an order in the objects that are potential goods; some have merely a character of service, are means to reach higher, more human goods. But it is clear that one good, one aim, must be the highest, to which all other aims are intermediary stages. Experience tells us that what we always aim at is happiness. Therefore happiness must be the highest good and last aim, at least *formaliter,* however much man may disagree about what concrete object may *materialiter* fulfill this intention. But before objective reason there must be an objective fulfillment independent of the often treacherous desires and uncertain longings not controlled by reason. Aristotle, in his metaphysics, said that the formal cause, the essence of a thing, is, in its process of becoming and growth, its final cause also. This means, applied to man, that the final cause is the most perfect expression of his nature or essence and that it thus becomes for the will the last aim, the highest good, giving happiness.

Now it is the exercise of the rational, intellectual activity of the soul that is the real core of man's essence. Man as a moral subject achieving this intellectual life reaches his highest aim and becomes happy; the activity of the sensual and vegetative part of his nature cannot give happiness. The isolated man cannot live an intellectual life, because the satisfaction of the wants of his sensual and vegetative life would wholly occupy all of him. A favorable surrounding. economically an order of organized cooperation, must be created to afford man the intellectual life. Neither the individual nor the family and the neighborhood (village) can provide that order; only the self-sufficient "city," embracing all necessary social, moral, and economic functions, can do that. It is the perfect society. The idea of man is fulfilled in the citizen, and he who is not a citizen is either an animal or a demigod. This Aristotelian alternative is valid for all time for the political being, and not only for the social animal; restricting it to the latter is to a certain extent a mutilation of the Aristotelian concept.

Consequently it is the object of the political order to help the citizen to become virtuous and thus able to lead the intellectual life, and so to enable the individual to reach happiness. Hence the "city" becomes the great pedagogue. The citizen does not belong so much to himself as to the state. His specific life is the public life; the private life is essentially inferior. The state, the public life, the order of the common good, is the highest and sovereign form of morality because it makes the intellectual life of the citizen possible.

This theory gives rise to a certain ethical socialism, for which Aristotle has been justly criticized. For Aristotle does not fully appreciate the human person and its subjective, inborn rights antecedent to the state. For him the end of the state and the end of man coincide almost wholly. The Sophists were the first defenders of human rights, but spoiled their theory by too much individualistic utilitarianism and even by a strong materialist strain that was as repulsive to the more democratic Aristotle as to the aristocratic Plato.

In the main trends of Aristotle's political thinking, only a few features are conditioned by specifically Greek social and economic conditions. The Greeks since Heraclitus have shown a remarkable tendency for the universal human feature, for the *koinos,* the universal as against the *idios,* the particular, the tribal features. True, Aristotle is an intellectualist; he may overstress the contemplative life. Thus in Aristotle's sociology the philosopher with his contemplative thinking is the highest form of human existence, just as Plato would give the monopoly of politics to the wise men: the ideal state is where the philosophers, not the sophists or the businessmen or the demagogic orators, are the leaders. But this sociological figure of the philosopher, who holds business and handicraft in contempt, is correlated to a society that rests upon the institutions of slavery—a natural institution for Aristotle—and upon the contempt of manual labor so characteristic of the ancient world that it needed the Carpenter's Son to reform the social pattern of society. Similarly the idea of the absolute self-sufficiency of the state and the state-socialism that follows from this idea is typical of a pre-Christian world and could therefore not be received by Christianity. It is of immense importance that the leading type of Greece is the thinker, the philosopher who remains secular, while in the Christian era the saint becomes the leading type and with him that supernatural world and aim to which he is correlated. For Aristotle there existed no problem of religion and state, which, by the way, is a genuine problem only if we mean revealed religion and not indifferent religious sentiment. It was Socrates and his death for his conscience, transcending the "city," that always attracted the early Fathers of the Church and that led a modern writer to make the statement that Socrates is a witness for Christ: Socrates the just, not Socrates the philosopher.

Yet the important concepts of the essentially social and political character of man, the distinction between imperfect and perfect society, the idea of a teleological social process, the idea of the common good as more than the mere sum of the particular goods of the individuals, the self-value of the political order in relation to the perfection of the idea of man—these ideas could be adapted if the prerogatives of the supernatural order and of the other world were established.

Another pre-Christian political philosophy, that of the Stoic school, was of some influence, especially upon the early Church Fathers, who came to know Stoic as well as Greek political philosophy through the popular writings of the orator Cicero. This great eclectic writer imitated Plato in his book about the Republic, the Stoics in the "Laws," and Aristotle in the fragmentary *Dialogue of the State*. Thus for the first Christian centuries he became the mediary of the political philosophy of the past. The importance of the Stoics lies in the fact that several of their fundamental concepts could be easily filled with Christian ideas. The leading principle, for instance, of Stoic philosophy is life according to reason, which is virtuous life. Conformity with the eternal cosmic law, with the cosmic universal logos, beyond tribal limitations and national particularities, that is the essence of virtue. Their ideal of the ascetic wise man who in his *ataraxia* remains quiet and undisturbed by worldly ambitions and sensual unrests, though this ideal is subjected to the temptation of a pagan haughtiness, afforded the Church Fathers an idea that, by Christian interpretation, could serve them as an argument against the omnipotence of the pagan state of the Roman Caesars.

VIII. The Main Problems of a Catholic Political Philosophy

In the same measure as Christianity began its ceaseless controversy with the pagan world, political philosophy had to undergo profound changes. Christianity had not to adapt itself to the world; but the world, and the political world too, had to be adapted to the immovable principles of Christianity. Yet it does not follow that each concept and every form of thinking must mean something different from what it meant before. Political life belongs to the realm of nature which is not abolished by the new order of grace, but, on the contrary, is blessed and perfected. The great changes in meaning and import lay far more in the presuppositions, in the theology, and in the moral and legal philosophy of the new spiritual power. From this viewpoint the following principles and premises emerge: first, the idea of the Christian person; then the Christian idea that not earthly happiness in intellectual life alone, but the salvation of the soul and the glory of God for and in the life beyond are the last end of man and of ethics; and thirdly, that by the side of the only perfect society, the city of men of the ancients, the Church takes her place as a perfect society, the City of God, free and beyond the power and sovereignty of the state. From now on the idea of man no longer finds its absolute fulfillment in the citizen. Man's end transcends the state. Man's end is in the other world; the state's end is in this world. The state ceases to be the omnipotent, absolute pedagogue of man; it and its end become a relative value, a subordinated end in the new hierarchy of ends and values. The individual person is no longer bound to the state as to the exclusive teacher of ethics and happiness. What before was an absolute ethics established by civil law, is now put under the direction of the superior morality of love of God and neighbor. For all, Greeks and barbarians, slaves and freemen, are equal before God.

The state is not the only master of moral life. The contention that it is this sole master, is the only logical reason for the omnipotence of the state advanced from early times to the days of the Hegelian apologists of totalitarianism. Above the state lives and rules the realm of the eternal revealed verities and values. In so far as these are not regarded as invisible, lacking form, but find their adequate visible form in the Church as the visible organized community of the faithful, with doctrine and dogmas, with hierarchy and sacraments, another great theme of political philosophy is born in the Christian era.

This new sequence of themes dominates the history of the Christian era. These themes reappear in every generation, mark the climactic crises in universal history, and lie as the real issue today at the bottom of the struggle against totalitarianism. These themes are: the perpetual struggle of the individual Christian person against the ever-present abuse of power by those that rule, ranging from the trial of Socrates to the trials of Father Meyer or Pastor Niemöller or the martyrdom of so many who suffer and die without due process of law in the concentration camps; the theme of the justification of the state and its sovereign power to rule not beyond the order of law but as a servant of and in the order of law; a theme expressed in many forms, such as might and right, sovereignty and natural law, ethics and politics, political science and moral philosophy, the theme of Church and state, theology and politics, religious freedom and government, or whatever the historical aspects of that theme may be called.

Out of the treatment and discussion of these themes, out of the practical attempts to put into political reality the ideals that are involved in these themes and the ever-continuing discussions and evaluations of these attempts for historical realizations, Christian political philosophy evolves with increasing richness. With the realization of the theories that followed in the wake of the Reformation and in the growth of secularism, this political philosophy becomes "Catholic," this term designating the home and shelter where it grows.

It is in continuous controversy with the historical powers, and is developing in these controversies, but is never a mere empty echo of these powers; diverse in the solution of concrete problems, elastic in the treatment of the pressing questions in the changing historical surroundings, it is, however, never a suitable apologist for opportunist "power-politics" or the mute result of historical influences. At various times it develops and accentuates its diverse elements, with the historical situation as the principle of problem-selection. But it never releases these out of the systematic unity, and is therefore the image of the unity of its mother, the *philosophia perennis*.

PART I

PHILOSOPHICAL FOUNDATIONS

CHAPTER I

Social Being

I. THE REALITY OF SOCIAL BEING

BEFORE we arrive at the presentation of political philosophy, we must discuss the meaning of social being and the relations between social and political philosophy, political ethics, political science and the art of politics.

Even before we take up these questions, we have to clarify the following: A political philosophy has as its subject matter the essence and nature of the state, the political community, of its end, of its scope, of its properties. We are concerned with the state. But can the state be the subject matter when so many contend that there is nothing like the state, that in reality only individual persons can be observed? Is the word "state" as all nominalistic philosophies contend, only a conventional term of human language without a foundation in reality, a breath, *flatus vocis*, as Occam called the words by which we designate the universal concept? And is a philosophy of the state that by definition deals with universal notions and principles merely empty metaphysics? Or is there really not merely an amorphous conglomeration of individuals but a specific form of living together which, though it never exists apart from the individuals, is more than their mere arithmetical sum, is in fact an intelligible form that we can grasp by our abstract thinking? Thus the real problem becomes the following: To what extent is the form of community, of political community, of the state therefore, a reality? Is there such a form distinguishable from the mere sum of the individuals as its component parts, something beside them or even above them; a form, independent of an individual's subjective view, an objective reality and not merely a convenient product of the mind?

Catholic political philosophy asserts the reality of the state as a social form. The state is not a mere abstraction; it is not an abstraction of the legal order, a system of norms observed by individuals *hic et nunc*. However important these norms may be, they are never the state, the community. Against Kelsen's doctrine that makes the state a system of norms, one may rightly object that thus it formulates a philosophy of the state without the state. The state is a system of norms; but a system of norms presupposes a real authority issuing the norms, and persons who do in reality acknowledge and obey them; only by this real obedience, freely given or forcibly imposed, does the community exist. Thus "norm" presupposes *in abstracto* authority issuing orders and expecting conformity from free rational beings; "norm" presupposes someone addressed, and acceptance or consent and effective obedience to those orders by the individual persons. We may, therefore, say that community is not beside or above the individual persons, but in them all together. Therefore he who gravely disobeys the norms is "excommunicated," outlawed. These words have a sense only if we accept the view that the community is in the individuals, grasping them, organizing and integrating them into a whole which, though not existing separate from the individual members, is distinguishable, as a particular mode of coexistence, from the mere arithmetical sum of the individuals.

Scholasticism has used its fundamental principle of form and matter to describe the social forms, the community in general. Here the individuals as a mere multitude are an amorphous aggregation constituting the matter element. The form element is the specific bond, the order among persons which is characterized by its intentional object, the common end or the common good as *causa finalis*, not only as *causa formalis*. That the common end or purpose characterizes objectively, or subjectively at least, all forms of communal being or social existence and is as the value intended consciously, willingly or under an irrational urge by the members, is nowhere doubted. St. Thomas and Hobbes, Spencer and Marx, all agree upon this. The difference in the theories of these scholars lies in the following. For St. Thomas the end, at least for the so-called natural communities, such as the state, is objectively given in man's nature and in the order of the universe; furthermore, the end is consciously willed after rational recognition. For others like Spencer, the end is itself irrational, the aim of an irrational social urge. For Marx the end is always material, even if spiritualized by ideologies. For St. Thomas the end is the perfection of human nature, a spiritual and a material end. For Hobbes in his pessimism it is simply preservation of oneself from violent death. For St. Thomas the end is rationally recognized and is then a moral task for free persons. For Hobbes or for Spencer the end is irrational, and man is driven to it by unconscious social urge; the end is morally indifferent and beyond ethical categories. For St. Thomas the end is objective though realized by the subjective actions of individual persons; for others it is simply the psychological result of subjective actions and is ethically indifferent. The Thomistic approach is rational, moral, and objective; the opposing approach is irrational, causal, and subjective. But all agree that the end characterizes the communal forms, that the *telos* is the formative element, though many deny the logic in the end and thus deny the teleology, moral and objective, of the social forms.

II. THE END AS THE FORMAL ELEMENT OF SOCIAL BEING

Thus it is the specific end realized by common actions organized by a particular bond that gives us the criteria for distinguishing species and classes of communities, while the actual persons united by the specific bonds and ends are unessential for these distinctions. A state is formed by Frenchmen and Spaniards, by black people and Semites, by pagans and by Christians, in primitive cultures and in high civilizations; myths even speak of the Amazon state.

Furthermore, the state is not merely the result of a classification that we form by generalizations, without reaching by our scientific observation to the perception of its essence and nature. The essence of the state—and that is what we mean when we speak of the state—is not absolutely dependent on the empirical actuality of a state. True, we form the idea of the state by our abstractive thinking from empirical observations because the idea is visible for us only in the real bond and the persons united here and now. Therefore, when we subsume an empirically perceived community under the universal idea "state," we do so because we have the idea, the *forma* of the state; through all individualizations by history, anthropology, geography, etc., we perceive that what makes individual communities participate in the essence of the state, is the universal nature, the *forma*.

Political philosophy now has to deal with that essence, the *forma;* and as the *forma* is also final cause, where the *forma* is the object of human acts, political philosophy can never do otherwise than become political ethics. The idea becomes necessarily the ideal of human living together and it gives the critical norm and measure for these empirical acts realizing the state, in measuring them by the ideal. Political philosophy deals necessarily with the problem of what the concrete state ought to be. The state's end is a value, a moral good, and ultimately, an objective good, independent of the arbitrary will; it is the objective standard for our judgment measuring the observed facts. All our laboring for a true, necessary, unchangeable, stable knowledge would be a vain effort if, regardless of the changing phenomena that our senses experience, there did not exist something unchangeable, a lasting structure of being, of form, that our spiritual eye, our intellect, sees as intelligible form and essence, as metaphysically the idea, logically the concept; this idea is the proper content of the act of knowledge. And it is this idea that is the basis for our distinctions and our comparisons, our assents, our assertions, and our negations; in short, for our judgments. Against the skepticism of the Sophists who were disrupting the cosmos making not man but each individual man's mind the measure of all things, Socrates pointed out that this intelligible element in the things re-presented by the concepts of the mind, is the true and necessary basis of scientific knowledge.

III. Social Being, Not of a Substantial Character

Individual persons intending a common end and organizing themselves to realize it by a particular bond with a division of functions and acting thus as free moral agents, constitute a social form. What specific form of being have these social forms? The organicist theory and poetry make, for instance, the nations or the states substances, the poets make them personal substances, the organicist theory biological substances. Then the individual persons, in reality the only true substances, become mere members or cells without independent existence; they lose their individual personality, which is totally immersed in their being mere particles of that personified substance, the social organism. But if we apply the metaphysical terms "substantial being" and "accidental being," there is little doubt that only the individual persons are substantial beings, so that metaphysically the social forms should belong to the category of accidental being. But this does not help us very much because we think that the social form belongs to the personal sphere. The assertion that social or communal being is accidental being fits also the herd of animals and thus gives us not much additional knowledge. We shall have to derive the nature of social existence from the personal being, i.e., rational, free, active, individual substances. The specific being, the mode of being that we can ascribe to the state, is thus not that of substantial being. Neither the state nor the nation nor the Church is of the mode of substantial being so that there exists, over the substantial beings who form these communities, namely, the individual persons as such and as members, a separate substantial being, which may be even of spiritual substance. Such a hypostasis is not justified and is never proposed by the organic view of the state as it is familiar in Catholic political philosophy.

We can deduce this by considering the consequence of such a substantialization of social being, e.g., of the nation, as it is represented by one of the leading political philosophers of National Socialism.[1] Huber has the individual person so wholly determined by racial factors, by historical destiny, and other objective factors, that the individual person becomes wholly submerged as a mere cell of the organism of the nation, as a mere biological transmitter of the blood, a transitory and, in itself and for itself, valueless particle of that organism. Hence terms that stem from personal individual life, such terms as "conscience," "free will," "reason," and that only in a metaphorical, analogous sense, can be predicated of the nation, are denied by Huber to the individual person and reserved exclusively to that substantialized being, the nation. The national will ceases to be a term designating the common *intentio* of the many acts of individual persons uniting in consent for the common good with such methods as public discussion, appeals to reason, to the consciences of individuals. The national will, the collective conscience of the nation, becomes the "Leader"; not that the "Leader" is a representative, an agent, or organ of the nation. On the contrary the Leader is the nation; his conscience and his will do not stand for the nation; they are actually the conscience of the nation. The consequence is that no appeal is possible to a supreme moral law,

[1] Ernst R. Huber, *Verfassungsrecht des grossdeutschen Reiches* (Hamburg, 1939).

to the rule of conscience, to natural law. The nation, consisting of wholly determined cells, is substantialized and, in a mysterious way, materializes its will and conscience in the "Leader." Hence the "Leader" is a law unto himself. This, then, is the reason in Nazism for that outspoken political irrationalism and for that radical political opportunism, for which neither international law nor individual in-alienable rights exist, neither a supreme natural law valid for all men nor a moral law valid in politics. Any appeal to moral and spiritual values transcending the nation becomes treason. For such a view man-kind and history are a battlefield where, in a lawless state of warfare, mythical substantialized monsters, determined by irrational powers of race (blind biological forces), fight a senseless battle for conquest, the meaning of which is forever closed to the reason and consciences of the individual persons.

When we speak of the spirit or the mind of a nation, we do not mean a spiritual substantial being that expresses itself in the organized multitude, the nation. Even the *Weltgeist* ("world mind") of Hegel, that in historical development presumably expresses itself in the leading nation, cannot be considered such a substantial being. If it were so, then that could only mean a deification of these nations. It is equally wrong to speak of a world reason as a substantial being, of which the individual personal substances are only parts, as the Ara-bian philosophy taught. Nor does there exist as a substance an enig-matic mysterious power—nature or "life"—interpreted as personal or impersonal, of which the social communities are forms of appearance or modes of material self-realization. All these attempts to attribute to the communities, to the forms of social being, the character of sub-stantial being, lead to the devaluation of the individual person, to its instrumentalization by a supra-individual substance and hence to the destruction of individual free will and individual responsibility, to the utter demoralization of social life. It necessarily leads to the deification of that substantial being, the nation, the state, the *Weltgeist* ("world spirit").

IV. *Esse Intentionale* AS THE FORMAL BEING OF COMMUNITIES

What, then, is the specific mode of being that we may ascribe to the communities? Gundlach proposes the term "intentional being" (*esse intentionale*).[2] This is the formal being of all communities. By it all communities, all forms of social existence, are founded in the teleological order of the created universe so far as any community is formally destined for and intends the realization of a specific good which demands the solidarist cooperation of a multitude of persons and consequently is a common good.[3] We have thus to consider the order of being and the teleological order, the order of ends. In the order of being, the individual persons as the only substantial rational beings are first. In the order of ends, the community is before the individual; for, as the end of the community is necessary for the perfection of all members of the community, the end of the community is superior in the same rank of goodness: the earthly common good is superior to the earthly good of the individual person, but not to its eternal good. Thus by the term *esse intentionale* is best expressed the objective end and value of the content of every community and the lasting process of integration of individuals into the community as according with the end and as measured by it. We should remark that this is possible only as long as in reality the end of the community participates in the supreme divinely instituted teleological order in the universe. Therefore the end of the community in reality has the character of service to the only substantial beings, the persons, and for their perfection. Thus the persons are intentionally directed by their own nature and end to the community as a whole, but so that the community gets its own value actually from being linked to the perfection of the persons.[4]

Any community, especially the state, stands face to face with the

[2] G. Gundlach, *Soziologie der Katholischen Ideenwelt und des Jesuiten Ordens*, 1927. Cf. the same author in *Gregorianum*. Vol. XVII (1936), article "Solidarismus, Einzelmensch, Gemeinschaft." It seems that this term would fit also Hauriou's definition of society, which he describes as a tissue of which the woof is formed by the subjective wills and the warp by objective ideas: "It (society) surpasses human psychology inasmuch as it prolongs itself partly into the world of ideas which is external to the human person though the latter is in connection with this world through the categories of reason. Erich Kaufmann, in his *Règles générals du droit de la paix* (Paris, 1936), p. 170, quotes this remark of Hauriou and points out that Hegel in his *Philosophy of History* uses the same comparison. Kaufmann himself adheres to the teleological view very decidedly (*op. cit.*, pp. 168 ff.). Both jurists stress the two elements which Gundlach means by *esse intentionale*, first the objective ideas which as the ends to be realized by the community are intended, and the intentional acts of persons, the subjective wills.

[3] St. Augustine's definition of community: *populus est coetus multitudinis rationalis, rerum quae diligit concordi communione sociatus.*

[4] Cf. Gundlach, *Gregorianum*, XVII, p. 289.

perpetual question, *quid hoc ad hominem*. Therefore the justification of the state and of its power and authority which enforces the order is an unavoidable object of political philosophy. That explains why all biological theories, all non-moral positivist theories, are so unsatisfactory. They deny the teleological order, the order of values and ends, which is the deepest and most important foundation of any community because in the realization of these ends and values the human person perfects its very nature. However community may be demanded by individuality and its shortcomings, community belongs to the personal sphere; it receives its consecration by its service to the perfection of the persons. All successes of the social and economic civilization of our age are nothing if they do not contribute to personal perfection. Of what help is it humanly if the material standards of living are raised, but if personal internal happiness by virtuous life, by life unto God as the last end, is submerged in extrovert material life? It may be noted that here is the foundation of the principle that the spiritual is superior to the temporal because, in the order of ends, for the human person the spiritual is superior to the temporal as it is by far nearer to God. Thus the order of the objective ends, presented to reflective thinking by the intellect as a consequence of the order of being, is the basis for the hierarchy of communities. From this it would follow that any of the so-called naturally essential communities, to mention only the family, cannot be replaced by an other community (e.g., by the state) and that the specific principle of authority, i.e., the authority of the father or of the parents, must never be destroyed in favor of the state's authority. How true this is may be seen from the simple fact that the use of power given for the furtherance of the common good to private advantage is commonly considered a treason to the idea of the community. The internal principle, the form, of any community is thus its natural end because the end gives the unity to the amorphous multitude. The end is the common object of the individual wills and assents; it is the principle of unity and the object of cooperative social activity.

This emphasis upon the end of the common good, a good which is common to all personal members and is normally realized by their solidary cooperation and for their individual good life, is a fundamental feature of our social philosophy. The latter's criticism of divorce, of birth control, and of totalitarianism rests upon its view of the ends of the various communities of marriage, family, state. The order of law organizing the community is ruled by the end. The purpose or end of law to be realized by the moral will of the members makes the community a moral organism. This emphasis upon the end of the community makes possible the important distinction between office and person. We demand from a person in office, in public authority, a good service to the end of the community; we are less interested in his private affairs. As long as he faithfully fulfills the public functions in his office, we are less interested in his being privately depraved. The fact that the ruler, in his private life, is a libertine, does not free the citizens from obedience and allegiance as long as the ruler fulfills his public functions, his service to the common good, the end of the community.

What do we mean when we speak of "destroying a community"? This can be done by the physical extinction of all its members as the substantial elements on which the existence of the community is totally dependent. But the usual case of the destruction of a community is the destruction of its specific moral and legal bond, of its moral order which binds the individuals in their interdependent coexistence and organizes them for the independent free realization of their specific common good. Thus a state can be destroyed by force (*debellatio* in the sense of international law), and still the individual persons who formed that state continue in their substantial existence under a new form of political community or by being incorporated in another state. Nothing then has practically changed in the substantial existence; the towns and villages, the court buildings and other buildings that housed the governors and administrative officers with their files and cabinets, are still substantially identical. But what has changed, what has ceased to be, is the specific moral and legal bond, that specific moral allegiance among the members, their obligation to their *status politicus,* in other words, their political existence, their *forma* of this existence, leaving now only the subpolitical communities, the families, the neighborhoods, the factories (as social or economic forms of cooperation), the towns. But the specific form of political existence is destroyed; the multitude remains in the substantial identity of the individual persons, but the *unitas ordinis politici* is gone; they can no longer realize their common good in free self-determination. It is of utmost significance that the conqueror, to express this destruction of a real though invisible form of being, represented in symbols, marks his conquest by the destruction of the symbols of this political existence. And it is furthermore significant that the destruction is definite only after the members of the conquered community have, as the result of persuasion, of compulsion, or of propaganda, openly or at least tacitly transferred their moral allegiance—the legal constitutional order was of course at once destroyed—to the new political order of the conqueror.

V. "Social Relatons" Theory as Explanation of the Nature of Communities

The formal nature of social being is therefore not well enough defined if we simply call it interpersonal or interindividual relations. It is that, of course; but its very essence is what it is over and above that. If social being is not more than is implied in the term "relations," then it would only be a nominalist definition of psychological acts of identical character in the individuals, and the classification of social relations would be made from the intensity of these relations or their specific character of love, sympathy, or interestedness. Social being would be merely a nominalist classification of individual acts and interests on account of an identity of the psychological acts (individualistic interpretation). But the true social being, its form, can be grasped only if we take into consideration the intentional character of these psychological acts and their meaning, if we look for a true common aim or end of these acts. In other words, the forms of social being are determined by their objective ends, by their idea, by what the individuals with their acts intend, by the unifying purpose of their individual relations. That points to an end transcendent to the individual. It is the end that defines the community, not so much the specific social acts inasmuch as they are the same in all the related persons. The act of love may intend my family or my country. What then defines my duties in a conflict of love for my family and love for my country? The degree of intensity of my love to the two communities? There is no doubt that the intensity of love for my family is greater. Still there is likewise no doubt that in such a conflict I have to prefer my country, as every soldier in wartime proves. The answer to this problem is to be taken from the superiority of the common good of the state over the family and its end, however much ordinarily both ends coincide. So it is the end that is decisive and not the quality of the social acts as such or the relations between individuals produced by an identity of the acts in various individual persons.

It is the common end that distinguishes and forms the relations between individuals, the end which is transcendent to the individuals, though it can indeed never be realized without the acts of the individuals. Thus these individual relations establishing social forms of living together for something common, the communities, become more than individual by the intentional direction to the common object, by their finality to the common value. This object, this value, this directive finality of the acts of the individuals to the objective end, give the actual community its form. The acts between individuals as merely psychological data do not do so. The common good in its specific character, the end, is the form-giving element; the social relations are the means. That is the reason why all constitutional documents providing the legal organization of a community have as their first and most important part a declaration of the objective end which is intended to be realized by the establishment of the new order. And it is only a sign of the utter positivist relativism rampant in the last decades, when constitutional lawyers impute no value to this declaration of the end, but consider it a rhetorical ornament. The true view is, of course, that the whole constitution and each of its articles must be interpreted from the meaning of this solemn constitutional declaration of the end of the state. We should never forget that the law, the legal order, has essentially an end in view. What we mean by "the will of the lawgiver," is not the psychological act, but the end he has in mind.

Thus social being is intentional in its form, directed to an objective end beyond individual ends. And it is the end that rules and is the measure, not the subjective will. Of course the psychological acts and acts between individuals are necessary for the realization of the end *in concreto*.

Since it is the end that constitutes social being and differentiates essentially the various communities, we must, to be accurate, limit social being to rational beings, to persons. The individuality in abstraction from personality may, in its limitations, imperfections, and so on, be a powerful motive for living together; but the conscious will to live together in order to realize an end beyond individual ends, presupposes personality. We are conscious of this fact when we call the mob a headless herd, when we assert that the totalitarian beehive-state or slave-state contradicts the "dignity of the human person." [5] All this indicates that the forms of social being, especially the state, are necessary not on account of mere biological urges and instincts that we have in common with irrational animals, but in order to perfect our personal life, our human nature, not only our biological nature. If the latter were the exclusive basis, this would lead necessarily to depersonalization and would destroy human dignity. Only if social being is a form of living together of persons, can the end of the community be effected without the sacrifice of personal values. Only then is possible this coincidence of common good and private good of the individual person, the double character of all social being, namely, that it is above the individual, is common, objective, and still justified only by serving persons. Only so can we understand the idea of subjective rights, of inalienable rights of the person against the state, which *in concreto* is always the government. They arise from the service character of all forms of social being, but can find their actual content and active life only in the order of social being, for the forms of social being exist for the sake of persons. Hence we must regard this personal individual and this social being always as one and never in artificial abstraction, always as ordinated one to the other, never as absolutely separated forms of human existence. We shall later see why Catholic political philosophy had to uphold the free human will in the question of the origin of the state and in the formation of political authority, and we shall see why the very heart of its theory is the common good. We shall see why it accepted a form of social contract, however much it denied the utilitarian individualism of the natural-law doctrine of the Enlightenment and the unrestricted subjectivism of Rousseau.

VI. The Meaning of Political Symbols

To say that social being is materially invisible while only the individuals are visible, must not lead us to that positivist denial of social

---

[5] According to St. Thomas, this dignity rests on the fact that man is gifted with intellect, that he is *intellectualis substantia* and thus made after the image of God. *De potentia*, q. 11, a. 5 c.

being as a reality. Social being in its various forms is rendered visible
in symbols, in public acts, in outward signs; the flag, the throne, the
tiara, the national anthem, the uniforms and attire of public officers
in pageants and solemn gatherings, the statues, even the popular figures of Uncle Sam or John Bull. And it becomes visible, too, in those
public buildings, like capitols and memorials, the function of which
is not to house the lawmakers or to shelter precious memories but to
represent the community for which the memorials have a meaning,
a moral and spiritual content. They are the projections into visible
reality of the moral bond, of the inner allegiance of the consciences to
the common good. They represent in a particular form the durability
of the community and of its end over and above the transitory existence of the individuals.

The individuals die, the community and its representations and
symbols endure through history. History is not an accumulation of
data about individuals, but a record of the life and destiny of human
communities, their ideas, and their political existence, of the persons'
inner religious, cultural, and economic living and working together.
The biography of an individual is always also a record of the communities in which he lived. The faith in these symbols, however much
it may succumb to nationalist superstitions, is the best sign of the
vividness and power of the represented community, as is the eagerness
with which the symbols are venerated. The impious criticism and the
snobbish derision of these symbols or the attempts by parties to turn
party symbols into symbols of the whole, are sure signs of the progres-
sing disintegration of that invisible *unitas ordinis* which constitutes
the community. When the community, the actual form of social being,
ceases to exist, then these symbols that stand for it have lost their
meaning and become relics of bygone times, of interest only for the
historian. We can now understand why man takes these symbols so
seriously in social life. What is important is of course not the symbol
in its material form, the flag, which is materially merely a multicol-
ored piece of cloth. What is important is that for which it stands, the
unitas ordinis of a people, its political unity and freedom, its national
way of life, its dignity and majesty, its being an exaltation of life of
the individual person.

VII. Personality as the Foundation of Social Being

We have said that all human community is in the first place *unitas ordinis* between persons; that it is not only the limitation, the narrowness of individuality that calls for life in community, but even more the will, the urge of the person to let others participate and to participate in others' personal value and that by this is produced an exaltation of life in community. We may now add that the act of love is the most constitutive one for community life as Aristotle seems to point out in his *philia* theory. The act of love as the constitutive element, as important as justice, may have different forms, such as sexual love (marriage), comradeship and friendship, solidarist brotherhood, *pietas*, merciful love, and the various forms of sympathetic interest as the least intensive form of *philia*, or love in the most general sense. This means, of course, not a cognitionally blind love. It includes the intellectual cognition of the singular being that the other person is and consequently the singular personal value; it includes, too, the cognition of the common, ultimate end and the intermediate ends that give actual communities their objective classification. We have to stress love because the rational cognition cannot come to a full grasp of the individual person. Thus it seems that it is more the acts of *philia* that open to one person the inner values of another person, its very singularity, however much these values are themselves again representations of the objective values in the order of being.

These considerations lead us again to note the personal point of view. If we do not take account of this view, there is a danger that the material element will become too important, that biological, racial, economic, and geographical definitions will have an exaggerated importance.

Undoubtedly the individual being is immersed in these determinative factors. And they are powerful factors so far as they narrow down the sphere of freedom. It is significant that the word "nation" comes from *nasci* in a biological or even racial sense. It is significant that, with the wane of Christendom, with the overpowering of the Christian man by the *national* man, truth has been sacrificed too much to the relativism of the ideologies. Here the intellectual process is made a superstructure, a mirror of my racial, national, economic, social determination. The universal man, the personality, that is the image of God, is so immersed in these material determinations, that the most important communities, mankind and the Church Universal, either have disappeared or seem to be on the way to disappear at least as conscious genuine communities. These above-mentioned determinative factors are community-building factors, yet they are not supreme; they are transcended by personality, by which they are made relative, and thus they become servants to the person.

VIII. Nature and Scope of Political Philosophy

Human community is not a mere fact, the result of a blind natural urge, like the beehive or the anthill which are called allegorically animal states. Human community, and thus the state, exists by continuous human acts. Therefore a political philosophy is not and cannot be merely a study of the order of being in social life. The order of being in social life as a life that is active, practical life, as opposed to contemplative life, becomes necessarily for concrete rational free beings, the order of ends to be realized *hic et nunc*. The nature of a being is also its end to the practical reason and therefore the critical standard and exemplary norm for the will. Moral philosophy is but a prolongation of metaphysics. Political philosophy, whose object is the study of political life and its forms as being, has to work out the ends of these forms, and is necessarily a part of moral philosophy, and thus rests on the same basis, metaphysics. The modern but now dubious objection, that political philosophy has nothing to do with what "ought to be," [6] is evidence of a complete lack of philosophy in its true meaning, in particular of a wrong idea of science. According to this idea, the scientific approach imitating the principles of mathematics and natural sciences is merely of positive character, has as its only justified methods the inductive and comparative study of facts— facts being what various thinkers have thought and what statistics and laws and decisions of courts show. On the ground of such studies, all that is possible is certain more or less accurate generalizations and perhaps the working out of general types of social relations and atti-

---

[6] Cf. Edward H. Carr, *The Twenty Years Crisis*, 1940. According to Carr, political science has to deal with what "ought to be." Cf. also further A. Macfie, *An Essay on Economy and Value* (London, 1936). Macfie stresses the necessity of normative economics and especially of social ethics for a curriculum of economics (pp. 80, 85).

tudes. However, these are not norms for action or standards of value judgments, but merely an economizing cipher for the multitude of single facts to be classified, like the plants in Linnaeus' system. Of course this ascetic resignation of the fact-hunters accumulating a vast mass of facts cannot produce what makes the essence of a political philosophy or even a true science, which is necessarily about universals, and not about the particulars in their singleness, in their transitoriness.[7]

This modern idea of science has produced almost as many "systems" of science as there are professors in the field, but never one science. Science is thus no longer a system of necessary propositions elaborated by experience and thought, but rather an accidental collection of so-called facts, classified according to a preconceived subjectively chosen and therefore intrinsically indifferent principle of selection. No wonder that skeptical relativism sprang up. Relativism is bearable only as long as, for all relativist theories, there exists the same freedom of teaching and propaganda. When one of the relativist theories is made the basis of a totalitarian state, man is stirred to free himself from the pessimistic resignation that characterizes these relativist theories and to return to his principles. Many gave up metaphysics because too many systems of metaphysics began to sprout in the era of rationalism. So they turned to positivism as an intellectual habit that is concerned only with facts. But this concept of fact was already the result of a philosophical assertion, namely, that facts are easily discovered and can be classified univocally. True, this turning to the manifold, concrete world is explained by the sterility of pure thinking, not guided by reality, as it marked rationalism and idealism in the eighteenth and nineteenth centuries, when at every fair some new rationalist systems of natural law and political philosophy were offered. Yet this turning to the facts without metaphysics has outdone even rationalism in its production of vague systems. At the end of this era there looms up a despair in human reason that reveals itself in the acceptance of Marxism by "bourgeois" social science. Now these relativist systems have become quite sociologically determined and thus they are simply ideological cloaks for material political and economic class interests without any title to objective disinterested truth, without any unconditional moral obligation for social and political life. It was

7 St. Thomas, *Contra Gent.*, I, 1.

not, however, the work of assembling facts that was wrong, but the denial that in moral and social nature there exists an immanent order, an intrinsic finality of an objective normative character.

Against this we maintain that man, through his intellect, has access to truth, and that truth is the norm and critical measure for human acts in political life. We hold, therefore, that political philosophy and even political science must deal with what "ought to be" as the basis for politics, which is a system of human acts to realize by good or bad means a good or bad end. Moreover, man does not possess two separate reasons, one the theoretical, the other the practical. He has only one reason with two powers, theoretical and practical. Especially in political philosophy there is no mere *res cogitans*. There is, rather, man who thinks, selects, judges, decides, acts. No political philosophy and even no political science can be morally neutral or indifferent. Even the opposite contention is an assertion implicity including a moral judgment.

Political philosophy is not thinking in a vacuum; it is not a sort of geometrical rationalist deduction of propositions from some presupposed principles or innate ideas. Like all philosophy it is reflective thinking about that which experience and the empirical sciences offer as material. It acknowledges "Her Majesty the Fact" as truly as any science does, but it upholds the principle that man must get behind the facts of social and political life and down to the causes, principles, and origins of these facts which are by themselves not univocal but the results of human deliberations, judgments, and moral decisions, realized by free acts, by a choice between right and wrong, just and unjust, and therefore a problem of morality. Thus its concept of fact is much broader than the facts of empirical sciences. The end of man, the nature of man, the objective norms for man as a political being, all are as much facts as are the forms of parliamentary rule or totalitarian dictatorship. Thus political philosophy and political science are coordinated. St. Thomas, speaking of moral science, says: "It is necessary for anyone who wishes to be an apt student of moral science that he acquire practical experience in the customs of human life and in all just and civil matters, such as laws and precepts of political life." [8] This applies literally to political philosophy as a part of moral philosophy. It is the human acts in political life that the political

8 St. Thomas, *Comm. in Eth.*, I, 4.

philosopher has to take as the material object, and we attain knowledge of them by experience. All that political science, constitutional jurisprudence, sociology, and economics, history, comparative science of law and political institutions have collected, is useful information gratefully but critically accepted by political philosophy. There need not be a conflict between political philosophy and the political and social sciences. That conflict came into existence by justified reaction of the scientific spirit of the nineteenth century against the lifeless schemes of rationalist natural law of the Enlightenment and by the unjustified positivist philosophy that crept into the social sciences. Any science, being a systematic order, needs first principles or it will produce counterfeits of them. It is a hopeful sign that the general revival of metaphysics so distinctly felt today has found a new urge through the experience with modern totalitarianism and its blatant injustices, which make impossible that positivist indifferentism toward what "ought to be."

IX. Social Philosophy and the Social Sciences

We have now established a foundation upon which to set up the architecture of the social sciences. In earlier times these were called moral sciences. For they concern human free acts and their rational ends. Any social institution is generated and is kept alive by human acts and by human will which intend the ends or purposes of these social forms. Consequently the acts, the intentions, the ends, are open to moral judgments and not merely to morally indifferent judgments of instrumental or pragmatic fitness or the like.

The foundation of the architecture of the social sciences is social metaphysics.[9] This deals with the nature, forms, and properties of social being in the most general way. The meaning of individuality and sociality or of individual and society, the meaning of the adage *Ubi societas, ibi jus,* the nature and structure of the social acts, i.e., such human acts as are intrinsically ordinated to a thou or a we, acts

---

[9] The term has come into use lately. Cf. E. K. Winter, *Die Socialmetaphysik der Scholastik* (Vienna, 1929); Gundlach, *op. cit.* This does not exclude the fact that the matter itself has long been known under other names. Very often it appears under the name of moral philosophy or of that part of it which treats of man as a social being; it appears also under the name of "natural law."

that receive a fulfillment of their intentional nature only by an answer from another person, all such problems belong to this first science. Furthermore, the meaning of the order of authority, the distinction of human societies in hierarchic and consociate ones, are questions belonging to this science. As metaphysics is the foundation and crown of all sciences, so this social metaphysics is the foundation and crown of all social sciences. There is no social scientist who has not, either consciously and openly or subconsciously and uncritically, some form of social metaphysics at the basis of his systematic scientific effort. Before any social scientist begins to work he certainly has either uncritically or critically made some decisions about the most general questions, as, for instance, what the nature of social being is, whether there are objective ends for social forms, about the intentional character of social acts, etc. He must have an idea, however vague and blurred in contour, of the social nature of man, before he can adequately deal with the nature of the state. It is not necessary that he should first have this idea perfectly clear and distinct, because in studying the particular historical forms in which the idea of the state is expressed, in the multitude of individualizations and their study the universal idea itself becomes clearer. St. Thomas points out that the science which deals with the ultimate causes, i.e., metaphysics, comes last to man in the order of cognition. Thus it is that the foundation is first somewhat invisible and becomes visible only in the process of studying the actual social forms and institutions in which we live, into which we are born, and without which our individual life would become an impossibility. What Cicero says of art, that theory follows the works of art and not the works the theory, applies to all sciences and thus also to social metaphysics which is of direct concern to man's life in society. Before the philosopher of law comes the lawgiver, wise or unwise. Before the philosopher deals critically with the idea of the state, men live in states under statesmen; before moral philosophy rationally and critically establishes the principles of what is right and wrong, man lives, acts, and judges according to practical rules about virtues and vices. After all, man is by nature a moral and social being, and thus his life, his acts, his judgments according to some evident intellectual and moral principles innate in his very nature, that dowry of the divine Creator, are the primary facts, the "matter" of the reflective mind and of critical philosophical endeavor.

The next step of the reflective mind is an attempt to construct a philosophy of such social forms as are of the greatest import to the individual person. It may be interesting and at the same time quite indifferent to me to know what form of marriage contract tribes adhered to thousands of years ago. But it is of the utmost importance for me to know what elements, intellectual, moral, and economic, contribute to the dissolution of family ties today. Similarly I may be little concerned with the organization of street-corner gangs in city slums but deeply concerned with the form of government, the degree of civil liberty, the honesty of political leaders. These things, by their effect upon the perpetual form of the state and its immense power apparatus, directly concern my individual life. Thus, after reflective thinking and critical observation of the immediate facts of political life, arises the endeavor to construct a philosophy of the state, of the family, of political economy, of law. Yet it seems clear that these philosophies are not in a rationalist method deduced from some innate ideas, but that the reflective mind, after more or less comprehensive experience and after enough critical contemplation of the facts of political life, abstracts and clarifies the idea which more or less potently influences men when they practically make politics. Thus the critical reflective mind of the political philosopher starts with the facts and with some fundamental concepts that are traditionally inherited or that spring from a precritical understanding of the idea and the end that shines through the imperfect realizations and appears also by reflective meditation about man's being a political animal.

Thus it follows that political philosophy, as a part of social philosophy, and the political sciences like political history, constitutional theory, international relations, political economy and geography, law and what may be called political sociology, political psychology, and the like, are coordinated to one another. Every political scientist is, perhaps without realizing it, a political philosopher. Every political philosopher must use critically, weigh, and study the material which the political sciences collect, describe, and classify. The colorful political reality as in innumerable forms it arises in the stream of history, always producing new forms out of lasting elements and yet following identical ideas, is, so to speak, the raw material for the political philosopher, and also for the political scientist who first collects, organizes, and critically classifies this multitude of observed facts. Then either for himself or in personal union with the scientist, the political philosopher does his work according to philosophical method and in consonance with moral philosophy.

The modern separation of political sciences from political and moral philosophy, and the consequent aversion to political philosophy, are recent features. So is the recent trend away from moral sciences to social sciences with the proclamation of the method of natural, causal, sciences as the supreme and only admissible method. Hence we hear the contemptuous assertion that political sciences must abstain from value judgments, an assertion rooted in moral relativism that results from a positivist philosophy. It arose as a reaction against eighteenth-century rationalism, which sinned by neglecting experience and observation, on the basis of its theory of mere deduction from innate ideas, just as positivism sins by disregard of the objective moral rules and of transcendental ideas. The one despised the reality of the facts, the other the profounder reality of the transcendental ideas and the objective moral order. The one took man as merely a deductively thinking being, the other as merely a causally reacting being.

In reality such a separation (as opposed to distinction) and such a mutual rejection are both wrong. The political scientist may confine his scientific work to mere description. His advice may be limited to something like this: If you (the statesman) wish this end, you must use this and that means, and you must consider how you are to counteract this potential but undesirable effect; about the moral issue I refer you to the judgment of your own informed conscience, to moral philosophy, and to revealed morality, which will advise you as to the moral value of your intended ends, to the fitting means to be used and to the weighting of the potential effects, good or bad in respect to the common good. After all, human societies have not, like anthills, a coherence and integration based exclusively on the causal laws of nonrational nature. On the contrary, however much man may be motivated by mere material interests causing him to act as if controlled by physical laws, in the ultimate result the statesman must appeal to the moral conscience, to the eternal moral ideas; the social or political "engineer" is only the hideous product of a materialist era. The supreme sacrifice which may be required of the individual can be demanded only by love and for eternal moral ideas but never for material interest, for a rise of the material standard of living, or for any such things as concern the social "engineer." It is not the technical organization, the devices of integration, the forms of control and subordination which constitute the difference between a band of gangsters and an army or a state. It is the moral end, it is, to use St. Augustine's famous sentence, justice which differentiates a state from a band of gangsters. Consequently the fact that a social institution works, that it has technically a high degree of social efficiency, is not a sufficient proof of its moral goodness and philosophical truth as pragmatism implies. On the contrary, the moral rules and the philosophical truth are ultimately decisive in any judgment over the technical efficiency and working of the social institutions.[10]

The trouble with positivist political science is that, in its negation of objective morality, it entirely excludes moral considerations and takes into account only the technical fitness of what it regards as morally indifferent means for morally indifferent ends. Although such mere technical advice may be suitable for the natural scientist, who deals with irrational and therefore non-moral matter, it is wrong for the political scientist to deny the validity of value judgments. For what he deals with is human acts, which are either moral or immoral and not altogether and always indifferent. In reality only a few political scientists are able to refrain from value judgments, as their zeal for political reform shows. Often their assertion that they refrain from value judgments is only a device to exclude value judgments that they do not like.

A careful scrutiny of the particular function of the political sciences and of political philosophy shows that they are coordinated, that they need each other, however much their methods and immediate or direct ends may differ. Both are concerned with man as the political being who is intrinsically also a philosophical and a moral being. And

---

[10] The "truth" of a theoretical model, i.e., a theory elaborated to grasp the existential characteristics of a concrete social institution or of an economic system, must be distinguished from philosophical and moral truth. In the first case the social scientist constructs his theory after careful observation of the facts, on certain assumptions and conclusions (e.g., that under conditions of perfect competition and on account of the lack of any social legislation or opposing social customs, the wages of workers will be below the level of a living wage). This theory can then be checked or verified. If in further study of facts the theory coincides roughly with more and more facts, we say that the theory is true, since it works, i.e., that the assumptions and conclusions agree with the facts. But it seems clear that such a theory can be true as a mere technical model of the real economic world, and yet the conditions of the real economic world can be judged unjust, as irreconcilable with the philosophical truth of man's nature, man's dignity, etc.

if in the hierarchical structure of sciences a higher place, a more important influence, is granted to political philosophy, this no more degrades political sciences than the dignity of all sciences is degraded by saying that they all are founded and culminate in metaphysics. The various truths of the particular sciences are not disconnected fragments but parts of the one intellectual and moral cosmos of truth. All the concepts formed by the secondary sciences, in our case the political sciences, point to some higher, profounder, more comprehensive concepts. The undeniable fact that political scientists and statesmen involuntarily turn to political and consequently moral philosophy, bears witness to this.

X. POLITICAL PHILOSOPHY AND POLITICS

A last word about political philosophy and politics. As we have pointed out, political philosophy as a science in the Thomistic sense has to deal with the universal concepts, the objective ends, the immanent order, and the definite finality in man's social and political life. It uses the *singularia,* the concrete historical forms, of political institutions, as the observation material and as the construction material from which it derives the immanent principle, the idea, the necessary order, and the critical norms for any concrete political order. Thus political philosophy gives only the framework of general principles in which politics, as an architectonic art guided by prudence, builds up the always changeable concrete order.

Political philosophy is, therefore, unable to give advice in a casuistic way to the political leader in a concrete situation in which he has something to do or to omit. It will provide the framework of principles and norms in which the stateman can and must make his choice of practical means and immediate purposes. He does so on his own responsibility, guided by prudence. Prudence and its species, *prudentia regnativa,* necessitate two things: the knowledge of principles of reason and the knowledge of the actual situation, the appropriate means, the experience and counsels of experts about what has to be done *hic et nunc* for the realization of the immediate purposes put before the statesman in order to fulfill the last ends of political life: order, peace, and justice. Thus political philosophy and politics as an art are coordinated to each other. Political philosophy works out the principles, the critical norms for political action, the last ends, the frame-work. It is not its task in the first place to judge about the suitability of means, their technical value, their involvements with other fields of human social and spiritual life; though its task is to point to means that are intrinsically wrong, unjust, immoral. The positive evaluation of means for an ethically positive end must remain in the first place with the political leader, and the technical criticism of such means with the political scientist.

It is science that deals with universals. Politics has to do with the present, contingent situation, with the choice of the new suitable means appropriate to the situation and the immediate ends. It is prac-tical; it has to deal with the *agibilia*. Where the statesman acts without consideration of political philosophy and the immanent ethical norms for his activity, the issue will be Machiavellian politics, ethically indif-ferent, nay immoral.

CHAPTER II

The Idea of Man

I. Theories of Man's Nature as the Foundation of Political Philosophies

EVERY political theory, especially in its treatment of the justification of legal authority and political power as against individual liberty, has as its basis a certain theory of the nature of man, even though this basic theory is seldom openly discussed.[1] Going deeper into this philosophical anthropology, which most often is not clearly stated, we may even find as its presupposition a certain theology, in its literal sense a theory of the existence and essence of God. It was this truth that led Proudhon to make his famous statement that at the basis of every political problem one will find a theological problem.

Let us first discuss the philosophical idea of the nature of man, beginning with his moral nature: Is man naturally good or evil? Is he dangerous, driven not by reason but by uncontrolled passions, and yielding to the forces of evil? We find that all political theories which incline to radical anarchism or to an eventual "withering away" of the state answer the question of the moral nature of man optimistically. They either declare that "redemption" has made human nature good, or they believe that, with a change of the bad social or political pattern, the liberated good nature will need no "state." And again we find that all political theories which praise power and unrestricted authority, violence and dictatorship, are fundamentally pessimistic. Humanity is *massa damnata*. Man left alone is evil; he must be forced to a civilized life by ruthless power and deterring violence. And because man is corrupt he is to be a mere means in the hand of the ruler who works for superhuman values. All tyrants and absolute rulers are despisers of man.

[1] Thomas Hobbes is a notable exception. His *Leviathan* duly opens with the treatise "Of Man."

The social nature of man is also important. Is the individual man fully self-sufficient? [2] Is social life a mere incident, an accidental property of human nature, so that man does not need social forms for his perfection; or are social forms so essential that man has an existence exclusively as a member of a social form? And further, has the individual person an end which in the last resort places him above society and the state; or is man completely subordinated to society and the state? If we decide that man is an image of God, then the dignity of man is preserved and the state, however its end may be superindividual and necessary, has the character of service to the individual person. Only then does the idea of inalienable rights of the human person find a solid foundation, because all assertions about the dignity of man have their true legitimation in the metaphysical, universal fact that man's mind and soul are immortal and thus transcendent to any secular value, since the whole material world is as nothing compared with the soul.

The opposite decision is that man is only the highest developed form of the material biological world, a result of the blind non-rational, mysterious powers of biological evolution, or of the equally mysterious biological struggle for existence. If this view is accepted, then any assertions of the dignity of the human person become empty oratory that will be unable to stand a test. Wherever the transcendent value of the person is totally submerged in either the biological race or the economic class and the proper independent value of the person thus vanishes, we must not wonder that politically ugly and tyrannical totalitarianism arises. The attacks by the popes of the nineteenth century upon agnosticism and bourgeois materialist philosophy, so easily derided in the heyday of this complacent agnosticism, have proved more prophetic than was ever expected. What primarily counts is, indeed, not the political institution in its formal character, for example, the bill of rights, but the underlying philosophy, the idea of man's nature and end in the minds of peoples and their legislative and judicial authorities. Soviet Russia's earlier constitutions contain a fine declaration of the rights of the toilers (notice that not men but only members of an economic class have such rights), but their rights are

---

2 This full self-sufficiency must be distinguished from independence. The latter is a moral term, a legal quality, and does not preclude a basic and—viewed from the perfection of human nature—real interdependence of men destined to live together.

not based on an unconditioned belief in the transcendent value of the human person. Consequently their practical value and their interpretation is wholly dependent upon the political expediency and the utilitarian considerations of the monopolists of power, the Communist party, with its purposes, ideology, and lust of power.

Again, how in a Christian civilization does the theory about the relation of the natural to the supernatural status of man influence political theory? It seems clear that if in its natural status man's nature is evil, then the redeemed man may not need those political forms with compulsion, power, and punishment which are, it is granted, necessary for the unredeemed, who are not in possession of supernatural grace. This argument seems to explain why sects separating from the Catholic Church so often demand for themselves an almost anarchic freedom while at the same time subjecting the "unredeemed," the "heretics," or the "Papists" to cruel persecution. This fact is widely proven by the sectarian movements at the time of the Reformation, especially by the Anabaptists who, for instance, in Muenster abolished temporal power, only to use spiritual power more ruthlessly than ever a Christian state did against "heretics." It is worthy of mention that the idea of God held by most of these sects is that of the angry chastising, revengeful God of the Old Testament, not the kind Father of the Gospel. Thus all the real problems of political theory are influenced by the presupposed theory of the nature of man: the problem of freedom and political authority, of the end of the state, of the justification of political power, of the relation between Church and state, of the limitation of the state's supreme power or sovereignty, of the fundamental rights of man, and even of the superiority of monarchy, democracy, or aristocracy. If predestination is not a hidden mystery but positively recognizable, as was taught by the Calvinist groups, it would follow that the elect must rule as an aristocracy over the *massa damnata,* while this aristocracy itself would not be willing to recognize the absolute power of any monarch, especially one not adhering to their creed. The trend toward aristocracy against monarchy and against popular democracy in early Calvinism has here its basis.

We can now understand better that at the time when political theory was still philsophical, and not a positivist, merely technical science, the doctrine of the "pre-state" or natural status of man was very important for Sophists and Stoics, for Hobbes and Rousseau and

Thomas Paine. For in the natural status appears the "pure nature of man." And we can understand that for Christian political philosophy, for St. Thomas and De Maistre, for Donoso Cortes, and for Calvin or Luther the doctrine of the consequence of the Fall is equally important.

II. ROUSSEAU AND HOBBES

Rousseau describes the natural status as an idyllic Paradise in which the individual, as an autonomous, free, fully self-sufficient being, lived a perfect life of perfect goodness. A transition into a political status (*status civilis*) was by no means intrinsically necessary. If, nevertheless, the individuals prefer to live in the political status, this status must not only rest upon a completely free contract of the individuals, but its permanent existence must be based on the ever-reiterated renewal of this contract. As the original rights must be preserved—and with Rousseau they are very broad—the so-called will of the state has to be identical with the will of the free and intrinsically good individuals. Consequently the only legitimate kind of government is immediate democracy. Every authority is magisterial authority, that is, merely delegated authority, and any other kind of authority would be usurpation. The general will must therefore coincide with the will of all in so far as these individuals are actually free and can follow without restriction, i.e., usurpation, their autonomous enlightened reason. The crucial problem of authority is thus solved for Rousseau by an identification of government and governed. A striking consequence is that Rousseau has no place for a church, for a theology, or for a priest, since, in the last resort, all these exclude this optimistic view of the nature of man. Any genuine theology knows the forces of evil, knows that the nature of man is weak, inclined to evil, and in need of supernatural help and redemption. So Rousseau denies the Church. God is only the faraway deistic demiurge. The "civil religion" of Rousseau is anything but religion; it is a mere element of homogeneity for the state, a kind of laicist morality, of sentimental education for a secular end. The fundamental problem of the relation between the spiritual and the secular power, the independence of each from the other, the liberty of the Church from the state, and the necessary cooperation between Church and state, are simply not recognized because of Rousseau's optimism.

Very different was Hobbes' consideration of the nature of man. Like Epicurus in Greek antiquity, Hobbes thought that man is intrinsically evil, that he is driven by the reckless pursuit of selfish interests and passions uncontrolled by reason, that he is a lawless being.[3] The natural status, therefore, is the *bellum omnium contra omnes;* men are by nature like wild beasts.[4] Somewhat in contradiction to this thesis, Hobbes says that man nevertheless recognized that this status of permanent fear of violent death was very unsatisfactory and that for it should be substituted a contractual order of law. But because the evil nature of man is not reformed by the law, it is not enough that this social contract is made. There must be a transfer of all individual rights to the sovereign political power, a concentration of might which will forcibly uphold order and peace among men. Compulsion and obedience are the topics of Hobbes' theory. The state's power must be unlimited because man is selfish, reckless, and evil. Out of the surrendered liberty arises, then, the omnipotent Leviathan. There is only one will, the will of the state. There is only one power, the supreme power. Outside of this there is no right: not that of the Church as an independent society, not that of the autonomous groups such as feudalism or the medieval guilds had built. There is nothing but the Leviathan, and there must be nothing more, or else the forces of evil passions, the ruthless selfishness of man, would destroy this toilsomely established order. Thus the fundamentally evil nature of man is the origin of the state and its lasting justification. Therefore the enhanced natural law disappears behind the absolute will of the state. A political ethics becomes almost impossible, and political theory is a practical doctrine concerning the acquisition, preservation, and use of sovereign power. There must be order and peace. Truth is negligible, order alone is essential, and order is the product of an omnipotent will. The

[3] Cf. the opposite opinion of Thomas Aquinas. *Est autem omnibus hominibus naturalis, ut se invicem diligant. Contra Gentes,* III, c.117. *Inest autem homini naturalis inclinatio ad omnium hominum dilectionem (ibid.,* c.130).

[4] Cf. *Elementa philosophica de cive,* Foreword. *Homines malos esse* is his presupposition. Significantly Machiavelli says in *Discorsi* (I, 3) that whoever founds a republic (or a state) and gives laws to it must proceed upon the presupposition that all men are malicious and that they all, without any exception, would follow their internal maliciousness as soon as they had a good opportunity.

utilitarian Hobbes shows a remarkable contempt for the intellectualism of Aristotle.[5]

That the Church now on earth is the kingdom of God mentioned in
the Old and New Testaments, Hobbes regards as an erroneous theory
(*Leviathan,* 383). Need it be pointed out that Hobbes' idea of God
reveals only a revengeful, almighty God whose predominating attribute is unlimited will-power and that thus it becomes the duty of the
clergy to preach not so much truth, as obedience? This obedience is so
stressed that "the conscience, in fact, is bound to any religion the state
imposes." [6] Compare with this the Thomist doctrine that intellect is
superior to will, that obedience should be reasonable obedience, that
truth is superior to utilitarian order and peace separated from truth.
One may try to explain Hobbes' gloomy theory by his historical background of civil war and religious struggle; but what finally explains it,
is his deep pessimism concerning human nature.

The theories just mentioned, contradictory to each other on account
of their different anthropology, are in the last analysis unchristian.
The gentle gospel of the God-man is forgotten by the mere secular
humanism of Rousseau and has not overcome Hobbes' pre-Christian
contempt for the specific Christian virtues of truth, charity, and humility.

III. LUTHER AND PROTESTANT POLITICAL PHILOSOPHIES

The political theories developed in the different Christian denominations are influenced likewise by the theories of human nature: not
exclusively, of course, by a mere philosophical and moral anthropology, but by their theology of grace and nature.

No Christian can have such optimism about human nature as Rousseau exhibited, for the dogmas of original sin and redemption belong
to the essence of Christianity. It is, therefore, easily understandable
that all Christian political philosophers opposed Rousseauist optimism. It is a proof of the prevalence of Christian ideas, that the fathers
of the American Constitution, in striking opposition to the political

---

[5] *Works,* III, 85. "There is no such *finis ultimus,* utmost aim, nor *summum bonum,*
greatest good, as is spoken of in the books of the old moral philosophers. . . . Felicity is
the continual progress of the desire from one object to another."

[6] Figgis, *The Divine Right of Kings,* p. 319. For other remarks on obedience to law, see
Leviathan, VIII, 42, 43.

philosophy of their contemporaries, the Jacobins, during the French Revolution, were not in any considerable way influenced by Rousseau.

There exists in the different Christian Churches a notable difference in their political philosophies. An acute observer of the struggle of the national socialist state against the Catholic Church and against Protestantism remarks that the Catholic Church seems to have a great advantage over the Evangelical Church in possessing a consistent philosophy of law and of the state, as well as of society.[7] The Catholics, therefore, are able to oppose to the Nazi philosophy not only their theology, but also a well-founded social philosophy, too, while Protestantism bases its defense more exclusively on the integrity of the revealed word of God and on theology.

The reason for this difference, which ultimately seems to include the non-existence of a typical Lutheran social philosophy, is a quite different theological anthropology. Luther taught that original sin had so utterly destroyed the goodness of human nature that even grace did not reform its innermost malignity, but simply covered it (*natura deleta*). He denies that reason is able to recognize natural law and that will can strive for it. The universe is broken up: the realm of nature is evil, separated from the realm of supernature. There is no bridge between religion as grace and the world as the field of reason and natural ethics. The famous Thomist principle, that grace presupposes nature and perfects it,[8] has no validity, even though upon this principle is based the participation in redemption of the world of politics and social order. For Luther there is only one morality, the supernatural one. Therefore he has as his guiding principle for the world only the revealed Word. He does not acknowledge that human reason has its own way to a natural morality, to a natural law, and to a social philos-

[7] Cf. N. Micklem, *National Socialism and the Roman Catholic Church* (1938), pp. 56, 137; *National Socialism and Christianity* (1939), p. 10. For a denial of natural law, cf. also Helmut Schreiner (editor), *Nation vor Gott*, 1937: the introductory essay and the essays by H. Wendland. These writers are deeply influenced by Karl Barth's dialectic theology, which goes back to the original pessimism of the Reformers and consequently denies the idea of natural law, of the missionary task of Christendom in society and the state. It issues in the uselessness of Christian social and political reform on the basis of natural ethics, as its critics have satisfactorily proven. It is therefore more than amazing, when the father of dialectic theology, in his essay on the Churches' fight against Nazism in Foreign Affairs (January, 1943), criticizes the Catholic Church for its allegedly opportunist and condoning policy concerning Nazism.

[8] Cf. the striking formulation of this principle in the offertory *Deus, qui humanae substantiae* in the Ordinary of the Mass.

ophy based on the essence and end of human nature. Luther despairs of a reconciliation of the gospel and politics. The world is God's enemy, God's foe. Between God and the world there is an abyss which cannot be bridged; so the Christian restricts himself to the inner life of faith; good works in this world of political and social life are indifferent for redemption. "If all people were true Christians, that is, true believers, there would be no need for princes, kings, lords, sword, or law." [9] This attitude, that state and law are exclusively consequences of sin, has been well explained by a recent Dutch political writer and leader of the Protestant anti-revolutionary party, Dr. A. Kuypers, when he says that the state is an issue and consequence of the broken, sinful character of man after the Fall. The state lasts as long as this sinful status lasts; "the state is like a surgical bandage, the abnormal. . . . The state exists for the sake of sin." [10]

Luther, early horrified by the anarchic consequences drawn by some early Protestant sects which inclined in ethics to nihilism (Anabaptists, Adamites) and in politics to anarchy, as some thirteen centuries ago the Gnostic and Manichaean sects inclined for similar reasons, sought to evade these consequences. Therefore he asserted that the secular authority with sword and scale must exist on account of utterly corrupt human nature; thus political authority is instituted by God. But it is not produced by man's reason and free will under direction of and subject to natural law. The princes are instituted by God as his hangmen, and His divine anger uses them to punish and to keep external peace. Then, however, it would seem to follow that almost every existing political and social order is sanctioned, at least as long as the integrity of the gospel is not wholly destroyed. [11]

Thus the most valuable measure of the quality of legislation, which should take its legitimacy from the concrete realization of the common

[9] *Von weltlicher Obrigkeit*, Weimarer Ausgabe, 11, 249.

[10] In his book, *Antirevolutionaire Staatskunde*, I, 290, 305 f.

[11] Not to give a false impression, we must add that Luther himself sometimes, in practical questions, yielded to the traditional natural-law doctrine in contradiction to his leading theory. Cf. A. Lange, *Reformation und Naturrecht*, p. 19. Of course we might quote also sentences of Luther in which political authority is declared to be God's work, order, and creature. And he once boasted that he had taught that authority is the highest work of reason (Seeberg, *Dogmengeschichte*, IV, 261). But most authorities will agree with Baron (*Calvin's Staatsanschauung*), that Luther's pessimism is decisive and that he is more inclined to see in the world and in the state, above all else, sin (p. 19). It should not be forgotten that the Aristotelian Melanchthon alleviated this pessimism where and as far as he found influence.

good, is neglected. Probably the Lutheran theory of the nature of man induced Lutherans to recognize more than any others the "normative power of the fact"; in consequence of this, passive obedience and non-resistance against unjust government are preached. Here is the cause of the strict Erastianism [12] of the Lutheran Church in Prussia which today so greatly weakens a unified resistance to the national socialist *Weltanschauung*.

In Germany, at the beginning of the national socialist revolution, most of the parishes that yielded under the pressure to conform to the Nazi ideas were Lutheran, while the Reformed of Calvinist origin, especially in the South and the West, resisted almost from the outset. Moreover, it is interesting to find that the resistance among Lutherans like Niemöller rests on the fact that Nazism abolishes the Scriptures, the revealed word of God. Yet even a superficial reading of the encyclical *Mit brennender Sorge* (1936) will show that the resistance of Catholics rests upon both natural law and social philosophy as well as upon the Scriptures and the theological doctrines of the Church. This explains also the fact that in Catholicism the resistance was more unified and that some prelates who followed at first a policy of appeasement did so only out of a pardonable opportunism, while the "German Christians," the Nazified group, got practically all its recruits from the Lutheran denomination. A theory of natural law would have given a yardstick to measure the concrete acts of the political authority as to how, for instance, the common good ought to be realized, and thus would have given or refused moral justification to the acts of authority.

For without natural law Christianity becomes too easily only inner conviction, while the "world" remains subject to lust for power; politics is beyond morality, and the duty of the Christian member of an invisible Church is passive obedience and suffering. A remarkable combination of pietism and patriarchalism makes this bearable. Freedom based on reason is not for man whose nature is evil; this evil nature demands power and domination. Those who have power have it by the hidden work of Providence; they have acquired it mysteriously; their right is a kind of divine right, and resistance to it is immoral,

---

[12] Erastianism, according to Figgis (*The Divine Right of Kings*), has been best defined by Selden in the words, "whether the Church or the Scripture is the judge of religion? In truth neither, but the State" (p. 317).

unless they command something which openly contradicts God's will revealed in the Scripture. It is this characteristic view which produces a remarkable mixture of inner, private Christian religiousness and power-politics: the only secular foundation of a great state is its state egoism. The consequence is that politics becomes *Real* politics, exempted from natural law and ethics.[13]

IV. CALVINIST THEOLOGY AND POLITICAL THOUGHT

In our problem, Calvinism presents a most interesting picture. Calvin and all his faithful followers accept with Luther the theological doctrine that human nature has been utterly depraved by original sin.[14] But the redemption by grace, the definitive election, and the fact that the Old Testament particularly plays the role which in Thomism is assigned to reason, gives Calvin a less pessimistic attitude toward politics The realm of grace and the realm of secular life are connected by the predestinated men, who in order to have the certainty of their election must Christianize secular life. The state exists because of divine institution, as revealed in the Scripture, but is not a product of human nature and reason; and it cannot be, because of man's malignity. Yet the state becomes a holy gift of God. Thus not natural law (the light of reason and human will) constitutes the state and realizes the order of the common good, but the divine law as revealed in the Scripture, especially in Calvin's beloved Book of Judges and in the law of Moses. The Bible is so exclusively a source of political theory for Calvin that one scholar familiar with his theory states that Calvin found in the Bible a pattern of the constitutional life in its most minute particulars as instituted by God's will.[15] The state and its rulers have to do everything necessary for the realization of all the minute divine laws, as revealed by the Scripture. The safeguarding of public honesty, understood in the widest literary sense, as the later word "Puritanism" intended it, and the preservation of piety, these are tasks

[13] The point must be emphasized that this view is based upon a theory that human nature is fundamentally evil. This explains the amazing contradiction in Bismarck's personality, the individual piety of the private Christian and the ruthless "Realpolitik" of the man of public affairs. For further explanation, see E. Troelsch, *Die Soziallehren der christlichen Gruppen und Kirchen* (1912), p. 604.

[14] For example: *Institutio*, Bk. II, c.3, 1. *In se perditus est (homo) et deploratus . . . frustra in natura nostra aliquid boni requiritur.*" Cf. *ibid.*, c.9, 3.

[15] Hans Baron, *Calvin's Staatsanschauung* (1924), p. 35.

of the government. Calvin thoroughly affirms that the government has the unquestionable right to compel to a Christian life. To neglect this would be worldly indulgence.[16] Calvin's state is a theocracy, or a Bibliocracy. But it is not a priesthood that governs the Church and, through the superiority of the Church, also governs the state, as some writers in the Middle Ages taught. It is the holy people of the redeemed which lives in Church and and state together. The state, even though it originates in sin, is sanctified by the fact that its citizens are at the same time the holy people of God, the chosen people. In internal policy, therefore, the idea of predestination does not lead directly to democratic equality, but to an aristocratic government.

This is elucidated in Thomas Hooker's *Laws of Ecclesiastical Polity* (1594), where the principle of theological predestination leads to the political predestination of the noble, wise, and virtuous to govern by natural right those of servile disposition. The ideal state is the rule of the elect over the broad masses in an aristocratic, hierarchical government. This presupposes, by the way, that the elect are "visible." The virtuous life is public, visible, not private and hidden; it is a life ruled entirely by the observance of the minute rules of the Bible and by whatever the holy people institutes by its customs and laws; later, even economic success may be an additional sign of election, and poverty a sign of non-election; a Puritan pattern of life, very different from the ascetic life of the Poverello, is the consequence. Tolerance in its true meaning is inconceivable because the dissenting Papist, for example, denies not only one sector of communal life, religious unanimity, but the whole life-pattern. St. Thomas Aquinas can afford to be far more tolerant than the early Calvinists and Puritans. It is the accent upon the holy people, not upon a hierarchically graduated Church, that gives Calvinism a republican character, yet with distinctly aristocratic features. It is Calvin's Bibliocracy, his enthusiasm for the man of the heroic mind, which gives to his political theory the aristocratic character. But the aristocracy is not a feudal aristocracy of the blood; it is an aristocracy of the redeemed, chosen by God.[17]

Calvin's ideal was a real theocracy, as it had been established in Geneva, without any kind of tolerance. But precisely his strong ideal of the holy chosen people, his belief in predestination, and his original

---

16 Cf. R. Schwarz, *Calvin's Lebenswerk in seinen Briefen*, II, 426.
17 It is easily understood that most of the Monarchomachi are Calvinists.

republicanism were bound to produce in later Calvinism and its different communities a certain revolutionary power against an irreligious ruler. These made it easier to demand a religious tolerance, originating in social expediency but based upon the spiritual rights of the holy people living as a minority in an irreligious state.[18] It became possible to demand a minimizing of government, because the pious believers with the Scripture as rule of life were able to order their social life better than a government which did not consider the Scripture as its constitutional law.

And a further consequence ensued with the the idea of predestination: as soon as the rights of Christians could be formulated, the separation of the Church from the secular, religiously neutral state, would be easy. These rights were formulated and transformed into a political theory by the Independents under the influence of an enthusiastic subjectivism. The basis of this theory is the assumption of absolute freedom of the individual conscience, to which God reveals Himself directly and immediately, not by intervention of a divinely provided hierarchical office; consequently, the sacrament, the channel of grace, was, as the exuberant subjectivism of the Anabaptists taught, independent of ministry. These rights of a true Christian were certain to become the rights of man, as soon as, through Enlightenment and Deism, the idea of a chosen people had been secularized. The revival during the seventeenth and eighteenth centuries of the idea of natural law in an individualistic garb superimposed upon the religious individualism and congenial to the new naturalism of the deistic philosophy, contributed powerfully to this transformation. And all the more because the natural ethics of the eighteenth century—of Locke and Adam Smith, to mention only two—followed with their rational soberness the exuberance of religious fervor characterizing the seventeenth century.

A contributing factor to this transformation was also the development of a more peaceful and less militant concept of evangelical religion as it emerged in the various forms of Evangelism and of Pietism. The City of God is no longer an immediate political, external purpose. It is internal; the world of politics now becomes more indifferent. The

---

[18] We find this already demanded more or less expressly in Arminianism about 1610–20. Cf. D. Nobbs, *Theocracy and Toleration* (1938), chap. 2, §§ 2–5; chap. 4, § 4; and Conclusion.

Christian lives and works in the world. The Christian has to prove
true, has to stand the test by sober, assiduous work in the secular sphere
and in economic life. He has to use his chance not for success as such,
but for success as a proof of his goodness. If that is true, then it follows
that the Christian needs freedom and equal opportunity in that political and economic sphere. Thus the revival of natural law could be
amalgamated with the new religious ideas. These rights of man against
the government are valid *par excellence* in a democracy. They are
rights, moreover, against an alleged absolute power of majorities.
Rousseau would not have recognized rights against the general will
appearing in the majority decision, but the political theory of later
Anglo-Saxon Calvinism had as its aim to protect the rights of the
Christian against heretical or agnostic majorities.

For Calvinism, man is not good. Man's nature is utterly depraved.
Therefore, as long as state and Church are united, only God's divine
law and redemption and a strong authoritative state are necessary. If
there is separation of Church and state, the rights of man are necessary,
not on account of human nature, but for the redeemed, the saints, to
protect them against abuses by the secular power when the holy people
is a minority. Then the predestined saints, not the natural man, will
prevail in social and economic life. Every kind of regulation by a
secular, neutral government will be more to the advantage of the non-
elect. Calvin's fear of the *vitium, stultitia, et levitas* of the masses was
still vivid in the minds of some of the fathers of the Constitution and
in English Toryism.

V. Modern Agnosticism

What is common to all the Reformers is the separation of nature and
grace because of the theological thesis of the utter depravity of human nature through original sin. The state is therefore the consequence of sin and not of the social nature of man; at least this social
nature does not come strongly into consideration and cannot do so,
because in itself it is impotent for any morally good act. Only where
and when the theological basis of this doctrine vanishes and is replaced
by secularized human rights, by the more optimistic idea of the nature
of man as it appears in rationalism and Deism of the seventeenth and
eighteenth centuries, is the way open for liberal democracy.

This rediscovery of natural law, however individualistic, this emergence of the sphere of a nature perhaps not wholly corrupt, thus produced a natural philosophical basis for the new democratic forms, the new liberties, which by themselves were not representative of original Calvinism. Through this rediscovery of natural law and ethics there emerged, too, a kind of platform where citizens as such, upon the basis of their inalienable rights, could meet in the secular state which had now become somewhat neutral in matters of religion. A common basis of practical political institutions and frameworks derived from man's social nature, not from man's religious affiliation, was thus possible. We must stress institutions and working patterns because the justifications of these institutions, for instance, religious freedom—the non-establishment of a state Church—continued to be very different for the Calvinist or the Catholic, the Free Churchman or the agnostic. Nevertheless a true and durable *modus vivendi* in society and in the state could be found with the democratic institutions that were in themselves admissible from the political standpoint of all. But still the *homo religiosus*, upheld by all Christian communities, is of utmost importance in political philosophy. The religious sphere is sacred, for it is the sphere of conscience. If that sphere is shattered, and with it religion, then the ultimate ramparts of freedom against totalitarianism collapse.

The good pagan of the agnostic era and his purely secular culture have not enough resistance against the pseudo-religious political theories of our time. This good pagan, the ideal of Comte, of Bentham, and of so many modern writers previous to the World War, grew by fighting against revealed truth, against the influence of the Church and the clergy in education and in public life, and against the "superstitious creeds stemming from pious but stupid, unenlightened medieval monks." And this good pagan fought as a rationalist and humanitarian for autonomous ethics, for self-redemption, for infinite progress by ethical culture, unaware that his ideals would become idols, false gods for the broad and unrefined masses in the monster cities of our industrial age, whose instincts are cruder, whose emotions are more erratic, than those of the elect few of the cultural upper class.

The good pagan, too sure of himself, did not know that he lived upon a Christian inheritance, that even his ideals were secularized Christian ideals. He thought highly of the Sermon of the Mount just as he thought highly of the sayings of Confucius and the advice of Socrates or Marcus Aurelius. But the divine authority of Christ did not count for him; Christ was merely one of the sages and perhaps, as the daring biblical criticism claimed, He never existed to bring valid testimony of His own divinity and the will of the Father. Yet the good pagan's ideals, ultramondane and absolute, separated from their nourishing root, the Christian faith, began to be decomposed by the rationalist criticism of that very one who had first dissolved positive religion, the good pagan himself. So the agnostic of the nineteenth century abandoned his smiling optimism about infinite progress and became a mild skeptic, a somewhat disillusioned relativist. But the broad masses laboring in the factories and offices, surging through the desolate canyons of the industrial cities, and banished through the good pagan's propaganda from the protective shelter of positive Christendom, fell into cruder forms of materialism. The good pagan himself, now a skeptic, was frightened by that crude materialism, but he could not change it. Only in its youth had his philosophy something of an ethical effort, of an inspiration from truth and a love for truth. But then he had given up philosophy, the love for truth and wisdom, and had surrendered himself to the busy collection of facts in a positivist sense, or to methodical problems that left the quest for truth unsatisfied, or to unobligating, cynical, yet elegant discussions.

The first signs of despair began to show themselves. Spencer, the promoter of a biological political theory that must result in the enslavement of the individual to the absolute, irrational power of the state, became alarmed.[19] Edward von Hartmann developed his philosophy of pessimism. Nietzsche, the most powerful critic of the good pagan's saturated complacency, developed his cruel, anti-humanitarian and power-drunk dream of the superman, the roving blond beast. So the idea of man changed, and with it the political philosophies of the late nineteenth and the early twentieth century.

The First World War, the initial period of a historical era which is not yet finished and will some day be remembered as at least as portentous as the era of the Reformation, burned out the last remnants

---

[19] *Social Statistics* (1902), p. 10. "What must we think of this wealth-seeking age of ours? Shall we consider the total absorption of time and energy in business, the spending of life in the accumulation of means to live, as constituting greatest happiness and act accordingly? The real heaven sought dips far below the horizon and has yet been seen by none. Faith, not sight, must be our guide. We cannot do without a compass."

of the good pagan's secular optimism and belief in immanency. Now the religious sphere, if such a figure is permissible, was burnt out. All the ideals that had animated and inspired the fathers were gone. Youth, unable to return to the fallen gods of their fathers, began to feel the *horror vacui* represented by the emptiness of the religious sphere in the individual soul and in the "soul" of civilization. The young intelligentsia grew cynical; they "debunked" the dimmed ideals of their parents. But that *horror vacui* continued to trouble them. So they longed for the new "myths," as a substitute for a repentant return to the faith. They wanted something to live for, but they had lost the causes of life and did not know what to do with it. They grew tired of the individualist and autonomous ethical culture of their fathers and that serene egocentrism which appeared so utterly foolish in the trenches of the First World War.

The *horror vacui* drove them to the new myths of quasi-religious collectivism, whether racial, economic, or national in its irrational transcendency. They wanted something to live for, they longed for causes of life, for a missionary call in following which they could lose themselves, immerse their useless individuality in community and comradery. Their barren loneliness cried for the "gang." So the myth-making pseudo-religious political creeds, Fascism, Nazism, Communism, succeeded in conquering souls. Fascism confesses that mysticism is its form. So the unsuccessful self-redemption, the useless autonomy, turned into redemption by the individual's unconditional surrender to irrational mass-feelings and to the sacrificial idolatry of the leader, to a blind, inhuman, and utterly unchristian, irrational obedience not to a moral authority, but to power beyond law and reason. Thus the new political philosophies show that their deepest roots are in a specific idea of man as an unfree particle of the masses, depersonalized, without individuality, self-responsibility, or individual reason and conscience. Whenever the religious sphere becomes empty, whenever the belief in man's individual reason and consequent self-responsibility disappears, the dignity of man disappears, too.

This "political" pseudo-religious mysticism lacks one essential element of religion: the interior life, the sanctification of the soul, the interior mystical union with God; that vivid feeling of finiteness and imperfection and consequently the longing for redemption through atonement, asceticism, and spiritual discipline; that consciousness of the incomparable value of the soul and of the primacy of the kingdom of God. On account of the lack of this element the "new faith" becomes extrovert, secularist in the full sense; its discipline, its vaunted "asceticism," becomes external uniformity merely instrumental for irrational and vague "historical processes" without rational justification before personal conscience and reason. The new politicized faith is anti-intellectual and consequenly non-moral. It becomes an aimless political dynamism, i.e., nihilism for which fight and war become ends in themselves. The inner restlessness becomes external destruction.

There exists an invisible but quite real connection between man as a religious being and man as a rational being, between the faith in a personal supra-mundane God and political philosophy. Without that faith, without that transcendent religion, the *horror vacui* of the *anima naturaliter christiana* creates its own God, the God-state, in order to avoid complete anarchy and an unbearable emptiness of soul. Any political philosophy neglecting the truth that man is "religious" (*homo religiosus*) cannot avoid the alternative of either anarchy or God-state with all its consequences. But it is the change in the ideas about the nature of man that is basic.

VI. Man a Rational Being or Merely a Member of a Race or a Class

Leaving the theological ideas of man's nature in their influence upon political philosophy, let us turn to the idea of man in philosophical psychology and its consequences upon political philosophy. One example may suffice. From the time of Greek philosophy the answer to one question has influenced all philosophical psychology: Is the intellect superior to the will, or the will to the intellect? This question later took the form: Is man primarily reason, or is he ruled by irrational passions, by the subrational elements of his nature, like blood or race? If we accept the first alternative, we can find a philosophically sufficient basis for democratic institutions. The fundamental forms of political life in democracy, majority rule, representation and general franchise, free speech, public opinion, and party regime, all rest upon discussion, deliberation, and persuasion as the outstanding processes of political integration.

These same processes proceed from the presupposition that man is first and predominantly an intellectual being, gifted with reason to control his actions, and not controlled by the irrational passions, by the subconscious power of blood or race, or *Volkstum,* or by his membership in an economic class. This process of integration by reasoning, argument, and persuasion means the active participation of all men of reason in the political life; it must therefore protect the rights of man as means by which, as a reasoning being, he participates in the forming of politics. It follows, further, that government should predominantly be government by consent, government not only for the people but by the people. For this philosophy, law is, in its essence, reason; the *ratio legis* is more important than any mere will of the authority. Any political philosophy that has as its presupposition the thesis that man is essentially intellect and reason, and that intellect and reason are superior to the other elements of human nature, cannot accept antidemocratic principles. Of course, such a philosophy must also abhor that mechanical concept of democracy which we find, for instance, in Kelsen's relativism or in the idea of the mind as a bundle of associations (sensualism). In this concept, democracy is an irrational process by which, without any higher moral pretentions, a majority decision is mathematically calculated without valuing its truth. Hence democracy becomes the political form of philosophic, skeptical relativism.

The other alternative puts first the subconscious, the irrational, nonintellectual elements in man's nature, such as blood, race, *Volkstum,* and nationality in a biological sense, or the impersonal, irrational powers of history or the class situation. If this alternative is accepted, then, of course, the common blood or the common race is the power which with inevitable force integrates men into states, or the common class situation, our being a proletarian or a capitalist, fixes our political philosophy but never our being a rational substance, an individual person. Consequently the political process of integration needs nothing like persuasion, discussion, deliberation, majority decision, and whatever political institutions are fitted to them. The blood, the racial soul, the inexorable forces of history, decide, and we respond to their appeal with the irrational powers of the soul. It is natural that such a political philosophy can see in any form of dissent only treason and hence must demand uniformity; that it derides intellect and extols feeling and sentiment; that it appeals to the passions of the masses and praises the "intuition" of the leader; and that its unity is a uniformity of passionate feeling.

The appeal to reason is evidently treason because it sets up the principle that the individuals as persons deliberate, argue, and decide by the merits of objective reasons and not by the inner subconscious voice of the blood, the race, etc. Our personality, our individuality, is consequently nothing compared with that irrational power of blood. The highly praised inalienable rights are a democratic illusion. As the individual is not master of his feelings, his blood, his race, or his class situation, he cannot decide, cannot stand above these elements by force of reason, but is immersed in the inexorable current. All the values of the other political philosophy appear to this one as vices. It speaks for itself, and for the use of words, that these believers in blood, race, and class talk of "fanatic faith," while the Christian theologian speaks of "reasonable faith" (*fides rationalis*).

Totalitarianism in politics is the necessary consequence of this philosophy as is the domination of the masses over the individual person, of passion over reason, and of race or *Volkstum* over humanity and the Church universal.[20] It also follows that there exists in the world no metaphysical order which is for every concrete order in socio-political life the exemplary and critical rule; no idea of a natural law, but the law of the jungle, is conceivable. The political order cannot be a moral order of reason and for reason. It can only be an orderless struggle of races, classes, and other masses. To speak of an international order between legally equal and free nations is thus nonsense. The only rule perceptible between nations is the power of the strongest nation, or the master race, and conquest by it. The Hobbesian natural status is the international status; peace and order can be instituted only by conquest and subjection. The dream of a *civitas maxima* is to be ful-

---

[20] Note the praise of the irrational voluntaristic element in the philosophy of activism of Giovanni Gentile, the once foremost Fascist philosopher, who is representative of a time that is devoid of all eternal ideas and unchangeable moral laws, despising a timeless truth; who is elated by aimless, senseless activity, by the delusion of irrational life that speaks in the mystical voice of the equally mystical blood, nation, or whatever one may call this new substitute for what a more pious, more prudent, wiser generation called Providence, the Divine Logos in the history of the human mind. The irrational nonsense of the official philosopher, A. Rosenberg, in *The Myth of the Twentieth Century*, need not be mentioned, nor the venomous books of other Nazi philosophers; they really spit upon reason and seem to think that intellect is a democratic degeneration of man.

filled only by the absolute and irresponsible power of the strongest
nation and the servitude of all weaker nations. And this conquest and
rule carry their justification irrationally in themselves; just as in internal politics the absolute tyrannical power is vested in itself, in the
superhuman intuition of the leader.

VII. The Rational and Social Nature of Man

The idea of the nature of man, as developed in the *philosophia
perennis* and in its perennial home, the Catholic Church, must be decisive for Catholic political philosophy. In the history of Catholic
thought, even though there may be some oscillation about the nature
of man, there is a distinct doctrine concerning it, and never are the
essential elements of this nature abandoned.

The origin of the state lies in the rational, social nature of man. In
the nature of man. This means that it is not original sin, the fall of
man, which gives birth to the state. Since St. Augustine, it has been
common doctrine that, even if Adam had not sinned, there would be
state and law, and that in the state of pure nature before the Fall men
would have organized themselves in a state. State is therefore independent of grace. This doctrine means further that the state remains necessary, too, for the redeemed; for grace does not destroy nature or make
its essential socio-political institutions superfluous, as some sects think.
The citizen's loyalty to the government is, moreover, independent of
whether or not the ruler is a Christian, and the duties of subjects to
the political authority are duties of natural law, which are independent of the quality of a citizen as a Christian.[21]

The state originates in the social nature of man. Not merely on account of expediency or utility do men build states, nor on account of
some psychic disposition, so that the social life is something which is
merely an unessential addition to nature. Sociality (*socialitas*) is as
essential an element of man's nature as is rationality. To human nature
belong essentially certain acts which intentionally find their end in
community, such as love, piety, friendship, and language. Even our
innermost thinking, which we should suppose an absolutely individual
affair, is touched by sociality; justly, therefore, has it been said that

---

[21] St. Thomas, *Summa theol.*, IIa IIae, q.12, a.2; Suarez, *De leg.*, III, c.5, n.5–7;
Defensio fidei, III, c.4, n.5; Bellarmine, *De laicis*, c.11; *De S. Pontifice*, IV, c.16.

"Cogito, ergo sum" should be *"Cogito, ergo sumus."* For we think by *verba mentis*, by words of the mind. Therefore a sphere of absolute solitude is not separable from the social sphere of the person; it is the last, indissoluble essence of the concrete man's ego that there is no experience of the community through which individuality does not shine, and no experience of individuality which is not borne by community and open to it. Man is born by the lasting community of the family into social life. He is educated in that community and grows up in it; he is formed by various communities and he forms them as a free agent, and his social nature finds its fulfillment in citizenship in the state and in that of mankind, which is transcendent to the state. The political life belongs to the nature of man, so that a definition of man's nature which would omit this element is imperfect.

The state has its origin in man's rational nature. Hence there is no immediate establishment of the state and of the form of government by God. Man being a free rational agent, no state is established without consent, without the free and rational action of man. The authority of the state in the last analysis originates in God, but no political authority comes into existence without the consent of the men associating for political life. And political authority can demand only reasonable obedience. The law is a rule of reason and for rational beings.[22] A blind obedience is contrary to this idea of human nature. To demand unquestioning obedience from a rational being being presupposes on the side of the authority the full possession of truth. That belongs only to God. Human authority can demand only reasonable obedience; that is, its commands must be justifiable before reason.[23] Thus the dignity of the human person is saved. Freedom never means licence: to be free, to act as a rational being, means to follow reason; the opposite of freedom is the arbitrary, unreasonable use of authority in questions in which human dignity is concerned.

In this idea of man, therefore, the whole content of the concept of natural law is preserved, and with it, human dignity. Thus the human person never can become a mere means or instrument in politics.

---

[22] Cf. the opposite opinion of Hobbes, that law is the command of a sovereign which, though it may be iniquitous, cannot be unjust. *De cive*, chap. 6, pr. 15; *Leviathan*, 26, pr. 4.

[23] Of course there are orders which demand obedience even if they are arbitrary; "drive on the right" is arbitrary; in certain countries the rule is to drive on the left. But these are things indifferent.

It follows, then, that the *unitas ordinis,* which is the specific form of social being and especially of the state, is not the exclusive product of authority for which the subjects would be like an amorphous object, mere passive matter. The *unitas,* i.e., the enduring will to live in the state, is concretely the result of cooperation between authority and subjects. The subjects, as rational beings, participate normally in some way in the formation of the concrete common will. When St. Thomas praises the *regimen mixtum* as the best, he intends to point out that normally the unity in the multitude is produced by cooperation of rational beings, who by a rational consent obey the authority because of the reasonableness of its commands. Reason is in all citizens; and the best way of government is by appeal to that reason common to all men. Consequently there is not much room for the modern "Elite"-theory. One cannot say that, by recognizing the death penalty and the obligation of the citizen to sacrifice his life in a just war, Catholic political doctrine contradicts these statements; the human person is not destroyed by bodily death.

Capital punishment is atonement on the part of him who suffers the extreme penalty for the grave injustice he has committed against the unity of order, against the common good. As long as we believe in immortality this idea of atonement, apart from the idea of determent, justifies the death penalty. The evildoer atones, and thus he can be received into paradise. That the priest accompanies the condemned person to the portal of eternity, is what makes such death penalty bearable. The socio-political order that has been gravely disturbed is restored by the sacrifice of life, so that in his death the condemned person helps to restore that order. Thus he has not become a mere instrument of determent. But evidently the belief in immortality is the reconciling fact. As soon as that belief has vanished, there is no longer any justification for the death penalty if we will preserve the idea of human dignity. Yet is that idea of the dignity of the human person conceivable without belief in personal immortality? Experience shows that wherever the individual person is wholly submerged in the above-mentioned "mystical" entities of blood, race, or class, personal immortality as the foundation of human dignity is denied. The death penalty there loses its moral element of atonement and becomes annihilation or extirpation in the true sense, and is for that reason so irreverently and eagerly imposed. No witness of the other world, into which the condemned man is to be transferred, is admitted. It is therefore quite consistent when the Soviet jurists, according to their materialist philosophy, speak not of the death penalty, but of a "social opera- tion," in executing a criminal.

The sacrifice of life by the soldier on the battlefield is justifiable only if by that sacrifice the political life of his country is protected, and if the soldier by his death discharges an objective ethical duty that per- fects him morally and can do so because his soul is immortal. The sacrificial death on the battlefield does not ennoble an abstract idea, but it perfects the personality, the immortal soul of the hero. When- ever personal immortality is denied, there remain but humanitarian sentimentality and consequent radical pacifism, because life on earth becomes absolutely the highest value; or there may recur an utter despising of life in a depersonalizing, fanatical submergence into a mystical whole of which the individual is a valueless particle.

The coincidence and reconciliation of freedom and order, of reason and authority, of human dignity and political power, in Catholic poli- tical philosophy may appear to outsiders as a *complexio oppositorum*. But it is nothing else than a consequence of the idea of man's nature in which is found the same polarity: even after the Fall, human nature is not destroyed, human reason can still find truth and is ordained to truth, and human will is directed to the good. But human nature is in- clined to evil, to a selfishness threatening the just, peaceful order of things, to immoderate indulgence, to passions that endanger the dig- nity of man and the order in which alone this dignity can be realized. That is the basis for an often criticized, because misunderstood, elas- ticity of Catholic political doctrine, which can accept almost all his- torical political institutions, all political forms as they appear in the history of nations: monarchy and republic, aristocracy and democracy. This philosophy embraces Donoso Cortes, preaching the necessity of dictatorship to halt the process of decay in modern civilization on the one hand: and, on the other hand, Lacordaire, Ozanam, and Montal- embert, the best of the liberal Catholics in France, the lovers of polit- ical freedom and of democratic institutions. This philosophy may appear in its struggles against socialism as a mobilization for the de- fense of property, and yet may appear as a revolutionary doctrine in the Irish priest who inspires striking workers to brave the abuses of propertied capitalists. But he who studies more deeply will find that this specific idea of human nature is what gives to Catholic political doctrine that universal feature which understands and evaluates concrete historical circumstances and social expediency, and the almost unconditional value of order. Yet it subjects every concrete order to criticism from the standpoint of invariable ethical principles, and in solemn solitude often stood for the normative might of natural law when brutal might or the theory of the normative power of facts seemed to rule the world and thought.

VIII. The Doctrine of the Fall

This idea of human nature utterly denies the contention that the origin of the state and a legitimation of its power beyond good and evil must be based on the fundamentally evil nature of man. Catholic political theory holds that this idea of the nature of man is only a basis for that abominable kind of polity which sees its essence in violence and compulsion, in absolute power outside every moral and legal law. For this kind of *Realpolitik* right is might. Justice, natural law, and moral values are empty shells of mere propaganda phrases. They are excellent masks to veil lust for power and violence. They afford good catchwords for the mob, to give its actions the dignity of righteousness. But behind the mask there is this stupendous non-morality of political action. And the non-moral use of power is considered necessary because the *massa damnata,* the *bête humaine,* the rabble, could not be kept in order by a use of power restricted by moral and legal law. If this power could not be used unrestrictedly, on the basis of expediency, it is held that the war of all against all would be waged every moment.

But what gives to the rulers, who obviously participate in this presupposed malignity of human nature, a right to use such power? Strange myths have been invented to justify this contradiction. The *de facto* ruler proves through successful ruthlessness that he belongs to a higher kind of man, that his is the better blood, derived from the gods; or that he is the representative of the master race; or that Providence has called him. Can there be a moral appeal of bad blood against good, an appeal of slave races against the master race, an appeal of man's reasoning against Providence?

The Catholic thinker contends that man's nature is not evil. His theology tells him that the original goodness has not been utterly destroyed by the Fall. But it tells him, too, that, as a consequence of original sin, man is always tempted to perfidy, selfishness, and uncontrolled passions which help dissolve the human community. However, the life in community—in family, neighborhood, state, and economic and social order—is not a consequence of man's inner malignity, but of man's social nature. Only the right of authorities to compel with physical force, and the duty in conscience to respect human, i.e., imperfect, law are based on man's inclination to evil.

Absolute freedom would give these destructive urges and the blind passions and the destructive vices prevalence over the commands of reason and of the virtues. For this continuous struggle of the inclination to evil against the rules of reason and the commands of virtue, this existence of the two laws in man's heart, of the *thymos* and the *psyche* (the fiery, boiling soul, and the cool, detached soul; cf. Aristotle, *De anima*, I, 405 a), is the condition of man's existence on account of his *natura vulnerata*. Yet through its relation to reason and the objective end of the state, political authority and power are measured by a moral yardstick. Authority and power receive no absolute legitimation from their function of constructing and preserving order, because human nature is not absolutely evil. Evil is not a quality in itself; it is lack of a good which ought to be and could be. Evil is a negation of this good. Therefore authority must be legitimated, must justify its actions before the idea of the good in man. And this good, demonstrable for reason, is the legitimation of a right use of power. Moral law gives the last decisive, irrevocable judgment in politics, too.

IX. Man, an Image of God

Man's nature as a rational, essentially social and political, and morally free, being (each word to be understood in its full meaning and bearing) remains the foundation of Catholic political doctrine. This idea of man now receives a further yet more exalted meaning from the fact that for Catholic thought the human person is an image of God. This is the typical Christian definition and excels the Greek definition, as Christianity excels Hellenism. But the Christian definition is of incomparable importance for political philosophy in any civilization, *post Christum*, even if that civilization is a secular one, as ours is to a considerable degree. For the dignity of man as a rational and free being receives its true sense through this definition. The whole world, with all its material wealth, its civilizations, its works of art and literature, is less than the soul of man, the immortal person in the likeness of God. This addition by Christianity, then, gives to man that supreme and most profound dignity of which there is so much talk. Man, every man, is the image of God, gifted with an immortal soul; this idea truly was revolutionary. With it is born a new concept of freedom. Now man transcends essentially all earthly social and political classes and qualifications. Now arises a realm in which all, king and peasant, free-born and serf, Greek and barbarian, knight and burgher, are equal, not in a quantitative sense, but in a qualitative sense. Now the idea of a sphere of definitive freedom is born; the Spirit blows where it will. In Christ all are free.

True, this freedom remained in rather embryonic form during the Middle Ages with their social system of strict, frozen social status and classes. But it began to work quietly, that idea of the upright dignity of the Christian person which everybody is, however poor and weak his social and political standing. It would be wrong to idealize the society of the Middle Ages as a society of democratic equality. Medieval society remains predominantly a hierarchic society of socially and politically unequal static estates. But the Aristotelian idea that some are born to be free, some to be slaves, could not endure in Christianity. The popular preachers in the Middle Ages indefatigably stress the equality of all children of God, and declare that there is only one true nobility, that of Christian virtue irrespective of social standing. There is only one freedom, found where the Spirit of the Lord is (II Cor. 3:17). It is the service to the common good that makes the nobleman, not succession, blood, or knightly vows, says a preacher of 1475 in a collection of sermons, *Origo nobilitatis*.[24] Every *officium* (occupation) has its own dignity. It is the right moral sentiment that counts, not social esteem or the rank of the *officium*. Against the encroachments of the ruling classes this Christian idea of the dignity and freedom of the person and the Church enforced the freedom of the matrimonial contract of serfs, the liberation of those who entered a religious order from the brutal ties of pagan slavery, and the access of all, irrespective

---

[24] Wilhelm Schwers: *Stand und Ständeordnung im Weltbild des Mittelalters*, 1934, Paderborn, p. 64, a work that is to be recommended to those who all too quickly contend that the Middle Ages were "democratic" in the sense of modern egalitarian theory.

of their membership in servile classes, to the ranks of the clergy. True, it is not justifiable—as is done all too easily by well-meaning people without the necessary historical knowledge—to put the modern ideas of social liberties and political rights into the strictly organized medieval society with its closed ruling and servile classes, with its legally and politically privileged upper estates and its patriarchally ruled obedient lower estates.

Yet the revolutionary ideas of an ultimate equality of all men, children of the same God, and of freedom and dignity of the Christian person, were put into the world never to disappear until our time. But now anti-Christian forms of political and social rule have arisen from the deteriorated soil of a non-Christian materialist doctrine. At the same time that they destroyed the root, Christianity, they destroyed also the flower, the freedom and dignity of the human person as an image of God. They would not have succeeded, had not secular materialism already theoretically dissolved the idea of human dignity by teaching that man has no immortal soul, but is only the most highly developed animal; that man is not a free being, gifted with creative initiative, but that his mind is only a result, a bundle of reactions to the sovereign conditions of economic production; that man is not the image of a supermundane, supreme Intellect, but that his soul is an image only of his subconscious *Triebleben*, of an all-penetrating libido. Whenever man, the free, rational, political being, the image of God, is so degraded, it is no wonder that with his personality and his dignity there disappears also the state as a moral institution. What remains then is a brutal tyranny, "the cold monster," the moloch. The destruction of the idea of the Godlikeness of the individual person must produce the diabolical, omnipotent God-state of mortal tyrants.

Perhaps the student of the history of political theories will object. He may point out that Donoso Cortes, De Maistre, and De Bonald in their antidemocratic sentiments, seem to prefer absolute power and defend dictatorship or praise the unlimited power of monarchy. But Donoso Cortes overstressed the wounding of human nature by original sin. He fought with theologians about the degree of injury, stating that this injury was so severe that it came near to destruction. De Maistre, the traditionalist, did not think highly of human reason and its ability to control dangerous passions. Both, therefore, distrusted the liberal ideas in government which were of rationalistic, Rousseauist origin and showed a deep dislike of democracy. They rejected the vaunted superiority of persuasion over compulsion and were very pessimistic about the consequences of the theory of the rights of man, general suffrage, and the majority rule. In opposition to these men the student of history may point to Lord Acton, the famous historian, to Montalembert and his liberal Catholics in France, to Archbishop Ireland and Father Hecker in America, all known as stout adherents of just such political principles as were strongly opposed by Cortes, De Maistre, and others.

A skeptical student may say: "This is the typical Catholic *complexio oppositorum*. It enables Catholic theory to defend or to reject every political system, as expediency and the temporary political interests of the Roman Catholic Church demand. There does not exist an inner unchangeable principle, but only an unprincipled opportunism."

The student without prejudices, on the contrary, will see that the reason for these differences in political theory rests on that universal polar tension between two opposing ideas which strive for unity. In theology this opposition is evident in the two systems of Thomism and Molinism. In ethics the dispute is between the doctrines that law is reason and that law is will. This contrast itself rests on the existential way of human thinking which is discursive and dialectic. Yet as long as we are conscious of these contrasts and are aware that we must strive for a concordance,[25] this opposition means dynamic life. Only if we lose sight of one of the contrasting poles, overstressing the other, do we fall into false theories. If we deny the original value of truth by despising intellect while exalting will, the result must be a destruction of metaphysics, the promotion of positivism in philosophy, and the destruction of natural law in politics as well as an exaltation of absolute power. If we deny that there is still left some goodness and truth in fallen man, a cooperation with grace is impossible. In the last analysis, all heresies deny this polar tension in all things human, and exalt one of the contrasting polar tendencies. But "Catholic" means an embracing of these contrasts; it means a perpetual striving to produce

---

[25] Every high point of Christian theory is a time of concordance: St. Thomas produced a concordance of Aristotle and Christian tradition; the late Scholastics, of Thomism and Augustinianism; modern times have produced concordances in social philosophy.

the *concord-antia* as it lives in God, who is pure intellect, omnipotent will, perfect goodness, and unlimited love. There is a deep truth in the thesis that all political problems are at last theological problems and that there is a parallelism between the idea of God and of state.

Man is a rational, free being, not a passive instrument of God's act. Certainly, God always bears man in His almighty hands. No human acting is possible without God's active cooperation. But this cooperation follows the mode of being of the creature; in man, according to his freedom. The natural powers of man, developing from his intellectual, social, free nature, are able to produce a social order. This social order is based on the unchangeable nature of man and aims at its permanently more perfect realization. As realization occurs in history, in concrete life, it is concretely influenced by biological differences, by national culture, and by geographical situation. St. Thomas' moral philosophy always recurs to circumstances and their influence in the concrete realization of the perennial principle.

It is just this historical view underlying the above-mentioned differences in political theory that gives to Catholic political philosophy its elasticity. It is just this idea of man which enables us to esteem an active attitude of man in the realms of culture and politics. In this world man works for his salvation. The Christian is aware that he fulfills God's command when he pursues his own happiness. Must it be said that his happiness is not an animal's happiness, but the happiness of a free, rational being? The perfect life, therefore, finds its coronation in contemplation, not in seclusion from the world, or in immersion in worldly affairs.

To work for his salvation man ordinarily needs a favorable environment. He needs a good social order which guarantees his freedom and personality and produces an environment for their preservation; an order which enables him to develop his nature and to promote the use of all his faculties. He needs a socio-economic system that affords him a basis for his cultural life. He needs a political order for the protection and preservation of this social-economic order. St. Thomas Aquinas often remarks that to live in virtue, a sufficiency of temporal goods is necessary; this demands a stable order in political, economic, and social life. Environment and morality have a kind of interdependence. Hence there cannot be an absolute indifference on the part of the Christian to things temporal. They become important according as they are able to create an environment favorable for the work of salvation.

This, then, is the reason why the Church cannot resign its interest in the world. This is the basis for a cooperation of the spiritual and temporal powers. The Church cannot be a private affair, nor can it restrict itself to a social quietism. Justin Martyr (A.D. 155) in his *Apologia* told the Roman Emperor that the better Christian a man is, the better citizen he is.

These ideas enable Catholic political theory to remember always the innermost metaphysical connection with God, especially in political life. At the same time Catholic political theory can be open and unprejudiced toward historical development and the free will of the nations to decide their political life as it suits them best. Christian political theory does not adhere to a passive conservatism, nor is it enamored of progress. It is conservative in principles, but progressive in application of these principles to the ever-changing circumstances. In the struggle between the passionate urge for limitless freedom and conservative order, Christian political theory stands on the side of order. In the struggle between man's longing for freedom and dehumanizing absolute power, it will fight for freedom. In the struggle between social justice and reactionary defense of the vested interests of selfish classes, it will unite with justice. Faced by the choice between the dignity of the human person and political expediency, it will defend the dignity of the human person.

X. THE NATURE OF MAN AND THE IDEA OF PROGRESS

The importance of the idea of man is seen also in the fact that it is the basis of the concept of progress in Catholic political philosophy. The spirit of the nineteenth century indulged in a concept of unlimited progress in all fields of human endeavor. This idea of progress is profoundly secular and optimistic. It issues from a philosophy of history and of development according to which man rises from a brute, crude form of animal existence to ever more perfect forms of intellectual, moral, and socio-political life into the infinite, where in a far distant future man will become godlike and human civilization will produce an earthly paradise without such institutions as compulsory laws, political authority, social classes, and Churches. Comte's dreams of a conquest of the theological and metaphysical status of man by the positivist philosophy with humanity as a deity represents such a form of infinite progress. The idea of such progress is distinct in the philosophy of liberalism as well as in the philosophy of communism and of the various forms of socialism. They all agree formally in their faith in a millennial reign of a most perfect sublimation of man's nature, without the intervention of God's grace and of religion—in its very nature supernatural and transcendent to all mere human natural development. They transfer into history, into the world and human will that which according to true religion is supramundane, beyond human will, beyond history, belongs to other-worldly eternity. This nineteenth century chiliastic belief in progress and in the parousia of a final earthly paradise reached through man's natural development is actually a secularized form of the Christian's hope in a future perfect life in the other world—in the eternal union with God, never to be attained by man's natural power but only to be received as a gift (*gratia*) of God.

In political philosophy such a secular millennium means the "withering away" of the state as a compulsory order, of authority as a moral force demanding obedience and thus restricting perfect individual freedom. It means consequently that the Rousseauist political ideals, all those technically democratic institutions that do away with authority and compulsion by an identification of government and governed, are the most important factor in making superfluous any compulsion. In the end the *civitas maxima* (humanity) appears not as an old-fashioned *civitas* but as a perfect rule of unlimited individual freedom. To be sure, here again the underlying idea of man is wholly optimistic. If anything is wrong in human affairs, it is the effect of imperfect socio-political institutions or economic environments, and it will disappear with the progress of evolution. The government is bad, the people are good. The aim of progress is the regeneration of the people alone without government. Yet even the more brute ideas of the biological evolutionist theory in political philosophy founded upon the Darwinian principle of the struggle for existence or the Spencerian principle of the survival of the fittest are of the same kind of pattern of infinite progress. History here is also an unending production of more and more perfect forms of political life destined to reach for a status of absolute perfection.

On the opposite side we have the pessimistic philosophies, for instance, that of Spengler. In regard to the "goal of humanity," he is thoroughly and decidedly a pessimist; for him humanity is a zoological quantity; he sees no progress of human nature, no "goal of humanity." Man is a beast of prey; ethics is a utilitarian ideology for those interested in an ever transitory *status quo*. History is an irrational wavelike surge and fall without ideals. Politics is only the brutal will of a nation to preserve its strength and its own form of existence by means of war, which is the everlasting form of human existence in a never-ending change of cultures and civilizations. Progress, therefore, is a fake. And history is always the history of warfaring states. The consequences of such an idea of man for political philosophy are best illustrated by the influence of Spengler's ideas in the formation of National Socialism. History is not the immanent progressive perfection of man by himself nor is it the revelation of God's providential guidance; it is senseless, irrational, eternal return, endless dashing of the waves. There is no better or worse form of government as there are no unchangeable standards to judge by. There is only one subject matter to study in political philosophy—which, by the way, is not a philosophy at all but merely a collection of facts—and that is might; might as absolute value, might with its technique and its migration from one conquering state to another, from one elite in the state to another elite. All other things—justice, equity, righteousness—are intrinsically meaningless ideologies, and are of value only as instruments for political might.

Between these perennially recurring extremes, Catholic political philosophy stands. Its idea of man is specifically different, though at a superficial glance one may think it only a balanced mixture of these opposing extremes. Such a view is just as wrong as to make Christian social philosophy the middle and the balanced mixture of individualism and socialism. For Catholic political philosophy the nature of man is the *terminus a quo* and the *terminus ad quem* of political development. It is the *terminus ad quem*. This means that never will the *status politicus*, authority, compulsory order, might, be unnecessary. The state with all its essential elements will never wither away in any possible form of the perfection of human nature. So there is no possibility of a stateless earthly paradise, a mundane millennium as the goal of history. That goal of history is the final supernatural redemption of all creation; the finis of history will be: doomsday, the last judgment, and heaven or hell.

However, in history the goal of man upon this earth is the continuous perfection of man's nature but as an essentially political nature. So the state will never wither away; it still is necessary for the perfection of human nature at any degree of progress. Catholic political philosophy is not overpessimistic as is the original Lutheran political theory and again its newest form under the influence of the dialectic theology of Karl Barth which, overcoming theological liberalism, returns to Luther's doctrine of the *natura deleta*. Catholic political philosophy is humble and does not indulge in that modern titanism which makes man the autonomous creator of order and the measure of all things. Man's existence is essentially contingent and finite. By none of his efforts will he be able to produce an earthly paradise. All too often man attains a progress in material wealth with a regress in spiritual wealth; an advance in intellectual endeavor with a regress in virtuous life; an all too proud effort in moral progress with a regress in virtue on account of lack of humility.

And yet this awareness of finiteness, this consciousness of unfulfillment of his longing for progressive perfection, does not lead to social and political quietism. On the contrary, the Christian is aware of sin and the continuous threat of destructive passions inimical to the peace and progress of his political existence, and he is also aware that it is his divine vocation to work incessantly on the slow perfection of the City of Men, because thus he helps to improve the external conditions in which he can work for the salvation of souls. And he knows also that any progress in the perfection of the City of Men is an approach to the never realizable prototype of his City, the City of God.

The Christian convinced of the intrinsic dignity of human nature will work for political progress to more and fuller freedom; yet he will be aware of the necessity of legitimate authority equipped with compulsory power to be used, however cautiously, whenever the use of freedom leads to the impairment of the order and peace which, under human existence, is the condition of freedom. The Christian aware of the divine call to perfect the socio-economic order by social justice, however much he may be aware that charity is no substitute for justice, will know that "the poor you have always with you." Consequently he will know that justice always needs helpful charity, not only humbly seeing human dignity in the poor and unhappy ones, as did the Stoic philosophers, but seeing Christ in them.

The Christian trusts in man's vocation to liberal progressive organization of humanity to produce "world peace to abolish war." But he does not indulge in the illusions of modern perfectionist progressivism: that as soon as a world government, an international police force, and a body of positive international law with a world court are established, humanity will enjoy eternal peace. The Christian is aware that the legal forms themselves can easily be made subservient means of political struggle for power, if the spirit of peace, the moral will, and the vivid sentiment of being obliged in conscience to keep the peace and realize justice, the *telos* of the legal forms, are not alive with internal power in the body of laws. Nations wax and nations wane, the positive *status quo* "sanctified" by the legal forms cannot endure. The contingency of human existence effects changes in the *status quo;* justice demands and charity urges to change the legal *status quo* even against the will and the armed resistance of the *beati possidentes.* Legality and patriotism are not enough. The inner will to sacrifice vested rights in the interest of the paramount common good of the community of nations must influence international life. Thus it is the intellectual mood or the moral temperament that distinguishes the Christian from the modern apostles of infinite immanent progress. They can agree in many particular matters and projects, and yet they differ in the underlying philosophy, a fact that baffles the progressive optimist again and again.

CHAPTER III

Political Theology

I. The Concept of God and Political Philosophy

In primitive societies theology and politics, priesthood and statecraft, are fused into one. The state and the laws, the king as the representative of the hidden God, all are considered divinely instituted. All laws are sacred. All authorities are divine. As the link between the gods and the visible world of the political offices, the priest-king is supreme. Every act of government is imbued with religious ceremonies which give the act its fundamental legitimacy. The two characteristic qualities of the religious world, according to Rudolf Otto—the *fascinosum* and the *numinosum*—are also characteristics of the acts of political government in primitive societies. This fact points to the identity of the tribal gods and the state, of priesthood and political authority, of sacred law and civil law.

Even the Greek communities, with their worldly political philosophy, their rational enlightenment, and their "humanization" of the gods, were still aware of this influence of the divine power on their laws and politics. The law, the *nomos* of the city-state, retained even for some skeptic Sophists this theological aspect. The state of the ancients was, to repeat a truism, at the same time political and religious community. The divine worship of the Roman emperor, so scandalous to the Christians, was a consequence of this identification.[1]

In the Christian era the old identification could, of course, not endure. Yet the influence, the interdependence and the interrelations, to use the most general terms, between the dominant concept of God and the idea of the state, and consequently between theological doc-

---

[1] Cf. Ulrich von Wilamowitz-Moellendorf, *Staat und Gesellschaft der Griechen* (Leipzig, 1923) pp. 41 ff.; Lily Ross Taylor, *The Divinity of the Roman Emperor* (1931); Erik Peterson, *Der Monotheismus als politisches Problem* (Leipzig, 1935).

trines and systems of political philosophy, must not be regarded as indifferent. True it is that, with the rise of rationalism, political philosophy emancipated itself from the doctrines of natural and supernatural theology just as the state became religiously indifferent. And even more, political philosophy treated its subject matter as if God did not exist. But such an abstraction could not satisfy, and has never satisfied. Proudhon, himself an unbeliever, could not deny that at the bottom of every political problem lies a theological problem. The idea expressed by Shakespeare, that there is a mystery about the soul of the state, resisted all those easy attempts in political philosophy to separate that stupendous and fascinating being, the state, from the idea of God and thus from theology.

It is therefore understandable that after the energy and the influence of secular rationalism began to decrease there awoke a new interest in regard to the interrelation between the specific idea of God and the tenets of the state held by a political philosopher, and that the problem of theology and politics or of a "political theology" began to be studied anew. This problem had naturally interested such minds of the Counter-revolution, of the Romantic Restoration, as the Catholics De Maistre, Adam Müller, Donoso Cortes, and the Protestant philosopher of the monarchic principle, Julius von Stahl. These men had made use particularly of theology in their battle against Enlightenment and Revolution, but were looked upon with derisive contempt by the nineteenth century, which indulged in the departmentalization of sciences and in agnostic positivism.

Only in recent decades did political philosophers other than the disciples of this romantic philosophy begin to be interested in "Political Theology," in the "Theological Presuppositions of Politics," in "Theology of Politics," in "God and the State." [2] The political philosophy of Charles Maurras, for example, commended itself to Catholic Frenchmen by subtly putting in the foreground Catholic theological doctrines in the interest of an only slightly concealed positivist political philosophy.

[2] The words in quotation marks are the titles of books by Carl Schmitt: *Politische Theologie* (Leipzig, 1922; 2nd ed., 1934); of Alfred de Quervain: *Die theologischen Voraussetzungen der Politik* (Berlin, 1931); of Nathaniel Micklem (Oxford, 1942); of Hans Kelsen's Essay, "Gott und der Staat" in *Logos*, 1922. It would be easy to give a long list of books regarding political theology or theological politics from early Gnosticism until today. In spite of its title, Spinoza's *Tractatus theologico-politicus* does not strictly belong here.

What is common to all these recent works is the thesis that theological doctrines and the fundamental concept of God which a political philosophy holds are of greatest influence on its ideas, principles, and elaborations, however little this theology may be openly expressed. This fact makes it necessary to discuss these questions of political theology.

II. The Potential Meaning of Political Theology

To clear the field, it is necessary to establish what is meant by these writers when they use the term "theology." At the beginning we must discard the idea that they treat religion (and politics) in the sense of William James or in the sense of that general subject matter of "the science of religion." What is meant here is either natural theology, i.e., God revealing Himself in His creation to the human rational mind, revealing Himself in the conscience, or supernatural theology, the doctrine of God, revealing Himself positively in Christ and the inspired Sacred Scriptures, interpreted by the infallible doctrinal authority of the divinely instituted papacy or, as in Protestantism, by divine guidance of the individual conscience, with or without the assistance of tradition (*quod semper, quod ubique, quod ab omnibus*) and of the consensus of theologians. Thus it is not religious experiences, religious sentiments, or irrational feelings, but doctrine that is meant here. (The theology of the Church can enter here only if the Church's constitution is considered to be of positive divine law and not the result of merely human acts and consents or of historical development.) The writers mentioned may contend that a certain affinity exists between the methods of theology and the methods of jurisprudence; and most political philosophers come from the study of jurisprudence. For the lawyer, the constitution, the written statute law, and the customary law play the same role as the canon of Scriptures, the dogmas, and the tradition do for the theologian. Furthermore, their methods are akin so far as the science of jurisprudence acts like the science of theology in elaborating on the meaning of the "texts," working out the interrelations between parts and individual tenets, explaining from the tradition the import of a principle or a conclusion; for both, "texts" issue from a sovereign authority: in the one, God revealing Himself and legislating; in the other, the sovereign

state legislating without appeal. Hence the expression "juridical dog
matics." The affinity between theology and jurisprudence comes ou
distinctly if one compares the role which Cardinal Newman attribute
to the consensus of theologians in relation to the papal dogmatic au
thority and the role which is attributed to scientific jurisprudence i
relation to the laws of the state.[3]

More important than the affinity of method, however, are suc
questions as the following. What analogies exist between theologic
concepts and doctrines and political concepts and doctrines, and wh
is the nature and import of these analogies? To what degree do di
tinct political doctrines follow positively from certain theologic
doctrines, or in how far does a specific political idea or ideal follo
from a distinct concept of God? For instance, what implications h
Deism upon problems of political philosophy; what consequence fo
lows in political philosophy from the tenets of modern liberal theolog
or from the dialectic theology of Karl Barth [4] and his school? T

[3] Cf. Wilfrid Ward, *Life of Cardinal Newman* (1912), I, 653 f.; II, 376, 406, 556.

[4] The dialectic theology of Karl Barth, or as it is also called, the *Theology of Cri*
(this is the title of E. Brunner's English book; New York, 1929), is the violent reacti
of Protestant (reformist) theology against the "liberal theology" of the nineteenth a
early twentieth centuries and against the "Social Gospel" theology. Liberal theolo
through biblical criticism, through the "historical Jesus" research, through its historic
evolutionism, had diluted the substance of faith which the Reformers held. Th
Christianity became a religion among many other religions; Christ became an ethic
philosopher like Confucius or Socrates; the Bible became a religious document like t
Koran. Thus theology became general religious science, religious psychology, religio
ethics. Or it became a social ethical doctrine regulating secular life; or, in the one-sid
Social Gospel enthusiasm, Christianity became a theory of social reform in competiti
with socialism. Thus the very substance of the Christian faith—word of God, revelatio
redemption from sin—was step by step diluted so that any difference between the go
pagan and the Christian almost disappeared. Christianity became an atmosphere, a set
useful ethical rules for the secular sphere. The activism of the one-sided Social Gos
theory with its aim to "Christianize" secular society threatened to secularize Christiani
Against these currents in Protestant theology and ethics Barth arose with a revival
the Reformers, Calvin and Luther, in their prime when neither was yet compromised
Melanchthonism. Some of the main theses of this theology of crisis are: The absolu
transcendence of God, of the hidden unknown God who is not first cause, legislator
natural law in our hearts, but who is Totally-Other. We have no way to God; neith
by the Thomistic *analogia entis*, i.e., in natural theology, nor by our being created af
God's image. God only speaks to us. (The finite is not capable of the Infinite). Wor
man, finiteness, all this is sinfulness. The reformist doctrine of the *natura deleta*
emphasized; so, therefore, is the *sola fide* doctrine of redemption. (A sympathetic presen
tion of Barthian theology is given in the following: John McConnachie, *The Barthi*
Theology (London, 1933); Walter Lowrie, *Our Concern with the Theology of Cr*
(Boston, 1932), with a bibliography. The theological "climate" in America is somewh
unfavorable to this Theology of Crisis as Adolf Keller points out in *Karl Barth a*
Christian Unity, (New York, 1933), pp. 177 ff. The best books by Catholic theologia

vhat extent do theological doctrines or a distinct idea of God nega-
ively influence a political philosophy by prohibiting the approval of
ertain political ideals? For instance, how does the faith in revelation
aught and preached and interpreted by a divinely instituted authority
nd guided by the Church qualify the principle, as distinguished from
he practice, of freedom of religion? How does the concept of a divinely
nstituted universal Church influence the legal status of this Church
vithin a particular state (the theory of the relation between Church
nd state)?

That all these problems are also ethical problems should not lead
o the contention that they do not belong to political philosophy. For,
s previously stated, since political philosophy concerns matters result-
ng from human actions and since it concerns human ends to be at-
ained by man as a free and rational active agent, it becomes implicitly
thics. And it is this very fact that produces the problems to be dis-
ussed here. The objection that political philosophy should have
othing to do with political ethics would imply that political philos-
phy is a part of natural philosophy which concerns "nature" as op-
osed to reason, mind, free will. Yet it is true that political philosophy
no more simply "moralism" than theology is "moralizing" in the
nterest of subordinate and ephemeral interests.

The literature of political philosophy is filled with analogies be-
ween theology, the idea of God, and the pattern of thinking of polit-
al philosophers. A wide range of examples may be noted: the analogy
etween the idea of a transcendent God and that of the king of divine
ght transcendent above the state; the analogy of the miracle-working
od who suspends the laws of nature when working miracles to the
overeign king who suspends the laws of the state in granting a par-

---

out the Theology of Crisis are those of Erich Przywara, S.J., *Ringen der Gegenwart*
reiburg, 1929); *Analogia Entis* (1930); *Christliche Existenz* (1934). It is understandable
at this theology, rejecting natural theology, natural law, the *Imago Dei*, and the
alogia entis doctrine, offers scarcely a possibility for a political philosophy and ethics
sed on human nature and reason. If it treats political ethical problems at all, it must
se its theories on supernatural revelation. Cf., for instance, Emil Brunners, *The Word*
d the World (New York, 1931), which indirectly proves this thesis; Adolf Keller, *op. cit.*,
. 100–104. If, therefore, on the basis of this theology, a political philosophy and ethics
ould ever be constructed, it will be truly a political theology. A first though rather
eager effort is the book of De Quervain. Another example is found in some essays of
ineth-Schreiner, *Die Nation vor Gott* (5th ed., Berlin, 1937). Even a superficial com-
rison of these essays with the encyclical of Pius XI, *Mit brennender Sorge*, will show
e difficulties which the *Theology of Crisis* finds in political philosophy.

don or a legal privilege; and the analogy which Karl Marx stressed as existing between the theological doctrine of religious liberty in the sense of religious individualism on the basis of personal interpretation of the Scriptures and the sway of free competition within the field of economic production. The fact that theology is considered supreme in the divine rights theory and the political ideal the reflex, whereas in the Marxian analogy the social pattern of economic production is considered supreme and the theological doctrines only the reflex, shows that here the analogy rests in the first case upon a wholly spiritualized philosophy and in the latter case upon a materialist philosophy, each denying the other and thus depriving the analogy of any worth.

The subject matter in which this problem arises is mainly the study of the so-called state forms like monarchy and democracy. Furthermore, such constitutional problems as sovereignty and its monarchic and popular forms and, in the international order, imperialism and the chosen-people theology; further, the theological doctrines concerning natural reason and supernatural revelation and the nature of man already discussed in a previous chapter but to be evidenced here from the aspect of political theology.[5]

In order to organize this discussion, it is well to make some distinctions: first, between natural and supernatural or positively revealed theology, or between the idea of the God of the philosophers and the God of revelation; and secondly, to distinguish the analogy that is constitutive as the result of an identical fundamental structure of theology and political theories, the analogy that is effective because it is determinative and therefore exemplary from such analogies as are merely illustrative and more incidental.

III. NATURAL THEOLOGY AND POLITICAL PHILOSOPHY

Let us first discuss the influence of natural theology on political philosophy. And let us remark at the outset that this natural theology must be sharply distinguished from theological doctrines, properly so

[5] Leo Strauss (*The Political Philosophy of Thomas Hobbes*, Oxford, 1936; pp. 59 ff. points out that Hobbes originally based much of his political philosophy on natural theology, which he later gave up on account of his change to materialistic metaphysics. He then based some of his rather extreme theories on a pretended supernatural theology which brought about many important changes in his whole political philosophy.

alled, which result from supernatural revelation. Writers who propound the idea of political theology usually have in mind the latter.
In the field of natural theology the main doctrines are monotheism as
against polytheism, pantheism, deism, and atheism (the denial of
natural theology). In the history of political philosophy each of these
doctrines has had its influence upon political theories.

In the first Christian centuries the analogy between the monotheism
in theology and the monarchy of the Roman emperor in politics,
between the divine monarchy of God in the universe and the political
monarchy of the Roman emperor on earth, was widely used by the
Christian apologists against the pagan philosophers with their polytheism. Celsus severely criticized the Christian monotheism as a revolutionary doctrine in politics.[6] The Roman Empire is, in his eyes, not
a monistic structure but rather a political organization of many peoples and nations, each with its own national particularities, living
according to their national laws. Each of these nations has its national
gods and, though there is a supreme god, he is not jealous of the national gods; he reigns over the world as the national gods rule over
their nations. The monotheism of the Christians refuses to honor the
national gods and so threatens to destroy the Empire.

Among many others, Eusebius answers this attack. He tries to prove
that the Roman Empire, overcoming the superstitions of the nations
and transforming the pluralism of national entities into the one Empire, is, so to speak, a historical proof for the Christian monotheism.
He points out that the incessant wars among the separated nations
and the civil wars inside the nations, i.e., the absence of peace, are the
result of polytheism. Consequently the Christian monotheism is not
a revolt but results in peace; and the universal Roman Empire is, as
it were, the political result of monotheism. Thus to the one God, supreme monarch of the universe, and to His rule of law and peace in
the universe, corresponds the one monarch upon the earth, establishing one law and abolishing wars in the *pax Romana*. Eric Peterson
quotes many other authors who hold the same idea, namely, that in
political life the Roman Empire under the one emperor corresponds
to the divine monarchy of the one God in the universe. Thus the
monotheistic idea was used to establish the superiority of the mon-

[6] We follow here the excellent study of Eric Peterson, *Der Monotheismus als politisches Problem*, 1935.

archy over other forms of government, to prove the eminence of the world-state over national separatism, and to point out that, politically international peace is the effect of monotheism, whereas incessant war result from polytheism.

With the victory of the Trinitarian dogma over Arianism thi "political" monotheism as the theological basis for the Roman Empire became impossible. Arianism, denying the divinity of Christ and hence the apostolic dogma of the Trinity, became obviously the politica theology of the Roman emperors. The Trinitarian theology, feeling the Jewish origin of the Arian monotheism, gave up any politica theology. Thus Christianity became disengaged from the politica form and historical destiny of the Roman Empire. It was now eviden that there are many states and nations, independent and free; and the idea of a world-state, as the Stoics favored it, is not favored by St Augustine; nor does he believe in the *pax Romana* which in fact, h says, never existed. The one apostolic universal Church above the na tions is the new Empire of God, the *Civitas Dei*. Furthermore, there i no need for such a worldly Empire as was the Roman. The natural law valid for all men, pagan and Christian, barbarian and Greek, is th common rule and law of the community of nations which are actuall or at least potentially united by Christianity.

Yet we should note one point of this monotheistic political theology namely, that monotheism with natural law as the universal law for al mankind, and peace, order, and international cooperation, are as much interdependent and related concepts as are polytheism, war, and in ternational anarchy. Under polytheism, whether of the pre-Christian or the post-Christian kind (the national gods of modern paganism, e.g. Wotan of the radical Nazi faith), all wars are necessarily religious war as any kind of religious community between such nations is implicitly denied. On the other hand, monotheism may, at least in its Jewish Old Testament form, be politically abused in the form of the chosen-people ideology. It is at least to be noted that this ideology arises when the Old Testament overcomes the New Testament in religious life. The Calvinist overstressing of the Old Testament gives a better foundation for the chosen-people ideology than does the New Testament and the Catholic theology; these latter make the ideology of a chosen people politically impossible from a theological standpoint.

In this connection a question ventilated by writers of early Chris ianity and again by the adherents of political Romanticism in the nineteenth century, is this: Does monotheism in religion necessitate monarchy as the only admissible form of government or at least as the best form; does monotheism in the universe demand monarchism in the state, and does polytheism demand democracy, i.e., political polyarchy? Such analogies have been made, but they do not carry far. Monarchy as opposed to anarchy and polyarchy does not necessarily mean the absolute monarchism of the divine right of kings, a doctrine so familiar from the sixteenth to the eighteenth century. For Aristotle and for the Middle Ages, monarchy meant the unity of the political order, the concentration of authority and sovereign decision in one person. *"Principium,"* the Latin word for the Greek *arche, princeps,* and our word "principle," all mean primarily "origin," "primary cause," then "rule," "supreme authority." Thus monarchy means that there should be one clearly defined personal authority. Its opposite is not so much democracy, or as Aristotle called it *politia,* but either anarchy, i.e., no authority, no sovereign decision at all, or polyarchy, the rule of many opposing principles which make unity and sovereign ultimate decision impossible.

When Aristotle, at the end of Book XII of his *Metaphysics,* quotes the Homeric verse (*Iliad,* II, 204), "One be the Lord," he was less concerned with the political form of monarchy than with the Platonists. For the Platonist philosophy accepted a dyarchy, a good god and a bad god, and Speusippus even accepted a polyarchy, several unrelated, unsubordinated principles (*archai*) in the universe. Thus "monarchy" means that the universe is what the name points out, a unity issuing from one principle and ruled by one divine mind. Thus monotheism would demand only clearly defined authority, sovereign decision and the rule of a common law; but not that form of monarchism which is typical for the theory of the divine right of the king, the hereditary absolute king as opposed to the elected king or emperor so familiar to the Middle Ages. The divine right theory knew this distinction and therefore it based the rights of the king not on the metaphysical principle of monotheism but on its own interpretation of supernatural theology and especially on the Old Testament, i.e., on the Jewish theocracy of one God, one people (His chosen people). Such ideas, in truth, lay far away from the thought of the Middle Ages that would say one God, one Church, one Christianity; but never one

God, one people. It was left to the neopaganism of Nazi "God-believers," to use the slogan, "One (sc. German) God, one Leader, one People," in a starkly polemic sense against the Christian Church, which lives above the peoples and races under God ruling the universe. Thus from a sober and reasonable standpoint monotheism is indifferent to the various forms, monarchic or democratic, by which the sovereign authority and the *unitas ordinis* is established in any state.

IV. DEISM, PANTHEISM, AND ATHEISM

Deism, pantheism, and atheism, the last in the form of militant positive atheism or in the milder form of skeptical agnosticism or positivist relativism, undeniably have had a far-reaching influence on political theory. It is, of course, not true that political philosophers have always been aware of this influence nor is it true, as the political philosophy of Romanticism and especially of Donoso Cortes argued, that their theories of justification of political institutions, e.g., of democracy, must lead to the condemnation of such institutions. Nevertheless the influence of deistic natural theology upon political philosophy is undeniable and has been shown in a bitter polemic way by such philosophers of Romanticism as De Maistre, Adam Müller, and Donoso Cortes. The latter, in their polemic criticism, have in turn developed "political theology" as they tried to show the influence of the doctrines of deism and pantheism on political philosophy. They ascribed to Protestant supernatural theology the rise of political institutions which they utterly loathed, thus inferring that the political institutions they preferred were owing to Catholic supernatural theology.

In this discussion one of the main problems is sovereignty as regards its origin, its holders (the monarch or the people), its extent. Historically, from the sixteenth century when in the Protestant countries the absolute king united in his hands political and spiritual sovereignty, the outstanding problem of Protestant political philosophy became the following. Protestantism, i.e., the principle of the religious sovereignty of the individual conscience, produced, in stark contradiction to this sovereignty, a new theocratic monarchy with the prince as chief bishop. It produced the absolute king of divine right and the state Church in which the king was "pope." Consequently in

Protestant countries we find absolute sovereignty quite untrammeled by independent ecclesiastical law, by the power of the pope, by the competency of the bishops of the universal Church. Such a condition implied the destruction of the medieval restrictions on royal sovereignty exercised by the Church. Yet the individualistic principle of the Reformation contradicted utterly such an all-embracing absolutism of the identity of monarchy and national Church, since in its extreme form this principle had to lead to the dissolution of the Church as a divinely instituted community with her sacramental law, her hierarchical order, and her ecclesiastical government.

Now that the monarchy and the established Church (state Church) were united in the absolute king of divine right, i.e., of unrestricted sovereignty, it was again from the individualistic principle that the problem of sovereignty had to be attacked. On the other hand the personalism of the Renaissance with its enthusiasm for the personal freedom of worldly wisdom, of an aristocratic republicanism, brought forth this same problem of the origin and restrictions of sovereignty. Thus the centuries are filled with discussions about divine rights, that is, absolute sovereignty of the king and chief bishop versus popular sovereignty and freedom of religion. The question of freedom of the individual from compulsory membership in the established Church arose.

From this original freedom of religion, other freedoms were later derived, such as freedom of the person, of speech, of association, though these "civil liberties" do not rest exclusively on this individualistic concept of freedom of religion. It was not Man versus the State, but the individual conscience against the summepiscopus and absolute monarch, and civil liberties and constitutional rights of participation in soverign legislation against unrestricted princely sovereignty. To use modern terms, it was civil liberty, representative government, and popular sovereignty versus conformity and subjection in spiritual and secular matters to an unrestricted monarchic sovereignty which was ultimately justifiable only if divinely instituted. Thus the civil liberties and the democratic institutions in the eyes of the writers of political Romanticism seemed to be founded upon the Protestant principle of religious individualism. This conclusion was not cogent, since these rights and institutions can be considered also from the standpoint of natural law. Yet the romantic political philosophy was induced to see in the opposite political institutions (e.g., in monarchy) a consequence of Catholic theology. Thus they fought one pretended political theology by constructing another one just as precarious as the first.

Once this religious nonconformity, founded on revelation, had been secularized in the natural religion of deism which, after all, is little more than secular morality, religious freedom became a civil liberty. And all the claims for freedom in the philosophy of the Enlightenment rest, of course, upon the idea that man's nature is intrinsically good, that in his acts he is psychologically guided, if enlightened, by rational or utilitarian, that is, reasonably calculable, motives. The necessary consequence is that such a man needs no sovereign transcendental rule to direct him. The sovereignty of the king must be restricted by two devices: First, the governed must participate in the use of the sovereignty, i.e., legislation must be made by the king *and* representatives of the citizens; secondly, a bill of rights (human rights) should fence off a sphere of individual self-activity, religious, scientific, moral, economic, impenetrable to an act of the sovereign. From this optimistic view of man's reason and will, of this substitution of natural common religion instead of supernatural religion and organized Churches, there follows an inherent consequence. This is the idea that in the end the sovereignty should rest as an inalienable right in the totality of the citizens as inferred by Rousseau in his theory of the general will, an idea that corresponds in natural theology to naturalistic pantheism.

Political theology, developed, e.g., by Donoso Cortes,[7] regards as parallel to the theological and religious decadence, this development of political government from transcendent royal sovereignty restricted by divine and natural law and by the prerogatives of the Church and the papacy to the immanent sovereignty of the people. But it is asserted that the religious decay is what causes the political decay. So Donoso Cortes infers that to theism in theology corresponds in politics the full constitutive sovereignty of the king, which is truly transcendent in relation to the people, i.e., divinely instituted by providential guidance and restricted only by divine law and by the Church. In his *Protestantism as Political Principle*, Julius von Stahl

---

[7] *Ensayo sobre el catholicismo, el liberalismo y el socialismo* (1851). German translation by L. Fischer (1933) under the title: *Der Staat Gottes*.

says that Protestantism is the straight counterpart of the principle of rationalism and revolutionism. Protestantism, i.e., justification by faith alone, as a political principle embraces two grand political consequences: the independent divine right of the princes and the higher political freedom of the nations; that by "higher political freedom" he does not mean "representative government, democratic bills of rights, etc., follows from the outspoken "anti-revolutionary," i.e., anti-democratic and anti-liberal, tendency of the treatise. Furthermore, divine Providence guides the destinies of kings and nations, and God alone judges the kings and punishes their abuse of sovereignty. Consequently there exists a close analogy between the God of theism and the sovereign monarch. As the theistic God is transcendent to the world, so is the sovereignty of the king transcendent to the people. The theistic God by His providence guides the secondary causes in the universe, so the sovereign monarch guides his subjects. As the theistic God intervenes through miracles in the course of the affairs of the world which run according to the laws of the divine Legislator, so the sovereign monarch can, as the exclusive source of the laws, repeal them or grant exceptions.

According to the deistic view of God, He is indeed the creator of the universe, but He has now left it to the rule of the laws of nature, which govern the universe in a mechanistic way. The deist brooks neither miracles nor a continuously guiding divine providence. The deist God reigns, but He does not govern. A similar position, Donoso Cortes informs us, is held by the king in the constitutional monarchy. He is legislator only, not an absolute sovereign; he cannot work juridical miracles, grant exceptions, or repeal laws; he, too, reigns but he does not govern. Liberal democracy, on the basis of a moderate popular sovereignty, is regarded by the romantic political philosophy as the political analogy to the God of pantheism. As in pantheism God is immanent in the universe and not transcendent, so in liberal democracy sovereignty is immanent in the people. As the law is the will of the people in liberal democracy, so the laws of the universe are the will of the God-nature, which in its identification of God and universe corresponds to the political identification of sovereign and people, of ruler and ruled. The political theory of socialism with its radical popular sovereignty, its denial of objective truth, its contention that the sovereign state is only a tool for the oppression of the proletariat, is considered analogous to atheism. Here the sovereign state itself is denied. The consequence is a political anarchy that will turn into social despotism. Donoso Cortes again and again points out this analogy between the theories of natural theology and those of political philosophy. Like the other authors of the Era of Romantic Restoration, he shows that the deistic, pantheistic, and atheistic systems presuppose man as intrinsically good, controlled by reason only or at least by calculable utilitarian considerations.

If that is true, the existing evils must be caused by bad political institutions. And so the enemies of sovereignty—so runs this argument—first contend that monarchic sovereignty is bad and can be improved by constitutional sovereignty. But this is only an intermediary solution just as deism is only an intermediary solution in theology. The radical solution is the sovereignty of the electors, the citizens, or of the majority. But even the political institutions of this sovereignty of the majority, a majority qualified by sex, race, or property-conditions, is not flawless from the standpoint of the principle that man is good, and sovereignty and authority are bad. Any political form is bad, even those of liberal democracy, because they still preserve sovereignty for social classes and do not effect the full identity of rulers and ruled. Hence the millenial paradise is realizable only when, with the destruction of sovereignty and of the state, a socialist stateless and classless society is established which necessarily is atheistic.

In brief, then, the deistic God is only the legitimation of that liberalist constitutionalism which gives power to the privileged classes of property and of bourgeois education. The pantheist God is the legitimation of popular sovereignty with majority rule, which still is not freedom full and untrammeled. Nothing remains, then, but the classless society without political power-apparatus, without even a remnant of sovereignty, i.e., anarchism in politics and atheism in religion.

These theories have received an unexpected help from some modern writers in political philosophy. Anybody who characterizes let us say democracy as the political form of philosophical relativism or of religious indifference unwillingly accepts this political theology. So does one who, denying natural law, turns positivist in law and attributes to the majority in democracy the sovereign power to define what is just and what is unjust; he transforms the majority decision into a metaphysical act that creates the objective good, thus claiming the prerogative of God and making the state, through its majority decision, God. So does the agnostic optimist who blindly believes that by social and scientific progress an earthly paradise can be formed without authority, power, and obedience. For he, too, transfers the evil from man's nature exclusively into political and social institutions.

V. CRITICISM OF POLITICAL THEOLOGY

Though the criticism of the adherents of political theology is often illuminating and, like a flash, points out the weakness of their opponents, they themselves are not without blame. First, they try to prove too much. However tempting these analogies seem to be, it is going too far to make certain political institutions, like monarchy or democracy, the necessary conclusions from doctrines of natural theology. These analogies, even if they were complete and convincing, do not issue into necessary logical inferences.

Even if historically democracy and its institutions had been produced as is contended, this fact would not prove that democracy and its institutions can issue only from the causes which the Romantic writers contend have once in history produced them. By confusing the polemic theories which deistic or pantheistic philosophers used to justify the destruction of obsolete forms of government and the revolutionary introduction of democratic forms, they forgot that monarchy, aristocracy, feudalism, liberal or social democracy, bills of rights, popular sovereignty, and representative government are in themselves theologically indifferent. They arise in the current of history from various and involved causes, economic and social, philosophical and moral. They arise from the weakness of the existing systems or the sins of the rulers or on account of the obsolescence and inadequacy of political forms in a changing economic world. They arise from changes in the temperament of generations or in the style of living and thinking. They may arise because of a wrong theology and philosophy, and they have done so. But with the exception of extreme forms of despotic absolutism, of totalitarian dictatorship and Rousseauist popular sovereignty, most of the historical forms must not be tested by the malicious designs or wrongness of their producers; rather their test is the concrete realization of the common good, *hic et nunc* in the framework of natural and divine law.

Thus the paralellism or correspondence of theological systems and political systems so emphasized by the adherents of political theology may be interesting for the historian. It may be an appropriate warning against blind acceptance of innovations, and may even be a good critical standard against unreserved enthusiasm about modern democracy. But the correspondence cannot compel us to object to these new political forms as such; because objectively the primary question is the realization of the common good in the framework of natural and divine law. The political theologians should not forget that their own beloved political form, monarchy, is perhaps in its historical origin as much tainted with wrong philosophies or with violations of justice as are the regimes which they so utterly condemn.

Secondly, many criticisms of the political theologians rest upon a theologically doubtful basis. When they pointed out that their opponents were rationalists they were so far right. But they themselves approached the theological errors of traditionalism or even fell into these errors. By rightly castigating the rationalist tendencies of their opponents, they were too easily prone to disparage the rationality of man. They depreciated individual reason, even excluded it, and instead introduced their idea of original revelation. Their principle of certitude is not individual cognition, and in their eyes the judgment of the individual conscience is always unreliable. Consequently in reply to the question, What are we certain of? they answer that we are certain of whatever is held true by the *sensus communis,* the human race in its totality, by virtue of the original revelation, embodied in the language. To the question, Why are we certain of this? they answer: Because God has revealed it. They would consider St. Thomas a rationalist or at least a semi-rationalist in theology. Thus history, which their opponents of Enlightenment in their rationalism so much neglected, becomes for the political theologians the vehicle of revelation. Time is the prime minister of God, who continuously reveals Himself in history to faith, and not so much in the universe to human reason by the *analogia entis.* The sphere of human freedom, moral and political, is thus as much limited as is the sphere of human reason.

When we ask for the reason of this diffidence in individual reason and freedom with the corresponding overextension of confidence in faith and authority, we find an outspoken pessimism regarding human nature. All these writers, though not so radically as Luther, exaggerate the consequences of original sin upon the human intellect and will. Bernhart points out: "While the Revolution overthrew the altars and the thrones, traditionalism overthrew man for the sake of the thrones and altars." [8]

They destroyed that carefully established harmonious system of St. Thomas which gave nature its place, reason its certitude, and will its freedom in socio-political life without impairing the sphere of grace, the authority of revelation, and the necessity of redemption. Because they had too great a distrust of natural reason, of the intellect for cognition, and of the will for the execution of cognized truth, the adherents of this political theology had to look for other secure standards for political ethics and prudence. These, they said, were obviously given either in the original revelation or in the positive revelation, but never in that which the Schoolmen call the "natural revelation." No wonder that the political theologians had little use for that heart of Catholic political philosophy, natural law. Rejecting this, they missed also the objective measure for a judgment of political forms, the lack of which has led them to their regrettable identifications of Catholicism (their idea of *sensus communis* in the Church) with monarchy, of democracy with unbelief, and of civil liberty with heresy.

VI. Supernatural Theology and Political Philosophy

We discussed the problem of actual or potential correspondence of systems of natural theology and systems of political philosophy. Does such a correspondence exist between the doctrine of supernatural theology, i.e., the theology of positive revelation, and systems of political philosophy? We have already pointed out how much influence the theological doctrines on original sin have exerted in political philosophy. Whoever adheres to the Lutheran doctrine of *natura deleta* cannot, of course, accept either natural theology or natural law. Both are then of no avail in political philosophy and can give no basis for political ethics. Thus the foundation of a political "philosophy" and a political ethics can be found only in the Scriptures, in the revealed order of creation as given in the first article of the Apostles' Creed and the Scriptures. Hence in Lutheranism either the state is

[8] Cf. Joseph Bernhart's essay on De Maistre's *Vom Papste,* translation of the famous book, *Du Pape.* (Munich, 1923), II, 288.

left alone in the sphere of the lost world, and the Christian, knowing that he cannot "Christianize" this piece of fallen nature, has a more passive attitude toward the state, or the state, basing its activity and life on the Scriptures, on the order of God, turns to certain theocratic forms.

This it does the more as the Church of Lutheranism is not itself a corporate visible community distinct from the state. Consequently Lutheran theology, as long as it is not superseded by liberal "theology," which is more a philosophy of religion than true theology, stresses the origin of sovereign power immediately from God and hence docile obedience to authority. Political authority, if it is Christian, that is, if it observes the revealed word of God in the Scriptures, is then responsible only to God. Not only the state *in abstracto* as now, but the historical concrete state and its constitution must be considered as instituted directly by God without the intervention of free human act based upon natural law. Thus the historical form of government, that is, predominantly monarchy, cannot be considered the result of mere natural circumstances and free decisions of the citizens. Then, too, the traditional form of government (Christian monarchy) must be regarded as directly instituted by God, who reveals His will in the providential guidance of history. Such is the representative political theology of Friedrich Julius Stahl in his *Protestantismus als politisches Prinzip*. There he stresses, as the two great ideas, the independent divine right of the princes and the higher political freedom of the people. The latter he considers rather in the sphere of international life than in internal constitutional life.

Yet the Scriptures contain not only the Books of Kings but also the Book of Judges. So, even if the doctrine of *natura deleta* is preserved, there exists the possibility of a republican theocracy when and where the abolition of monarchy is made necessary by historical circumstances, national character, and the fact that a Catholic (i.e., "heretical") king rules. So, too, on the basis of this political theology derived from the Scriptures, a republican form of government can find theological legitimation though of a theocratical character, as is found among so many Independist movements. (It was of far-reaching importance that after some hesitation Anglo-Saxon theocratic republicanism under the influence of Calvinism and of the common law incorporated into its doctrine the idea of natural law and thus found a non-theological basis for political philosophy and political ethics.)

Luther surrendered the Church rule and morality to the worldly government for which he had little room in his theology, and he taught non-resistance, humble obedience, and patient submission even under unjust and despotic government. But Calvin, on the basis of his characteristic unification of *lex naturae* (state) and *lex spiritualis* (ecclesiastical community), erected his theocratic republic. He taught active resistance and the militant religious use of the state as *bracchium seculare* for the preservation of purity of doctrine from heresy and for the austerity of civil morality against sectarian individualistic freedom. In the beginning the Old Testament as a statute book of divine law served as the moral code. Later when, through the influence of the milder personal religion of tolerant revivalism and through humanistic Bible criticism, Calvinism lost this austerity, the idea of natural law automatically came into the foreground and made possible a political philosophy and ethics on its basis. On the other hand, when Lutheran theology lost the biblical basis and became liberal theology, it offered no basis for natural law and so its political philosophy became positivist and relativist.

The question whether this rediscovery of natural law and natural ethics has been bought at the high price of the secularization of religious life, of the substitution of a secular morality for supernatural faith, of a sentimental, vague religiousness for genuine theology, is another trying problem.

From all this it follows that the genuine problem of a political theology concerns, not so much what forms of government the various political theologies have positively favored, but what forms of government and what rules of political ethics they have categorically rejected as opposing their specific theological doctrines or their characteristic theological temperament. All theologies adhering to the doctrine of *natura deleta* and consequently rejecting natural theology, natural ethics, and natural law, have a characteristic trait. They have either a positive political theology of monarchic or republican theocracy or the passive quietist abandonment of the state, of the power, of the world, to itself as incapable of being "Christianized," with a retreat into a personal individual religion or into a religious group-life separated from this "world," forever surrendered to the power of evil. Thus this theology of original sin does not acknowledge any autonomy of political life, any natural political ethics, but either "theologizes" the historically given political institution or surrenders it to an absolute autonomy never to be restricted by theological doctrines.

An interesting example of political theology is offered by Taparelli d'Azeglio in his refutation of general suffrage.[9] According to Taparelli its genealogy is as follows: The French Republic of 1848, introducing general suffrage, is born of the revolutionary Convention of 1789; the latter is born of Rousseau from Mirabeau; Rousseau is born of Calvin, and Calvin of Luther. Once the Lutheran principle of free and private interpretation is admitted, then any state must become a republic, and any prince an elective magistrate.[10] Any impartial student of history, however, will point out that such a genealogy is not cogent. Actually the Lutheran states remained aloof longest from general suffrage, e.g., Prussia and other states of the German Federation.

Taparelli fought against the ideologies of the promoters of general suffrage such as Mazzini. And it was they who based their demands on an exaggerated individualism and on the optimistic view preached by Enlightenment. But from this it does not logically follow that general suffrage as a political institution is wrong or that it rests by philosophical necessity on that genealogy previously given. For it is one of the many historical forms, intrinsically indifferent in ethics, by which a working government may be formed. General suffrage is far more the result of economic and nationalist trends than of religious individualism, however much in historical causation the latter may have served as an ideological factor among many others. And even if Taparelli's genealogy were historically true, that is, if really general suffrage had been produced causally by the alleged "heresies," this would not prove that general suffrage can philosophically be derived only from these heresies. We would have here a confusion of historical causation and logical inference. Against this we need merely to point out that philosophically general suffrage may be derived, and with more justice, from the idea of personality, from a Christian humanism, and from the idea of natural rights quite familiar by inference to the *philosophia perennis*. Thus a reference to theology is not necessary.

Another theological doctrine which resulted in political theology is the doctrine of predestination. If this doctrine is applied to whole

[9] *De l'origine du pouvoir;* translated from the Italian (Paris, 1896).
[10] *Ibid.,* p. 94.

groups of predestined Christians organized into a corporate body, it may easily lead to the scriptural idea of the chosen people in its numerous historical manifestations. The Calvinist idea of God was that of the Omnipotent Will and Absolute Freedom choosing and rejecting sinful man according to His free election and not according to any acceptance by man of the grace offered. Such a dominantly Old Testament idea of God results in that tremendous mystery of predestination. Christ sacrificed Himself only for the predestined. They are already now visibly marked. They are the holy people of Christ the Lord.

The elect are equal to one another. Popery and episcopal hierarchy, then, are destined to appear in their eyes as vicious diabolical machinations. In the people of God ecclesiastical synodalism and Presbyterianism prevail. Consequently, instead of the hierarchical principle, representation and majority decision are introduced as institutes by which the religious community governs itself. So a new spirit of the historic vocation of the holy people is possible. If an identification of this idea with a concrete nation is made, then the political struggles of such a chosen nation become crusades, religious wars. Power politics of a mere secular character are then considered detestable. In Cromwell, this crusader idea and the idea of the chosen people are most powerful. More often than we expect, either such specific theological doctrines of a divine vocation of the nation or their secularized form determine the political actions of political leaders and nations, or at least the moral justifications of such actions. A comparison, say of Bismarck and Woodrow Wilson, would very likely lead to different theological doctrines, however rationalized and secularized, as determinant factors for the policy of both men. It would perhaps show that Bismarck would reproach Wilson for "cant," and Wilson would reproach Bismarck for non-moral power politics, though considerations of power politics quite naturally are not absent in Wilson's foreign policy, nor are moral considerations absent in Bismarck's.

VII. Negative Attitude of Catholic Philosophy

From the standpoint of Catholic theology a specific political theology cannot be held. St. Thomas bases political philosophy on natural reason and natural law, not on revelation and supernatural theology. Natural theology in the form of theism is indeed involved, but theism is based on natural reason and not on a traditionalist original revelation nor on a subjective spiritual revelation. Thus it remains that the rights and duties of the citizen are not changed in substance through supernatural theology or through baptism; they are perfected and exalted. The natural motives are strengthened through supernatural motives, but they are not superseded by the latter. The divine law that issues from grace does not abolish human law that issues from natural reason.[11]

In its field the state and the citizen have therefore a genuine though not absolute autonomy. Theology has no direct and immediate influence on political philosophy and political ethics. In the theory of the forms of government there exists no theologically founded predilection or preference. Political institutions are not to be judged by the theological errors which ideologically called them into existence, but by their conformity to natural law. As long as they so conform, they belong in the sphere of free human decisions. This explains the fact that St. Thomas in the *quaestiones* dealing with political philosophy and ethics more often quotes Aristotle and Cicero than the Scriptures, whereas Luther and Calvin must always quote the Scriptures. (Calvin, rejecting natural law not to the degree that Luther does, chooses to quote the Decalogue as the substance of natural law rather than any of the ancient or Stoic philosophers, a fact that must be explained by the Occamist concept of natural law in Calvin's thought).

"Political" theology, with theology understood as supernatural theology, is a product of the antirevolutionary romantic movement. It is ideological in this sense, that it turned against the newly rising democratic institutions of representative government and tried to point out, not their political weaknesses, their practical shortcomings, their possibly dangerous consequences (i.e., all the perfectly legitimate task of the conservative mind in politics), but their alleged contradiction of theological doctrines. It succeeded only in showing that many of the ideologies which helped as historical midwives to produce these democratic institutions, were contradictory to theological doctrines and were influenced either by wrong theological doctrines or by rationalist philosophies decidedly in contradiction to theology. By this excessively hasty identification of abstractly indifferent political in-

---

[11] *Summa theol.*, IIa IIae, q. 12, a. 2 c. Cf. Peter Tischleder's monograph: *Ursprung und Träger der Staatsgewalt*, etc. (1923), pp. 37 ff.

stitutions with their generating ideologies, the political theologians, however, could not avoid making their own political theology and ideology one of "reaction" rather than of conservatism. They misused their theology for the defense of legitimist monarchism, for the defense of the medieval feudal patrimonial state as the God-made state, for the continuation of feudalist agriculture as a "Christian" institution, etc.[12] The attempts to exalt one form of government over another, e.g., monarchy over democracy, by an appeal to ecclesiastical and theological doctrine were blamed by Leo XIII as inadmissible, and he called it an abuse of religion to draw the Church and her doctrine into the party struggles about forms of government.[13]

Most adherents of "political theology" underestimate human reason and nature. They consider the Thomistic system as semirationalist. They suppose an original revelation in their traditionalism and so come to a divinization of history. Furthermore, they are inclined to see in the medieval Christian feudal monarchy, allegedly formed after the example of the papal monarchy, the necessary consequence of Catholic doctrine and theology. They come thus to this dangerous view: The Catholic system is, according to the *sensus communis*, the best, the exemplary, socio-political system; the monarchical constitution of the Church ought to be the model for political constitutions. They forgot that history contains two elements, a perennial and a transitory, the latter tending to become obsolete. Because of their distrust of human reason and of natural law, they neglected the perennial being, coordinated to human nature and to human reason, i.e., "natural reason and natural law," in favor of supernatural revelation. The transitory and obsolete was all too easily exalted and considered perennial. Hence their attempts to salvage traditional values often degenerated into salvaging the obsolete. The ultimate form of such a political theology may well be that of Charles Maurras and the *Action Française,* in which theology is replaced by positivism, and Catholicism is debased to a mere instrument of a rather agnostic political philosophy of monarchism and nationalism.

That political theology which grows from certain theological doctrines peculiar to the individualism and enthusiastic subjectivism of

12 Cf. Adam Müller, *Von der Notwendigkeit einer theologischen Grundlage der gesamten Staatswissenschaft* (Leipzig, 1819), *passim;* A. von Haller, *Restauration der Staatswissenschaften* (Wintherthur, 1820–25), *passim;* De Maistre, *op. cit., passim.*

13 Cf. P. Tischleder, *Staatslehre Leo XIII,* pp. 242 ff.

the Protestant sects falls into similar pitfalls. From its theological principles of individual examination and interpretation of the Scriptures, of private revelation and subjective spiritual enthusiasm, it derives the denial of the visible Church authority divinely instituted. So it extols the elective and representative forms in ecclesiastical life as the necessary consequence of that subjective spiritual individualism. Transferred to the political stage, this theology leads to the theory that only democratic and representative forms of government and an exaggerated individual freedom embodied in an expanded bill of rights are the exclusively legitimate and the absolutely exemplary forms of government. All too quickly the historical, and to some degree transitory, forms of democracy, typical of the rugged individualism of the nineteenth century, are made absolute. The result is that the label of "Fascism" or "authoritarianism" is quickly laid on any conservative criticism of the lack of consciousness of social duties, and the uncritical faith in the competitive automatism of its egalitarian social philosophy.

Hence the conclusion that "political theology" is subject matter for the student of political history and the critic of ideologies; but that, as a systematic and scientific aid to the development of political philosophy and ethics, political theology (in the sense of supernatural theology) seems to be a futile effort and, as Erik Peterson says, a "theological impossibility." [14]

This repudiation of political theology follows the traditional Thomistic doctrine of the distinction between nature and grace, between philosophy and theology, and between natural reason and revelation. This distinction does not mean "separation" as if "theology," the revealed word of God, and the positive divine law as distinguished from natural law, were under no circumstances of any influence on political philosophy and political ethics and on political institutions. Nor does this distinction mean that the various theories of natural theology must be devoid of any influence. For example, the rights and

---

[14] *Op. cit.*, p. 158. It deserves mention that, in their disappointment about the reserve of ecclesiastical authority, some adherents of a political theology prefer their theories in the case of a conflict of their politico-theological theories with Catholic doctrine. Others did not show that necessary critical attitude toward political movements which, in their "conservative Christian" propaganda, disguised their secret non-Christian (Facist) if not anti-Christian (Nazist) basis. Those who deny political theology have usually shown more critical reserve toward such movements on the basis of their definite philosophy of natural law.

duties of the citizen and of those in authority do not in their substance change but are exalted and sanctified by acceptance of the Christian faith; yet it is obvious that the doctrine of the Church as a divinely instituted and hierarchically organized body narrows down, so to speak, the potentially broad, autonomous sphere of political authority. The positive divine law demands from the state that it respect the liberty of the Church, that it do not interfere with the administration of the divine task of the Church, that it recognize the marriage of Christians as a sacrament, and that it recognize the sphere of religious life which by positive divine law is a prerogative of the Church, as will be discussed extensively in the chapter "Church and State." But here again historical research speaks against "political theology." One cannot be sure whether the political theologians and their disciples of the romantic period, with their identification of Catholicism and monarchy or at least of antiliberalism and antidemocratism, tried only to serve Catholicism impartially and devotedly or saw in the theological doctrines suitable instruments for the refutation of their political adversaries and the promotion of their own political ideals, accidental though these were.

Nevertheless one should not assert that adherents of "political theology" have no merits at all. However much their antagonism to modern liberalism and egalitarian democratism was abused to extol their own political ideals as true Christian and Catholic political ideals, that antagonism preserves the student from an uncritical acceptance of and a blind devotion to modern democracy and its institutions. In the books of De Maistre, of Donoso Cortes, of De Bonald, of A. Müller, and even of Charles Maurras and Carl Schmitt (though the latter are rather the literary and intellectual successors of the first mentioned), the student will find many sound criticisms of the consequences of a secularized liberalism and of a relativist democratism, of the misinterpretation of the democratic institutions by agnostic positivism and anticlerical laicism. The merit of "political theology" lies, then, in certain aspects of its criticism and not in its positive system, which is inadmissible.

Such a repudiation of "political theology" must not be interpreted as if supernatural theology had no influence whatever in matters of political life. Theology will always be of help and assistance to political philosophy. But that does not exclude the fact that the latter's principle of knowledge and its starting point of speculation is reason and experience, that it is natural revelation and natural law, not primarily and essentially theology and faith. This repudiation does not deny that positive theology or supernatural revelation is a most efficient help, practically a necessity for propagating among men with their *natura vulnerata* the cognition of those verities which belong to the natural order of knowledge, to reason. Now that we have received the truth of revelation we are, so to speak, in possession of the truth independent of speculation, of the discursive processes of reasoning. Thus a repudiation of political theology does not mean that theological supernatural truth is of no corrective and directive influence in political philosophy or that ecclesiastical authority has no right to teach in this field. It means only that reason and experience are the principles of knowledge sufficient for its speculation. For the believer, obedience to political authority is based first on natural law and in addition on God's revealed word, whether in the Scriptures or in the authoritative teaching of the Church. This does not imply that the believer is consequently more docile and more subservient to political authority. On the contrary, he has now a second critical norm for judging about the obligation of orders of political authority. That we must obey God rather than man, was a revolutionary criticism of worship of the state. It was, therefore, a salutary step forward to human freedom when St. Thomas and the doctors of Late Scholasticism based their political philosophy upon reason and natural law, took away from the state its sacred, theological majesty, its divinity, with which paganism had consecrated it.

VIII. Influence of Natural Theology on Political Philosophy

Far different, however, is the case for the influence of natural theology on political philosophy. It is obviously of the most profound importance in political philosophy if the student of the latter is a theist, a pantheist or an atheist. Most anarchists, i.e., men who deny the state as a necessary form of human social existence, are atheists.[15] That ap-

[15] There have existed and there may still exist religious sects which in politics hold rather anarchist views. But they do so mostly on account of Manichaean doctrines. According to the latter the redeemed disciples of Christ or the personally inspired faithful do not need the state as a necessary form of human existence. Because redemption or inspira-

plies to Karl Marx, to Proudhon, to Bakunine, to Lenin. This fact is not strange because the openly admitted or silent premise of all these men is the deification of the individual or of (communist) society. The consequence of this atheism is that, in the interest of the divinized individual *in abstracto*, the individuals *in concreto* must be subjected to an utterly tyrannical rule. The denial of true authority derived from a transcendent God who is perfect reason and supreme Goodness, degenerates to the despotism of oligarchies and their changing and arbitrary opinions, dreams, and plans.

This militant atheism is to be distinguished from the more pacifist skeptical agnosticism of the modern intelligentsia. This agnosticism, steeped in humanitarian sentimentality, is not filled with that militant zeal of the atheists. It smiles condescendingly upon the superstition of the masses concerning the founding of human authority upon divine authority. It substitutes for God the belief in infinite progress, the blind biological urges of nature, or the impersonal powers of historic development, of the "growth" of civilization, without ever giving an objective measure or critical standard. So this agnosticism itself falls easily to materialistic standards and is able to establish the Rousseauist tyranny of compelling people to be free, i.e., the despotism of infinite progress. In both cases that specific dignity of man, namely, that he transcends history, biological urges, and material progress by his immortal soul and by his destiny of union with God, is sacrificed for the absolute subjection of man to some concededly relativist standards of progress or growth. Here, too, is found that inevitable divinization of man, or of progress or growth. Man, having lost God, invents his own deities. Feuerbach's thesis that the gods of men are created by their wishful dreams would rightly apply for the agnostics.

One of the worst consequences of agnosticism for political philoso-

---

tion has so exalted human nature, the faithful, wholly immersed in the religious self-sufficient community, have no longer any need of the state. As a matter of fact, in such cases the religious community itself assumes all the functions and characteristics of a body politic. Such communities turn into a form of theocracy, as their spiritual tenets and their religious customs take on the functions of a political constitution and of legal norms ruling the life of community, family, and person. This theocratic identity of religion and socio-political existence often leads to disillusion of the initial religious enthusiasm that for a short time could do without the state. Then such communities dissolve or their members, as simple members of a politically indifferent denomination, are reintegrated into the existing body politic from which they originally emigrated, because as redeemed or inspired faithful they thought it wholly superfluous.

phy, besides its inability to give authority an ethical basis, is its degradation of democracy.

Kelsen himself has pointed out that to the wane of theism, the idea of a transcendental God above the universe, corresponds the wane of the metaphysical foundation of the state; and that to agnosticism in natural theology corresponds positivism and relativism in moral, legal, and political philosophy. The state loses all ethical objective value; and democracy becomes the political expression of positivist relativism in philosophy and ethics. Democracy is formalized, becoming an indifferent receptacle for anything. Thus it loses its dignity and becomes a mere slogan abused by politicians and misconceived by politically superstitious if not yet disillusioned masses. It must strike the impartial observer that the powerful attacks of Pius IX on a democratism of that kind thus finds a late justification.

Pantheism in its various forms, if it accepts the state at all and if, in a sentimental naturalism it does not hope for a withering away of the state as a product of degrading civilization in favor of a return to peaceful nature, cannot avoid extremes in political philosophy. Let us suppose the principle of pantheism—the theological identity of God and the universe, the absolute immanence of God in nature—to be applied in political philosophy. Then authority, objective and morally dependent ultimately on the objective end of the state and not wholly derived from changing majorities or the whims of absolute monarchs, must be wholly immanent in the body politic and identical with it. The result is the contention that rulers and ruled are identical, a view which Rousseau, the strongest propagator of this total identity and immanence, brought forward with all the sophism he was capable of. Or pantheism leads to the following sequence of conclusions from the principle that God and the universe are identical. Then the universe is the self-expression of reason; reality then becomes actual reason, and in history reason expresses itself in all forms, of which the idea of the state is the highest form and thus becomes the representation of Reason, i.e., of God. In both instances some vital problems become insoluble, especially those of the ultimate origin of the state, of the autonomy of the religious sphere, (the sphere of the transcendental *par excellence*), of personal and communal rights. Against the God immanent in the general will expressed by majority decision or against the "*repräsenter Gott*" there are no rights or limitations.

There are other doctrines of theology which, implicity at least, exert an influence on political philosophy. One of the most important is the doctrine of individual life after death (personal immortality), of God as the supreme judge in the Last Judgment, and of eternal reward or punishment for each soul according to its personal responsibility for its acts and omissions. There is little doubt that the intensity of a conviction of these truths exert a profound influence on problems of political philosophy. If the governing powers are convinced of these truths, they cannot act in the same way as they would if they were not convinced. Sovereign authority held by a person who believes in these truths is necessarily limited by the demands of natural and divine law, and nobody can become intoxicated with power so long as he takes such truths seriously. Reverence before the dignity of the individual person and its self-responsibility in moral freedom will be the greater the more these truths are acknowledged. On the other hand, history and experience prove that the great unbelievers in this eschatology have often little reverence before the individual. For their worldly eschatology of an earthly paradise or of a secular progress to a deification of man, the individual is only a means for their grand political illusions. Surely the dictators of our time, with their secular eschatologies of an eternal *Reich* or of a socialist paradise of a classless society, have sacrificed the happiness and the lives of individuals more eagerly than any ruler believing in the other-worldly eschatology ever did.

Furthermore, before such an eschatology what can become of politics and reputation and states and kingdoms and warlike glory, more than a relative value, something that is less important than the four last things? And is not that strange craving for power over men for its own sake only a form of escape from the inexorable semi-consciousness that every one, even kings and tyrants, must die, and then render an account to an incorruptible Judge? How unimportant becomes the *polis* on this earth and how enormous becomes the responsibility of the rulers of that *polis*, if they believe they must stand before the divine Judge before they can enter the heavenly *polis*?

It is a remarkable fact that the question of death as a philosophical problem arose only in recent years. Death as a new problem was due as soon as the Christian idea of death, being only the entrance to life everlasting, was given up and the idea of personal immortality disappeared under the impact of a materialist philosophy or when death was embellished by the pantheist idea of an impersonal immortality. This notion was in the form that the individual through death was immersed in the nirvana, the formless life of the pantheistic worldground. It is likewise a remarkable fact that of the foremost German philosophers only Martin Heidegger, the philosopher of death, found an easy way to Nazism, with its romanticizing of death for the thousand-year realm, its macabre intoxication for death as the restful immersion into the collective, impersonal "soul" of Germany, its glorification of death on the battlefield as the meaning of human life. Heidegger is the philosopher of death, because according to him human existence is existence to death, because man is thrown out of nothingness and rushes to nothingness (*ex-sistens ex nihilo in nihil*). Human existence is, then, senseless because the eternal question, What after death? is simply declared superfluous; after death is the *nihil*. This astounding coincidence points out that there exist open or hidden interrelations between the philosophy of death, immortality, and the theological doctrine of eschatology on the one hand, and problems of political philosophy on the other hand. This may be concluded from the ideas of another philosopher, from Thomas Hobbes. In spite of the Christian disguise, Hobbes became a materialist. But materialism implies denial of immortality and Christian eschatology. His stressing the fear of (violent) death may well have led to his demand for political security and unconditional obedience to absolute sovereignty as the only means of order and security.

There are other observations. Behind the optimistic belief in infinite progress and behind the outspoken restless activity of secularist social reformers for unceasing reforms in the hope of this-worldly perfection, the secret power may be actually the persistent problem of death, which by this immersion in social reform activism should be shouted down.[16] The modern escapism from death, the conventional hiding of death and what it means, or its pagan embellishment as an unconscious yet beautiful dream, and the concomitant secularism, is often the real source of the ever busy reformers' "activities" which are so different from the calmness with which the Christian accepts the imperfections of this life. On the other hand, in some eras and places, for instance in Orthodox Russia, we often find a social Quietism, or

---

[16] Miguel de Unamuno, in his *The Tragic Sense of Life* (London, 1921), p. 96, elaborates the idea that without faith in immortality all our activism is only empty busibodiness.

less radical, a certain indifference to human distress, poverty, and social injustices. These conditions are often caused or at least gravely conditioned by the vividness with which death and the last things and eternal happiness in personal immortality are grasped. The Christian perspective of eschatology, in which some problems of reform are considered, is different from the perspective of a modern secularist who argues away death and the last things or romanticizes immortality in a pantheistic immersion in the nature god.

It is true that the Christian eschatology, the faith in a future life of happiness for the good, of eternal punishment for the wicked, is never an excuse for putting off those who suffer from social injustices and political oppression with the doctrine of the future life. Yet the Christian attitude to social evils and political imperfections will be different from that of the merely secularist humanitarian. The latter easily condemns the demands of Christian ethics in such problems as divorce, birth control, war, and a certain reluctance to cure injustices by violent revolutions. The secularist humanitarian condemns because he implicitly denies God the Judge, personal immortality, and individual moral responsibility in favor of a social or historic determinism. And so it comes that he is readily tempted to the worship of the state, to uncritical belief in the reforming power of the state. The secularist liberal of the early nineteenth century, with a strong bias against the state, may easily become the promoter of an intolerable growth of government interference in the sphere of personal and communal liberty at least as long as democratic formalities are observed. The expectance of *vita venturi saeculi*, once for all, makes impossible the divinization of the state or of the classless society as the ultimate meaning of history. It makes impossible the destruction of individual liberty and moral responsibility, those necessary suppositions to put the state into its right place in the universal order of values.

There is no way out. The state as a moral entity, political authority without regard to its historical form equipped with the indubitable right to demand moral obedience and not simply shrewd external conformity, the rights of man, all these problems of political philosophy can find a satisfactory solution only from the standpoint of theism. If the rights of man and the duties of authority, and the duties of man and the rights of authority, do not ultimately originate in a transcendent God who is perfect Intellect, infinite Goodness, omnipotent

Will, gracious and just Providence, then there is no escape from anarchy or from tyranny. So invincible is this argument that from time immemorial philosophers have deduced a proof of the existence of God from the nature of man as a political and legal being, from the existence of the state and of the law.[17]

17 Cf. P. Klein, *Der juristische Gottesbeweis* (1917).

CHAPTER IV

The Organic View of the State

I. The Basic Aspects of Community in Social Philosophy

EVER since man has endeavored to grasp the essence and the being of the enduring forms of social life, especially of the highest and most comprehensive one, the state, there have been two fundamental ways of perceiving, of understanding, and of comprehending these social forms. One is the mechanistic, individualist; the other, the organic, solidarist. These terms themselves are modern; the ways of comprehension which they designate are as old as brooding speculation on the essence and nature of human social forms.

For a distinct grasp of these two fundamental views, we need only to let pass before our eyes the colorful succession of systems of political philosophy, systems of social philosophy, and systems of natural law that are in themselves systems of social philosophy. For they are general views not only of forms of social existence but of life and of living being itself.

It can be shown that an organic view of the state is the consequence of an organic, teleological metaphysics, as a mechanistic view is the consequence of either a mechanistic metaphysics or of the denial of all metaphysics. So far as we may call the metaphysics of the *philosophia perennis,* an organic teleological one, to that extent the conception of the state by this political philosophy is likewise organic, teleological.

II. The Mechanist-individualist View

Whenever the contemplative mind approached the problem of man's community forms, especially the so-called natural ones, such as the family and the state (the functional social group for continuous community), it had two points to start from: the individual and the group. In starting from the individual it may begin with the idea of the individual as a fully self-sufficient, perfect being, autonomous in itself, a being for which sociality is only accidental, an external relation, useful, but not essential for its internal perfection and a higher form of good life. If that is the starting point, there is no specific category of "social being," "social being" is only a sign or a symbol, without anything real behind it, and it is futile to speak of the reality of the state, of the common good, as something qualitatively different from the quantitative sum of the particular goods of the individuals forming the body politic. Then the state has no objective end. Then, too, all these words do not mean something real, but are only symbols used economically, signifying simply the individuals as a sum, as a quantitative aggregation. Then all so-called "social being" (*ens sociale*) has no value as such, but is a simplified expression for the material utility which the individuals derive from the social form. And so all these social forms and institutions are produced by the arbitrary will of the individuals without any internal necessity.

These forms, then, in their being and content, are absolutely at the mercy of these individuals whom no objective teleology controls. What unites the individuals is not an objective end, but the utility of the form as a mere sum of the fractional advantage, quantitatively equal for each of them. The individuals, of course, cooperate. But the motive is exclusively their self-interest, their profits. Each seeks first himself and his own advantage; the others become a mere means for that self-centered purpose. The individual does not devote himself to the community interest, the common good; his personality plays no part in his relation to the community. He "invests" in society only his carefully calculated "interests" and preserves for himself, so to speak, the right to rescind what he regards as always purely contractual relations controlled by self-interest. The rationality of calculable legal forms, the rationally expected behavior of the other individuals as agreed upon by contracts, constitute the typical element. The unselfish social virtues aiming at the common good as a higher form of life and love, as an ennobling unselfish search for higher objective values, are all foreign to this attitude.

The powers of love, of devotion, and of altruistic sacrifice for the common good become sentimental unrealities. Consequently the discussion within such a pattern swings about the "rights" of the individual because these rights grant the free functioning of self-interest. Duties to the community, the social balance of rights, are less perceived, and when perceived are again subordinated to self-interest as a fair price for rights. From this point of view, the idea of objective duties independent of any paying return to the person, that is, as a categorical imperative, is inconceivable. There exists only one duty, to observe the freely enacted contracts. Other duties are not considered necessary because the rights of the one contracting party are balanced by the equal rights of the other. The self-interest of the one is controlled by the right of the other to effect his self-interest.

Of course the philosophers of this individualism teach that, in spite of the fact that self-interest and profit are the motives of social relations, a peaceful pattern of social life can still be reached. Because of the pre-stabilized pattern of the laws of nature, social harmony automatically arises out of the pursuit of self-interest by each, checked only by the right of others to pursue their self-interest. As previously noted, the point from which all this individualistic thinking starts is the intrinsically self-sufficient, perfect, autonomous individuals who, controlled only by their self-interests, freely form a network of relations represented by revocable contractual forms. This they do so only for their own advantage and at their own risk, sociological monads that they are. It is significant that this philosophy draws its figures of exemplification from the world of mechanics and that its appropriate natural theology is deism. This takes a mechanical view of the universe as a watch, and the Creator as a rather disinterested watchmaker.

III. MECHANIST-INDIVIDUALIST VIEW APPLIED TO THE STATE

If these concepts are applied to the body politic it follows that the state originates not in the social nature of man, not in the will for a fuller and more perfect realization of man's nature, but in a free contract of autonomous, self-sufficient individuals with the sole motive of a more successful pursuit of self-interest. The end of the state is this self-interest and nothing else; it is not objective and transcendent to the individuals. The state is not intrinsically a higher form of human life. It is only the protector of the contractual relations of the individuals. If the expression "common good" is still used, it is used only

as a conventional symbol; it is a concept that has no basis in reality
but is a purely nominalist *flatus vocis*. The compulsory power of po
litical authority, authority in the strictest sense, demanding obedience
is explained exclusively as the sum of transfers and concessions o
rights by the individuals and revocable by them at any time and a
their subjective pleasure. Authority, therefore, has no proper objec
tive power arising out of the objective end of the body politic, which
itself issues from man's social nature. Consequently the relations be
tween subject and authority are ruled by commutative justice. As in
private law, the contract form is the basis of these relations; hence the
fundamental principle of the legal bond between individual and state
authority is that of equality [1] and private utility.

Likewise the general tendency, as it has developed in marriage and
family law, is to subject the relations between individuals and the
state to the typical forms of the private law and of commutative justice
of an individualist society; that is, to a strongly contractual subjective
interpretation of law without much understanding of the objective
status. A consideration of marriage law will throw light on this ten
dency. Matrimony is undoubtedly initiated by a contract. But the
performance of this contract results in the fact that the partners enter
into a new objective status wherein not the subjective will, agreements
and interpretations of the partners prevail, but the end of man in his
social nature, and the interest of society and the children, or at least
these should prevail. It is modern individualistic thinking and sub
jectivism that, by forgetting the status character of matrimony, has
overstressed the subjective interests of the contracting partners and
facilitated divorce as if matrimony were in its whole content abso
lutely at the mercy of the contracting partners. No wonder that mar
riage and the family are considered not as an objective form of man's
social life essentially independent of the changing subjective pleasures
and whims of the members, but as an easily soluble contractual rela-

[1] It should be remarked that there are, of course, such relations between individual
and state authority; the bill of rights is intrinsically subject to the rules of commutative
justice. Thus in the modern state the citizen can sue the government in the courts, and
the state appears as if it were an equal. But the presupposition in such suits is always
that the state does not appear here as the protector of the common good but as a partner
in a private contract; the state has stepped down into the sphere of the private law and
is to that degree subject to the *ordo* of the private law.

ion serving exclusively the subjective interests and caprices of the partners, therefore to be dissolved as soon as sacrifices are demanded n the interest of something greater than that of the individual.

This kind of individualistic utilitarian thinking manifests itself, oo, in regard to the relation between citizen and state. And this thinking is also responsible for modern attempts to do away with the conepts of a distinctive public law, of legal justice, and of distributive ustice. It treats problems of eminent social and political importance s if there were at stake only interests of A and B unconnected with he common good. It has no understanding of the sovereign intervenion of the state in the form of social legislation for the sake of the ommon good and of distributive justice, because it consistently sees nly individual interests. And these are to be left to the free, unindered contracts of the partners in the labor contract. To read Ricardo's chapter on wages is to see at once that his reasoning is trongly controlled by the mechanistic philosophy of deism and conequently has no room for the intervention of the state in behalf of ocial justice. The ultimate form of this thinking is the normativism f Kelsen and his school, which regards the state as exclusively a ystem of norms; norms, furthermore, ruled by the conceptions of ommutative justice. What remains is then a system of norms without uthority, and a legal order without justice; because any objective measure of the positive norms is lacking, and the whole profound roblem of the *just* law disappears before the problem of the mechnism of norm-production; democracy, which we consider the ighest form of political status, becomes the political form of philoophical relativism. It is the market of a free competitive economy and ts rules that set the pattern for this thinking in social philosophy.

For such thinkers the sole and sufficient motive of social life and rganization is found in the self-interests of individuals. These selfnterests, under the conditions of liberty of contract and property and f formal legal equality, automatically produce an optimal social armony that results from the free forces of the individuals. With this elief is connected, at least by the optimists, the conviction that proress in economics and technique will so promote human perfection hat eventually the specific political element, the state with its overeign authority and compulsory power, will wither away in an economic world-society. This society is, as it were, a *civitas maxima*, though it is anything but a *civitas* in the traditional sense; rather it looks like the machine that the deists, in their mechanistic theology, conceived the world to be. Thus the specific political life, the authority that decides sovereignly and intervenes by appeal to the common good and to social justice, is regarded as something strange and inferior in relation to the automatism of socio-economic life ruled by self-interests and free competition everywhere; it is but a stage of social development that will be outmoded by continuous enlightenment. Then there will be needed no positive order, no authority, no compulsory power, interfering irrationally in the smoothly running apparatus of society. This dream of bourgeois individualistic optimism, this chiliastic belief in an unlimited progress, is but one of many similar fancies that have been dreamed by men since the Sophists in Greece dreamed of a stateless paradise on earth. It is striking that this mechanistic view of the state takes its parables and examples from the realm of technical science or individualistic economics. The state is a mechanical apparatus or a mutual insurance corporation. The taxes are insurance premiums, the state and its government a kind of property-owners' protective association.

IV. Totalitarian Collectivism

One should not think that the mechanistic view of the state sketched above is the only one. True, it rests on the fact that in the antithesis of "individual" and "state" the process of thinking starts from and cares only for the individual as such, already internally perfect and morally self-sufficient. But if the process starts from the other pole (the state) and concentrates round it, the resulting totalitarian collectivism is an equally perfect expression of mechanistic thinking in social philosophy. Collectivism in its antithesis "individual-state" makes the state all; the individual becomes a qualityless element, a mere numerical concept, empty of any value. All other social forms through which and in which man lives, such as the family, the vocational group, and the religious community, and the rights of man to them and in them, become empty words.

There must not be any other loyalty than that to the state. The individuals are nothing, the state is all; they are, therefore, beings without rights, unrestrictedly subject to an omnipotent state which holds even the idea of God an unfair competitor and which, therefore, either atheistically denies God or pantheistically identifies itself with God. The individuals are mere tools, and are kept by propaganda in the condition of masses without independent minds and free wills. They are simply "matter" for the supreme power. As atoms, these massed individuals are moved, united, separated, and again united into new social combinations by ordinances and commands. They do not plan their own lives; these are planned by an irresistible, unlimited, and therefore irresponsible power. Concretely they are planned by men with megalomaniac dreams and limitless lust for power. These men strive for a realization of perpetual human dreams by inhuman means, however much they conceal this lust for power in such propaganda terms of justification as "the incarnation of the race," the "froth on the top of the wave of the future," the "tool of the dictatorship of the proletariat." The higher-sounding the phrases, the more worthless is the individual person.

The concept of politics has been changed from that of the leadership by wise men to a more perfect life into that of control by the skill of the social engineer, and by the cleverness of the experimenter in propaganda who uses lies, fear, bribes, and betrayal to extinguish the reason and will of the individuals molded into the rigid forms of mass organization. The idea of the people, the nation, as a coordinated living unity in the *ordo* of political existence, as a teleological universe of diverse social forms for free persons, where each person and each social form has its own function and independent rights in the order of the whole, where everybody finds his own perfection and happiness in the free service to the whole—this idea vanishes and is replaced by the idea of the impersonal mass, without will, without critical reason, the object of infinitely changing organization in accordance with the changing demands of a non-moral, anarchic, frigid "reason of state." "Mass" is lack of individuality and personality, lack of all stable organization of forms and groups originating freely in the social process; it is atomistic uniformity of always interchangeable individuals, mere matter without souls and rights, tools of the social and political engineers.

V. Mechanist Philosophy as the Basis
of the Mechanist View

At the root of this view of social forms lies a mechanistic philosophy. It is the belief that a scientific causal method with its presupposed atomism, its necessary limitation to the quantitative measurable element, is the only admissible means of interpretation of the phenomena of the world and of life, of the biological, vegetative and sensitive life as well as of the intellectual and moral life of man and of the forms of his social life.

Man himself is regarded as if he were something like a machine. The psychology of this philosophy is likewise mechanistic. The principles that Newton's atomistic natural philosophy used appropriately to explain physics, are applied to the psychophysical "apparatus." There is a striking affinity between the Ricardian pattern of the *homo economicus* with the laws under which the mechanism of the market works, and the psychology of David Hume, for whom the soul is a bundle of associations, a diverse pattern of reactions to stimuli from that external world which later captured the attention of mechanistic thinking under the name of "milieu." Thus the psychic life is an intricate apparatus, moved according to the principles of scientific causal epistemology. Consequently that only which can be comprehended as experimentally provable cause-effect relation, or as measurable by number and weight by the calculating intellect,[2] that only exists as a true object of scientific perception.

The application of this principle to the social life produces an atomistic social philosophy which, with emphasis on the social form, leads to Hobbes' Leviathan or modern totalitarianism, with emphasis on the individual, it leads to individualistic theories, ranging from Bakunine's anarchism to the liberalist individualism of the Rousseau-Ricardo type. This way of thinking has no place for a genuine perception of the life of the soul, of love and hatred, of sympathy and charity. This world of innermost social life, the world of virtues and vices, the world of the heart, is beyond "sciences." Therefore to thinkers of this school it is inferior. It is "unscientific," just as the religious world, imaginary and unreal as it is held, is unscientific

---

[2] "Intellect" is not quite the right word. The Germans distinguish *Verstand,* as the calculating, means-discovering power, from *Vernunft,* the intellect proper.

and is to be overcome by "sciences." It is truly striking that after the spread of rationalism no true philosophy of love appeared until late in the nineteenth century, when the tide against rationalist philosophy began to turn.

VI. The Biological Misinterpretation of the Organic View

The direct opposite of that "atomistic" social philosophy is the so-called biological one. This has become popular since Herbert Spencer, applying the evolutionary theories of Darwin and Lamarck to social and political philosophy, with astounding industry and somewhat incautious enthusiasm drew analogies between the biological organism and the social organism. Romanticism had already used these analogies to interpret the state as a being created by the irrational powers, the subconscious historical process. But it did so in its bitter polemic against the political philosophy of rationalism and against the mechanistic interpretation of economic life by Ricardo and the other classical economists. The romantics, therefore, were still aware that the life of the mind is neither rationalistic nor biological. But the new theories of biological evolution as distinguished from reverently contemplated historical life were applied in an irresistible hasty ardor of analogy to social and political philosophy. According to their theories, the states are regarded as natural biological organisms, true hypostases; political history is a natural process, a prolongation of natural history, as Gumplowicz tried to show. Of course, "natural" means here the opposite of mind, of free will directed by reason; it means the impersonal organic life of animals and plants; the theology of this school, if it has one, will be an impersonal pantheism or monism.

Though it may seem as if this biological theory in political philosophy is infinitely removed from the mechanistic theory described above, they are more akin than appears at first sight. For in the last resort, the biological theory also rests on a similar concept of nature and on a similar method, the causal-quantitative one, of the natural sciences. Thus, for instance, Darwin's principle of selection by the struggle for existence, the milieu theory, is in the last analysis likewise mechanistic. As utilitarian, therefore measurable, motives are the basis of ethics in the other theory, so here usefulness or harmfulness to the hypostasized social organism is the basis of an ethics in which the traditional terms "good" or "bad" become merely a sign, an irrational reflex of the basically useful or harmful. So the new theory rests on the same mechanistic concept of social life as did the individualistic; the latter, however, was rationalistic, whereas the biological theory is bitterly antirationalistic; its concepts of nature and the natural exclude the intellectual-moral world, making it merely a reflex of the biological one. The individualistic theory at least acknowledges the world of the mind, though it narrows it down to a rationalistic one, a mere instrumental means to be employed by the individual for his self-interest and utility. For the biological school the ethical imperatives are only "signs" of behaviors useful or harmful to the impersonal life of the social organism.

This seems to be the place for a remark about the often misunderstood attacks of Pius IX and Leo XIII upon individualist liberalism, Manchesterism, etc. It shows an excellent sensitiveness in these popes and in many Catholic writers that they were so seldom carried away by the nineteenth-century enthusiasm for natural sciences and the philosophy of individualist liberalism. They felt more than their contemporaries the noxiousness of the partly hidden principles on which the new "civilization" rested. They also saw with a clear eye that Marxism and the other forms of collectivism could be built upon the same principles as liberalist economics and could use the same methods to produce disastrous results for our Christian civilization.

After the highwater mark of the biological theory was reached, modern political philosophy, resigning itself to an ascetic research and accumulation of "facts," ruled out all "philosophy" and gave itself over to positivism. Any mention of the organic view of the state or an attempt at a transcendental, teleological interpretation was considered unscientific, as beyond our experience and empirical methods. This empirical or positivist method, in a rather fruitless modesty, restricted itself to a mere mechanical collection and arbitrary classification of sociological and scientific "facts." It despised the *theoria* of the old metaphysics and rejected any kind of intrinsic and transcendental teleology.

VII. THE ARISTOTELIAN-THOMISTIC PHILOSOPHY
AS THE BASIS OF THE ORGANIC VIEW

The resurrection of metaphysics, the turn of the philosophical mind, dissatisfied with a mere hunt for facts, to the world behind the facts and phenomena, the growth of the antipositivist currents in Bergsonian vitalism and Driesch's philosophy, in Husserl's phenomenology, in the revival of natural law and the rise of the institutionalism of Hauriou against the positivism of Duguit or Kelsen, and finally the powerful revival of Neo-Scholasticism and Thomism brought about a great change in the picture. The methods of the natural sciences, however fruitful in their coordinated field, were recognized as insufficient for the full interpretation of social life, as unable to grasp exactly the innermost essence and meaning of social life. The "understanding" sociology, the Ganzheits-psychology, the vitalistic biology, the philosophy of life of Bergson and Dilthey, and hundreds of concomitant attempts, all show the limitation of positivism, however successful its work in experimental psychology, in the accumulation of factual studies, and the like. No wonder that a new, or in truth very old, view of the state, an organic social philosophy, arises.

The history of philosophy shows that vitalism in biology is accompanied by an organic view of the state in political and social philosophy. It may show further that the mechanistic view in biology finds its counterpart in a mechanistic social philosophy. The reason for this parallelism seems to be that the rationalistic epistemology, if applied in the biological and social sciences, must become an exact-causal method. It easily turns into a mechanistic view, because the exact-causal method is not apt to grasp the non-rational life powers of love and hatred, of sympathy and antipathy, the emotional, the "unreasonable" part of life. This part of human life is not wholly coordinated to the measuring, calculating, exploiting, rationalist mind. That which naturally is not calculable, measurable, or useful, such as love, the spirit of sacrifice, obedience even if not useful,[8] is declared "irrational," therefore unreal; it is metaphysical dream or imaginary reflex of the only reality, that recognized by the exact-causal method.

---

[8] Thomas Hobbes explained obedience in a utilitarian way; he had to do so on account of his fundamentally utilitarian philosophy.

It is left to the poets or to the saints, who are supposedly unrealistic dreamers. But this part of life takes revenge. Rejected as incomprehensible and unscientific, it forces itself upon us in the philosophy of life or in that strange psychoanalysis, which uses the dream as a way to the innermost life of the person, as a philosophy of the unconscious or subconscious or the libido. (Let us hope that we will be saved from a political philosophy that has already revealed itself in some predecessors of Hitler and makes the Oedipus complex or homosexual abnormality the foundation of a political philosophy.)

With the resurgence of this organic philosophy, our problem was put anew: What form of reality has the social community, the state? what is its essence? is it really a whole, distinguished from the sum or any mere summation of those physical beings that form it? if so, what are the fundamental relations of the whole and the members? what is the objective end of the whole and how does it relate to the ends of the parts?

Though the use of the word "organic" as signifying a main feature of the nature of the state is comparatively recent, that quality which is meant by "organic," is very old. That the term itself is new is owing to the fact that only late in the seventeenth and in the eighteenth century did the mechanistic view become the rule in modern political philosophy. In controversy raised by this view, the word "organic" received a kind of polemic point, and in some writers of the romantic and antirevolutionary school this polemic character became so distinctive that its real meaning beyond polemics was in danger of being lost. This does not mean that we should give up the term; its use is sanctioned by most eminent Catholic theologians and philosophers. To mention only a few: Joseph Mausbach, Peter Tischleder, Delos, Wilhelm Schwers, Theodor Meyer. Delos in his book *La société internationale et les principes du droit publique* gives a broad list of Catholic political philosophers who prefer the organic view. Thus we must try to elaborate its true meaning. And we may say that the metaphysical basis of the organic view of the state is itself "organic."

Aristotle made the problem of becoming, of movement, the core of his metaphysical endeavor in trying to explain the enigma of life: the unchangeable in an ever-changing thing, the active forming power that continuously forms and reforms the world around us. Is there at work a meaning, a *ratio*, therefore an intelligible force? Or is all this movement, this evolution from imperfect to more perfect status, the result of changing, blind, chaotic powers that can produce only anarchic disorder and not a cosmos, an order? Aristotle, in opposition to Plato's dualism, the world of ideas separated from the phenomenal world, lets the idea, the form, the essence realize itself, or be realized, in the existing thing (*universale in re* became the medieval formula). The idea thus becomes the forming agent, the active element, while the formed, the changeable element, is passive, determinable but, as the potential element, as "matter," disposed, open, to the form. Any existing thing, therefore, is the result of a union of form and matter. The form, the idea in lifeless nature, is expressed by an outside "forming" agent, or expresses itself in animated nature.

Aristotle thus finds that in two different ways the union of form and matter can be preformed. First, through an outside agent; an already existing agent infuses or expresses the form in matter: so the artist forms the marble into the statue. Secondly, from within; here the form as an internal moving principle forms the matter. This is the way of the animated, the living, substance, the way of organic growth. The form organizes the matter. Such an active, organizing form expresses itself. The end of the process is the perfect expression of the form, or the "nature." The form as active agent is the nature, the final end, that which is to be expressed. Wherever, then, the form is self-moving, self-expressing, self-organizing, there the form as *causa finalis* is the end of the process. And such a form is, for Aristotle, one that is the end of itself, that has its end in itself. The form is not only the beginning but the end of the process of growth. The form is not only the principle but the tendency, the intentional end, of the process of growth; the *causa formalis* is the *causa finalis*. The idea, the essence of a thing, now becomes for the practical reason the norm, the critical norm by which the existing thing can be judged, as also its growth, the degree of perfect expression of the end by the form. The most perfect realization of its nature, of its idea, becomes thus the end of a thing. Teleological perfection is thus the property of the living being. Life is the self-expression of the idea. That is the reason why the order of nature becomes for practical reason the norm of doing, acting, performing: the ideal order. To act against nature (in the sense of the ideal order, not in the abused, denuded popular sense) is therefore wrong, it is a disturbance of the natural order.

VIII. The Organic View Applied to the State

These conceptual forms apply to man and his communities. Man himself is the union of the forming principle, the soul, gifted with reason and free will, and of the formed element, the matter, i.e., the body. It is man's nature to perfect himself in an active life, the end of which is a life corresponding as perfectly as possible to the idea of man, to a life according to reason.

Aristotle thinks this end cannot be reached by the solitary man. It can be reached only by men living in that community, to which all the essential properties and the very nature of man point. Social life (i.e., living in community with one's like) is a necessity arising not out of "wants" but out of the intentional perfection of man's nature. Thus community is an intentional form of life for the individual. "Community" is here used not in the sense of a general, nondescript, sentimental, and undefined way of living, but rather in the sense of certain definite and concrete social forms. Of these forms at least two are fundamental and necessary, serving directly and immediately for the generation, the exaltation, the perfection, and the transmission of life, life in its full sense: the intellectual, moral, cultural life as well as the "biological" life. These fundamental forms are the family (the community of husband and wife and of parents and children) and the state (the community of political life, of an order among families and persons). The individual, though unique, is still not perfect, and has in isolation no chance for the perfect life, the realization of the idea of man. The individual's very individuality points to membership in communities. Man comes into existence as a fruit of the family, cared for and protected during the time of tender growth until he is equipped to fulfill his destiny, to realize concretely his personality. and to become man, to attain the state of happiness for which each one strives, as long as passions and greed for inhuman things do not cloud his mind. And when the individual is not submerged in the community as a soulless, unconscious organ, but retains his individual personality, and becomes a member in order to develop his personality more fully, then life in community enlarges, exalts, and perfects the individual person, and cures the shortcomings and wants that are connected with mere individuality and isolation. Any kind of seclusion from the fullness of community life ultimately means for the individual a personal loss, a self-mutilation, an atrophy, a defect in self-realization.[4]

The guaranty of the fullest perfection of the idea of man is the state, the public order among families and persons. In it the social process finds its earthly culmination. But precisely because the state is the end of an internal teleological process of the social nature, it is not a merely artificial, casual aggregation, or a mere network of legal relations created by and voided by arbitrary will at its pleasure, enacted by self-interests alone and legitimated by the utilitarian and material motives of individuals. No, the state proceeds by inner moral necessity from the social nature of man for the sake of the more perfect life, the fuller realization of personality for all its members in a working sovereign order of mutual assistance and mutual cooperation. This is an order of solidaric responsibility for that perpetual task on earth, the attainment of felicity, in the secure perfection of human nature according to the will of the supreme Creator of this nature to whom ultimately it longs to return.

Thus the political life is also God's ordinance to man revealed by man's nature. Political life originates not in nature as a blind irresistible urge, but in "nature" as a teleological, intentional form of human existence morally necessary for the realization of the idea of man. Nevertheless it is still *in concreto* the will and the reason of concrete men that creates, organizes and institutes the particular state. The political life *in concreto* demands man's freedom of will; men create their state in freedom, however much the idea is the critical norm of the realization of the particular state in history. Because the state is thus both a natural and a morally necessary consequence of man's social nature and in concrete individual existence a free creation of man's free will led by his intellectual reasoning about the necessity of political life, Catholic political philosophy likes to call the state a moral organism to signify the teleological predisposition to it in man's nature.

The end of political life is the perfection of man not only as an individual in an abstract sense but as a person living in community and only thus reaching his personal end. Thus the end of political life is

---

[4] Against this view one should not cite the anchorites of the early Church. Apart from the fact that they lived in close community with God and the saints, they form an exception, whereas the communal life and worship of the monasteries is the rule.

a wholeness with a teleological independence, which is more than all the individual ends summed up together.[5] This end is the realization of the public goods: law, the *ordo rerum humanarum*, the security of the lower communities, their peaceful functioning, the furthering of their self-initiative by the creation of legal institutions and public offices as a help and assistance (but not as their substitute), and the assurance of their peaceful development by protection against internal disorder and external disturbance. Men achieve their happiness and their destiny not as separated individuals but as coordinated members bound by solidaric responsibility for one another as mutual usufructuaries. Hence, although the state serves its members and gets its mark of perfection by the excellence of its service, it is not the servant of the individual citizen to be exploited by him. For under certain circumstances it is the individual good that has to be sacrificed and not the common good, that belongs to all so far as they form the body politic. By the very fact that the end of the state, this common good, is qualitatively different from the mere sum of the particular goods of the individuals, the state as the form of political life has dignity and majesty. Therefore its power can be and should be moral power that legitimately demands obedience in its rightful sense of a morally free acceptance of the *imperium*, not a compulsory external conformity to overwhelming force.

Now we can understand the seemingly enigmatic Aristotelian thesis that the whole (the state) is before the individual, a thesis fully accepted by St. Thomas. If we consider the metaphysical order of ends derived from human nature, then community, especially that perfect and necessary community, the state, stands in the foreground as a form of human existence without which the individual cannot become perfectly man and therefore cannot reach his end, the perfection of his essentially social nature. For sociality is as essential to human nature as is rationality. Thus the end of the individual and the end of the state, though different, coincide with a prevalence of the common good. If, on the other hand, we consider the order of being, then individuals as such are in the foreground; they alone are beings of substantial character, natural persons, rational substances, yet destined

[5] St. Thomas (*Summa theol.*, IIa IIae, q.58, a.7 ad 2) points out that the common good is essentially different from the private good. Similarly in discussing commutative and distributive justice (*ibid.*, q.60, a.1; Ia IIae, q.60, a.3).

and directed by their very social nature to combine into a *unitas ordinis* in community life in order to realize perfectly that social nature.

The bond that characterizes the community thus produces this significant reciprocal interaction and direction: the individuals are by their end bound to the whole that logically is prior, but only in such a way that the whole receives its dignity, its *raison d'être,* and its justification by its very service to the individuals. Its value is never *in concreto* abstracted from the personal values, or from the dignity of the persons as members. It is a solidaric bond expressed best in the slogan, "Every one for the whole and the common good; the whole and the common good for every one." The double character of the whole (the state) may be represented thus. It has a self-value when opposed to the individual as a member and therefore can demand the sacrifice of the life of the individual as a member. But it may do this only on condition that it is at the same time of service character *in concreto;* that is, by its form and acts it must actually serve the general end of all the individuals as persons, i.e., the perfection of their nature, the development of their eternal personal values. An organic view of the state thus helps us to understand this continuous living interaction and interdependence of the whole and the members.

The active element that achieves the direction and coordination of the members to the whole in the *ordo* is not an external principle, but an internal one. And the *ordo* itself is not a mechanistic, automatic result of the motives and acts of separated individuals, looking only to their self-interests. The active principle is not the directive authority and its commands alone. Political authority is not the *forma rei publicae* which only from above externally organizes the matter, the mere amorphous multitude of individuals. The *forma* is the common good, the *ordo.* And this is the result of the acts of the directing authority and of the free rational consent, that is, the moral obedience of the citizen. Authority and subjects meet in reason and devotion, and by mutual cooperation realize the common good, which is consequently the norm of the legitimacy of the authoritative ordinance and of the obedience of the citizen. Hence there is an interdependence, a mutual completion, between political authority and its orders, and the obedience, the loyalty, or the allegiance of the citizen. It is the common good as the *ordo* that guarantees the perfection of the idea of man. The perfect political form is therefore democracy so far as this appeals to the citizen's free obedience to laws which have been enacted because they best serve the common good, laws which are based on mutual consent and have been adopted after free deliberation of reason. Thus it is not the technique of consent that matters, but the form of consent as the best means to realize the common good in harmony with man's dignity as a rational being who should exercise a reasonable obedience, not a blind one.

That is what is meant by saying that the state is a moral organism. The word "organism" is not merely allegorical. It represents, indeed, an objective fact and rests on the knowledge that the organism in the organic world and the moral organism in social life are both built according to analogous metaphysical principles of order. The biological organism stays totally and absolutely under the law of organic life in the way of an unconscious, unfree "must." The moral organism lives under the moral law before which man is free; its teleology is not blind, but normative; its "ought" is clear and cogent to reason and intellect, as the rule of free acts and for free beings to the end that coincides with the ends of the individual persons, i.e., happiness in peace, justice, and order.

Thus Catholic political philosophy proceeds inversely as compared with the biological theory of the state. For this latter the physical organism with its instinct and urge for life, lacking reason and self-conscious will, is not only a starting point and a source of analogy; it is the actual form of social existence, too. The state is not a macrocosmic man; it is actually only a more complicated physical organism, a sort of animal "state," a beehive or an anthill. As self-consciousness in addition to animated organism cannot be denied, this self-consciousness has to be explained not as a result of the thinking process but as a rather unreal reflex of the only real life of the organism. Consequently ethics consists of signs for acts that are useful or noxious to the organism; ethics is nothing but a reflex of the natural blind urge of life into its mere emanation, the consciousness of the individuals. Not the spiritual and moral superstructure, but the biological substructure is the real thing. The consequence of such a theory is the separation of politics from ethics. Politics becomes the field ruled by the non-ethical urge and non-moral instinct. This urge, or better, its volume and force, is the only reality, the might of the strongest; right is merely the sign of the stronger life urge.

Catholic political philosophy thinks quite differently. It knows that to a deeper intellectual insight the laws that govern the physical organism and the moral laws for free rational beings are not contradictory but correspond to each other in their basic teleology. But it regards as the ultimate cause of this correspondence that general world law, according to which the order of the world is established and continuously preserved or re-established by the blind "must" in the life of creatures without reason, and as a free "ought to" in rational creatures. For Christian philosophy the entire cosmos is a well-ordered whole, a real cosmos from the highest to the lowest forms of created being. The higher stage of being contains what the lower contains normatively and causally; and what is contained in the lower intentionally points to the higher.

The organic view is, therefore, not a mere working hypothesis without a true basis in reality. It may be formulated thus: We can, of course, not reach an inner teleological understanding of the state, because that transcends our cognitive faculty; but, since we have to develop some hypothesis of cognition, we tentatively try to conceive the state as if it were an organism, though our experiments demonstrate only that the thing called "social organism" is in reality an utterly complicated apparatus, the conception of which as an organism is not fully guaranteed by facts. Any exact empirical method applying the technique of natural sciences must fail in trying to understand the mysterious hidden life of human communities. For we are of course unable, by geometrical method, to grasp these powers of love and devotion, and that spirit of sacrifice and unselfish service for others, which are so opposed to calculable self-interest. Yet the human communities live by the power of these social virtues and, if selfishness extinguishes these virtues, the human community dies. The principle of self-interest may give a sufficient explanation of the mechanistic laws which Ricardo sought in a competitive conglomeration of individuals aggregated in an exchange market, but that is all it can explain. And even here it is unsufficient, because the presupposed *homo economicus* does not always behave even in the market as a dispassionate, reasonable individual. And further, self-interest as the only motive of social intercourse does not afford a full understanding of what it has to explain: the actual cooperation and mutual help, the unselfish devotion to the common good, the community-forming powers. Moreover, self-interest is separative; that "invisible hand" which the mechanistic theory presupposes in order to explain the coherence of the community, is evidently an even greater riddle than anything else.

According to the organic view, law is neither the sign of the power of the stronger nor a device by which a balance is achieved between liberties of one individual and the self-interests of the others in the political order without arbitrary interference by authorities. In the organic view, law is that part of the general social order which is considered necessary for the existence and preservation of the community and of the individual members, its necessity being judged by its service to the end of man. Law is the order in which and by which the faculties, the external acts of the individuals, and their natural or free associations and groups recognized by the law but not created by it, are directed toward the common good. Thus the order of law, the state, surrounds the individual persons and their groups and forms of social life, giving them protection in their existence and furthering their full and perfect functioning for the greatest good of each of them and of all together. For the state does not create the persons or their social forms. Either these grow naturally out of the social nature of man, or they are produced by the initiative of free persons for the more perfect realization of their ends and purposes. Law is not a mere mechanism, nor is it such an order that its property would be compulsion, as the mechanistic view must conclude. Law rests far more on moral free acceptance and consent, on reason and confidence, than on actual compulsion and menace. And it rests on these moral virtues so strongly that they are the very soul of law, so that law becomes mere compulsion in the same ratio as this soul vanishes.

IX. THE ORGANIC VIEW AND THE PROBLEM OF PLURALISM

The independence and autonomy of these intermediary forms, their rights and sphere of self-government, self-organization, and self-direction in their social functions do not mean a pluralism dangerous to the unity of the political order or to the supreme loyalty to the body politic, the form of existence of the people as an independent community. A dangerous pluralism is bound to develop only in modern class-society where classes with truly totalitarian claims arise precisely because these functional intermediary forms have been abolished under appeal to the wrong antithesis, individual versus the state, which made the state the exclusive lawmaker. The juridical monism of the positivist doctrine destroyed all self-governing organizations with particular ends in order to create the free and equal citizens, who were subject only to the law, the positive law of the state. Leo XIII saw that this juridical monism threatened to develop into a kind of tyranny. The secularized state, preaching indifferentism as a gospel, not as a merely expedient policy, would, like Rousseau, compel the citizen to be free in the law, free therefore from anything that is not state law.[6] Thus the workers' unions were at first treated as states within the state, as conspiracies against the freedom of the individuals. Thus the Church was considered a foreign body in this monistic concept of law, as if real freedom did not consist in the fact that the individual is free to worship not only in the seculsion of his chamber but also publicly, and that he is free to organize with his fellow men institutions for social and economic mutual help, for moral and spiritual progress. The pluralism of social self-governing institutions so feared by the defenders of the Third Republic is not to be confused with a pluralism that actually dissolves the unity of the political order by putting loyalty to the union or the professional group, for example, beyond loyalty to the state or on a competitive level with such loyalty.

As opposed to this kind of dissolving pluralism, Catholic political philosophy knows a genuine pluralism. This grows up from the plurality of social forms and of cooperative spheres that proceed from the person, serve independent particular ends in the order of the common good, and therefore have their own rights and duties. It is not the law of the state that creates these ends and therefore the institutions and rights. In their essence they are before the state, and, however the law of the state may afford them the legal hulks, their essential contents are independent of the positive form that the law gives them. And it is their essence, their ends, that control the legal forms, not vice versa. Thus the state may provide the family with its family law,

---

[6] How this positivism as a creed can lead to a ruthless persecution of religious communities even under democratic government and under a bill of rights, can be seen best in the laicist legislation of the Third Republic in France, especially from 1901 to 1904. Cf. Lecanuet, *L'église de la France sous la troisième république*, Vol. III.

but the essence and the end of the family form the critical norm for the legal forms. Thus likewise the state may furnish the legal form to the vocational groups and professional organizations, but their very ends and their rights and duties are not created by the state; they exist by their own merits as fruits of the social process. They are not evolutionary stages of this process, the functions of which will, with the progress of social evolution, be taken over by the state, the totalitarian state.

This genuine pluralism does not result from that ultimately wrong polemic antithesis, individual versus state, which necessarily leads either to a pluralism destructive of the unity of the state or to all-devouring totalitarianism. For this pluralism the state is the existential sovereign unity of order. Family, home, neighborhood, town, homeland, as also vocational, professional, educational, and religious institutions: in these and through these man lives for his final transcendent destiny. With regard to their specific ends, all these are irreplaceable, however changeable and adaptable may be their concrete legal forms in the different stages of historical development and national culture. However loosely or tightly they may be interwoven into the public order of the state, they have their own functions and their intrinsic value. The function of the state is to produce and preserve the public order among these spheres and institutions; the state is not their *raison d'être*. The task of the state is furtherance and protection of their coordinated, their "organic," symbiosis. Therefore the nation, the people, can, at least for a time, live in them without its own political, free order. Thus the state may in a conquest be suppressed for the time being, but the families and the other institutions continue. The Nazis knew that the only way to destroy a people is to destroy not only their political form of existence, but also these social organizations and institutions. The breaking up of families, of neighborhoods, of parishes, and of educational, cultural, and economic organizations and institutions, entails the atomization and therefore the final destruction of a people. The "dismemberment" (our natural language is an adherent of the organic theory) and the destruction of the forms are the final destruction.

The intensity of social life is greatest in the family and decreases gradually in the larger communities. When, as in totalitarianism, the opposite concentration is striven for, when the state is considered the most intensive form of social life and social interdependence, freedom is impossible. It is the envy and jealousy of the totalitarian state that compels it to destroy or minimize the loyalties in the lower, smaller communities, in order that there shall be one exclusive loyalty. This constitutes the essence of the totalitarian state: such a social intensity and density in knitting the individuals into state organizations that no choice and no initiative remains to the individual, because he has become a tool without right, an instrument for the almighty state. The more freedom the individual person possesses to institute lower communities and to participate in their work, that is, the greater his freedom to form associations and the greater the freedom of the associations themselves in self-initiative and self-government, the freer, actually, is the person, although his bonds and ties increase in these associations. But this is the proof for our contention of the excellence of the organic theory. This theory implies the recognition of these intermediary forms of social life, their freedom and their right and duty to perform their particular functions, the subsidiary function of the activity of the state, and universal order in this diversity which produces an exalted existence of men in the body politic.

X. Other Advantages of the Organic View

There is no question that in the last analysis the difference between the mechanistic and organic view rests upon a difference in the idea of God. Deism looks upon the world as a machine, an almost perfect machine which, once put in motion by the Creator, continues to run on according to the laws of nature. God no longer participates by His providence in this mechanical running of the world machine: He is far away, a quiet restful Contemplator, either amused or cynically disinterested. To this idea of God corresponds the idea of the state as a kind of machine. To the mind nothing is left except to discover the laws as did Newton and let the invisible hand do its work. To think of the state as an organism, or of man as the free producer for better or for worse of the *ordo* as a realization in history of the eternal order of ideas, is a very unsuitable conception. Even less than deism could the nineteenth century, with its materialistic philosophy and its atheism, grasp the organic view. For it discarded the idea of the pensioned deistic God: it also discarded God Himself, and left the world a senseless, ever-changing result of power and matter. In the biological view, it made life the great unconscious, enigmatic mover. Both views can regard the state only as a mere apparatus, a sum of unceasingly and senselessly moving atoms, an automaton; or the revelation of an equally senseless growth without reason and without end, moving unconsciously and blindly beyond good and evil to an endless progress in a senseless history, a growth which cannot be grasped by human understanding. Consequently either the ego or the state becomes God. Ethics in the sense of a rule of the free acts of a rational, responsible, personal being, becomes meaningless. The arbitrariness of the autonomous ego or that of the omnipotent state destroys all order and authority. The result is either the anarchy of Bakunine or the totalitarian destruction of the human person in the omnipotent state.

One essential result of the organic view of the state is that it opens the eye of the mind to the "irrational" powers from which and by which any durable human community really lives. Nothing stands in greater need of these powers than the self-sufficient community, the state.[7] It lives by the social and political virtues of justice, of faith, of devotion, of allegiance, and of sacrifice. These virtues are indispensable. They are the soul of the body politic, whatever its legal form may be. Whenever the very existence of the body politic is at stake, there follows an appeal beyond the legal formalities, the mechanical apparatus (the "red tape"), to the spirit of self-sacrifice, to unswerving allegiance and unselfish devotion. The acknowledgment of this appeal shows that in a center beyond the legal forms the state lives as a being, whose end is not only the protection of individual rights, but the exaltation and the perfection of man, the good life of a higher form. As a person, the individual is unique but still, as individual, he is a limited realization of the idea of man. That is why man, driven by his urge for a more perfect life, strives for society, for a life in family, neighborhood, and state, searching for that completion and happiness which teleologically is shown in the very idea of man, in a consciousness of "ego" that intentionally demands a "thou" to live as "we."

Life can be kindled only by life, through self-devotion and love, when the individual finds himself again in a higher, more perfect form in the community with others of his kind. The first form is mar-

---

[7] Suarez must have had this in mind when, in obvious analogy to the Church as the *corpus Christi mysticum*, he called the state "*corpus politicum mysticum*."

riage and family, the cell of all communal life. Not only in the biological sense is the family the cell of the state. It is—and this is more—the nursery of all those social virtues from which the state lives: obedience to paternal authority, authority mitigated by self-forgetting love; solidarity among the members, mutual help beyond narrow utilitarianism, and the spirit of the honor of the whole obliging the members to stand together. There exists a direct ratio between the health of the family, mental and moral health primarily, and the health and well-being of the state. An impairment of the family that produces individuals looking only for their own advantages will result in a deterioration of the body politic.

The organic view makes us more clearly grasp the lasting duration of the body politic as contrasted with the continuous change of the individuals, the families, and the other social forms, which live and die and are replaced by new lives. The state, the body politic, existed before the present generation was born, and it is destined to exist when the grandchildren are buried beside their ancestors. The ruler is not the state, nor is the family of the ruler; nor is the majority in an election, or even the sum of all living citizens. The people form the state; but as an historic entity, generations bequeathing to later generations what the former inherited from their ancestors, all building in a spiritual succession of inheritance to perfect the body politic, the existential form of the people. This inner meaning of the state as an organic, lasting unity can never be understood on the rationalist basis of individualist utilitarian, materialist motives. Why should treason be considered the lowest, meanest crime? The Quislings, the mean sellers of their own and their country's honor, can be judged only on a basis beyond considerations of utility. What they violate is the inner life, nay, the principle of life, of the body politic, which transcends rationalist concepts as does the life of man.

XI. LEGAL AND DISTRIBUTIVE JUSTICE AND THE ORGANIC VIEW

Catholic political philosophy teaches not merely commutative justice, which intrinsically treats men as equals, as individuals, centering their concern upon self-interest and separated by self-interest. A social philosophy that considers nothing but commutative justice becomes individualistic, self-centered and separative, and loses any true understanding of the state. Capitalistic individualism centered round the open competitive market, in which individual profit was supposed to be restrained automatically by the mechanism of competition and the self-interests of others. This individualism had only contempt for the state if the state could not serve as a tool for the imperialist expansion of the markets. No wonder that capitalists, if ruled only by profit motive and property interests, financed the armaments of dictators and, in the final emergency, preferred to make one per cent under the foreign conqueror than to make nothing working for the salvation of their state and the preservation of the common good.

In addition to commutative justice, a true and full justice in its appropriate field, the exchanges, Catholic political philosophy takes account of distributive and legal justice. Distributive justice prescribes duties and rights between the state, represented by political authority, and the citizens. In it the state protects and furthers the diverse functions of the individual citizens, and of their organizations as social functions of the whole. This it does, not only for the exclusive benefit of the individual, abstracted from his function, but for the individual as a member, as a functioning part, of the organic whole. Therefore, in the field of distributive justice, what matters is not the fundamental equality of the citizens as persons, but the difference, the inequality in their functions.

Only the organic view and the concept of distributive justice can provide an adequate moral basis for social reform. This reform is not sufficiently justified by the statement that there should be some kind of mitigation of shortcomings in the economic system because otherwise social upheavals would threaten to destroy this supposedly fine system. Such a utilitarian explanation has always been disapproved by Catholic political philosophy. Social reform is considered necessary because the true form of the common good has been distorted, because "parts" of the whole did not get back, in the form of individual happiness and participation in the rich life of the whole, all that was demanded by their dutiful functional contribution and the dignity of their persons.[8] Economic liberalism, against its principles and after a

---

[8] The slogan of the "forgotten man" receives its resounding appeal precisely from the presupposed idea that he, though contributing to the whole and having been guaranteed his dignity, was forgotten by the community and did not get back in wealth and happiness what by his service he contributed to the whole.

long resistance, accepted social legislation, only as a kind of free alms for the weak, as charity for the unfortunates, or as a kind of insurance against the insurrection of the mob, but never as a strict duty of distributive justice.

Furthermore Catholic political philosophy knows about legal justice, which regulates the mutual duties and rights between the individual and his associations and the state. And again this justice is not based on self-interest and quantitative equality. Legal justice requires from the individual, as member, loyalty and allegiance, even the sacrifice of life when the sacrifice of one's life is necessary under given circumstances and on account of one's specific function in the whole. A soldier who is derelict in his duty in order to save his life is despised, while the subservience of the individual citizen to a ruthless party boss is held quite pardonable. The specific loyalty is related in kind and in completion to the specific functional membership in the body politic and is not the same for all individuals.

To all these aspects the organic view opens the understanding. It perceives the state as a living whole, as the consequential progress of man's social nature and its purposive evolution. The state is not entirely the product of mere considerations of utility for autonomous and intrinsically self-sufficient individuals. Nor is it an unconscious, blind urge of life, irrational, endless, aimless. In no way does the individualistic, mechanistic view perceive and explain the very essence of the state as the form of political existence of the people. In truth, its starting point, that is, the individual, is such an abstract notion, such a qualityless point of imputation of social relations, that we cannot understand how from this aimless abstraction the complicated system of manifold relations could be explained. It has been forgotten that the concept of "individual" had at first a distinct polemic meaning as used against a concrete, historical political system, and that, therefore, the concept of "individual" mirrored a distinct philosophical content. But this modern abstraction without its counterpart, the European ancient regime, does not mirror anything and thus is so fully an abstraction that it is unable to explain reality. For in reality there is no abstract individual opposed to an abstract state as a system of norms; there is man, born, brought up, and educated in the family, participating in the economic process of society, furthering his very concrete happiness in many social forms, joining a religious community, and, through all this, living in the well-ordered protective, comprehensive sovereign community, the state.

Only so does the instrumental apparatus, which the state also is, find its place. The state is not a mere bureaucratic machinery, oppressive at any rate, or a cold monster. The administrative bureaucratic machinery is the state as it encounters the citizen in everyday life in the market, in the streets, in the offices and factories, in education and cultural life; it is the police, administrative supervision and regulation, tax-collector, etc. This machinery is bearable because it serves the higher end, the metaphysical end of the state as a community in which man may grow into a form of higher, more perfect life, in which he is enabled to perfect his own end, to be man in the full sense and to work for the salvation of his soul and the glory of God.

If this bureaucratic apparatus serves not the common good, but only the particular interests of a group, or if it makes itself the very essence of the state, it is of course unbearable. Typical of the individualist view is its conception of the state merely as an instrumental apparatus, therefore always somewhat oppressive, something that may wither away as soon as the individuals by further enlightenment in a better evolution of society can take care of themselves without this kind of state. Here again individualism and collectivism touch each other, seeing only the instrumental apparatus: the one, perhaps as a still necessary servant of a not yet fully developed society of free and equal; the other, as the omnipotent dictatorial machinery organizing as pure matter by command and specific ordinances the mass of equal and unfree for the final establishment of a stateless society beyond want and necessity.

The organic view offers, too, the best basis for a satisfactory relation between authority and freedom, right and might, individual, intermediary, but independent communities, and sovereign order. Of course, authority, to be morally justified in exacting obedience by man from man, must have its last source in God. But its mediate source is the objective service to the common good. This objective legitimation of political authority, founded on the service to the common good, the *raison d'être* of the state, protects liberty, at least as long as we agree that life in the political status is necessary for the full realization of the idea of man as a "political animal." Authority and state then serve the individual as a concretization of the idea of man, though not always his particular longings and the aimless urge for anarchic freedom. For then the very dignity of the human person, its incomparable transcendent value and self-interest, can never disappear in mere membership, in mere instrumental service to the state. In the last resort the state and political authority serve the human person. Authority can, therefore, be objective and genuine, and must not be a mere sum of rights transferred to it by individuals and revocable at their pleasure. Nor must the basic rights that issue from the person be sacrificed to totalitarian absolute authority for ends and aims beyond the person. Authority and the freedom of the person are both measured, not by power, successful subjection, or unlimited urge, but by the metaphysical end of man as the supreme rule, and consequently by God's will revealing itself in the order of creation.

Similarly, might without right, that is, without reason, is inhuman and unable to bind the conscience, which is the final arbiter. On the other hand, right without compulsory power is a chimera. It is unable to establish, protect, and restore the concrete order which, in relation to the idea of man, is a necessity.

Moreover, Catholic political philosophy does not consider the state a mechanism constructed from below, from the atomistic will of abstract individuals. And it does not regard the state as an omnipotent bureaucratic apparatus constructed from above, regimenting the citizens, organizing the abstract particles of the masses without rights, for a meaningless dream of world conquest by the proletariat or by the master race. At the basis of the organic view lies the idea of a cosmos (in the true meaning) of the spheres of life, from the individual personal one, through the intermediary ones, which serve partial aims of man, to the comprehensive political sphere, a cosmos in which authority is the boundary of freedom, and freedom the boundary of authoritarian might; a cosmos in which the law as the general rule has the might and in which might serves the moral value of the right of the *ordo* against disturbance by the chaotic, anarchic tendencies that exist wherever men live.

These are the ideas that Catholic political philosophy regards as inherent in the organic view of the state. Therefore it can build upon them a true political and social ethics, whereas individualism knows only about an individualist ethics, an ethics for individuals as such, and hence inapplicable in decisive political problems. And this limitation has the paradoxical consequence, as facts are more powerful than bloodless theories about them, that the era of political individualism, misunderstanding the true nature of the state, became the era of international power politics.

CHAPTER V

Origin and Growth of the Idea of Natural Law

I. ORIGIN OF THE IDEA

IN CATHOLIC thought the political theory is based on natural law. There are two specific reasons for this. First: the state is by necessity the product of human nature. Although not created without the intervention of the free will of man, it is never merely the result of an arbitary act of human discretion. The concrete state, on the other hand, does not originate by an immediate act of God, but gets existence and form through human activity and is therefore in its constitution and historical form dependent on various merely human factors. Neither democracy nor monarchy, neither the nationalist principle nor the federal principle of state structure, therefore, can be of divine right. Second, even though the concrete formation, constitution, and activity of every state are of mere human law, not of divine law, the formation, constitution, and all internal and external activity of the state are subjected to the rules of one natural law, derived from the idea of man's nature and man's end. These rules are immediately evident and have their sanction in God's eternal law. Thus we have one of the crucial problems of every political theory, the relation between right and might.

In the beginning of their historical awakening, people in primitive culture do not distinguish between an unchangeable divine law and a merely human, changeable law, between legal laws about external behavior and moral laws directing consciences. All laws are of divine origin. The whole order of social and individual life is a divinely instituted order, sacred and protected by the tribal gods. For the ancient Greeks as well as for the tribes in Gaul, Germany, and the British Isles, all laws (legal, moral, and ritual) were divine laws. They had a

sacramental character. There is no distinction of laws in primitiv
times. All laws are divine laws, unchangeable, beyond all human re
soning. In all primitive cultures, therefore, it is the priests who cult
vate jurisprudence as a kind of secret science and act as judges. Thu
in the Bible, the Book of Judges, who were priests, comes before th
Book of Kings, as with the Romans the pontifices were also the ac
ministrators of justice, in primordial times. What distinguishes thi
original theological or sacerdotal form of law is its immutability.

The idea of a natural law can arise only when reason discovers tha
not all laws are unchangeable, that different peoples live according t
different laws, and that the law almost imperceptibly changes. Th
conclusion must be that not all law is divine law, unchangeable an
sacred, and that there exists also human, changeable law. The ritua
or sacred law of worship is now distinguished from the law governin
the socio-political and civic order. This human law, originating i
human will, demands actual and moral obedience and vests huma
authority with power to enforce. Whence comes this moral authorit
of human law and the moral obligation to obey it? The mere will, th
arbitrariness of rulers, cannot be sufficient to oblige human reason
once reason comes to self-consciousness. Were it so, right would simpl
be the arbitrary will of mighty rulers. Obedience would be a non
moral, actual, and efficiently ruthless compulsion, not a moral obliga
tion of loyalty to conscience and reason.[1] But this is an impossible de
mand on human reason especially if it has just freed itself from th
early hierocratic status of law. Human reason must ask for a justifica
tion of its obedience to human law. Consequently this leads to ques
tions about the best organization or form of public political authority
or the best form of the state. It leads also to some kind of "enlighten
ment" which dethrones the mythical tribal gods and leads reason to
the idea of an eternal unchangeable law of an omniscient lawgive
who is at once omnipotent will and perfect reason, hidden behind the
images of the tribal gods, which are not the last and perfect form o
the religious idea. If we do not accept this reasoning, there are lef
only two contradictory solutions, namely, anarchy or the so-callec
positivism of the historical school with its stepchild, historical ma

[1] Since the time of Socrates and Antigone this antithesis has been represented thus
Power makes law, truth makes law; or, the will makes law, reason makes law.

terialism. Anarchism despises every kind of law and recognizes only the "Ego and his own." [2] Positivism declares the search for a moral or natural basis of the positive laws to be inexpedient. It explains, or perhaps we should say it describes, laws exclusively as a result of historical factors like race, environment, cultural development, defense of economic interests, class struggles. Historical materialism declares that right is merely an ideological reflex of the only reality, the economic condition, and the social relations of production. All of these dubious and, in the last analysis, inhuman theories cannot stand muster before human reason seeking last principles.

Consequently there must be a law from which all human laws derive their validity and moral obligation. There must be a right which is paramount to all rights of the state, one on which the state itself bases its authority. The wisdom of the Greeks and the legal genius of the Roman lawyers have held this law, the natural law, to be of divine origin. Since their time the idea of natural law has been the inheritance of mankind. There have been times when this idea seemed to fade away because fatigued skepticism or a cynical attitude of science denied the ability of the human mind to attain to the knowledge of truth and metaphysics. But, as the history of ideas so convincingly proves, there is an eternal return [3] of the idea of natural law in general. And at least in Christian philosophy, in the *philosophia perennis*, natural law has always been at home and found there its refuge in the times of philosophical despair over the human mind's ability to penetrate to the truth. No wonder, therefore, that we are witnesses of a resurrection of metaphysics in a revival, for instance, of Thomism, in all countries which are in any way heir to the Christian and classical culture. We are witnesses, too, of a revival of natural law. Never, for generations past, has the idea of natural rights found so many and such manifest professions, as since their denial by totalitarian governments has awakened the minds of men to their eternal value. In the last analysis our whole argumentation for the inalienable rights of man, for the subordination of politics to moral law, for the rights of small nations, for independence, liberty, and security, rests as firmly

---

[2] Cf. Max Stirner, *Der Einzige und sein Eigentum.*

[3] The author has devoted a special study to this eternal return in his book *Die ewige Wiederkehr des Naturrechts* (1936).

on the idea of natural law as does the argumentation of the papal encyclicals for social justice against communism and for the natural rights of the individual person above the state, against Nazism.[4]

II. RISE OF IDEA OF NATURAL LAW IN GREECE

Every philosophy of law faces the alternative: Law is arbitrary will, or law is reason. Law is a rule *of* reason and *for* reason. If we accept the first alternative, we really deny a philosophy of law and restrict ourselves to some merely instrumental and abstract concepts in law, to a behaviorist theory without any claim to value judgments. If we accept the second alternative, we come to the conclusion that the philosophy of law is intrinsically interwoven with the idea of natural law; that it is a part of a perennial moral philosophy which in itself, as Sertillanges says, is a prolongation of metaphysics.[5] This will appear clearly enough in a short survey of the idea of natural law. Our sketch will show also the intimate connection and evident interdependence of natural law and political theory. The principal task of the idea of natural law is twofold: to give a solid foundation for the necessity of the political order for man's social existence; to give us a principle from which we can derive limitations of the sovereign and concentrated power of those who govern and are thus all too much subject to the temptations that power over men involves.

The active genius of Greece first developed the idea of natural law in what we may call the history of Western civilization. Heraclitus, popularly known on account of his principle "all is in flux," is the first who praised a general unchangeable law. There is, he explains, behind the perpetually changing world of outside phenomena, a divine *logos*. It constitutes the law of harmony which the wise man is able to discover behind the changing phenomena. "It is the highest virtue and true wisdom in speaking and acting to obey nature that is the common logos. Therefore all human laws are nourished by this original divine law." [6] The human laws of the different peoples are attempts to realize this eternal law. This eternal law is *logos*, is reason. Therefore human law bases its authority on the eternal law, for man is a rational being.

---

[4] For a powerful demonstration of this, see the encyclical *Mit brennender Sorge* of Pius XI and *Summi Pontificatus* of Pius XII.

[5] A. D. Sertillanges, *La philosophie morale de St. Thomas d'Aquin* (1916), p. 15.

[6] Diel, *Fragmente*, no. 112.

It is this theory of natural law which induced St. Justin Martyr to call Heraclitus a Christian.[7]

Heraclitus inveighed with bitter scorn, as Plato did later, against the Sophists, who were the radicals in the Greek *polis*. But some of the Sophists were better than their reputation. Of course, many Sophist demagogues uttered theories that sound quite modern in their radicalism. But some taught convincingly the doctrine of a natural law superior to the laws of the *polis*. They said that the authority of these laws depends on the fact that they are exemplifications of the natural law. When Heraclitus, a conservative, preached the natural law, he did so because he wished to protect the laws of the *polis* as realizations of the natural law, from the radical criticism directed against them by some of the mob-baiting Sophist orators. The moderate Sophists for their part used the same idea of natural law to criticize the laws of the *polis* as mere means, devised merely to protect the power of the ruling classes. When Callicles, therefore, says that might is right, he is not making a cynical statement. On the contrary, he implies that the ruling class, contending that their laws are a realization of the commonly accepted natural law, are abusing the idea of natural justice in the interest of their rule.

There are three ideas that we find heralded in the Greek spiritual world by the Sophists. First, that the laws of the *polis* serve the interest of the ruling class, contradicting the natural law which radiates from human nature as a free rational being; secondly, that all men, not only the Greeks, but also the barbarians, are free and have equal natural rights. In the eyes of Hippias, for instance, all men are relatives, and fellow citizens by nature even though not by law. "Deity," says Alcidamos, "has created all men free. Nature has made nobody a slave." [8] It follows that above the *polis* there exists a *civitas maxima*, humanity, the cosmo-polis. Thirdly, that the individual *polis* is the outcome of chance, not of nature. It comes into existence by some kind of human resolution, by a free social contract. Thus the *polis* has been preceded by a natural status in which the natural law in its purity ruled. Some

---

[7] *Apologia prima*, no. 46; Migne, *P.G.*, VI, 397, 399.

[8] It may easily be understood that such a revolutionary statement aroused Plato and Aristotle. They believed in the excellence of the laws of the *polis*. They saw a great difference between Greeks and barbarians. They defended slavery, the economic foundation of the philosopher's contemplative life, because nature has made some men slaves; all that without denying, of course, the idea of natural justice and law.

Sophists considered this natural status optimistically. With them the *polis* could exist only under recognition of these original rights. Other Sophists, like Epicurus, had a pessimistic idea of this natural status, as Hobbes did later. Therefore, even though they were utilitarians, they were inclined to an exaggerated valuation of laws and authorities and, like Hobbes later, began even to deride the idea of natural justice. It is striking to observe how, from that time on, these ideas begin a triumphal way through history. Yet it should be kept in mind that the idea of natural law can become a mere slogan and that its understanding depends entirely on philosophical environment and on the metaphysical basis on which the idea of natural law grows.

Throughout the centuries Aristotle has been called the father of the idea of natural law.[9] This is true not so much in a historical sense as in a philosophical sense. His metaphysics, on account of its acceptance by St. Thomas Aquinas, and his influence on Stoic philosophy and through it on Roman jurisprudence formed the spiritual stream that carried the idea of natural law down through history to our time. It was not a favorable era for jurisprudence and the philosophy of law when historical circumstances compelled this stream to flow underground.

Aristotle's leading idea is that the very essence of a thing is at the same time its end. All creatures are in a never-ceasing process from the rudimentary state to the perfection of their idea. It is the essence of man to be a free, rational, and social being. Therefore the highest law governing man's acting and living is: to realize this idea of man, to realize the universal form, the essence in his individuality. For in this fulfillment of man's nature consists man's happiness, that for which all strive, in a life conforming to virtue, virtue being the full realization of man's rational and moral nature. The measure of morality, therefore, is perfect human nature as the final cause of man's intellectual and moral growth. Consequently all acts which correspond to the essential idea of man's nature are good, and the opposite ones are bad, not because the law makes them so, but because nature makes them good or bad. Thus Aristotle distinguishes, discussing the virtue of justice, what is just by nature and what is just by positive law, the recognized concrete law of the *polis*. What is just by nature is invariably so, because nature is perennially invariable. Furthermore, it is

9 This is now denied. Cf. Hertling, *Histor. Beiträge* (1914), p. 77.

universal as human nature is universal. It is independent of the law-makers. The positive law is, indeed, in its obliging power, dependent on the natural law. Every human law must be an attempt to realize the natural justice or law. This is the yardstick of the justice of all human laws. Hence that law essentially is reason, a rule *of* reason *for* rational beings. For Aristotle, accordingly, each positive law, so far as it is just, is a more or less successful attempt to express the idea of law. That is its essence and its purpose which ought to be realized in every human law.

Aristotle's theory of natural law is conservative. It is not used against the laws of the *polis* as is the theory of the Sophists. The laws of the *polis* are presumed to be good. Furthermore, the *polis*, with the common good, is so much in the foreground that its laws are to a degree sacred. The *polis* is the omnipotent pedagogue destined to make men virtuous. The idea of man is realized in the citizenship of the *polis*. With some reason one may therefore say that Aristotle and, in an even stronger degree, anti-Sophist Plato, are state socialists; they practically do not recognize that man's end is beyond the *polis*.

We should never forget how mightily the idea of a paramount law, to which the laws of the rulers must correspond, influenced the mind of the Greek people. The unwritten law, coming from the Deity, and obedience to that law even when it meant disobedience to the law of the *polis*, have found their most striking expression in Sophocles' *Antigone*. Here the genius of Greece for true tragedy, while clearly feeling that man's end is superior to the *polis*, shows in the final suicide of Antigone, its impotence to solve the contradictions. The tragic annihilation of both Cleon (the defender of the laws of the *polis*) and of Antigone (who appeals from the human laws to the natural unwritten law) shows that the Greeks were unable to find a final solution of this tragic dilemma.

III. Growth of Natural Law in Stoic Philosophy and Roman Jurisprudence

Very important for the development of natural law has been the influence of Stoic philosophy. It created the word channels through which the eternal imperishable heritage of Greece came to early Christianity. The background of Stoicism is the decaying ancient society with its proletarian city mob, howling for bread and games, with its monied bourgeoisie mingling with a rotten aristocracy devoted to shameless debauchery or to Oriental mystical cults, ruled by the despotic tyranny of blasphemous emperor-gods. Out of this background steps the figure of the Stoic philosopher. Knowledge is the basis of his ethics. Unity of knowledge and acting is the unchanging ideal of the sage. The sage, austere and undisturbed by passions, surrounded by the twilight of the waning culture of antiquity, is the most all-embracing representation of the spirit of the Stoa which, indeed, comes nearest to the greater representative of Christianity, to the Saint.

For the Stoic philosopher virtue is right reason, that is, the correspondence of actions to the rational concept of man's essence and nature. Nature means here the pure idea of man, the ideal of man's moral and intellectual striving, such as, perhaps, has never yet been reached. It has no reference to that empirical sense we have in mind when, disappointed in our moral expectations, we ask: Can anything better be expected of human nature? The moral rule therefore is: Live in accordance with human nature. This rule, as part of the divine law of the world, is eternal law for man, something greater and nobler than the laws of Greeks or Romans. Thus the innate unwritten law is the basis of all positive laws. This innate law is not a mere generalization and abstractions from positive rules like the Law of the Twelve Tables or from the judicial decisions of the praetor. It is invariable, valid at all times, because it emanates from the divine reason. Fraud, theft, adultery are not illegal and wrong because the decision of judges or the will of the legislator says so; but these men declare fraud illegal because fraud contradicts the natural law. Therefore laws admitting slavery are for Epictetus "laws of the dead," an abyss of crime against the dignity of man's nature. All men are relatives, free sons of the Deity, equal citizens of the *civitas maxima*.[10] "In so far as I am Antonius, Rome is my fatherland; in so far as I am a man, the world is my home." The *polis* of the Greeks has lost its power. Ideas of the Sophists, those foes of the narrowness of the *polis*, came to life again in the Stoic philosophy. The Greek distinction between Greeks as superior men and the barbarians as inferior men disappears. The idea

---

[10] Concerning the Stoic world state, cf. J. Bidez: *La cité du monde et la cité du soleil chez les Stoiciens* (Paris, 1932). This idea lives also in Seneca's wonderful saying: *Homo sacra res homini.* (Ep. 95 § 33).

of a natural law arising from the nature of man and common to all men, without regard to their national or tribal membership, prepares the world for St. Paul's idea of a Christian equality of all men (Rom. 2:14; 3:29).

The genius of Stoic philosophy, the last comprehensive and most impressive emanation of the ancient world, poured this idea of a natural law into the greatest juridical system, the Roman law. Roman law reached its highest perfection when the lawyers were at the same time Stoic philosophers. For the lawyer-philosopher the written law must be interpreted on the basis of the innate natural law. In the case of a conflict the natural law has precedence. This enhancing of natural law gives the Roman law of Gaius, Ulpian, Paulus, and Papinian something like a sacerdotal character. They held that the jurists were like priests administering the knowledge of what is just and unjust.[11] A great consequence followed from this teaching. Not only the Roman citizen is a subject of inalienable, original rights; but each man as a member of human society, of the Stoic *civitas maxima*, is a subject of rights derived from natural law. Therefore, for the philosopher-jurists, slavery is against the natural law, a tenet which is in strong disagreement with Aristotle. Here we have the first tender buds of the idea of human rights. It is true that the jurists and the philosophers almost despaired when they compared the world around them with their own ideal world. It is understandable that they began to distinguish between an original status when the pure natural law ruled with equality, liberty, and the rule of reason, and a secondary kind of natural law where reason, counteracted by passions and bad customs, cannot dominate the order of society.

It is to the lasting glory of the Roman jurists under the influence of Stoic philosophy that they tried to subject the positive law of the state to the control of the eternal natural law, emanating from a divine reason as the paramount ruler. And whoever asserts this truth must, in his political philosophy, deny any despotic or absolute government as he must deny any totalitarian claim of the state to the individual person. The true perfect sovereignty belongs to the natural law and the world-logos. All human sovereignty is restricted and measured by that supreme law, that is, by reason. Yet this Stoic world-logos remained

---

[11] Cf. *Corpus juris civilis* (ed. Krueger and Mommsen); *Dig.*, I, I, 1. *Juris prudentia est divinarum et humanarum rerum notitia justi atque injusti scientia.* (Ulpianus.)

vaguely understood. It was not viewed in a merely pantheist sense nor was it clearly recognized as a personal God. A satisfying solution could be found only when the natural law, paramount to the will of the state, would be founded in the idea of a personal God, who is at the same time supreme intellect and omnipotent will, perfect wisdom and supreme authority, perfect justice and supreme power.

IV. DEVELOPMENT OF NATURAL LAW IN EARLY CHRISTIANITY

This new idea was given to the world by Christianity. God, perfect intellect, supreme will, is the Lawmaker of the world. Human reason is the light by which this law is seen. This law is engraved in man's heart; its basic principles are self-evident; its conclusions can be found by the human mind from the knowledge of the created world in which the Creator and supreme Lawmaker reveals His will. Human personality, the immortal soul of man, is paramount to all secular things, even to their highest embodiment, the state or *polis*. Man's end is beyond the state. The state is not omnipotent. The Christian conscience demands its freedom and resists Caesar in things that are not Caesar's. A new religious society arises, the Church, with its own God-given rights beyond the power of the state. The Christian is more than a citizen, and the state is not the omnipotent pedagogue, as it was for Aristotle and Plato. The *civitas maxima,* dreamy ideal of the Stoics, becomes the Christian society, the Church above the *polis,* the tribes, the races, the Church for all peoples.[12] From now on might had to justify itself before right, before conscience and natural law. Law must be a rule *of* reason and *for* reason, it cannot be merely arbitrary will. And even higher than right is charity. Every man is thy neighbor.

The early Christians, soon setting aside the hope of an early reappearance of the Lord as the world Judge, stood face to face with the problem of Christian ethics in state and society. Celsus, the pagan defender of the pagan totalitarian state, reproached the Christians with disrupting the Empire, with trying to form a state in the state. Thus the Christian apologists had to show that a Christian can be, even must be, a good citizen in the state and that the citizenship in the *Civitas Dei* does not hinder or diminish the duties of the Christian as a citizen in

---

12 Cf. Rom. 2:29.

the secular state, but enhances them. Thus the first rules of a Christian political ethics are formulated. We find the gospel and the idea of natural law as their basis. The power of Christianity begins to transform the world. To do so it has to incorporate in its ethics the rules for the Christian's active life in the secular sphere.

In the teachings of the last philosophy of the ancient world, Providence provided expressions to be filled with the new ideas. According to St. Justin Martyr, these teachings are particles of eternal truth not originating from the mythology of Dionysus but from the original revelation. The Stoic distinction of a primary and a secondary natural law could be used to explain the perfect rule of the original natural law in the status before the fall and the dimmed rule of natural law after the fall attributable to the disturbed reason and the weakened will seduced by uncontrolled passions.

This influence of Greek and Roman tradition must, of course, not be exaggerated. The use of the old words and concepts must not lead to the opinion that this doctrine of natural law and political ethics is a mere syncretism of different pagan theories. On the contrary the adoption of these ideas into the Christian thought transformed their meaning. They were adapted to the original Christian ideas; the latter were not adapted to the former. Besides, in the epistles of St. Paul, the Church Fathers found the idea of a natural law clearly expressed.[18] The teachings of Christ offered the new ideas also. The Old Testament contained them. What the Fathers, therefore, took over was the perennial imperishable idea, not merely its expression by Aristotle or the Stoics. Because the Fathers taught that human reason fundamentally could arrive at truth and had not been completely darkened by the Fall, they did not need to adapt the new Christian moral ideas in a bad compromise to a sinful "world" in which the spirit of the Sermon on the Mount could not be realized.

The Fathers, of course, did not try to systematize their ideas on natural law in a juridical and political theory. Theirs was not a time for the medieval *Summa*, for the construction of a whole system. Theirs was the time of hundreds of Oriental mysticisms threatening revelation. Their problem was the protection of the faith against the Christological and Mariological errors. Their task was the practical care of

18 Cf. Rom. 2:14 f.

souls, the preservation of the sparse lights of the faith in times of per-secution, and the conservation of spiritual life in the collapse of the remnants of pagan antiquity.

St. Augustine, exceptional in all things, is the exception here too. Heir to the spiritual treasures of the ancient world, adversary of the Pelagian heresy, which taught that reason could substitute for faith, foe of Manichaeism, which held that nature and the world were de-livered to evil, witness to the collapse of the Roman Empire, the *civitas terrena*, St. Augustine was forced to occupy himself with prob-lems of political theory and of the philosophy of law. To him, Plato's ideas become ideas of God. The impersonal world-reason of the Stoics becomes the personal all-wise and almighty God. The rather deistic divine intellect, the *nous* of Aristotle, becomes the transcendent Crea-tor of the world, the eternal intellect, the omnipotent will holding the creation in His hands, directing it with His providence, ruling it under the eternal law. This eternal law is God's innermost nature and essence; it is the divine reason, which governs the inner life of the Deity and His activity in the created world. It is the essence of God which is reflected in the eternal law, in the perfect order of all beings. The nat-ural law, moral as well as juridical, is a participation in the eternal law. It is the same eternal law revealed in the nature of man, written by God into man's free conscience, cognizable by the light of reason as the Creator's will, as the order of the creation for rational creatures. Therefore the authority of each human law depends on the fact that it does not contradict this natural law. Therefore human authority re-ceives its dignity from its obedience to God's law, and may demand obedience because it realizes and preserves the divinely instituted order, as it appears in the natural law.

In St. Augustine, therefore, are formed all the decisive ideas for a philosophy of law and of the state. There is an eternal law ruling the universe. It originates in God's very essence and creates the order of the universe, the logic in all being. This eternal law becomes for free rational beings the rule of their acts, the natural law. And this law again is the source and the standard for all human law. Human law can bind in conscience because and in so far as it is derived from nat-ural law. The order of the universe, constituted by eternal law, pre-sents itself to reason as the analogy of all being to God the Creator.

Human reason, even after the Fall, is able to discover this eternal law. For human nature is not altogether depraved as the Manichaeans contended. The Stoic idea of a happy original status of man and of an imperfect one later, unexplained as to its cause, is clarified by St. Augustine as the status of human nature before and after the Fall. The imperfection after the Fall is recognized as a consequence of original sin, but a positive legal and political order would have existed also in the state of pure nature.[14] Only some attributes of the political power, its use of coercion for instance, are a consequence of the Fall.

Since St. Augustine there has thus existed, in the framework of a Christian social philosophy, a philosophy of law and of the state, based on the concept of natural law and natural reason, along with a theology of the state. It was the privilege—a dubious one—of the Reformers to be satisfied with a theology of the state. But the great secularization in liberal theology, in the last resort a religious relativism, has done away with both under the impact of so-called historicism.

Ever since St. Augustine the idea of a natural law as the basis of a morally acceptable political philosophy has remained a lasting heritage of Christian civilization. All subsequent political philosophies have accepted either formally or tacitly the theory of natural law in some form; or they have denied it and cannot rank as a genuine philosophy of politics however meritorious they may be in the elaboration of specific partial problems or in the factual historical study of political institutions and leading ideas. True it is that the idea of a natural law, though banned from the public universities of a Europe inclined to political absolutism, found shelter in the *philosophia perennis*. But it is also true that this idea never again wholly disappeared. When in the decay of Scholasticism it was almost destroyed through Occamism, it returned in a more perfect form in Late Scholasticism. When it was ruined by rationalism in the era of Enlightenment and was deposed by the nineteenth-century positivism, it returned after the secure bourgeois world was shaken by the revolutions of the twentieth century following the First World War.[15]

---

[14] Cf. Rommen, *Staatslehre des Fr. Suarez*, p. 325; O. Schilling, *Naturrecht und Staat in der alten Kirche, passim.*

[15] Pope Pius' encyclical against National Socialism (*Mit brennender Sorge*) is mostly based on natural law. Is not the applause it received valid, too, for the theory of natural law?

V. Interdependence of Natural Theology, Metaphysics, and Political Theory

The student of the history of natural law will notice that there exists an interdependence between natural theology, metaphysics, and political theory. He will also notice that the idea of natural law flourishes when law is defined as the rule of reason and for reason and that it recedes into the background when law is defined as will. The definitions proceed from a presupposed answer to the question: In God is the intellect superior to the will, or is the omnipotent will superior? Only if we accept the superiority of the divine intellect over the will can we call the eternal ideas of things in God's intellect the exemplary causes of created things, only then can we assert that the natures or essences of things and the order among them are unchangeable. Only then can we assert that man's intellect can come to true necessary knowledge in the *analogia entis*. If the second alternative is true, then human reason will be unable to recognize the nature of things and their natural order. For creation is then not the natural revelation of God's nature; there is no *analogia entis,* and all our knowledge is contingent, and positivism is right. Then only by supernatural revelation do we know about God's nature and His will. The idea of a natural law becomes impossible. Occam, a positivist, exaggerated the omnipotence of God's will in relation to God's intellect in theology; he denied that human reason could penetrate to the nature of things in epistemology and so in the last resort dissolved metaphysics as the basis of moral philosophy.

We find here an antithesis recurring over and over again in history. One side maintains the superiority of the intellect over the will; consequently the ability of human reason to recognize the nature of things and to recognize a natural order which, as a moral order, must be observed by all human will, hence also by political sovereign authority. This means in the last analysis that truth makes the law and that law is reason; this again means there is a natural law. The other side contends for the superiority of will over intellect, of the irrational intuition over rational knowledge; in other words, it denies that reason can penetrate to the nature of things and their invariable order. This means relativism in ethics and agnosticism in epistemology because of the denial of metaphysics.[16] It means positivism in jurisprudence, non-morality in politics, denial of the natural rights of men, and the acceptance of absolute power of the state. It leaves no alternative but to profess that might is right. It must lead to the contention that international law originates exclusively in the will of the states, and that what is decisive is, not the rule of the law, but the changing interests of the state, so that international treaties are expedient means of diplomacy and strategy and, apart from that, are mere scraps of paper.

This antithesis is found also in the theory of constitutional law, wherein democracy stresses persuasion and discussion, wherein it is presumed that law is a rule for reason, that the governed should consent as a result of reasoning and not blindly obey an irresponsible decision of arbitrary will. Absolute governments glory in the opposite, the will of the ruler. He needs no justification because God's irresistible will is supposed to reveal itself in the absolute king, the vicegerent of God, or because there is some irrational mystical power in him which makes his will always right, however utterly unintelligible this may be to the reason of the governed. The idea of natural law and the view that truth makes the law constitute the insurmountable contradiction between totalitarianism and the Christian political theory. Let us observe that the control which, in the United States and in countries of similar constitutional structure, the Supreme Court holds over the legislative body, measures the latter's acts not only with the mere literal text of the fundamental law, the constitution, but also with basic rules and the idea of law. This points to the conviction that beyond the will of the earthly lawgiver there is an unwritten law of which the inalienable rights of man are, in a predominantly individualistic era, more strongly pronounced examples.

In the Anglo-Saxon judiciary, for a long time educated by the philosophically and theologically eminent priestly heads of the Chancery, the idea of natural law practically never died, as any history of Anglo-Saxon law and judiciary proves. Only in the nineteenth century under the impact of continental positivism, especially that of French and

[16] Very illuminating is the skeptical essay of Justice O. W. Holmes on natural law (in *Collected Legal Papers*, New York, 1920.)

German origin, do we see a recession of the idea of natural law even in Anglo-Saxon countries. But here, too, in consequence of the World War, a revival is visible, as may be indirectly shown by the assent to so many utterances of the last popes in matters concerning social justice, the international order, and against Nazism and communism —utterances that are based upon natural law and justice.

CHAPTER VI

The Idea of Order as the Philosophical Basis of Natural Law

I. Philosophical Presuppositions of the Concept of Natural Law

WE MUST now develop the metaphysical foundation of natural law. The conviction about natural law and its validity do not depend wholly on this philosophical reflection. The common man knows more or less definitely about natural law: the voice of conscience in his social relations with others. St. Paul uttered a commonplace when he spoke of the law that is inscribed in the hearts of the pagans (Rom. 2:15). And the juridically non-educated is fully aware that there is a difference between what is just and what is formally legal, between what is unjust and what is illegal. This appeal to the idea of justice, to "the law" as distinguished from the mere factual will of the lawgiver, is an irrefutable witness to the conviction of the existence of natural law. So our reflection is not designed to convince the juridical specialist given to skeptical positivism, though it often happens that, when grave issues of justice are at stake, we see the most determined positivist changed into a believer in natural law appealing to the idea of justice as superior to all statute books. It is intended to deepen and clarify that undeniable conviction of common sense concerning natural law.

The idea of natural law rests on the following presuppositions. 1. A last and profound unity of mankind, a unity of conscience in the last and least of human beings. However darkened or enlightened by primitive civilizations and progressive cultures, by deleterious habits become traditions and by lack of serious efforts to live up to the demand of critical consciousness,[1] there exists a unity and a community of human conscience, of human nature through all the epochs, in all races, in all nations. 2. The ability of the human intellect to perceive the essential and the unchangeable nature of things, in other words, the actual objective reality. The measure of our knowledge is the thing in its essence; it is not the categorical forms of the subjective mind, induced by the phenomena of the things that produce order out of the chaos of the phenomena. 3. Granted that the human mind recognizes the nature of things, this nature is for the existing thing at the same time its end and perfection. It is the degree of realized idea in an existing thing that determines the degree of its goodness. 4. Superiority of the intellect. The intellect recognizes the nature of things and presents to the will the concrete thing as a good that ought to be striven after.

The human mind recognizes the nature of things through the senses. The things are first; they are as individual, existing beings perceived by the senses, which are passive. The intellect, an active power, though objectively dependent on the things, recognizes the nature and essence, the general substantial form, of the thing. This is what the thing is (*essentia*), not only that the thing is (*existentia*). We can now compare the intellectual content of the knowledge in us with the nature and existence of the thing outside. On that rests the fact of true knowledge. It is therefore the actual essence and nature in the existing thing which is the measure and control of our knowledge. Hence our knowledge is not a mere generalization of similarities in different things, giving us mere types or symbols with the logical limit of "thus far experienced." For this would mean that we perceive only the existentials, not the essentials of things.

On the contrary, we recognize what the thing in itself is, its essential nature. To do this would be impossible if this essential nature were not invariable. Furthermore, we not only recognize the nature of the different things, but also that they are related, that there is an order, a hierarchy of things. We recognize that there is a progression from the imperfect to the more perfect, and that this progression is dependent on the intensity of being in the things. The things of the inorganic world are less perfect than those of the organic world, and in

[1] Cf. V. Cathrein, *Die Einheit des menschlichen Gewissens;* W. Schmidt, *Ursprung der Gottesidee* (1922, 6 vols.).

the organic world there is a progression of perfection from the plant to the animal and up to the crown of creation, the rational free man. The "world," the universe of things created, is order, it is cosmos, not chaos.[2]

This order established in the invariable natures of things is a rational and a constituted order, not an accidental, or a merely arbitrary order. Its creator is not a dark, mystical, irrational power, but *Logos, Nous,* Supreme Reason, Intellect. The things are imperfect exemplifications of the ideas of this supreme intellect. The nature of a thing is the divine idea of it. Therefore the things and their nature are the measure of our knowledge, because the things themselves receive their essence and nature from God's creative supreme intellect and receive their existence by God's will, either immediately or mediately by the activity of secondary causes. Therefore the things and the universe depend for their existence absolutely on God's preserving omnipotence. Yet the essential forms in the things are as ideas of the perfect supreme intellect of God independent of God's omnipotent will. When Occam, emphasizing God's omnipotence, taught that God ought to be able to will that a creature should hate God, he utterly destroyed the possibility of a natural law. It is the primacy of the intellect in God from which we conclude the invariability of the essential nature of things and their order in the universe. And it is this invariability which enables us to say that moral acts are good because they conform to nature, and not simply because a supreme will commanded them.

All being is good. The evil is not a quality of being but a lack of being which ought to be. The divine will, creating and preserving all being, could create and preserve only the good, not the evil. Therefore a creature is the better, has the more goodness, the nearer it comes to its nature in its concrete existence. It is the degree of being what it should be, that determines the degree of goodness in a thing. A house is a better house the more perfectly it serves its end. To be is to be of value.[3] But there is no mere passive, aimless being. Furthermore, for living entities, to be always means to act, to be in movement. It is the movement, to the ideal or away from it, it is the dynamic life, that is

---

[2] St. Thomas, *Contra Gentiles,* II, 39; *Quaest. disput.,* II, q.3, a.16. The Greek word *kosmos* signifies originally the "right order" in a community.

[3] St. Thomas, *Summa theol.,* Ia IIae, q.18, a.1. *In rebus autem unumquodque tantum habet de bono quantum habet de esse.*

the real object of the philosopher, not the mere passive existence. There is, therefore, no genuine philosophy without metaphysics; and ethics or philosophy of law without metaphysics is without a basis.

The nature of a thing, that by which the thing is what it is, is the forming power *(causa formalis)*, as it is the aim of rational knowledge. Its nature is the end of a thing, is its *telos*, the *causa finalis*. Every being is striving toward its perfection, and the most perfect realization of its aim. However, if there is an order of being, there is necessarily also an order of aims and of values. That is no useless abstraction, but simple common sense. In economics we call a useless detour an uneconomical use of things; we speak of waste when things are not used according to their objective purpose, that is, according to their nature and properties.

It is this coincidence of the order of natures and the order of ends that is the basis of ethics. The human mind recognizes speculatively this order as an order of being and necessarily, too, as an order of aims and ends. But as all things point to a perfect, pure being, the divine being, so the ends of creatures point to a last, supreme, infinite end, God as the aim of all creatures.

Man is a free rational being. He has reason and will. Therefore St. Thomas says the theoretical reason becomes necessarily practical reason. The speculative order of things as recognized by reason becomes to the practical reason, to the free will, an order which ought to be and ought to be realized by man's activity. The ontological order as recognized by reason as an order that ought to be becomes the moral order as a law for man's will. We call it natural law in the broadest sense because we recognize, too, that it is God's will. The ontological order is the eternal law, which becomes natural law for the free rational being. The basic rule, therefore, is: act according to your essential nature; be what you ought to be; be your nature perfectly as possible; be true because you are rational; be good because you are free; be social because to be perfect you need certain social organizations which help you to become perfect. The structure of a moral act proceeds, therefore, from the recognition by the theoretical reason of the nature, the idea, as the end of the thing, to the perception by the practical reason of this nature as a good that ought to be and is then proposed to the will to be realized by acting.

Therefore it is profound wisdom when Socrates speaks of knowledge as the way to virtue, when he contends that truth must be the basis of law.[4] Truth is adequation of the intellect with being. As truth and being are one, so are truth and justice in the last analysis one. Justice, the eternal law as St. Augustine puts it, demands that all things should be in perfect order.[5] In this sense of a unity of truth and justice we may say that the truth makes us free. The binding in and by justice is genuine liberty.

II. The Ontological Order and the Moral Order in the *Philosophia Perennis*

This idea of a universal order of being, though not essential for the common-sense concept of natural law, is fundamental for its philosophical foundation. Any system of natural law is based on the presupposition that the universe, the world, is an "order" of being; from this order of being, from the *ontological* order follows then the *moral* order. This ontological order leads to God as the Creator of being and of its order, and thus to God as the legislator of the moral order. So the basis of natural law is not "human nature" in isolation, but surrounded by the order of natures, of created things.

The idea of order is not specific to natural-law philosophies. Any philosophic effort is an effort for order. Even the relativist, to understand the outside world of phenomena, must understand or construe this mass of phenomena as an order. Thus the difference between these philosophies is not the abstract and formal idea of order; the difference concerns the origin, the nature, and the material content of order, in particular the ability of the human mind to penetrate to the natures of the objective things, to reality as the natural revelation of the Creator.

If, as Kant declared, the "thing" in itself, in its essence, is inconceivable for the human mind, then an ontological order of nature is inconceivable, too, and likewise inconceivable is a moral order as the object of practical reason and as a rule for the human will. From his epistemology stems Kant's formal and ultimately empty categorical imperative. As the order in things is inconceivable, so also is the moral

---

[4] Truth gives or denies to human laws their highest crown; and they draw from truth their genuine moral power.

[5] *De libero arbitrio*, I, 6, 15.

order as an objective rule for the will. For Kant, consequently, the world with its phenomena is not a universe, is not objectively an ontological order; it is an order that man produces by the subjective forms of his mind. For St. Thomas, on the other hand, who asserts that the natures of things are conceivable for the human mind and that the natures are invariable, an ontological order of the natures is conceivable. And this order which is created by the divine intellect is therefore neither the product of blind chance nor of men's subjective willful mind.[6] The world is thus ontologically an objective order. Since, for the will and the practical reason, being is a good, the ontological order becomes necessarily a moral order in which all beings teleologically are ordered to the supreme end, to the supreme good, to God, just as in the ontological order the beings in their various degrees of perfection point to the *ens purissimum*. Thus the degree of being is fundamental for the degree of goodness. The world is, therefore, a cosmos, an objective universe that presents itself to the will as a moral cosmos to be realized by human free acts in the greatest possible perfection of man's nature in this moral cosmos.

Only if the world is in some way objectively an order created by God's will under the direction of the divine intellect and only if man's mind can get "intelligence" *(intus legere)*, can "read" this order by the process of cognition, only then have we a reliable philosophical basis for natural law. We must stress the philosophical. In practical life common sense may be greatly blurred by vicious customs and prejudicial traditions, and conscience may be darkened by passions, material interests, and traditional *mores*. Yet both have retained a rudimentary idea of what is right and just in itself. Often both common sense and conscience have appealed in dire stress to that unwritten natural law of which they were sure, when the professional philosopher had long since undermined the philosophical basis of natural law, the idea of the world, the universum (not *multi-versum*) as an ontological order.

[6] Cf. *Contra Gentiles*, II, chaps. 24, 39, 42. The interdependence between the concepts order, truth, justice, the foundation of natural law, is mentioned by St. Thomas on many occasions. The order of the universe as it appears in natural things as well as in voluntary matters demonstrates the justice of God (*Summa theol.*, Ia, q.21, a.1). The distinction of things, the order itself in created things exists by the intention of the first agent, God (*ibid.* q.47, a.1, 3). The justice of God which constitutes the order among the things in conformity to God's wisdom, which is the law of the order, may appropriately be called truth (*ibid.*, q.21, a.2).

The parallelism of metaphysics, realistic epistemology, and natural law that we can so distinctly see in the history of philosophy, seems obvious. Thus natural law could find its perennial home in the *philosophia perennis,* that "educated sister" of common sense, as it has been aptly called. Therefore the idea of natural law in the history of modern philosophy began to fade away with the waning of metaphysics, brought about by sensualist or subjectivist epistemology. It may be objected that this conclusion does not agree with the historical facts since Kant, for instance, upheld the theory of natural law. but this he did in spite of his destruction of metaphysics and of his subjectivist epistemology. Furthermore, we must never forget that the concept and a certain consciousness of natural law were preserved against "the philosophers" by the incorporation of the principles of natural law into the body of traditions and thoughts that we call Christianity, Christian civilization, or the like. But then again the idea continued to live and to influence socio-political life in spite of the modern philosophies.

The purpose of any philosophical attempt is to come to a system, to an order by which the truly entangling amorphous mass of empirical facts is ordered. The human mind strives for cosmos. Any philosophy is systematic. Even the denial of truth is systematic skepticism. The order, then, is either objective and created by the divine intellect so that the distinction of the natures of things and their definite finality is the basis of the ontological order and consequently of a moral order to be produced by free agents; or the order, though objective, is the result of blind causes. If the latter is true, the ontological order cannot become the basis for a moral order, unchangeable and divinely instituted, and the corresponding ethics must necessarily be hedonist making the amount of pleasure or pain the ultimate criteria of what is morally good or bad. A third possibility remains. According to this the human reason, in autonomous autocracy, subjectively "creates" the order out of the chaos of phenomena since objective order is inaccessible to the human reason. As long as such a theory exists under the shadow of positive Christian religion, the necessary chaotic consequences may be avoided. The faith for which Kant would make place by restricting knowledge can of course balance the faulty consequence of such a philosophy. But in the measure in which the power of the positive Christian religion gives way under the impact of such a theory in favor of mere secularism, the consequences of such a philosophy become rampant with chaos, moral and philosophical. The most sensitive minds of the nineteenth century felt this distinctly as, to name only a few, Thomas Carlyle, Cardinal Newman, and E. Rénan did. Rénan, the typical skeptic product and representative of the chaotic philosophy of the nineteenth century, perceived that religion alone would be able to counterbalance that philosophy. But he grew pessimistic on account of the waning of religion. "After we are gone, on what will people live?" he asked; surely not on the philosophy of chaos of which Nietzsche's deranged mind is as good a product as is pragmatism and the passivist philosophy of uncritical adjustment.

As has been already pointed out, whenever in medieval philosophy the validity of the universal concept was denied, as was done by Occam, then the disappearance of the ontological order led to the denial of the natural law. This was not always so much in words as in matter. Consequently for Occam the natural law is the will of God revealed in the Scriptures. Thus the idea of the moral order as the sequence of the ontological order disappears. Luther and most of the Reformers, till their disciples rediscovered the concept of natural law, likewise conceived as the only rule of morality and law the will of God revealed in the Scriptures. The reason for this moral "supernaturalism" was their want of confidence in the human intellect, in its ability to find the order of being in the world, its finality, and the natures of things as the final causes of the order of ends culminating in the divine Being.

Yet, as long as we preserve faith in this divine will supernaturally revealed in the Scriptures as the norm for moral life, the order idea is still vivid though it may be already paralyzed. But take away the revealed will of God, as deism and rationalism did, then truly there remains nothing but chaos. If we discharge metaphysics and objective epistemology, as Hume did to the great grief of Kant, the continuous longing for order produces the idea that man, by his sovereign will, has to create order out of chaos arbitrarily because no standards of judgment are given. Or again, there are in "nature"—and "nature" becomes now the physical and biological "nature" of the natural sciences—rather mystical forces of a mechanistic kind that as efficient causes blindly produce order to which man, himself a part of that mechanistic world, has to subject himself. The *causae finales* disap-

)ear from the philosophical discussion in favor of blind *causae ef-*
cientes.

III. Separation of the Ontological and the Moral Order in Modern Philosophy

For modern philosophy the world is not an objective divinely instituted order; hence it is not accessible to the human mind, it cannot
be the measure of the intellect, and it cannot be for free acts the moral
order of final causes. For modern philosophy the world is principally
a chaos of phenomena, but *sine fundamento in re.* The *Summus
Artifex* of St. Augustine—the idea of God revealing His essence by
the *analogia entis* of the created universe and thus establishing the
moral order of natural law in the natures of things as *causae finales* in
the total order of finality of the world to God—disappears in modern
philosophy since Locke, Hume, and Kant. Man now becomes the
measure of all things and of all acts, but it is man not in the Thomistic
sense, human nature as *causa finalis* and *exemplaris,* but man as an
empirical entity in its factuality. With this thinking, the idea of order,
metaphysically and morally objective, disappears in favor of perpetually changing subjectivist order ideas. The human mind is now
a sovereign versus the world, and especially versus the social and
moral world. For Kant it is the thinking subject that produces its
world in autonomy as the object of possible experience in space and
time. Moreover, man is subjectively even the creator of God; the idea
of God is merely a product of our reason.

Thus the human mind, in its historical contingency, produces, and
even finally creates, not only its objects but also its moral rules. Man
is above all laws, not under that old natural law. The world becomes
for Schopenhauer, and likewise for Auguste Comte, a product of a
more or less mystical will, as for Nietzsche the moral laws are products of human longings, enigmatic, irrational, and sovereign. It is not
moral obligation that determines the will, but the arbitrary will determines obligation. Man, free and autonomous, creates for himself a
subjective order of ends. The objective ideas of the older philosophy
(God, immortality, human freedom), if they are accepted at all, become hypothetical ideas of a regulative character for the practical
reason. But that shows only their unreality, their impotence to bind

the human will. For it is this will, unlimited in its acts, unrestricted as to its objects, that produces in arbitrary sovereignty any order at all, with the one restriction that the maxims of the one must be able to become the maxims of general legislation. The will of the autonomous individual is absolutely free.

What these idealistic philosophies do is to deify human reason. It is human reason that measures the world. The idea of God as the Creator of the recognizable ontological order in the world is transferred to the sphere of practical reason as a necessary postulate and so is the moral order. They are necessary conditions, realities which are to be believed. The moral law and the natural law, based on the autonomy of man's practical reason, must be conceived as if it were divinely instituted and sanctioned. Thus the original creative power of God is confused with the creative autonomy of the human mind and is replaced by that autonomy. Thus no recognized objective order of being controls human reason, is the measure of its acts. Thus the link, the connection between *ens, bonum,* and *verum* is torn asunder. The moral autonomy of the pure ego is established, as it is subject only to its own law.

Consequently man may produce any order. There is no intrinsic reason why the state should not destroy the family. There is no intrinsic reason why the autonomous individual should accept the state, why economic freedom should be established. There is a good reason for the fact that the followers of Kant gave up the concept of natural law as soon as the pietistic aura which surrounded Kant faded, and also for the fact that they became positivists in legal philosophy and empiricists in political philosophy. The austere heroic formalism of the categorical imperative proved itself empty and impotent to give a material rule for human acts. And why? Because the link between being, intellect, obligation, and will had been broken.

In Anglo-Saxon civilization the sensualist and the utilitarian philosophy and the biological philosophy of men like Spencer served the same purpose of disrupting the link between the divinely created natures of things and their order of finality, between being and the moral order as moral obligation. Here the foundation of morality (of good and bad) is not the objective order; but the quantitative amount of pleasure and happiness, plainly in a sensual sense, or of pain, becomes the measure of good and bad. The whole object of human life becomes the augmentation of utility and sensual happiness; of course it is left by necessity to the individual to determine the objects of pleasure and happiness. When thus the subjective increase of a rather abstract and ultimately meaningless "pleasure" becomes the measure of good and bad, then we must not wonder if all institutions, even the most necessary ones, are judged by the amount of pleasure they offer, the amount of sacrifice of pleasure they demand. From this utilitarian philosophy one can defend totalitarianism if he but shows that it is more efficient in the production of material goods and sensual happiness. The measure of all human values is their ability to increase the material living standard. Very easily economic success becomes a derived rule of ethics. Economic success covers the wickedness of the successful, as Luther's grace covered the sinfulness of man. Such utilitarianism crushes the spiritual and sensual human happiness of families in the slums, disregards the dignity of the human person, preaches the prevalence of material property rights over personal rights. Thus it produces an order in which sensual values are highest, and spiritual values are judged according to their ability to increase sensual values, or better still, with a pharisaic self-righteousness, to console man, disturbed by the voice of his conscience. Religion becomes social respectability or a safeguard for the protection of his property rights or even a kind of week-end psychotherapy for the painful remorse aroused by the unjust mammon. Still, what is at the bottom of all this is the lack of an objective order idea as the true measure of values and of their hierarchy.

Things may go on with such a philosophy prevailing in universities and among the ruling classes as long as the Christian tradition is still a potent influence. Yet the more that tradition vanishes, the sooner utilitarian philosophy becomes crass materialism for the broad industrial masses, when they have slipped away from religion in which the moral order is preserved and hallowed as the revealed divine word in the Scriptures. The more the lack of an idea of an objective order becomes conscious to man in a chaotic world, the riper that world will be for any pseudo-religion like communism or Nazism or some other ism. All of them have in common the denial of natural law, of an objective order. For them, too, the world is the dead material object of a titanic, unrestricted will of an elite or of a leader. The aging Spencer felt the insufficiency of utilitarian ethics. "What must we think of this wealth-seeking age of ours? Shall we consider the total absorption of time and energy in business—the spending of life in the accumulation of means to live—as constituting greatest happiness and act accordingly?" he asks skeptically and continues pessimistically: "The real heaven sought dips far down below the horizon and has as yet been seen by none. Faith not might must be our guide. We cannot do without a compass" (*Social Statistics*, 1902, p. 10).

The biological philosophies with their ethical systems, the consequence of Charles Darwin's *Origin of Species*, also lack the idea of an order in the sense of the *philosophia perennis*. Of course they do not say that the order has to be arbitrarily created; they are satisfied that they have found an order. But what an order! The blind biological forces work without an objective norm in a senseless struggle for existence, the result of the survival of the fittest. Fittest in what sense? Obviously not in the sense of the Christian idea or in the sense of the virtuous citizen of Aristotle or of the intellectual and moral perfection of the idea of man as humanism conceived it. Such an order would, therefore, be anything but a human order. And the ethics following upon such a concept of order is one of utility and noxiousness in reference to the struggle of existence or the survival of the fittest. Any political philosophy built upon such a basis must lead to mere positivism for which the state is an instrument of that struggle, an indifferent means. For such a philosophy sociology becomes the queen of sciences. No objective standards for our moral life and for our laws are possible when once the traditional Christian rules that preserve the essence of natural law are consumed.

The last and most anemic theory of an order arbitrarily produced by man we find in the neo-Kantian juridical theory of Kelsen. To understand the world, i.e., the contents of consciousness, we assume it to be an order of meaning. We think, that is, we construct the amorphous mass of impressions as a unity and as an order but *sine fundamento in re*. That order is then an ideology rather sovereignly produced by man, and it enables us to systematize the impressions, the contents of our consciousness, according to principles that we simply and arbitrarily posit. The "world" is not an order. By means of the subjective categories of his reason man produces a necessary but intrinsically arbitrary scientific hypothesis, which creates an order, because man has that inexplicable inclination for systematization of the host of his impressions. There is no doubt that positivism in legal philosophy is here the necessary consequence. Natural law is either merely one of a dozen of potential ideologies, each of them relative, or it is simply an unscientific dream.

We must give up that titanic idea of man so rampant in modern civilization. The immense energy of the aggressive intellect, the wild living intellect must be rescued from its own suicidal excesses (Newman, *Apologia,* p. 221). We awaken to this fact rather late now that we see to what this idea has led in its pure isolation in modern totalitarianism. We must give up the idea that the world is chaos to be ordered by man following subjective arbitrary standards or that it is an irrational, unintelligible order mechanically produced by the struggle for existence or the survival of the fittest. We must restore the sequence—objective being, intellect, moral law, will. Otherwise we cannot come to a genuine natural law as the basis for political philosophy that is more than a collection of trite indifferent facts that are by themselves only the raw material for science, but not a real science, even if classified according to some arbitrary standard.

IV. The Idea of Order in the Universe and Natural Law

Let us repeat: The universe is order, cosmos not chaos. It is the eternal law, the divine reason, that has instituted this order. Since free rational beings can intellectually grasp this eternal law and through it the will of the divine legislator, for them this order becomes the natural law. In the light of reason man recognizes the order as one that ought to be realized by himself. Therefore St. Thomas speaks of a participation of all creatures in the divine law. But this is a participation according to their nature. Hence the non-intellectual creatures follow their nature blindly without moral responsibility. Intellectual free beings ought to realize their free, rational, and social nature, in freedom. In the last resort, accordingly, there is a coincidence of the laws of biological life and the natural law. Natural ethics or the natural law and the human law are not a mere reflex of the biological or racial, irrational and blind law. Ethical propositions are not mere tokens of acts that are useful or detrimental to the biological existence of that animal called man. Ethics is not an unreal superstructure over the animal life of man which naturalism has made the natural life of man as opposed to intellectual life. Man is *homo sapiens* and, as St. Thomas in the first chapter of the *Contra Gentiles* says, it is the office of the wise man to institute order. From this it follows that politics are subordinated to ethics; that a real irreconcilable conflict between *ethos* and *bios* is impossible; and that, in the long run, a moral policy is true and more useful than non-moral policy. From this point of view alone can we refute the modern biological or racial "inhuman" basis of polity as it is expressed by H. St. Chamberlain, Gobineau and, in a crude and unintellectual way, by the Nazi *Weltanschauung*.

The natural law is the supreme standard for all human acts. Every human authority is subject to it. No human authority can demand obedience against it. All human authority remains such only so far as its commands do not contradict natural law. Both the subject and authority are subordinated to natural law. This is the moral guaranty of liberty. An absolute authority whose will and act would be right simply because it actually wills this or that would destroy liberty. The dignity of the human person demands the subordination of authority to natural law, because this itself is the basis of human dignity. An authority freed from natural law and following only political expediency is no authority at all. Therefore the commands of authority must justify themselves before human reason, for it is the reason in the law and of the law that makes it just and legitimate. Never can mere actual will give these qualities to law. This is common conviction. What is the basis of the bill of rights, of the distinction between constitution and legislation? Nothing but the fact that legislation derives its authority from a paramount law, neither from the will to obey nor from the mere fact of obedience. When Lord Hale said that the English Parliament could do all, that it could make the wife of A the wife of B, but that it could not declare adultery to be lawful, he meant precisely the above. Every human law must rest on a moral basis.

St. Justin was right when he said that Heraclitus could be called a Christian, because he held that all human law must be derived from the divine law. Experience and history show us that the freedom and dignity of the human being cannot be preserved when the conviction vanishes that both the subject and the human authority, whether the state or any other human authority, are subjected to the same paramount law. But again this paramount law is an empty phrase if it is not synonymous with that which for millenia common sense and the *philosophia perennis* have called natural law. And in natural law any possible conflict between power and authority, will and reason, truth and expediency, is abolished because natural law originates from God, who is at once perfect reason and omnipotent will. An indirect evidence of this is the fact that tyrannical dictators either put themselves in God's place or, denying a personal God, speak of their power as emanating from the authority of the racial community or of the proletariat or of other such mystical superhuman entities. If a person does not consciously or unconsciously accept natural law, how can he define abuse of authority, tyranny, crime in international policy? [7]

[7] An interesting illustration is presented by the situation of the courts and the judges in Nazi Germany as compared with the judges and courts of the common-law countries. Here the judges were led by the ideas of natural law. There, in consequence of legal positivism as cherished by German universities since about 1870, the judge considered law to be what the state commands, because the judge feels he is a mere official of the state, unable to resist unjust tyrannical law since, on account of the prevailing positivism, he lacked any distinction between just and unjust law.

CHAPTER VII

The Contents of Natural Law

I. THE THREE FORMS OF JUSTICE

ST. AUGUSTINE remarks that without justice states are nothing but organized robber bands.[1] This may lead us to a further discussion of the problem of natural law, of justice, and of the state. This will lead us again to an appreciation of the contents of natural justice and to the problem of natural law and human positive law.

Justice has to deal with the coordination and subordination of men in relation to one another and with the relation of the individual person to social bodies, to the different forms of social integration. Three basic relations are possible. There is the relation of one person to another person, of persons simply as such and on the basis of equality in participation in human nature. The second relation is that of the individual person as a member of a natural or of a voluntary social unit, e.g., the family, the state, a labor union, to the person or persons vested with the directive authority of this social unit. The third relation is that of the person or persons vested with authority to the members constituting the social unit and subjected, therefore, to the directive and coercive power of this authority.

This network of relations as a social fact would be impossible among free, rational beings without a moral and juridical rule. Each human society is not an amorphous aggregation, a mere mass, but a *unitas ordinis;* it has a constitution, a framework of rules by which the *ordo* and the *unitas* of the wills of the individuals are produced and their functions are integrated to an organic whole. Four or five persons at different distances walking independently over a road do not form a society. But they may form a society at once if they have the same purpose and follow the authority of one among them in the search for a lost child. It is the unity of purpose and the coincident resulting order

[1] *De civ. Dei,* IV, 5.

in the functions of these persons, with one leading and the others obeying, which constitute a society. And those individuals are a society, though it may be a very shortlived and weak one, because as rational beings they acknowledge a set of rules of coordination and subordination, led by the objective necessities of their common purpose and consequently the finality of their acting together and of each act serving this purpose.

Justice deals with these rules of coordination and subordination. These rules are made not just because a person designated by convenience, personal excellence, tradition, or agreement as "authority" declares that they should be obeyed, but because they are reasonable and useful for the purpose of the society and of men so far as they are members of the society.

Therefore we have three forms of justice.[2] Commutative justice considers persons as equals before the law and regulates their relations, their exchanges, and services from the standpoint of equality of the exchanged goods or of the remunerations for services. This is the field of justice concerning prices or exchanges. This justice presupposes at least an equality of the persons as owners or exchangers. It presupposes that they are free and self-determining beings. Thus the Roman law, logically correct, held that the slave acquired for his master, because the slave was legally no person but a thing, an exchangeable good. The relationship of members of a group organized for a specific purpose to the persons in authority is ruled by legal justice. Here it is the moral and reasonable purpose, which in the last analysis and objectively rules the relationship and makes the commands or laws of authority just and requires just obedience from the members as long as they are members. Of course it is supposed that the end itself is not unjust and that the acts for the realization of the purpose are not intrinsically unjust. Inversely the moral and reasonable purpose together with the fact that the members of the society are persons is what subjects the will and the commands of authority, in its dealings with the members, to a specific kind of justice, to distributive justice.

All these factors, the purpose, the rules, the relations, must be just. It is not uncommon to hear members of a band of gangsters speak, though quite improperly, of justice when they distribute their booty,

---

[2] Aristotle introduced these distinctions; since then they have been familiar in the *philosophia perennis.* Cf. St. Thomas, *Summa theol.,* IIa IIae, q.58, 60, 61.

even though the purpose of their band is utterly unjust. And again it is commonly agreed that a just purpose does not justify immoral commands and rules, because an immoral command or rule would destroy justice in the relationship of members among themselves or the just cause for the existence of the society itself. We all agree habitually, though perhaps not always actually, about these forms of justice. We may demand a just living wage, but we would not, even as communists, object to a judge of the supreme court getting a higher salary than a charwoman on account of his more important social function. We all agree that in taxation the principle of ability to pay should be applied. The controversy over the progressive income tax does not refer to the principle of progression so much as it does to the degree of progression and to the social expediency of this degree.

This discussion shows that never does mere will make a rule, a command, or an order just. It is rather the conformity of these with human nature, with the purpose and personal dignity of the members of society, which does so. The rationality and the freedom of man's will are the basic a priori ideas. The non-personal beings, subordinated to man, are under his dominion for his use. To attain his end, to come to the perfection of his essential social nature, man realizes this nature in family, state, and human race, in religion, in culture, civilization, economics, arts, and sciences. This fact is the starting point for the discussion of justice. It is the divinely instituted nature of the forms of social existence as the ideal goal of human activity that makes commands and rules, authority and obedience, just. They are just if they conform to that nature, and unjust if they contradict it.

II. Natural Rights of the Person and of the State

From this standpoint the old saying that justice means, "to each one what is his," *suum cuique*, is right. This *suum* is what is generally or individually related to any specific person or to any organized group of persons. Man as a person has natural dominion over non-rational beings; they may serve his needs. But that one man may serve another man in the same way as an animal does, it is logically necessary to deprive this man of his personality, to say he is not a man but a thing. The *suum* is, therefore, not a mere truism; it has a metaphysical content. Of course we must distinguish between a perennial philosophical content and the ever-changing factual contents as they are concretely determined by the legal systems of different peoples at different times. Yet there is a perennial *suum* and *justum*.

The first and proximate principle of knowledge for this *suum* is the rational, social, free nature of man. The *justum* is that conformity to human social nature of social acts and relations between persons and between persons and things. We always make the following syllogism either positively or negatively. What is just and what is *suum* ought to be, because it follows from human nature, is conformed with it. This fact, this law, this act is in contradiction to the idea of human nature, therefore it is unjust. The difficulties are not so much in this syllogism as in the implications of the more concrete notions: this fact, this law, this act, the idea of human nature.

Each human being is a rational free entity, that is, as a person, the holder of rights. An animal has no rights.[3] The individual person is the presupposition of justice and right. To be a person means to exist for oneself, to be free, to have an intangible sphere of one's own initiative and self-direction externally in time and space, safe from obtrusion by any other agent, person, or society. But from this metaphysical truth there arise immediately certain personal rights. These are not given by the state; they are pre-existent to the state. Therefore they are called natural rights. Neither the state nor the constitution invent or create them. The state regulates their use; the constitution declares and guarantees them. A tyrannical government may refuse to recognize them, but they claim their power and validity against oppression.

There is, therefore, a right born with us, the right to life and liberty. There exists an inviolable sphere of intimate personal life for each individual, a sphere that is sacred according to natural law. And this is typically a juridical sphere. The commonly accepted rule of *vim vi repellere* rests on the existence of this sphere. This is the first *suum* for each man inasmuch as he is a person. It is also the basis of personal honor, or good reputation. What is this but a kind of radiation of our personality into the juridical and moral world?[4] This honor is rooted

---

[3] Cruelty to animals is not punished like assault and battery because a right of somebody else has been violated. An animal has no rights. Punishment is meted out for this kind of cruelty on account of its effect on man, as a violation of moral standards of a community of men, beings that participate as rational animals in the nature of animals.

[4] This gives us a good illustration of the essence of the order of justice as compared with the order of charity. The order of justice is cold, sober, separative; it separates

in personal being; only persons and associations of persons have honor. It is essential for our membership in the community, because the dishonored is the outlawed in all legal systems. This honor is, therefore, pre-existent to a positive legal order. The latter does not give honor but guarantees it, and institutes working rules and instruments for its protection and for reparation of violations against it.

Similarly this *suum* of the personal sphere is realized in the right of personal liberty. This liberty is acknowledged, at least in its essentials, by all legal systems, especially since the personal sphere has been hallowed by the Christian idea of the priceless value of the immortal soul. The positive legal order, as we are taught by history, may regulate the use of this liberty, may narrow or enlarge the issuing specific rights of liberty, e.g., the concrete liberties. But to annihilate this liberty completely, to deny the personality of man by making him a mere instrument, is rightly called tyranny. It is against the natural law and it is in open contradiction to the essence of personality that one person should become a mere tool of another, for then that person would existentially be destroyed and would become a non-personal creature. Here again, the positive legal order presupposes this personal liberty; it may guarantee it, but it does not create it. When the legal genius deprived the slave of his legal personality, making him a thing, it indirectly acknowledged the principle of natural law, the freedom of the *person* as a presupposition of the legal order, not as its creation.

Liberty is closely connected with property; this is true philosophically, not only in our bills of rights. It is common theory that the idea of property follows immediately from the idea of person. It is philosophically a necessary consequence of it. The right to property is simply an enlargement of the person, and the right of liberty is realized in the right of property. Therefore the institution of property, the *suum* as related to things, is presupposed by the legal order. The bills of rights do not create it, even as they are not competent to destroy it. The institution of property is like a dowry of the personality.

---

personalities and then organizes them into a community with retention of their existence for themselves. In the order of charity the persons strive for union, for self-sacrifice. The *suum* in justice is devoted to the other person. Therefore in Christian philosophy the order of justice is accomplished by the order of charity; where the latter is lacking, *summum jus* becomes *summa injuria*. It was the clear distinction between these two orders which made Christian philosophy teach that the heroic sacrifice of life for one's country is a duty not so much out of justice as out of *pietas*.

Today this truth is easily proved. Where the institution of property is completely abolished, as in Soviet Russia, man has ceased to be a person and has become a mere tool of the superstate, a mere cog in a nonpersonal machine. Rightly, therefore, Leo XIII (*Rerum novarum*) speaks of a slavish yoke that has been imposed on the *propertyless* modern proletarian.[5]

It is morally impossible to exist as a free person without property. The sphere of freedom increases directly with the sphere of property, or contrariwise, as Linsenmann [6] so ably put it, the man who has no property easily becomes himself the property of another man. It is, therefore, a conclusion from the principle of natural law that the institution of property ought to exist. The positive legal order guarantees the pre-existent right to property; it may regulate the use of property; it may constitute certain things to be public property, and so on. The capitalist and the feudalist property orders are but transitory; the institution of property is perennial. We may thus see that there exists a perennial kernel in the concept of *suum* which precedes its concrete determination in positive law.

These rights followed from the idea of the individual person which every man is. The old saying, *Unus Christianus nullus Christianus,* reminds us that necessarily there is a plurality of persons and that to live in society in some manner or other belongs to the nature of man. There are essential acts of the person which intentionally presuppose other persons. To love, to speak, to own things, can be understood only when other persons exist. The "I" demands the "thou." The "we" is as essential for human existence as the "I." The individual person and community are ordinated one to the other. Social life is equally as original as individual life; it is not merely accessory. Only

---

[5] Private property as an institution is meant here as being according to the natural law. A state whose constitution prohibits private property in all forms would thus violate the right of man to property based on natural law. However, individuals and groups have a right to renounce property, according to the evangelical counsel, as the natural right to marriage is not weakened by the vow of chastity on the part of the clergy or members of religious orders. Even in the case of the vow of poverty the group at least owns property, and the Church has rejected any radicalism in this question as will appear from any study of the great controversy about poverty in the fourteenth century (cf. Denzinger, *Ench.*, nos. 494, 577). The *Code of Canon Law* (can. 1495, 1499) states that the Catholic Church has a *nativum jus* to acquire property in all just ways according to natural and positive law. The actual distribution of property in any given society is, of course, made by positive law; yet the institution of private property exists by natural law.

[6] In his famous *Lehrbuch de Moraltheologie* (Freiburg, 1878), p. 666.

through life with other persons and with God, with the Trinity of divine persons, does the human person live. The union of men with God is the union of men among themselves. Among the various communities through which man accomplishes his end, the perfection of his nature, there are at least three that follow necessarily from the nature of man. They are the family with its basis in marriage, the state, and the human race. Essentially they cannot be absorbed by one another, for they are perennial societies each with its independent end. Each of these necessary communities has its own *suum* by natural law and not because one of them, the state, creates it.

The essence of the family, for instance, is presupposed by the laws of the state. The family and the essential network of rights and duties constituting it are older than the state.[7] Its natural, essential functions cannot be absorbed by the state, and the parents have a natural right concerning the education of the children. The state can regulate and can order the use of the rights, but it does not create them. If we allow the state to abolish these rights as institutions, how can we distinguish a state, an order of justice, from tyranny, the disorder of arbitrary violence? The civil power enforcing a positive law and interfering in the parental rights on account of some abuse of these rights by an individual father, does so only because it acknowledges such a natural parental right antecedent to the state. St. Thomas says that even the Church has no right to interfere with these parental rights.[8]

If the will of the state were the creator of these rights, how could we protest against their suppression, when the state thought such a procedure expedient to its interests? Our refutation of totalitarianism, and our opposition to Nazism or to Bolshevism rest logically upon the acknowledgment of such natural rights, independent of the state.

The citizens owe respect and reasonable obedience to the state. Political life is a third necessary sphere of man's social life. It is, there-

[7] Cf. Aristotle, *Nic. Eth.* (Berlin ed.), col. 1162; St. Thomas, *Summa theol.*, IIa IIae, q. 50, a.3.

[8] *Summa theol.*, IIa IIae, q.10, a.12. St. Thomas protests against the contention that the Church has the right to baptize the children of Jewish parents against the will of the parents. He says that to do so is against natural law, because the child as such is under the care of the father. Cf. further, the letter *Postremo mense* of Benedict XIV, the great canonist, to the Governor of the City of Rome concerning this matter. Here the Thomistic theory is strongly upheld against the theory of Duns Scotus (in IV *Sent.*, dist IV, q. 9, n. 2), who contended that the baptism of Jewish children could be ordered by a Christian ruler even against the will of the Jewish parents. See Denzinger, *Enchiridion* (21–23 ed., 1937), nos. 1480–90.

fore, natural law that induces man to live in states, and this perfection of the idea of man in political life to achieve the common good, a higher form of social life, is the basis of political authority. Loyalty, allegiance, and obedience are duties of the citizens, and they represent rights of the state, a *suum* of the state. The positive law with regard to these rights and duties does not create them, but only determines their forms, their execution, the concrete circumstances under which they arise and are to be realized. But this allegiance presupposes justice on the part of the state, justice arising from reverence for the natural rights of the citizens. When we speak about abuse of authority, we can do so only because we have an objective measure for use and abuse. If there were only the positive law, the will of the state, we could not logically speak of an abuse of authority by the state, for the tyrannical government could not be distinguishable from the just government.

We hear much today about the right of small nations to independence. This right is not a creation of international law, but rather its basis. Therefore the Constitution of the League of Nations contains the declaratory rule expressed in Article 10, i.e., that the political independence of the member states is guaranteed.[9] Any treatise on international law as the rule of the community of nations cannot omit statements about rights and duties of the members of the community of nations. These rights are not created by the agreements of the members nor do they exist because they are acknowledged by the members. They are the logical and metaphysical presupposition of the existence of the community itself. Agreement about these rights has a merely declaratory character, but does not constitute these rights. Conventions and treaties concern only the use of those rights, but not their essence and validity. It is an indirect proof of this thesis that the founders of the theory of international law elaborate the doctrine of the state as a person, as a subject of original rights and duties which are a supposition of the cooperative yet individually independent existence of the state.[10]

These natural rights are the basis of any legal order; the legal order is not like a divine creator, the author of these rights. Pope Pius XII insisted on these rights, noting expressly liberty, integrity, and se-

[9] According to this Article 10, the members bind themselves to respect the territorial integrity and political independence of the member states.

[10] Cf. Rommen, *Staatslehre des Franz Suarez*, p. 285.

curity, in his Christmas Eve allocution of 1941. The *Osservatore Romano* (January 4, 1942), in a report of this allocution, said: "States have natural primordial and fundamental rights which arise from the very fact of society; liberty, integrity, and security belong to the category of rights which are immutable and inalienable." Thus the *suum* of the state as a member of the community of nations is clearly discernible and generally accepted even by those who deny the natural law or think it is a worthless romantic dream. The principle of natural law as it is expressed in the phrase, *suum cuique,* is therefore not at all an empty formalism to be filled with every potential content by positive law or by the arbitrary will of the state. On the contrary, the *suum* has a metaphysical, substantial content, the nature of man which comes to perfection through living in various necessary forms of social life. Of course our contention is dependent on the idea of an ontological order which, for the free will of rational man, is the moral order; the metaphysical nature becomes the end of the being. Therefore we need not emphasize that the idea of natural law flourishes when metaphysics, the queen of sciences, rules and that it fades when the human mind, despairing of its power to attain truth, restricts itself to a vain, hopeless hunt for mere "facts" in positivism and empiricism.

III. Correspondence of Rights and Duties

We have discussed chiefly the natural rights of the person either in its abstractness as person simply or in its natural functional status of parenthood, citizenship, authority, and we have dealt with natural rights of moral persons such as the state. This emphasis on the rights must not be interpreted in the modern excessively individualist sense. As the person is a self-sufficient autonomous being, but directed to communal life, so, too, these natural rights cannot be understood as isolated and wholly independent. They are by far more coincident with the order among the socially connected persons. No right has a meaning if it is not a right positively to act with other persons, or negatively to be free from interference by other persons. Consequently the rights receive their intended meaning from the social order in which the persons live and they are necessarily counterbalanced by duties. Any order among persons thus involves rights and duties, emanating from the social nature of the persons and the necessary teleology of their coexistence. But this implies the objective order in which their separated individual existences become necessarily social coexistence. Thus to any right in the order belongs a duty to the order. To any right as opposed to another person belongs the duty of the other person to regard the right of the former.

The fruition of the rights in an order is coincident with the loyalty and obedience to the order. Thus the rights have not abstract and independent meaning but a complementary and interdependent meaning in reference to duties; and both rights and duties in reference to the order in which the persons live. This is so because, in the ultimate analysis, the end of the persons and the end of the order coincide.

To give an example: The right to freedom from state intervention is conditioned by such a use of that right in the social sphere as not to violate the freedom of others and the end of the state, the common good. The right to vote is today dependent on the duty, a moral not enforced duty, yet a duty, to serve the common good loyally and actively as a conscientious citizen. This is merely another formulation of the famous saying, that eternal vigilance is the price of freedom. And further: The fight for my natural right and its defense must be a fight for and a defense of the rights of all other persons in the order. At the same time it is intrinsically a fight for and a defense of the order and its end, the common good. Consequently such a fight may well become a duty to the common good, because my right is not an isolated matter subject to my arbitrary whims, but is itself part of the order. Thus, for example, the right to life is not my absolute property but involves my duty to God who gave that life and to the order, the state, the family to which I have a duty. Therefore suicide is a sin against God and a violation of my duty to the order.

IV. Right and Might

There is a deep reason why the Catholic philosophy of the state so strongly emphasizes the idea of natural law. It holds that this is the only solution for the unavoidable and critical problem of the relation of right and might. From a superficial standpoint, positive law evidently comes into being by the will of the state, whether represented by a monarch or by a parliament or by the citizens themselves in a

plebiscite. If we have no objective standards of right and justice independent of the will of the human lawmaker, then the actual will of
the legislator, on account of his might, would always be right. The
essence of law would then be not justice but compulsion, that is, the
ability of the lawmakers to enforce the law by whatever means, to compel the citizens to external conformity. This would then be the exclusive note of the law. The internal, the morally free, obedience to the
law for conscience' sake would be wholly irrelevant. Yet our own experience tells us that it is this moral obligation to obedience which
makes us obey, and not the compulsory apparatus of enforcement, however important the latter may be against a small minority of selfish
individuals. But nothing is more evident than that, under all circumstances, we demand that might must be subject to right, that right must
be the superior rule. We demand also that the state shall live by the
rule. To observe the law: that is to rule.[11]

If the mere arbitrary will of the state could create the justice of the
law, there would be only one rule, national self-interest or political
expediency. But it is the common conviction of all civilized nations
that both the authority and the subject who must obey are subject to
a higher law. The existence of this higher law gives to authority the
right to demand obedience, and to the subject the right to protection
against arbitrary abuse of authority. Both the dignity of the person as
a subject of authority and the legitimacy of the authority are preserved
by the common acknowledgment of the higher rule. That is what
Heraclitus meant by saying that all laws live on the supreme divine
law. That is the reason why logical thinking leads to God as the supreme Lawgiver, the highest authority, because in Him reason and
might, justice and power, are one and perfect. That is why the pattern
of the social contract always returns in political philosophy, because
through it the state's authority and the citizens are both active elements of the new order of justice and are both subject to it. Might can
legitimately act only in the framework of the order of justice, of which
the positive law is merely a declaration or a determination. The historical process of democratization can be characterized briefly as the

---

[11] Erich Kaufmann in his *Règles générales du droit de la paix* (1936), p. 266, agrees
fully with this view. He says that this theory was discarded under the sway of positivism
as belonging to fictitious natural law, but it is now revived by such eminent bodies as the
American Institute of International Law, the Union juridique internationale, and the
Institut de droit international.

growth of the rights of the subjects and the control of might and its inclination to arbitrary expediency by a superior rule of law and reason.
On the contrary, all lawless might is compelled to appeal to non-moral
justifications, such as the interest of the proletariat, or the "right" of
the biologically stronger (physically or racially). As these justifications are beyond the ideas of justice, no wonder that their champions
cannot acknowledge the equal "rights" of others to independence,
and cannot consider themselves bound by their pledged word, since
laws are only means in a lawless struggle for unlimited might.

V. Ethics and Politics

Another reason why the Catholic philosophy of the state emphasizes
the principle of natural law is the relation of ethics and politics. In
this connection we may point to a new theory about the essence of
politics, promoted by Carl Schmitt,[12] a theorist of the Nazi philosophy
of law. He holds that, as in other human realms, likewise for politics
there must be an antithesis which in its assertion and negation gives us
the basis for the concept of polity. As now, for instance, in art we have
the antithesis beautiful—ugly, in economics productive—useless, in
epistomology true—untrue, in jurisprudence just—unjust, so, he says,
we must look for a similar categorical antithesis in order to discover
the essence and nature of polity. He thinks he has found it in the formula: friend—enemy. Hence the nature of politics would be for a
state to distinguish between its friends and its enemies.[13] It should be
remarked that Schmitt is strongly influenced by modern antiliberal
thinkers like Sorel, Cortes, and Maurras, and by writers such as Hobbes
and Machiavelli. Words of refutation are unnecessary. This theory
itself has found its expression in the actual negation of peace and international law, and in the reintroduction of the law of the jungle
into international life, a kind of natural status where states live in
perennial war.

The essence of politics seems rather to be found in the opposing
concepts, order—disorder. Every body politic strives to organize for

---

[12] *Der Begriff des Politischen,* first published in *Archiv für Social-wissenschaften und
Socialpolitik,* 1927. Later, with some remarkable changes, it was published separately
(1932, 1933). Cf. the able criticism by Hugo Fiala, "Politischer Dezisionismus" in *Revue
internationale de la théorie du droit* (1935), pp. 101 ff.

[13] Schmitt, *op. cit.* (1933), p. 7 and *passim.*

order and to avert the danger of disorder, to preserve the established order against disturbers, and to reform or adapt it when the underlying powers of social life, the changes in the economic, moral, and cultural forces and classes, demand a reform. Otherwise the minimum of order and unity, necessary for the bare existence of the classes themselves, would disappear. It is the *unitas ordinis,* more strictly, the unity of a sovereign order of any one people in a distinct part of the world, which constitutes the individual state. Men are organized by this order, which is the order of law, the order of political action, the order of the spiritual, socio-economic, and cultural life of this people. This sovereign order implies that there is authority and obedience, leadership and allegiance, legislation and courts with a supreme court to settle disputes between constituents in the order. Therefore it is a durable order not based on the changing moods of individuals but on the everlasting common will of the citizens to live in this order and, within it and by its help, but not against it, to solve their problems of ever-present conflicting interests, contrasting social ideals, and disagreements. Community is possible only so long as such a *unitas ordinis* exists. Of secondary importance are the constitutional methods by which it is continually produced, protected, and reformed. Members may disagree with some parts of the order; for instance, socialists may not agree with that part of the order which makes capitalism possible and lawful, Catholics may not agree with laws that are a part of the order, which facilitate or even promote birth control. But they recognize that they are bound by this order as a whole; they do not oppose the *unitas;* they will defend it against threats of disorder from without or within.

This very primacy and this necessity of the political order, of the state, make it impossible to accept the pluralist political theory. The state, the trade-union, the political party, and the nationality are not on the same plane. To the political order belong a superiority and an eminence compared with those other orders and communities. Trade-unions are transient forms of socio-economic organization with partial ends in the state, not such ends as international proletarism wants beyond the state; they are correlated to the capitalist form of economic production. However important the trade-union may be, unlike the state, it embraces only the socio-economic status of man, not his human status. A person can leave his trade-union without being compelled to join another trade-union; but no one can live outside a political unit; whoever emigrates from one state comes under the sovereignty of another state. Man can live without trade-union affiliation or that of party or nationality, but he cannot live without the state.

The *unitas ordinis* is not a blind physical "must" or the product of an instinctive irrational power like the instinct of animals. It is a spiritual thing worthy of rational beings. Its existence is a spiritual one, and it needs visible representations. The flag, the national anthem, the capital, the courts, the uniforms of army and police force, the solemnity of robed judges, or the regalia of the king, and the formalities of legislature and the protocol of the diplomats. Yet this order and unity is always endangered by the disordered passions of individuals and mobs. Its human concord is threatened by the human vice of discord. The persons in power readily abuse it for the advantage of vested interests. Its ideal, the coincidence of private good and the common good, is realized only by continual virtuous effort of governors and governed: yet private interests may force the public servants of the order into their selfish service.

The unity endangered by disruption, the order threatened by dissolution through reckless, selfish, antisocial interests, by passions and vices, must be protected to be preserved. This unity must be adapted to the perpetually changing life of the people. There must be authority, and authority with might, to protect and to reform. This is polity. St. Thomas in his wisdom called it an *ars architectonica*. We call order "peace," because peace means order, to be secure from disturbances. Polity means to realize order. But there are two kinds of order: one effected in freedom by free obedience to a freely acknowledged authority on the foundation of natural law; the other effected by violent power and enslavement of the subjected. Only the first is human.

But even this political order is not under all circumstances an ultimate end and the supreme value. The order itself serves higher ends, as do arts, science, economics. Sienkievicz is said to have declared that the real meaning of polity is the creation of conditions (perhaps he might better have said the creation of an order) under which Hermann and Dorothea could love, marry, beget children, and educate them for a true human life. Now he might add that in doing so they were working for the salvation of their souls in another world. This, then, is what Aristotle meant when he taught that man's social nature finds its perfection in citizenship; or the Scholastics in saying that the external bliss, the sufficiency of this life, is the purpose of the state.

With all this granted, it is clear that the sovereign order, the state, the preservation of law, and the protection and reform of the order, get their final justification and measure from the nature of man and from the divinely constituted *ordo mundi,* witnessing God's justice, as St. Thomas says. But this means that the ultimate rule of polity is natural law. This is clarified further when we consider what happens in the state of siege. Then the common order of law is abolished on account of an emergency; even some fundamental rights of man are set aside. But why? To preserve the community, to preserve the *unitas ordinis.* Are the acts of an emergency power then simply beyond the law? Not at all. We still apply some rules and demand recognition of such rules by the authority.

We all agree that not all the acts of the emergency power are right. When we do so, we always recur to basic ideas of justice and reasonableness which are given by the necessity of the *unitas ordinis* for human social life and the perfection of human nature. Thus, even in the case of the temporary abolition of the order of positive law, we still hold that political power is not absolute but is bound by the rule of justice. At this juncture, natural law appears as the solid basis of the whole social framework. If we lacked this idea of an unwritten. nonpositive law, how could we distinguish a tyrannical dictatorship from the emergency power, necessary even in the most genuine democracy? The *ordo juris* may change, may even for a time be abolished in favor of mere measures and commands. But still these measures and commands are themselves not absolute, but are measured by the *ordo justitiae,* that is, by natural law.

This fact, then, is the salvation of human dignity. Only if the *ordo justitiae* remains, can this dignity be preserved. There have been cherished, from ancient times to Machiavelli and modern materialism, theories which deny the validity of such an *ordo justitiae* and contend that every concrete *ordo juris* is simply a truce in the materialist struggle of class interests or the consequence of a mere biological superiority of one race. But most of those who hold such theories refute themselves. In Karl Marx's *Capital* there burns a genuine feeling for an *ordo justitiae*, as every reader will remark.[14] In Machiavelli we find a real understanding of this perennial justice.[15] Hobbes never denied that even the Leviathan is bound by the divine and the natural law, however much his theory destroys those ideas. And in our days we can see that attempts are made to justify even the most unjust acts of tyrannical government with an appeal to a justice beyond the positive order of law, because human life is impossible without this *ordo justitiae*, this appeal to natural law as a divinely instituted law. So even the greatest cynicism of tyrants is compelled to bow before this deeply human idea, without which man ceases to be human. Natural law is, therefore, the moral basis of every political authority. Might without right is mere violence, inhuman and destructive.

VI. Natural Law as the Basis of Unity for All Positive Law Systems

The necessity and function of the idea of natural law becomes clear in the problem of the unity of various kinds of law, especially of the municipal (internal) law of the sovereign state and the external law of the community of nations, and also in the problem of the relation between morality and right.

This problem of the unity of national and international law seems to involve a dilemma. The national law, because of the absolute sovereignty of the state, is supreme. Therefore international law can be considered only the creation of the will of the states in the form of self-obligation. Hence it is revocable at any time, whenever the states, by arbitrary decisions, see fit. Thus international law could be nothing objective, independent of the will of those who subject themselves to its order. Consequently international law could not be law in a true sense. For, whatever else law may be, its essential property is that it

---

14 It was this protest against the injustices of laissez-faire capitalism which made that clumsy book, *Das Kapital*, the bible of the socialist labor-movement in continental Europe. The laboring masses were released from the traditional rural order and crowded into the slums of the barren and monotonous industrial cities. They were seldom cared for by the Churches; or if so, then often in the wrong way in a condescending attitude of almsgiving. These laboring masses thirsted for justice, for redemption from the proletarian status. They drank the wine of wrath that Marx offered, because all too seldom the consolation of religion and of justice was given them.

15 Cf. his eulogy of religion in *Discorsi*, I, 11 f., 55.

rules independently of the will of the persons who are subject to it as individuals. Evidently, then, law is valid and must be enforcible even against the will of the individuals subject to it. Essential to a rule of law, is that it is enforcible against those subject to it.

Furthermore, the international law is supreme. Then the municipal law, the national law, cannot be considered sovereign. The very existence and extent of national law would be at the mercy of international law. The sovereign decision even in what is still called "domestic affairs" would be controlled ultimately by international law, enforced by international agencies. The various states would thus become provinces (less than dominions) of the *civitas maxima,* of the only sovereign international law. Practically this would mean that the agencies instituted by international law would assume a right of continuous intervention in the domestic affairs of the states, a right that would be governed only by international law. This is, of course, an extreme formulation, because presumably the international law would be created by the states themselves. But this presumption is not valid if, in a given case, the international rule to be applied is not produced by unanimous and formal consent of all the member states of the community of nations, in which case the subjective self-obligation theory would arise anew. But if the international rule is only common legal conviction, if it is merely customary law, with the implication that not all but a great majority of the members are convinced that they are bound by it, then the self-obligation theory would not work. We would have a case of superiority of the international law against the will of one state or of a small minority of the member states.

Of course, it is easy to say that the international law is superior to the national law *in abstracto.* The problem arises when we ask whether this superiority goes so far that the international law (i.e., its authorities) can decide arbitrarily (law is will) all or any matters, even such as the state considers to be its domestic affairs. If so, we would have not merely an international law, but an internal law of a world state or world government with absolute sovereignty, equipped with the right of intervention without any restrictions. We may safely say that such a world state built upon a positivist will theory would not be acceptable, when we consider the difficulties that arose on account of paragraph 8 of Article XV of the League of Nations' constitution. This paragraph said that if in an international dispute one party contends, with the recognition of the Council, that the dispute concerns matters which by international law are solely within its domestic jurisdiction, then the Council has to state this without proposing a solution of the dispute. The superiority of the international law seems here to be clearly established, because it is to define what is or is not a matter of exclusive domestic jurisdiction. Should international law itself be merely will, arbitrary will, of a partial majority, then the very existence of an individual nation could be at the mercy of such a majority. It is understandable that very self-conscious powerful states would prefer to live in a kind of natural status even at the risk of war.[16]

But this danger exists only if we adhere to the positivist principle that all law is will. On the other hand, if we recognize that law is reason, if we include an objective finality in the concept of law, there exist matters which by their nature are domestic because derived from the nature and end of the state as a perfect society. Then it would be possible to state in individual cases and *in abstracto* at least a minimum content of the domestic sphere of the state which is sacrosanct from international intervention. In any federation, to save the existence of member states, it is necessary to presume or positively to state the reserved powers of the states against federal intervention. International law holds to this. The growing idea of fundamental (natural) rights of the states or nations, and of the international natural rights of minorities, is proof of it.

So we may conclude that the whole legal world is built up out of social spheres in which a specific community freely and independently develops its positive legal order to effect its specific end, an objective common good. However much matters may vary according to cultural, economic, and social changes, there remains a legal minimum of matters that must be domestic. Otherwise this community's objective end would be unattainable and would itself become an empty shell. The unity of the different spheres, domestic and international, would thus be established by the fact that the will of each, the authorities in each, national and international, are bound ultimately in legislation and in decisions by the natural law which rules both supremely. An empty formal statement that "agreements must be kept" is insufficient; only an objective rule will do. And this rule can be found in

[16] This problem was one of the reasons that induced the United States Senate to reject the League of Nations.

the principles of natural law, emanating from the objective ends of the various legal orders, from their necessity for the existence and development of human nature to its most perfect realization in and through the various communities.

By developing his own nature, man forms mankind, nations, states, families. Each, in its relations to man's end and nature, has an objective end and a protected unassailable sphere of rights and duties in a specific *unitas ordinis*. Like the state, existing for the sake of persons and families and having the character of service to them, so the *civitas maxima* must have the character of service to the states and to the individual persons. The unity of the legal cosmos and its various orders rests upon the universal natural law. Not without reason have the popes declared that without the restoration of the universal rule of morality, that is, without the acceptance of the principles of natural law, an international order of peace and justice is impossible.[17] By founding the legal orders upon the natural law we can also avoid that pernicious strict separation of morality and right, instead of a distinction between them. Both belong ultimately to the moral order, the prolongation of the ontological order. All right must stem from morality. There is no non-moral law, a law absolutely devoid of morality. Such a "law" would be no law, no rule for reason, for a rational free being. The natural law is the seam by which all positive law is connected with morality; both municipal law and international law rule human social life and both receive their authority from the natural law revealed in its divine institution in man's nature and in the order of the universe. *Fundamentum totius juris Deus est.*

17 Cf. Encyclical *Summi Pontificatus* (October 20, 1939).

CHAPTER VIII

Natural Law and Positive Law

I. Destruction of the Idea of Natural Law through Rationalism

BECAUSE the end of politics is the constitution, the preservation and historical adaptation of the sovereign order as a unity, the main function of political sovereign authority since the time of Heraclitus, Plato, and Aristotle has been legislation, the establishment of the *ordo juris*. This fact leads us to a discussion of the relations between natural law and positive law.

In the nineteenth century in almost all countries, we find a definite turning away from the idea of natural law. In the Anglo-Saxon countries, Austin denied it in favor of a practical positivism in law. Savigny, founder of the historical legal school in Germany, elevated customary law emanating from the living soul of the people; then Bergbohm devoted all his vigor to a tremendous attack upon natural law; and Oliver W. Holmes, with skeptical doubt, rejected the idea of natural law as romantic. This was owing partly to the widespread desertion of the realm of metaphysics and to skeptical empiricism, which values only the scientific method of the natural sciences. Consequently the traditional metaphysics and ethics appear as unscientific disciplines. But apart from this influence of the *Zeitgeist,* the desertion was owing also to the so-called natural-law theories of the Enlightenment and of rationalism in the seventeenth and eighteenth centuries.

At that time the various holders of university chairs of natural law issued books about their ideas of natural law. They began to derive from various principles—like sociability (Pufendorf) or utility (Hobbes) or inborn ideas (Chr. Wolff)—complete systems of natural law. These contained a minute description of supposedly natural-law rules about property, contract, tort, inheritance, family, in other words, the whole civil law. Those professors began to consider natural law as that law system which they imagined had ruled the natural status of man before the formation of states. And so, in their abstract rationalism, they developed a complete law system down to the rules of procedure, sequestration, and execution. And they developed such systems solely by reason. It is most remarkable that many of these promoters of natural-law systems had only a slight connection with the ancient tradition, often lacked a sound philosophical basis, and sometimes regarded the great teachers of the past with open contempt based partly on simple ignorance, partly on the inability to understand their basic ideas.[1]

For these thinkers the *status naturalis* in an imaginary form is the main subject of interest. This is the age of Defoe's *Robinson Crusoe*, of the glorification of the peaceful life of the primitives, of Rousseau's *Emile*. The different systems—and they were as different as the philosophies of their originators—had of course a polemic purpose. They served, for instance, to reduce the universal Church to a private religious association ruled exclusively by the law of the land or by a department of the state administration.

On the other hand, they served to reform the savage usages of popular customary law full of magic belief in sorcery and demons in favor of a more humane penal law. They served to undermine the feudal aristocracy in favor of a bourgeois society of free men. Furthermore, they led the way for a liberation of property rights from the various legal ties characteristic of the *splendor familiae* idea of a feudal society; for the liberation of serfs from their bondage to the soil in order to put upon them the mask of free labor; for the liberation of the economic forces of the entrepreneur-manufacturer from the manifold ties of the bureaucracy of a mercantile economic policy; for the final coming of age of that new economic giant, capitalism. Thus these various theories and systems began to describe a sphere of individual rights versus the state. But, on the other hand, they could also easily develop arguments for the Leviathan, for the state as *Deus mortalis,* and for the enlightened despotism of the absolute princes. They could even serve Rousseau to formulate an almost anarchic revolutionism.

This is the conception of natural law as it is commonly known to its opponents in the nineteenth century. This, too, explains why the

[1] Kant knew very little about Aristotle and almost nothing about St. Thomas Aquinas.

polemic and political natural law succumbed as soon as its legal reforms and its political demands had been realized in the constitutional revolutions of the late eighteenth century and the nineteenth
century. This also explains why, nevertheless, the idea of natural law
did not vanish but lived on in its old stronghold, the *philosophia
perennis,* which, in its essentials, is beyond the transitory political
polemics of the ages.

II. NATURAL LAW AND POSITIVE LAW IN THE *Philosophia Perennis*

The conservation of natural law was possible in the *philosophia
perennis* because natural law was not considered a polemic weapon
or a rationalist system of all civil and penal law, of minute rules of
procedure, of specific forms of constitutional and international law.
Rather it formulated only a few general principles. All human law—
that is, the positive law, statute law, and customary law of the state, the
Church, the international community, and the rules of autonomous
bodies in the state—is a determination or consequence of these
principles. In other words, all human positive law is derived from
natural law or is determining it. Natural law thus remains the
paramount measure and the superior critical norm of judgment for the
justice of human laws. But human law itself is necessary. Natural
law calls for positive law, for concretization and individualization of
the perennial principles according to the circumstances. Natural law
leaves plenty of room for discretion; therefore legislation is the most
essential political function. The state, with its sovereign order of
positive law in this nation and for this era and culture, is necessary by
natural law.

Whereas the theoretical reason starts with the individual fact
presented by the senses and, by the process of abstraction, strives for
the general, the practical reason applies a few evident principles to the
particular, the contingent, the individual, the "case" in the final
sense. Usually there is a plurality of means through which the general
purpose can be realized; there are various circumstances which concretely condition the realization of the principle *hic et nunc.* The
more the practical reason descends from the height of principles to
conclusions and to their applications to individual situations, so much

the more does the possibility of diversity increase, certainty weaken, and agreement cease. St. Thomas rightly says that to realize justice in economic life and in the manifold relations among persons is harder and more laborious than to define the right diagnosis and therapy in medical art.[2]

The fact of a variety of means and methods for a commonly acknowledged goal and the difference in the historical situations require a definite decision especially since we live under continually changing circumstances. Whenever such a decision must be made, it is made by authority; whenever there is no appeal from a decision, there is sovereign authority. Authority is likewise necessary for a decision about the conclusions from the principles; the farther the conclusions go, the more uncertain they become. Here, again, a decision is needed; otherwise uncertainty and discord would arise and neither unity nor order would ensue. We know that the farther we are removed from the evident principles, the more our individual interests, our passions, and our class preferences and prejudices influence our reasoning in regard to remote conclusions. For man is not the angelic being, the merely thinking and reasoning being that rationalism thought him to be. Without a determination, without a decision upon derivations from conclusions, without a positive law governing concrete situations and deciding thus between a plurality of purposes, ways, and means, there would follow only endless discussion, which is unpractical for beings who live in time.

Furthermore, there must be a positive sanction, an actual compulsion for man to obey the natural law. This is the more necessary the farther away from the principle are the conclusions to be applied in the circumstances. True, in the long run history provides a sanction of natural law. A nation despising the first principles of natural law will perish; justice remains the foundation of the state. Wherever a nation, in contempt of natural law, lets the crusaders of birth control or the cynics of libertinism corrupt the sexual and family life, this may produce in the short run easy solutions of economic or social dilemmas. But once loose practices become national habits, such a nation will become senile, will become extinct by losing its identity through subjugation or immigration by more vigorous nations. Natural law has stood at the deathbed of many a nation which had

---

[2] *Comm. in Eth. Nic.*, V, 15; *Summa theol.*, Ia IIae, q.14, a.3 ad 4; q.94, a.4.

contempt for that law in the heyday of materialistic hedonism. History is to some extent the last judgment. Direct compulsion against those who despise the principles and ordinances of the natural law and of the *ordo rerum humanarum* there must be.

The inclination to selfish egoism and the destructive force of the passions of disorder are unfortunately as strong as the inborn will to order. Man's life is always threatened by chaos. Yet man is the more himself, the more he lives in order. It is in contending against chaos that man builds the state, the law, the courts, the police, his civilization, and culture. The *philosophia perennis* could never accept the groundless optimism of Rousseau's natural-law philosophy. It is mindful of the demonic potentialities of human nature, of the dark powers that ever threaten with destruction and anarchy.

It may be evident to all that theft is against the natural law. Nevertheless the retributive justice of positive criminal law is required that the crime may be promptly expiated by actual punishment. What this punishment should be, must be determined by competent authority. Private property is a natural-law institution, but in practical life there would be a ceaseless struggle and collision of property interests if the lawmaker did not define the use and limits of property, the forms of property transfer, and the legal circumstances and conditions for the loss of property. Historically, manifold forms of property —feudalist and capitalist, for instance—are possible; but they are so by positive law. Not nature, but the legislative authority, whether king, customary law, or parliament, has decided upon these contingent forms.

Repeatedly St. Thomas points out that justice and prudence are proper for the lawmaker. Prudence now refers to expediency, to the right choice of the means most adapted for a certain purpose. St. Thomas calls this prudence an architectonic virtue. This prudence must govern the decisions of the lawmaker. Prudence manifests itself in acting; intelligence, in thinking. Prudence, which according to St. Thomas is derived from *providere* ("seeing ahead"), is not so much concerned with the intelligible and general end but with the best and most useful and efficient means by which, in acting and doing. we reach the end. Prudence has to do with concrete realizations. with judging dispositions and circumstances, with producing favorable conditions for the realization of the moral ideals. Natural law tells man, living in time and space, in the contingency of his existence, the general principles and the essential objective and transcendent ends. Prudence, of which experience and good counsel and learning are integral parts, tells us about the ways and means, about their rectitude, their efficiency; it tells us about the concrete possibilities of realization, etc. Thus we recognize the necessity of the ruler and lawmaker, i.e., authority which determines the general principles of natural law in concrete situations, authority which decides by legislative decisions upon particular ends and particular means. The positive law, therefore, is a necessary consequence of the idea of natural law.

Jurists often depreciate the theory of natural law because they think that by continual appeals to it the security of the legal order would suffer. They may ironically vary Aristotle's appeal to the unwritten law [8] thus: When you have no case according to the law of the land, appeal to the law of nature and quote Sophocles' *Antigone*. So they conclude that the whole theory is futile and can only disturb a good administration of law. Such an attitude would be justified against the revolutionary natural-law doctrine of the eighteenth century.

But the perennial philosophy made this careful distinction, between prohibitive and permissive rules. Only prohibitive rules always demand obedience; positive law prescribing acts which contradict a prohibitive law is simply no law. Evidently no law can make murder, adultery, lying, or perjury lawful. Nobody will regard as despisers of the law, Christians who refuse obedience to laws which prescribe idolatry. Such laws are utterly non-obligatory. On the other hand, a tax law contradicting the principle of justice and proportionality, though unjust, gives to the citizens no right to illegal tax evasion. Here it is not immediately the order that is endangered. And here, the preservation even of the imperfect order is preferable to resistance to an unjust law of this kind.

This precedence of order allows, therefore, to the judge and to the administrator the application of the unjust law and does not give the individual citizen a right to resistance. The right thing to do is to change the law. The fact that a positive law commanding an act in itself unjust is rightly considered to be no law, is based on the assumption that the prohibitive rules of natural law protect the essence of the social and political order. When sworn oaths are no longer sacred,

---

[8] *Rhetorica,* I, 15.

when the honor of our neighbor is despised, when adultery is lawful, and no legal distinction is made between marriage and concubinage, when authority is powerless, all possibility of a social order ceases, the existence of an *ordo rerum humanarum* is impossible.

III. The Fallacies of Positivism and the Revival of Natural Law

It is no wonder that the idea of natural law always returns after its banishment from the universities and law courts on account of the dominance of positivism. Positivism is a paltry philosophy and may satisfy the human mind at times of sensual and material saturation. As long as the socio-economic system produces enough material goods to build a comfortable civilization and afford the intelligentsia economic security and leisurely discussion, such a civilization may be able to live for a certain time without the moral foundations of human existence being consciously preserved. It is easy for the sons of successful businessmen to discuss the merits of communism and the sins of capitalism. They may even indulge in romantic dreams of going back to primitive life, or they may play the role of the cynical skeptic for whom there is no truth, no morality, no duties: nothing but dreams, interests, instincts, and pleasures.

Yet man does not live by bread alone. The self-satisfied mind of nineteenth-century positivism proved inadequate, when the material basis of this positivism, the optimistic faith in its endless progress and its easy solutions of all life-problems by sciences, was suddenly shattered in the first years (1914–19) of that world revolution in which we are still so deeply involved. Thoughtful minds outside of the *philosophia perennis* and the Church had already felt the insufficiency of positivism in all fields of intellectual and moral life. The philosophies of life (Dilthey), of intuition (Bergson), of vitalism (Driesch), to mention only a few, were a sign of this. A certain humility instead of the unbridled pride of the nineteenth century is beginning to be evident. From the subject-centered sensualist attitude, we witness a return in many fields to the object. We see a new interest in the Catholic Church, which the nineteenth century regarded as a ridiculous or antiquated and therefore venerable relic of bygone times. This initial turning away from positivism began to produce a favorable atmosphere for a renaissance of metaphysics and of the *philosophia perennis.*

On account of the intrinsic connection between metaphysics and natural law, there followed a new evaluation of the eternal idea of natural law. As now in psychology after the rampages of materialist or sensualist psychology without psyche (soul), the soul was rediscovered, as in natural philosophy the organic vitalist principle began to prevail, so now in legal philosophy which, under the rule of positivism, had produced a legal theory without a philosophical substance, there gradually occurred a return to the idea of natural law. The weaknesses of the presuppositions on which we had built our life have now become evident. That legal framework under which capitalism, the modern secular state, and the materialist civilization were taken as self-evident, has now become dubious under the impact of class conflicts, devastating depressions, and social revolutions everywhere. The divided Christian bodies have seen the inner power of their common inheritance wasted away in modern secularism and they have felt themselves threatened by a common enemy, the growing paganism of the masses in our civilization. At the same time the situation for a revival of the idea of natural law has become more favorable.

It is an old truth that, as long as man is materially sated, he thinks he can live by bread alone. But in times of social and political upheaval, when the customary framework of the socio-economic and legal-political order is shaken, when the positive law becomes doubtful, man turns to what is behind the now doubtful positive law, to the idea of natural law. In such times the simple definition, that law is what the state wills, is utterly insufficient. The revolutionary forces unable to appeal to positive law will appeal to the idea of a natural law; the conservative leaders in power, feeling the moral weakness of positivism, are likewise compelled to appeal to the idea of natural law in order to justify the present order before reason.

These circumstances, in themselves inconsequential for the true substance of natural law, opened at least an approach to its idea and its necessity. Legal philosophy, by its criticism of positivism in the theory of the sources of law—of the Kelsenian pure theory, of the Duguit school—had also somewhat lowered the barriers to the idea of natural law. When the theory of the sources of law shows, for instance, that the will of the state alone is not a true source of law, that there are always lacunas in the positive law issuing from the will of the state, and that these must be filled by the judge, then, of course, there arises the problem of what the rules are that the judge has to apply in such a case. The answers may be worded differently, yet substantially they point to natural law. The pure theory of law (Kelsen) with its Kantian basic norm *(Grundnorm)*, a hypothetical, formal, and empty variety of the "categorical imperative" in Kant's *Ethics*, is, of course, not natural law. But the construction of the positive law, being derived from such a *Grundnorm,* which remains unexplained, has an amazing formal affinity to some tenets of the natural-law theory. Duguit comes nearer to the Thomistic concept of natural law than he would ever have conceded. Yet the attentive reader of Duguit's works, if he know St. Thomas, will be amazed by some essential similarities. Of course, these are not devaluated by Duguit's fervent protest that he is not a metaphysician. Duguit's principle of social solidarity as the source and critical norm of the positive law is in fact one element of the Thomistic *natura* as the basis of natural law.

Modern positivism, held up against the gaps in the positive law, introduced the theory that in the case of such a presumed gap the judge had to find out what the lawmaker's will had been. In the search of that will the judge, of course, was not looking for what we may call the psychological act of willing in the soul of the lawmaker. What he looked for did, from a positivist standpoint, not even exist. But the judge took refuge in contending that, whatever the lawmaker may have psychologically willed, he had willed reason, finality, justice. So it happens that the will often disappears; reason, finality, and justice appear, essential elements of the idea of natural law. The judge assumed, indeed, that the lawmaker had willed what is just.

Scholars and jurists who otherwise show no enmity toward natural law or who even recognize its metaphysical basis, often say that natural law as a body of ethical and political ideals, to be desired *de lege ferenda* for future better legislation, is intrinsically too general. They say it is too vague, and lacks that clarity and preciseness of positive law which the practical jurist and judge needs for his guidance in his profession. In this view, natural law thus becomes an ideal program for the lawmaker but it lacks all validity until it is vested in positive law. Consequently natural law has not that essential quality which tradition attributed to it, namely, that it is the critical norm for existing positive law and for the judges' decisions under the latter. The strict obliging character of natural law is thus denied.

This objection is prejudicial. The demands of natural law are not vaguer than the fundamental concepts of positive law, civil and constitutional. The opposite opinion apparently flows from a positivist interpretation of the general principle that the judge is independent of the other powers, legislative and executive, and is subject only to the law. The positivist here interprets law in the formalist sense as emanating technically correct from the lawmaker. Duguit, though confessing himself a positivist, objected vehemently to this opinion, which is quite familiar in German, French, and Italian positivism. If everything that emanates from the lawmaking power correctly according to the constitutionally prescribed technique is a rule of law, then the study of law does not deserve a moment of intellectual effort. Then the judge would be only an automaton of mere logical subsumption: Put the case with its evidence into the slot, and the juridical mechanism of logical subsumption of the individual case under the general rule produces the decision. On the contrary, the judge has to measure the positive law with the critical norm of the higher law of the Constitution, and the latter with a paramount law, the natural law, the rule of reason. Natural law is by no means merely an ideal program *de lege ferenda;* it is obligating, independent of the fact that its rules have been vested in the cloak of positive law. Otherwise it would be a *jus inutile,* which Hobbes' concept of sovereignty made it.

From the standpoint of juridical positivism, the vital distinction between legality and legitimacy is impossible, though the so-called natural rights, the concept of loyalty and of moral obedience (not simply compulsory external conformity, to legitimate governmental authority as distinguished from merely compulsory power) depend on that distinction. It may be true that natural law recedes into the background when democratic forms of government put the lawmaker and the administration of law under the vigilant control of the governed. Nevertheless, in cases of emergency when artificially produced majority decisions oppress natural rights, the idea of natural law arises again from the background even in our modern states with highly developed legal systems of positive law.

In such cases the issue is legitimacy (the justice of the law) and not legality (technically correct law). Our modern dictators are masters of legality. Hitler aimed not at revolution but at a legal grasp of power according to the formal democratic processes of majority vote. And when he had legally grasped power he destroyed legally the natural rights of political, religious, and racial minorities, and the rights of individuals as they are embodied in natural law: freedom of consciences, freedom of speech and of association. From a positivist standpoint it is hard to object to Adolf "Légalité" as a witty scholar called Hitler. The genuine problem that so arises is that of the legitimacy of the legally correct acts of totalitarian government.

This question can be answered—and is answered thus even by jurists who profess themselves as positivist—only from the acknowledgment of an unwritten paramount law which since the time of Aristotle has been called "just by nature," i.e., natural law. Legitimacy, that eminent quality of government, cannot rest on technicalities or formalities, on the simple fact of majority vote. The political legitimism of the monarchist theory sensed this. Therefore it did not base the right of the monarch on the constitution. But it based the constitution on the divine right of the monarch or on tradition, on duration and trial through centuries. The legitimism of De Maistre made time God's prime minister and thus based the rights of kings on providential guidance, that is, on God's will. We think this legitimist principle is wrong. But this is not the same as saying that now democratic legitimism is right, that a just law is what the majority decides, that the majority is the exclusive origin of authority and legitimacy. Legitimacy lies deeper. True, the democratic acceptance of a government's laws is eminently important from a psychological point of view. But this fact of acceptance is not enough. It cannot explain as an obligation of conscience the moral obligation (the consequence of legitimacy) to freely obey authority. Legitimacy, so we must conclude, is accordance of a government and its laws to the principles of natural law; and natural law obliges because it emanates from God, who is perfect reason and omnipotent will.

If we do not accept natural law, we cannot make that important distinction between legality and legitimacy in politics. Thus we lose the basis of any distinction between lawful political authority and tyranny, between the moral obligation of the free conscientious citizen to loyalty and obedience and passive external conformity, cowardly and undignified, to the illegitimate yet technically legal orders of tyrannical government. Thus the idea of natural law, however much it may be buried under complacency and saturation of peaceful times, rises again as soon as the problem of legitimacy arises. And another conclusion follows from our discussion. In the ultimate analysis God is, as Leibnitz put it, the foundation of all law (*Totius juris fundamentum Deus est*); and this makes obedience and allegiance concordant with the dignity and freedom of the human person.

The resurgence of international law after the First World War contributed notably to a revival of natural law. The reason for this is clear. In international relations, the positivist demand for a concrete will of a rule-maker is often practically impossible. Some of Wilson's fourteen points, the Atlantic Charter, the common conviction that all nations, small and great, have a right to independence, liberty, and security, are as much natural law as is the bill of rights. Today we frequently behold the strange spectacle of philosophers and lawyers denying natural law in their textbooks and proclaiming its main principles whenever they have to deal with international relations, today so utterly devoid of justice and equity. Just as frequently, stirring appeals to the rights of man, to justice, to liberty as an absolutely metaphysical and therefore undoubted principle, are made by men who never tire of stressing relativism in ethics, positivism in legal philosophy, and sensualism in epistemology.

We may take this as a proof that man, by his rational and social nature, is always an adherent of natural law and that he must be under the sway of a wrong philosophy in order to get rid of natural law. Karl Bergbohm, who vehemently attacked the concept of natural law in the second half of the nineteenth century, had to confess that all men are born adherents of natural law (Introduction of his *Rechtsphilosophie*, 1885). He is quite right, but he thinks this fact a proof that the natural law is unscientific. This attitude, that common sense is wrong and that only the "scientific" mind as understood by positivist scientism is right, is an outspoken anomaly. Any true philosophy is critical, educated common seense; if a philosophy, especially moral, social, legal philosophy, blatantly contradicts sober common sense (not to be confused with the changing fashions of the intelligentsia of our uprooted half-educated urban mediocrities), there must be something wrong with that philosophy.

The present revival of natural law, however slight it may be, is caused also by the great upheaval in our increasingly secularized society and by the paganizing of its institutions. The substance of our common Christian revealed inheritance is slowly being consumed. This means that the age of controversy between the divided Christian Churches, which somehow presupposes a substantially Christian society, is definitely gone, and that we have entered an era of cooperation, against paganizing influences, between the Churches and all who are of good will. Upon what basis is such a cooperation possible? Upon what basis is it possible especially in the field of socio-economic, political, and international action? Upon such a basis as can be shared by all cooperating members.[4]

This basis is natural law. Passions, class conflicts, wrong philosophies, too optimistic reliance on endless progress, secure under the rule of nineteenth century materialism, have dimmed many principles of natural law. The expression itself has been purloined, and its eternal appeal to man has been abused by the modern totalitarian regimes. Yet, that leaves us burdened only with the task of clarifying its meaning and elaborating its concepts. Let us get rid of the notion that our poor will, disturbed by passions, selfish interests, class envy, and national presumption, can by itself produce order in our world. The order we have to produce must be an imitation of the divine order of the moral universe as it is revealed in the principles of natural law. It is a law that can say: "You would not have searched for me if you had not already found me." As certainly as the soul is *naturaliter christiana,* so certainly is our idea of justice in all the fields of social life *naturaliter christiana.* There is no other way out: we must anchor our secular, earthly order in the throne of God. The "oughtness" of that divine order revealed to our reason in our very human nature and in the universe surrounding us must be the foundation and model for the concrete order *(ordo juris)* in which we wish to live.

[4] Cf. Max Pribilla, S. J., *Um kirchliche Einheit* (Freiburg, 1929). An excellent review of this work is given by John C. Murray in *Theological Studies,* IV, 100 ff.

Part II

THE PHILOSOPHY OF THE STATE

CHAPTER IX

The Origin of the State

I. THE MEANING OF THE PROBLEM

EVEN for the highly civilized men of our rationalist age the origin of the state and its deepest root are surrounded by mystery. Indifferent skepticism and rationalist utilitarianism could only decompose the allegiance of citizens and vilify the symbols that stand for the state. They could dissolve but not explain the state and the politico-juridical order with its compulsory power and supreme authority demanding obedience. On the other hand, a theory which finds the origin of the state in irrational, uncontrollable biological forces is no more satisfactory. States do not rise, blossom, and wither away like plants, blindly ruled by the unconscious powers of nature. A poetical figure is not a philosophical argument. Man is a rational being, an independent, self-conscious person. And the state carries as symbols of its power the sword and the scales; it has the *jus vitae ac necis,* the *jus belli et pacis:* the right over life and death, over peace and war. The right, the moral power! Whence comes such a powerful community, with this moral and juridical power? That is the question ever rising before man as a rational and moral being.

This was the question before the simple mind of primitives, and it is the most exciting question for the modern mind. The primitive mind sought a theological origin. To the primitive mind political organization originates in the tribal deity. The king, the patriarch, is the son of the tribal deity, and the primitive state shows a hierocratic origin. Authority, power, and law are immediately transferred by God to the king or the rulers. Another explanation, found especially in monarchist theory up to Lord Filmer's and recent legitimist arguments, employs the idea of the patriarch. The power and authority of the king, and therefore of the state as kingdom, originates in the paterfamilias and the patriarch. As it is senseless for a child to doubt the origin of the family and the authority of the father, so it is sense-less for men to argue about the origin of the state, or the power and authority of the king.

The primitive hierocratic myths and the patriarchal theory have lost their enchantment with the progress of thinking. The Son of Heaven has been deposed, and patriarchalism as promoted by Lord Filmer is ridiculed. But the problem remains: Where does the state come from? It is not so much a question of how this or that actual state came into existence in the course of history. It is the problem of the ideal, moral origin of the state endowed with sword and scales, with majesty and power, demanding from the citizen almost uncondi-tioned allegiance and the sacrifice of life in the emergency of war, for the continuing life of the state. In the attempt to cope with this problem, fantastic theories of the divine right of kings have been de-veloped; tired and disillusioned human thinking has ceased to strive and has tried to explain the state as the outcome of blind natural forces, the product of irrational, fortuitous developments of history or the outgrowth of class struggles with the millennial hope of a withering away of the state in a classless society. But all this gives to the rational mind and the moral conscience of man no answer to the problem of the moral authority, juridical power, and compulsory force of the state.

II. Human Nature in the Origin of the State

Catholic political philosophy asserts that in human nature is the origin of the state. Here it must be stated that "human nature" should be understood in its full philosophical meaning. Human nature does not mean the empirical, psychological nature as the politician or the advertising businessman sees it. The state originates in the bodily and spiritual nature of man. Nature or essence is also the end of man's activity and striving. Therefore the political status is necessary for the fulfillment of man's end; the state is an intentional disposition of human nature.

Two important things are thus made clear: that the state has its origin in human nature as a relatively independent secondary cause; that it emanates necessarily out of this nature in developing it to a status of perfection belonging to this nature in the political status.

And this development is natural; that is, the state is not the outcome of a special superhuman act of God; the state is not a supernatural, immediately divine establishment. Yet, as originating in human nature, divinely established, the state is part and subject of the order of the Creator. To live in the state is therefore God's order. To obey legitimate political authority is God's will, and the legitimacy of every political authority is measured by God's will as revealed in natural law. Further, the origin of the state in human nature does not mean that the state grows out of human nature as by physical law, on account of blind, unfree compulsion, but following human nature, that is, free nature. The origin of the state cannot be without the cooperation of the free will of men. There must always be some form of consent of men to form a state.

Again, as human nature is not completely destroyed by original sin, but only wounded, it follows that the state is not a consequence of sin, but that some kind of state would have been formed by man even if he had continued to live in the state of pure nature. And lastly: for the redeemed Christians, too, the state is necessary. The state will never wither away, for it is a lasting and necessary form of social life. It will never be submerged in the Church, as Dostoevski proposed, nor in international society, as Karl Marx thought; nor will it be useless for the redeemed Christians living in the grace of God as again and again Christian sects since the Manichaeans have contended, in denying the relative independence of both the Church and the state, of supernature and nature.

The origin of the state lies in man's nature. Man is a social and a political being. His bodily nature makes him more dependent on beings of his own likeness than are animals. The idyllic natural state of the solitary man as Rousseau depicted it, or the brutal natural state of the solitary warrior fighting against other solitary warriors as Hobbes described the "natural" man, is utterly unreal. This is conceded by Hobbes himself when he openly says that he will contemplate men as if they sprouted like mushrooms into maturity. Compared with this, Leo XIII's statement is realistic: that as man in isolation is missing care and welfare and as these are necessary for life, God in His wise providence has ordered that man be born into a human community; first and immediately into the family, then into the political community, for only the latter can afford to man a perfect sufficiency

of life.[1] St. Thomas again and again points out that man has not full
equipment like other animals, to whom nature has given sufficient
clothing and nourishment.[2]

III. MAN AS A SOCIAL AND POLITICAL BEING

But the insufficiency of the individual man with regard to his bodily life is not alone the root of social life. As integral a part of the
essence of man as the acts of thinking and willing, are the acts which
intentionally aim at other men as their object, like love and other
so-called sympathetic acts. Aristotle, in his admirable chapter on
friendship in the *Nicomachean Ethics*,[3] stressed this point against the
utilitarian philosophy of the state held by the Sophists. The bodily
expressions of the inner life of our mind, the eyes sparkling with
anger, the lips radiating joy with laughter, the "language" of our
gestures, are intentionally directed to another being of our own likeness. The "you" is therefore equally original and simultaneous with
the "I." In other words, perfect self-consciousness is reciprocal to
"we-mindedness," as was once well expressed in a variation of Descartes' famous thesis, *Cogito ergo sum: Cogito, ergo sumus* ("I think
therefore we are").

Likewise language, as all scholars from St. Thomas to Leo XII
argue, shows that sociality, and not only sociability, is an essential
part of human nature. Every attempt to explain language in a merely
utilitarian way, based on a mere biological desire for exchange, must
fail. Language is attached to mind and reason. Therefore only in a
figurative sense may one speak of a language of animals. When a mind
expresses itself it intentionally addresses another mind. This has
been admirably set forth by Thomas Aquinas: "Language is a property only of man, because in comparison with other beings it is the
privilege of man to have the knowledge of good and evil and consequently of the unjust and the like, of what can be uttered by language. As, therefore, language is by nature due to man and has as its
natural end that man may live in community for good or evil, for
right or wrong, it must be concluded, on the strength of the axiom

1 Leo XIII Allocutiones, Epistolae, etc. (Brugis et Insulis 1887–1901), II, 147.
2 *Summa theol.*, Ia IIae, q.95, a.11; *Contra Gent.*, III, 117, 128, 136.
3 Books VIII and IX.

that nature does not produce anything for nothing, that man im-pelled by nature shall live in community." [4] In another treatise St. Thomas explains the spiritual character of language in interpreting the word *verbum* as *verum boans* ("crying out the truth").[5] Hence language is not the product of a mere utilitarian, unnecessary so-ciability; for in language itself the innermost social nature of man reveals itself. Leo XIII once rightly called language the principle of outstanding power in forming community.[6]

Proceeding from the end of man, the perfection of his nature, the good life achieved by knowledge and virtue, we arrive at the same result. In isolation the perfection of mind and of heart is for the individual man out of reach. The philosopher and teacher there-fore employs dialogue and the dialectic method. Human nature has not merely a disposition for a social life, to participate in which is left to the arbitrary decision of the individual who is supposedly self-sufficient; for human nature itself is social, so that Aristotle will be right to all eternity: A man who by nature and not merely by fortune is cityless, is either less than man or more than man (cf. the clanless, lawless, homeless, solitary warrior, the Cyclops of Homer).

Thus from all points of view man is a social being. He builds up and lives in different kinds of communities: in the family, in villages and towns, in factories and shops, in churches and cloisters, and in the innumerable associations for innumerable purposes in economic life, in spiritual life, for arts, for science, for knowledge, and for research.

But Aristotle's dictum meant and expressly said more; namely, that man is by nature a political being. The stateless is for him the lawless and homeless. This means that the social nature reaches its perfection in political life, in the state. Man's social nature reaches its perfection in citizenship in the state. In the process of self-reali-zation of the social nature there is a state of development where self-sufficiency is achieved. One of the social forms is self-sufficient; it is a closed circuit where the social process comes to its natural end, in a community which is sufficient for all social wants and dispositions, a perfect society. This society, representing and enforcing an all-embracing order of law, deciding what is in the common interest and

---

[4] *Comm. in Pol.,* I, 1, *quod autem;* cf. Aristotle, *Pol.,* I, 1, 10–12.
[5] *De veritate,* q.4, a.10.
[6] Leo XIII, *Allocutiones,* I, 213.

what is just in men's dealing with one another,[7] is "state," wherever it appears. And this state has its origin in man's social nature. It is therefore eternal; it will not wither away. This lasting truth is proved by an argument *e contrario* before our eyes. There has always existed in man a kind of presumptuous longing for a stateless society. In earlier times, and here and there in later times, religious sects with a strong antistate bias, attempted to live without political bonds. They almost all degenerated into intolerant theocracies without freedom, and went to a quick doom in complete dissolution.

In our days we have seen a powerful revolutionary movement prophesying that, with the realization of a classless society, the state would wither away. There would be, as Lenin said, instead of necessity, meaning coercion, to obey the laws of a supreme authority, only adherence to simple, fundamental rules of everyday social life, very soon to be transformed into a habit.[8] Thus necessity, the coercion to obey laws, would be "state"; the habit of obeying simple rules would be stateless society, which would exist on the basis of complete equality and which would exclude any kind of conflicting interests, opinions, and ideas about justice in production, distribution, and consumption. To produce these habits, coercion would be necessary. And not to preserve them? These totalitarian habits would certainly not produce a state, but an unbearable tyranny, for man has reason in addition to habit, and man only.[9] And reason, not habit, is the outstanding criterion of man. Enforcement of habits is necessary, but, by the way, far more cruel and unjust than enforcement of laws that necessarily appeal to reason. Against this kind of stateless society one may refer to Aristotle again: "The state exists for the sake of good life and not for the sake of life only; if life were the object, slaves and brute animals might form a state, but they cannot, for they have no share in happiness or in a life of free choice."[10] To destroy the state for the sake of liberty means to destroy liberty and to produce a hideous monster state.

All these attempts to make the state superfluous by more religion or a new religion, or by a change from a class society into a classless society, arise from that perpetual longing of man's dreams to live with-

---

[7] Aristotle, *Politic.*, VII, 8, 7.
[8] Lenin in *The State and the Revolution*, 1917.
[9] Aristotle, *Pol.*, VII, 13, 12.
[10] *Pol.*, III, 9, 6 (Jowett trans.).

out force and compulsory power, to live without an enforcible "must." But so imposing is this "must" and so necessary is the state that all attempts to have a social life without the typical form of state have failed. For a being like man, living in time, dependent upon the active cooperation of others and the forceful protection of his sphere from the intrusion of others, social life is possible only if the individual member can with certainty rely upon a behavior of others following commonly acknowledged rules and norms. It is not the habits that make social life enduring. It is the fact that there exists a power which, when appealed to, will enforce the "habits" that will in turn enforce a behavior of all in accordance with the norms. We base our security in society upon the certainty that the rules or, if you like, the habits, of the members will be observed voluntarily and that if not so observed they will be enforced. In this way only can man living in transitory time live in society for secular happiness and se-curity. Thus society, so far as it lives by habits, necessarily demands the state as the enforcing sovereign order. There can be no evasion: social life demands the political form, the state.

IV. PERFECTION OF HUMAN NATURE IN CITIZENSHIP IN THE STATE

The state originates in man's nature. The social process of man's nature teleologically finds its final perfection in life in the state. The political status has its root in the finality of human nature. Now the concept "nature," having lost its traditional preciseness, needs some clarification. Modern sociologists of the so-called biological school are inclined to speak of a development into the state brought about by natural forces. Their idea of nature implies necessity produced by blind, laws of nature, as opposed to the spirit or mind that is freedom. For them the state is a product of nature like a beehive or an anthill. This idea was vigorously rejected by Aristotle long ago. It could never have entered the mind of Thomas Aquinas. It could arise only after the old doctrine of the essence of man as a compound substance was abandoned by Descartes, either for the one-sidedness of rational-ism, with the consequence of an exaggerated individualism making the state exclusively a product of the arbitrary will of individuals; or for a kind of open or sublimated materialism, explaining the state as a product of the blind forces of mindless nature. So the state becomes a physical superorganism.

When we speak of nature or of natural teleology we understand by it the essence of man not in the static sense, but in the dynamic sense as the final cause, as the operative principle inducing man to realize his essence as perfectly as possible in practical life; in other words essence is called nature as a dynamic principle proceeding to perfection. Hence arises the difference between moral law, which says what ought to be, and physical law, which simply states what by blind causality must be. The family has its natural basis in the difference of complementary sexes, in the sex desire, in love, and in the mutual devotion of all its members to a higher and better form of life by living together.[11] Yet marriage and family are *hic et nunc* the work of a free decision by reason and will. The root of the family, marriage originates in a free contract.[12] Similarly the state cannot come into existence without the intervention of reason and will. Man, contemplating his very social nature as the final end of the good life knows that to fulfill this end he needs certain forms of sociality These, therefore, appear before his moral will as social forms that ought to be; he is obliged to produce these by the very nature of his essence, because of the moral natural law.

The state is based on the moral necessity and the stimulation of natural law. But this itself presupposes freedom, which is an essential of man's nature. Natural law is now related to the free will of men it is nothing else than the eternal law of God, the Creator of that human nature which is not destroyed even by original sin. Therefore, in the last analysis, the state is based on God's will. "God has created man for life in community and has put man into associations of like beings so that he (man) may find in community the satisfactions and perfections of his nature which he cannot find in solitude. Therefore the political community especially, in so far as it is community, ought to accept God as father and originator."[13]

Thus the progress of thinking returns to its origin. God is the

---

[11] For this reason religious, celibate communities speak of their community as family; the orphanage tries to awaken family spirit.

[12] The Church successfully emancipated woman from the barbaric marriage-law by stressing that the marital contract must be a free contract of the bride, not of the father of the bride.

[13] Leo XIII, Allocutiones etc., III, 109 (Encyclical *Diuturnum Illud*).

primary and principal cause of creation in the order of its different natures. It is *processio Dei ad extra*. . . . But this "process" goes on according to the nature (essence, in dynamic expression) of the creatures, even though they are always sustained in their being by God, the First Cause. The secondary causes, real causes at least so far as they are rational beings, operate according to their nature; that is, rationally and freely. Theirs is not the necessity of a blind "must," but the moral necessity of a rational "ought." Human nature taken in its full content is thus the cause of the state. But this in itself means that the ultimate cause of the state is God.

The ideal process of the growth of human social forms culminating in the state may be sketched as follows: It is necessary for man to live in community to reach his perfection, which with essential finality is revealed in man's nature; man is "the" social being. Hence the realization of this nature occurs in at least two necessary social forms: the family (in a very general and broad sense) and the state.[14] The family has no substitute; any attempt to dissolve it and to transfer its social functions to other social forms will, in the long run, destroy society and man himself.[15] But the family itself in all its historical forms (e.g., the patriarchal expanded family or the tribal kin) is measured by the aim of social life: order and peace, imperfect for a life of happiness and the full expression of man's nature; it points to a higher social form essentially different from the family. The family intentionally postulates, from the fact of its imperfection as concerns man's social nature, a higher, a perfect form of community. Families living together side by side, composed of generations and based on the independence of the family heads, need for a more perfect life a specific new kind of order for their common life, a specific new authority directing the realization of their common interests in peace and order, deciding the conflicts and solving the tensions which arise out of their living together.

This new order is superfamilial. It is preserved and protected by a new authority, excelling the authority of the simple family head

[14] Family including the husband-wife, parents-children, master-servants, relations. *Oikos* (the house) and *economia* (the economic life) are essentially related to the family; so is education.

[15] An interesting proof of this statement is afforded by the futile attempts of Soviet Russia to dissolve the family, which it considered a hotbed of egoism, inimical to socialism. After years of experimenting, the Soviets practically returned to the "bourgeois" concepts of family.

or the sum of their authority all together. Only in this new form does the social process, the realization of the social nature of man, reach its end, the perfect life, the *felicitas externa* in the political order, the state. This new order comes into existence because of a moral impulse that is not realized without the free action of man himself. So this process shows the state to be a necessary consequence of the God-given nature of man, as well as the free work of human action so far as the concrete realization of the new order and its preservation are concerned.

V. The Fall of Man and the Origin of the State

This doctrine of the state's origin in human nature and its coming into existence not without free action by man is made possible by the theological doctrine that by original sin the metaphysical nature of man has not been destroyed. In other words, so deeply is the state rooted in human nature that it would have grown also in the *status naturae purae*, i.e., without the Fall. The state is not a consequence of sin. The doctors had to uphold this proposition against several sects which declared that the state originated in sin, and which contended that the redeemed Christian is free from the state. He does not need the state because the religious communiy is wholly self-sufficient, has full human, moral and, legal self-sufficiency, so that the state as the order of secular life becomes superfluous. In history, these religious communities could live in such a self-sufficiency only in the first flower of religious exuberance and of emotional exaltation. As soon as this began to weaken, these communities either disintegrated or turned into theocratic forms of political government. And from such a theocracy the step was never far to a rather tyrannical, therefore shortlived, community. The sinner, the non-conformist, or the dissenter lost not only all rights as a citizen; all too easily he lost even bare human rights. Tolerance under such a theocracy is impossible. This supernaturalism destroys nature and its justified sphere, and must be carefully distinguished from the ideal of union between Church and state, nature and supernature.

The great thinkers have maintained that the state would have developed out of human nature even in the *status naturae purae*. This doctrine was elaborated especially by late Scholasticism after the

Reformation contended that the origin of the state lay in sin.[16] It is true that the masters taught that some qualities of the state originate in sin; for instance, its coercive power. But they taught, too, that in the state of pure nature political authority would have been necessary, though only a directive, not a coercive, one. There is no need to explain the origin of the state by the Fall, because this philosophy has the state founded in the metaphysical nature of man, not in an abstract, empirical nature of man, as have later theories.

VI. The New Social Contract Theories

The more recent theories of a natural status preceding the political status (*status civilis*) have another meaning. In them there is no moral ideal necessity to change from the *status naturalis* to the *status civilis*. Their concept of human nature would allow the man of the *status naturalis* to continue in that status, but for purely utilitarian purposes. In the doctrines of Hobbes or Rousseau the theory of the *status naturalis*, brutal or idyllic, is essentially a practical theory with immediate political purposes. Such theories are by no means empty juridical fiction.[17]

On the contrary, the *status naturalis* is considered a historical fact. The *status naturalis* is abstracted from the empirical state in which these scholars live and from the idea of state itself, an ideal, or at least real, form of human existence. The origin of the state, therefore, must be founded exclusively in a free contract between men. And further, the new order, civil or political, is in its whole content at the mercy of the contracting partners. They are free to change the order arbitrarily or to abolish it, as it suits them. The new order in its wholeness is not an objective order, independent in its essentials

[16] Suarez, *De legibus*, III, 1; *De opere sex dierum*, 7. *Defensio fidei*, III, 1. Bellarmine, *Comm. ad Summan theol.*, IIa IIae, q.96. Franz X. Arnold, *Die Staatslehre des Kardinal Bellarmin* (1934).

The Reformers usually misinterpreted St. Augustine, *De civ. Dei*, IV, 4; XV, 1; XIX, 15, overlooking the antithetic style of St. Augustine, who often calls *status naturalis* what later was called *status supernaturalis*. Mausbach (*Ethik des hl. Augustinus*, I, 331) rightly blames R. W. Carlyle (I, 167), since the famous sentence, *remota itaque justitia, quid sunt regna nisi magna latrocinia* (*De civ. Dei*, IV, 4), must be translated not "because justice is made remote," but "if justice," etc. St. Augustine himself (*De Gen. ad lit.*, 8, 9, 17) seems clearly to contend that the state would have evolved even in the *status naturae integrae* or *purae*.

[17] Cf. Defoe's *Robinson Crusoe* and many other literary pictures of the gentle savage.

of the will of the partners. Nor is the social contract really a status contract which takes its validity and power from the objective end of the community. The new order is not a necessary product of human nature for its own perfection. Its authority is not an objective one, deriving its power from God, the Creator of man, and its teleological idea; it derives that power from the actual will of the partners. Therefore the *status civilis* is not a necessary outcome of human nature, but it is useful, even most useful. Authority, therefore, does not receive its power from an objective fulfillment of its objective end, but is the sum of the individual rights which the contracting partners have transferred to the person or persons in authority. Such, at least, was the teaching of Rousseau and many others of his kind.

The political purpose was to have the freedom of the individual guaranteed by making those in power dependent at every moment upon the actual will of the individuals, not upon a law binding both authority and subject. Hence there is only one justifiable form of government, the sovereignty of the people: there are not authorities, but only revocable magistratures; the state is a kind of public service. As the individual is autonomous, so the sum of the individuals must be autonomous by the identification of the governed with the governing.[18] The majority, therefore, is just as absolute a ruler as the detested absolute tyrant; there are no rights of dissenting minorities. Actually the rights of the individuals that they had in the natural status are sacrificed here as completely as they are in Hobbes' *Leviathan*. As in *Leviathan*, all rights are at the arbitrary will of the supreme power, whether a prince or the magistrates of a republic, as Hobbes taught, or the majority in a democracy, as Rousseau taught. This fact becomes evident when we see that both demand a nationally

[18] Rousseau saw the contradiction involved in his aim: to find a form of association which defends and protects with total force the person and the goods of each associate, yet which enables every one, uniting with all others, to obey only himself and remain as free as he was before. (*Contrat social*, I, 6). Hence his frantic attempts to reconcile the will of all and the general will. That attempt could not succeed upon the subjective and psychological basis of Rousseau's philosophy. Thus no objective end of the community, no objective idea of man's perfection, nor the will of God revealing Himself in nature could form the end of the state. On account of the lack of such an objective criterion the majority rule as the technically true expression of the general will remained the only admissible criterion of just and unjust. Consequently only one form of government was good, formal democracy in the technical sense, without an internal protection of dissenting minorities and with a great urge for total homogeneity that necessarily narrows down the sphere of freedom, as there exists no objective measure for what is arbitrariness and what is reason.

unified religion and think that only thus can the homogeneity and the unity of the state be guaranteed.

In other schools of thought the juridical figure of the social contract has the purpose of protecting the inalienable natural rights against any willful infringement by the government. Here the social contract serves the purpose of defining a sphere of substantial freedom of the citizen and a sphere of free, discretionary governmental action. As the government exists to protect the freedom, its regulations and its authority can only regulate the use of freedom, or put up an order for freedom of the individuals, but cannot touch the substance of freedom itself.

VII. Other Non-juridical Theories

We may distinguish several theories concerning the actual coming into existence of the state. One proceeds from a purely biological concept of human nature without consideration of reason and free will; another proceeds from the free will and only from this; and a last one proceeds from human nature in the philosophical sense. About the coming into existence of the state, there are two chief varieties of theories which exclude the moral free will of men. One has as its basis Darwin's evolutionism: the state develops out of the family by the blind forces of biological life just as the family developed from a state of sexual promiscuity. Not an objective idea, but the milieu is the creative factor. The state is only a sociological form produced without any intervention of the moral free will of man, an independent result of adaptation to biological milieu. Beehive and anthill are prototypes of this biological theory.

At the end of the nineteenth century this biological theory got a racial companion. The race, a sum of diverse social and biological characteristics, is the basic concept; the state is the blind result of the struggle of those biological groups called races. So the state becomes the visible expression of the superiority of a biologically better equipped race.[19] This theory has today become of tremendous power in Hitlerism. It explains the contempt for the idea of state as a moral

---

[19] Typical of this theory are the writings of L. Gumplowicz: *Geschichte der Staatstheorien* (new edition, 1926) and *Der Rasseukampf* (1927). Representatives of this theory are to be found among the evolutionists in practically all modern countries.

institution which Hitlerism shows; it explains, too, the utter contempt for the rights of other "inferior" races and of an international
law among states, because there is no "law" in the biological struggle of races.

Marxism, with its materialist conception of history, seems to have
a similar theory of the state. It is not the biological nature or process,
but the process and manner of production that creates the classes and
therefore the class struggle which produces the state. Where the
racial theorists say that history is the history of race struggles, the
Marxists say that history is the history of class struggles. The state is
a non-moral instrument of this struggle and will wither away as soon
as the struggle is decided. For both theories the state is the product
of blind, non-moral forces. It does not belong to the moral sphere; it
is an indifferent, lawless weapon in a material struggle. Consequently
the use of this weapon is subject to no moral law.

Another theory denying the will and reason any initiative in the
origin of the state came to the fore after the French Revolution and
gained influence among adherents of Romanticism. As a reaction
against the political theories popularized during the French Revolution, there developed in Europe an anti-revolutionary political theory
which delivered invaluable arguments to the statesmen of the Restoration. Since the revolutionary theory made the state exclusively dependent in origin, task, and order upon the autonomous wills of the
individuals, the Restoration looked for a theory that made the state's
origin as independent as possible of the will of the individuals. The
state then becomes exclusively a result in essence, origin, and continuance of irresistible natural forces revealing themselves in political
history. Of course, these natural forces had to be understood not as
merely biological, blind forces in a materialist sense. Still, human
will, human conscious action, had to be excluded.

Karl Ludwig von Haller's theory, advanced in his widely read,
voluminous work, *Die Restoration der Staatswissenschaften,* is the
best example of these anti-revolutionary theories. The real basis of
the state, he maintains, is the great indestructible law of nature,
namely, that only the superior and more powerful shall rule. To express it more clearly, wherever power and necessity meet, there arises
a relation in which the first will achieve mastery, and the latter will
have to obey in subservience. This relation arises necessarily as soon

as human beings live together, yet it is likely to be ruled by justice and to confer mutual benefit. The state, therefore, is the highest gradation of the natural relations of subservience in which all social relations consist. There is never equality and consequent coordination, but natural inequality and subordination. This is the outstanding law of social life given by God, compelling to obedience, and proved by every page in political history.

The feudal family was considered the best expression of this law. The natural authority of the father, never doubted by the children, was Haller's favorite idea. As the children do not owe the father obedience on account of a covenant, but on account of their being children, so the citizen, or better the subject, owes obedience to the mighty, the owners of lands, and the kings. The king is an enlarged father and, one is inclined to add, rather the paterfamilias of the old Roman law, with his absolutely unrestricted power over the members of the family. Quite justly Joseph von Görres called a theory like Haller's a naturalistic theory. Historically this theory of the Restoration,[20] widely accepted by political Romanticism, is understandable as a strong reaction against the revolutionary theory of the social contract and as an apt ideological basis for the policy of reaction against the political trend of "emancipation" from that very political paterfamilias-king. Although this theory found a few adherents among Catholic thinkers, it was so utterly irreconcilable with the traditional strict distinction between family and state, paternal authority and political authority, that it was soon forgotten.

VIII. THE RADICAL TYPE OF SOCIAL CONTRACT THEORIES

Contrasting with all these theories are those which deny any teleological necessity for the origin of the state from the nature of man and assert that the state comes lawfully into existence exclusively by a free social contract. The outstanding features of this radical type of the social-contract theory are individualism, utilitarianism and antihistorical rationalism.

The belief in the social contract itself is very old, and there has

[20] It was the "Restoration" of the spirit of enlightened despotism, which had always treated its subjects as feeble-minded children and spoke contemptuously of the 'limited intelligence of the subject.'

been no time when it did not find adherents. It is easily understandable that when a new order appears, with new duties and rights and with a new authority, if immediate creation by God or blind development is excluded, there must be in some way a legal act of the constituents as the cause of this new institution. But this problem is not the only one. Another problem is how and why the new order was produced. This means, too, the question of what purpose is served by the new order transcendent to either the family or a mere factual aggregation of various families or individuals.

One point is significant. One type, the radical or pure type, developed since the sixteenth century, presupposes individuals or, as Hobbes once said, adults sprung out of the soil like mushrooms, while the other type, familiar in Catholic political philosophy, always presupposes the family, and not incoherent individuals, as the first social unit.[21]

The radical type has as its main problem: How can we explain and justify the power and authority of the state over the individual, an autonomous, self-sufficient individual? There is no inner dynamic finality in human nature demanding a life in the state as the perfection of human nature; for the individual as such is regarded as spiritually self-sufficient.[22] Consequently, this type asserts that it is merely utilitarian purposes and individual motives that lead to the formation of the state. As a result, all the authority of the state is a mere bundle of conceded rights revocable at the whim of the individuals, and the common good is simply a nominalist word for the sum of the private goods of the individuals. The dangerous consequence, namely, a permanent revolution, was already clearly seen by Aristotle and Plato when they rejected this type of social contract as it was proposed by some Sophists. Another consequence of this purely subjectivist type would be that, from an optimistic conception of human nature such as Rousseau had, only immediate democracy would be admissible, and a representative democracy would be almost a tyranny. Again, from a pessimistic Hobbesian point of view, an all-devouring state absolutism would follow, because by this alone could

---

[21] The Pilgrim Fathers of New England were not adherents of the radical type.

[22] Similar thinking is found in some Protestant doctrines. No intermediary Church is necessary for the salvation of the soul, since the individual is religiously self-sufficient A Church, therefore, is not essential; a mere association for utilitarian purposes is enough. The true Church is invisible, beyond any legal forms and external social manifestation.

the naturally decomposing tendencies of the individuals be checked. What is then common to both, to the Rousseauist and the Hobbesian types, is that in the end the very purpose of the social contract is lost, that is, the rule of the law of nature in the *status civilis* and the perseverance of the inalienable rights of the individuals. With Hobbes they simply disappear in the *status civilis* in favor of the absolute power of the state. With Rousseau they are subject to the absolute will of the majority.[23] Rousseau, of course, would tell the outvoted minority that they should try finally to see that their "genuine" will agrees with the general will as uttered by the majority. As the general will is presumably a revelation of reason, that should be easily possible, because the minority's will must be unreasonable.

But the greatest difficulty of this individualist type of social contract is for it to answer the unavoidable question: How can there be an obligation to keep the original contract by those born later, who are not active partners in the original contract, by the succeeding generations which are born in the *status civilis?* Again the only available explanation would be that the very content of the social contract is reason. Thus, by the social contract every one binds only himself and obeys only himself as a rational being. But the office of every acting authority is not to discuss endlessly, but to decide which of a sum of more or less reasonable solutions of a pressing practical problem should be applied and enforced. It can be said with certainty that no logical merits of this type of social contract have given it importance, but that it found followers so far as it could ideologically help revolutionary movements against the divine right of kings or other kinds of political absolutism. Its real meaning lay in its explosive power of ideological decomposition and political destruction of absolute and therefore oppressive forms of government. Its startling weakness lay in its inability to provide constructive power, to build up a sound authority, a durable political order, because logically it means only permanent revolution.[24]

The state is essentially an order of a community of families and in-

[23] It must be remembered that Rousseau was far more totalitarian-minded than is usually thought. One has only to mention his idea that there must be a civil religion of the state. Cf. *Social contract,* IV, 8.

[24] It is interesting to contrast in this connection the ephemeral constitutions of the French Revolution, based on Rousseau, with the United States Constitution, the authors of which were influenced by Montesquieu and the Christian type of the social contract and, with very few exceptions, not by Rousseau.

dividuals in which the purposes and interests of the whole must be reconciled to the good of all and to the good of the single persons. The radical type of the social contract in the Rousseauist form was interested only in the rights of the individuals; in the Hobbesian form it was interested only in preservation of order and unity, and sacrificed each and every individual right. The radical type, therefore, is merely ideologic; it has to serve, for the immediate political purpose of a singular historical situation, either the absolute right of political authority (Hobbes) or the absolute and abstract right of the individual against a very concrete political oppression. The rights of the individuals in Rousseau's thought were actually the rights of the third estate, the bourgeoisie, as Karl Marx derisively called them, for their revolution against the ancient regime; as the rights of the individuals became in the late nineteenth century, and are still today, the rights of the workers (the fourth estate) in communist ideology against the now conservative bourgeoisie interested only in the preservation of the existing order of capitalist property. The entirely political, unphilosophical character of this radical type of the social contract is apparent, as is the theory of the so-called natural origin of the state current in the political theory of the Restoration or of the biological school.

IX. The Social Contract Theory in Catholic Political Philosophy

Against the background of the foregoing we can now come to an understanding and appreciation of the legal figure, in Catholic political philosophy, of "social contract" as the legal basis of the rise of the state, a theory which has been misunderstood and misinterpreted *intra et extra muros*.

Catholic political theory insists that the state originates in human nature. The state arises with moral necessity out of this dynamic, teleological growth of human nature that finds its self-sufficiency, the good life, in a social life possible only in the sovereign political order of the state. But the concrete coming into existence, the concrete new order of political life, the concrete organization, is actively formed by man's free and rational will. The view of the state as a moral organism is the universal view of sociality and individuality at once, of the realization of man's nature by free will, led by the idea of man as the teleological aim of human activity. Human nature is not just a blind, working, efficient cause, but is the consciously recognized final cause of man's free activity in socio-political life. The state is thus the result of a driving power of man's biological life and of the free rational activity of man recognizing his nature's realization as the ideal of his moral existence. The elements which the radical type of the social contract and the biological theory about the origin of the state in their respective one-sidedness exaggerate or forget, are seen here together. It is neither *bios* (life) alone nor *logos* (reason) alone that produces the state, but both together in interaction, as man is essentially a compound of *bios* and *logos,* since he is a rational, political animal.

The great masters doubtlessly stress the sprouting and growing of the state out of the family. But they contend that the new order of political life is essentially different from all preceding forms of social life, and needs free human acts and human initiative as the condition and cause of its birth. There is only one choice: free human initiative, or the assertion that the state, every concrete state, is the result of an immediate act of establishment by God. But to support this last there was only one historical fact traceable: the people of Israel and its covenant with God.

Thus there remains only one solution. The state individually and under ideal conditions is established by a contract, a covenant, a pact, or whatever term is used to denote that the transfer from the pre-political state to the political state ideally cannot occur without human, free action and initiative. The legal figure of the social contract means nothing else. This is what Leo XIII in a masterly fashion expresses: "Diverse families, without abandoning the rights and duties of the domestic society, unite under the inspiration of nature in order to constitute themselves as members of another greater family, the civic society." [25] The members constitute the state, they unite themselves; that means that they do so as free rational beings. The rise of the state out of a mere aggregation of independent families is at the same time a natural development of human social nature, but

25 *Acta Sanctae Sedis,* XXIV (1891–92), 250.

proceeding in the light of reason by free human activity, showing thus the twofold human essence of biological and rational life, both participating and cooperating in the origin of the state.

As the legal figure of a social contract meant no more nor less, evidently the great teachers were not eager to construct an expressive, solemn, and formal contract, such as it was necessary to construct for the rationalist individualism of the seventeenth and eighteenth centuries. One must keep in mind that the natural state was not and could not be thought important as soon as human nature was considered to be fundamentally political. Therefore no specific form of that contract is necessary: it may be a solemn covenant, as with the Pilgrim Fathers; it may be simply the silent but legally important acceptance of the leadership of the outstanding head of one of the families; it may be a simple acclamation. But some form of covenant and consent is morally and juridically necessary.

The figure of the social contract gets its importance from the fact that its necessary content is the institution of a political authority and a definition of the form and organization of government. Thus its real importance is recognized only when the origin of political authority is explored and the question arises about what in the seventeenth century was called the *pactum subjectionis*. For Catholic political theory these were the same. The social contract had as its second main purpose the institution of a definite form of government and political organization. Otherwise the new order of legal justice would not be a working order.

But theoretically the doctrine that the state arises out of human nature, but not without free human activity of the members constituting the new civil community, was of great importance, because, by refusing to exclude the free will of the constituents of the new *status civilis*, it did exclude all those theories of a divine right of kings. A basis was found for a repudiation of the traditionalist theories as propounded by the antidemocratic political theory of the Restoration (De Maistre, De Bonald, etc.), according to which divine Providence, without intervention of free secondary causes, destines the political forms, especially monarchy, in which nations ought to live. Similarly, the emphasis laid upon the necessary intervention of free will resulted in the recognition of the paternalistic theories, of Haller, for instance, as naturalistic although they had a strong and tempting appeal in their antirevolutionary cloak. But what is most important, the scholastic theory of the social contract made a historical view possible. Whatever may be said against the radical form of the social contract (especially Rousseau's), the strongest objection must be its unhistorical and rationalist argumentation, which would make immediate democracy the only just form of government. Such a statement would actually deny the individuality of nations, of phases, and of epochs in political development. The Scholastics' particular conception of the social contract left open to them the way for the appreciation of the historical developments of the individual nations.

On the other hand, the faults of the radical form of the social contract are avoided. The difficulty of this form is that it cannot constitute authority in a human moral sense. The leviathan of Hobbes is simply an absolute non-moral coercive power in which the question of a justification of its acts simply does not arise.[26] The purpose of the Rousseauist social contract is to preserve in the new political status the liberty of the individuals that they enjoyed in the natural status of Paradise. Rousseau's problem is to find a form of social community that makes it possible for the individual, though living in community, not to obey anybody but himself and to remain as free as before the joining.[27] This is the anarchistic denial of authority, and not a solution to the problem of why men ought to live in the *status civilis* and be obedient to the authority even when they themselves were never active partners at the conclusion of the social pact.

The Catholic theory is that the state originates in human nature. Human nature is a dynamic concept. The perfect realization of human nature is possible only in political life. And further, the end of the state is coincident with the individual end; therefore again, obedience to authority and authority itself are measured by an objective end, the perfection of man's nature. Authority is not a value in itself and must never be arbitrary. To live in a state, then, is a command of natural law and of God as the Creator and supreme

---

[26] It is true that according to Hobbes the leviathan is subject to natural law, but this natural law actually becomes a *jus inutile*, as with the conclusion of the social contract all rights of the individuals perish after being transferred to the "power." For Hobbes, after the conclusion of the contract, there remains only one norm of the natural law: *pacta sunt servanda.*

[27] Cf. *Contrat social*, I, 6.

Lawgiver. Thus, to be obedient to the new order, which does not derive its authority from the free will and is not a transfer of individual natural rights but a protection of them, is of natural law.

The perfect life to which human nature is intentionally and teleologically directed, requires the state. The social contract is, therefore, a status contract: by it is produced the necessary new order of political life. But though the moment of conclusion and some concrete features of that status contract are still left to the free decision of the constituents, the basic elements are beyond human will. They are preestablished in human nature and follow objectively from the purpose of the new order. The state is of the objective moral order, that is, an order by itself independent of the will of man. All social institutions have a moral substance independent of the will of their constituents. Such was the philosophical basis of Lincoln's statement that the United States as a higher form of political life is an indivisible, indissoluble union independent of the will of the states, once they had constituted the union.

X. The Controversy

We can now better understand the controversy that arose among Catholic political philosophers in the nineteenth century but that has subsided since. The controversy circled round the legal figure of the social contract as a means of representing the free human acts and initiative in the birth of the state. We have already pointed out that the antirevolutionary political theory of Romanticism disputed any free human intervention in the birth of the state. Haller spoke of an indestructible natural law, by force of which the state originates from the natural inequality of man in power. The state thus is the non-intentional outcome of power and want; power of the powerful owner, and want of the weaker for protection and fruition of the goods of life under the rule of the powerful. For both the powerful and the weak, this brought advantages and the resulting domination and subordination was open to justice. A more reasonable theory is represented by De Maistre and his followers of a conservative traditionalism. In this theory the state does indeed come into existence without conscious, intentional intervention of human free will.

Every kind of sovereignty, that of the father of the family as well as that of the ruler, is the immediate result of the will of the Creator. Every political constitution, because it is creation, surpasses the power of man. To say that a people has given itself a government is, in De Maistre's eyes, as foolish as to say that a people has given itself its character or its color. No people has chosen its government; it is Deity that has intervened directly and immediately in the establishment of government.[28]

De Maistre thus founded the state upon the direct action of Providence, denying that men, as secondary free causes, had any activity in the birth of the state. Thus monarchy, as the oldest time-honored government, becomes one of divine law freed from any constitutional limitation, even from the law of reason. For De Maistre the monarchy, and that is for him the exemplary state, is founded in the *sensus communis*, the *opinion universelle*. The secular monarchical state is similar to the papal monarchy. The latter is the creation of God by supernatural establishment; the first as well is an immediate creation of God as majestic Providence without the petty intervention of human will. As was already pointed out, Catholic political philosophy found out early that such a theory must lead, not so much to the defeat of rationalism, of the philosophism of the eighteenth century and the ideas of 1789, but to the dissolution of the Christian philosophy that had so carefully established the realm of human liberty, of natural reason, and of the temporal and the spiritual.

Traditionalism, the underlying philosophy of this theory, making the act of human reason an act of God, could easily lead to a confusion of human and divine reason in one, and would make the king's will and law, God's will and law. De Maistre's ideas were not widely accepted. But his theory in its antirationalist, antirevolutionary, and antisecularist fervor, has influenced many Catholics of the nineteenth century to disclaim the scholastic theory of the social contract. To distinguish their political theory from the prevailing individualism and subjectivism, to fight what they considered wrong in the new political theories, they played down the social contract as the legal

[28] Monsignor Germain Breton, Rector of the Institut Catholique of Toulouse, has published in *Bulletin de littérature ecclésiastique* (1927, nos. 3 and 4) an excellent criticism of De Maistre's theory.

cause of the state. They minimized the human initiative in the origin
of the state. They began to stress, even to overstress, the natural as
opposed to the intentional element in the origin of the state, its organic plantlike growth and the providentially directed forces of history: all this in an apologetic zeal against modern political ideas.
They would not, of course, follow De Maistre wholly, but they
thought that the old scholastic theory, which made the consent of the
families, the social contract, a cause of the new political order, was
an outgrowth of the particular position of late Scholasticism.[29] The
doctors of this had, so it was said, in opposition to Lutheran theology,
stressed the importance of nature, natural reason, individual activity,
and human free will as against the supernaturalism of Luther and
the other Reformers, for whom nature, because of sin, was impotent
even in the sphere of secular life.

Several nineteenth-century political philosophers, though they did
not simply deny the *consensus,* the *pactum,* as a legal figure for the
freedom of the act of political union, made it merely an external condition. They would thus point out two things. First, that the order
of legal justice, the political order in its essential substance, should
not be at the mercy of man's will. The order of legal justice embracing the fundamental rights of authority and the duty of the citizen
to obedience in furtherance of the common good, that pre-existent
order emanating from man's nature, should be withdrawn from the
power of human arbitrariness. Making the *consensus* merely the external condition for the establishment of the new public order of
political life, these philosophers thought they had so protected authority against the dangers that the Rousseauist social contract necessarily included. Secondly, they thought that thus the problem of how
to obligate those born later, not personally participating in the consensus, was best solved; for this obligation was made independent
of the consensus if that were only an external condition but not a
cause of the birth of the political order with its new duties and rights.

---

[29] Typical, for instance, is Bellarmine: *Respublica ab hominum consensu originem
habet.* Cf. Suarez, *De leg.,* III, c.3, n.1: *Ipsa communitas medio consensu et voluntate
singulorum coalescit.* And *De op. 6 dierum,* c.7, n.8: *unio politica, quae non fit sine
aliquo pacto expresso vel tacito; De leg.,* III, c.2, n.4: *Alio modo consideranda est
hominum multitudo, quatenus speciali voluntate seu consensu communi in corpus
politicum congregantur.*

XI. Legitimacy of the "Social Contract" Theory

However, these reasons do not seem to oblige us to give up the older theory of the social contract as the cause for the birth of the political order, as long as "cause" is here understood as a proximate cause and not, as Rousseau and rationalism intended, as the exclusive or sole cause. For the consensus itself is motivated as a necessary act to institute the political order for the perfection of man's nature and thus rests upon natural law and upon God's will.

We must, furthermore, not forget that the condition theory intended to avoid also the principle of popular sovereignty, since it would withdraw the political order as the element of stability in social life as much as possible from the volatile masses bent upon novelties and momentary material advantages promised by irresponsible demagogues. This was an era of materialism and relativism, of wild claims for uninhibited rights and no sense for implied duties of an economic system whose very essence seemed to be instability, of a progressive secularism that long since tried to restrict religion to the private sphere. This was an era when tyrannical majorities on the basis of popular sovereignty seemed to overturn all traditional values, thrones and altars. In such an era—it was thought—one should avoid even any words that would lead to misinterpretations of the old theory of popular sovereignty and of social contract. So arose the tendency to minimize human free will in the origin of the state, which the elder philosophers had cloaked in the legal figure of the social contract.

Yet it seems that all these considerations need not force us to give up the older theory, that the consensus is the next cause of the birth of the state. Costa-Rosetti, who always held to the older theory, protested that, when human activity as represented by the legal figure of the *pactum* of social contract was minimized, the pitfalls of legitimism could not be avoided and that the birth of the new order of legal justice remained a juridical miracle. Morally and metaphysically, the origin of the state is human nature divinely instituted. But that *hic et nunc* an individual state comes into existence, is born into life, presupposes a human free act, however strong may be the urge of natural instinct for social life and the motivation of the will by the idea of man's perfection. If we minimize human activity, we may succumb to the danger of biologism: that the state is produced by the unconscious social instinct. And that would be a contradiction of the organic view of the state. For it would overlook the fact that the state is a moral organism and therefore in idea and existence implies the element of freedom, that its principle of unity is not a blind law of nature but a free though necessary moral bond intending the common good as the condition of the perfection of man's social nature.

A true organic view will see in the state a necessary community that originates metaphysically in man's rational and social nature and comes into existence *hic et nunc* as a political body, as a new public order transcendent to the lower communities of the families and neighborhoods in ideal view by a willing covenant, a decision of free rational beings. Thus the juridical figure of status contract that gives rise to a new social status of the associates is ruled by the idea of the state. Thus the contract form does not destroy the idea of the state, but is the realization *hic et nunc* of the timeless idea. What Bellarmine said concerning the laws, we may, with slight change, say of the contract theory. "All things that concern their *existence,* depend upon him who acts (*ab agente*), but are in their *essence* (or idea) independent of him, because the essences are timeless and are a kind of participation in the divine Being. So is the political order of legal justice with its positive mutual rights and duties of governor and governed in its existence dependent upon the consent, the *pactum,* the free acts of those uniting for a body politic. But the foundation and the final cause of the order and the natural-law basis of the duties and rights in the order, that is, the *essence* of the political order, is independent of human will. That which obliges and empowers is not the juridical fact of the contract or consensus, but the natural law which is eternal and immutable as a kind of participation of the eternal divine law, which is the first and supreme rule." [30]

The above-mentioned difficulty about the obligation of those who are born into the state without being partners of the contract, is thus solved. So far as a state must exist in order that they may reach their end, earthly happiness, they are bound by this end to observe the positive rules of legal justice. Furthermore, we should not forget

[30] Bellarmine, *De laicis,* chap. 2.

that the state is not a ready-made external form, but lives and is kept in existence by the exercise of the political virtue of all its citizens. It is thus kept in existence by a perpetual plebiscite, the continuous will to live in community, in peace and justice, in order to reach the end of man. Perhaps this may become clearer if, with all necessary reservations, we compare our problem to that of the family or of marriage.

The rules of natural law for family and marriage are pre-existent, immediate data from the idea of man in their essence, therefore independent of human consent or assent. But, that these rules establishing concrete duties and rights should bind two human beings in a new social status, the marriage contract (a free status contract) is necessary as its cause. *Quoad existentiam,* the concrete marriage and family depend upon men; *quoad essentiam,* that is, what concerns the objective end and meaning, and the consequent rights and duties, marriage and family are independent of human will, however much positive family laws may vary. Continuance and validity of the essential norms, those that make the connection of man and wife a marriage, are beyond the reach of the will of the spouses.

The contract theory will become clearer, when later on we discuss the origin and coming into existence of political authority. Thence a full light will fall upon our problem. For Catholic political philosophy does not separate the *pactum unionis* from the *pactum subjectionis,* the formation of the state and the organization of political authority, the constitution. The will to a common life in a body politic realizes itself in the institution of a constitutional framework; the will to order in peace and justice is *in concreto* the will to a definite working order.

It may be held that all this discussion about the social contract, the consensus, etc., is rather futile and at least very unhistoric. But that is not so. We must distinguish between the *quaestio facti* and the *quaestio juris.* For the political philosopher the latter is the more important. And this *quaestio juris* is: How must we explain the origin and the coming into existence of the state in a normative way (*idealiter*)? And even supposing that brutal usurpation and reckless power historically have produced more states than ever were created in the ideal normative way, the problem of justice remains, that only by a consensus and acceptation by the people, and never by itself, may that brutal fact become an obligating moral rule.

Thus this Catholic theory avoids the extremes of romantic political philosophy on the one hand, and of the individualist theory on the other. Each of these exaggerated either nature or will. Romanticism, too much enamored with the unconscious organic growth, with the silently working powers of history as the providential direction of political history, lost all too easily the sense of a rational natural law in general during its fight against the rationalist concept of natural law popular in the era of the Enlightenment. Thus it reached a kind of irrational conception of historical development that leaves hardly a place for human rational will. In the historical school of law, it finally came to a negation of natural law itself. Tradition, history, and duration, the test of centuries, were enough proof of the value of institutions, which plantlike grow up from the irrational power of the life of the people. Tradition and the length of time are the sufficient and best tests of legitimacy. Political romanticism and those Catholic political philosophers who are influenced by it draw near to political legitimism. Therefore they are unable to master the problem of revolution and, fearful of the potentialities of popular sovereignty and democratic instability, they embrace authoritarian ideas, whether these are the ideas of monarchy, or of the so-called authoritarian state.

The individualist natural law of the era of Enlightenment fell into the opposite extreme. Animated by the belief that all forms of sociopolitical life are the free and rational production of human will supposedly quite free from any objective rule and metaphysical finality, it suppresses nature, the urge of nature, and nature as the final cause of the social process. Socio-political life in all its forms is the ever-changeable result of the arbitrary decisions of free individuals. All relations in social life are nothing more than contractual relations dependent in their content upon the free will of the individuals. Natural law becomes a mere form to be filled with any content; it becomes, moreover, a set of subjective individual rights wholly abstracted from the socio-political order; the end of the state becomes utility, not the perfection of the already self-sufficient, autonomous individual. While legitimism freezes political life into formalism, individualism succumbs to perpetual revolution and ends in legal and political positivism, sanctifying all political forms and facts. The oratorical pathos of the revolutionary rationalist natural law, after it had delivered its services to the bourgeois revolution, gave way to a somber contempt for justice and morality, and surrendered to the relativist acceptance of any political fact, with the contention that it had nothing to do with what "ought to be."

Precisely here it becomes evident how important it is to stay in the fruitful polar tension of natural urge and freedom. If we leave this tension, we then come either to stiffening conservativism or to perpetual revolutionism. In both cases we descend from political philosophy to a mere instrumental utilitarianism or political pragmatism, and lose the only lasting foundation of political life as well as of political philosophy, the idea of justice.

CHAPTER X

The State as a Perfect Society

I. FAMILY AND STATE AS NATURAL SOCIETIES

WHEN we showed that the origin of the state is in human nature, the basic elements of the state were thus already determined. We can best come to an understanding of the nature of the state by repeating the process of the development of man's social nature. Likewise the different opposing theories about the origin of the state will show different ideas of the nature of the state and will accordingly, by comparison, lead to a clearer understanding of the nature of the state as presented by traditional Catholic doctrine.

Man by his very nature is a social being requiring various forms of communal life with his equals in order to approach and realize that perfect form of life, the intended goal and the final purpose of his very existence, to which his nature directs him. This purpose is life according to reason, life in order and peace to realize a happiness for which he longs with an irrepressible desire. Ultimately this desire will find its fulfillment only in rest in God. This life on earth is the way to God. To live in virtue, to perfect his nature, and to work for the salvation of his soul, constitute the aim of man. But ordinarily the life of virtue or the realization of man's ideal nature requires a favorable milieu, a stable order, a certain satisfaction of the wants of a being composed of body and soul. He needs an order of peace, justice, and security in which and by the help of which this good life, this earthly happiness,[1] is reached through a virtuous life as a necessary step to the ultimate happiness.

There are at least two necessary communities in the process of the

---

[1] In this connection there is no difference between Aristotle, the Stoics, St. Thomas, Washington, and the fathers of the United States Constitution and of the Constitution of the Weimar Republic. (Cf. the preambles of these two constitutions.) St. Augustine rejected the "Gloria" ideology of the Romans, just as Christians today must reject the racial-superiority ideology or the class ideology. All are against the Christian tradition.

development of man's social nature. The first and the most natural is the family. It takes its origin from marriage, the community of man and wife. The purpose of marriage is twofold: the propagation of the race by procreation and, equally important, the education of the children; secondly, the mutual assistance and cooperation for a life of happiness in the sphere of the home by husband and wife. But the family is not only the community of spiritual and sexual completion of the husband and wife; it is also the community of education for the children. Furthermore, the family is the basic economic community, for even in a society of far-reaching division of labor, such as we have today, the family and not the individual is the basic economic unit. That is the reason why progressive social legislation demanding a living wage refers always to the wage earner as the father of a family. That is why our advertisements appeal to the mother as the head of the basic consumption unit, even in an age when complaints about the dissolution of the family are frequent. Thus the life of the individual is embedded and immersed in the family. Ordinarily each human being is in some way a member of a family, and thus it is of real significance that religious orders, whose members forego marriage, still retain the idea of the family, calling their superiors "Father" or "Mother" and their community a family of brothers or sisters. For the same reason we demand a spirit of brotherly love in our intercouse with one another.

Thus the family is a genuine and necessary community with its specific non-transferable ends, the procreation and education of children and economic activity; the family, in a broad sense, may thus be perfect for these ends of the economic life.[2] But the families increase in number; their original self-sufficiency is only ephemeral. The division of labor and social functions begins early in primitive cultures and shows that the family has not that self-sufficiency which

[2] *Oikonomia* is the science of the rules of the house, the center of the family as the producing and consuming unit. Our modern "economics" is still influenced by this idea. Any demand for freedom in the economic sphere is based on the idea of the specific and social proper value of the economic life, which is not identified and should not become identified with the state in totalitarianism. When the independence of the family and the indispensable authority of the father are made futile, the destruction of freedom will follow. It should not be forgotten that, speaking of individual freedom, we actually mean man's freedom as a member of a family or as an adult but potential founder of a family; at least the freedom of a bachelor is not meant intentionally. Inviolability of the home, freedom of the person, freedom of association, of education, all these center on the home and the family far more than on the abstract individual.

human nature demands as the ideal. The living in a neighborhood, the cooperation by families in the economic field, with the beginning of functional specialization in production, require a new community order regulating cooperative activities, protecting justice, promoting common interests by combined efforts. This community needs a new authority greater than that of any of the fathers as such. Such a community, establishing a social order, administering justice, imposing rules for its members independent of the family authority, preserving order among the families, and promoting the common interest, is the germ of a rudimentary state.

II. Self-sufficiency of a Perfect Society

The outstanding feature of this state is that the new political order with the authority administering it is a self-sufficient one. Under certain circumstances, this means an economic self-sufficiency, that the society of families and individual members are able to satisfy, by their own coordinated production, all economic wants of the community. But it also means more than that. This new political community, its order, and the decisions of that authority administering the order are legally self-sufficient, i.e., sovereign.

Ever since Aristotle the chief distinction between the economic life with its prototype, the family, and the political life with its organizational form, the state, is that the former is imperfect and therefore calls for a perfect form of social symbiosis. The state is a perfect society. We may recall what we said about the end of man as a political animal and about Aristotle's idea of the social process. It is the end of man to come to happiness in the good life which is a life of reason, of the activity of the soul according to virtue. But this virtuous life cannot be realized in the sphere of the family or of the economic life. This is engrossed too much with concern over bodily wants.[3] Furthermore, we recognize the great danger of identifying happiness with wealth and pleasure.

There is also too little opportunity for the contemplative life, for the life of reason and according to reason, a life aimed at spiritual,

---

[3] The ancients to a certain extent despised economic activity. The philosopher was a man of liberal arts, the lawyer in Rome was not paid like an artisan, but received a gift in the form of the honor-arium for his advice.

divine happiness. Thus, over and above the imperfect societies, above the family and the economic associations, there must develop a new form of social life where the contemplative life is made possible, at least for the philosopher, freed from solicitude for the economic life. And this new form is the political life, the city-state, where all functions of human life, all professions and vocations, are rendered attainable in a well-established order that securely rests in itself and gives to man social security (especially to the philosopher, the "wise man"), and affords the freedom to realize the idea of man. Thus, therefore, in the political life the social process reaches its perfection.

III. "Self-sufficiency" in Pre-Christian Political Philosophy

This idea of the state as a perfect society, as Aristotle developed it, would make the state the omnipotent pedagogue. Hence it has been criticized as a kind of state socialism, for his idea of man reaches its highest and last realization in the citizen of a *polis*.

It is evident that this teaching could not be taken over unchanged into a Christian philosophy of the state. The highest end of man in Christianity is not to be a citizen in the earthly city, but in the city of God. Man's ultimate end is the glory of God, the participation in divine life, the salvation of the soul. Therefore, if the idea of the state as a perfect society were to be taken over by Christian philosophy, that notion must undergo a change.

Yet even in ancient Greece and by the Stoics of Rome this change had been at least inaugurated. St. Justin Martyr once said that Socrates could be called a Christian,[4] because his knowledge and wisdom went beyond the political life to a contemplation of being itself. What St. Justin meant is best revealed in the death of Socrates. Up to the time of his last trial, he accepted the common Greek doctrine that man's nature is to reach its happiness in political life; therefore that the laws of the *polis* are the ultimate rules of human life and human virtue. In his trial he was accused of godlessness and of violating the laws of the state in his teachings. He answered that the *daimonion* (his conscience, we may be allowed to call it) demanded his acting against the laws, his following rather truth and virtue. This was shocking to

---

[4] In *Apologia pro Christianis;* Migne, *P.L.,* VI, 397, 399.

the Greek mind.[5] It meant nothing else but that the *polis* is not the last end of man, that man is transcendent thereto, and that the "political animal" is not the final concept of man. Man, that is, his soul, his conscience, tends to a higher life beyond the state. Socrates could have fled from the *polis* of Athens as others had done when accused in the same way: Anaxagoras and Protagoras, for instance. He chose death, thus announcing his new discovery, and giving to the Greeks, who knew only of the hero's death on the battlefield as a "happy" death, the spectacle of the happy death of the philosopher, of a man who taught for the first time that the immortal *bios theoreticos* is beyond the *bios politicos*.[6]

From the Stoics the Greek concept of the state, the ultimate stage of social development, suffered further important change, after which it could be taken over by Christian philosophy. Theirs was the idea that, beyond the state and its self-sufficiency, there is a broader community: the human race. Marcus Aurelius thus put it: So far as I am Antonine, Rome is my home; so far as I am man, the world is my home. Moreover, we shall remember that from the Stoics the Roman jurisprudence took the idea of a natural law as the constitution of the *civitas maxima,* embracing as a larger unit with a larger end the Greek city-states, "We are members of one body, equals among equals" (Seneca). Thus, even before St. Thomas took over the idea of the state as a perfect society, this idea had undergone a great change and could consequently then be adopted without much difficulty.

IV. The Transformation of the Idea of Self-sufficiency by Christian Political Philosophy

The idea of a Christian personality, the belief that one must obey God rather than man, that the things of Caesar are different from those of God, that the ultimate end of man is the salvation of his soul which is beyond the reach of the state, and that the states themselves, though self-sufficient and sovereign, exist as coordinated equal members of a community of nations, all this had from now on to be considered when the state was called a perfect society. Thus was the way

[5] The same conflict occurs in Antigone of Sophocles' *Antigone,* which also points to the fact that there are unwritten laws higher than those of the state.

[6] I follow here the interpretation of Socrates' philosophy by Karl Bucheim in his profound book, *Wahrheit und Geschichte* (Leipzig, 1935).

made ready for the Church as a perfect spiritual society, beyond the state and correlated with the ultimate community, the human race. The Church moves at the side of the state, independent, related to the citizens of all states, to the members of all cultures, races, and civilizations.

But we can still uphold the characterization of the state as a perfect society. But it is secular happiness that is the end of the state; the perfect sufficiency of earthly life, then, grounded on the basis of the new Christian idea of man, is its goal.

The state ceases to be the omnipotent pedagogue. But it still has a pedagogical task, to make a good citizen, which is one of the necessary forms of human existence. But this task of the state is now absorbed into a new hierarchy of human tasks and is no longer the final and supreme goal.

The state thus becomes a unity and an order (*unitas ordinis*), a unity of man's social activities, an order of man's associations for specific purposes. Under the protective order of the state, man's social nature develops in morals and law, in culture and economy, in civilization and sciences. Not that the state is creative. Rather, the individual persons, in their free associations and in their group life, are creative. But the state as an order existing among free creative persons protects and preserves the creative powers of its citizens; it makes order and freedom possible for them; it strives that none of the endeavors of human social nature prevail hypertrophically over the others, but that they all grow as balanced parts of a well-organized order in unity. The state is a universe whose constituents, without sacrificing their individuality, achieve the common good. This they do by converting to unity something which is more than they themselves could reach in disconnected efforts. The state, therefore, is unity in diversity; but it is not uniformity.

The self-sufficiency of social life must not be understood in the first place to be economic self-sufficiency. It is rather the social and political self-sufficiency of unity and order. Economic self-sufficiency is claimed not for itself but as a means of political self-sufficiency: for legal and moral self-sufficiency in internal affairs and for independence in foreign affairs.

Hence the state is a self-sufficient, legal, and social (therefore economic) order of families and of individuals so far as they move from their individual sacrosanct spheres to form associations for satisfying human needs and economic wants, for mutual help in charity, for the pursuit of happiness in their physical and mental life, in truth and justice, in the realization of the idea of man. Seen in this light, the *unitas ordinis,* the state, is the concrete order of law under which the individuals devote themselves in liberty to realizing the good life.

The state, as a concretely realized unity of order organizing a multitude of families, individual persons, and groups, is necessarily related to a certain territory as the permanent living space of these families and persons. Likewise, for the creation, adaptation, and protection of the concrete order, to make effective the unity of order, there is needed a supreme power of judgment and decision concerning this order. This is equivalent to saying that within the order there is need of a closed circuit of decision, a sovereign authority. Since, therefore, the *ordo* is the result of the willing consent of the people and the supreme power (the government), this latter is not above the order but in it. Actually the state may be called a daily plebiscite. The state as *unitas ordinis,* creating unity in the multiplicity of families and persons and affording this unity a forceful common will able to direct the multitude to the common good, in its moral aspect is essentially the result of conscious cooperation of the associated persons and exists concretely in the constitutional order. It is the constitution, as the historical result of the *consensus communis* of all the constituent members of the multitude, that gives to a state its individuality. Hence self-sufficiency is integral to the political order. This self-sufficiency constitutes the supremacy of the order. The formulation, functioning, and competence of the sovereign will of the state is always related to the order and the common good. But the order is created anew each day by the consensual cooperation of its members. Therefore a state is rightly called tyranny when this cooperation is merely the consequence of detailed commands of the government and is attained only by compulsion, terror, and espionage.

Hence self-sufficiency is not, like sovereignty, a formal property of the will; it is rather an actual mode of social being, of social existence, which from the very idea of man ought to exist.

Self-sufficiency, then, is a political concept signifying the completeness of a comprehensive order, essentially independent from any other order of the same kind. Only as a tendency and under given historical circumstances does the concept embrace economic self-sufficiency, and this tendency is bound to recur under an international order that is weak. In fact, there seems to exist a proportion between the likelihood of its recurrence and the strength or weakness of the working of the international order. Furthermore, this self-sufficiency is legal inasmuch as the state reveals itself as an order with all the original rights, competences, and powers that are necessary to produce the secular sufficiency of community life. This it should do in regard to material life (social, economic, and technical organization), in regard to the intellectual and moral life (the legal order, legislation, law-enforcement, and administration, the secular moral order of civic and social virtues, of culture and public welfare), and in accordance with the concrete geographical, climatic, and historical conditions.

V. Self-sufficiency and Sovereignty

These original rights and powers make it possible for the state to reach its purpose independently, that is, without subordination to any power like itself, of the same nature. Consequently the international order is an order of coordination and not of subordination; and sovereignty, as we said, is a formal property of the will, whereas self-sufficiency is the material content of the idea of the state. It must be noted that this self-sufficiency regards its independence not in the light of absolute isolation like that of the leviathan. It is rather a potential openness to other units of the same order; nevertheless this self-sufficiency works within the body politic and not outside it. The states themselves, however, as a plurality, form the international commonwealth with its own end, the international common good. Now it should be clear that it is the functioning of this international order as such, its security, and peaceful working only which is the precondition for a relaxation of the completeness of the self-sufficiency. But the latter tends most surely to tighten up again as soon as the working of the international order becomes ineffective. Accordingly in total war the self-sufficiency is absolute, because total war denies international order absolutely. If, then, a nation makes self-sufficiency its absolute goal, this can mean only that the existing international order is utterly weak, or that that nation is preparing for total war, is denying the validity of the international order.

Moreover, this self-sufficiency, as the content of the idea of the state, excludes the idea of an absolute sovereignty, though it necessitates the idea of a relative sovereignty related to the common good or of a supremacy *in suo ordine*. Though within the sphere of the state, the individual person, the family, the socio-economic groups, the administrative self-governing bodies rooted in the neighborhood, town, or county or in the national divisions of the component parts of the body politic, all are original entities and original social organizations. These the state did not create and may therefore never destroy, just as the loyalty to them is original and ordinarily is not engulfed by the loyalty to the state. The state as an order of subordination may direct these associations to the common good. To destroy them would mean to rob the persons of a protective shield and to transform them into social atoms, into indifferent objects that now, without intrinsic rights and freedoms, are subject to a centralized bureaucratic power. Such a power substitutes its commands for the ordered activities and free initiative of the persons, families, and groups therein governed. Such absolute sovereignty in the interior is opposed to the Christian idea of the state, because the state is order among persons, their free organizations, and original groups.

On the same basis, sovereignty cannot mean, just as self-sufficiency does not mean, absolute exclusiveness, unchecked absolute power in relation to other states. Out of the plurality of states in which the whole human race dwells, a community is formed, though its existence is naturally in no way so intense and immediate as that of the state. Upon the states and the individual persons as citizens of the world there falls a new loyalty to the community of nations to which the states are open and a new loyalty to all mankind, to every person who participates in the dignity of man.[7] The different orders and

---

[7] The strict pacifist is such from either religious or humanitarian motives. If from the first, he sees an open conflict between his loyalty to God and that demanded by the state; if from the latter, the conflict lies between the loyalty to humanity as a whole and that demanded by a part of it, the state. Both undervalue the state as a necessary order of human existence and show a somewhat anarchic trend, a fundamental distrust in any kind of power over men. The humanitarian pacifist would, of course, accept a world state because his loyalty is to humanity. But it may be feared that then the real problem would only have changed labels, the foreign conflict now becoming an internal conflict (civil war, secession) with a materially unchanged character of warfare.

their related loyalties are, of course, parts of the whole of the order
of creation and all ought to join in the perpetual *Benedicite* of all
creatures for the glory of the Creator. In correspondence with this
conception sovereignty has been defined as that dominion of a ruling
authority in a given territory over its inhabitants, above which only
the order of international law holds sway. The basic idea, therefore,
is that the states do not live in a Hobbesian *status naturalis* of warlike anarchy and selfishness. This essentially anarchic *status naturalis*
of the states as positivism conceives it—to construct the theory of international law that rests exclusively upon the arbitrary and absolutely
sovereign will of the states—is unreal. It is as unreal as the *status
naturalis* propounded by Hobbes with its war of all against all.

Against this idea, Christian philosophy opposes the idea that humanity, a real though less intense form of human social existence,
has its natural constitution in the form of the law of nature, in human rights, and in a bill of rights of the states and that it demands a
true loyalty from man as well as from the states, which are organizational members of the human commonwealth. Therefore positive international law, so far as it is natural law applied to the states, is
independent of their will. Hence sovereignty is restricted by natural
law (and of course by divine law). Only the positive determinations
and derivative conclusions from that natural constitution of humanity are created by the states.

All this may become clearer if we take into consideration that the
Church, the spiritual community, is called a perfect society with
spiritual self-sufficiency. And, because of its spiritual end, it has also
derived legal, moral, and temporal self-sufficiency. That this perfect
society is sovereign is expressly stated in canon law.[8] Since state and
Church are both self-sufficient, perfect societies, intended to live
peacefully together, but each sovereign in itself, this is understandable only if they dispense different orders: the temporal and the spiritual order. Moreover, their respective sovereignty is relative to these
orders, or relative to their ends, the temporal common good and
the spiritual redemption of man as two different and distinguished
spheres in which man lives. Self-sufficiency here means that, although
Church and state have a field of collaboration and of condominion,

[8] Can. 100, in connection with can. 196, 218, 1553 § 1, 1495. See *infra*, chapter entitled
"Church and State."

they have each a realm in which they are sovereign, because they fill and control that realm independently.

VI. Sovereignty over a Territory as a Property of the State

Our discussion of the meaning of self-sufficiency leads logically now to a distinctive property of the state, namely, its being essentially related to space, to a particular portion of the earth, as a geographical unit. In consequence of this property, the wrong organic theories of Kjellen, from which sprang geopolitics and the demand for living-space, have then to be discussed.

Most of the communities of men are predominantly personal communities, i.e., they organize persons without direct relation to and universal control of the territory on which these persons live. They are not personal units and territorial units simultaneously and they do not exclude other communities of the same kind from a particular piece of territory. Religious communities, for instance, are eminently personal communities; in the same state various such communities can therefore exist beside one another. Labor unions similarly are personal communities first and principally; so is the family. True, all these communities are related to territory, to space; but they do not exclude other communities of the same class from control of the space. Churches and unions have territorial divisions. But they follow in these divisions the primary territorial control of the state. Dioceses are circumscribed as a rule according to the space and the territorial subdivisions of the state; so are unions.

It is only the state that has territorial sovereignty. The state's end is as much related to space control as it is related to persons. Thus the territory which a state claims is impenetrable to other states; it is the law of a particular state that rules supremely in a given territory and thus excludes the validity of law, the competence, or the sovereignty of any other state. The supremacy of national law has thus meaning, too, in the sense that over a given territory this law is self-sufficient in origin, competence, and effectiveness. While the Church has an original sovereignty and self-sufficiency primarily over its members, the state has this simultaneously over its citizens and the territory, and consequently over all persons living or sojourning upon its territory. This sovereign rule over territory is essential for the state's independence. Hence we can undestand the demand by the papacy for sovereignty over a territory as the necessary condition of its spiritual independence.[9]

This original and direct universal rule of the state's law over a territory and through it over persons is what distinguishes the state from all other communities. Consequently self-sufficiency includes the universal and supreme rule of the state's law in a particular territory.

This assertion must not be misinterpreted in the sense of an absolute rule, or of the totalitarian principle: nothing outside the state, nothing except the state. It means: that the state's law is common to all residing in the territory; that it does not acknowledge the validity of laws of other states in this territory except by international agreement; that the state's law is supreme and universal, whereas the "laws" of other communities in the state are particular and subordinate laws, as are the constitution and bylaws of a union or of college, or the charter and ordinances of a town. Consequently territorial and personal exemptions from the jurisdiction of the state, presumably exclusive, are not a refutation of this rule, but are exceptions that prove the rule. In earlier times we find, for instance, that the clergy had a greater or smaller right of exemption from the rule of the state's common law on account of concordats. Then the canon law ruled over the exempted persons.[10] In yet earlier times, during the mi-

[9] Cardinal Gasparri (October 24, 1926) established as a necessity for the solution of the Roman Question that any agreement between Italy and the Apostolic See must guarantee to the latter full liberty and independence. He required that this independence must not only "be effective and real but visible and manifest with a territory in exclusive property and under the Apostolic See's jurisdiction, as it belongs to veritable sovereignty under all conditions inviolable." Cf. Charles Loiseau, *Saint-Siège et Fascism.* (Paris, 1930), p. 116.

[10] This juridical exemption of the clergy from the juridical sovereignty of the state, partly based on the fact that a truly common law was widely absent in the feudal structure of the medieval "state," must be distinguished from the acknowledgment of the canon law of the Catholic Church in matrimonial matters as we find or found it in Concordats with modern states. When in this way the state, (its law and courts) acknowledges the canon law in matrimonial matters and thus refuses suits for divorce by a Catholic citizen validly married according to the canon law, the state acts as the federal state does in reference to the autonomy and right to self-government of the member states, acknowledging their rights to self-government and refusing to review the acts of such states as long as these remain in their constitutionally established field. The difference lies in the fact that the validity of the canon law rests legally on an international treaty, the concordat, and the rights of the member states rest on the federal constitution.

gration of nations and just after, i.e., before the new nations were definitely established, the personality principle ruled under the influence of rather primitive Germanic law. This principle means that the tribal laws, so to speak, are personal appurtenances, wander with the member of the tribe, and have no territorial validity; therefore it demands no validity over members of another tribe though they may live in the territory of the first tribe. A person's law wanders with him.

In more recent times we find the exemption of consular jurisdiction and international settlements which Christian nations exacted for their citizens from the law of infidels, especially of the Turkish Empire, of China, and of Persia. These exemptions, originating in international agreements, arise from a distrust of the "foreigners" in the jurisdiction and administration of justice in those countries. They are an application of the personality principle, and thus the law of the foreigner, so to speak, permeates into the territory of the "non-Christian" state, or the "non-civilized" state, i.e., a state which does not acknowledge or is unable to apply those general legal principles which are common to all "civilized" nations. It is quite understandable that in our time nations like China consider such exemptions of foreigners from their national law as an unjustified penetration of foreign law in the territory of their common law, as an insulting discrimination and as a diminution of their legal self-sufficiency and their sovereignty.

Still another fact illustrates the essential relations of state and territory: the exclusiveness of political loyalty which supersedes *in suo ordine* all other loyalties. It was against this loyalty that Hitler's blood-nationalism was directed. This form of nationalism contends that a personal loyalty to the nation of birth, like an indelible note, follows the man of German blood and supersedes all other loyalties, especially that which is owed to the state in which the German national settles and of which he becomes a citizen. Such a principle of primeval loyalty to the nation of one's birth is rightly considered an illegitimate penetration of the territory of a sovereign state by loyalties that in case of conflict must dissolve the political order of the state, the common law of which the immigrant citizen accepts.[11]

---

[11] Cf. Raymond E. Murphy et al., National Socialism. Basic principles, their application by the Nazi Party's Foreign Organization and the use of Germans abroad for Nazi aims.

From this political loyalty which by its very nature is exclusive in relation to all other states must, of course, be distinguished the love and reverence the immigrant citizen may cherish for his national culture which is independent of the political existence of his native country. Thus it was the political loyalty which the founders of the United States denied to England; but the English language, the English literature and folklore, even to a large degree the English common law, continued to belong to the national heritage. Political loyalty, exclusive as it is against loyalty to other states, shows thus the nature of the self-sufficiency and of the essential territorial character of the state, distinguishing the latter from all other communities.

This discussion shows the error of a pluralism that puts, for instance, the labor union and the state on the same level. The state, as a self-sufficient territorial community with the supreme authority to decide without appeal all questions of a political, social, and legal order, has a pre-eminence which is not due to any other community, not even to the Church. For this has sovereignty and self-sufficiency in an order different from that of the state. On the other hand, the impenetrability of the territory of the state by the national law of another state does not exclude the fact that international law penetrates the national domain, and thus restricts the sovereignty of the national law. There exists, for instance, a tendency in international law to give to individual persons a bill of international rights, to grant them immediate access to international courts (especially in questions concerning the protection of national minorities). But it seems clear that international law is first and predominantly a law of nations, and only indirectly establishes claims of individuals.

If the state or its agent violates a general rule of international law and in doing so violates the person or the property of the citizen of another state, then it is not the national law of the latter state that rules, but objective international law which is superior to national law. If, therefore, one state protects the person and rights of its citizens living in another state, the basis for this protection is international law itself. To realize this international law is the obligation and right of each state as a member of the juridical community of nations. And if one state or its agent has violated such rights of a

---

U.S. Government Printing Office, 1943; Part II, pp. 67 ff., 93 ff., and the documentary evidence, pp. 178 ff.

foreigner as are acknowledged by international law (e.g., the right
to life, liberty, property, access to the national courts and protection
by them), this represents a violation of international law and establishes primarily the liability of the violating state in international
law and before international courts.

Thus self-sufficiency and sovereignty, the impenetrability of the
state's territory to the national law of another state, do not exclude
international law. The international rights of man, living as foreigners (or even as stateless) are, as demands of natural law and as
legal reflexes of objective international law, superior to national
law. The various orders of law—natural, positive national, international, and ecclesiastical—order the social life of man simultaneously and according to their proper spheres: natural law, as fundamental and general, rules and protects man as person; positive
national law, as determination and derivation of natural law, rules
and protects man as citizen of the state, in his individual personality,
and in his many associations; international law, as a determination
of and derivation from natural law, rules primarily the community
of nations and its members, the states. But as the state consists of
persons and for their sake, it becomes their rule and protection as
men. Apart from these other systems, ecclesiastical law embraces man
as a religious being. This law does not serve the glory of an extra-
individual, substantial being, the Church, but it serves man for the
supreme task, the glory of God and the salvation of man's soul. Natural law and ecclesiastical divine law are supreme as God-made law;
the other laws are as man-made laws relative. But this fact does not
hinder these man-made laws from being supreme and independent
in suo ordine under God-made law.

VII. Geopolitics

The territorial character of the state, self-sufficiency, and sovereignty, can lead to errors about the nature of the state, as can be
seen from the theories of "living space" and absolute economic autarchy, the biological theory in the sense of Kjellen, and their newest
upshot, geopolitics. Like other political "heresies," these theories
take one element, and not even the most important one, of the complex idea of the state, isolate and exaggerate it. Then they make it

the exclusive basis of their theory, thus dstroying the due order and weight of the elements which form the whole idea.

Thus the demand for living-space (*Lebensraum*)—another name for full economic self-sufficiency—exaggerates a quite natural longing of the nation to be in its political existence free from the economic power of other states. Two extremes are to be avoided. The one is full autarchy which actually no state can claim though there exist states with geographical and climatic conditions that may potentially afford a policy of full autarchy. Even where autarchy is possible, historical developments, political reasons of alliances or affinity, time-lags in economic and technological development, or particular advantages of other nations in production, make full autarchy actually a regression in international life. The other extreme would be represented by a country which is economically almost wholly dependent upon a single product, because it one-sidedly developed only that at the expense of other more complex products. Such a country's political existence is too much dependent on factors entirely beyond its control for it to have a reasonable degree of independence.

The demand now for full and actual autarchy cannot be realized without the destruction of economic interchange, the material basis of the community of nations. It cannot be realized without conquest and subjugation of other nations or their ejection from their traditional living-space, guaranteed and protected by international law.

Consequently such a demand for living-space and full autarchy implies a Hobbesian *status naturalis* of a war of all against all and is the denial of a community of nations. On the other hand, the community of nations and each of its members have the duty to help in solving a genuine living-space problem of an overpopulated state. Such overpopulation in the historically occupied territory of a nation is a possibility. But the right solution is not war and occupation of other nations' territory but promotion of international trade, liberalization of immigration into undeveloped districts (colonies) or into countries with empty spaces. There exist states that cannot territorially expand, if overpopulated, without destroying the equal rights of neighboring nations. If geographical situation, climatic conditions, historical development, and lack of natural resources produce overpopulation in a nation, i.e., when the nationally controlled territory is insufficient as the economic basis for national existence, then other nations, the "Haves," have the duty to help such a nation by exchanging their raw materials for the finished products of the overpopulated nation, by admitting its people to undeveloped colonial territory, etc. The right to independence and liberty of all states, small and great, is intrinsically counterbalanced by the duty of all states to mutual help in the development of economic interdependence as the material basis for an international community of ideals and morality. The economic nationalism of naturally wealthy states, able to indulge in autarchy, provokes in less fortunate states the demand for living-space by conquest.

The theory of the nation as a biological organism is connected with the question of space, and it exaggerates the territorial element. It unites geography as a descriptive science of the earth's surface, of the flora and fauna, of climatic conditions, and of the natural resources of different parts of this surface, with the biological concept of the nation, which is hypostasized into a non-moral being, animated by an enigmatic vital force which is the substitute for the reason and free will of man. It is the theory of the struggle for existence and the survival of the fittest applied totally in a most inhuman way to the state as a form of life.[12] Consequently an irrational dynamism of growth and an insatiable urge for territorial aggrandizement are considered the very nature of the state beyond the moral categories. Clothed in the scientific language of the philosophy of life and of biologism, this insatiable urge for power is declared the law of political life. "No really great power can ever be satiated." Another camouflage of this theory of lawless power politics is that of so-called natural borders and that of full economic self-sufficiency, which logically of course contradict the thesis of the insatiability of the really great power. Wars are then a non-moral biological "process"

---

[12] Kjellen's title for his book is *Der Staat als Lebensform*, wherein life is not the life of the spirit or the life of a soul and body compound ruled by the intellect and subject to moral law, but is law unto itself. Kjellen is not the only promoter of this theory though he was perhaps the most popular. It would be easy to give the whole genealogy of this application of a fundamentally anti-intellectual naturalist philosophy in politics and political philosophy which developed in the same ratio as men abandoned Christian faith and its philosophical *praeambula* in the *philosophia perennis*. Edmund Walsh, S.J., has published a competent *Essay on Geopolitics* in *Political Economy of Total War* (School of Foreign Service, Georgetown University, Washington, D.C., 1942), pp. 93 ff., where he gives attention to the philosophical background of geopolitics and of the biological theory of the state more than other critics do.

beyond reason and free will, beyond justice and the moral law.

Kjellen explains the First World War in saying that Germany "needed" the Suez Canal and the Dardanelles. Because the other powers refused to satisfy this "need of life," war had to be the result. This theory is simply a rationalization of the thesis that might is right, expressed in the scientific terms of nineteenth-century naturalism and thus made palatable. Machiavelli is more honest; and he was more "human," too, because politics was to him still human acts, free and rational, of individual persons however motivated by selfishness, lust for power, and other human passions, and not the impersonal life-process of an inhuman superorganism.

Geopolitics, a word we find already in Kjellen's book (*Geopolitik*, i.e., geography and the state, is one of the main parts of the book), became more popular through the German general Haushofer who, picking up the more casual remarks of earlier political geographers, integrated them into a system. In this system the territorial element of the state is united with the Nazi thesis of the racial nation-state and the myth of blood and soil. It serves in a scientific garb to justify world conquest by the Nordic superior race, not by the well or badly reasoned decisions of fallible statesmen, but by the mystical laws of the blood that supremely rule over the impotent minds of man.[13] The

[13] Numerous books and articles have been published about geopolitics; e.g., Strausz-Hupé, *Geopolitics* (New York, 1942); Hans W. Weigert, *Generals and Geographers* (Oxford University Press, 1942); Johannes Mattern, *Geopolitics* (Johns Hopkins University Studies in History and Political Science, 1942). Heretics induce the orthodox theologians to study again and to formulate anew the truth which the heretic distorted. So the serious political philosopher and scientist can learn valuable lessons from the fallacies, distorted theories, and open frauds of the living-space, biological, and geopolitical theories in picking up the little grain of truth that is found even in the greatest error. How could such theories otherwise be humanly bearable? Though political philosophy may incline to forget about the geographical situation, the security of border lines against foreign attack, the free access to the freedom of the seven seas, and the economic potential of war as a material basis for genuine political independence, these facts are nevertheless of utmost importance especially for the practical statesman. Political philosophy does well to take such facts into consideration, because the realization of its moral ideals depends not only upon good will but also upon an appropriate weighing of these facts. If political philosophy forgets, for instance, the urge of countries for national security behind natural frontiers, the demand for the freedom of the sea, the urge for a free access to the seas for a land-enclosed great power, if it forgets the industrial resources as potential of war of one country as against the lack of an equal potential of war of a neighboring country, political philosophy will become utopian, bookish, and ineffective. The "heresies" warn us against satisfaction with easy generalizations, against acceptance of truisms as profound wisdom, against the evasion of practical tests of our principles.

determining function which economic classes and economic conditions of production have in Marx' historical materialism, these same
determining functions in the life of mankind are here attributed
to the races and geographical condition. Geopolitics is, then, the
study of the relationship that exists between the various social and
political sciences and the geographical situation, the space relations
of nations. It studies the relation between power, geography, and
military strategy as earlier writers did, but it studies these not in a
detached and merely demonstrative sense. On the contrary, they all
serve as means for the dominant practical purpose of telling the leader
of the superior race how he must act. Geopolitics asks an outspoken
dynamic question and answers it by practical advice, by drawing
blueprints for conquest. Thus it has a remarkable affinity to Machiavelli; he, too, gives advice, draws plans for political action, teaches the
tricks of statecraft. But his study is man as a passionate selfish being, not the mysterious biological forces of superorganisms.

Geopolitics thus was at the same time a practical political plan of
conquest and a mighty instrument of propaganda ridding man of
moral inhibitions, justifying power politics and ruthless suppression
of other states by the mystical appeal to the supra-individual life force
of the racial nation-state. The individual person, who alone has a
conscience, can now submerge in that enigmatic being, the superorganism. Thus he is relieved of all moral responsibility in the degree to which he, as individuality, disappears to become a fully
embodied cell of the superorganism while the latter becomes a non-
moral vital process determined by geopolitics. Politics as a moral
science, the state as a moral person, the statesman as subject to natural
law and justice, to charity—all that disappears. Earlier times saw in
the education of the prince the main task of politics. Our democratic
modern times sought to see it in the education of the citizen. Now
these "heresies," isolating and exaggerating one element of the state
and combining it with false biological theories of the nature of the
state, have degraded politics to an immoral technique of conquest
and tyrannical power. Thus they deny that the state is justified only
as the *ordo rerum humanarum* to which vital forces, geography, and
space serve as means and never as ends.

VIII. THE RELATIVE CHARACTER OF SELF-SUFFICIENCY

Hobbes was the first, since the beginning of the Christian era, who made sovereignty legally and morally absolute, without intrinsic limits,[14] engulfing man in his entire existence. Against this sovereignty, accordingly, there is appeal neither to God and to the law of nature nor to the people. The only appeal is to internal war, and Hobbes does not tire of pointing out that the sovereign must therefore be so powerful that an appeal of the subjects to arms will have no chance to succeed. In Hobbes' concept of sovereignty there is lost the essence of relative sovereignty, the idea that it involves, in the case of abuse, a legal or moral appeal to the law of nature, to the dignity of the human person (expressed positively in the bill of rights), to God and the divine law against tyranny. He ignores all these vigorous distinctions, for he abolishes natural law, he lets it disappear in the will of the sovereign. He does not acknowledge inalienable rights of the person; such rights are alienated by conferring them on the sovereign in the pact of subjection. He does not acknowledge the spiritual body, the Church, as a perfect society; he makes it a department of the state. He forgets about the rights of the intermediary organizations between the individual person and the state: the family, the vocational and professional groups, which he compares to worms in the body of a living man. Hobbes' ideal state became interiorly the prototype of absolutism, the centralized police state, regarding the Church as a gendarme useful for policing the minds; exteriorly it expressed itself in power politics in foreign affairs.

Since the eighteenth and nineteenth centuries this Hobbesian concept of sovereignty has been losing ground. Modern constitutionalism has taken up the earlier tradition, and sovereignty begins again to be related to the content of social life, making the distinctions in that content once more workable. The spiritual order is recognized as transcendent to the temporal order. The bill of rights, with its positive formulation regarding the proper sphere of self-initiative and

14 It is true that Hobbes, like Bodinus, lets the natural law and the divine law limit sovereignty. But, with Bodinus this actually had a substantial meaning; with Hobbes it has none whatever. For with Hobbes the *jus naturale* dies, becomes a *jus inutile*, as soon as the sovereign power is established. The sovereign power is the final interpreter and dispenser of natural and divine law. Thus the difference between natural law and positive law disappears and monolithic, total sovereignty is born.

integrity of the individual person and his social patterns of existence, such as the family, and free organizations for education and for economic purposes, is now an integral part of our civilization. The whole field of arbitrary power-decision in international relations has been restricted by the growth of international institutions and juridical bodies with competence to decide authoritatively. Such are international courts and commissions of arbitration, treaties concerning international economic and intellectual collaboration, the League of Nations, international labor organizations.

Thus the idea of the inalienable rights of the person or of national or racial minorities now permeates the rigid, impenetrable borders of sovereignty and makes their acknowledgment the condition of membership in the international community. It is indeed true that, since modern totalitarianism lifted its ugly head, all this has been destroyed, at least so far as the totalitarian states are concerned. But this very fact has compelled the states of Western civilization, still nourished by their age-long Christian tradition and substance, to reconsider the basis of their common life. We may also hope that it has made them morally fitter for the rebuilding of a Christian order based on an invigorated, rediscovered tradition.

This is a tradition which stresses self-sufficiency as the character of the state but denies absolute sovereignty, conscious of the "openness" of the individual state to the community of nations. It is aware of the service character of the state in relation to humanity, eager to cooperate in the establishment of an international order: the consequence of the natural pluralism of the states. Thus, as there exists a hierarchy of moral ends, there follows a hierarchy, a teleological order of human communities to accomplish these ends and a hierarchy of loyalties of man to these same communities. Ideally, a conflict of loyalties is possible only when this hierarchic teleological order is disturbed. All human endeavor works ceaselessly toward an order without conflicts of loyalties. The purpose of law and order, from the family on to the international community, is to give each loyalty its place.

CHAPTER XI

The State and Other Social Groups

I. THE QUALITATIVE DIFFERENCE BETWEEN FAMILY AND STATE

THE concept of "perfect society," designated as an essential criterion of the state, contains a qualitative difference between state and family, whether the modern two-generation family or the clan, the tribal group, the kindred. Even though a state arises out of the growing clan or great family in the course of historical evolution, that does not hinder us from conceiving a qualitative difference between state and family, just as the oak is teleologically preformed in the acorn. This qualitative difference is ascertained from the end as well as from the origin and the specific competence of the powers in family and state.

The metaphysical principle states that the essence of a thing is defined by the end. Now the end of the family is the propagation of the human race, the mutual completion of husband and wife, the care for the children and their education. The specific authority that orders the life of the family is the paternal authority, which has here a kind of sovereignty. However, the civic family-law regulates and determines this field in the interest of the common good and against any abuse of paternal authority. But the civil law presupposes and honors the paternal rule; it cannot take the place of the natural and moral basis of paternal authority, which ends with the children's coming of age, though piety, love, and reverence continue.

The ends of the many intermediary organizations between family and state, such as economic enterprises, professional groups, institutions of learning, and those for the promotion of a particular interest, are in their nature self-governing. But they are partial and represent merely partial goods, not the common good. Hence the specific authorities that direct them to their ends are imperfect, though still true authorities in their special fields, however democratically they may be instituted and however ephemeral their end may be.

But the end of the state is the common good: the enactment of an order of tranquillity, justice, and peace among the families, the persons, and their many social institutions and associations for individual and group welfare and interests. The end of the state is the preservation of the order, its adaptation to the ever-changing conditions of community life, its protection from disrupting elements from within and without. All this, however, is done not in the interest of authority but exclusively in the interest of the common good. Therefore, in case of conflict, the interest of the common good always precedes that of the holder of authority, whereas in the family it is the very opposite in a case of conflict: the interest of the father precedes the interest of the children. Paternal authority rules by individual commands, and the children, not yet fully in the possession of the use of reason, obey in filial confidence without scrutiny of the commands as to their reasonableness.

But law is essentially general rule, not individual command. The law, therefore, addresses the adult, fully in command of his reason and will; the law is a rule of reason and for reason; accordingly it must be reasonable, not arbitrary. Moreover, the political common good is not created by the organs of the state, by its bureaucratic, administrative agencies, as the good of the family normally is created by the paternal authority. The administrative and legislative organs produce only the durable framework within which is realized the common good. The state defines the different orders, determines the forms, in which its members, the citizens, out of their own initiative work for their own material and spiritual interests. Thus, in an organic cooperation and symbiosis, they daily create the common good by their active or passive consent, by their duty-bound obedience to the *ordo*, together with the organs of the state.

II. PATERNALIST IDEA OF THE STATE

In accord with the end of family and state, it follows that the nature of power in each is different. St. Thomas says that the paternal authority may dispense only corrective punishment, a punishment strictly limited to the purpose of correction and not embracing retaliatory power such as the king has.[1] The reason for this is that the family does not represent a public, self-sufficient, sovereign order. Such an order is the state, which therefore can go so far as to use capital punishment against a member who by his acts gravely endangers the order of the common good. This order must be preserved in the interest of all, whereas the need for preservation of order in the individual family is not so stringent. The perfect society requires sovereign authority whose decisions are definite and without appeal. The imperfect society and its partial authority does not need it, because its authority, if abused, is subject to correction by a sovereign authority. Intimately related to these differing authorities are the dispositions we see in them toward their subjects. Whereas the partial authority of the father must be completed by love, the sovereign authority of the state rests on justice. From paternal authority we expect love in the first place. From the political authority we demand justice in the first place. We acclaim paternal kindness and praise the father's mercy to his prodigal son, but from the state authority we demand justice, objective justice without consideration of such qualities as appeal to us in the father.

Here, in the last analysis, lies the distinction between public and private law. However the line of distinction may have been blurred in the course of history and however questionable may have been the ascribing of one or other legal matter to public or private law, the distinction itself is of perpetual value. Moreover there is hardly any legal system that lacks it, that fails to recognize the individual person and his associations, especially the family, as values in themselves, substantially independent of their recognition by the state.

Without this distinction, then, either the substance of the state, the typical existential status of the political life of a people as a unity, gives place to the family and its controlling ways of life, thereby weakening the stability of the public order and endangering liberty through an abnormal growth of obedience, or the substance of the family, that essence of privacy, disappears before the overpowering state as in the totalitarian systems and with the same effect, the loss of liberty, the excessive fostering of blind obedience, the lack of justice. Thus the integrity and validity of this distinction is necessary for the preservation of liberty. Therefore, in opposition to many mod-

[1] *In Sent.*, IV, dist. 37, q.2, a.1 ad 4; *Summa theol.*, IIa IIae, q.65, a.2 ad 2.

ern political doctrines, Catholic political philosophy has always stressed the importance of this distinction, which it had received as a cherished heritage from the legal mind of Rome.

The abandonment of this distinction and with it of that essential difference between family and state, between paternal and political authority, leads to dire consequences, as may be shown by the so-called patrimonial state theory of C. L. von Haller or by Lord Filmer's patriarchal theory. In defense of royal absolutism, Lord Filmer contended that royal authority has its legitimate origin in Adam's patriarchal authority as the father of all men, not in any kind of popular election or transfer of rights. It is not completely absurd so to argue. We should be aware that the consequence must be absolutism and that the absolute prince, in addition to sovereignty, now demands the whole content of those emotional values and moral justifications that belong rightly to paternal authority. The subjects become children who have no privacy before the father-prince. The subjects, with immature reason, treated like minors, have no claim to strict objective justice. Moreover, whereas now, against abuse of paternal authority a person may appeal to the courts, against the acts of the father-prince, however arbitrary they may be, there is no appeal except to his mercy. Consequently, there is no limit to the interference of the father-prince in the private sphere, supposedly for the sake of the welfare of the state; all security and liberty of the citizens are subjected to the good pleasure, the arbitrary will of the father-prince. Thus the transformation of all public law into private paternal relations of the father-prince to the subject must lead to destruction of liberty.

This distinction has important bearings, too, on our problems of today. The modern democratic state, with its growing bureaucratic apparatus, is in danger of indulging in paternalism, of substituting bureaucracy and command for free initiative and self-governed control on the part of free associations for their specific purposes in the fields of economics, social welfare, and education. Thus we have a state that assumes care for all, a state that provides everything for everybody. The people, longing more for economic security than for the preservation of liberty, begin to regard the bureaucratic state as a father whose duty it is to give. All too easily the people then forget that the benevolent father-state wants control over all their affairs and thus may become a tyrannical father. It must never be forgotten that bureaucracy, in that disparaging sense in which it is used here, was the creation of the absolute prince and that it represented his supreme control over the lives and goods of his subjects.

In that deteriorated absolutism returning in modern totalitarianism, we can easily find another proof for our contention. Here all law is public law in essence, if not in label, for the individual is nothing, and the state is all. If, in addition, private property is abolished and the family as an essential social form is discarded, the state becomes all, bureaucracy penetrates every sphere of individual life, religious, intellectual, and material, and freedom becomes an empty phrase, for it loses its social basis, the family as an independent protected sphere of the human person. Then we see citizens regarded as a mere mass of subjects without rights, the objects of bureaucratic management. The reverence of the old Roman law for the family and its private, free sphere, Mommsen considers the greatest contribution of the distinction between private and public law. No community was so omnipotent as the Roman city-state; but in no community did the law-abiding citizen live in such unconditioned legal security, both in respect to his fellow citizens and to the Republic itself.[2]

The distinction between private and public law is not merely a legalistic, philosophically irrelevant invention; it is one based on the essential difference of the social forms and on the dignity of the human person. The supereminent meaning of a bill of rights is the preservation and protection of that field of the family, and the individual persons, which is ruled and ordered by the institutes of private law. And private law is essentially the sphere of individual initiative and of the self-governmental activities of groups of individuals, of families. All bills of rights establish first a sphere of freedom against state intervention. Therefore they delineate a sphere in which the state may interfere only under strictly formalized and unequivocal conditions, and it is the state that has the burden of proof. This line of demarcation is marked by its posts, freedom of the person, freedom of worship, of speech, of education (parental rights), of association, of property, of contract, of freedom from intrusion into the home, and so on. Thus it establishes a realm free from state intervention for the person, the family, the paternal authority,

[2] Mommsen, *Romisches Staatsrecht*, I, 75.

and the associations of the persons produced by their own initiative for any purpose not contradictory to the common good, that is the public order, and to the basic religious and moral values that concretely form the fundament of the public order. Other rights that are sometimes inserted in the bill of rights and that actually are rights not of man, but of citizens, like the right to vote and to have equal access to public office, are related to that demarcation line, in so far as they establish a government by consent. Thus they give the people control over the government that is always in danger of falling into the temptation to intervene arbitrarily. This is the meaning of the modern growth of the judiciary, which has to deal with justice, whereas bureaucracy deals with expediency and efficiency and is by its nature prone to yield to the temptation of paternalist expansion.

III. Society and State

From what has been said we can distinguish society and state. Society is the multitude of citizens and aliens, of individuals and families, of innumerable short-term or long-term associations of different kinds. All of these are connected with one another by their free initiative, directed by their particular ends and interests, in everyday efforts for the preservation of spheres of life, for individual and social improvement, for economic cooperation and social progress. These social relations may be informal and merely factual, or they may grow in social intensity from loose, friendly relations to contractual, legally enforcible connections, to the establishment of institutions and corporate bodies of stricter organization, like parishes, free institutions of elementary or higher learning, corporate enterprises, cooperative associations of all kinds, labor unions, societies for humanitarian purposes and adult education, charitable institutions. What distinguishes these is that they are created by the initiative of individuals and groups of the same. The state affords legal hulls, formal standards, and prevents violation of the public order, the common good and its basic moral values. The state does not create them nor has the state a right to destroy or confiscate them without due process of law. The state may regulate them, but it cannot command them. The state reigns here, but it does not govern.

The state is not society, but rather the public order as a living action in society; likewise the state is not identical with race, nation, or religious community. The racial, national state or religion-state is a historical form of political life but not a necessary form from the philosophical standpoint. Race, nation, tribe, and religious group are but "matter" of the real "form" of political existence, the state. The state is thus the new thing, the form that is the unity of order. The bond of law is added to the already existing unity of blood, of tribal coherence, of national group consciousness, of religious common faith. These prestate unities may form a specially apt "matter" for the political form, they may even bear in themselves a strong tendency to produce a political unity, but they are not necessarily the cause of political unity. The state carries its justification in itself, not in the greater consistency of earlier bonds of unity. To appeal to the "matter" and its prepolitical unity as tribe, race, or nation is not a necessity for the state. For centuries citizens of different nationalities have lived in the same state. The nation-state is merely one of the many historical forms of political symbiosis. As history tells of the nation-state, it tells also of the nationality-state, like Switzerland and like the Austro-Hungarian monarchy with some of its successor states, Czechoslovakia and Yugoslavia; and it tells of the interracial and nonnational state like the United States of America. Seipel, the eminent Austrian statesman and excellent political philosopher, thought that the non-national state was a higher form of political organization than the nation-state. The doctrine of the nation-state is actually rather narrow and easily becomes the forerunner of the modern racial state, the rather materialist kin of nineteenth century nationalism.

IV. NATIONALISM AND TOTALITARIANISM

Behind all these identifications, as a political leitmotiv, runs the problem of homogeneity of a multitude to be organized into a *unitas ordinis*. Nationalism and racialism regard the state as the fruit from the mysterious depth of an irrational, national soul or of an even more irrational, naturalist power of the blood. State, consequently, is not the creation of reason for reason but appears as the outcome of unfathomable, irresistible moving forces of the godess Life that is married to Death and bears these reckless, lawless, faithless, irrational, and power-seeking regimes that find their real end in the battlefields, in the intoxication of conquest and subjugation. Catholic political philosophy, on the contrary, upholds the thesis that the state is the rational clarity of law, the result of the daily renewed free resolution of the citizen to live in the *ordo*, in the working organization for the common good, which has arisen out of the social nature of man as a reasonable being and for the perfection of his nature.

Nevertheless the problem of homogeneity has to be treated. In the abstract order we need not concern ourselves with it, because the fundamental homogeneity for the state is human social nature. In the concrete order, however, the problem is most important, because the actual state is also a creation of history adapted in its actual constitution, written or unwritten, to the specific features that individualize the "matter" at least partially, the actual people, nation, or tribe, apart from the political individualization by its concrete political form, the state. It must further be stressed that *in concreto* the common good is not only an order individualized by the specific social structure, economic system and law; it is based also *in concreto* on a community of morals, convictions, interests, or even religious beliefs. This common content in the minds of the citizens, what may be called their common culture, represents the homogeneity of the people in its political form of existence.

We see at once that there is possible a wide variation of homogeneities as the concrete foundation of political unity; but there must be at least one in addition to that abstract homogeneity of human nature. And there may even be propounded a complete all-embracing homogeneity as we find it in totalitarianism, where really the race or the nation or the class in an all-embracing, all-penetrating homogeneity is the actual basis of political existence. No room is left for neutrality or dissent. Only one loyalty, breaking all others, is valid: that to the race, nation, or class as the sole basis of political and individual existence. Men not homogeneous either in fact or by will are necessarily foes of the state. Then, of course, no sphere of freedom is left, because no individual choice or initiative can be allowed, for that may lead to dissent and is therefore too hazardous. The description of such a totally homogeneous state as a monolithic state speaks for itself.

While this represents the maximum of homogeneity and is totalitarian, we also find in history a minimum of homogeneity, like the liberalist theory with its tendency to minimize all that is government and state to the advantage of the free society. The sole homogeneity of this is the observance of contractual relations and that honesty necessary for the functioning of the economic system of capitalism. The minimum of homogeneity is the belief in the principles of the capitalist system. However—and therein lies the difference—it is not enforced by political means but by ostracism and economic persecution, just as deftly as is done by political means. Yet even this minimum, namely, homogeneity as to the law and abiding by the law, is never merely abstract, is never merely formal, because no positive law is absolutely open to any and every content; nor is a constitution a merely formal code of political organization and government activities, but embraces rather a concrete material decision about certain common values that are presupposed as the homogeneous basis of the political unity.

The bill of rights is not mere formalism but has as its basis certain clearly discoverable convictions. Freedom of speech presupposes a belief in the ability of the individual mind to find objective truth. The consequence of freedom of speech (discussion and deliberation) presupposes the conviction that a plurality of men viewing a problem from different angles has a better chance to find the best solution than even the best educated absolute monarch, who, by the way, appeals to counselors, too, for his decision. Freedom of conscience presupposes a deep regard for the dignity of the individual person and the sanctity of the intimate religious sphere. Freedom from arbitrary search of premises presupposes the home of the family as the free sphere of parental authority, for in an Amazon state this rule would be void.

Thus these fundamental rights are not mere formalities but they presuppose a material moral homogeneity. Only people who have forgotten this can go so far as to allow even to subversive individuals the full use of these rights. A Nazi or communist, who denies the substance of these rights and thus the material homogeneity of a free democracy in regard to such basic moral values, has no claim to the free use of these rights, for he practically says: As long as you rule, I demand these rights on the basis of your principles; if my revolution succeeds, I will deny them to you on the basis of my principles. It is with telling force that our language denotes totalitarianism as subversive. What does it endanger? An empty form? No, the moral and philosophical basis that forms the real moral homogeneity of democracy. The state is *in concreto* always a moral being, too, for it lives by the actual exercise of social and political virtues, which concern the common good, the *status politicus*. The measure of moral homogeneity and the actual will to political unity are the measure of individual liberty. The demand for justice, for observing the order of law, is the minimum of this homogeneity. The quest for a government of law means this, as far as the law itself represents the minimum of political, moral homogeneity. This quest, indeed, also means that law is not intended as a mere formal element open to every and any content, but that its content should be the minimum of enforcible homogeneity that guarantees the preservation and protection of the state.

The problem of homogeneity of the "matter" of the state (metaphysically a *materia secunda,* of course) appears in many historical situations as most important. When Philip II used the Spanish Inquisition for political purposes, it was not so much religious fanaticism that ruled him, but his conviction that religion should be the homogeneous basis of the state which he intended to build. Therefore, at least in the beginning, conversion to the Church was enough to avoid the Inquisition, while apostasy from the Church delivered one to the Inquisition. Similarly the conviction that religious homogeneity is the only secure basis for political existence led to the execution of heretics in the Roman Empire in the Middle Ages, while there are enough proofs that Church leaders thought this practice wrong.[8] At other times, other kinds of homogeneity will be considered necessary, and dissenters will be prosecuted and persecuted. The history of capitalism shows interesting features of such persecutions of

[8] The issue is very complicated. Emperor Justinian (in *Novella* 132), like Emperor Theodosius before him and later that agnostic Emperor Frederick II, imposed heavy penalties upon the heretics. The *Sachsenspiegel* (1215–35) similarly threatens heretics with burning (Bk. II, art. 12, § 7). Bishop Wazo of Liège in 1045 declared himself against it. St. Thomas holds that the state has the right to inflict capital punishment on the pertinacious heretic (*Summa theol.,* IIa IIae, q.11, a.3; cf. Bellarmine, *De laicis,* III; *Controversia,* c.21). Usually the secular rulers are more savage in their ideas and acts than the churchmen because, in a community that took faith as its basis of political existence, heresy was considered a rebellion against the state; just as the early Puritans in New England also thought. For further material, see Eduard Eichmann, *Acht und Bann im Reichsrecht des Mittelalters* (1909) and P. Hinschius, *Geschichte und Quellen des kanonischen Rechts* (5th ed., 1890).

more or less "radical" labor leaders called "disloyal" to the state or nation because they endangered the tacitly presupposed economic homogeneity of a capitalist system by propagating heterogeneous economic systems.

The homogeneity problem is important in foreign policy also. The difficulties of the so-called nationality-state (state with national minorities) in a nationalist era is the following. Such a state thinks it lacks homogeneity on account of its national heterogeneity. Instead, therefore, of looking for a different kind of homogeneity, it too readily is inclined to establish national homogeneity by enforced nationalization which has as a consequence a continual growth of government intervention and bureaucracy in stark contradiction to the democratic, therefore tolerant, constitution. Furthermore, states surrounded by strong, covetous neighbors try to increase the field of homogeneity in order to make themselves less penetrable from without and thus stronger by removing any possibility of dissent.

In the last resort this problem is connected with that of loyalty. Loyalty is more than external conformity to legality. It does indeed signify that. But in addition it includes an active moral assent to the values and moral convictions that form the moral unity and prelegal homogeneity of this concrete political form, the state. Hence it is internal and subjective and can be but insufficiently shown by an outward conformity to the law. It needs special expression by the use of political symbols, by a readiness for voluntary service and sacrifices in the interest of the common good. By exaggeration it may show itself also in the discarding or voiding of loyalties to something other than the state, for instance, to the pope. Thus in England and in the colonies, but in Germany too, the Catholic was often considered a rather doubtful citizen and was kept from office and from the ballot because his publicly professed loyalty to the pope was thought to weaken and diminish his loyalty to the crown or the state. He was considered not homogeneous enough, measured by the standards of the supposedly homogeneous majority.

In the interest of human dignity and liberty, this concrete demand of homogeneity must be controlled. One way to do so is by federalism or regionalism. The single political units that form the federation can more readily reach a tolerable homogeneity than can all of them together. Loyalty is the easier, the less it is outwardly enforced by conformity, i.e., adoption of homogeneity. Thus the supreme loyalty to the federation is strong enough for the protection and preservation of itself and its members, while the loyalty to the member states may have a good homogeneous basis in their more local traditions, in their native character and culture.

A further restriction upon an exaggerated demand for a homogeneity which actually often threatens to issue in uniformity arises from the principle of subsidiarity. According to this principle the state should leave all social tasks and activities which can be performed by smaller communities to such communities. Any task that free (private) cultural or economic or educational organizations and institutions can perform, in the framework of the public order of law, by their own initiative or by their own service to ideals which often transcend those of the state, should be left to their discretion and competency. For example, any demand by the state for a monopoly of education in order to produce such a homogeneity as nationalism considers ideal, is intrinsically vicious. We may grant that the state has decidedly an interest in the education of its future citizens; we may grant that the state has a right to demand certain minimum standards, certain supervisory and advisory functions. Yet the state has no right to monopoly in education, for many educational aims, religious education, character education, the formation of the moral conscience, are transcendent to the state. They aim at higher values than the state itself is, at values in relation to which the state itself is a servant. If the state, in disregard of the principle of its subsidiarity in education, establishes a monopoly of education under appeal to fullest homogeneity of its citizens, the schools are turned into barracks of the mind, where perhaps robots, uniform particles of masses, are molded, but where the moral wells are dried up, the sources from which the state as a moral organism really lives.

It can be stated, therefore, as a principle that a state is not the better the more homogeneity it has. Otherwise the totalitarian state would be the ideal· the principle should be: Have as much freedom as is possible, as much homogeneity and therefore only as much compulsion as is necessary in any given situation of history. And furthermore, loyalties are necessarily many. The loyalty to God and to the Church, to the family and to "my people" (not necessarily identical with all the citizen members of the state), the loyalty to my professional or my vocational group, union, and the like, and the loyalty to the state: ordinarily they can and do exist together without conflict; and the less a constitution or a state produces such conflicts, the better is that state under the supreme loyalty to God.

CHAPTER XII

The State as a Moral Organism

I. THE STATE NOT A MERE SYSTEM OF LEGAL NORMS

THE state, as we pointed out frequently, is not a mere legalistic entity, a system of norms, but a moral organism. It is the nature of man to live in a sphere of tension. Not in a dualistic world, like Gnosticism that once was and still is potent in heresies contending that there are two principles, two worlds strictly opposed and separated. What we mean is a tension arising from a polar opposition of diverse principles. Man's task as an individual and as a member of social bodies is to unite these principles. Such antithetical concepts, though always leading to synthesis, are the following: freedom—subordination; authority—autonomy; nature—spirit; reason—will; society (state) —individual; power—law; economics—ethics. These are the poles out of which life comes, between which arise its stress and strains, between which it goes on. To overcome this restlessness in the restfulness of God is the longing of man. Christian philosophy has ever marked this tension, this antithetic character of man.

All perfectionism and all progressivism have tried to do away with this essential mark of human existence. These systems deny ethics and believe in the laws of economics. They glorify freedom and, in detesting subordination and order, dream of an anarchic future; they deify nature and race or matter and despise the intellect and the things invisible which only faith grasps. They adore power but "debunk" the moral tradition and the law which for them are merely clever expedients to fool the innocents. Christian philosophy is aware of this antithetic character, too, but it also knows that it can be overcome by showing the hierarchy of values and the synthesis, the *concordantia discordantium*. Thus it understood the necessity of balancing the opposing pressures of these haunting antitheses in human life, it understood their destiny to become reconciled in the moral effort till they are definitely overcome in the life beyond.

Thus it conceived the state as a unity in multiplicity, as a moral organic entity. Here were bridged the opposing poles, each of which means only a part of the full life. Already its "vitalistic" metaphysics, as opposed to mechanistic, its psychology that sees in the soul the "form" of the body, both constituting one substantial entity, man; all these gave the opportunity to see both lines of ideas united. It is striking to see how, since the breakdown of Thomistic philosophy, the intellectual life destined for unity goes astray, thinking, so to speak, in a linear way. The overemphasis of individual liberty produces an exaggerated subjectivism to which all "power" and authority must appear as heteronomous and therefore arbitrary. The pendant of this individualist concept of liberty is the thesis that all authority and power is arbitrary and thus immoral. Consequently the idea is developed that the state belongs to a lower form of human social existence and will wither away. Or the power and authority are, as in Hegel's philosophy, raised to the substance of morality itself. One could write an interesting history of political philosophy showing how, since the Renaissance and Reformation, a philosophy of separation, of antimonies, has replaced the great harmony of Thomism. To no small extent the longing for a harmonious philosophy, felt today after the heyday of separative specialization, is traceable to this.

For Catholic political philosophy the state is not an arbitrary, unnecessary institution, entered into by individuals so that they may remain as free as they were before. That idea is a contradiction. Nor is the state the unconscious outgrowth of biological life, of an involuntary, unintellectual, blind drive of a mysterious force, nature. The *ordo* is essentially for reason and by reason, though actually it is instituted and preserved by the will of the authority and by the continuous will of the citizen to realize the order. Yet a full picture of political life *in concreto* is impossible without an appreciation of the power of vested economic interests to sway moral conscience by confusing private interests and the common good. But this realistic appreciation must not lead to skepticism but rather to the full apprehension of moral values in social and economic life and to the clear vision of the common good as the controlling measure for the sovereign intervention of the state in the free economic society. One cannot say that the state is more important than the individual person absolutely, for the state is essentially of service character. However, the state, as the highest form of the good life, may demand from the individual even the sacrifice of life for its continuance. This it may do because the state, as the objective framework of the good life for all, is more than one individual's private good.

II. The Social and Political Virtues

Sovereign authority is a necessary property of the state. But as it takes its legitimacy from the concrete service to the common good, it cannot destroy the *ordo* in which the lower groups in autonomy perform their ends protected by the *ordo* and realizing it just as much as does the authority. The idea of political life, as the temporal perfect form of human life, is not only an efficacious principle, it is also intrinsically the end and the norm of existence and growth, but an end that is realized by free men, a norm that rules moral activity not compulsory, blind, animal growth. According to this view, free, independent individual persons are at the same time members of families, of professional and vocational groups, of many other free associations, of national civilizations, and finally of the whole, the state. In this view the state is the necessary form of human existence on account of the essential end and freedom of man. But this existence and this freedom are realized in concrete institutions and organizations engendered by history, by geography, by economic and cultural surroundings. This, then, means the acknowledgment of the political existence of this people, this nation, preformed as the "matter" for the political life. This cannot be understood fully as a logical thing, but remains somewhat irrational in its affective ties of sympathy, of love, of passionate affinities. Yet these, incapable of self-direction, require a rational guidance and a conscious governing to a rational end, measured by the norm of natural law. The state is thus not an abstract, formal order or system without regard to material content, an empty shell to be filled with any content. It is order and is the sum total of the persons and things ordered. The state does not live by the law alone. It is more than a logical system of legal norms although, as the concrete order of persons and for persons,

t lives in the law and not beyond the law, as the biological and
ociological schools contend.

Catholic political philosophy is aware of these interdependencies.
That is why it extols those social and political virtues which live be-
ond legal minima and legalistic formalities, such virtues as fidelity,
piety, and loyalty, that are akin to legal justice. Hence the rationality
of the formal legal system is considered not the only essence of the
tate; that rationality of the law seems rather to be like directing rays
rom a lighthouse, which arises out of the waves of social life. This
universe of a thousand diversities of spirit and blood, of past tradi-
ion and present improvisation, of the upsurge of rising masses and
erenely ruling elites, of emotional preferences and irrational dis-
ikes, all this life cannot be caught and held merely by legal forms.
The true communities of life (the family, the Church, the state) live
ot by legal form; they live and are nourished by the power of love,
aith, loyalty, piety, obedience, grace. They are endangered by the
pposing vices of egoism, treachery, lust for power, revolt, selfish-
ess, infidelity, treason against mutual trust.

These good forces are not produced by the legal system; nor are
he vices completely suppressed by it. The virtues are protected by
he law and directed to the right end, the common good. The vices
re repressed, are made harmless for the order; to destroy their harm-
ulness is the work of education, of religion, an incessant work and
n indispensable one. It is the task of the state, giving it dignity and
majesty, to direct to the common good these blessings and mischief-
making powers that arise out of the inexhaustible fountain of life.
These forces are in themselves undirected and may be used for a good
r a bad end, as all virtues have their opposing vices, or, if they are
misdirected, become vices. They must, therefore, be directed to the
ommon good by the legal order in the interest of all, and the vices
must be checked as a menace to the order.

Man is not good in himself. The powers, even love and loyalty
nd obedience, can destroy as well as construct. To direct them to the
onstruction and preservation of peaceful order among individuals,
families, and their associations born of common interest, of sym-
athies, creeds, cultures, and traditions, and to prevent a war of all
gainst all, is the task of the state, of politics, that is, the education of
he people to be itself the state in an active sense.

The state is the *ordo rerum humanarum* and politics is the unre lenting task to preserve, readapt, and restore this *ordo* in a world everchanging social relations, in a life of the many which, if left to i self, is chaotic and would become more chaotic the closer men actu ally lived together. Thus politics is the perpetual task of man; it the original, unavoidable form of human social existence. It is wron to say that economics is destiny. No; politics is destiny, the concret political order, for law is frozen politics. We should always be on ou guard against the false view, that politics must give way to economi or business, as liberalist theory puts it. This is the great heresy the nineteenth century, liberalism: the substitution of the econom categories of utility, production, and profits for the political cat gories of order, law, and sovereign authority, this devaluation of th political concepts of the state, in favor of economic concepts an business practices. But these fields of human activity thrive und different stars and values.

It was in part a base move, this devaluation of the state. It was a excellent means to construct the domination of the bourgeois typ over all fields of human life. It minimized the state in order to ru the community for itself. In place of law as the rule of human exis ence, it substituted the efficiency of business. For the state as the fine creation of the constructive human mind, for the good life of th perpetual human community, it substituted the well-oiled machir for producing profits, without regard to how they were gained an from where they came. Consequently, not unselfish service to th community but economic success became the standard of social rep tation. Full moral and public responsibility, that complementa concept of authority and power, has vanished in favor of the limite responsibility of invested money. The anonymity of the private corp ration, the perpetual interchange of replaceable individuals in the ec nomic process, has, even in the economic field, destroyed the value social responsibility. This it has done to such an extent that the sta must increasingly intervene and, by force of law, realign econom power and public responsibility, because business ethics, individuali as it was, had tried to accomplish the impossible, the separati of economic power and public responsibility. Indeed, business do not become better when we call politics an ugly business.

The pursuit of happiness is a political concept and it means, to he happiness of the whole, the good order among the citizens that engenders the individual happiness. Furthermore, this happiness is not measured by the number of modern gadgets that blatant advertising forces on us, but by the peace and good order of community life, the development and cultivation of human values, of virtues, of arts, of religion, of justice. In the metaphysical sense economics is the matter that needs the form of order. Its categories therefore depend on the political categories, the form-giving concepts that have to do primarily with man, and with the economic values only as service values, not as the controlling standards. Therefore the end of politics is the state, the *ordo rerum humanarum,* the form in which the people, conditioned by its biological inheritance and fatherland, by its sagas and spiritual tradition, recognizes itself and exalts itself, expresses its hidden soul in symbols and in the form of its definite political existence, in a higher, more perfect form of communal existence. Economics is a subordinate feature of this community life and essentially a servant to the *ordo* that lives by justice, piety, loyalty, and charity as the specifically human values. That is why the state may justly demand the sacrifice of life from the individual citizen, whereas it does not make sense to talk of dying for greater profits. Man perfects himself in being a citizen in the *status politicus,* not by being a successful *homo economicus.* Therefore again, the legislator holds the highest human office, next to the priest who cares for souls, for, as the Roman lawyers expressed it, law means the knowledge of things divine and human, the science of what is just and unjust. Therefore, as Ulpian rightly says, the jurist is called a priest.[1]

III. Political Freedom and Morality

And again, freedom, the generous gift of God to man as a person, is so fundamentally a complementary concept of order that economic freedom is merely a reflection of political freedom, but it may easily become enslavement when not all the members of the community are politically free and independent from their capitalist breadmasters. Hence there exists a certain complementary relation between freedom and compulsory law as the minimum of legal behavior among the members of a community. Any community lives on into the fu-

[1] *Institutiones* (Gaii), I, 1: *Digest.,* I, 1.

ture by the fact that the individual members can expect a law-abiding behavior from one another, that all will keep the rules they have agreed upon as the constitution of their community life. Only thus can man overcome the hazards of his existence. Man desires a secure future for himself, his family, his property. He can secure it only by continuous war (the might of the stronger) or by the introduction of an order of moral and legal, that is, compulsory, rules. But for the sake of more material security or for better mechanical efficiency, these legal rules of compulsion may expand so much that no room is left for freedom. This happens when the rules are transformed into individual commands dominating all activities of the citizens who are now passive instruments of the sole free one, the tyrant. Freedom and law, as a general rule, are therefore not mutually opposed; but freedom and arbitrary compulsion, or freedom and individual commands, are definitely so. In an army there is less freedom than in a club or a college; that is why suspecting democracies are against compulsory military service since they see in it a nursery of militarism, a foe of freedom for all; that is why in free democracies, even in war time, the military power is subordinated to the civil government.

Therefore law in connection with freedom means chiefly not statute law, compulsory law; it means rather moral law; and this law is not the opposite of freedom but rather the protector of freedom. The compulsory law enforces such standards of behavior as are deemed necessary for the mere practical existence of the community; they have been called ethical minima, that need to be transformed into compulsory legal rules. But beyond these rules there exists in the minds of the citizens a body of rules not formally enforced, especially the ethical rules that are at least as important as these minima. Freedom as distinguished from license means, then, that the citizen, in free acceptance of these laws, realizes for himself and the community a higher and more perfect life. Therefore any growth of such freedom calls for the growth of more sensitive and more highly developed moral laws.

Man is the freer the more he is ethical. A state can be freer the more its citizens cultivate social and political virtues.[2] And we can declare the following as a universal principle. In the more integrated interdependent social and economic life, state intervention, that is

[2] Montesquieu therefore made virtue the basis of the republic.

increase of the compulsory minima, grows in the same ratio as social and political virtues fail to grow. If the bankers of a country with a complicated credit economy do not themselves develop a high standard of professional ethics, then in the interest of the bank customers (the public), the state must intervene by narrowing down that sphere of freedom which was not determined by the necessary standard of professional ethics. Unions may be free in bargaining collectively; but when their leaders are lacking in the presupposed ethical standards, then the state must intervene with compulsory legislation. Freedom, therefore, is possible only on account of corresponding ethical responsibility and obedience. No cynical critic may appeal to the freedom of science, because this freedom is in direct ratio to the serious, impartial, ethical standards of the searcher for truth. Plato grew incensed against the Sophists because they demanded freedom but declined responsibility to truth and the coordinated ethical standards. Nobody can demand abstract economic freedom for employers and overlook the need for ethical restraint in the pursuit of profits and self-interest. The practical outcome would be and has been the enslavement of the working classes, if not legally so, at least practically. We see the evidence in the revolt of the workers and in their demand for industrial democracy.

The test of modern freedom in democracy is not freedom of enterprise or an abstract economic freedom, but economic freedom for all citizens by securing the rights of the worker and a stronger cooperative spirit, instead of one inspired by narrow self-interest. The more the cooperative spirit is fostered, the more equal obedience is furthered as a rendering of service to the objective purpose of increasing the standard of living for all, the better can freedom be preserved. On the other hand, the less the cooperative spirit prevails, the more will narrow self-interest grow and the more the state, as an administrative bureaucracy, will reach out into the field of freedom. Thus the state will become more totalitarian under the necessity of furthering the common good. Undoubtedly this is not the best way to protect the common good, but rather the worst; yet there is no other choice. Freedom, then, will be deserved and won by virtuous service to the common good. Hence politics is destiny, not economics; and politics belongs to the moral sciences.

IV. Power an Element of the State

Here another problem looms upon the horizon: the problem of state and power or might. The history of political thought exhibits a colorful galaxy of theories: from the cynical worshipers of violence, from the pessimistic glorifiers of power as the essence of the state, to the utopian dreamers and the optimistic prophets of a chiliastic society, where there is no state, no compulsory law, no "power," but only a free society. History even shows us noble experiments especially on the ecstatic basis of sectarianism, that tried to realize these dreams, only to disappear after a short time or to degenerate quickly into a ruthless despotism.

The sociological theory of the state by such scholars as Gumplovicz the Marxist theory, and the Machiavellian doctrine, together with that of Hobbes, all regard the state exclusively as a power organization beyond law and morality. Law and morality appear to them as mere camouflage or as an ideological, unreal superstructure for the only real thing, the lust for power. This lust for power may be that of individuals following the Machiavellian *Principe* or of classes like the bourgeoisie according to Karl Marx or, to go back to earlier times, like the Athenian patriciate according to Trasymachus, who was the first to propound the cynical phrase: "Might makes right."

In opposition to these theories there have always been doctrines regarding power and might as intrinsically bad. These doctrines endeavor utterly to eliminate the power element from the state or they demand elimination of the state itself. To the first class belong some Stoic philosophers and Christian sects, like the Waldenses or the Fraticelli and in modern times radical liberal theorists who contend that the state is merely a system of legal ordinances and nothing else. To the second school belong all the anarchists (literally, "no government"), whether of Christian extraction like the Manichaean sects or the many experiments of religious communist groups like those of Robert Owens, Brook Farm, and so on.[3] These Christian sects all in some way assert that, because the state is caused by sin, redemption makes it superfluous for the elect and redeemed. Of course, it must not be forgotten that seldom were those doctrines objective and philosophical. Oftener, they are practical political theories di

[3] Cf. Francis Calverton, *Where Angels Dared to Tread* (1941).

ected against an actual government that arbitrarily used its power against the disciples of heresiarchs or political leaders in an effort to suppress their movements which frequently voiced a justifiable complaint against the ruling powers. Thus Christian sects oppressed by the orthodox powers would contend that power and compulsory application of laws are necessary and adequate only for sinners and not for the holy ones.

Thus we have two opposed views: the state is power and nothing else; the state is law, a system of ordinances, and nothing else. This opposition of views is based to no small extent on a certain anthropology and even theology, as we have already shown. It may even lie deeper: in a longing of the individual to be absolutely free and undisturbed, to grow like a flower in a wilderness, to roam through the woods and plains in perfect freedom and independence in a state of innocent nature. These are all longings that fill the books and dreams of the romanticists in stark opposition to the Greek philosophers, who considered the stateless and lawless man a barbarian.

Catholic political philosophy could not accept any of these opposing principles. For it the antithesis could only become: law without power; power without law. Humanly speaking, both are nihilistic. The synthesis is: power controlled by law, by natural and divine law, determined in positive law, the order of law enforced against the lawbreaker by power. State and power are indissolubly connected. Power, the application of force as a factor serving the end of the state, is one of its essential elements. As a result of original sin, man was left darkened in understanding and weakened in will. The individual reason, therefore, cannot always and under all circumstances come perfectly to truth, the inner essence of law.

Especially in what concerns the best ways and means for a commonly agreed upon purpose, a thousand different opinions are possible and all may be equally worthy. The necessary unity of endeavor to reach the end would be impossible, and the end would never be realized, if not by persuasion and subsequent free submission of the dissenting minority; and if persuasion is insufficient, by power and enforcement the unity of endeavor can be completed. Even for one who is a fanatical democrat, the application of power and the enforcement of unity is unavoidable. A perfectly democratic government, after being empowered by the electorate, the true sovereign, to attain a certain aim (e.g., the introduction of social legislation), must have the right, after the parliamentary process has produced the choice of means, to reach the accomplishment of this end by forcibly suppressing any attempt to obstruct the use of the legally approved means. In an emergency the essence of the state, as indissolubly connected with power, becomes even clearer. Here the ruler or government has the right, must have the right, to apply force *extra* or *praeter* and even *contra legem* in order to protect the unity of the order. But one thing is clear. The use of force must be controlled by the moral end and the adequate licit means to the end.

The reason for this need of power is that man is intellectually and morally imperfect. Catholic political philosophy is aware of the almost tragic existence of man, of his undirected passions, of his urge for unlimited selfish pleasure. It knows about those passions destroying the unity, rebelling against the order, selfishly neglecting the community, which are all opposed to the social and political virtues of justice, piety, loyalty, honesty, and charity. It knows that the actual *ordo,* the framework of individual and common happiness, cannot be realized without sacrifices. It knows that the order is incessantly endangered by selfish lust for power, by uncontrolled self-interest, by the temptation of rulers to abuse of authority for selfish ends, by political corruption. It knows, too, that the actual *ordo,* through the shielding of vested interests, can become unjust, that the changing circumstances in social and economic life demand the abolition of unintended privileges protected by the existing order; it knows, in other words, that the positive order may contradict the ideal order of peace and justice.

The order of laissez-faire capitalism thus has become unjust, creating unwarranted privileges of vested property rights against unjustly suppressed personal rights of the working classes. Formal right can, under our mode of existence, become material wrong. In these conditions the state needs power and must apply force for the sake of its own end. It must enforce the law against the lawbreaker; it must forcefully change parts of the actual order which have grown unjust, even against the will of the privileged interests; it must use force against the selfish resistance of the privileged interests that range themselves above the new and juster order. All men are not consistently led by intelligent understanding of the necessity and reasonableness of a just change of the existing order, particularly if the latter benefits particular interests and thus offends the interests of the other members. Therefore the state, as St. Paul says, carries the sword; not for glory's sake or for superhuman pride and lust, but for the sake of the order of the common good. The state has power to use it morally, and that use is moral as long and as far as it is made for the realization of the common good.

V. Political Power and Private Economic Power

We must distinguish between power and violence, though the practical use of these words is rather confused. Violence is unjust, is lawless, is unordered, is wantonly aggressive. George Sorel glorified it against the bourgeois order; Lenin and Mussolini confessed themselves as his disciples. Power in some way includes the quality of justness, righteousness. Power has the direct relation to the end in itself just. Violence is uncontrolled, unlimited, aimless. Power, on the contrary, means service, responsibility to the moral end. The liberalist tendencies in political philsophy, which minimized power and tried to divest the state of any trace of power, have for some time been proved self-deceptive. They disputed the power of the state, they tried to abolish as superfluous the concept of sovereignty, they tried to harness all state activity to cumbersome formalist rules of procedure; they promoted a kind of panjurism. They tried to do away with any power relation, dependence, or subordination in the state's sphere.

This they did because they had no idea of the common good as a value in itself, not exclusively representing the mere sum of the particular goods of individuals. Consequently to them the *ordo* is not a *status* to be created and continuously upheld by the authority and the power of the state, but is the order of the society, an automatic natural one. It is created by free individuals on the basis of their freedom of person, of property, and of contract. The individuals, for themselves and by their free contractual relations, create substantially the positive order; that order, if undisturbed by state intervention, which presumedly is arbitrary, will at any time be the natural order. This is the order that corresponds perfectly to the individual gifts, skills, and abilities of the free individuals, who are also equal as to opportunities. A free competitive society is the ideal, a society which, undisturbed by state intervention, weaves its web of contractual relations by individual private initiative, directed only by well-considered self-interest. This competitive society thus creates automatically at any time and produces as if with an invisible hand the right and just order, where everybody holds that place which corresponds to his individual gifts and abilities.

The result was not a natural order, or equality, or the abolition of power, subordination, and dependence. On the contrary, in that society so undisturbed by state intervention, the power of wealth, of capital, and of high finance was established. And while equality before the law was somewhat reached, the economic inequality, the cleavage in society between a few rich and the broad masses of poor grew continually. The political privileges were abolished, but the new economic privileges grew more scandalously. The political dependence was done away with; but, as an individual, actually living on a short-term labor contract, enacted as a result of his weak bargaining power, the worker in his life and person was more dependent on the decision of indifferent, impersonal estimates of cost accountants or financial operators, than the journeyman had ever been dependent on the master, the subject on the sovereign. Thus that power which liberalist theory argued away in the political sphere, returned aggrandized and rather more non-moral as private power, yet as politically irresponsible power in the economic society.

Thus the outcome is not a peaceful and justly ordered society of free men and equals, but it is the modern industrial class-society. In this society capitalist and financial interests may easily form a kind of invisible government, strong and ruthless behind the fair screen of democracy. The outcome is the modern class-society, the injustices in the social and economic order that are the more felt as they are in such contradiction to the solemnly propounded political principles of human rights and democracy. This contradiction became so strong that the laissez-faire abstention of the state had to be given up. Social legislation, which is state intervention, was called for because the class-cleavage turned into political issues; revolutionary or reformatory socialism demanded, even from the most inveterate partisans of laissez-faire, legislative and administrative intervention on the part of the state. But everything depends now on the kind of state intervention. If it cures symptoms only, but not the roots of the evil, then there arises the danger that the state's administrative intervention simply substitutes state bureaucracy and planning for insufficiently coordinated and cooperative self-initiative. The result may be an enormous growth of the state's bureaucratic apparatus of social and economic control and not the reconstruction of a stable order of self-government and cooperative self-control in liberty. But then the basic fault, namely, the class cleavage, the class consciousness, and the class struggle, continues, and the classes begin to strive for the control of the bureaucratic apparatus. Each class tries to increase it as a means of social and economic control of the opposing class. Thus, wherever the class struggle outbalances the consciousness of political unity, or wherever the destruction of political unity is the accusation hurled successfully by the one class against the other, there the bureaucratic apparatus, growing with every shift in election or Cabinet change, becomes the prize of political party struggle. Consequently parties organized or at least crystallized round class interests, are interested in the control of an increasing bureaucratic apparatus than in the fundamental cure of this situation, in the reconstruction of the social order, or in the limitation of the state to its proper field.

No wonder then that this cancerlike growth of bureaucracy in society produces a quasi-totalitarian state, a mixture of mercantilist and socialist bureaucracy. With the advent of this evil, all began to seek the strong state, strong against the class opponent. They had forgotten that the really strong state is not the bustling bureaucratic state but rather the reserved state that rules above the busy citizen. It reigns in solemn majesty, the imperial arbiter of interests, the protector of the common good. This majesty is typified not by busy bureaucrats but by the sublimity of political symbols, by the flag, by the national anthem, and by the calm dignity of the legislators, the Supreme Court, the President, where the venerable office and the esteemed institution is more important than personal ambitions and individual weaknesses. The state is majesty, dignity, sublimity. What is symbolized, what is invisible to the bodily eye but so visible to the eye of the intellect and dear to the heart and mind of the citizen, that is the state, though skeptics and cynics try to argue it away. We may add that consequently state and religion are more closely related than modern laicism thinks. It is not a mere custom, but rather a profound symbol of the biblical sentence, "By Me kings reign," that our legislative assemblies are opened with prayer. Power is thus submerged in a feeling of responsibility before God and before the people. Here is the best protection against arbitrariness and abuse.

The theory that started out to do away with the "political animal" has produced the "economic animal." What a strange result! A weak state because subservient to strong class interests; a meddling bureaucracy doing away with the self-government and self-control of the natural social, professional, and vocational groups; a concentration of social, economic, and "public" power. This power controls the whole community but is vested in private individuals and in private organization. It is ruled by private interests without the counterbalance and the justification of power, namely, public responsibility and subordination to the common good, responsible to the people, the public, the *respublica*.

VI. The Weakening of Social Ethics

The first cause of this development is the neglect of morality and an exaggerated individualism that forgets the basic principle of subsidiarity and of self-government.

Wherever men live and work together there arises the problem of power. Though it is a wholesome thing to channel the use of that power by the imposition of legal rules and of formalized proceedings and standards, what is decisive is the moral restriction, that restriction and responsibility which make power and powerholder alike subject to the end of the organization, the common good. This philosophical teleology of power becomes moral restriction and is stronger than the finesses of legalist proceedings, which are, as history shows, only a weak element of resistance against the temptation to abuse of power.[4] There is much more wisdom than modern man suspects in the volumes so frequently published in the sixteenth and seventeenth centuries concerning the education of princes. They were directed against Machiavelli's Prince who is a cunning, clever, amoral politician animated by lust for power, recognizing only one standard· success. In these books e.g. in Ribadeneira's *Princeps Christianus*

---

[4] The modern Caesarist tyranny, resting on the principle of popular sovereignty, plebiscites, and even general franchise, shows this distinctly.

adversus Macchiavellum or in the more famous *De rege et regis institutione* of Juan de Mariana, just the opposite is taught. Piety, religion, nay self-interest teach the prince the just policy. He is taught that he may be rightfully deposed, if he abuses his power; for the people is greater than the king and the king's authority and power is derived from the people for the sake of the common good and the popular liberties.[5]

We in our times are again aware of this problem. Therefore we try hard to educate for democracy, meaning of course an ethical political education of the citizen to prevent the abuse of power by the modern sovereign, the people, especially by a controlled part of it, called the majority, which may establish mob rule and then prepare the stage for the tyrant. This task of education, an ethical task, is the best proof that the decisive problem in power is the moral one.

The second cause we have called exaggerated individualism. It appears in the opposition of individual and state. This opposition omits the most important intermediary communities: the family, the free, religious, neighborhood, professional, and vocational groups, the free educational and cultural organizations, by narrowing the freedom of assembly to political groups. The opposition of individual and state is in a way the secularized opposition of individual conscience and Church, religious individualism, which was at the root of the Reformation but was somewhat corrected in practical life, as even appears in the history of the individual dissenters in the congregations of the dissenters. This opposition of individual and state or, to use Spencer's famous formula, man versus the state, though it represents a kind of perpetual process, took on a note of acrimony at the time of the revolt against the absolute state.

For the absolute state had practically done away with the old intermediary organizations, the guilds, the professional organizations, the self-government of towns, and so on. The absolute state did this in order to have under itself only subjects, some of them privileged ones because they were the necessary bureaucratic functionaries of the police state. With the bourgeois revolutions the modern citizen turns against the absolute prince and seeks freedom in a decided polemic antithesis of freedom for the individual against the state. So strong is

---

[5] As the old saying is: *Nunquam libertas gratior exstat quam sub rege pio.* Nathaniel Micklem, *Theology of Politics* (1941), p. 140.

that idea of the individual's untrammeled freedom that the democrats of the French Revolution and to a certain extent of the English Revolution eagerly pick up Hobbes' invective against the "corporations," the intermediary organizations. The French Revolutionary Assembly abolished the political privileges of nobility and clergy in its first resolution. Then followed the abolition of the guilds and the professional organizations, and soon the enactment of the Civil Constitution of the Clergy. In England likewise the old economic organizations were sacrificed to the principle of free, i.e., individualist, competition. Attempts of workers at unionism were punished on the score that they were an illegal conspiracy. Even in the United States an individualist interpretation of the rights of man served well to keep the individuals truly individuals, for some time at least.

The trouble was, of course, that the great pleadings for actual liberties against actual oppressions in the police state became one great pleading for liberty against the state. But this justified liberal attitude, stressing the dignity of the individual and his rights to self-government against the collectivism of the police state, turned into Liberalism, which exalts abstract liberty as a dogma, as a creed, as an absolute value. The substance of community life, then, and its forms become relations between individuals without an objective, transcendent end as the standard of value. Social ethics, social justice, social philosophy must give way to new sciences independent of values, to economics, to political science, and to sociology. Forgetting that all human life oscillates in tension between opposing poles (here liberty versus *ordo*, individual versus community), only the first links are considered, and the social world must be interpreted in their light.

"Old-fashioned" philosophers, poets, and thinkers, such as the popes from Pius IX on, began to deplore the destruction of these intermediary organizations that surrendered the weaker individuals, now isolated and defenseless, to the callousness of the economically stronger. They deplored the dissolution of the family, the pouring of great masses of rural families, torn from their customs and protective morals that helped them to live, into the slums of the great industrial cities. They deplored the disparaging of moral values by the skeptical realists and the cynical naturalists of modern literature, the vanishing of social virtues along with their nursery, the dissolving family. Furthermore, they deplored that these individuals were now so individual that they could not see beyond their narrow self-interests and, when in trouble, cried for help to the state. For not much else was left between the individual and the state, which thus threatens to turn paternalistic. In such a highly integrated society as ours, this means totalitarianism. They deplored that these aggregated individuals might easily become emotional, vague, and amorphous masses and, through the diffusion of general franchise, might become a political mob, an easy prey for ambitious politicans or a popular Caesarism, a new tyranny. Such fears were expressed by Hegel, Newman, Pius IX, Ketteler, and not a few of the fathers of the American Constitution.

It may be that here and there these men have exaggerated, that they have been rather conservative and have not clearly seen that brighter side of this individualist civilization. Still their criticism is wholesome and by far not so wrong as that of those contemporaries whose sons all too eagerly now begin to glorify Fascism, or seek communism. Today a new evaluation of the criticism of these conservatives, but a short time ago still being shouted down, begins to put in its appearance. A return to first principles is always a good thing. Let us not forget that what is worth while in our civilization has its roots in the leading ideas of Christianity: God, the sovereign Creator and Lawgiver, the dignity of the human person, and the salvation of the soul for the world beyond through a virtuous life here. What is worth while in modern civilization is precisely that Christian heritage. To the extent that we live humanly, we are nourished by these values, now long since secularized.[6]

VII. The State as a Moral Organism

Catholic political philosophy considers the state an organic unit, in which, under the preservation of their metaphysical, substantial equality and independence, the members of the moral organism in different, unequal, concrete functions form that organism. Thus the dignity of the person always exists even in the humblest function of the organic whole. Precisely this is the most perfect expression of per-

---

[6] I find in Renan's *Feuilles détaches* (pp. X, 17 f.) a striking illustration. This somewhat tired, somewhat resigned skeptic, doubtful of himself says: "L'homme vaut en proportion du sentiment réligieux qu'il emporte de sa première éducation et qui parfume toute sa vie. . . . Les personnes réligieuses vive d'une ombre. Nous vivons de l'ombre d'une ombre. De quoi vivra-t'on après nous?"

sonality in the service of the whole, which exalts the individual and perfects the community. This organic idea of the state as a cooperative whole of mutually complementary functions, with preservation of the substantial independence and specific dignity of the person, has been rightly called the active, the forming, the measuring, and sometimes even the revolutionary principle of Christian social metaphysics. And further, the function itself as a forming principle, too. Actually the state does not find as its matter an unqualified, atomistic aggregation of individuals formally equal. Its matter is the individuals living in their natural and free organizations like the family, the neighborhood, the religious community, and the various organizations of cooperative economic and cultural activity. The quality of individuality is, moreover, a negative one, abstract and therefore easily egalitarian. But the human being, apart from being an individual, is always a father or a mother, a son or a daughter, a brother or a sister, a farmer or a townsman, a member of a certain profession or vocation, or a member of a religious group, a believer, and so on. And these qualifications constitute his social life. Whereas the individual personality is the basis of equality, the source of inalienable rights, the sphere sacred and inviolable against any intervention from outside and from the state, the differentiation in situation and in function is the positive social qualification in social and political existence.

Therefore the polemic antithesis of individual versus state as the total problem of political philosophy is not acceptable. Catholic philosophy felt not only that it was much too abstract and unreal but that it contained dangerous dissolving tendencies, if put in a radical form. It suspected that this antithesis would lead by fanatical conclusions from the individual pole to the dissolution of all community, to a mere social utilitarian interpretation and subservience of the community values: family, marriage, profession. These would appear as exclusive service values to the profit and interest of the individuals. Marriage would appear as a contract not much different from a sales contract; all and anything in marital relations would be at the subjective pleasure and will of the individual. The *status* character would disappear in favor of a bundle of contractual rights and obligations, merely for the benefit, interests, and subjective pleasure of the partners, who must consequently be allowed to void the contract, if the "merchandise" does not measure up to the expectations, or if the partners cannot get

along without a specific moral effort. Similarly the rights and unlimited freedom of the individual would be stressed against the state
as an *ordo*, while the duties and obligations of the misunderstood
status of a citizen would be minimized and limited, thus delivering
the forms of social life to the wanton selfish and subjective utilitarianism of the individuals. This is what Catholic philosophy foresaw as the
outcome of the attempt to base political philosophy on the one pole,
the individual. If one sets out in linear fashion from the other pole of
the antithesis, one comes necessarily to totalitarianism with the complete surrender of the individual person, who now becomes an indifferent instrument of the leviathan. The individual is nothing, the
state (or the nation or the race or the class) is all, in opposition to the
other dictum, that the individual is all, the state and the family and the
communal groups are nothing. Again and again Catholic political
philosophy, from the days of the French Revolution on, has tried to
show how closely related are individualist Liberalism, the Ricardian
economic philosophy of individualism, and modern collectivism in its
different totalitarian forms of communism and Nazism.

For the organic conception, the social process, as we have repeatedly
said, develops in different stages. They are: individual person, family,
neighborhood (town, city), professional and vocational groups, religious, national, cultural, educational organizations, and finally the
state as the *unitas ordinis,* itself again a member of the community of
states or nations, humanity. All organizational forms have their intrinsic values and their objective ends, the upper form does not make
the lower one superfluous; it must never abolish it, nor may it take
over its functions and purposes. The individual in actual life does not
nakedly confront the state, the sovereign concentrated power, and
enviously strive to protect himself, to stress his rights, to minimize
power. In a society highly integrated by a division of functions, these
social forms confronting the state and protecting the rights of the individual safeguard the individual in the protection of the intermediary
groups: the family as a unity of parents, children, and grandchildren
and as a unity of generations, the town as the unity of neighborhood,
the professional and vocational economic and cultural autonomous
groups. Hobbes, the glorifier of the state, the despiser of individual
rights, was instinctively more correct than many modern individualists, when he hated the "corporations," the groups and organizations

under the state. His leviathan became more powerful in proportion as it did away with these intermediary self-governed groups. And it is of profound significance that St. Thomas calls the paternal authority a *quasi-regia potestas*. When Aristotle protested against Plato's proposal of communism of wives and property for the ruling class of the warriors, he did so because this "emancipation" from family and home would constitute a tyranny of the warriors, who would become the state.

Thus the social process shows the end values of the intermediary organizations and their right to realize their ends in the *ordo* of the state. Thus it is once and for all established that the state may not substitute itself for these organizations because it then degenerates into the meddlesome, bureaucratic, and paternalist state, the last step on the way to tyrannical totalitarianism. Correlated to this is the principle of subsidiarity, especially noted in *Quadragesimo anno* in a most forceful manner. "Of its very nature, the true aim of all social activity should be to help individual members of the social body, but never to destroy or absorb them." Consequently "it is wrong to withdraw from the individual and commit to the community at large what private enterprise and industry can accomplish." [7] From this it follows that "it is a disturbance of right order for a larger and higher organization to arrogate to itself functions which can be performed efficiently by smaller and lower bodies." Thus the principle of subsidiarity applies also to the different natural or freely created communities in the social order. Social life is governed by the principles of autonomy, of hierarchy and intervention. The individuals in their free associations and natural communities are organized by natural instinct and reason into an order with a unity represented by the state as a sovereign organic community. In solidarity of existence, aims, and actions, men live in this community to perform their highest task, the salvation of their souls and the glory of God.

The hierarchy of ends is mirrored in a hierarchy of functional associations designed, directed, and measured as to efficiency and good-

---

[7] The Latin text has here: *propria marte et propria industria possunt perfici*. The text is here concerned with a general principle applicable to all social activity not, as may be interpreted from the English version, only for the field of economics. The ambiguity of the English word "industry" does not attach to the Latin *industria*. The principle generally opposes bureaucratic centralization and propounds autonomy and self government in the social order as the principles counterbalancing centralized authority

ness by their objective ends. As these ends, though parts of the whole moral order, are still real ends, it behooves rational, free beings to organize themselves and to act in performing the end by their own initiative. Consequently the lower communities are truly autonomous; man has a natural right to self-government, in actual organizations and activities, to perform the objective ends in the *ordo*. But, in his hazardous and transitory existence in time and space, with his inclination to egoism, to passions disturbing the order, to imperfection in the execution of purposes, with his difficulties in realizing the metaphysical order of ends in a historical situation, man himself may become a danger for the right functioning of the lower societies. Vested interests may abuse them; lust for power may divert them from service of the common good to the selfish advantages of politicians. The concrete form and constitution originating under specific historical circumstances and serving well for a time may become too rigid and thus hamper the right function or even be totally inadequate to reach the objective end. Thus a distortion in the social organism may disturb the balanced functioning and welfare of the whole. If this should occur, the supreme protector of the order, whatever its form, the state in that significant sense, has the right and the duty to intervene.

The purpose of this intervention is the reconstruction of the order, the rehabilitation of the function, not the abolition of the part or the substitution of the state for the lower society. To illustrate: Economics is the production of wealth not as an absolute end, but as a service end to bring the whole community to a fuller and more perfect life measured by the metaphysical and religious ideas of man's destiny. Therefore the production of wealth is more than a problem of technical efficiency, of the most economic means; it is also a problem of order, of justice, of charity. For wealth is produced for men. Thus the individual and functional distribution of wealth and of the national income, always produced by cooperation among the individual members and the economic groups, is of utmost political importance; any order in society and state is an order of production as well as one of distribution. Every member should participate as much in this material part of the common good as it contributes to it.

But this is a question of social justice, of the right social and economic order. In some parts of the social and economic field, the rule is not that of the objective standards of justice and charity, but rather the rule of unequal bargaining power. Or the abstract forces of supply and demand operate in contradiction to the quest for justice. Or again, because of the commercialization of labor-power, the property-less proletarian, in his life and social existence, is subject to the blind and morally indifferent forces of supply and demand. Thus he is unable to participate fully in the advantages of the common good: a standard of living above the level of poverty, an economic security for his existence, a family life worthy of human dignity. In all these cases there arises a situation, a social and economic disorder that cries for an intervention of the state. A readjustment of the economic system by political decision is necessary if all the participants themselves are not able to readjust the mistakes by their own initiative, either because they cannot cure the distortion of the order or because they are not willing to cure it on account of a lack of true appreciation of justice. But this intervention can never be more than readjustment, reconstitution, of the order of self-initiative, of property, of free functioning of the individual persons, their associations, and functional groups in the social and economic field as a *status* of the economic society to be enacted and enforced by the political authority, the state.

The order of justice is thus the measure of intervention. Consequently the state has to restore the malfunctioning parts or help in their self-restoration. It must help to abolish the unjust distribution of bargaining power, the abuse of social and economic power against one group; because such an unjust distribution or abuse is against the common good. But the state has no right to substitute a bureaucratic apparatus for the functioning of the free associations, nor has it, by reasons of social perfectionism, a right to meddle continually in petty tutelage in the affairs of its citizens. A. Smith was right when he stressed the importance of self-interest against mercantilist bureaucracy. He was wrong when, by a rather individualist interpretation, he declared that self-interest controlled by free unrestricted competition would be able in a mechanical, automatic way to produce a true social order of justice and harmony.

The organic view of the state offers thus the critical standard, too. It measures the right and wrong developments in every historical situation. The basis is the natural law as the supreme rule under which the state and all its powers function. It may be that practical jurists scoff at the idea of natural law. But we should learn from experiences. Modern totalitarianism grew most readily in national cultures where for generations the idea of natural law had been ridiculed and where the rule of judges had been substituted by a picture of the judge as a mere automaton, applying in court any rule that the sovereign commanded. It grew most readily, too, where the mind of the rulers was not dominated by the vision of an unchangeable order to be realized by each generation in changing historical circumstances. These rulers were dominated rather by the usefulness of everything for the flawless functioning of the ant-state or the materialistically conceived race (or class state). This attitude disregarded the eternal values and the human dignity of the individual person; a person destined for more than wealth, power, efficiency; destined for happiness, for freedom in justice, for the perfection of himself and the salvation of his soul.

CHAPTER XIII

The Nature of the Common Good

I. The Objective Purpose of the State

It is the privilege and duty of man over and over again to ponder the end of the social institutions and forms that give shape to life. Life is a perpetually changing stream of noble and ignoble impulses, of love and hate, of ardent striving for justice and recurring betrayal of spiritual values for material advantages. Thus the actual forms of social life are always in danger of being abused or of becoming obsolete or unfit to reach their objective ends and thus obnoxious to the very end which they ought to serve.

It is, therefore, always necessary to measure the actual forms in their historical working by the ideal philosophical end of these social forms. Moreover, this re-examination is needed to justify, before the human mind and the urge for freedom, the restricting bonds which these social forms always carry.

Now just this very question in regard to the end of the state is, more than any other question, dependent on the philosophical background of him who tries to answer it. The basis for his answer is a complex one. It depends on his idea of man, of man's end in this earthly life and beyond. It is dependent on his ideas about the existence and nature of a universal order in human community, about life and the respective moral values to be realized or at least guaranteed by that order. It is the question of freedom and compulsion, of the rights of man and the extent of governmental authority, of individual initiative and superimposed government interference with this sphere of individual initiative. It is the question of the independence of the family and the religious community from the sovereign body politic. And lastly it becomes the problem of the existence and necessity of a real community of nations as the highest form of human social life.

This problem is thus twofold. A mere study of facts may be interesting and helpful. It may even be sufficient if the political and social order is not at stake. A bourgeois society may thus not arouse any doubts in the mind of the bourgeois capitalist who derives a good income from his vested interests, however much the factory worker and the moral philosopher, the progressive statesman and the liberal jurist, may have grave doubts concerning the sufficiency and excellence of that order. But, when the fundamental institutions of the existing political order become doubtful, then a mere study of facts is not sufficient. With irresistible force the philosophical question of right, or we may say of justice, arises and demands an answer. And this is what we have to consider now, always of course being aware that we do it for the practical reason of measuring the value of the existing order and getting a foundation for answers to the practical questions put before us.[1]

By these statements we have implicitly said that the state has an objective purpose, ultimately in its very essence independent of the mere factual will of its constituents, just as we have explicitly said that the idea of the state, its essence, is of a supra-individual character, that it is a moral, legal, and objective institution and not merely the sum of its constituents. On the other hand the end of the state is not absolute according to Christian philosophy. It is inserted into the universal order of human ends, into the order of creation, therefore subordinated to the supreme end of all creation, the glory of God.

II. The Service Character of the State

When we say that the end of the state is an objective one and is not the mere sum of the ends of its constituents, it should not be concluded that man's end is wholly subordinated to the state; the ends of the state and of man really coincide. Human life is possible only in the framework of the state; from this fact the political authority derives dignity and majesty. True as it is that man is not a slave of the

[1] These distinctions are today of greatest importance. The totalitarian state can be refuted only by a clear view of the end of the state. The distinction between power and authority, eminently important especially in the conquered nations, the principle of subsidiarity, the distinction between de facto and de jure recognition in international law, of legitimacy and mere legality, all these problems rest on a clear idea of the end of the state; likewise the idea of eminent domain, of the domestic affairs left to the sovereign decision of the state under international law (Covenant of the League of Nations, Art. 15, 8).

state, just as true is it that the state is not a servant of the individual citizen. Therefore the sacrifice of the individual citizen's property, of his rights, and even of his life in defense of the state, is justifiable, when we agree that the end of the state, the common good, is superior quantitatively and qualitatively to the life and property of the individual citizen as such. How otherwise could we concede to the state the *jus vitae ac necis,* the right of conscription, the authority to send the soldier-citizen into war? This is an inescapable conclusion from the fact that the end of the state is not identical with the individual end of the private citizens or any sum of them. It is true, as we shall see, that normally there occurs a coincidence: the common good of the state and the private good of the citizens are interdependent; normally the common good and the citizens' private good cannot widely diverge; they converge so strongly that we rightly speak of a coincidence.

This can easily be demonstrated by the following considerations which have great practical bearing. The state does not exist outside or over and above its citizens. It is not a substance. It exists only in its citizens, by them, and with them. The sum of the individuals is the "matter" of the *unitas ordinis politici,* of the state, whereas the form is the moral end, expressed in its laws, customs, and political constitutional organization. It is the common purpose, usually stated in the preamble of modern constitutions, that unifies, that forms and organizes the individuals into a distinct political community. The people, therefore, as distinguished from the state, as a sum of individuals and as a cultural or racial unit, may continue to exist as a social group while, through the destruction of the constitution and of the constitutive power, the order of law and the political organization is destroyed, e.g., by final conquest by another state.

From this standpoint the state, as distinguished from the whole of the individual citizens and their families, is a servant. Its end, the common good, can be realized only by enabling the citizens to fulfill their ultimate and transcendent end, the salvation of their souls, in pursuing their secular task in peace and security and in mutual help. Therefore it is not true that under all circumstances the end of the state must prevail in case of conflict. The state normally cannot demand every sacrifice. There exist genuine limits to the sacrifices of the citizens for the common good, and the acknowledgment of such limits distinguishes the Christian idea from the paganism of the totalitarian state. In a genuine conflict between natural law and the positive law of the state, the natural law prevails. In a genuine conflict between the salvation of man's soul and a positive demand of the state, the salvation of the soul prevails. Besides these qualitative conflicts we have what we may call the quantitative conflicts. Even a just war may not be continued, if it would mean the destruction of, let us say, 70 per cent of the male population. For what is then the state, the concrete *unitas ordinis politici,* when there are no more citizens? [2] Furthermore, because the end of the state is relative, never can there be demanded from all the citizens the renunciation of their basic rights of family life, of their freedom to direct the education of their children, to fulfill their religious obligations. For it is precisely to enable them to live up to these individual rights and duties all together in the peace and security of communal life, that the state is produced.

The idea of the "reason of state" as something beyond morality is therefore irreconcilable with the Christian idea of the end of the state, because it ignores the service character of the end of the state.

The genuine Christian contribution to the philosophy of the state has been the doctrine of this service character of the state. The Greeks, especially Plato in some of his dialogues where he praises Sparta, looked to the *polis* as the supreme absolute master of the citizens. Against it there was no appeal to the gods, political gods as they were. For the Greeks human nature and man's last end found their absolute perfection in citizenship.

Therefore it was revolutionary to say: We must obey God rather than man. Here "man" meant the pagan state in its all-embracing power. It was a denial that the state's end, the common good, is the pinnacle of all human ends and values, and that it must prevail in all conflicts, moral and religious. The state's end now became relative and limited. If the state was not any longer the moral order itself, it had to become a part of the transcendent moral order emanating in reason and in revelation from God, above nations and states and races and cults of tribal deities.

[2] This may have been the conflict which the King of the Belgians faced in May, 1940. Before any emotional quasi-heroic judgment of King Leopold's surrender, we must at least view the genuine conflict.

III. Definition of the Common Good

Since the ultimate end and highest perfection of man is not citizenship in the *polis* on this earth but citizenship in the city of God, the early Fathers had to recoin the inherited classical word for the purpose of the state—*felicitas*—and limit it to the *felicitas externa* or *politica.* It corresponds to the Christian idea of the mortal state, of the state as a framework during the *status viatoris* necessary for this *status* and belonging to its perfection. Thus the end of the state becomes immanent, belonging exclusively to this world; it becomes the felicity of this life as opposed to eternal felicity beyond. The state ceases to embrace the moral world entirely; it is no longer the objective morality. Not everthing that man has, does he owe to the state, as was held by Hegel, in whom the ancient political philosophy found a late renaissance. But as little as nature loses its innate dignity and its intrinsic value through grace but rather reconquers it in an elevated and sanctified form, just so little does the state and its end lose dignity and majesty. Now on the contrary there falls upon it a ray from the divine Majesty by whom all rulers rule.

Since the time of the Greeks the end of the state has been regarded as the common good, or the political felicity, a status in which is reached a perfect satisfaction of all the wants of the community and thus, as the community does not actually exist without its members, of all its members To quote merely Suarez' definition: It is a state of affairs, a *status,* in which men live in an order of peace and justice with a sufficiency of goods that are related to the conservation and the development of the material life with that probity of morals which is necessary for the preservation of external peace and felicity of the body politic and the continuous conservation of human nature.[8]

The common good is the prevailing principle that controls any other interest in its order. It is the creative principle, the conserving power of the body politic; it is the final cause of the state, its intimate end; it and nothing else gives the political, sovereign power its moral authority and legitimacy. Therefore the common good is the directive rule and the last unappealable norm of the acts of the sovereign power, as the object of this power is nothing but to produce, in collaboration

[8] Suarez, *De leg.,* III, c.11, n.7.

with the citizens, the actual realization of the common good. The common good is the first and the last law. (*Salus populi, bonum commune, suprema lex.*) It turns the external amorphous mass, the mere conglomeration of individuals, into a solidarist body of mutual help and interest, into the organically united nation. The laws receive their justice exclusively through their service to the common good.[4] Under no circumstances can it be conceded that public authority, the end of which is to serve the common good, should be put into the service of private interests; for public authority is instituted for the common good of all citizens; and a law that does not serve the common good is not "law" at all.[5]

IV. THE COMMON GOOD A RELATIVE VALUE

Yet the common good is not an absolute value. It remains in the sphere of the secular life and is viewed from the ultimate end of the human person and from the final purpose of all creation. Hence it is a relative end; its place is not on the pinnacle of the Christian hierarchy of values. Man's end is beyond this world. His last end, the salvation of his soul, is transcendent, and that institution which furthers this last end is therefore beyond the end of the state. The common good has to deal with the external secular felicity, yet by this the end of the state and the state itself are not degraded. In Catholic theology nature through original sin is not destroyed and is not made absolutely valueless. Thus the "world" retains its original value. Similarly the state and the common good in the sphere of nature belong to the order of creation and thus are in themselves values, in so far as they participate in the end of all creatures, the glory of God; all political power is derived from God and gets its majesty from God. The state and the common good are not the whole of morality; they are parts of that hierarchy of moral values which culminates in God. Therefore religion with its divinely instituted form, the Church, is beyond the state, and the common good of the religious community is different from the common good of the state, just as both communities are independent and sovereign in their respective orders.

---

[4] Leo XIII, especially in *Au milieu* and *Notre consolation*, makes a number of solemn declarations about the common good. Cf. *A.A.S.*, XXIV (1891–92), 519 ff., 641 ff.

[5] St. Thomas, *Summa theol.*, Ia IIae, q.90, a.2.

When in the nineteenth century secularism took on a militant anti-clerical air, the contention that the end of the state is relative and is a part-value but not the chief value of the moral order, was described as a sinister attempt to subject the state, its legislation, and administration to the Church, in particular to the pope, whom the Vatican Council had just declared to be the infallible doctrinal authority in matters of faith and morals. Thus the authority of the Church represented by the pope, it was said, becomes actually the soul of the whole system of human, secular community life, and the state will always be endangered by clerical parties, because the decisive loyalty of the Catholic citizen is owed not to the state, but to the religious authority, i.e., the pope.

Such a contention is understandable only against the background of the nationalism so typical for the nineteenth century. According to this nationalism, to the national state is owed exclusively and to the whole extent one supreme loyalty, that of the citizen. Even the famous ideal of separation of Church and state, in particular the principle of freedom of worship, actually became a creed, a material dogma of religious indifferentism that was considered a necessary basis of national unity. There is a difference between the practical policy of neutrality of the state in religious affairs and the creed of neutrality as it was shown in the Third Republic in France and in republican Spain. Neutrality and religious indifferentism became a political creed, a kind of civil religion which even liberty-loving Rousseau deemed necessary.[6] An ardent anticlerical militant agnosticism, so different from the private agnosticism of private individuals, becomes a public creed. The agnostic nation has its own table of values and either it tries to enforce them—then farewell to freedom—or it indulges in relativism. Then the marrow of social and political consistency is destroyed by the disease of partisan struggle, by corruption and great infidelity to any supra-individual, supra-material values. No, we should be well aware that the best protection of liberty is this doctrine: that the common good, the end of the state, is only a relative value and that there are other values higher than the state and beyond its competence.

---

[6] *Contrat social*, Bk. IV, chap. 8. This chapter should be read by all who think that continental liberalism (France, Italy, Spain) is as peaceful in matters religious as Anglo-American liberalism predominantly is.

It has been said with much justice that the struggle for the freedom of the Church from state domination and state interference, a struggle that issues from a doctrine of the independent common good of the religious community, has contributed more to human liberty than all the declamations of the Jacobins in the bourgeois revolutions. The reason is that this struggle rests on the belief that the common good of the state is not at all the supreme value, but is so only in the political order. It rests on the confidence that human reason is able to grasp the fundamentals of natural law; that consequently the end of the state is recognizable and distinguishable from that of the persons and that of the religious community.

Thus the profound meaning of assigning this relative value to the end of the state is not a depreciation of the moral nature and value of the state. On the contrary, this insertion of the end of the state into the supereminent moral order gives to the state a moral dignity as a servant to the eternal, transcendental end of man. We must never forget that any attempt to give to a creature, whether to a man or to a state, absolute sovereign value means simply to deify that man or that state with the consequence that its necessarily arbitrary will becomes the final measure of right and wrong, of just and unjust. Then freedom is impossible; because freedom presupposes reason, and free will informed by reason. Thus the freedom of the citizen is actually protected by this relativity of the end of the state, because now those in authority must be aware that they speak not as a sort of divinity, but as men, subjected to the supereminent law of nature. Thus they have to be mindful of the great temptation which authority over man brings with it, that lust for unlimited power. The idea of the reason of state regarded as the highest value means nothing but that all other values become relative. The rights of the individual person, of the parents and of the family, of the Church, and of the professional and vocational organizations, all become instrumental values for politics.

When thus the state or the men who are in authority are made gods, then not only the positive law but also the idea of law itself must serve as a well-modeled mask for arbitrary power. Religion, the Church, is made a servant, a tool of mass psychology to be used against the liberties of the people. Then the state becomes the cold monster, and the statesman that kind of calculating cruel power without moral restraint, without moral guidance, as Machiavelli described him in *The Prince*. To insert the end of the state into the realm of morality, to deny that state and morality are identical, is therefore not a danger to the state as the anticlerical thinkers and parties used to tell us, but it is precisely the basis for genuine political ethics. Omnipotence and supreme perfect morality are one and the same only in the infinite God beyond the created world. If man tries to confer omnipotence and supreme moral authority upon his equals or upon finite human institutions, he only creates molochs that devour him.

V. Individualist Interpretation of the Common Good

The common good, which is the end of the state, is in the secular order independent and autonomous as compared to the end of the family, and of that other perfect society, the Church. But it is independent, too, so far as it is not simply the sum of the private good of the individuals composing the state. It is not a mere nominalist concept invented by man for the sake of an economy of thinking, without reality and objective foundation. The presupposition of such a view would be that the idea of the state itself is only a *flatus vocis* and that the state exists exclusively for the private benefit of individuals; that the term "common good" is merely a simplification for the rather complicated phrase, greatest utility of the greatest numbers, as the individualist school of utilitarianism teaches and has taught from the Sophists in Athens down to our days. Against this, Catholic political philosophy has always upheld that the common good has reality and is essentially different from the private good of any sum of individuals.[7] Suarez even goes so far as to say it is not the task of the state to take care of the private good of the individuals inasmuch as they are private persons; on the contrary, the end of the state is the good (*felicitas*) of the perfect society; and the state has to take care of the individuals only so far as they are members.[8]

The individualist interpretation of the concept of the common good is the following. The state is not a new reality but a nominalist statement of the fact that the individuals have agreed to live in certain social relations, exclusively in order to promote their individual

[7] St. Thomas, *Summa theol.*, IIa IIae, q.38, a.7; cf. q.31, a.3.
[8] *De legibus*, III, c.11.

purposes and ends as individuals, not as members of a qualitatively different *status politicus*. As the state is nothing more than a free and rather arbitrary network of relations between individuals without an objective reality or true essence beyond these actual relations, thus what is called the common good is only a name for the sum of the private particular goods of all the individuals. It is not an objective and qualitatively different reality. The state has only a service value and is consequently a utilitarian institution exclusively for the interests of the individuals as inherently self-sufficient beings. It is founded by the individuals merely to further their interests as individuals.[9] Therefore what is called the *common good* is not really distinguishable from the mere sum of the particular goods of the individuals. The individuals are the only reality. The individual is fundamentally autonomous and self-sufficient. Anything beyond his individual existence can be only of service character, can be only dependent means subjectively valuable for the individual. In the view of liberal individualism, the individual citizen appears as essentially self-sufficient and perfect. He agrees to live in a political community only so far as his individual purposes are thereby served. Any binding restrictions that seem still to be necessary are regarded as a loss of freedom, and are expected, through progress, gradually to disappear.

The typical individualist believes in the final overcoming of any form of society that demands any kind of sacrifice of his individual subjective interests and any restrictions of his liberty. The individual remains a social monad in Leibnitz' sense. Man is *per accidens,* not by intrinsic nature, a social being and a political being. Consequently the common good, which is presumably the end of the state as a specific form of social being, has no objective value or independent reality. What is called common good is merely a distributive sum of the interests and private goods of the individuals.

In the opposing view, that of socialist totalitarianism—and all totalitarianism is somewhat socialistic, and all kinds of socialism become necessarily totalitarian in trying to become actual—the individual and his objective ends are completely submerged in society or

---

[9] Rousseau (*Contrat social*, Bk. I, chap. 6) has stated the view clearly: "Trouver une forme d'association qui défend et protège de toute la force commune la personne et les biens de chaque associé et par laquelle chacun s'unissant à tous, n'obéisse pourtant qu'à lui-même et reste aussi libre qu'auparavant."

state and in its ends. The individuals are mere marionettes in the service of impersonal powers of economic productive relations or of a mystical and irrational spirit of the nation revealed in a deified leader for ends and purposes that are utterly foreign to the individual. All socialisms say in one way or the other: the individual is nothing, the nation, the party, the proletariat is all. But still they have the same Messianic complex as has liberal individualism, namely, that in the end that dreadful institution, the state, will wither away and a new paradisaic millennium of freedom will appear; a state of freedom where everyone gets what is due to him and what he individually and subjectively wants.[10] Socialism is really socialistic only as a means, as a historical function for the transformation from capitalist to socialist production. Teleologically, regarded from the angle of its chiliastic dreams of the perfect socialist society, socialism is utterly individualist. That final society is non-political, without authority and compulsory laws, without family and a functional division of classes or groups. These are only historical stages of a blind causal development of materialist productive forces. Thus this final society is an amorphous multitude of socialized individuals, classless and egalitarian.[11]

VI. NATURE OF THE COMMON GOOD IN CATHOLIC POLITICAL PHILSOPHY

Against these doctrines Catholic political philosophy contends that the common good, like the state, is not a mere sum but a qualitatively different entity, that the common good is a new objective good essentially different from the sum of the goods of the individuals. Of course this is a consequence of the idea of the state as a distinct higher form of social coexistence of persons. The state is an objective reality. But does this mean that the common good and the authority of the state, which has as its object the common good, are

10 This chiliastic dream, revealing the character of socialism, has led acute observers to say that fundamentally the modern forms of socialism are equally as individual-minded as liberal individualism. Capitalism and socialist collectivism are the one the legal, the other the natural, son of the same philosophy; agnostic individualism. "Agnostic" because both acknowledge nothing beyond the material sphere; "individualism" because they indulge in the same chiliastic dreams of a stateless existence of individuals.

11 Undoubtedly there exists a multitude of shades in socialism and individualism, with different approximation on to the extreme expressions. But the gist of individualism and socialism as systems may still be represented in a sketch like the above.

under all circumstances and always the superior value and the controlling power in relation to the individual? Or is the whole discussion an empty one, so far as in reality the common good and the interests and particular goods of the individuals are identical and thus the discussion is mere hair-splitting? Against the first contention Catholic political philosophy decidedly stresses the fact that the state has also a service character. Against the second contention stands the fact that the readiness for the sacrifice of life itself in battle is a duty of justice for the citizen conscripted for military service in wartime, not merely a free voluntary act of *pietas*, and hence is demanded for the common good and is commonly approved. If that is to be upheld, then in the secular order, in the order of secular felicity, we must acknowledge that the end of the state, the common good, is qualitatively different from the good and the interest of the individual person. How are we to find a solution? And a satisfying answer to this problem is necessary. Without a clear grasp of the idea of the common good as the end of the body politic, neither a social ethics nor a political ethics can have a sound foundation.

We have now to refer to what was said about the nature of the state. If the state is a reality, a specific mode of being, namely, social being, then of course it must have its specific end and purpose. And consequently this end, as St. Thomas says, is qualitatively different from the private good of the individual and any kind of summation of such private goods.

The common good is formally the good order. It is the order among persons as individuals and as social beings inasmuch as they already live in families and other free organizations for religious, cultural, and social welfare and for economic purposes. The order, therefore, among persons embraces not only mutual services but material goods in relation to persons and to their individual or social purposes. Now an order, if one abstracts from persons or things ordered, is nonexistent; just as health can be predicated only of an organism as the order of the whole in its parts. Thus Suarez says that the common good *consurgit ex bonis singulorum.*[12] Hence it is impossible without the individual members fulfilling their own particular good. The existence and the development of this actual order, that is, of the felicity, of peace and justice in the body politic, is in itself a value and is not

[12] Suarez, *De leg.,* I, c.7, n.3.

exclusively a mere means for the interests of the individuals. The music of an orchestra, the beauty of a mosaic, the flourishing life and well-proportioned structure of an organism, cannot be explained exclusively by the interests and independent value of the parts, whether these are the musical instruments, the little stones, or the limbs and organs of the organism. Beauty, melody, structure, the order of the parts forming the whole, are values in themselves.

Of course, the big difference between the biological organism or the bee-hive and the anthill state that we may by analogy call animal states, and the *civitas humana* is that, whereas their order is one of blind obedience to their instincts, the political order is in its actual form the result of free human acts under the rule of reason and under direction by rational authority. It is a conscious process that produces that order. And as the parts or members that are ordered are persons, the order must be of service character. A common good, a concrete order, that would destroy fundamental rights or infringe on them would be disorder, a mutilated common good. If, therefore, on account of the failure of the concrete order a whole group of the members should suffer injustices and intrusions into their personal sphere, offenses against human dignity, then the order is disturbed. Not only do those suffer who are immediately concerned, but the whole suffers, too, because the common good is not realized.

This thesis agrees with our common experience. Whenever the community to which we belong (e.g., town, parish, club) does not fulfill its purpose by letting injustices and blatant contradictions to its end continue, then all the members feel ashamed and hurt, not only those whose individual particular good is actually and directly hurt (for example, people living in slums). This is a strong proof that the whole as an ordered entity suffers because the whole, the town in this case, tolerated a state of affairs that, while hurting only a part, showed that the whole did not fulfill its end as intended by its nature, its *raison d'être*. Revolutionary forces will then arise with the claim to restore order, or to produce a better order. All really political problems are those of a concrete order, of a durable, just, and peaceful order. And all deep differences between the political creeds are differences of their ideas of a just order of peace, internal and external, and of how to construct and preserve it.

VII. COMMUTATIVE JUSTICE

The relation between common good and individual good will become clearer by a discussion of the different forms of justice. Aristotle, and later Scholasticism, distinguished legal, commutative, and distributive justice as parts of the virtue of justice. This doctrine is of the utmost importance for political philosophy. That it was put too much in the background in an era of exaggerated individualism has caused much wrong thinking, and the preservation of it has been and is one of the most important contributions of Catholic political philosophy.

Commutative justice or the justice of exchange presupposes the equality of price and service or merchandise, of equality of debit and credit; it presupposes also the formal equality and freedom of the partners in the contract. What produces a violation of commutative justice is the actual inequality of contracting power in bargain or inequality of mutual exchange values. Inequality or lack of actual freedom in bargaining power or inequality of exchange values or conceptions about them is at the bottom of the complaints of injustice concerning the labor contract in modern times, as inequality between price paid and goods received is at the bottom of every market complaint. But the essential presupposition of all such complaints is that equality, formal equality, is considered always essential. Thus this justice regards all contractual partners as equal; to do so, it makes them persons and, so far as the contract is concerned, free and equal persons.

That this kind of justice is necessarily individualist needs no further explanation. A glance now at our civilization will show us that this justice, or rather the submission of all human social relations to this specific form of justice, is dominant and consequently concerns the interests of the individuals. Thus the popularity of divorce is based on the belief that the marriage contract is similar to any other private contract that is exclusively dependent on the interests of the individuals. That by marriage one enters an order, a status, as the old Christian tradition upholds, and that the family has its own interest or common good to which individuals have to sacrifice, is a view which is practically forgotten. The fundamental error of Rousseau is similarly the application of the rules of commutative justice to the relations between government or political authority and the governed. But in his system the necessary and well-founded equality and freedom leads to perpetual revolution, attempts to void the social contract or to enforce it, thus abolishing freedom even where it is justified.[18] Likewise the liberal theory of the labor contract, considering labor as a mere commodity with mere exchange value, applied exclusively the rules of commutative justice, but it failed to see that the vaunted freedom of contract and equality in bargaining power did not exist.[14] It failed to see that the question of a just wage is not only a question of the forces of demand and supply in a casual market situation and thus of commutative justice, but also one of distributive justice.

From the standpoint of strict justice—and commutative justice is intrinsically such—separating rather than unifying, the idea of a living wage or a family wage is a rather insoluble problem in the liberalist social pattern. True it is indeed that at least the more optimistic adherents of this individualist economic school presupposed that the prices (and wages), established by free competition on the basis of freedom of contract and legal equality in the market, would be just prices and wages. What was forgotten is the fact that this could be presupposed with some degree of certainty only if, in addition to freedom of contract and legal equality, a true equality of bargaining power would exist in the market. If that is not the case, as is undeniable, then the prices and wages are so much determined by inequality of bargaining power, freed from moral considerations, that often from the standpoint even of commutative justice such prices and wages cannot be considered just according to the quantitative equality of the exchanged values.

A labor contract, whether we like it or not, founds a community,

18 The deep aversion of Catholic philosophy to Rousseauism is not owing chiefly to his vituperative attacks against revealed religion and especially the Catholic Church, in the fourth book of the *Social Contract*. Rather it is prompted by the feeling that Rousseau's starting point is disruptive of all human institutions or must lead, in the name of freedom, to oppression of dissenters even where dissenting must be tolerated for the sake of human dignity. The history of anticlericalism proves this and, though one may try to explain this anticlericalism by a preceding clericalism, there remains everywhere in the theory and practice of continental liberalism a residuum that can only be explained by the wrong start of Rousseauism.

14 Unionism, when it goes into the labor market, is the attempt to do away with inequality of bargaining power.

and intentionally at least a durable community of interests, because its issue is a cooperative effort of employer and employees. Economics does not serve for the production of abstract wealth irrespective of its personal distribution, but it serves to satisfy the material wants of all the members of society who cooperate in its production. We do not mean, of course, that commutative justice should not rule the labor contract, the mutual rights and duties of the partners in the wage contract. We simply point out that the wage problem, especially the problem of the just wage, the family wage, cannot be treated if we exclude distributive justice, or as it is preferably called today, social justice. When in an actual economic system, because of the mechanism of this system, a family wage cannot be paid on account of the competition of female labor or child labor, then the market price of labor will fall far below the level of a family wage. The individual employer is now in an unavoidable dilemma. On the one hand, general justice requires that he pay a family wage according to the social nature of wealth-producing labor. On the other hand, owing to the mechanism of a competitive market system in which the wages are determined by the impersonal uncontrolled forces of supply and demand, the employer is unable to pay for any length of time more than the substandard (the family wage being the standard) competitive wage. What is the solution of this dilemma? None, if we acknowledge only commutative justice in all social relations. But if we agree that there exists a different kind of justice, social or distributive and legal justice, controlling specific relations, we may then find a solution.

Social and distributive justice refer to the public authorities who have to take care of the order of the common good, the welfare of the community. Their obligation according to social justice is to bring about such a social order and such economic conditions that the individual member in the community is enabled to fulfill the demands of commutative justice, e.g., pay a family wage. Thus the first obligation here is for the public authorities to bring about by social legislation such a change of the social and economic order that the individual members, the employers, are enabled to fulfill their obligations. Restrictive legislation for child labor and female labor would thus be a demand of social justice or, as it is sometimes called, common-good justice. We may even go a step farther by giving social justice a larger content than the traditional legal or common-good justice.

For social justice adresses the individuals as members of the order of the common good, too. Not only are they forbidden to circumvent for their selfish interests the measures of social legislation enacted by the public authority. Would it not equally be a demand of social justice in this broader sense not to use one's greater economic and social power against the efforts of labor to build up by unionization a stronger and less unequal bargaining power for the effective demand of a family wage? As long as the law of the land admits freedom of organization, one must conclude that such a demand not to interfere with the efforts of labor for unionization is, even without a specific prohibitive law, a demand of social justice. So at least do the social papal encyclicals approach this problem determining a strict right of labor for unionization, which means of course that all other groups in the economic society have to acquiesce. What now follows from this is that in the social and political field commutative justice and its specific object are not enough but call for a different form of justice with the order of the common good as its object. And this presupposes that the common good is a value in itself and not merely a sum of private goods.

If we try to apply the rules of commutative justice to the relation between state and citizen, we are soon at an impasse; yet this is actually the liberal and individualist effort. We may be able thus to destroy the privilege-state of the ancient regime. But how can we build up a new state? That new state of laissez-faire was a weak, passive onlooker at the markets, the markets where goods, services, philosophies, educational opportunities, and even religious creeds were offered with all the clamor of the trader. And the only task of the state was to keep the market in order, to protect freedom and property and to enforce the contracts of individuals. "Watchman state" was the appellation given to such a state by Lassalle with the approval of Bishop von Ketteler. In the matter of taxes such a state would acknowledge only a cold equality. In the matter of social legislation this individualist theory, that only recognizes commutative justice, would say that the protection of the market is enough, and social legislation would then mean inequality by giving one party privileges that, from the natural conditions in the labor market, were unjustifiable.

In the relation between state and individual according to this theory, there must be the same quantitative equality as presumably exists, and rightly so, on the market, the place of commutative justice. Hence the furious attacks against a progressive income tax that does not fit into that quantitative equality. Hence also the resistance to social legislation as an attempt against freedom of contract and for the creation of inequalities in giving favors to one group in the labor market. The idea that the rights of authority are the mere sum of the conceded rights of the individuals, is the root of all this.[15] Thus, that which since olden times was regarded as a value in itself, qualitatively different from the private good of the individual and called the common good, appears as merely the sum of the interests of individuals. A remarkable process of juridification, of a panjurism, begins thus to develop. Without doubt this theory in its polemics against obsolescent legal privileges, arbitrary abuse of absolute power, and unjustifiable inequalities, was initially quite plausible. But, driven too far, it simply dries up the life power of the political community, which lives not alone by legality but also by piety, fortitude, allegiance. And, while the claim is general equality, we see that the individualist theory, if it controls politics, produces almost greater inequalities in social and economic power among individuals and also produces classes with deep-seated conflicting interests.

VIII. DISTRIBUTIVE AND LEGAL JUSTICE

But the idea of other forms of justice, for example, of distributive justice, changes the picture. Here the political authority distributes the fruits of the order that it organizes, among the individual persons and groups, not exclusively on account of a quantitative equality, but according to the basic dignity of human persons and their position and importance in the social organism. Thus if the market order does create a blatant inequality in bargaining power so that, e.g., family wages are economically impossible, the unionism of workers must be promoted by the state. Thus the state authoritatively intervenes in the sphere of economics, granting protection to workers, women, children, farmers, and small businessmen, in the form of

---

[15] One may ask why this disruptive doctrine did not destroy the state. Nationalism was a kind of antitoxin. And the old traditions did not die so quickly, but continued to sustain the political framework. As in all communities, the spirit of sacrifice of a few often saved the whole.

social legislation. Thus the state distributes the tax burden, following the principles of ability to pay and of equality in sacrifices. Thus is promoted the idea of a living wage and a family wage inaccessible from the standpoint of the individualist theory of commutative justice. Social legislation has been promoted for years by Catholic social reformers from Buss and Ketteler, Ozanam and Le Play, Hitze, Leo XIII, and Cardinal Manning, H. Pesch, down to leaders of our days like Monsignor John Ryan in this country or Monsignor August Pieper in Germany, because these men live in the tradition of distributive, social, and legal justice as well as of commutative justice.

Social legislation is not owing to magnanimity nor is it something done merely out of charity; it is the fulfillment of a true obligation of justice. It is due on account of the services that the worker contributes to the common good; it is not to be explained as advisable for utilitarian reasons because otherwise revolution might ensue. It is not a selfish insurance against social unrest, but it is due out of justice. The difference in the services which the state renders to the groups and classes that do exist—and no abstraction from reality can do away with these differences and therefore inequalities—corresponds to the difference in importance of the services which these groups contribute to the actual common good. This is the good order in which persons work and contribute their goods and services to one another in peace and justice so that the community has felicity. Here again is evident the eminence of the common good and its difference from a mere sum of the private goods of individuals, though the common good grows out of the particular goods, and in the normal state of affairs coincides with the particular goods of the individuals. It follows, too, that in the case of conflict the private good of an individual has to step aside, though one cannot say that the private goods of all have to step aside, because without them a common good is in reality impossible.

This qualitative difference and eminence of the common good appears especially in the discussion of the term "legal justice." By that is meant the specific justice that controls the relation between citizens and the body politic, in particular the common good and the political authority that protects and guarantees the realization of the common good. It is that specific moral attitude which is called loyalty or allegiance and which found perhaps one of its finest expressions in St. Bernard's idea of the *homo fidelis,* the example for the religious orders of knights. It is more than a compulsory obedience exercised because it is wise to accept a naked, overwhelming power. It means the very opposite of such a mere factual compulsory external conformity. It is a free obedience, a keeping faith with the purpose and the very life of the body politic. It is devotion and fidelity to authority and to those in authority on account of their service to the common good. Thus this becomes the real object of this virtue. It is not a personal allegiance to the person who chances to hold authority; it is allegiance to the end of the state as the *forma populi.* This legal justice is what obliges the citizen to sacrifice even his life for the protection and continuation of the common good. This duty is not a consequence of the virtue of piety that we owe to our family and to our country as distinguished from the state; this duty is not the consequence of the doctrine that it is better that one man suffer than that a hundred should perish. In this numerical manner it cannot be demanded by justice but only by charity. Still to sacrifice even life is a clear duty of legal justice, because the life of the community in the order of the common good is a higher form of life than is the bodily life of an individual.

Professional honor requires of the doctor, the policeman, and the professional soldier that they be ready to sacrifice their health and their life in the fulfillment of their duties. The judge, too, by his professional honor is required to let justice prevail even at the cost of his fortune, position, and life, against the abuse of power by the executive authority. We do not demand such strict ethics from the ordinary citizen. The reason is that such professions, in regard to their immediate ends, are nearer to the common good and its order than is, for instance, the work of the cobbler or the mason. These ends are higher in the hierarchy of values than the economic goods. They are such because they are more essential to the functioning of the order of the common good, as are law and the forcible protection of law, health, and life. The relation of these professions to the common good is so obvious in all cultures and civilizations that the members of these professions are protected in their livelihood by privileges in the true sense. They are in some way placed beyond economic competition by means of licensing systems, tenure, a higher protection of their professional honor, a stronger self-government of their associations even in a strongly competitive and egalitarian society. Their livelihood is guaranteed to them by social institutions far more than is the livelihood of a worker, a craftsman, or a storekeeper, especially in a competitive society. But the reciprocal demand of the community is a higher allegiance to the common good. To the privilege corresponds a higher duty and, in the case of conflict between self-interest and common good, a higher obligation to the common good.

In earlier societies this fact led to a hierarchically ordered state with the professions as the leading classes, enjoying legal and political privileges. Aristotle was so inclined to underestimate the craftsman and the merchant, those who take care of the economic goods, that he was not in favor of letting them participate in the government. It needed a long educational effort of Christianity to make the "occupations," servile work for the provision of the economic goods, a "vocation" and thus to hallow the workingman, the merchant, and the craftsman and his work. So they, too, were conceived as contributors to the common good and therefore entitled to receive their share from the order of the common good by distributive justice. That the individualist idea of capitalist society, with its excessive regard for economic goods and consequent making of the businessman the leading social type, did not accept the living wage in its theory of labor as an economic commodity, is an argument *e contrario*. This capitalist egalitarianism transformed all values into measurable market values; so the economic value became all important. The service character of all human labor and social activity was so much veiled by commercialization that now the self-interest of the individual became the exclusive stimulus of social life, and consequently the justice of exchange on the market, commutative justice, became dominant. The common good logically had then to become a nominalist concept and not the object of the specific virtues of legal and distributive justice. The social harmony of economic society became the automatic result of the work of that invisible hand, free competition of individuals exclusively looking for their self-interests under an order of commutative justice.

IX. The Good of the Individual

The sacrifice of one's life can have meaning only if by it man serves his own good, too. That would mean that in reality there is no conflict between the common good and the rightly understood private good. The sacrifice is only obedience to a law that is even higher again than the common good, to God's law. Thus we can truly say that in the ultimate sense common good and individual good coincide though they do not absorb each other. The actual good order is the best guaranty of the private good of the individual; and the righteous realization of the private good by the citizen is to the advantage of the common good. To such a degree is this so, that any grave violation of the private good of an individual by another is a violation of the common good with the reaction of punishment on the part of authority, the aim of which is the protection of the common good. Though man's social nature reaches its perfection in his becoming a citizen, man does not become a mere part of the state, but as a member retains his inalienable personal independence, his substance. Similarly the qualitative difference and the prevalence of the common good do not do away with the private good. The common good is to be conceived like the health and the vitality of the organism, which are different from the members but are of benefit to each of them as something animating them, connecting them so that each participates in it, and still no member has it wholly and separately.

The basis of this doctrine is, first, that the political life is a necessity for man considered from the idea of the perfection of his nature; secondly, that, as the end of the individual person is in eternity, the state remains in the secular field; therefore the sacrifice of life on the part of the individual person does not mean destruction but rather fulfillment of his last end the salvation of his soul and the glory of God by fidelity to a duty founded on a law which itself still controls and rules the state and its life. Where this immortality of the person and the mortality of the state are not considered or are not included at least as a presupposition, this combination of common good and individual good, this golden mean between the extremes of socialism and individualism, is impossible.

If once the transcendent end of the individual is denied, then there remains only a dilemma. Either the state and the common good are mere names for the individuals taken together, and these latter are the only reality; or it is a mere biological organism, where the individual is nothing but a member, having no reality and independent value separate from that organism. Then the sacrifice of life is merely a natural event, not something that needs ethical justification as ful-fillment of a moral duty. To put it in other words: Capital punish-ment ceases to be intelligible for the moral conscience if man finds himself in that above-mentioned dilemma. The mere agnostic skeptic, from the standpoint of his individualism, cannot conceive a justifica-tion for capital punishment, as he also cannot understand war but is radically a pacifist; if there is no life beyond the grave, if there is no living faith in God, and if political authority is not in the last resort from God, then to demand the sacrifice of life or to mete out capital punishment or to conduct even a just war is utterly futile and un-justifiable. For the communist state and other totalitarian states founded on economic or racial materialism, capital punishment is no punishment, for that presupposes guilt, a moral immaterial cate-gory; but it is an operation on a material organism. That is why totalitarianism is so reckless in destroying human life in a nihilistic rage. Not with impunity can man organize the state apart from God in an agnostic secularism; the fruits are bitter.

CHAPTER XIV

The Common Good as the Measure of State Activities

I. THE TASK OF THE STATE IN MORALITY

SUAREZ, describing the common good, called it *felicitas externa*. The common good, the end of the state, is an affair of this world. The spiritual values are beyond the state, its power, or its end; but that does not mean that they are unimportant for political life. Life is not separated into compartments, as man is not a mere bundle of incoherent functions. This confining of the state to the secular field is the consequence, e.g., of the fact that God has established the Church as the perfect society for the realization and dispensation of the spiritual values. Hence the state has the duty to guarantee the liberty of the Church and of worship.

This *felicitas externa* is a status in which men live in peace and justice. Is is the *ordo rerum humanarum*. Peace is order without disturbance. Justice signifies that it is an order where the original rights of all the members and of authority are protected and guaranteed. For only thus is human life worthy of itself. Only thus can the individual, secure in his personal life, his family, and his occupation or profession, devote himself to his transcendent end, the salvation of his soul. Only as an order of peace and justice can the common good and its protector, the state, participate in the great Benedicite of all creatures to God, who wills justice and peace and perfect order as an image of His own essence to be realized by His free creatures. It is in this order of peace and justice that the citizens produce for themselves in various forms of mutual help and collaboration the amount of material goods that is necessary and desirable for the preservation of themselves and for an increasing perfection of their nature as beings composed of body and soul. The economic life and the procuring of economic goods also belong to the contents of the common good. Men should own these goods with such probity of morals as is necessary for the preservation of the external peace and the continuous existence of the state, the framework of the good life.

Compared with the Greek idea that the state ought to be the all-inclusive pedagogue of man for virtuous life, this thesis is a certain restriction of state activities in moral life. The end of the state is not virtuous life as such, but only inasmuch as the exercise of certain virtues is necessary for the existence of the state and the preservation of the public order and the common good. Thus the activity and the jurisdiction of the state in moral matters are restricted to public morality, to those virtues that immediately concern the common good. Personal individual morality and education to that end are not directly the concern of the state. Thus the virtue of justice in its general form and in its particular forms as legal, distributive, and commutative justice, is directly the concern of the state, but other virtues only so far as they are actually related to the common good and to justice.[1] St. Thomas therefore restricts the legislative and punitive power of the state to those virtues and vices that are related to the obvious advantage or disadvantage of the common good. We may call them the public virtues and vices, meaning by "public" what directly concerns the *respublica*, the common good. As an example, the great doctors usually refer to the problem of prostitution. They hold that it is the task of the state to prohibit, not all the vices, but only those from which the majority can abstain and especially those that are an infringement on the rights of others, are harmful to others, and are such that without their prohibition human society cannot thrive. Consequently as long as, in the individual state, prostitution is not a public scandal but remains in the private sphere, it may be better that the state tolerate it, because its coercive suppression and the punishment become mere chance. Then the dignity and the power of the law suffers. The attempt to enforce the law, on the other hand, may make necessary intrusion and spying into the private sphere of the individual as would destroy the sanctity of this sphere. No Jansenist rigorism could excuse the actual destruction of this private sphere under the allegation that the state must suppress all vices. For the

---

[1] St. Thomas, *Summa theol.*, IIa IIae, q.61, a.1; q.99, a.3; q.100, a.2.

measure of the rights and of the task of the state is not the prohibition and suppression of all vices, but only of those that directly or indirectly have a discernible relation to the common good, of those that, unless suppressed, would prevent the community from existing or the common good from being realized.

In this question what rules is the virtue of political prudence,[2] not abstract perfectionism. But prudence is right reason concerning things to be done. It deals with the application of universal principles to actual situations under actual circumstances, and it deals with the right means to reach the end, so that it is the end that advises, judges, and prescribes the means. That is the reason why, directed by the concrete task of the realization of the common good, the ruler may, according to circumstances, refrain from prohibiting all vices or commanding all virtues, restricting himself to the suppression of those vices that more directly concern the order of the common good. Here we have the field of right selection of means directly necessary for the preservation of the common good, for we are here in the concrete order of *agibilia* and *operabilia,* the field of social expediency. Justice and prudence are the supreme virtues of the ruler, and it is of profound significance that the jurists are disciples of *jurisprudence.*

With this moderation in the problem of the moral task of the state, Catholic political philosophy is equally distant from two extremist views that were popular in the nineteenth century. One is the ideal of liberalism, that the state is merely a legalistic order, the only end of the state is to be an order of law having neither a moral character nor in any way a moral end. The other extreme is the Hegelian ideal, that the state is a moral absolute, the divine representation of absolute morality itself. The first theory leads to a minimizing of the state; the other theory, especially when impregnated with nationalism as a secular religion, leads to the deification of the state and to the doctrine that, as the state is the absolute good, it also is the absolute master of morals. The state lives and reigns beyond all morality because existentially it is all morality. It is only a confirmation of the old adage, *Les extrêmes se touchent,* when we see how in continental Europe we find in the nineteenth century a coalition between these

---

[2] Political prudence is distinguished thus: as *prudentia regnativa,* that belongs to the ruler; *prudentia politica simpliciter dicta,* that is the right direction to the common good on the part of the citizen. *Summa theol.,* IIa, q.47, 50.

extremes in nationalist liberalism. This political doctrine proclaimed, on the one side practically against the traditional institutions and on the other side theoretically against the Christian doctrine, liberty from all religious, moral, and customary restrictions of the individual in a militant anticlericalism, better called antiecclesiasticism and antimonarchism. It declared itself for total religious, moral, and economic freedom; but at the same time it oppressed the Church and her institutions. Out of the neutrality of the state it made a new secular agnostic religion and, inspired by imperialist nationalism, produced a state that was as absolute and beyond any general rules of morality as was Machiavelli's Prince.[8]

The juxtaposition of these extremes may again help us in understanding the relation between common good and individual good. Though qualitatively different and each having its own value, they actually coincide or, as Suarez said, the common good arises out of the individual good of the citizens. Therefore[the common good *in concreto* is the better realized the more all the citizens can perfect their individual good. In other words, it is a clear sign of an imperfect realization of the common good if a group of citizens suffers from institutional injustices, that is, from injustice arising from the improper functioning of the public order or from its failure to function at all. To live in peace and justice: in an *ordo rerum humanarum* this is the specific form of human social existence. An existence without order is lawlessness; it is inhuman. But order does not exist for its own sake, because those ordered are rational beings, persons. Now persons are ends in themselves and are not under any circumstances mere instruments. Therefore the *ordo politicus,* though a value in itself, can never be regarded apart from its service function on behalf of the ordered persons. That *ordo,* therefore, *in concreto* must serve the transcendental end of the human person, which is beyond the sphere of the state and thus establishes the specific dignity of the person before which the state must bow. Therefore the main function of the order is the preservation of personal freedom, of inalienable rights,

[8] From the standpoint of this coalition and not as abstract doctrine, must be evaluated the often misunderstood and misinterpreted condemnation by the popes in the nineteenth century of the "modern" theories in politics and law.

The states of Anglo-Saxon culture have been mostly—though not completely—spared the effects of these "modern" theories partly because no militant anticlericalism sprang up in the form of anti-Christian Freemasonry of the Grand Orient kind and partly because they were less infected by that heated nationalism of continental Europe.

of the initiative of individual persons, and of their natural and free associations in furtherance of what is their teleological essence, the perfection of human nature. Thus there does not exist a philosophical antinomy between the common good and the individual good of the citizen. A conflict is possible only between the common good and an interest, not the existence, of an individual person. A real conflict between the common good and the interests of a greater number of persons or of a group of persons is therefore nothing but a sign that the order has become unjust and that the common good is violated. That is what led Leo XIII to call for the intervention of the state in the social and economic sphere to cure the institutional social injustices against the proletarians, because the wretched existence of the working class proves a great violation of the common good. And he demanded this intervention as a claim not of charity but of justice, because of the common good and of the violated rights of the working classes, since they were not given their part in the common good.

II. The Order of Law, the First Task of the State

To come to a more definite understanding of the end of the state, it is usual to distinguish different tasks of the state as the contents of its end. Thus we speak of law, welfare, culture, and education as rationally distinguished parts of the one end of the state, the common good. They are pheonomena, distinguished and yet, in the conception of the common good, amalgamated properties of the one end of the state, political felicity, the good life as a form of existence, as an existential status of the political community.

The first and fundamental task of the state is the law as the form of justice. The state has as its final cause the *ordo juris,* the sovereign order of law and peace. Every state is a state of law and is a state only so far as it is an order of law in the positive form of the realization of justice and peace. To develop, to protect, and to preserve this order of justice and peace, to decide continuously in conflicts according to justice, is the task of the state as legislator and judge. This task it performs by enacting positive laws that endure and are respected. Very justly the natural law doctrine calls the prestate existence of man the *status naturalis,* a status of lawlessness, and the *status civilis* a status of law. Still we must note that, as the state is not a mere order of law, its end is not simply the production and preservation of a system of legal norms. The concept of order is broader than that of law. Along with justice, according to the great doctors, the end of the state includes tranquillity, security, and peace. Thus the political and social order is more than the system of positive norms as compiled in statute books or court decisions. The law is merely one form of that order, though the most important because on its function immediately rest tranquillity, security, and peace. Nevertheless integral parts of the social order are also the traditional usages and customs of a nation, the moral preferences and evaluations in economics, culture, and social life, all that the Romanticists called the *Volksgeist* ("spirit of the folk"). These attitudes, values, and customs stand as mighty powers behind the more visible legal order, and influence and determine it. The end of the state, therefore, is not merely law. The legal order is rather a form for something that stands behind it and speaks through it. It is like the bed of a river, the form through which the life of the people flows. Therefore the state does not live and the common good is not realized by the law alone, but they live and are realized in the legal order as the positive, living form of justice, the continuous and persistent will to give to each one what is his due (*suum cuique*).

We might discuss at greater length this problem of the state as a mere system of legal norms, because it is most important for the problem of state intervention in the sphere of moral and economic life, especially in the form of social legislation.

III. The Liberal Ideal of the "Watchman State"

The modern liberal idea of the "state of law" has its origin in a powerful reaction against princely absolutism and enlightened despotism in the seventeenth and eighteenth centuries as it was carried out by the economic policy of mercantilism, by the strict supervision of all private life both moral and religious, of family life and economic activity, on the part of the paternal police state. It is best portrayed by some principles controlling this despotism. In religion it developed from the abominable principle, *cujus regio ejus religio,* into the practice of embodying the Church as a department of the state administration and of endeavering to treat the Church as a kind of spiritual police force, not so much for the sake of religion as for the sake of stricter control over the minds of the subjects. The priest and the minister become a sort of spiritual gendarme, more influential among the peasants and burghers (the third estate) than is the armed police. Frederick the Great, himself an unbeliever, and Voltaire as well, to name only two, were convinced that the homogeneity of the state, that fundamental unity, requires religion. This religion, however, is to be controlled by the "reason of state," subservient to the political interests of the absolute prince. Though not necessary for the enlightened nobles and clergy, it is regarded as necessary for the people, especially for the children. And the priests are the best teachers of morality for the protection of the absolute authority of the prince and for the safety of the property-holders.[4]

Similarly mercantilism destroyed, in the prince's interests, the old and perhaps too brittle forms of an economic society built on the principle of guilds to make room for the manufacturers. Yet it meticulously supervised and regulated the economic activities of the manufacturers and by an elaborated labor legislation, but one without regard to the just rights of the workers, controlled labor in the fast growing factories and mills. This strict control of economic activity in the interest of the prince's policies, especially his wars and war coffers, had no care for the sanctity of private property or personal rights. The *jus politiae* and the *jus eminens* gave a right to confiscate private property for state purposes without a duty of compensation. It gave the prince the right to intervene in judicial procedure, to decide any suit arbitrarily by his sovereign authority. It invaded the personal sphere by star-chamber trials, by *lettres de cachet* and arbitrary imprisonment, banishment and seizure of property, as the prince, with a very arbitrary idea of the interest of the state, saw fit.[5] Thus the fundamental distinction between public and private law disappeared and similarly the idea of rights of the people, of the individual

[4] The much vaunted "tolerance" of the Enlightenment does not grow out of a reverence for the individual conscience, but is a mere principle of political expediency. Neither Montesquieu nor Voltaire nor Rosseau, nor the Puritans and other nonconformists in England and in New England demanded tolerance or gave it to dissenters as a basic human right. Cf. Waldemar Gurian, *Die politischen und socialen Ideen im französischen Katholizismus* (1928), pp. 18–20; Thomas O'Gorman, *A History of the Catholic Church in the United States* (New York, 1907).

[5] Under appeal to this *jus politiae* endowed with the absolute *jus eminens*, the absolute prince could really say: *L'etat c'est moi.* No sphere of personal rights, of the Church, or of rights of property could withstand this arbitrary power.

person as an end unto himself. Justice disappeared in favor of social expediency or of utility for the state, actually for the interests of the prince.

Education, too, was subordinated to the interest of the absolute prince, who regarded the primary schools as nurseries for subservient loyalty to himself, and the universities as professional schools for the breeding of efficient administrators for the extensive administrative apparatus of the police state.[6]

But the Enlightenment, in its doctrines of natural law, had already constructed the basis from which to attack this unlimited totalitarian competence of the absolute prince. The time-honored rights of men embodied in so many sacred instruments like the Magna Charta or the liberties of the medieval towns and cities, the struggle of the Church to free itself from the tutelage of Gallican and Febronian or Josephinist practices, the fight of dissenting religious minorities against the oppressing demands of religious conformity as a basis of political homogeneity, the rise of natural-law ideas though in an individualist garb, all these contributed to the rise of a new spirit. The longing for liberty and tolerance grew stronger and stronger. The Church demanded freedom from the unworthy tutelage of the state. Religious minorities proclaimed the right of religious freedom or tried to establish it in their new homes on this side of the Atlantic. The third estate, the manufacturer, speaking through the mouth of physiocrat writers and A. Smith, demanded economic freedom from molesting state control. They contended that the wealth of nations could be better and more quickly increased by a laissez-faire policy than by bureaucratic planning. The eternal process, man versus the state, went into a new phase.

The third estate arises allied with individualist natural law, the new science of political economy, but not without the time-honored tradition of Christianity along with its antiabsolutist, personalist tendencies. The third estate, the classes of industrial employers, and the lay intellectuals, not all of them anticlerical, come of age. They are tired of the fussy tutelage of paternal absolutism. They want freedom. All the great minds, Catholic and Protestant, philosophers and

---

[6] The growing pre-eminence of the law faculty and the jurists over the theological and the philosophical faculties and their graduates is caused by the absolutist government's demand for administrators.

lawyers, employers and economists, the new scientists, plead for liberty. In their attitude, moral and intellectual, all of them are for liberty, for the rights of the individual person, for tolerance, for constitutional government, for free enterprise and for safeguards of property and person, for equality before the law. All of them are tired of the absolutist principle: all for the people, nothing by the people. They wish participation in the government and the construction of a sphere of freedom from state intervention.

They were all liberals in their attitude, but they differed widely in their arguments. Though founded by Catholics, the Colony of Maryland had first pronounced the freedom of worship as a political principle, not as a philosophical one. Pius VII introduced the freedom of enterprise into the Papal States. At the beginning of the French Revolution a majority of the Catholic clergy stood for constitutional government and the rights of man. Thus the new political institutions (e.g., bill of rights, representative government, liberation of the individual from oppressive intervention in the religious, economic, and social sphere) were the ardent desire of all. Men had come to the conclusion that an end should be put to the existing political, social, and economic order of a rigid feudalism, of an arrogant absolutism, and of privileges that had become senseless because their holders had no longer any worthy social functions but had turned into social parasites, into inefficient exploiters of senseless privileges. Thus in their polemics against the antiquated order all were united. All pleaded for liberty and liberal institutions. It is significant that institutions are somewhat influenced and shaped by the philosophical arguments in their favor. To use an example: freedom of worship can be defended as a political principle from the standpoint of tranquillity of the public order and the common good,[7] of the intrinsic wrongness of compulsion in faith on account of a profound reverence for the ultimate arbiter, the conscience. But it may be and in reality has most often been propounded as a consequence of a wrong philosophy. In this event freedom of worship can become the cause of polemic enmity against Christianity, especially against the Catholic Church. Then in the name of this freedom, the freedom of the Church and of religious orders together with their schools and hospitals may be

---

[7] Thus St. Thomas (*Summa theol.*, IIa IIae, q.10, a.11) defends tolerance of Jews and infidels on the basis of the idea of the common good.

abolished, as happened in the anticlerical Third Republic and in republican Spain. Thus the philosophy of militant agnosticism does away with the neutrality of the secular state as a practice, and the so-called neutral state turns to militant, anti-Christian secularism.

Without exaggeration we may contend that in the bourgeois revolution, especially on the European continent, it is philosophical individualism and liberalism that prevail. Thus after the new institutions were created they were backed by individualist liberalism. But after the "enemy," absolutism, had been abolished, it continued to shape the new world and to interpret the new institutions according to its individualist meaning. It became the ruling social philosophy demanding absolute sovereignty in the form of doctrinaire liberalism.

Here the tendency is to depreciate the state and unduly to minimize its activities according to the laissez-faire doctrine. The state is not an active element of social life with the common good as its proper end. This kind of liberalism is distrustful of government: government is bad; only the people, the autonomous free individuals, are good. Thus the legal order is not a genuine stable order, but a mere system of formal norms with the help of which the individuals construct their relations led by their self-interests. The legal order, especially the constitutional order, has as its exclusive purpose to guarantee and to protect a sphere of individual initiative as broad as possible. The state ceases to be a social being of specific form and is nothing but an apparatus to be used for the interests of individuals; especially in economics the state has no right to intervene. Parallel to this aversion toward the state goes the idea that political power and authority are almost intrinsically bad.

IV. CONSEQUENCES OF THE "WATCHMAN" IDEAL

Thus an essential part of the program of liberalism is its idea of the function and essence of the legal order. Liberalism knows only abstract, therefore equal, individuals. It treats problems of eminent political and social importance as if they were private, indifferent affairs of individuals. The whole world of law is built upon the idea of free contracts of free individuals, beginning with the lawgiver and the state and proceeding to marriage and other social forms. Of utmost importance is that the material contents of the contracts are left wholly to the free decisions of the individuals and their changing self-interest. Law becomes a formalism, indifferent with regard to its contents. The range of this field of individual activity, which is soon ruled by economic interests as the controlling forces, must be enlarged as much as possible. No outside authority has a prerogative to interfere in this field, whether on account of moral demands, religious teaching, or political exigency.

Such an idea is possible only in consequence of an extreme optimism in the power and wisdom of the individual. This is really evidenced when the classical economists who, with the exception of a few clerics like Malthus, are mostly optimists, say that the individuals, if only left free to follow their self-interests in autonomy and to bind themselves by free contracts, would produce an order of social harmony, as it were automatically. The social order is thus considered to be controlled by perpetually changing economic interests and by continually renewed short-term relations without the stability of vocational groups or of functional corporative organizations of persons. In this scheme the contracting individuals, led by their momentary interests, constitute by their contracts a social organization that is the best possible for the present. It is so because the greatest possible number of individuals will so establish their greatest possible happiness, which is based on the successful realization of their self-interest. Hence there is no stable organization of society, which is merely a name for a ceaselessly changing network of contractual relations. The state's only function is the protection of the individual fundamental rights, especially in their economic bearing, and the legal protection of the contracts and of what is disposed by contracts, of property.

Consequently society is organized around markets: markets for commodities (and labor is considered a commodity); markets for credit and capital; markets for philosophies and sectarian doctrines; markets for amusements and literature. The successful businessman, with an uncritical indifference as to how and where he made his money, is the leading type of this society. Economics not politics is the accent. The state, so honored by the ancients and so praised by the Christian doctors, the state which Suarez called *corpus politicum mysticum*, becomes a mere public service. The Aristotelian and Thomistic principle that life in the state makes man better, is utterly strange to this society, because the individual is already good. The state has, therefore, no right to intervene in the sphere of society. That would be an irrational interference, destroying the calculability of economic activity, disturbing the automatically produced and sensitive balance of interests. The ethics of such a society is necessarily individualist and utilitarian. The form of justice that is accentuated is commutative justice, that justice which controls the contractual conditions of exchanges on the markets; distributive justice is a forgotten concept.

The accent, the attention of intellectual curiosity, does not fall upon man, upon politics in the Aristotelian and Thomistic sense, upon metaphysics, philosophy of law, and invariable ethics. No, it falls rather upon the individual as a qualitatively indifferent social atom, each equal to all others and not vested with such qualifications as are acquired by the specific social functions of the cleric, the monk, the guildmaster, the father of a family. These qualifications remain more private; on the market, in the economic sphere, there appear the impersonal forms of the businessman, the seller, the buyer, the capitalist, the worker. Or the depersonalization goes even so far that we begin to speak only of producer-consumer and employer-employee relations or even of the relations of finance, capital, and labor. What is meant here is that abstract capital, abstract labor, and abstract money rule and dominate human relations. What counts is the magnitude of abstract profit, that is, a profit without consideration of its character as a social premium for a positive contribution to the common good. Furthermore, it is the abstract labor power that counts, rather than the indisputable fact that the seller of abstract labor power is a father, a mother, or a bachelor. Yet these social concrete characters of individuals are of the utmost importance for the persons themselves and for the good life of the body politic. The reason, of course, for this abstraction is the optimistic belief that social happiness will automatically arise by the free competition of those abstract individuals.

What is common to all these terms is that they are somewhat empty of concrete life. The picture of economic society—and on economics falls the accent—is one of free and equal individuals, each for himself pursuing his self-interest, exclusively motivated by it and standing against any restrictions but those necessary to guarantee this chase on the basis of equal chances. Thus this society is essentially atomistic, dynamic, ever changing, an immense but unstable network of shifting short-lived relations in the form of private contracts. These contracts are motivated not by a common good but by their private interests, subject to mere formal rules of the law of contracts.

This society has an organization, but only in the sense that the individuals at their will organize themselves through short-term contracts for the realization of the self-interest. Critics have rightly spoken of the anarchic character of the capitalist market-society. Especially in the economic world do we see these features prevail. Individualist liberalism, it should never be forgotten, fought against the rigid vested interests, representing the stable organization of guilds in their corrupt form. But they fought also against all stable social forms that are intermediaries between the individual and the state and that were the real protection of the individual and his rights in the medieval society.[8]

What this society demands is initiative, alertness, daring, speculation, a sharp legalistic mind, and a jealousy for all the rights of the individual. What it does not favor is charity, unselfishness, social restraint, contemplation, fidelity to ethical ideals; these traits do not pay. It is economic thinking that controls it; it is the virtues useful on the market that count. That enigmatical being, man, living in the *polis* for the better life, man as typified in Socrates or in Thucydides, in St. Paul or in St. Augustine, in St. Francis of Assisi or in Gregory VII, in Pascal or in Spinoza, man as the religious genius, as the saint, as the philosopher, as the man of letters, such is not the ideal and the measure. Rather, this ideal and this measure are material success, market values, money. The ideal of youth is not the statesman, the *pater patriae,* but the successful money-maker or the corrupt politician, without social responsibility, as also the business executive without responsibility but to the impersonal capital interests. This does not mean that other types of man—the saint, the faithful servant of the common good, the philosopher, the unselfish educator—do not exist, for such a statement would be nonsense. Without them society could last but for a short time. No, what is meant here is that the economic values and the practical virtues that pay are the decisive

---

[8] A striking illustration is the prevalence of the capitalist corporation with the negotiability of its shares the highest point of impersonality, as opposed to the cooperative guilds and the like, which are essentially personal organizations where the common interest is visible and demands personal loyalty by its very nature.

thing. Material success alone is what counts. Men are measured by these things first and are pardoned many wrong acts if they but succeed. Wealth, material wealth, however acquired, is the measure. If it is acquired honestly, that is well and good, but it is not absolutely necessary. Hence this kind of society develops in its sociology an evolutionist theory of the survival of the fittest that of course is non-moral and has no room for the unselfish virtue of charity. Thus this society has, as its adequate philosophy, positivism and pragmatism where the measure of truth is efficiency and where ethics is utilitarian. That is why this society is unpolitical, is for the minimizing of the state as the framework in which man reaches a more perfect life, a good life. That is why this type of society has use only for commutative justice, the justice of the exchange values of the market, as we pointed out earlier.

V. The Contradictions of the Liberal Ideal

Distributive justice and legal justice presuppose a functionally organized society of different groups. But individualist liberalism tells us that under free competition the organization of society is automatic and at every moment the best possible. Therefore liberalism is against intervention of the state in this self-regulating society. In its concept of the relations between state and citizens, this liberalism has the tendency of protecting the individual against unreasonable use of the police power, against the sovereignty. But we find also among the jurists the tendency to juridify even the essentially sovereign act which concerns the common good immediately and directly. The concept of sovereignty (the supreme act beyond the law and subject only to the objective idea of the common good) is argued away. The judge becomes the master of the legislator and the arbiter of the government; he gets the *imperium*.

This control by the judge over the representative body, which is a reflection of changing popular opinions, is in itself a good thing. But we should bear in mind that what controls is not so much the institution as the philosophy and opinions of the majority of the highest court. Thus the highest court's philosophy becomes the decisive fact, the sovereign rule. He who authoritatively and without appeal interprets the law, is the true sovereign. Oliver Wendell Holmes in one of his many dissenting opinions concerning labor legislation, an out-growth of distributive justice, criticized the majority because they still clung to the ideas of Adam Smith and Ricardo when the social and economic system had already undergone enormous material changes. They continued to apply specific rules of commutative justice, the justice that controls the relations between equal and free individuals, to facts that required the application of distributive justice.[9] Thus, as we have seen, the ideal of an individualist and liberalist society becomes the depreciation and minimizing of the state and the exaltation of the laissez-faire philosophy which implies the total subjection of the sovereign power to the rules of commutative justice. Yet such a total subjection of the sovereign power under the rules of commutative justice contradicts the very idea of the state, of common good, of *ordo* to which is coordinated distributive justice. And this justice concerns subordination, obedience, and authority. The longed-for ideal of individualist liberalism is the prospect of a progressive development that will end in a perfect society without the state, without politics, sovereign will, or autonomous common good, without authority or government, which all are, compared with this ideal status, presumably avoidable evils.

The whole thing is of course contradictory. The same authority that condemned in various utterances nineteenth-century liberalism as the destroyer of true liberty—the Pope—could in the twentieth century with the applause of the children of nineteenth-century liberalism affirm that the state had been weakened, and that that abominable thing, power, had conquered as private irresponsible power the economic field and therewith controlled the destiny of thousands of small property holders and proletarians. Behind the weakened visible government rules an invisible and therefore irresponsible government of financial interests. The concentrated economic power of great combinations in international cartels is even able to have its own foreign policy, to the people invisible, along with the foreign policy of the visible government. It truly is historic irony that at the end of individual liberalism stands the totalitarian state.

The grandsons of the great liberals, anxious to protect their economic privileges against the labor-movement that demands—if for a

---

[9] On the individualist spirit of the common law, cf. Roscoe Pound, *Spirit of the Common Law.*

while we discount labor-czars and labor-bosses—from modern society
and state just the same things that the Third Estate, the bourgeoisie,
demanded a century and a half ago; these grandsons hire the wor-
shippers of absolute state-control against their antagonists in the
labor-market. And yet this is only the consequence of their wrong
principles. For they could indulge in their contempt for politics, for
social ethics, for social justice and pharisaically propound their
"market-justice" because they were the state, because indirectly they
owned the government. Now the fourth estate or the proletarians or
—call them what you will—find that they and their children remain
on this side of the labor-market. Therefore they use the same slogans
that were earlier devised by the bourgeoisie: liberty, equality, fraternity, for themselves and for their organizations. Actually that individualistic society begins to become socially organized around the
labor market. The place in the labor market becomes the nucleus of
new, very powerful organizations either for the change or for the upholding of the status quo of social power in capitalistic society.

These powerful concentrated group-interests begin then to fight
for or against social legislation. The consequence is, unless traditional
ethics or a strong spirit of national unity counterbalance, that both
parties try to control the state which presumedly has the monopoly of
power. For its own sake and in the interest of unity, the state sends
out more and more its controlling tentacles into the struggling
society. In an industrial society, without self-governing intermediary
institutions similar in function to the medieval guilds, the bureaucratic state arises. Cancerlike grows that state with the approval of
both groups if and as long as each of them controls alternately the
bureaucratic monster. Finally there comes a point where one of the
groups loses patience or hope and delivers the state over to predatory
pretorians of the totalitarian ideologies. This group sells out to them,
because it hopes to form an invisible government behind them. But
though one can buy pretorians, one cannot control them. They will
be and they are the conquerors.

The solution of this problem—and the earliest signs of that solution are now visible—is a new functional organization of society.
This society will have self-governing autonomous groups to regulate
and deal with their own problems in a spirit of cooperation, motivated by their respective partial common good. That is the essence of

Pius XI's proposal of a vocational group order, that is, of a stable, legally circumscribed, visible order. For what is needed is a realization of the general principle that wherever there is crystallized power, social or economic, there also must be linked to it visible public responsibility. This is the only justification for wielding power, because power is never an independent autonomous value. It is justified only as a means for a morally good purpose. Since power is here social power, its end must be good according to social ethics. The trouble in individualist capitalism is that economic power always crystallized around capitalist wealth and around labor organizations, but that no open, clearly circumscribed, and public responsibility to the community or the nation is bound to that power. When someone has such social power that his decision means happiness or distress and poverty for hundreds and thousands of his fellow citizens, then his decision must be controlled, it must be an openly responsible one. Here, too, we need today a fresh application of the principle of government by consent.

I am fully aware that in this sketchy presentation some features are put in relief while others have been neglected. Still, as a presentation of dominating tendencies, this picture is valid. The best proof is the situation in an actual militant conflict. As everybody knows, a tendency on the part of each group is to use other social values and institutions as their allies and especially as their servants. Religion, the Churches, and the idea of the nation are brought into the discussion as allies, each group identifying its limited interest with justice, with religion, with the national common good itself. Thus strikers, in particular their leaders, may be called reds, atheists, internationalists, foes of the unity of the nation, and all this is declared without evidence being adduced. On the other hand, a sinister conspiracy of high finance, the interests of money, are decried as the true power behind the scenes. As often in other instances, it is the emergency situation that best reveals the true antagonisms. Furthermore, it may be said that this society lives on because there are still big reservoirs of moral and religious ideas inherited from the past, ideas which somehow counterbalance the disruptive tendencies. We should not forget that Sodom would have been spared if ten just men had lived there. It is these unnamed thousands in our nation who, faithfully serving the common good, keep the social fabric together.

VI. Duty of the State to Intervene

But let us return to our original problem. As we have shown, Catholic tradition always upheld the idea that human social and political life, apart from other virtues which likewise were neglected by individualism, is controlled not only by commutative justice but also by distributive and legal justice. Consequently it accentuated the public welfare as the end of the state. Thus it opposed to the liberalistic idea of the emasculated "watchman-state" the idea of this "welfare-state." By that it meant an existential concrete status of happiness (*felicitas politica*) of the whole body politic, as health is in the biological organism. Of course, it never denied that the state and its authority must live in the law and under the universal norm of morality, since the state is neither the substance of law nor the rule of morality itself.

To Catholic political philosophy the state is more than a disinterested automaton that produces and protects a formal legal order for the functioning of commutative justice alone as the condition under which the individuals are the perpetrators of their self-interest and so construct a kind of order in their contractual relations. Catholic political philosophy recognized these truths: first, that the formulas or the doctrines of liberalist individualism concerning the pure "Rechtsstaat," liberty, and equality, for the propertyless proletarian masses are fictitious, that these formulas develop into a questionable domination by the propertied class, into an unrestricted avarice and heartlessness of the masters, which leaves the workers propertyless and undefended.[10] Now in the social and economic field, as distinguished from the political field, the relations between finance and productive forces, between employers and workers, become necessarily relations of economic power, supraordination and subordination. Division of labor, the prevalence of property and financial interests in a capitalist society, and the existence of vast numbers living on the basis of short-term labor contracts and without property produce these subordinations. Thus the relations actually threaten to become lawless power-relations of 'domination by property and finance over labor and small business.

Because of the liberalist, non-interventionist idea of the mere

[10] Leo XIII, *Rerum novarum*, § 2.

"watchman-state," the balancing elements (public responsibility of the economically powerful and public protection of the economically powerless) cannot be realized. This condition leads to an abominable contradiction. Politically the rights of democracy (freedom, equality and fraternity) are professed. But in the economic world where actually the property interests rule, such concentration of economic power, unrestricted by the ideas of distributive justice, arouses bitter feelings of hostility. The dominated classes begin to feel they are wage-slaves, the farmers and small businessmen develop a glowing hatred against high finance or international finance. Thus, instead of the longed-for society of free and equal individuals, a class-society appears with strong opposing interests, where socialist theory demands, in the name of liberty and equality, the expropriation of the expropriators. On the basis of the same rights of liberty, labor justly claims the right of organization. The more that economic concentration of capital grows, the more must grow the power of labor organization. The hoped-for society of free individuals and of social harmony becomes a society where there emerge enormous mass collectiva, organized around capital and labor interests, agricultural and industrial interests, that by their very nature stress predominantly antagonistic tendencies and not unifying forces. And as the individuals are organized according to their conflicting interests without direct regard of their common interests as citizens, no social harmony emerges. Rather, we have hostile classes kept together only with great effort in the framework of the state. We have conflicting allegiances, where the allegiance to the class interest may too easily supersede the allegiance to the state, the alleged instrument of the class enemy. Under such conditions capital may prefer an alliance with a foreign power if that power promises to suppress labor. Labor, on the other hand, may transfer its allegiance to a foreign power that appears as the international champion of the rights of the proletarians. The paralysis of their own state in the protection of the common good is the result.

This outcome of the liberalist illusion was early and fully grasped by Catholic political philosophy. But it recognized also that the Marxian socialist theory, acting as a new social gospel for the oppressed, offers no genuine solution. Socialism contends that the private dominating power of capitalist and financial property-classes must be destroyed and that it can be destroyed only by destruction of private property as a legally sanctioned institution and by destruction of that bourgeois "watchman-state" in favor of a dictatorship of the proletariat. But socialist thinking originates in the same presuppositions as does liberal capitalism: in an excessive regard for material wealth, in a negation of the original dignity of the human person, in a dream of a stateless paradise of the future. Thus socialist Marxism and all its variations claiming the elimination of private property as an institution tend to the destruction of the freedom and dignity of the person and of the family in socialistic totalitarianism which, like individualist capitalism, subordinates the person to values and institutions that are essentially service-values compared to the intrinsic value of the person.

Against these socialist and liberalist aberrations, Catholic political philosophy upheld the idea of distributive justice with its obligations to the common good and to the groups within the state. The "good life," the "perfection of the order," implies that the state (i.e., the political authority), on the basis of distributive justice, has a right and a duty to intervene in the economic order just as the citizens have by legal justice a duty to contribute to the state. This contribution is not on the basis of formal equality (commutative justice) but in proportion to their personal gifts and economic power. The common good is the ground on which rests the right and the duty of the state to intervene in economics and in social relations. To this right, particularly this moral duty of the state to realize public welfare, a just order, or whatever we may call it, there corresponds, on the side of the violated interests of the citizens, a right to the re-establishment of their rights by a change of the social order and its institutions.

Leo XIII strongly reiterated this duty of the state in the face of social wrongs produced by capitalism. He refutes the socialist claim to solve these social problems by the abolition of private property as a legal and economic institution. But he blames the liberalist concept of the "watchman-state," showing that it has forgotten the protection of the personal rights of the lower classes and especially of the workers. The "watchman-state" destroyed the protective institutions like the guilds and the journeymen associations and so isolated the modern wage-earner and left him without social institutions to protect and defend his rights and interests. Thus the exigencies of an economic system and material wealth were put above the happiness and the dignity of human persons and of families. Yet the common good is the result only of the work and pains of all members of the community in the framework of the social and legal order. Therefore the state must, in proportion to the hierarchy of values and the contribution of the members, afford protection and care. If it protects especially the property rights and the freedom of contract without regard of the nobler and higher ranking rights of the human person, of the father of a family, the result will be an unjust privilege of the propertied classes. Thus the essence of the equality will be destroyed. Yet even the humblest worker not only has his human rights but, by his daily work and by fulfilling his duties as a conscientious father, citizen, and Christian, he also contributes in a considerable way to the common good.

If the economic system renders either the fulfillment of these duties or the realization of these rights more difficult, or if the system deprives the worker of these rights, then the order of the common good is gravely violated. When this violation is caused, not by merely individual incidents but by an institutional inadequacy of the existing economic order, of its institutions and group relations, there arises for the state a binding duty to reform the order so that it can more perfectly promote the common good. For everyone has a right to participate in the use and enjoyment of the good life, of the common good, as a member and in proportion to his contributions to the realization of the common good. The state exists for man's sake and not for any class or simply for the production of wealth. And this improvement, this reform of the economic order on the part of the state, is a duty arising from distributive justice.

The need for this reform amply justified the great Catholic social movement that developed in all modern countries after the liberalist and individualist ideas proved their sterility when they produced the modern proletariat, the propertyless wage-earner. The whole existence of the wage-earner depends on his ability to make a short-term labor contract and on the price he can get for his labor on a labor market which is ruled over not by human dignity, justice and fairness, but rather by the impersonal, blind, iron laws of supply and demand. It was a ridiculous contradiction to put on the modern worker the mask of a free seller of labor power and then, without social power such as property can offer, leave him to the play of these impersonal forces of the labor market. An even more disastrous consequence of abstract individualism is that the concrete circumstances and nature of the fictitious "free worker" were of no consideration on the labor market. There one hires a kind of commodity without considering whether the owner of that commodity is a child, a father, a mother, or a single man. The buyer is interested only in the impersonal objective commodity, labor power. That at least is what the classical liberal economic theory brought forward. The consequences of this view are to be noted in the reports of factory inspectors and of poor-law administrators, in scholarly research work, and in gloomy poems like Hood's *The Song of the Shirt*.

From the standpoint of distributive justice that is an intolerable condition, a grave violation of the common good. This violation of the common good gave the oppressed masses a right, on the constitutional and natural principles, to form organizations of mutual help like unions, beneficiary societies, and cooperatives. It also enjoined on the state the duty to reform the economic order by social legislation, by intervention.[11] This intervention has first to protect the personal dignity of the worker as a man: as the father of a family, as a woman, as a child, as a religious being, as a citizen. This protection is afforded by laws regulating minimum wage and maximum hours, by regulation of work on Sundays and religious holidays, by regulation of the work of women and children, and still further by protection of the right to association in unions and in cooperatives, as well as the right to political activity. It has then to protect the health and life of the worker by forms of social insurance, such as those insuring against accident, sickness, unemployment, disability, and old age. Here, too, it is the task of legislation to promote the family wage, though this problem may belong rather to the more basic task of a real reform of the economic order, which is especially urged by *Quadragesimo anno*.

Here what is discussed is not so much the improvement of an existing economic order, but the reform of that order itself; for the subject of that encyclical is the reconstruction of the social and eco-

---

[11] In Catholic social philosophy in the late nineteenth century there existed two schools. The school of Angers (France) was against state intervention; the school of Liège stood out in favor of state intervention. In the general trend since the earliest propounders of social legislation from von Buss and Ketteler to Hitze and Manning, Leo XIII, in outspoken manner, approved the interventionist school.

nomic order. It treats the problem of self-governed vocational groups as the bearers and the effecters of social justice. It urges participation in industrial property and in management and thus the redemption of the proletarians from their weak and insecure economic situation. Especially since the monopolist concentration in industry, this condition has grown worse and has led to tendencies of state paternalism that are perhaps a step nearer to state socialism or state capitalism, both of which are wrong.

VII. Limitations of State Intervention

All social legislation is "practical" and consequently will be different in various modern states as the capitalist systems differ according to a variety of circumstances. Still the principles are the same. First, the right, even the duty, of the state to intervene if the common good is violated, through failing institutions in the social and economic order and through the denial of the rights and dignity of man. Secondly, the measure of intervention is based on the idea of distributive justice: namely, what each contributes to the common good, the state has the duty to return in an equal amount of participation in the enjoyment of the common good. For only under these conditions have those citizens who fully participate in the use and fruition of the order a right to demand from the worker the fulfillment of the duties of legal justice: obedience to the law, active participation in politics and honorary offices, protection of the peaceful order, military service and defense of the nation. The cry that the proletarians have no fatherland, that they must be international, has some foundation as long as the proportion in those things owed them by distributive justice actually remains a great disproportion.

When we speak of social legislation we think mostly of legislation about labor. But that is a narrow concept, because it does not consider that social legislation intervenes wherever an institutional failing occurs which violates the common good. Therefore any legislation to protect the homestead of the farmer, tax laws according to the ability-to-pay principle, anticartel legislation having as its purpose the protection of the small business man, laws that privilege cooperation of farmers, of borrowers, of small businessmen are all equally the outgrowth of distributive justice as is indirectly recognized by liberal capitalism, which considers them irreconcilable with the system of non-intervention. Similarly modern economic legislation for the averting of bankruptcy, for honesty in the capital market transactions (Securities and Exchange Act) for the protection of the small depositor and saver, and for tariff policy, all this is social legislation. It is controlled by the need of equal protection of all rights and by the importance of all these things for the common good. It is an ironical fact that in our modern economic society, where many legislative problems involve power problems of different group interests, each group interest if endangered cries for "social" legislation under appeal to the common good. But it is eager to deny the same appeal to other group interests if such action would change the *status quo* of social-power relations. This proves merely how little these groups are united in basic principles and how clamorous they are for participation in the common good when their interests require it.

In social and economic relations it is a general principle that quantity may change the quality and nature of the social body. Social legislative intervention may likewise, as soon as it reaches a certain quantity, change the quality and nature of the state. The social-welfare state, as opposed to the watchman-state, may by exaggeration grow to be a paternal, care-for-all state which, because of its spreading administrative bureaucracy, turns into totalitarianism.

Therefore it is not enough to proclaim as a principle the right and the duty of the state to intervene by legislation in the social and economic order. We must at the same time try to find the limits of state intervention. The limit is again the common good. That A makes bankrupts on account of a wrong speculation, or that B, who is a bit querulous, often loses his job, or that Farmer C's uninsured barn is struck by lightning, has nothing to do directly and immediately with the common good. Only if the whole community or the interests of whole groups have suffered damage, only when a grave danger threatens which cannot be helped or hindered in any other way even by organized self-help, only then may we speak of a damage or danger to the common good and of a right and duty of intervention.[12]

Four conditions must be present to justify state intervention. First, there must be some harm to essential interests and rights of the whole community or of one of its functional groups, because their right

12 Leo XIII, *op. cit.*, § 28.

functioning represents an essential contribution to the common good, to the happiness of the whole. Negatively it follows that the state may not intervene if the public order and the cooperative functioning of the groups is working in security and successfully; no mere utility, no profitable expediency for itself, which the state expects from an intervention for administrative purposes, confers a right of intervention. This limitation protects the public order against any perfectionist who, clamoring for the most perfect world, confers on the state powers of intervention which, if realized, would do away with freedom and initiative. Under the paternal police state of the enlightened despot we have had such a perfectionism, where the absolute prince, like Joseph II in Austria, intervened in the most intimate relations of families, between individuals, and in ecclesiastical affairs, in order to educate all according to his standards. In consequence of this policy, just on account of his well-meant interventions, he died as a hated despot.

Secondly, that damage must have already occurred or it must at least threaten proximately. The point is that the state must not deem its intervention as necessary without a compelling reason. It should not intrude upon the groups, the families, and the individuals, even from a paternal interest in their better development. For to do so would be acting like a guardian putting them into a state tutelage. That would be offensive to their liberty and their initiative.

Thirdly, it must be clear that the institutional emergency cannot be met by any means or effort of those that suffer, especially by freely enacted measures of self-help and by the help of other groups in a cooperative effort. Thus the state intervention must be a kind of last resort to master an institutional emergency.

Fourthly, the limits of state intervention are fixed by the emergency itself; only what is necessary to meet the emergency may be done by state intervention. Leo XIII, who cogently teaches these limitations, especially stresses this last point. No more matters must be regulated and no further must the intervention extend than is necessary to right the existing wrong or to avert the present or threatening danger.[13] It seems that Leo XIII knew something about bureaucratic perfectionism which, allured by chiliastic dreams of a worldly paradise, prefers to compel people to be perfect and happy even if doing so

[13] *Ibid.*, § 29.

reduces them to the status of children or minors. He may also have known that this bureaucratic paternalism creates vested interests for administrative bodies which, to prove their right of existence, in a vicious circle continue to discover new possible improvements and therefore new causes of intervention. Finally a totalitarian management by state administration of all social and economic activities is reached with the loss of freedom for the citizens in their free associations. At the same time this policy works to the advantage of an all-embracing political and economic tutelage that slowly strangles all independence, freedom, and initiative in the interest of a managerial, privileged group of officials. The interests of these officials have been substituted for the genuine common good.

All these restrictions presuppose that the existing order is not in itself wholly unjust or built on utterly wrong principles. Yet this problem need not disturb us because, if an order should deteriorate so as to deserve such qualification, it would simply be overthrown by revolution. Moreover, man as a reasonable being will not live in an absolutely unfit order. He will always build on that order, improve it, restrain hypertrophies, for life outside the *ordo* is really inhuman.

VIII. Autonomy of the Lower Communities

Catholic political philosophy thus adheres neither to a stubborn principle of nonintervention like the classical liberal economic and political theory nor to the equally stubborn principle of socialist all-embracing intervention. It is likewise sure of the necessity of the state as the requisite framework for the realization of the good life, and sure also of the genuine limits of this intervention. Thus, for instance, intervention of the state in property rights and their regulation must never go so far as to do away practically with personal, individual property as a social legal institution; for, as property is an emanation of personality, the destruction or excessive restrictions of property would result in the abolition of individual liberty. One of the sad facts of modern society is that there are so many proletarians, people living on short-term labor contracts; their liberty is therefore more endangered than that of a society of farmers and craftsmen. Whoever owns no property becomes easily the property of others. Similarly all public social help to the underprivileged, to people who for any reason cannot support themselves, should know that its very purpose is to make that very help unnecessary by strengthening the self-help and self-responsibility of the underprivileged. Its purpose can never be to form an institutional substitute for the family as a community of mutual help. This produces that degeneration of the helpers and the helped, which we call paternalism.

As the basis of this argumentation about the limits of state-intervention, we see the famous principle of subsidiarity, which we have discussed above. As Leo XIII pronounced in such a masterly way, the limits of state intervention lie in the emergency that leads to the intervention. Therefore no more matters should be regulated by the state and no intervention should go further than is demanded for the cure of the grievances or the defense against the danger to the common good.

This conception is based on the idea of an economy of all the social virtues and social instincts and their coordinated original forms of community life. Thus the state cannot take over all or the most essential functions of the family and the coordinated task of education and care of home-life without thus destroying the specific social instincts and those social virtues for which the family is the cradle and nursery. Among these instincts and virtues we note the love of parents and children, of wife and husband, originating in the simple fact of family life; the sacrificing love of the mother, the mild authority of the father, the willing obedience of the children, the solidarity of all the members of the family and their common honor and readiness to sacrifice for one another; the responsibility and self-respect corresponding to the authority in the family that orders and directs the home. So much are these virtues rooted in the family and in the home as their nursery and their place of schooling, that, wherever the state or any other institution in an emergency must substitute for the disrupted family, as, for instance, in an orphanage, into such institutions the words and the forms of family life are adopted. So strong is this tendency that in religious celibate communities the specific forms of the family present the model for their direction (The father abbot, the mother superior, the sons and the daughters of St. Francis).[14]

14 An interesting and striking illustration is offered in the *Codex Juris Canonici* (can. 2214 § 2). Though here an original and independent coercive and penal authority of the Church is proclaimed in the spiritual and the temporal field, it is strongly stressed that

Nothing has endangered the whole social fabric of our modern nations so much as the progressive decomposition of the family, the ease with which divorces are granted, the cancerlike growth of birth control. In the same ratio as these tendencies progressed, the above-mentioned virtues, with their powerful radiation into social life, regressed. Thus a divinely ordered balance and growth is on the way to be destroyed. And still we wonder about the disturbing increase of selfishness, of revolt against authority, of the irreverence and the irresponsibility of youth.

An indirect proof may be taken from the communist experience in Russia. Following the Marxist doctrine, the family as a residuum of bourgeois suppression had to be destroyed. This was accomplished, at least in the lawbooks and in social work, by freeing divorce from any restrictions, by the introduction of communal nurseries for babies, by putting the mothers into factories, by debasing marital love to a mere biological effect. And the consequence? A rapid demoralization in the social life beyond the family, a brutal selfishness of irresponsible begetters, a general decrease in public morality, so much so that these "social engineers" after a short time returned to some of the despised rules of "bourgeois" family ethics.

The religious community of divine worship, the Church, is the nursery of such social virtues as neighborly charity, brotherly humility, a deep feeling of equality of all who are children of God, in a common worship and an equal need of redemption. The worship of God is the elevation and glorification of all individual and social natural virtues by which the people, the body politic, lives even more than it lives by natural wealth. The worship of God gives to political authority its dignity, admonishes obedience to the law, which it regards as emanating from divine authority. To make the Church the servant of the state means nothing less than to rob her of her contribution to the welfare of the body politic. An indirect proof of this is that all the agnostics from Voltaire on and all the disciples of *Realpolitik* from Machiavelli on, made their obeisance to this truth by hypocritically declaring that religion must be preserved for the people. The subjection of the Church to the control of the state pulls

---

the *monitum* of the Council of Trent (session III. *de ref.*, chap. 1) must be considered. The *monitum* says that the bishops are pastors not prosecutors, that they should not dominate but love those subject to their authority as "sons and brothers."

down, the liberty of the Church builds up. When Napoleon tried to compel his prisoner, Pius VII, to become his dependent court chaplain, Pius answered that in such event Napoleon would have in his power not the Pope, but only the poor monk Chiaramonti.

Economic society with its innumerable free associations and groups rests upon initiative and self-responsibility and an ethical code of just equalization of interests which is absolutely necessary for the good functioning of production and distribution of material wealth. In this realm the state may regulate but not command; by its laws it may fix the minimum of honesty, lawfulness, justice, and reliability. But it is in the field of economic activity that the virtues of cooperation, conscientiousness, fairness, and good administration find the field of their application.[15] In the acquisition, augmentation, and good use of property, the material basis of the freedom of person and family, here again we exercise the virtues of prudence, honesty, trusteeship, liberality. If instead of this initiative and self-responsibility, of trusteeship and liberality, the command of the bureaucratic state is heard, then these virtues wane while the passivity of state serfs and the insolence of bureaucrats triumph in the emergence of the slave state.

There is need of freedom for all these virtues supporting the social framework by their growth in their natural nurseries, the lower forms of social life, but ranking with the state, and their procreations, religion, culture, science, and economics. Hence the state has only a regulative function in relation to those forms of social life in which these virtues flourish. The state (the government) does not create them; it is not creative. The creative power rests in the people as a whole, within these forms, as the perpetual foundation of the state.

The state, however, while it orders and furthers the flourishing life of these forms of social life in freedom by instituting a true *ordo rerum humanarum,* justifies itself by the realization of the common

---

[15] We speak here abstractly. What we mean is, therefore, not acquittal of capitalist abuses. What must be seen is that, if the members of the economic society do not by self-control develop these virtues and thus show themselves worthy of freedom, the state intervenes more and more and thus, in a vicious circle, the growth of state intervention at the same ratio diminishes the scope for the exercise of economic virtues, thus necessitating again an increase of state intervention and so on. The solution is not state intervention but self-government, self-control by freely adopted ethical standards in the economic society. Freedom in this field is possible only according as moral rules, freely accepted, control the pursuit of happiness and of self-interest of the individual participants in collaboration.

good before the citizens and their free associations. Thus it acquires dignity, reverence, and majesty. And while the state subordinates itself to the hierarchy of moral values and lives in the law and under the universal norm of morality, a shining ray of participation in the divine rule of creation falls upon it.

CHAPTER XV

The State in Relation to Education and Religion

I. THE TREND TOWARD STATE MONOPOLY IN EDUCATION

IN THE Middle Ages formal education from the teaching of the three R's to that of theology, philosophy, and the liberal arts in the universities was the commonly accepted task of the Church. She it was who educated the barbarians of the North and the Latin nations after the destructive march of the migrating tribes; she it was who led them to the treasures of ancient civilization which her monks had preserved. With untiring effort she amalgamated and integrated ancient civilization, Christian faith, and the folklore of the rising nations into the new medieval universal civilization of Christendom.

In the sixteenth century this universal Christendom dissolved. The modern nation-state moved as an independent power at the side of the Church. In the countries of the Reformation, along with the nationalization of the Protestant Churches and their control by the absolute prince as *summus episcopus,* it even assumed control over the educational institutions which the Church had created and sustained. In the Catholic countries a less radical yet still considerable control over education developed under the influence of the Gallican theory and of movements like Josephinism and Febronianism. As the modern state with its intense national sovereignty grows and the Churches become departments of government or are established as state Churches or even sink to the state of private religious organizations, to the same degree formal education on all its levels becomes more and more a prerogative of the state. The schools cease to be *seminaria ecclesiae,* institutions for the education of Christians, of members of the Church. Under the control of the absolute state they become primarily institutions in which the absolute prince, not without a high moral impulse nourished by Enlightenment, attempts to produce good and industrious subjects able to execute the economic purposes of mercantilist policies and increase the political prestige and power of the state. The schools thus become part of the administrative state machinery. The purpose of the higher schools is to furnish efficient servants for the administration in the state Church, the state bureaucracy, and the state schools. The lower schools are intended to produce skilled and loyal subjects.

In the growing American colonies also education began more and more to be considered a task of the state; but here, while the religious element was at least as important as in the schools of the absolutist prince, the school was considered a necessity on the basis of a democratic philosophy; the school had to educate the citizen who was not a subject but an active partner for political self-government. Thus the national state, united under enlightened absolutism, and the growing democratic movements both worked in the same direction: schools and formal education are a task and a responsibility of the state rather than of the Church. With the victorious bourgeois revolutions this principle triumphs. Thus the meetings of the National Assembly in revolutionary France are filled, under the influence of Condorcet, with discussions about public education from the elementary level to adult education. Now that the people has become sovereign it must be as well educated as the princes were in earlier times. Formal education thus became the prerogative and the responsibility of the state.

Concomitant with this progress of state control in education runs a progressive secularization, since rationalism and Enlightenment began to substitute reason and philosophy for faith and theology, a religion of reason for Christianity, and nationalism for the universal civilization of Christendom. This process began with the unbelief and skepticism of the educated classes. In the rise of the egalitarian tendencies of the bourgeoisie, it produced the class of secular education and economic wealth and resulted in the modern apostasy of broad proletarian masses, which were drawn into the slums of our drab industrial cities.

With the decay of the proud belief in reason which Enlightenment conceived as a source of eternal truth greater than the dogmas of the Church, the new philosophical systems of utilitarianism, naturalism, and positivism impressed themselves upon educational philosophy. The purpose of education then becomes a secular humanism, i.e., antiquity plus nationalism but minus Christianity, or it becomes training for specific useful adaptations of the individual in a world controlled by economic wealth and technological civilization. In a world without a faith in things invisible, without a belief in eternal truth and unchangeable moral laws, everything becomes relative and instrumental. So become the educational institutions. The state as the stable order and the nation as the form of political homogeneity seem to be the only firm elements. So it happens that the liberalist mind which in the nineteenth century favored nonintervention of the state in economic life, proclaims, with strange contradiction of its gospel of liberty, a state monopoly in education. This monopoly was demanded by the anticlerical nationalists in the European countries. They wished a secular nationalism as a civil religion according to Rousseau and therefore were hostile to the freedom of education that the Catholics in those countries demanded. They were unable to conceive that the great danger to true civil and personal liberty is not the claim of the Church for freedom for her denominational schools but the monopoly of the state or of the ideology of the ruling educational bureaucracy over the schools. The true danger to liberty is a ministry of public worship and popular enlightenment with too complete a control over education. The mere existence of free schools of the Church has done more to protect the liberty of education than all the oratory for freedom.

Since the state, with few exceptions, became secular, i.e. separated from the Church, and since the Church on principle assumed the right to found schools for elementary, secondary, and higher education (C.J.C., can. 1375, 1379), and since separation of Church and state made the public schools non-religious or religiously neutral, a real problem now arose. This problem became aggravated when the rising modern state, controlled by a minority of the educated classes steeped in secularism and presumably speaking for the people, demanded an exclusive right of the state in the field of education and began to oppress the many private schools which the religious teaching orders had been developing for centuries.

II. Catholic Reaction against State Monopoly of Education

Thus it is that, especially from the middle of the nineteenth century on, a struggle between Church and state arises about the mutual rights in the field of education. In many countries this strife has been settled by concordats with the respective states; in other states a genuine freedom of education has led to a tolerable *modus vivendi*, though in yet other countries the struggle is still going on. Some states have what is called the confessional or denominational public school; others have mixed schools with a Christian atmosphere and an obligatory instruction in religion for the students, separated according to religious affiliation; others again have non-religious or non-sectarian public schools but give to denominational schools, which have to be founded by municipalities after a sufficient number of parents demand it, full equality in financial support from taxes and full rights such as the non-denominational public schools have; others again have only non-denominational schools as tax-supported schools but leave full freedom to denominations to establish their own schools, which rank equal to the public schools but receive no financial help from the municipalities or from the state and thus must be supported by the denominations though their members pay taxes to support the public schools which they do not use. Some states, like Russia, Germany (since about 1938), and Turkey, recognize only non-religious state schools and do not allow denominational schools at all.

There is no doubt that according to Catholic educational philosophy the denominational school is the ideal. A religion which rests on the principle that grace presupposes nature cannot do otherwise. For this principle means that the spiritual life permeates all fields of secular life, sanctifying and consecrating them without robbing them of their relative autonomy and of their intrinsic value. It means further that a full separation between the spiritual and the secular is impossible, however much the distinction between their particular ends, forms, and methods of realization are stressed. Just as man, as a Christian, i.e., as a member of the Church destined for salvation, and as a citizen of the city of man, the state, is a single whole unity, so education cannot be considered exclusively the task of one of those fundamental societies, of the Church or of the state. A religion built on the principle that grace presupposes and perfects nature can thus not concede that human life should be so divided that the Christian belongs on workdays wholly to the world and on Sundays to the Church. Education cannot be the exclusive prerogative of the state.

At least as important as this negation of an absolute separation in this question is the contention of Christian and natural law that ultimately it is the parents' right to educate the children. This thesis of the parental right as the primary right has ever been held in Catholic philosophy. This right is a natural right. All other agencies which men form to promote education are basically auxiliary agencies, their rights are derived rights. This does not deny that the parents, as citizens of the state formed for a more perfect life, have a duty to promote education by the help of private and public schools. Nay, the state authority has an immediate interest in promoting education. This interest is the greater as, on account of a progressive division of labor and of social functions, the parents are more in need of the help of other voluntary organizations or of state agencies (public, state administered schools) in performing their educational duty which becomes more and more a complex task and less and less a possibility for the family and the parental authority alone.

It is undoubtedly a natural right of the parents to determine the education of the children. In the interest of the common good the state has indeed a right and even a duty to regulate the performance of this parental right and to help wherever the task becomes too great for the family. The state has furthermore a direct interest in the education of the children, its future citizens, who must be equipped with civic virtues, political knowledge, and vocational and professional training in order to be able to promote the common good. This they do by realizing their own personal perfection in the pursuit of happiness and in their functional services to the community. On the other hand, the parents as members of the Church have the natural and supernatural duty to see not only that the education of their children is harmless to their faith, the gift of God, but that the education itself is engendered and permeated by the spirit of Christian piety.[1]

---

[1] Leo XIII, encyclical *Affari nos*, December 8, 1897. For the whole discussion, see Otto Willmann, *The Science of Education in Its Sociological and Historical Aspects;* translated from the fourth German edition by Felix M. Kirsch, 2 vols. (Beatty, Pa., Archabbey Press,

III. Various Types of Schools

The ideal type of school for Catholics is therefore a school in which only Catholic teachers are appointed, where only such textbooks are used as are approved by the ecclesiastical authority (the bishop). Thus a full right and an unhindered influence and codetermination of the whole education is preserved to this authority in order that all learning and teaching shall agree with Catholic faith and morals. These demands are not satisfied by a few religious instructions, while otherwise the whole instruction is non-religious or neutral.

Whenever these demands are not or cannot be fulfilled, the Catholic parents must have a constitutional right to institute their private or parish schools, which enable them to fulfill their duties to their children and to their faith. Consequently a compulsory attendance in mixed schools or in non-religious secular schools is a violation of the natural right of the parents and of the democratic right of freedom of conscience and of teaching. After all, the school is not merely a drilling place for the intellect and a means of acquiring useful information and vocational skills. The school is an institution for the forming of character and of the moral will for a good life of intellectual and moral virtues. A teacher's religious belief is by no means a mere private affair of his private life; teaching in its true vocation is not a mere imparting of technical and useful information, but a meeting, a dialogue between personalities, the one mature and learned, the other growing and learning. The dignity of the teaching profession is in the fact that every teacher ought to become a model, a master for his disciples.

Nevertheless, under modern circumstances and in consideration of the necessity of education by state and municipalities and of the character of the modern state as a religiously neutral state with the separation of state and Church, the attendance in neutral public schools may be tolerated as the only practical means of getting an education. But here a genuine neutrality is the necessary supposition. Unfortunately it often happens that the political authorities, under the pretense of neutrality, actually promote a naturalist educational

---

1921-22), *passim*. One of the best works on parental rights in education is the historically and systematically excellent book of Joseph Schroeteler, S.J., *Das Elternrecht in der katholisch-theologischen Auseinandersetzung*, Munich, 1936.

philosophy or conceal behind the word "neutrality" a consistent anti-clerical educational policy, i.e., a policy which denies or contemptu-ously disparages the Christian truths as superstitions to be overcome by reason and science, and promotes a relativist morality and philos-ophy. A striking case is that of the educational policy in some Latin countries, especially in France of the Third Republic. Under these conditions any denial of freedom of education and any actual compul-sion or economic pressure upon Catholic parents to send their children to such state schools, must be considered a grave violation of the natural rights of the parents to determine the education of their children and a denial of the freedom of conscience.

What lies at the bottom of this urgent demand for respect of the right of the parents and of the ecclesiastical authorities is by no means a disguised attempt to subject education to clerical control. It is a clear view of the intrinsic limitations of the state; it reflects the freedom and autonomy of the lower communities according to the principle of subsidiarity. It is in the competency of the state and for the common good to produce such an order and such institutions as enable the citizens individually and in their associations to realize the good life for the persons. If anywhere at all, then certainly in this field of education is the service character of the state most clear. Any pretension of the state, under appeal to the common good, to the spirit of the nation, etc., to an exclusive right to determine the con-tents and character of education smacks of totalitarianism, as appears from the fate of education in Nazi Germany, in communist Russia, and in Fascist Italy. The same conclusion is evident from the attempt to abolish educational autonomy in these countries, and also the courageous contest of Christian parents and of the Church against these pretensions.

Furthermore the elimination of Christian doctrine and Christian ethics must lead to the almost inevitable temptation to substitute for these either a nationalist or a merely humanitarian philosophy. The consequence will be that the common Christian supernational moral values disappear and narrow nationalism with all its separative forces destroys the common Christian inheritance and with it the basis for international cooperation and understanding; or mere naturalist humanitarianism, separating man from God, will fall into pitfalls of utilitarianism or an emotional relativist glorification of abstract freedom. All of these will lead to anarchy either by lack of moral strength or by an exaggeration of separative elements or by a reduction of man's spiritual existence to the material values of the useful and the profitable. The spiritual crisis thus indicated and the spiritual problem which they vainly try to solve cannot be met by material, economic, or political remedies. This problem can be solved only by a view of man as the image of God and a sensitive awareness of the limitations of the state in this field of the formation of character and of the education for freedom of persons who live for purposes transcending the state.

IV. The Duties of the State to Religion

This chapter should not close without some remarks about the relation between the common good and religion. The state as a moral person has duties to religion, to God. The state is not wholly an arbitrarily created institution of free individuals but is, considered from the point of view of the teaching on the end of man and on man's social nature, a necessary community. Inasmuch as the state is the result of this nature, it is of mediately divine origin. Therefore, as Leo XIII says, the political community has to recognize God as its Father and Creator and owes to Him reverence and public worship; a godless state is in contradiction to justice and reason.[2] In addition, Leo XIII rejects also the principle of indifferentism and its consequences; that, since all religions are relative and no true religion exists, it is right to introduce, on the basis of the principle of freedom of religion, the free public cult to all immigrants into a wholly Catholic country or to give all religious groups in a Catholic country the right of public worship.

As is evident from Leo XIII's letter to the Emperor of Brazil (July 10, 1889), the rejected contention is that even in a purely Catholic nation the state or the government is not obliged to profess the nation's creed or to privilege it; instead the state should be strictly neutral, that is, non-Christian, and treat all creeds equally. Leo assuredly does not speak here about the political expediency of tolerance but about the *philosophical principle* of indifferentism that puts truth and error, faith and heresy, the Church of Christ and any

[2] *Alloc.*, II, 109.

arbitrary human association, on the same level because there is no truth, because there does not exist a divinely instituted Church; there exist only opinions, equally right or wrong. What is here attacked is the philosophical and theological doctrine of agnosticism, which demands this kind of neutrality, not out of reverence for conscience but on account of a militant and often persecutory theory of philosophical agnosticism and theological relativism. For, as history has shown in Mexico, in the France of the Third Republic, and in Spain, this theory actually has been made a political creed itself resulting in more compulsion of conscience against the dissident faithful than ever before was applied by a Catholic government against heretics.

To interpret Pope Leo's meaning we must, as he does, distinguish between the state as order, and the people as that which is ordered. It is only in a figurative sense that we can speak of a Catholic, a Christian, a secular, a neutral state. What we mean is that the order of the state, its constitution and laws, if it is a Catholic state, give to the Catholic Church a public privileged position; that all anti-Catholic doctrines are banned from state-owned institutions of learning and education, that the canon law where it proclaims precedence and sovereignty (e.g., in matters of matrimonial law of Catholics) is acknowledged by the temporal law, that the institutions and doctrine of the Church enjoy legal protection against libel and public degradation while the state laws censor and suppress the free circulation of heretical propaganda. Such a "Catholic" state presupposes that the people in overwhelming majority are themselves Catholics. Only thus can one in a proper sense say that the people, the matter of the state as *forma populi*, is Catholic. The state, as *forma* and order of such a Catholic people, merely acknowledges this fact positively by furtherance of Catholicism as the public and established religion and negatively by repressing in public what is opposed to Catholicism. But we see here that the fact of the Catholicity of the people is decisive.

When a people has lost its unity in faith, as happened after the Reformation, and beside Catholicism other Christian denominations became a fact, the Christian state of denominational parity emerged on the European Continent. In each country one of the Christian denominations prevailed as a kind of state religion, though all Christian Churches participated in the privileges of a public-law corporation. Another practical solution of the problem resulting from the fact that the people were religiously very much divided, was the neutral state with neutrality toward all creeds so far as they did not reject in their doctrines the natural ethical basis of the state. Yet this neutrality can become and has become (e.g., in the Third Republic in France) a militant anticlerical, that is, anti-Catholic, quasi-creed by declaring agnosticism a kind of new state religion of the secular state. Today great masses of citizens are practically non-Christians in the theological sense. Of course they still live in a certain Christian atmosphere, in a civilization that tacitly acknowledges traditions grown on a Christian soil. On account of this factual situation, the state may be, in a practical sense, neutral, and out of political prudence keep religious freedom for its rule. The law, as the general rule of the people, can protect only what concerns all citizens and it can promote only what concerns all.

V. RELIGIOUS TOLERANCE

On the other hand, the practice of tolerance as a political expedient means something quite different from the militant neutrality, improperly so called, of the Third Republic in France. It recognizes first, as an indisputable fact, that in place of a unified *orbis christianus* we have today a secular civilization diversified in religious creeds and in social and political morals. The basis of political homogeneity in most modern states is no longer the religious creed, as was the case till the late eighteenth or early nineteenth century.[3] That homogeneity is today formed by the moral standards of Western civilization, by some common beliefs in natural theology and natural law and by the whole body of secular national culture. Accepting this fact and acknowledging the doctrine that none may be compelled to embrace the true faith—for, as St. Augustine says, man can believe only with his free will[4]—and furthermore considering the

[3] This condition was instanced by Catholic Emancipation in England and by the removal of all political restrictions against Catholics in the United States. Rousseau and Voltaire both believed that religious homogeneity was necessary for the full realization of the common good. Rousseau's theory of a civil religion would perhaps have produced more intolerance than a "Catholic" state, as we see in the suppression of the Church under the Third Republic or by Nazism in the Third Reich.

[4] *Tractatus 26 in Joh.*, no. 2.

democratic principle of equality before the law and equality in franchise, equality of control by all citizens in a government by consent, we see that the necessary consequence is the practical neutrality of the state as a principle of political prudence, because the law as a general norm for the body politic can protect only what concerns all. Therefore it will retire from a field where not all are unified and where also the application of compulsion would be in contradiction to the common good and to the dignity of conscience.

We must bear in mind that the state as a moral person has not always and under all circumstances the same obligations as has the individual person by his being a rational substance endowed with intellect and free will, which is the basis for the duty of immediate spiritual devotion of the individual person.[5] The moral person under abstraction from its members has as such no inner duties, no conscience, because it acts only through its constituent individual members, and when it acts there are only external acts that are performed. A wrong act is imputed to the state only inasmuch as the individuals forming the state have either positively agreed or at least acquiesced without counteracting, though this was possible and they were aware of the wrongness of the "public" act. We may now accept the fact that the state, on account of its necessity, its sovereignty, and its end (the common good), is thus all-penetrating so that the state and its end are not indifferent to morality and religion but show positive relations to them. Yet we must see, too, that these relations can be actively expressed only by its members, its citizens, that is, mediately and indirectly, not as in the case with the individual, directly and immediately. This conceded, it follows that, since the end of the state is not spiritual but secular, the state, even if it should be not a neutral but a Christian state, needs only to take into consideration the supernatural in so far as the common good is concerned.

As Suarez says, the Christian ruler fulfills his duties when, as lawmaker, he faithfully observes the demands of the common good and apart from that does not hinder the supernatural end of the citizen. To direct legislation to that supernatural end is not a matter of duty but of counsel.[6] Consequently only when the state *in concreto* is the

[5] H. Pesch, *Lehrbuch der National Oekonomie*, I, 143.

[6] Suarez, *De leg.*, III, chap. 2, nos. 9 ff. A modern canonist, Cavagni, in his *Institutiones*

political form of a unified Catholic people does religion, this specific religion, become a public affair and participate positively in the realization of the common good. But when the citizens are not unified by religion, religion is not the basis of political homogeneity as an actual fact. When the citizens are divided into a multitude of denominations and non-religious groups, then the establishment of a state religion or a public exercise of it by the state becomes impossible. This impossibility arises from the fact that the state can *in concreto* express a faith only through its citizens as a whole because only through them can it act in this field. Thus religious neutrality, a retreat of the state from the field of religious activity, becomes a practical necessity. For, should the state compel its dissenting citizens, should one group, perchance controlling the state, force the dissenting groups, though they behave as good citizens, to confess publicly a faith they do not accept, that would be a violation of the common good by producing hypocrisy, violation of consciences, and disturbance of the public order. The "contents" of the concept "common good" must be common to all citizens.

Thus we see that freedom of worship and freedom of conscience can be defended by Catholic political philosophy as a practical political principle out of deference for the freedom of the act of faith, out of reverence for the individual conscience, on the historical fact of the division in faith, and lastly because of the exigencies of the common good. That is why Leo XIII praised the situation of the Church in the United States where Catholicism, it is true, is not privileged by the government but where the laws and the practice of the government do not at all disturb its freedom.[7] That is why the Apostolic Delegate Satolli, inspired by the American way, asserted that the Magna Charta of humanity comprises the Gospels of our Lord and the Constitution of the United States.[8]

---

juris publici ecclesiastici (Rome, 1906), says that the acts of the state must be *ordinatione objectiva et negativa*, be directed to the ultimate end, that is, the state must at least create such conditions as do not hinder divine worship and religion and that it must refrain from acts that are against the universal norm of morality (I, 1).

[7] *Alloc.*, IV, 14 f.

[8] Ireland, *The Church and Modern Society*, I, 127.

CHAPTER XVI

The Theory of Political Authority

I. Problem of the Justification of Political Authority

FROM the earliest times political authority with its supreme power appeared to people living in political unity of any kind as something sacred. It was the gods of the tribe from whom the power and the glory of the ruler came. The early history of Rome, for instance, shows that the origin of political authority and majesty is the priest-king in his mysterious connection with the Divine. Crude belief would have the political power transferred from generation to generation in the royal family by the magical, mysterious force of the noble blood of the royal family. Even where we find the convention of the family-fathers as the ruling authority, even there in the sagas and myths of the people the political power belongs to a sacred sphere. As originally the law was the mysteriously revealed will of the gods, so the supreme power preserving the rule of the law and the order of peace by wielding the sword and the scales was thought to be of divine origin.

This divine origin, which we find in practically all the sagas and myths of old times, was the answer, satisfying for a time, to one of the greatest questions put to men: Whence originates this supreme legal and moral authority with unquestioned power to compel, supereminent above the power of all others, such as that of the family-father over wife and children, of the master over slaves or servants?

When man grew out of the age of sagas and when the myths lost their lure before the unceasing questions of the individual reason, the problem of the origin of political power arose anew. Thus to the philosophers in Greece, the jurists in Rome, the successors of the priests as teachers of the people, this problem of origin, import, foundation, and right of the supreme political power may well have appeared as the main subject of their political ethics and philosophy.

The fact that after the democratic revolutions not kingly families, but conventions of citizens or senators ruled, did not change the gravity of the problem. Even after the cyncial criticism of the state and its sovereign power by Marxism, which regards the state as an instrument of capitalist exploitation, and by a materialist philosophy, which regards the state as a non-moral organization in which the ruling class devotes itself to lust of power, an easy life, and conspicuous consumption, we cannot rid ourselves of the mighty influence of those symbols that represent the now rather depersonalized supreme power. And we see in an amazing reaction in several nations a corrupt revival of quasi-sacral theories of a mysterious origin of the supreme power surrounded by absurd crazy symbols, personalized in a quasi-divine "Leader," who is worshiped as never a primitive man worshiped his fetish. Losing one's mind is all too often the reward of cynical criticism.

When Christianity appeared in a political world that had begun to worship Caesar as a god set over the plebs of degraded, once proud, citizens, the problem of the origin and the extent of the political power was put afresh to human reason. Two new and independent ideas took their place beside the idea of supreme political power: the spiritual power of the Church, immediately derived from God Almighty; and secondly, the idea of the Christian person, who has an end for himself in another world beyond the state and its power, an end to whose fulfillment the state now becomes a servant. The theory of a natural law to which the supreme power is subject, thus received new force. It had flared up in antiquity in Socrates' daimonion theory, in Aristotle's distinction of what is just by nature and what is just by positive law, in the teaching of some Sophists, and later in the venerable eternal law of the Stoa, and now took on a new, deeper, and wider meaning. Not all belongs to Caesar. Men must obey the laws of God—and the natural law is divine law—rather than men; and Caesar is man, not God. Thus the once unchecked supreme power of the state was opposed from two sides: by the right of the spiritual power and by the right of the Christian person, the mother of the rights of man. Now the supreme power itself is put into the divine cosmos of moral ends. It has lost its "divinity" without being made wholly profane, for it receives a new consecration. All power that is, is from God. Never would the political power of man over man be moral, therefore, demanding obedience and loyalty even to the sacrifice of life, if it were not ultimately delegated from the Creator of man. Thus the *potestas temporalis* continues to exist in Christianity. It retains its majesty and dignity, and it may demand obedience and loyalty in its sphere.

II. THE PROBLEM OF POLITICAL AUTHORITY

During the almost two thousand years of its history, Catholic political philosophy has elaborated and expanded its teaching about the supreme power ever more profoundly and more perfectly. Its foundations remained the same, though the political and intellectual environments of its great teachers may have formed selective principles of a kind for problems which in each era found a more extended treatment. Thus the Church Fathers, though their interests were chiefly practical, pastoral ones, had to fight against the totalitarianism of the pagan emperors in Rome, as well as against the attempts of the Byzantine emperors to make the Church a department of their administration in a complete misconception of the state and its limits as well as of the Church and her rights. St. Augustine and St. Leo the Great are two outstanding examples of this. On the other hand, many early Christians, filled with the idea of an early Parousia of Christ the Lord and other chiliastic dreams, delivered themselves over to a kind of anarchism, condemning any political form and authority as anti-Christian. Against these theories the Church Fathers had to defend the legitimate rights of even a pagan political power, the Christian duties of faithful loyalty and cooperative citizenship. They utterly rejected the assumption of all political anarchism based on a wrong interpretation of the freedom of Christians (*libertas christiana*), namely, that temporal power over Christians is intrinsically wrong and that the community of Christians needs no coercive political power, the origin of which is sin. Thus we see the Church Fathers already fighting a two-front dispute: against any intrusion of the state into the field of the Church and into the religious sphere of the individual conscience, and against a depreciation of the state as an exclusive consequence of sin, therefore not necessary and without legitimacy for the redeemed disciples of Christ.

In the Middle Ages, the ruling idea of which was the *Imperium christianum,* the great problem became that of the relation between the temporal and the spiritual power, expressed, for instance, in the theory of the two swords. The German emperors, the Most Christian Majesties, lured by the glory of the Roman emperors, claimed the absolute sovereign power in the *Imperium*. They demanded the right to wield the temporal and the spiritual sword, transforming the Church and her law into a mere dependency of the divinely advised ruler. Between Gregory VII, Aegidius Romanus, and Nicholas of Cusa, on the one hand, and Henry IV, Occam, and Marsilius of Padua on the other, ranges this discussion that finds its answer in the teachings of St. Thomas Aquinas and its best formulation in the doctors of Late Scholasticism. The Angelic Doctor, by his reception and adaptation of Aristotelian philosophy and political theory, gave the best foundation for a solution of these problems.

At the time of the Reformation new problems arose. The national state, under the lead of the absolute prince, and the Reformation, and sometimes also the Counter Reformation, had disolved the idea of the *Sacrum Imperium*. The princes demanded spiritual allegiance from their subjects, excluding any kind of allegiance to the pope.[1] This practice culminated in the brutal principle of *Cujus regio, ejus religio,* abolishing any vestige of freedom of consciences. The prince could demand such an allegiance only when his supreme power was of divine institution; at least not less divinely instituted than that of the pope. At that time we find the theory of Lord Filmer, that, as the kings are successors of Adam, the father of mankind, their power is thus the paternal power of Adam; or the theory of Hobbes, who holds that only the sovereign pastoral authority is *jure divino* and that the civil sovereign, if a Christian, is head of the Church in his own dominions.[2]

Against this theory the great doctors of the sixteenth century, Suarez and Mariana, St. Robert Bellarmine and Molina, wrote their volumes. It was the origin and the boundaries of the political power that were under discussion. In their times the *orbis christianus* was extended through the discovery of America; the missioners went to China and Japan even while the religious wars in Europe disrupted

---

[1] Typical of this are the oaths of allegiance to the king of England after the separation from Rome. The subject swore that in his conscience he declares that only the king is the ruler in all things spiritual and ecclesiastical, and that nobody else has ecclesiastical and spiritual authority in England. Cf. Rommen, *Suarez*, p. 354. Bacon consequently addresses James I, *Memento quod es Deus seu vice-Deus*, and Hobbes says that the king is a *Pro-Deus*, (ibid., p. 355).

[2] Hobbes, *Leviathan*, Part III, chap. 42. Filmer's *Patriarcha* was published in 1680.

the idea of the *orbis*. Thus the problems of the international order, of the law of nations, of the *jus belli et pacis,* demanded a profound discussion. This was afforded by Vittoria and Suarez decades before Hugo Grotius, acknowledging his dependence upon these philosophers, wrote his famous book, *De jure belli et pacis.*

After the overthrow of absolutism by modern revolutions, the new ideas of individualism make a new study necessary. Inasmuch as this individualism is negative, demanding freedom of conscience because there is no truth, is too optimistic and therefore unlimited in its confidence in self-interest and in free competition, thinks that progress will make authority superfluous, and contends that all rights of public authority are nothing but the sum of delegated rights of and from individuals, Catholic political philosophy defends the "immortality" of the state, the intervention of the government in the social struggles of the labor market, and the duty to enact social legislation. Similarly, against positivism and sociologism, which deny the existence and obligation of a universal law of nature, the obligation even of the sovereign majority in the state and of the states among themselves to natural law has to be established anew. Against the anarchic strain of individualism this philosophy defends true democracy as well as the rights of the supreme power, whether its holder is a king or a parliament, by elaborating the thesis of the divine origin of political authority.

In our time even a superficial study of encyclicals and the literature of Catholic thought shows that against modern totalitarianism, whether of the nationalist, the racial, or the Marxist kind, it is the rights of man, the service character of the state, and the rule of law in the international community which are stressed.

Historical problems as principles of selection and development in Catholic political philosophy may, at least for the superficial observer, at first sight seem to exhibit great differences in opinion and teachings. They may even produce an impression of contradictions, especially in modern times. It would be easy to quote rather disturbingly contradictory utterances from Bossuet and Suarez, from Father Hecker or Archbishop Ireland and from De Maistre or Taparelli, as to the origin of political authority. We may find one writer condemning universal suffrage as anarchistic and another praising it as truly Christian. Nevertheless, after a careful study, we would also find that in their basic teaching both writers agree. Their conclusions, influenced by their political and social environments, differ. Frequently it is not so much the new political institutions, such as popular sovereignty, universal suffrage, or state intervention in social and economic life, which are fought against, but the revolutionary justifications of these institutions by false philosophies. Thus a person may accept the principle of freedom of conscience because there are only irrelevant opinions without objective truth, or he may come to accept it because he believes in the dignity of the human being and his ability to find truth. The Christian would accept the last justification and yet utterly reject the first one. And it may be that in condemning the wrong justification a writer would go farther and say that the institution itself changes its tolerable and admissible form, on account of its justification. We will find here the same oscillation between two poles, the difference in accentuation conditioned by historic environmental problems, that we found in other chapters. The outsider, looking to more or less ably argued theories, sees an open contradiction, exemplary for the *complexio oppositorum;* or, looking to the basic principles always the same, he sees an unconvincing and valueless repetition of principles, however impressive. Only the insider sees the *unitas in diversitate.*

III. The Person, the Family, the State

Catholic political philosophy distinguishes three essentially different circles of human existence, each of which has its own ends, its own rights and duties, and consequently its own organizing and order-producing power. But these circles are not utterly separated. They live in a kind of symbiosis and are equally necessary that man may realize his end.

Man is first an individual person, free and self-responsible, and so far autonomous. Yet he is a social being, too, and in the light of his nature and of the end of his being, necessarily so. He is a social being in a twofold sense. He is a sexual being, that is, male and female. Men and women are coordinated for the sake of propagation and preservation of their kind as well as for mutual help and completion. For a better and higher life they do and must form the community of marriage and family, consisting of man and wife, parents and children.

Each human being is man or wife, father or mother, son or daughter, each is in some way the member of a family. And even where we "leave father and mother, brother and sister, for the kingdom of heaven," we enter a spiritual community that speaks of itself as a family, where we are brothers and sisters. Thus even where the natural form of the family is sacrificed, the spirit of the family, the moral order and the affectionate bonds of the family, are still a kind of prototype. The plurality of the families and their mutual coexistence now lead to a second and higher form of social life, to the political community. Its end is to produce a sovereign order of peace and justice under the protection and furtherance of which the preceding and pre-existing forms, the family and the person, can live and function according to their own essence. The common good, the happiness on earth (*felicitas externa*), the right life (*recte vivere*) of families and individuals and their associations, are the end of this political form, in which the process of social development first of all reaches its end, though again the states themselves form a looser but not less real community: humanity.

The center of the first circle of human existence is the individual person as such. It is the realm of the most personal and individual life and work upon ourselves and for the end of ourselves, the salvation of our souls and the work of this salvation in the order of this world. Every person has his own self-interest, his own self-love, which is so justified that it is made the measure of the neighbor's interest and the measure of charity. The status of a person, immortal and in himself an individual and irreplaceable value, is the starting point of all social philosophy. And out of this status grow natural rights which the order of law presupposes and therefore does not create; and which it has the duty to protect and never the right to destroy. But equally out of this status grow duties, without the fulfillment of which this status cannot survive. Christian teaching gives, as the basis of all this, the fact that man is created after the likeness of God. The power that controls this intimate sphere of the human person is reason and free will; it is conscience. To have reason and free will, to have conscience, establishes the dignity of the human person and is the origin of human rights. Their legal formulation may be different: in a materialist society their interpretation may be wrong and self-contradictory; in an individualist society they may be overstressed, with a frivolous forgetfulness of the equally important duties. Yet a being with individual reason and free will, conscience and self-responsibility, subject to the divine law of the Creator, has his indestructible rights. The absolute prince spoke of the dull reason of the subject; the totalitarian of our times has made the individual a mere particle either of an aggregation or of a master race, in both ways denying personality to the individual and consequently abolishing his rights.

The second circle of human existence is the circle of the family. The Schoolmen called it *vita economica:* life around the house, the homestead of the family. Its end is the preservation of kind in the procreation of children and in their care and education by the parents. Apart from the care for material economic goods, that embraces the care for spiritual goods, the education of the mind and of the will to the virtues, individual and domestic, to charity and to obedience, to piety and to sacrifice, to justice and to love. There exist, therefore, original rights for the parents in order that they may fulfill their duties: the right of the parents to define the education of their children; the right of the sacredness of the family's home; the rights of paternal authority. But they are not now absolute as they once were in pagan laws; for instance, in the laws of the Roman Republic. They are limited by the fact that wife and children are individual persons. Even these rights disappear when the children reach the full status of self-responsibility. May we here say that the Catholic Church has done more for the liberation of women than any other influence, by declaring marriage a free contract of husband and wife, nullifying any marriage the consent to which was not free on the side of each party, and thus breaking the absolute *potestas patrifamilias* of the pagan laws with, e.g., their marriage of purchase.

Around the household and brought into existence by it expands the social and economic life. Here the fathers, as equals or at least as legally free subjects, and the adults beyond paternal authority enter into numerous contractual relations in order to produce economic goods, to deliver socially necessary services, and to transfer produced goods from producer to consumer. Here the free individual producers have the field of their natural rights: the right of a free choice of their professions and vocations; the right to the fruits of their work; the right to private property and to freedom of contracts. But again this new set of rights and powers includes the duty to honor the formerly mentioned rights. Practically the dignity of the human person prevails over contractual rights for profits; the duty and right of the father to take care of his family precedes any contractual rights of the employer derived from an exploitation of his superior bargaining power in the labor market. The protection of property rights must never prevail over personal rights in case of genuine, irreconcilable conflicts. The fathers and the other adults may further organize themselves freely for cultivation of higher interests, such as literature, arts, and education. All this is essentially a sphere of individual freedom, of personal initiative and responsibility.

But we see at once that the multiplicity of these social relations between families and individual adults, with easily aroused conflicts of interests and rights, demands a protective, coordinating, and mediating organization with supreme authority to put an order into effect and to decide conflicts. Thus arises the political circle. It has its own end, the common good, the order of peace and justice, the sufficiency of life for all those it embraces. To accomplish these tasks the political form has its own authority or power to govern, and the citizens who by cooperation live the political life have their new duties and rights as members of the political community. As has been pointed out, the Schoolmen distinguished three orders of justice. The order of commutative justice regulating the relations arising from contracts between persons who for this purpose are legally equal. The order of legal justice (loyalty, allegiance) regulating the duties of citizens to the political authorities. The order of distributive justice regulating the duties of the political authority to the citizen. But again, the political order does not and may not supersede or abolish the sphere of the individual person, of the family, or of the associations of individuals. Such substitution would be a perversion of its end, for it does not exist to substitute for them but to coordinate and to protect them. And this requires a political authority, a supreme deciding authority.

Though these circles are, to their own benefit and to the benefit of the persons, thus sharply distinguished, they form a *unitas ordinis*. So strong is their interdependent unity that where one suffers the *unitas ordinis* is endangered. No sound political life can exist where the rights of individuals are denied. No protection of the individual rights can exist where, instead of an efficient and honest authority, political corruption and administrative anarchy prevail. No sound family life can exist where the individuals care only for their own enjoyment, repudiating their duties as parents, or where the state, enlarging its sphere in a paternal manner, substitutes state agencies for the fulfillment of tasks that belong to the families and the free, self-governing associations of the citizens in social life. Thus the state consists neither of families nor of individuals. From the state's point of view, the family is seen to be not a mere plurality of individuals or a mere matter to which the state gives the form. So the social life moves in indestructible concentric circles: the circle of the individual person surrounded by that of the family, the circle of free, autonomous social activities of persons in their cultural and economic life, and then, embracing these and affording peace, justice, and order among them, the state as the *unitas ordinis*.

To this differentiation of the social life and its relative autonomy corresponds a differentiation of order producing genuine power. Thus the political power is not at all the sum of transferred rights originally possessed by the individuals or the family heads, nor is it a kind of enlarged power of the father, as the political theory of patriarchalism contends. Political authority is an authority *sui generis*, as is its task, the realization of the common good.

IV. The Terms "Authority" and "Power"

The terms "authority" and "power" are used almost synonymously. Yet they have a different meaning, like *auctoritas* and *potestas* in Latin. When we use the word "power," i.e., *potestas* (from *posse*), *puissance* (from *pouvoir*), *Macht* (from *machen-können*), we must note that, like its Greek original *dynamis*, the term has two meanings. In one sense it means moving, determining energy, according to the usage of natural sciences. It is that which as a cause determines the effect. In another sense it means the actual ability of a person to determine the will of another person by strong psychological motivation, even by the threat of applying force to produce an external conduct according to the will of the first person. In this sense, power means the ability of a person to find obedience to his imperative demands. It is the fact of obedience by others, that constitutes power. *Obedientia facit imperantem; vel potestatem,* we might add to that famous adage. But this ambiguity of power, its physical and political double nature, is not yet exhausted. We imply most often a normative element, too; we are not content with the mere definition that power is the ability, by whatever means, to determine another person's will so that this person obeys. When we imply the normative sense, power means that a person, as an organ of a social group, of an organized social entity, has a moral or legal competence, in some form acknowledged by the members of the group, to determine the will of other persons, members of the group or persons outside the group, and has at its disposal such means as regularly and calculably will be able to enforce obedience.

Thus power endowed with legislative quality, means first the competence, the right, of the power by the constitutional framework that every organized group has, rudimentally at least, to demand obedience. It means secondly that availability of means to enforce obedience to its commands. Such means may range from psychological motivation through tradition, habit, propaganda, to actual compulsion, the application to the subordinated persons of a greater evil than any evil obedience could bring them, ultimately the choice between the loss of life and property or obedience. But as obedience is an obedience by free rational beings and can never be "blind" obedience, a new problem arises, because the persons in power are human beings, too. Only if an existential superiority of the person in power existed, only if this person were superhuman, would there be no problem. Obedience to God, the omnipotent Power, is no problem at all; neither is obedience to a person who has power immediately from God, unmistakably revealed by God. Precisely in order to found royal power absolutely and to enable it to demand exclusive obedience, was the theory of the divine right of kings invented. Yet in the political field power is not directly transmitted from God to the person in power. Political power is concretely power of men by human law over other human beings. And then this power, its use and its means as well as its objective end, is subject to moral standards. The use and the means of such a power are measured by the end for which power is wielded and by the rule of reason. Obedience in rational beings must be reasonable, must be ultimately determined by the reasonableness of the end. So the imperative rule issued by the power must be a rule of reason and for reason.

Thus the power itself, however much natural law and, mediately, the supreme power of God may be its origin, is subject to natural law and is wielded usually under a constitution of the social group itself. Thus we arrive at the qualifications of power: abuse of power, arbitrary power, is a wrong use of power against the rule of law, the constitution of the social group, and a use of power that is against reason and against the end of the power. Power must be ordered to the objective end of the social group in which it is wielded; power must have the qualities of reasonableness, expediency, and proportion of its use and means in relation to its end. An absolute power of man over human beings as persons, is morally impossible because absolute power presupposes perfect, infallible, i.e., divine, reason. An indirect proof of this statement is the tendency of all absolutist princes and modern dictators to claim that they are divine or have received special revelations from God so that actually not they themselves command, but God. There is no appeal and no right of resistance or of revolution against God.

We said that the opposite of arbitrary power is reasonableness of power or of its use and means for an end, legitimized by reason. Instinctively we expect from those in power two things: greater insight, experience, and knowledge, and a certain degree of sincerity and honesty specific to the end and the use of the power. All laws demand from those who wield power over others a higher degree of honesty, impartiality, and moral responsibility than from private persons; namely, those persons who have no power, but are subject to power. And that demand is as valid for the president of a union or a club as for a monarch, the president of a republic, or a judge. The obvious inequality between those in power and those subject to power, irrespective of the democratic origin of the power, requires a specific intellectual and moral qualification for those in power. And here enters the term "authority."

In the Roman Constitution there was originally an obvious relation between the older, more experienced, wiser senators (*senatus* = assembly of old men) and legislative power. The *patres,* the fathers, are considered the *auctores* of the laws. Their *auctoritas* gives the resolution of the *comitiae* the sanction, the binding power. Even the emperors Augustus and Tiberius felt themselves to be under the *summa auctoritas* of the Senate. "Authority," moreover, is always used in relation rather to personal, intellectual, and moral qualities than to the technical holding of an office. So we may speak of the power of wealth, but to speak of the authority of wealth is ridiculous. Authority is, therefore, rather a moral power, not so much of the office or of the availibility of means of enforcement, as of personal experience, wisdom, greater insight and integrity. Power may be abstracted from persons; authority is never so. Therefore we speak less of the power of the judges, but more of their authority founded upon their higher legal knowledge, their honesty, and their integrity. Yet the authority of the judiciary is enormous. We speak further of the authority of experts, scientists, and scholars, meaning their greater experience and knowledge. An elder statesman may have no power in the strict sense, yet he may have an enormous authority. Augustus says of himself that he never had more power (*potestas*) than he possessed on account of the offices transferred to him, but that he excelled all in authority.[8] St. Augustine says that he would not believe even the Gospel unless he had the authority of the Church for it (*Contra Manich.*, 5).

In all these examples the relation between authority and greater insight, wisdom, and integrity is evident. The term "authority" includes implicitly a certain opposition to the judgment, knowledge, and wisdom of the subjects, of those who obey. The judgment of the authority is accepted more readily because of its higher qualities, as compared with that of the subjects, generally speaking. It is substituted for the imperfect judgments of the subjects, not so much because that judgment can be enforced by power, but rather because it has qualitative superiority. A person has power, legal competence, to command and enforce obedience externally, on account of the fact that he holds office or exerts social power by the fact of his wealth. But a person has authority because of his insight, experience, knowledge, and moral qualities. Power, therefore, means chiefly the simple fact of being obeyed. Authority means to find obedience on account of the qualitative superiority of a person, implying also a largely voluntary, never blind, obedience. We trust, we believe, in this superiority, and therefore we obey.

There is no doubt that the ideal government is the union of power (competence) and authority in all those who demand obedience. So

[8] *Res gestae*, chap. 34. Cf. R. Heinze in *Hermes*, LX, 348 ff.

we are instinctively inclined to use the two terms without distinction. Any government should, in that sense, be aristocratic, the rule of the best. Aristocratic government, so understood, is not in contradiction to democracy, for democracy's purpose is to guarantee to the people the best possible government. It is not in contradiction to equality, for true equality can never mean qualitative egalitarianism. True equality is more negative: it means absence of legal privileges and the accession to office or position of the better man simply because of his personal superiority in wisdom, experience, insight, and moral integrity, irrespective of his wealth, birth, or creed. Democracy is thus friendly to authority and more critical of power in the merely factual sense. It is based on civil virtue and public morality and therefore demands these qualities more than other forms of government. The term "authoritarian government," used by Fascism, on the other hand, is a misnomer. In the traditional nomenclature, Fascism is rather despotic, related to "power" and not to "authority."

V. Political Authority as Public Authority

Political authority is public, as distinguished from private authority. The Roman lawyers defined "public" as that which refers to the *"status rei Romanae."* [4] Authority is always fundamentally moral power; if it is legalized, it still draws its power from morality. Thus it becomes a problem of the objective end and purpose it has to realize. The allegiance that authority demands, as distinguished from mere psychological or physical compulsion, is a free assent motivated in the last resort by some personal confidence in the moral goodness either of the person in authority or of the act required by the authority. Thus one may rely on the judgment of the authority and not exclusively on one's own reason. Authority, at least if it appeals to adults, necessarily appeals to reason, and we can easily see that even dictators, and perhaps they most of all, attempt strenuously to explain and justify their commands by cloaking their acts in moralizing propaganda. No "blind" obedience to human authority is possible. Only the authority of God and that of His divinely instituted representative, the Church, are absolute. Even in this connection we find the saying that faith, which is assent to authority,

[4] Gaius, *Institutiones*, I, 1.

must be "reasonable." Cardinal Newman, in discussing the dogma of papal infallibility, without doubt the highest possible concentration of authority on earth, says that the pope cannot demand "absolute obedience"; for if he did demand this, "he would be transgressing the laws of human society" (Letter to the Duke of Norfolk, chap. 4).

In the light of human dignity this is necessary because otherwise it would not be possible to place upon the individual the duty to examine the positive commands of human authority with the help of natural law or of God's revealed will.

Political authority refers necessarily to adults or to men who have come to the use of reason. The child is a citizen, but his active citizenship is dormant in the lap of the family. It is the sphere of the family, usually closed to state action, in which the child lives, and it is the parents' authority, especially that of the father, which is the point through which the state authority reaches the child. The child has no active or passive vote, he is not responsible for illegal acts, and he cannot sue before the law courts, because he has not yet the full use of reason. This makes the obedience of the child different from that of the citizen, and makes state paternalism wrong. The presumption that the subject is stupid and the authority wise in its exclusive opposition of qualities was the oblique basis of enlightened despotism, a kind of regime that is anything but ideal.

Political authority is public. "Public" means the opposite of the private sphere of the individual citizen. The private sphere is the sphere of the individual conscience, the intimate sphere of personal life, the sphere of the family, and the sphere of the acquisition, use, and consumption of property in the economic sphere.

We find the distinction of public and private also in penal law. Thus, for instance, only public offenders can be prosecuted in canon law, and only for public offenses can public penance be imposed (can. 1935 §1; 2312 §2). A crime is further characterized as *ordinis perturbatio*. What is meant here is the external legal order as distinguished from the moral order. Thus every crime as a disturbance of the external order is morally a "sin" because it is violation of the moral law expressed in the juridical law, but not every sin is a crime or a rupture of the external order. The canon law distinguishes thus the *forum internum* and the *forum externum;* the latter is the public sphere. Here either the existence and the dignity of the authority is concerned, or the social order among the members of the community and thus the common good.[5] Furthermore, this disturbance, besides being external, visible to an indefinite number of the community, is of some danger to the common good, i.e., the order of the community. If a person does not fulfill the duties arising out of a private contract, this failure is in all civilized countries a civil private wrong but not the affair of the state as such; it is not a crime, because it is not a violation of the order of the community.

On the other hand, a grave violation of one's honor, which is a social, public category, by libel or slander, may become a violation of the order because the order is not a mechanist thing but a sum of active acts by the honest members, who by their active collaboration every moment keep the order in being. One's honor before the public is therefore an integral part of the order and thus demands public protection. Again, the idea of political representation includes the idea of a public as distinguished from a mere sum of private individuals. The House of Representatives represents the United States; the people, not able to act together, make themselves represented, "visible" in the Representatives, to perform a duty toward the common good which they themselves are unable to perform. "Public," therefore, in the strict sense refers to the community as such, not to individuals or agglomerations of individuals without a common formative, organizing purpose bearing on the order of the community. And we may even say that "public" always refers to the political unity made concrete in the common good, made concrete in an individual people's political existence. "Public" refers to the state and the common good.

This differentiation is of the utmost importance. When Mussolini says, "Nothing outside the state, nothing beyond the state," he actually destroys this differentiation, and the totalitarian state and tyrannical sovereignty appear. National Socialism and Bolshevism alike deny the existence of a private sphere. Thus their penal courts try

[5] F. X. Wernz (*Jus decretalium*, VI, 13) defines a *delictum* as an act or omission "disturbing the social order of the Church." We imply of course the validity of natural law. Positivism and totalitarianism cannot say that every crime is morally sin. The former cannot consent because, according to its view, crime is merely a forbidden act to which follows as effect punishment without regard of an intrinsic immorality of the act. The latter, claiming also the mind and its innermost thoughts for itself, must give up any distinction between the juridical and the moral sphere, between the internal *forum* and the external *forum*, between the private and the public sphere.

to sentence the accused because of their private opinions. There is no distinction between external forum and internal forum, and so neither justice nor morality nor freedom.

The object of political authority is thus not so much the individual as such but the people in its political existence, as a living whole, and its order, the common good. Political authority meets the individual will, demanding obedience not on an equal footing as a coordinated party,[6] not as a mere majority of summed-up individual wills, but as a will, as a power of a higher kind, fundamentally different from the individual will or any sum of such wills. It not only represents but is the order-producing higher will, as the political existence of the whole is higher than the individual.

Political authority, instituting and preserving the *ordo rerum humanarum* after the pattern of the eternal order, gives to the individual persons the possibility of performing their purpose. If we regard the state as the concrete durable order among individuals, families, and their free associations for economic, cultural, and educational purposes, then without the state man would be either an animal or a demigod. Thus the political authority guarding the common good offers to the citizen, too, the social and cultural environment in which he is enabled to strive toward his final goal, the salvation of his soul through a life lived in order and according to reason here on earth.

It is this which gives political authority the dignity, majesty, and sublimity always granted it. Even the most informal people yield to the symbols of political authority and to the persons who by free election exercise it a reverence which they are unwilling to give to the executives of even the biggest enterprise.

To it, therefore, exclusively belongs vindictive justice: the prerogative and duty to punish criminal action, that is, culpable violation of the social order which political authority is called to protect as a realization of the common good. This prerogative, especially the death penalty, can never be the right of an individual.[7] The individual's right of self-defense is not an issue of vindictive justice; it occurs

---

[6] It is interesting to watch how the formula "coordination, not subordination" in early Puritanical New England led practically to a kind of theocracy, making the Bible, i.e., those interpreting the Bible, as powerful an authority as the subordinating authorities of old had been.

[7] Where individuals or associations of individuals usurp such a *jus necis et vitae*, it is only because there is not yet a social order and an unequivocal authority established, or because these are so weakened as to be in a state of dissolution.

in the private sphere; but the accusation, the trial, and the sentence of a criminal take place before the people as a whole. Especially when the crime is grave, it is the jurors, representatives of the people, not the official judge, who find the accused guilty or not guilty.[8] The right of pardon and amnesty is a typical public act and therefore belongs to political authority, never to private individuals.[9]

[8] The wholesale perversion of justice and words alike can be seen in the Nazi "People's Court," which is not attended by representatives of the people and does not proceed in public, but secretly.

[9] It is an unmistakable token of true federalism, that is, of true statehood of the members of a federation, that their highest executives retain the right of pardon.

CHAPTER XVII

Sovereignty

I. History of the Term

Since the time of Aristotle the state has been called a perfect society because the social process reaches its goal in the political life in the self-sufficient community. The idea of autarchy or self-sufficiency is not an exclusively economic concept, as it may seem to be for Aristotle and as it is again propagandized today.[1] It is—and Aristotle does not ignore this—a moral and political concept. It refers to the social order of a community, meaning that this order is self-sufficient, embraces all organs and power to perform the community end on its territory.

Now the order, as we have seen, is not a mechanical, compulsory order, but an order among rational, free beings; it is a continuous moral effort of the authorities and the subjects. And it is an order necessary for the fulfillment of the end of man. It exists in time and space, necessitating a decision *hic et nunc* if conflicting opinions arise about the order or parts of it. Even in the most democratic assembly, discussion takes place only to assist deliberation and to prepare for the deciding vote; an endless discussion would paralyze political life and produce anarchy, unless it were simply a hypocritical means of preserving the *status quo*.

It is an order among rational beings subjected to egoism, envy, and violence, the vices destructive of this necessary order. If the order is to be lasting, workable, and perfect there must be power preserving and promoting that order, adapting it to the continual changes of social life, deciding upon the just, the expedient, and the futile, upon necessity and indifference, distributing social power among conflicting interests, and protecting the territory on which the order exists against disturbance from without. If such a power, a consequence

[1] In the self-sufficiency policies of Fascist Italy and Nazi Germany.

of the purpose of the state, which is the realization of the common good, did not exist, how could we call such a community perfect, or self-sufficient?

Thus the authority of such a community is a sovereign authority. The idea of sovereignty is very old, although the name came into use, especially in its polemic sense, comparatively late, almost at the time when the old words *republica, regnum,* and *civitas* gave way to the modern word "state." Like so many of our political concepts, that of sovereignty has its history and its change in meaning produced by political polemics and by the changes of the concepts that influence it.

The word "sovereignty" became popular after Jean Bodin made it the main topic of his definition of the state.[2] Even then Bodin's purpose was not so much to repeat the truism that where there is an order there must be a system of rules for human acts, that there must be imperium and obedience, and that any perfect, self-sufficient order requires a supreme, decisive power. His purpose was rather a concrete political one. It was to solve the problem whether the supreme power is subject to the law, or is *legibus soluta,* that is, absolute, unlimited power. Of course it would not occur to Bodinus or even to Hobbes to include in this concept "law" the divine and the natural law.

The Middle Ages upheld the theory that law, as a rule of reason and for reason, not mere will or command, is beyond the king. It is the law that makes the king (*lex facit regem*). To rule means to serve the "law"; *audiat rex quod praecipit lex, legem servare hoc est regnare* (Wippo). Law is the outcome of a process of reasoning in which those to whom the law is addressed, the subjects, cooperate. It is their answer of moral acceptance of the inner reason in the law that makes them obey. They obey not so much the mere positive will as the objective reason in the command.[3] The law is essentially an act of reason aiming at the common good; only because it is so, can the individual conscience be burdened with an inquiry as to whether the law is just and therefore binding. Only the law as having an objective rational purpose, the opposite of arbitrary, has the power to bind. In the regular course of events there exists, of course, a strong

---

[2] Johannes Bodinus, *Les six livres de la République* (Paris, 1577); Latin translation in 1586. Cf. Bk. I, chap. 1.

[3] St. Thomas (*Summa theol.,* Ia IIae, q. 17, a. 1) says that *imperare* is an act of reason.

presumption that the will of the authority is reasonable and therefore binding.[4]

Especially does tradition, handing down the wisdom of the fathers,
have this presumption. There is much wisdom in Disraeli's famous
saying that it is necessary to govern either by tradition or by force;
and it is equally evident that the more new laws a government must
enact, the worse a government is. The concept of law in the Middle
Ages reached an understanding that the law is something like a
covenant, which, when enacted, is beyond the will of the ruler. It is
thus the objective end of the law that is decisive, not the indifferent
psychological will of the ruler.[5] The dictum of the Roman law,
stressed by Bodin, that the prince is *legibus solutus* is usually interpreted as meaning that the prince is not under the law coactive yet
very much directive. A change of the law or a dispensation from the
law is never, according to this idea, based on *car tel est notre plaisir*,
but on the objective interest of the common good.

Especially under the feudal system the idea of the law as a pact,
therefore valid only by the assent of the representatives of the estates,
was strong.[6] It was against this practice and doctrine that Bodin directed his attack.

The distance between law and right, Bodin affirms, is very great.
Right refers to *aequum et bonum*, law pertains to the majesty of the
ruler. Law is nothing but a command of the supreme authority (*De
Republ.*, I, 8).

Thus the medieval saying, the law makes the king, is turned into:
"The king makes the law." [7] Thus the prince *legibus solutus* is freed
from the covenants and the pacts originating in the assent or consent

[4] The positivist theory, making the law exclusively the outcome of the will of the
potestas (*voluntas facit legem*) and therefore something having no objective measure for
the justice of a law, still occasionally reintroduces "reason." This it does by interpreting
the assumed "will of the lawgiver" and declaring that this will could not have willed an
unreasonable, arbitrary thing. Thus it puts reason in the place of will again.

[5] A good example is the Magna Charta, A.D. 1218.

[6] Perhaps the strongest expression of this covenant idea may be found in the coronation formula of the kings of Aragon: "We (the Cortes) who are as good as you, swear to
you who are not better than we, to accept you as our king and sovereign lord, provided
you accept all our liberties and laws; but, if not, we do not."

[7] Against some popular conceptions, it should be pointed out that Bodin was not
simply a monarchist. He occasionally speaks of the *summa potestas* as belonging to a
single person, to an aristocracy, or to all the citizens.

of the estates, the representatives of the feudal barons, the higher clergy, and the towns. His is the *summa potestas,* he makes the law, his will is law. He is therefore beyond the laws, not only coactive but directive too. The king from now on stands no more under the order of law, but above it.

Sovereignty thus means to be freed from all the restrictive theories and practices of the medieval feudal order of estates. In place of this dualist scheme of political organization, is put the monistic system of the absolute prince, in the interest of the unshakable juridical unity of the nation. Consequently the attack was further directed against two other theories. First, the secular sovereignty assumes an authoritative interpretation of the natural and divine law. It tends to free itself from any restrictions from the side of the papal, the spiritual, authority. In the "reformed" states it puts itself in the place of the pope as *summus episcopus,* or in the forms of Gallicanism it tries to make the canon law and the authority of the spiritual power valid only by its own placet, thus transforming the Church universal into national branches forming a part of the state. Thus the unity of the national state, the impenetrability of its borders to any other law than its own, would be firmly established.[8]

On the other side, the *legibus solutus* meant the abolition of the customary laws of the regions, of the independence of the towns, and of the self-government of the guilds and the universities, the public privileged corporations of medieval society. Thus the colorful static and hierarchic stratification of medieval society step by step was transformed into a mass of subjects who, however privileged among themselves, became equal before the supreme power. It is true that the unorganized mass of the old quasi-sovereign rights of feudal lords, freemen, guilds, and towns made an efficient national administration practically impossible. It is clear enough that the political authority, which must have unity, was practically dissolved into particles of power, each conflicting all too often with the others. Thus it can easily be seen that the old-new theory of the sovereign power of the king over the national state came to be preferred for strong historical

[8] The subordination of the spiritual power to the absolute prince was especially strong in Spain. The Crown had the patronage of all spiritual benefices and strongly enforced the placet for all papal and episcopal bulls and letters. The *Cujus regio ejus religio* is another example of the absolute prince's power.

reasons.[9] From now on there exists for this absolute sovereignty no limitation or restriction by tradition, regional customs, or interpretation of divine and natural law by an independent spiritual authority. Only self-limitation or self-restriction is left. The sovereign unites all power in his realm in himself to the exclusion of any other, whether the spiritual power or the international power of the community of nations.

The absolute king permits himself to be called "vice-Deus." His power is a quasi-divine one, for he is the one and only interpreter of natural law and of divine law. The natural law, the foundation of the distinction between just and unjust positive laws, practically disappears. The natural law thus becomes actually only a *jus inutile;* it becomes law, according to Hobbes, by the declarative will of the sovereign power; so it disappears completely in the positive law. The role of the highly important concept of natural law cannot any longer be a protection against the unjust and arbitrary power of the sovereign as a standard and measure of this power. Its essence becomes such that we cannot appeal to it against the sovereign. The will of the prince is the law: *Voluntas principis suprema lex,* instead of *Salus populi suprema lex.*

Against this concentration of power, with the consequent granting of privilege to the nobility and the clergy as the powerless sentries of the absolute king, there arose a new element alongside the traditional philosophy of natural law expounded by Catholic political doctrine. This new element was the third estate, the bourgeoisie. With it came the new natural law of individualist morals, the longing for freedom of worship and religion, against the nationalized creed. This movement culminated in the bill of rights, and the declaration of the rights of man in *Liberté, Egalité, Fraternité.* These have a double purpose. They first proclaim again that the sphere of individual, private life is free from arbitrary intervention by the state; secondly, for better protection, they call for government by consent, empowering the citizens with political rights to vote, to elect officers, and to choose juries; this demand was directed against uncontrolled "cabinet jus-

---

[9] France, Spain, England. In Italy and Germany, the rulers of the great cities and the more powerful territorial feudal lords, not the central power, became the absolute princes. Only in the late nineteenth century were Italy and Germany transformed into national states.

tice," Star Chambers, and *lettres de cachet*. In other words, the tendency is to subject all the holders of power to the control of the citizens in various forms of democratic government based on the theory of popular sovereignty. This last theory, when robbed of its philosophical basis, the concept of the law of nature, has proved itself in recent times an excellent means for the rise of a new and far mightier absolutism in Italy, Germany, and Russia, with this deterioration: the divine legitimation of the absolute prince, which might limit excesses, has now given way to a nebulous legitimation by the sovereignty of race, class, or nation.

After many conflicts, the concept of absolute sovereignty is given up in the interest of the international community, so that a modern definition of sovereignty can define a state as an independent territorial community with supreme power, subject only to the generally acknowledged rules of international law.

II. THE POSITIVIST CONCEPT OF SOVEREIGNTY

We should keep in mind that the concept of sovereignty got a new and exaggerated meaning when its earlier systematic surrounding, the idea of its limitation by natural and divine law, vanished with the victory of positivism in jurisprudence and the growth of fervent nationalism in politics. Positivism, afraid of all metaphysics and transcendental ideas, and fond only of realities, produced in jurisprudence the theory that the will of the state is the exclusive producer of the law, unlimited by any transcendental idea or teleological or moral idea. It is a secularization of the teachings of Bossuet and other proponents of the divine right theory.[10]

Thus the exclusive criterion of law is now that it emanates from the legislative organ in the constitutionally prescribed form. No other criterion is acknowledged. This theory is not too dangerous so long as the law is formulated by a democratic process of public discussion and deliberation, and under the safeguards of an inviolable sphere protected by a bill of rights, a sphere protected even against the ma-

---

[10] This school flourished especially in Germany and Italy. There the Hegelian school after its decomposition in Treitschke, and the historical school with its underestimation of reason, had prepared the introduction of general philosophical positivism into jurisprudence. This school found many adherents in Anglo-Saxon jurisprudence under the influence of Hume's and Bentham's philosophy.

jority of the legislative body. But as soon as this specific method of legislation is destroyed, as in the modern dictatorial regimes, positivism shows its faults and inefficiency. The judge, especially when made dependent upon the "law," loses the sublime ethics of his profession and becomes an executive police-official and a soulless automaton. It should make us suspicious that those two countries (Italy and Germany) in which legal positivism ruled the universities for generations, did not show much criticism of tyrannical arbitrary rule on the part of a judiciary that had lost its profession as a dispenser of justice when it had no other criterion of law but what is the will of the state. On the other hand, in the common-law countries, the resistance of the judiciary to princely absolutism and even to democratic absolutism of majorities in the legislatures rests philosophically and morally upon the consciousness that the judge is bound by the unwritten natural law, superior to the positive law.

The growth of international law has led to the contention that the concept of sovereignty is superfluous and should be definitely abandoned. This theory has found many apostles and deserves some presentation. Let us discuss the sociological theory, the leader of which is Duguit.

Duguit criticizes nineteenth-century positivism severely; for, if the exclusive criterion of law is the mere fact that it emanates regularly from the legislative authority, then the study of law does not deserve a moment's effort.[11] He says that the law of a country is the whole of the rules that are effectively applied by the administrative officers and the judges.[12] He is convinced that there exists a law imposed equally on the government and the governed, on authority and subjects. But it is not the metaphysical natural law, as had been held by the jurists and philosophers from the time of the Greeks and the Roman lawyers to the eighteenth or nineteenth century. What, then, is the law? It is a norm of behavior, a moral rule understood *formaliter* as a mere factual rule of behavior. But how does this rule become a legal rule? By the fact that the mass of individual consciences has reached the knowledge that the enforcement can be socially organized. Can be, not ought to be; for "ought" would introduce obligation. It is merely as a precaution against unfavorable reactions by the

---

[11] *Traité de droit constitutionel*, 3rd ed., I, 174 f.
[12] *Ibid.*, 2nd ed., Preface, p. viii.

majority able to enforce its rules that one conforms to the rule (for one does not obey a duty). The law thus becomes a utilitarian indicative of a conformist behavior; it is not an imperative, since any kind of determining will has to be discarded.

The law as a kind of utilitarian indicative includes the consequence that it has a purpose, an end. The social norm as a law of purpose has as its end social solidarity. Hence we have here a nonpositivist criterion; for the positivist has only one criterion, the will of the state, and is confident that it wills in some way the good and the reasonable. But social solidarity as a mere fact in our city civilization has shown that it can be bad or good. Social solidarity we find in the gang, in the organization of the political boss, in unions controlled by labor racketeers, in political pressure groups just as well as in reform organizations of citizens for better government and in political parties. The school of natural law had a criterion, the common good, the *recte vivere,* the realization of the idea of man, the order of peace and justice. Duguit, contending against legal positivism which gives to the state absolute sovereignty, founds his theory on moral positivism. He abolishes the sovereignty of the state to introduce the less tangible sovereignty of the majority of the individual consciences. "Conscience," of course, is not understood as a moral concept, but simply as the psychological fact of approval or disapproval of behavior.

Thus a behaviorist rule becomes sovereign. Consequently the concept of the will of the state is superfluous, and so, too, the concept of the moral personality of the state. Therefore international law is no longer *jus gentium,* but becomes *jus inter gentes.* The state as a moral person and as having genuine authority and sovereign power is superfluous, it is a metaphysical, inadmissible idea. The facts are groups of individuals of different density in social solidarity, and there is no hierarchy among these groups, either in their ends or in the authority of their rules. The legal world is an undefined monistic entity. The old traditional distinction between public law and private law and the distinction between national and international law become futile.[18]

[18] Nicolas Politis (*Les nouvelles tendances du droit international,* 1927) and George Scelle (*Précis du droit des gens,* 1932) are outstanding defenders of this monistic theory of law based on moral positivism.

III. Sovereignty

Catholic political theory has always endowed political authority with sovereignty. It is the consequence of the concept of the state as a perfect society with self-sufficiency. Thus, from St. Thomas to Leo XIII, the great doctors agree that the *respublica* or the prince or the legislator has supreme power. St. Thomas says that the prince may be called *lex solutus* because he can change the law, and because against him no injunction or sentence can be brought.[14] Through the whole tradition this concept is upheld, the concept of a power against which there is no appeal and which is therefore supreme in the hierarchy of temporal powers. Suarez, Vittoria, Vasques, Bannez, De Soto, Bellarmine, Gonet, the Salmanticenses, Pius IX, Leo XIII, and Pius XI all ascribe to the *respublica* supreme independent power. The citizen has no formal and legal appeal against this supreme power; if he had, the power would not be supreme. Leo XIII again and again declares that the state has *potestas maxima, supremum imperium,* and that the state, like the Church, as a perfect society, is *maxima*.[15] He therefore compares the supreme power of the state to that of the Church. The canon law [16] declares that the pope has the supreme and full power of jurisdiction. It also states that there is no appeal from a decision of the pope to an ecumenical council.

The traditional definition of the sovereignty of the temporal power says that it is supreme power *in suo ordine*, that it is full power, and that there is no appeal from its decision.

This is the formal meaning of sovereignty. It means in international life that the *jus belli et pacis,* the decision as to whether or not there exists in a given case a reason for a just war, is the prerogative of the sovereign power. Only sovereign states may conduct wars. Suarez says that it would contradict the idea of sovereignty, if for arbitration of an international claim, a certain arbitrator or court of arbitration should be imposed. Arbitration can come only with the free consent of the states concerned. There exists no international arbitrator by natural law among the free and equal states. But when states have united, by their free, sovereign decision, to subject their

---

[14] *Summa theol.*, Ia IIae, q.116, a.5 ad 3.
[15] Herder edition of the encyclicals of Leo XIII, II, 229, 355; IV, 53.
[16] *Codex*, can. 218, 219; cf. can. 223 § 2.

conflicts to an international court, then of course the decision of this court is binding. But the *ratio existendi* of that court is the sovereign will of the states.

Bellarmine is of exactly the same opinion, that it is common to all absolute princes that in things temporal they do not acknowledge a superior. Even the term "absolute prince" was, therefore, not astonishing to Bellarmine.[17] In the age of the conquistadors the Schoolmen, on the basis of this idea, rejected the justifications of colonial imperialism current in the sixteenth and seventeenth centuries as taken from Aristotle (*Pol.*, I, 1); namely, that the *barbaroi,* the savages, were by nature slaves and that consequently their social organizations were no states and were therefore open to conquest. And they equally rejected the religious cloaking of conquest under the pretense that the purpose of the conquest was the propagation of the faith. For the Schoolmen the Chinese and the West Indian states were real sovereign states, to which this armed intrusion gave a just reason for war.

Is there no difference between the Catholic tradition and the modern concept of sovereignty?[18] To what has been quoted above we might add these important terms about supreme power: the state is supreme in its own field, or *in ordine ad eundem finem civilis gubernationis,*[19] in respect to the end of civil government or *in genere rerum civilium.*[20] These mean that the supreme power is not unlimited and in all respect supreme, but that it is supreme only in regard to certain matters and to a certain content. Moreover, the term "absolute prince" as used by Bellarmine refers only to such laws issuing from the prince as contain materially nothing against divine or natural law. This proposition accords with Bodin's concept of sovereignty and is familiar to St. Thomas.[21] The measure of the acts of sovereignty is to be derived, too, from their ends and purposes. The so-called modern concept of sovereignty has had since Hobbes' time no distinct content at all because it has potentially and actually all things as its content. The state does not belong to the *ordo rerum humanarum;* it is that order. It is the leviathan.

---

[17] Suarez, *De leg.*, III, 7; *Defensio fidei*, III, 5; Bellarmine, *De Summo Pontifice*, I, 2, chap. 2.

[18] Cf. Pius IX's characterization of modern sovereignty, in the Syllabus of 1864 (no. 39).

[19] Suarez, *Defensio fidei*, III, 5, no. 2.

[20] Leo XIII, *Immortale Dei.*

[21] Bellarmine, *De potestate S. Pontif.*, chap. 8; St. Thomas, *Summa theol.*, Ia IIae, q. 116, a.5.

Religion and worship become a part of the content of that sovereignty. The pastoral authority of the sovereign is *de jure divino;* that of other pastors is only *de jure civili.*[22] For Hobbes a heretic is not one who denies a spiritual truth of the doctrine of the Church, one who puts his individual faith above that of the Church; the heretic is one who obstinately defends some private opinion prohibited by his lawful sovereign.[23] The old traditional restriction of sovereignty, that it is subject to natural and divine law, becomes futile when Hobbes, distrustful of individual reason and conscience, says that between the law of the civil sovereign who represents the Church —for the Church is subject to the sovereign—and the laws of God there can be no contradiction. His reason for this assertion is that, if an individual should disobey the laws of the civil sovereign under appeal to the divine law, there would be no one but the civil sovereign to pass judgment.[24] Thus the informed individual conscience, the last arbiter in religious and moral questions, is entirely subordinated to the civil sovereign. For, according to Hobbes' theory, what is the worth of a distinction of natural and divine law from human positive law if it cannot be different? That most important limitation of sovereignty by natural and divine law which Bodin upheld, has become empty words.[25]

Like religious life, the sphere of family life was subjected to absolute sovereignty without any restrictions. The universities, which were so free during the Middle Ages, were transformed into schools for bureaucrats to fill the offices of despotic rulers, and the freedom of the guilds, of the economic organization, was equally suppressed. The administration of justice became simply a means of unlimited arbitrary policy. "Star chamber," *"Lettres de cachet":* these are the

---

[22] *Leviathan*, chap. 42, at the end; cf. chap. 20 § 17. The sovereign's power is a wholly unlimited power. Yet when men fear that evil consequences will issue from this lack of any restrictions and limitations, Hobbes consoles them by maintaining that without this unlimited power there would be the perpetual war of all against all, a thing much worse than the leviathan. And this unlimited power is inevitable, for "whoever, thinking Sovereign Power too great, will seek to make it less, must subject himself to a Power that can limit it, that is to say, to a greater."

[23] *Ibid.*

[24] The most outspoken legal formulation of this theory, showing that it was not the abstruse theory of a solitary misanthrope, but a political principle, is found in the principle, *Cujus regio ejus religio.*

[25] It is remarkable that Hobbes, eagerly quoting Scripture in his chapter 43, omits all mention of the famous "one must obey God rather than men." Or perhaps it is not remarkable after all, because Hobbes regards the civil sovereign as God, *Deus mortalis.*

headings of the chapters of political history. The paltry camouflage of absolutism by the paternal or the patrimonial theory of the state, according to which the sovereign is the father and has a father's power and is the owner of the state as a father owns an estate, only shows that in absolute sovereignty the fundamental distinction between public and private law, between the family authority (*patria potestas*) and state sovereignty, is forgotten.

The chief reason for the absolute sovereignty which continued under a nationalist cloak even in the nineteenth century and has found a satanic renaissance in modern totalitarianism lies in the fact that the idea of an order of human ends and of the diverse communities that are ordered to their realization, went astray. Thus the rise and the continued influence of absolute sovereignty is only a concomitant result of the general philosophical trend away from metaphysics and from its consequence, a material ethics, in favor of a general positivism. The latter is naturally unsuited to distinguish the right content of sovereignty and, furthermore, makes the principle that sovereignty does not include freedom from the law of nature and of God, an empty formula because the law of nature is denied and God is far away.

IV. LIMITATIONS OF SOVEREIGNTY

Catholic political philosophy has always been able to apply the necessary distinctions because it has a social metaphysics and because its law of nature is a *jus utile*, a working rule, not a *jus inutile*, a mere dead word. As the state is only one, though the most important, of the natural communities, and as the end of the state is one, though in the temporal realm the decisive one, in an order of ends, so the political authority has its natural restrictions concerning the other communities as well as concerning the ends. Thus the concept of sovereignty can be understood only in the surroundings of the *ordo rerum humanarum*. Political sovereignty refers thus to a partial content of that order, not to its whole. The spheres of the individual, of the family, and of the cultural and economic organization (society), represent genuine limits to sovereignty. And as mankind is a genuine community, too, the international order, the constitution of the natural community of the states, is a restriction of sovereignty. By thus relating sovereignty to certain contents and not permitting it to be a mere formal concept with all possible ends as its content, it is possible to retain the concept and yet uphold international law as more than a mere arbitrary self-limitation of the states. In this way, though *in suo ordine* supreme, sovereignty becomes elastic. According to the contents, sovereignty may expand or contract, and has done so and will do so according to the needs of the common good. But it can never become unlimited or absolute, because that would mean the destruction of the order of ends and the related communities and their specific powers, of which state and sovereignty are only parts. It cannot shrink to such a minimum as to be nothing, because that would mean the destruction of order just the same. Sovereignty is thus similar to property.[26]

Property is an original right of the individual but burdened with a changing social mortgage, depending upon the intensity of social symbiosis and the rules of social justice. In its definition, property is exclusive, supreme, and full ownership of a thing, although not all things can become property: not men, not spiritual things. But property and its use are always under the law restricting its use, and the owner himself may invest rights of others in his property, though he himself retains the property and remains the owner. Yet, though property and its use may thus be restricted, even very much restricted, it still continues to exist. If it should cease to exist as an institution, the natural right to property would be abolished.

Sovereignty as political independence within the bounds mentioned above has two elements: it is supreme power and full power. To realize the order of the common good, justice, and peace among conflicting interests, between diverse opinions about what in the particular case is just, and between social groups with heterogeneous ambitions, there must be a supreme deciding power. How would order otherwise exist if the conflicting interests were left alone? How would security be established when conflicting interests continue to fight and so to menace the unity of the order? In the interest of order

---

[26] There has always existed the tendency to identify sovereignty and property, especially in the paternal theory of Romantic political philosophy which, by such an identification, led to extremes.

and the continuation of social life, the conflict of interests must be regulated and decided. This decision and regulation must be a final one.

All questions of justice and order are concrete ones. What matters is the application of a general rule to concrete circumstances here and now. There is no time in human life for an automatic compromise of conflicting interests. Such conflicts do not settle themselves. Hence the very existence of an order and the realization of justice demand a final decision, the enforcement of which is certain; for this is the presupposition of order and justice itself. The state as *unitas ordinis* could be neither *unitas* nor *ordo* if it had not been given a supreme power to decide, that is, to produce unity and order with the use of force if necessary. The strong state is not that state which, as in totalitarianism, does everything by itself, but that state which stands above the conflicts of interests and groups as the powerful umpire, as the preserver and protector of the order upon which all groups depend.[27] An essential element of order is security. But precisely this again requires that questions of justice and equity be decided *hic et nunc* and be decided with finality. Without such a final decision beyond appeal, how could individuals and groups be secure, how could the member rely on the adequate behavior of all others? It is precisely this secure confidence, this calculability of the behavior of others in the future, that makes all secure in the fruition of their rights and the sure expectation of the fulfillment of duties by all others.

It is not unlikely that the liberalist attempt to argue away sovereignty rests upon the following reasoning. There exists a natural order in social life instituted by the God of deism corresponding to the order of natural laws in physical nature. The motive of self-interest to be realized in liberty, limited only by the liberty of the others, is the sufficient agent for the establishment of social and economic order. As soon as such conditions are effected, the order, an adequate and just order, representing the natural gifts and powers

---

[27] This explains why the tyrannical sovereign, who does not acknowledge the natural limitations of sovereignty, needs so much force. The more the sovereign power stays within its limits, the less force it needs to apply. The subject obeys most of the laws and rules of the state without actually being compelled to do so by force. Tradition, a certain insight into the moral necessity of the rules, a free assent to the justice, however imperfectly expressed, in the laws, are the primary motives of obedience.

of the individuals, will, so to speak, automatically arise. No authority needs to establish a specific social and economic order as in the Middle Ages; no elaborated constitution of society, no hierarchical, stable order is necessary. The world goes along of itself. Free competition is the only principle of order and it produces social harmony. Therefore a sovereign power with competence to intervene in that field of competition where social harmony comes by itself, is unnecessary. Sovereign power need not try to introduce an artificial order when the natural order of free competition already works so perfectly. The state's task is merely to protect the market against foreign political disturbance. So the economic society, organizing itself according to self-interest around the market, is actually sovereign, and the state appears simply as a market police. The idea of political sovereignty with competence to intervene under appeal to the common good, to distributive justice, and with competence to intervene authoritatively, must appear to such thought as improper, unnatural, and futile.

The contention that a decision beyond appeal is necessary to preserve the order implies two things. First, that the sovereign power is subject to the end of the order, which is twofold: the common good, and the preservation of the rights and dignities of the persons and their associations in the interest of which the order exists. The old adage that the individual should be sacrificed for the whole is valid only in a concrete case of existential conflict, but not generally; for this reason the totalitarian adage that the individual is nothing, the community all, is utterly pagan and materialist. Secondly, political expediency, overruling strict justice, and the coordinated virtue of political prudence raise a real problem that can be solved only when we assert the superiority of the existence of the concrete order to any partial justice in it; only then is expediency justifiable. The adage, *summum jus, summa injuria*, has to deal with this fact. The necessity of a concrete decision in recurring conflicts among beings who are free, though compelled to live in unity, makes the dream of a *civitas maxima* in the strict sense unreal. Most of the great doctors did not think highly of this idea.[28] History also teaches us that the great

---

[28] It is very doubtful that St. Thomas, when speaking about *civitas* or *regnum* as self-sufficient, means the medieval *imperium*, as some have held. Suarez actually ridicules the idea of a *civitas maxima;* Bellarmine, though toying with the idea of a universal Christian

empires of Alexander, of the Romans, and of the Christian emperors in the Middle Ages were of short duration because there was no security, no real order, and no unity, as the supreme power was more and more shared by the satraps, proconsuls, feudal overlords, and the like. We should never forget that unity and order in a community are the more possible as the members of such a community are personal and responsible. The concept of sovereignty, therefore, is not a contradiction of the international order; on the contrary, it is a *conditio sine qua non* for its existence and realization.[29]

Sovereignty thus means independence of another sovereign state from an equal; it means political freedom in the community of states. But freedom means always concretely freedom from a certain compulsion, or freedom to do, not all things, but certain things. Freedom does not mean arbitrariness or license. Therefore the general claim for freedom or absolute sovereignty is wrong. When we say that the state is sovereign, we say merely that it is independent of another state, of its equal, not that it is free absolutely. On the contrary, by saying *suprema in suo ordine* we logically include the idea that the state is dependent upon supranational values and that there are moral and legal rules which are transcendent in relation to its independence. By such rules the law of God and nature was clearly meant until there arose modern agnosticism and, especially, the deification of the state. The state has a service character in the moral world. Therefore the moral and spiritual values and purposes that form the moral world are superior to each and all of the states. Precisely in the recognition of these values and in its help in realizing these ends, lies the reason for sovereignty. Thus sovereignty becomes supreme responsibility for these purposes and values and service to them. This service alone gives sovereignty the majesty and dignity

monarchy, actually means a sort of world federation with the preservation of some kind of independence by the federated states. He was influenced by St. Augustine's idea that smaller states are preferable to an *imperium*.

29 When Irak was received as a member state into the League of Nations, the Council of the League required that, to be eligible for membership, a state should fulfill the following conditions: (1) to possess a *constituted* government and an administration able to assure the *regular functioning of the central services* of the state; (2) to be capable of maintaining its territorial integrity and its political *independence;* (3) to be capable of assuring *public tranquility* in all of its territory; (4) to have such financial resources as to provide regularly for the normal wants of the state; (5) to have a *legislation and a judiciary organization* that assure regular justice to all subject to its judiciary. All the italicized words could have been taken from the treatises of a Suarez or a Bellarmine.

and moral authority that lead the citizen to free obedience in conscience. Any abuse of sovereignty, that is, non-recognition of these moral and spiritual values, destroys the moral foundation of civil obedience and thus the state as a moral being. And it destroys also the external honor of the violating state. Only a state that respects the supranational order of values has a right to the respect of its citizens and of its coequals in the community of nations.[30]

The state does not live alone in the world. Its self-sufficiency is not absolute, but is embedded in a thousand interdependencies with neighboring states on the same continent, and, likewise with the world through an identical interest as well as through the recognition of the identical basic ideas of a common civilization. And from these facts comes a moral and legal duty to recognize these interdependencies, to work with them, to utilize them for the common good. Not without deep meaning has man, in almost all languages, compared the political art to the art of the pilot. The pilot's art finds the natural conditions of wind and sea, of storm and calm, this whole network of interacting, interdependent forces, already given; his art is to appreciate them, to judge them for his purpose of bringing the ship home. Similarly the political art consists in appreciating, judging, and using these facts of moral and material interdependence; its liberty or independence does not consist in independence of these facts, but in independence of an equal, of another state. Thus external sovereignty means that beyond the state is no secular authority but the international order.[31]

[30] The highest form of such consciousness we may find in the formula: *Servus servorum Dei.* A contradictory form was that of the thoroughgoing cynic, Frederick the Great, who called himself the first servant of the state, not of the moral values.

[31] One may say that the concept of sovereignty first became absolute with the deification of the absolute prince. James I was addressed, "Memento *quia Deus es seu vice-Deus.*" The caesaropapal trend developed after the Reformation (not only by the Reformation, for Louis XIV felt rather like James I and not like the medieval sovereigns, for instance, St. Louis or St. Henry). The second element that changed the idea of sovereignty was the regress of reason and the progress of will; will, which more and more became arbitrary will, not directed and controlled by reason. There is a clear tendency in the development of law from the old theory that law is a rule of reason and for reason, to the modern theory that law is will. It begins with Hobbes; then voluntarism grows through Hume and Kant to Hegel and Nietzsche, until in Fascism and Nazism boundless, unordered, arbitrary will with an utter contempt for intellect becomes the supreme value. A real anarchism flourishes, denying any objective, original natural order, thus leaving the world at the mercy of anarchic dreamers.

V. Political Authority Sovereign *in Suo Ordine*

Catholic political philosophy thus denied the empty formalism of the idea of sovereignty, by which any and all things can become the content of this idea. It is able to point out that in the internal sphere of the state there are fields of individual and social life which by their nature are not the object of sovereignty. Such are individual rights, the rights of parents to decide the education of their children, and the freedom of the citizens to organize for their legitimate purposes, legitimate by natural law, not by the will of the sovereign. Similarly, the fact that the states live in community and form the human community implies that there are fields of international life exempt from the field of sovereignty. Such are those that are essential for the existence and development of the international community without which the individual states themselves could not in peace and justice perform their own tasks, the promotion of their respective common good.

This understanding makes the idea of sovereignty elastic. We must bear in mind that historically sovereignty became "absolute" under the impact of modern nationalism where the principle of unity was considered to embrace an absolute homogeneity in all fields of social life: in economics (self-sufficiency), in culture (control of all cultural institutions), in religion (religious unity as necessary for political unity). But that is only one historical form and is not an ideal, as we are compelled to see now when this idea of absolute homogeneity has led to totalitarianism and its suppression of all freedom.

Only if we refer the term "sovereignty" to specific material contents, to specific fields of human social life, will it be possible to appreciate federalism, which stands or falls with the idea of a division not of sovereignty, but of fields of control under two sovereignties. If we cling to an excessively rigid and monistic concept of sovereignty, we can understand neither the sovereignty of the Church in *suo ordine* apart from that of the state, nor a genuine federalism. True, a federal constitution is the final product of a political process by which states formerly sovereign in all fields, now unite, or by which parts or provinces of a unitarian state grow from below into a sphere where specific fields of social life are definitely surrendered by the federal constitution to their sovereign control. The member states of a federal

tion, by the force of the federal constitution, have guaranteed to them a field where their power of organization and their authority of decision is supreme; where, therefore, the federal power has no right to intervene. How a federal constitution divides these fields between the federal power and the state power is rather indifferent, for this division will depend upon concrete historical circumstances.

Almost certainly the member states are the original holders of the sovereign powers in this field ascribed to them by the federal constitution. This constitution is usually produced by a status contract of the member states, which retire from certain enumerated fields of social and economic life, surrendering these fields to the federal sovereignty. In the residuary field the member state is free from all intervention by the federal government. A proof of this is that in cases of conflict, not the federal government, but a Supreme Court, working like an international court, decides the issues. A further proof is that the member states have genuine legislative powers *in suo ordine* and that their supreme courts decide in judgments beyond appeal in such claims.

Another proof is that the federal constitution guarantees, not creates, the right of full political existence to the member states, just as any international league must guarantee the territorial integrity and the political independence of its member states. And again, in the case of dissolution of the federation, the constitutional limitations upon the member states disappearing, their sovereignty expands instantly to its original size, as it existed before the formation of the federation. We must not be deluded by the fact that in history such was not always the fact. The state and all other forms of political life have no existence as forms without their matter, that is, the people as an historical entity and so a potential political body. In that sense it is the active will or the passive consent of the people which forms the definite political form of existence, on account of a pre-political homogeneity of nationality, economic integration, geographical neighborhood, religious unity, or whatever may be the potential matter of unity in the order.

The objection that there cannot be a divided sovereignty, that sovereignty is by definition one and indivisible, is not relevant. In the same order, in the same determined field of social life, quite naturally there cannot be two sovereignties. "The world does not wish to be governed badly. 'Let there be one ruler' " (Aristotle, *Metaph.*, end of Book XI). This means only that in the same field there must be only one ruler or decisive power; otherwise there would be anarchy.

The greatest difficulty concerning the idea of sovereignty is the positivist denial that there is a genuine order in the universe, that this order is an order of the ends of human social forms as represented in natural law, and that therefore there exist various independent circles of legal order. The positive law is not only geographically, but also in relation to basic fields of human social life, pluralistic and not monistic. The natural law as the basis and critical norm for all positive legal systems is monistic. What has made the concept of sovereignty so suspect is the modern idea of the state as an institution in which might is right. It is the idea of the identification of simple and pure power with legal and moral competence, together with the denial that the world is order. Along with this view is the contention that man or the state creates the order in absolute and untrammeled arbitrariness—that there is no metaphysical "end" of the state, that there are no natural rights before the state, and no natural rights of the states in the international community. Consequently that all order and law is considered purely man-made and essentially arbitrary and therefore free from any unwritten law arising from the order of the nature of things themselves.

But when the line of thought begins with the idea of man's social nature and proceeds to the idea of a perfect, self-sufficient society wherein man lives for his eternal end in peace, justice, and security, when thus the common good has philosophically a definite content, and when man lives under the order of natural law defining the fields of the rule of the various powers and their mutual rights and duties, then there is no insurmountable difficulty in the concept of sovereignty.

The question whether we should give up the term "sovereignty," as is today demanded, is futile if we do not see the things that matter. Without doubt the term is, after so much abuse by nationalism and philosophical positivism, much tainted. But most of the foes of the term would not return to material ethics as the foundation for a true understanding. They would, indeed, give up the sovereignty of the political power of the individual states and transfer it to a *civitas maxima*. But what they thus transfer is simply the same positivist sovereignty that they now deny to the states. The principle that law is what the state defines it to be would then be applied also to the super-state. As little as their ancestors did would they ever acknowledge the independence of the Church as in itself a perfect society with a definable field of sovereignty. Just as little would they agree that natural law imposes intrinsic limitations upon the sovereign power of the *civitas maxima* in the inalienable rights of the person, of the parents, and of the free associations of persons in the economic and cultural fields. All these would appear as mere concessions by the world-state just as they were concessions or arbitrary self-limitations by the individual states, and not as rights prior to and therefore immune from the sovereign. The *civitas maxima*, we fear, would finally look very much like the leviathan of Hobbes.

The concept of sovereignty is wrong when it is an empty formal concept open, according to the arbitrary will of the sovereign power, to any and all contents. The concept of sovereignty is right and not dangerous either internally or externally if it is put into its inter-dependence with the principle of subsidiarity and the hierarchical order of ends, and subject to the natural and divine law. If someone thinks that the word "sovereignty" should be given up, this does not matter, as long as its content, as it is traditional in Catholic political philosophy, is not lost; namely, that it is merely a term to define the state as a self-sufficient *unitas ordinis*, with the common good as an order of law, peace, justice, and security, and consequently with the competence to decide finally and authoritatively in conflicts arising within the order; that it means the liberty, the political independence, and the right to live of the member state of the community of nations, guaranteed, not created, by that very community of mutual inter-dependence.

There is some reason to suspect that the fight against the term has a deeper significance, that it is an attempt to do away with authority. As we have pointed out, the term "authority" has a personal and moral relation to value more than the term "power" has. Authority binds the subject by an appeal to ideas necessary for the realization of man's end; authority is related to fuller experience, to integrity of character and to greater insight; it is aristocratic. It can exist only where meta-physical ideas and moral principles, the ideas of truth and justice in their full meaning, are acknowledged. When no objective truth, but only relative verities, are admitted, when no ideal justice is acknowledged and when, for the lack of this, might becomes right, genuine authority is impossible and any obedience is heteronomous, in contradiction to liberty and dignity. Then are destroyed the personal and moral elements of authority as a fact, and also its binding others to duties not because of will but because of a greater insight into ideas and a fuller appreciation of moral values. Then the power to bind, to demand obedience, is pure arbitrary power, unless those who obey, obey only themselves in the general will, in an identification of government and governed. But from this it would follow that the majority decides not what is *hic et nunc* just, measured by an ideal justice, but what shall be accepted as just only because the majority so decides. The concept of authority is thus dissolved. No one obeys anyone but himself. The consequence must be a new leviathan, a revival of the absolute sovereignty of majorities that are, of course, not genuine statistical majorities, but the technical means of party machines and other small political groups. These rule by their use of the majority principle just as absolutely as ever an absolute monarch has ruled, or even more despotically, as the technically legal plebiscites in the totalitarian regimes prove. Authority and democracy with liberty and equality are not such contradictions. On the contrary, in any genuine democracy the citizen has the right to be ruled by the best or the better man. We mean the man of higher political prudence, of more impartial justice, and of higher integrity in respect to ideas, eternal and absolute, however darkened by human weaknesses. It is never unworthy for the free to obey the rule of the better man.

CHAPTER XVIII

The Main Task and Justification of Political Authority

I. THE CONSTITUTIONAL ORDER

To BE thus sovereign in its order, though it leaves a field of elastic expansion or contraction for sovereignty, means that there are genuine limitations for sovereignty. It means further that within these limitations there is a field which may be called essentially subject to sovereignty but which is itself surrounded by matters that out of historical circumstances may become contents of sovereign action.

To the essential contents belongs legislation. This means first, the setting up, the preservation, and if necessary the change of the constitutional framework that is the political order in which a people has decided to live in freedom and independence: the organization of the organic elements of the state—legislative, judiciary, and executive—their competences and the mode of their formal procedure (constitutional order). In states which constitutionally proclaim civil liberty, we find in the constitution itself or in the bill of rights a clearly defined limitation to the exercise of the sovereign power. Usually we also find an enumeration of political rights about such matters as the franchise and eligibility for office. The reason for these latter is the control of the organs of the state by the citizens; the reason for the human rights is the need for protection from abuse of power by the government.

These human rights are actually the more important. The so-called political rights, which constitute government by consent, the formal democratic constitution in a more technical sense, are important rather as an additional guaranty of the first rights. This view receives an indirect confirmation from the fact that human rights are valid for all, irrespective of their citizenship, sex, and age, whereas the rights of the citizen may be restricted to the adults, to the male adults, or to those who have established a legal residence. A further confirmation may be found in the way everyone watches jealously over human rights, while in the sphere of political rights, even in outspokenly democratic nations, we often find a considerable indifference among the potential voters, an indifference that gives oligarchical party machines their opportunities. On the other hand, the idea of human rights is intrinsically independent of the form of the government; these rights may exist in monarchies as well as in democracies. Therefore the problem of the form of government—monarchy, parliamentary democracy, or an aristocracy of education and property resting upon a qualified franchise—is usually one of secondary importance.

However, the problem of human rights and consequently of the service character of the state is the problem of all forms of government, because these rights are the boundaries that mark out the sphere of freedom of the persons, of the families, and of their free associations.[1] These rights, whether inserted in constitutional charters or not, are always valid. They express most distinctly the service character of the state. They are the standards by which we measure arbitrary use of power, right to resistance, autocracy, and tyranny. They are preferably meant whenever we use the term "democracy." They constitute a sphere of individual initiative and social freedom protected from destruction by democratic majorities as well as by absolute monarchs. Today they are doubly important under the formal democracy of industrial urban masses, economically so insecure and so prone to sacrifice liberty for economic security in state socialism; it is these rights that demand eternal vigilance. True, they can be abused. The right of property, the right of freedom of contract, especially when interpreted in an excessively individualist sense, have been abused in laissez-faire capitalism. And however much we may now favor state intervention designed to abolish these abuses, we must not forget that such intervention receives its measure from these rights themselves, not from the perfectionist idea of a paternal, bureaucratic, all-provider state.

Laissez-faire capitalism had, in fact, made these human rights of

---

[1] The four freedoms of President Roosevelt's Annual Message to Congress, January 6, 1941 (Department of State Bulletin, January 11, 1941, p. 7), concern only these human rights; the Atlantic Charter expressly adheres to "the right of all peoples to choose the form of government under which they will live" (Department of State Bulletin, August 16, 1941, p. 125).

liberty and property too much like an empty shell for the masses of industrial workers. But it would now be wrong to abolish these rights generally in favor of various forms of state socialism. The true cure is the restoration of these rights by social and economic reconstruction [2] in the sphere of society, as distinguished from the organizational framework of the state, in a formal sense, from the forms of government. The guaranty and protection of these rights is the state's task; since it has not created them, it cannot abolish them. The right of freedom of worship, the right to life and property, the right of due process of law and of equal protection by the law, the right to associate for common ends in the field of economic, cultural, and spiritual life, the right of the parents to determine the education of their children, and the right of the Church to freedom in her spiritual and organizational life, all these rights exist prior to the state. The constitutional law and the common law may regulate their use, yet may never destroy their substance. They are natural rights. When the Supreme Court of the United States upheld the Constitutionality of compulsory sterilization in the case of the Virginia sterilization law (274 U.S. 200), and Justice Oliver W. Holmes argued for the right of the state, Catholic political philosophy protested vehemently [3] against this intrusion of the state, just as some years later it protested against the more excessive laws of the Nazi Germany.[4]

From this point on, the importance of the principle that the sovereign power is subject to natural and divine law and that this law is valid, too, for the constituent power in popular sovereignty, for majorities, should be understood. The sanctity of these rights, or at least of some of them, is a time-honored tradition. Bodin taught that the private law, the civil law and the rights thereby acquired were immune from the sovereign power. In the absolute states of the German princes the *jura quaesita*, the well-established private rights, were thought to

---

[2] The encyclical *Quadragesimo anno* of Pope Pius XI speaks expressly of "reconstructing the social order," and does not say a single word about the corporative state. Whoever reads this encyclical will find that it has to do mostly with the re-establishment of this sphere of personal freedom and social initiative of groups, and of property rights for the proletarians, and not with the political problem of the so-called corporative state as opposed to democracy.

[3] Cf. F. S. Betten, S.J., in *The Catholic Mind*, XXXI, 381–92; John A. Ryan, *Questions of the Day*, chap. 20; and LeClercq, *Marriage and the Family*, trans. by Thomas R. Hanley, p. 272. Justice Holmes was a frank positivist in his legal philosophy.

[4] Cf. Nathanael Micklem, *National Socialism and the Roman Catholic Church*, 1939.

be sacred. The common-law judge established the content of what is today the bill of rights as superior to the statute law of the sovereign, be this the king or the parliament. These rights were thought to issue immediately from reason in the law, not from the will of the sovereign or from an arbitrary concession or self-limitation of the sovereign power.

II. The Legal Order

The second essential prerogative of sovereignty is the establishment of an autonomous order of law among the citizens, the order of civil and penal law with the judiciary and institutions of enforcement; this represents a part of the *unitas ordinis* as important as is constitutional law. The link between them is the bill of rights: liberty of the person, freedom of contract and property, freedom of association, and protection from arbitrary violent intervention, whether by lawbreakers and criminals or by public officers. On the basis of their fundamental rights and in the framework of civil protection by penal law, the individual citizens, by their own initiative, carry on in liberty their economic purposes, their family life, their cultural activities, their worship, and so on. It is the function of this order of law to direct the citizens while they follow their own individual and social ends to the realization of the common good. How far this order leaves the determination of the content of their contracts, their property rights, and their protection to the individuals themselves, or has them regulated and materially determined by the sovereign, depends upon culture, manners, nationality, and traditions. But this material determination finds its limits, in all circumstances, in the natural rights of the citizens as individual persons, as members of families and of free associations.

Out of distributive justice also arises a necessary function of sovereignty. As the individuals form an organism of functional groups in social life of different importance to the common good, as they are, though equal before the law, never equal in personal gifts, wealth, and economic and social power, they deserve, in order to fulfill their functions, a contribution out of the common good corresponding to the importance of their functions. Provided that the lower official, for example, the policeman, gets a salary sufficient for a standard of decency and comfort, the more important officers may be given a higher salary without violating justice. This proportionality between social and political responsibility and compensation, although it produces social inequality, is not unjust.

Similarly the contributions of the individuals to the common good should be graduated according to their wealth or their income, because these rest upon the existence of an order of law that ultimately depends not upon the police and upon actual compulsion, but upon the free consent and daily assent of all the citizens to the realization of the common good in their obedience to the rules of legal justice.

Moreover, a necessary consequence of sovereignty is that when, on account of adverse economic or social developments, groups of citizens fall into a distress that can no longer be relieved by private initiative or charitable aid, but only by a new institutional disposition, then the sovereign has the right and the duty of distributive justice to intervene and to change the economic institutions so as to relieve these groups from their distress. The fact of this distress is a token that the common good is violated. That is the philosophical reason why Leo XIII promoted social legislation and why Pius XI demanded a reconstruction of social economy; for what is owned by distributive justice cannot be supplied by the charity of individuals. Thus social legislation to give the working classes a reasonable participation in the productivity of the industrial plant, with the aim of a living wage, and to afford them a degree of social security corresponding to that afforded by property is truly in the sphere of sovereignty. So is legislation preserving and protecting the farming class in correspondence with its functional importance to the well-being and relative independence of the whole. Legislation to diminish excessive differences in wealth, income, and economic power by progressive income and inheritance taxation is clearly in the domain of sovereignty as long as it does not transgress the basic rights of liberty and property and the important principle of the subsidiarity for all activity of the state. Yet any attempt to produce economic equality by all-embracing socialization including the destruction of the institution of private property itself or by a really confiscatory inheritance tax which would make the right of property an empty shell, would represent an abuse of sovereignty.

All these normal contents of sovereignty depend on the fact that the political existence of the people is protected by it against external and internal foes. Thus the *jus necis et vitae* and the *jus belli et pacis* are necessary contents of sovereignty so far as without these rights political existence, the order of law, cannot exist. This is true even when the *jus belli et pacis* has, through a desirable development of international law, shrunk to the case of exclusively defensive war. For the state is mortal, and its end is secular. Therefore it cannot consent to its own destruction, differing thereby from the individual person, who can give up the right to resist because his existence as an immortal being is not destroyed by non-resistance. But states, not being immortal, must defend their existence by warfare as long as their existence is not fully protected by an effective international order.

Apart from these necessary contents, many other fields, dependent on historical development and civilizing circumstances, may become contents of sovereignty. Thus, after the education of the states had been promoted by the Church in the Middle Ages, the state began to organize cultural life by public education, the founding of universities, and the furthering of the arts and the sciences in competition with the Church. The state began to enter the field of economics by regulating economic activities which, left to themselves, would have become detrimental to the common good (protection of the consumer; bans against the abuse of economic power; licensing of certain economic activities such as the liquor trade; or prohibition of trade in narcotics). But let it be clear that the state regulates an already presupposed free activity of its citizens. Any establishment of the totalitarian exclusiveness of the state, in education or in economics, for example, is usurpation. For it is the free initiative of the citizen as scientist, as parent and educator, as artist or as producer that is creative, not the state or the government as such.

Never, then, can the order of religious life and spiritual law become the domain of political sovereignty, nor can the substance of the natural rights of the individual person and the family. Sacrosanct, therefore, are the freedom of worship, the freedom of conscience or, as we may better call it, the freedom from compulsion in matters of conscience, the preservation of private property as a general institution of the law of the land, the freedom to marry or not to marry, and the rights of the parents over their children. These rights and freedoms themselves are beyond the reach of sovereignty. Their use, their coordination, and their regulation to produce the common good, that is clearly the domain of the state. The "How," the "Where," the

"When," the conditions under which these rights and their presupposition, the free initiative of the citizens, are to be used and protected in the framework of the general rules of law, are left to sovereignty. But their substance as the prerequisite of the *ordo* is prior to the state. An order of law is a system of general rules for reasonable free beings. Legislation, that is, the producing of general rules, and the rule of law, presuppose these rights and free initiative; they are not substitutes for them. The reason for the deep horror of totalitarianism felt by Catholic political theory is that in totalitarianism there reign, instead of general rules for freedom, the individual arbitrary command and the empty mechanical discipline of a passive mass of subjects barred from free initiative but subject to the omnipresent intrusion of governmental bureaucracy. It is, therefore, evidence of a deep insight when Catholic philosophy speaks of a field of sovereignty belonging to the individual and the head of the family equal *in suo ordine* to that of the state.

It is the purpose and task of political authority to care for the realization of the common good. It is its duty to guarantee and to protect the *ordo juris* in which the common good is realized. It ought also to change that *ordo* if the changing social life demands a change of that *ordo* in which authority as directive and even coercive power and the citizens in cooperative loyalty and free consent realize the common good in and under the rule of law.

Thus the common good becomes the moral justification and the juridical legitimation of political authority. The common good is the final cause of legislation, that most excellent prerogative and highest task of sovereign authority and power. And this to such an extent that the law derives its binding power from its direct or indirect relation to the common good, so that St. Thomas declares that a law not related to the common good is rather violence than law, and does not bind.[5]

III. Basis of Political Authority in Natural Law

In Christian political philosophy the state is considered a moral organism. This means that there is an analogy in the metaphysical

[5] *Summa theol.*, Ia IIae, q.96, a.4 c.

structure, a unity in diversity similar to that of the biological organism, but on another plane. The unifying principle of the biological organism is the soul *(anima vegetativa et sensitiva)* yet working as an unfree agent blindly following the physical laws as the organizing and coordinating force. In the moral organism the unifying principle is the moral and legal end realized by the directive action of authority instituting the order and by the loyalty and free initiative of the members. The order may find an additional basis in national homogeneity or in a common cultural inheritance. But its essence is that it forms the individuals as members into a lasting unity of existence with preservation of their independence in the lower forms of their social life.

Political authority as the directive principle to unity, as the coercive principle in establishing and guaranteeing the *ordo,* is necessary. There is no natural liberty that makes political authority superfluous, though man has dreamed of such liberty for hundreds of years. As the social nature of man leads to the state, so it leads to political authority. And this necessity does not arise from sin. It is true that sects, as they split off from the Church from the early centuries on, claimed such a freedom from political authority because, they believed, they no longer needed the law and sword, since they were just, redeemed by grace and worthy of a Christian liberty from all political authority. But it is equally true that from the very beginning the Church Fathers, the great Schoolmen, and ecclesiastical authority taught that even without original sin, that is, in the *status naturae purae,* as there would have been the state, so there would have been political authority as a unifying principle. Of course, as in such a state human reason would have been perfect and human will unweakened, authority would have been only directive. For, since reason is the essence of law and order, the perfect reason and the absence of a will misdirected and distorted by passions would have made the coercive power superfluous. But as human nature is now, the coercive power is necessary, because the order is necessary. Men often individually disagree about the particular means for realizing the social order or about elements of the order itself, and human will is subject to passions inimical to order. The individual is too easily subservient to his own interests without due regard to the interests of others. There must, therefore, be an authority and a power that decide definitely and beyond appeal about means and measures, and compel all to subordinate their selfishness to the common good.

When it is said that political authority is founded on the law of nature, two things are meant. First, the ruler or, more generally, political authority needs no ecclesiastical approbation or legitimation, nor does the non-Christian ruler need any kind of specific consent on the part of his Christian subjects. There does not exist a *libertas Christiana* which forbids the rule of non-Christians over Christians, as sectarians since the early centuries of the Christian era have contended. The sole and satisfactory legitimation of political authority is the law of nature generally, and concretely the fulfillment of its duty toward the common good, the *felicitas externa temporalis*. Even the medieval Church, which anointed and consecrated the secular ruler, did not by such acts transfer rights to the ruler that he did not already possess by the laws of the secular order. Nor did the Church by these ceremonies take away such rights. Strictly speaking, political authority does not need baptism, and the medieval rites of coronation represented only a symbolic baptism of the temporal power.

It is a misrepresentation of the common doctrine when several writers, from Thomas Hobbes [6] to W. Windelband,[7] contend that according to Catholic doctrine political authority needs a sanction from the Church and that, in order to prove this, late Scholasticism especially had tried to rob political authority of its original dignity, of its metaphysical and religious foundation, making it a mere affair of arbitrary human will. Thus, it is contended, the superiority of the spiritual authority and the sanction of temporal political authority over Christians by the Church could be more easily established. This charge, however, is without foundation and can be understood only in the light of the preconceived idea that, as Hobbes, for example, declares, the civil sovereign, if he is a Christian, must at the same time be also the supreme pastor or pope in his realm. But this has nothing to do with the common doctrine, which simply states that the power of the state rests on natural law, and faith rests on the supernatural divine law. The one law does not abolish or impair the other; political

---

[6] Hobbes, *Leviathan,* especially chap. 42.

[7] W. Windelband, *Lehrbuch der Geschichte der Philosophie* (6th ed., 1912), pp. 358 f., directed especially against Suarez and Bellarmine.

authority does not rest upon faith, nor does the submission of Christians, even to the authority of a non-Christian, contradict faith. Political authority has a field of its own. When this was especially stressed by the Schoolmen of the sixteenth and seventeenth centuries, so was the chief reason for it: to strip from colonial imperialism its religious cloak. Colonial imperialism at that time tried to justify itself by the argument that its only aim in conquest was to relieve the native Christian converts from the tyrannical rule of their pagan sovereigns. Against this argument Vittoria and Suarez maintained that such a reason was not valid, because political authority rests upon nature.

The second reason for stressing this theory was the absolutism of the kings and their propagandists, such as Hobbes and Barklay. They contended that the authority of the king, or civil authority, as Hobbes called it, was all-embracing, was spiritual as well as temporal, was of divine law, and left no room for a spiritual authority of the pope or a Church apart from the state and independent of it. Absolutism and its philosopher-propagandists would not admit that there is a difference between the spiritual and the secular order and that different authorities could both exist, each supreme in its own order.[8]

This fight of Catholic political philosophers against princely absolutism in the sixteenth century has been resumed today against totalitarianism. In totalitariansim, too, there is no distinction between a spiritual and a secular order; here, too, only one loyalty is allowed; here, too, there is consequently no freedom. For the guaranty of human freedom, however strange it may sound, is the *libertas ecclesiae*, which means the distinction between the two orders. Only by this distinction is a peaceful separation (as opposed to the laicist, anticlerical, and militant separation of Church and state exemplified in the French Third Republic) between Church and state possible though such a separation may not be an ideal in principle. Wherever that distinction does not exist, either the independence of the state or, as generally happens, the independence of the Church, and with it the freedom of conscience, is sacrificed for a monolithic caesaropapism or papocaesarism.

One of the reasons for the identification of the two orders in the

[8] Hobbes again and again tells us that nobody can serve two masters and that consequently the civil sovereign must be the spiritual sovereign. He seems not to have perceived that the argument the other way round, namely, that the spiritual authority must be the supreme civil or political authority, was just as well founded.

sixteenth century and later was the Lutheran and Calvinist theory that the state and its authority had their origin in sin, as the natural order is sinful in itself. If that is the case, then indeed, to save the political authority of Christian rulers it becomes necessary to take them out of the depreciated realm of nature and vest them with supernatural authority and to affirm that the Christian ruler's power and authority come directly and immediately from God. Consequently even a peaceful separation is impossible, and the complete identification of Church and state, as in Erastianism, is unavoidable.

IV. Fallacies of Rousseau's Theory

The theory that political authority rests upon natural law has thus a twofold significance. It saves the state and its authority from becoming an unnatural supernatural competitor of the Church and a tyrannical intruder into the sphere of religion. But it maintains, too, that political authority does not originate in sin, but gets its dignity and legitimation, its power to bind in conscience, and its claim for loyalty, irrespective of religious affiliations, from the social nature of man and so, in the last resort, from God, the Creator of all natures, the Ordinator of all orders. Supernatural faith does not change civil loyalty: it merely gives new supernatural motivations; it deepens and exalts the natural duties and virtues of the citizen, as generally the order of grace perfects the order of nature. This, therefore, is the justification of political authority, that it arises out of the social process of human nature at its pinnacle in the *Corpus politicum mysticum* (Suarez). On the concrete realization of the common good, which is the guaranty of the good life and the perfection of the social nature of man, lies its legitimation.

Abstract, unfettered freedom, along with its preservation, is not the preliminary question for the justification of political authority, as is the case in individualism of a liberalist pattern. The mark of that kind of individualism, as expressed most clearly by its prophet, Rousseau, is the declaration that the free individual is self-sufficient. To live in society means to live under rules to be imposed by authority and to be applied by authority in cases of conflict among individuals; otherwise society would be a mere amorphous conglomeration. If men decide to live in society, the wills of the individuals as single persons must be identical with what Rousseau calls the general will. Rousseau certainly tries to distinguish between the will of all and his mystic general will. But the necessary identification of the sum of the individual wills with the general will does not solve his problem.

The anarchic consequence of this concept of freedom is circumvented by a logical somersault. As the coercive power of political authority cannot be denied, it is simply stated that practically the will of a majority is the right and just expression of the general will and that the dissident individual wills are therefore not the true wills of the outvoted minority. The strong opposition of Catholic political philosophy to Rousseauism rests on the fact that for the unlimited power of the despotic prince is simply substituted the equally unlimited power of the majority, the will of which can do anything, since it is restricted neither by the idea of the social nature of man nor by an objective and therefore will-controlling end of the state.[9]

Rousseau and all his followers cling to the doctrine that the essence of law is not reason, but arbitrary will, uncontrolled by a reason that is itself controlled by objective being and ends. Rousseau and all individualists of a similar kind have to accept such an identification of the wills of the individuals and the general will because that is their only possible justification of coercive political authority. And this justification becomes the center of their political philosophy. This voluntarist and individualist concept of the law of nature serves the sole purpose of practically establishing and legitimizing the absolute power of the will of the majority, as Hobbes' law of nature established and legitimated the absolute power of the ruler. After that, the law of nature becomes in both cases a *jus inutile;* it is submerged in the positive unfettered will of either the majority or the one.[10]

If we go a bit deeper, we shall find that the problem at issue is that of authority. Rousseau, as we said, argues authority away by his identification of government and governed. On account of the general will, everyone is now subservient only to himself, and is consequently as

---

[9] Rousseau's theory can be used in behalf of totalitarianism, too, in the Caesarian plebiscites favored by modern dictators. It was Rousseau who even demanded a simple civil religion as a necessary unifying force.

[10] One feature that shows how much Hobbes still had his roots in the medieval world, though they were rather dried up by the antimetaphysical character of his philosophy, is the fact that for him all power derives in some way from God; whereas in Rousseau we find a complete secularization of political authority and its separation from any kind of divine origin.

free in the *status civilis* as he was before in the *status naturalis*. As has been pointed out, among rational beings authority is established, if we omit God's revealed law in this discussion, on the fact that the person in authority possesses a higher intellectual insight, a greater knowledge, a higher moral integrity, or more political prudence. Of course, it is not simply this higher degree itself that matters, but the ideas and objective common values that have to be realized by the cooperative effort of the directive and even coercive authority and the obeying subjects; both, especially the authority, are therefore subordinated to these objective values. The moral problem of authority is thus dependent upon the assent to such objective moral values, because they are ultimately the measure of reasonable obedience and of the righteousness of the authority's imperative rules. In the case of a denial of the validity of such objective norms and ideas as the basis of the mutual rights and duties of both authority and subject, then necessarily, if liberty is stressed, the problem of authority must be dismissed by some form of identification. Or if authority is stressed by laying emphasis upon the concept of security and tranquillity, as Hobbes did, it becomes unlimited and unmeasured by such objective ideas and rules. The truth lies somewhere in the middle.

Authority cannot be argued away in political life. It is the very essence of the order of law that it is valid regardless of the fact that a smaller or greater number of the subjects consent to it and accept it willingly. But the dignity of the individual person, his moral freedom and self-responsibility, is not destroyed by obedience if that obedience is reasonable, if, in other words, the authority is subject to the objective ideas and moral rules by which all human life ought to be governed. In the last analysis, we do not obey blindly a heteronomous will, but we obey the eternal ideas and objective rules to which both authority and subjects are subordinated. Authority does not rule by its own original right, but by its being obedient to these ideas and rules. The source of all human authority, therefore, is ultimately God, through whom all rulers rule. If such ideas and rules are denied or skeptically doubted, there remains nothing but the illogical identification of Rousseau or the absolute will of Hobbes' leviathan.

Catholic political philosophy could solve this problem more easily because it made the preliminary question not one of an abstract liberty and its preservation, but of the end of political life itself considered as a natural outgrowth of men's social nature. The objective end of political life is the order of justice and peace, the common good, the good life as it appears in the idea of man. Thus the justification of even coercive political authority is found in its necessity for men to reach that end, and its legitimation lies in its concrete realization of the common good. Thus it is understandable that in Catholic political philosophy the problem of the forms of political authority, which since Aristotle have been distinguished as monarchy, aristocracy, and democracy,[11] is of secondary importance. Rousseau's philosophy, however, is nothing else than a rather demagogical auxiliary theory for the promotion of an abstract and egalitarian democratism, which resulted concretely in a rather doubtful capitalist plutocracy that has little in common with what we mean when talking about democracy as a political ideal.

V. GOD THE ORIGIN OF ALL AUTHORITY AND POWER

Catholic political philosophy lets both the state as the form of political existence of a people and the political sovereign authority grow out of the social nature of man, and thus founds it on God, the Supreme Authority, the Lawgiver of the universe. Political authority, therefore, is ultimately of divine origin. Catholic political philosophy got its program from two sacred texts. The first is Christ's reply to Pilate: "Thou shouldst not have any power against Me, unless it were given thee from above. Therefore, he that hath delivered Me to thee, hath the greater sin" (John 19:11). The second is St. Paul's admonition: "Let every soul be subject to higher powers: for there is no power but from God: and those that are, are ordained of God. Therefore he that resisteth the power, resisteth the ordinance of God" (Rom. 13:1 f.). The meaning of political authority is to serve the common good. Fundamental to it is the insight that nature, the world, is for man the *status viae*, the way to eternal beatitude beyond. This world, this status, must be "in order" so that, with the help of grace, men can achieve the salvation of their souls and manifest the glory of God. The state, as the order which is good by reason and for reasonable beings, belongs to that all-embracing order of creation which praises the Creator in an

---

[11] Aristotle used the term "democracy" for the deteriorated, corrupt *politeia:* our term "democracy" is his *politeia*.

everlasting *Benedicite*. The world as a cosmos, as a divinely created order, demands a cosmos in human social life, too.

The order of intellectual and moral goods, as well as of material goods (that is, the whole realm of social forces: religion, philosophy, the sciences, education, technology, and economics, integrated into a working order of law, into a *politeia*) is generally and essentially necessary in order that man in the created world may reach his end beyond. To live in a world without order, to live in chaos, such a condition of the *status viae* is utterly inhuman and certainly not divine. In chaos only the hero of virtue could live, he whose virtue is so strong that he could live without the framework of external law and order. But ordinarily man is not always and in all circumstances a hero of virtue. A hero is the exception. The life of virtue generally presupposes order and law and unity. It also presupposes, as St. Thomas says, a sufficient amount of earthly goods and their use, since they are needed for a virtuous life.[12] In another place [13] he says that these material goods, by the use of which the virtuous life is made possible and the last end of man, his salvation, is promoted, should immediately and directly be striven after, in the same manner as we strive after the increase of grace, or anything else that is useful for the realization of eternal felicity. But all this is possible only if there is law and order, peace and justice, for without them a secure possession, a just acquisition, and a profitable use of goods and opportunities would be impossible. Similarly the Church prays that men may be aided by a sufficiency of earthly goods so that they will be better able to strive after the eternal good; that the Lord may give peace [14] in order that we may be free from sin, with the help of His mercy, and safe from all perturbation (of order).

To live in "order" (to live in the different spheres of human life protected in the order, to have an *ordo rerum humanarum,* the inaugurator and lasting protector of which is political authority) is indeed a fundamental central idea of Catholic political philosophy and is therefore seldom expressly treated. It is so central that without it we cannot adequately understand the propositions of this philosophy. It is of such consequence that on it is founded the moral justification of po-

---

12 *De reg. princ.*, I, 15.

13 *Summa theol.*, Ia IIae, q.114, a.10.

14 The word "peace" comes from the Latin *pax*, which is derived from the Greek verb *pegnymi* ("to put together, to order").

litical authority in general and its legitimacy *in concreto.* That there should be a concrete order among persons and an order of things in relation to persons, an "incarnation" of the natural order as it appears in the law of nature,[15] is necessary for the realization of man's last end: the salvation of the soul and the glory of God. God's eternal law wills that all be *ordinatissima,* as St. Augustine says.[16] This order is so important that, according to the words of St. Paul, the authority of the state receives a kind of superhuman dignity.[17] Authority appears thus as a mirrored reflection of the divine might, of God, the Establisher and Protector of the general order in the universe. When St. Paul wrote his admonitions, his "authority" must have meant the regime of the pagan Caesars. Nevertheless he upheld that authority. Even where the person in authority is morally corrupt, an infidel and a sinner, even there, through that sordid humanity, shines a reflection of the divine majesty by which the rulers rule.

That authority is such a reflection, is also the profound sense of those myths of all nations which describe the sovereign secular authority originating in divine authority; it is the only legitimate sense of that often abused formula, "by the grace of God." The state, that is, the rule of law, the unity of order *(unitas ordinis),* and political authority that carries the sword not for nothing, has always been regarded by Catholic political philosophy as the bearer and protector of a grand moral idea. Hence it granted the state and its authority that obligating dignity and majesty which give to the authority the right in extreme emergency to demand the sacrifice of goods and even of life. But at the same time it bound this authority. Only as long as it preserves the concrete order and serves the common good of all the people for all the people, is it legitimate authority, and only then has it the right to demand obedience.

This explains why, in the period of a liberalist minimizing of the state and its authority, when fashionable theories made the state a nonintruding servant of "economics" and "wealth," Catholic political philosophy protested by stressing the dignity of political authority, its

---

15 St. Chrysostom (*Hom. 23 in Epist ad Rom.*) says: "I contend that divine wisdom has arranged that there be authorities, that some command and others obey, so that not everything shall be by chance and without deliberation and reason."

16 *De lib. arb.,* 1, 6, 15. An excellent commentary on this is that of Joseph Mausbach, *Die Ethik Augustinus,* I, 128.

17 Cf. Rom. 13:4; John 19:11.

ultimately divine origin, its majesty beyond the economic and technical values, and its moral power and duty to intervene whenever the common good is violated. The state is more than a handmaid of economics. This idea of the state also explains the opposition of Catholic political philosophy to absolutism and totalitarianism, to the excessive magnifying of the state. Here neither the law of nature nor the service of moral values binds the state's authority. The deification of political authority puts it beyond morals, makes it an arbitrary power destroying the objective order, a non-moral instrument of a so-called racial or economic or doctrinaire elite, not the servant of the people. Thus political authority loses its dignity and its moral legitimation. Being mere suppression, it begets hatred and revolt, the highest treason to its end, which is order. Let it again be said that in attributing to authority a moral character and the task of making the citizen virtuous, the authority itself is subject to the objective moral order. Consequently it cannot be arbitrary power, but must be bound by that moral order of which its legitimation is a part, and from which it gets its dignity, because it serves this moral order, and only so far as it does so. Absolutism and totalitarianism, since they declare themselves unlimited, are lawless and make lawlessness. As they do not serve the moral order, they produce non-morality within and without, a fact of which we are the unhappy witnesses.

CHAPTER XIX

The Origin of Political Authority

I. THE MORAL AND JURIDICAL PROBLEM

THE ultimate divine origin of political authority, and therefore the supreme legitimation of a power that transcends the sum of the powers of all individuals as a mere sum of individual wills, a power that wields the *jus vitae ac necis* or the *jus belli et pacis,* must be protected against any kind of misinterpretation. The greater the power, the more necessary is the rational clarity of its essence, its meaning, and its origin. The temptation of abuse and the danger of corruption are proportional to the degree of power and authority.[1] The greater the authority, the greater its responsibility before the incorruptible moral conscience and to the ideals of which it is the servant.

Thus Catholic political philosophy asserts the ultimate divine origin of authority. It asserts that political authority is founded on the social nature of man and on the doctrine of the living God [2] as the source of all order and of all authorities preserving and protecting that order. The divine source of authority must not be interpreted as meaning that God gives authority directly and immediately to the ruler himself; in other words, that God designates the holder of authority by a divine immediate act. Such a theory was held by some court theologians of the Stuarts and by a few Catholic writers in the era of antirevolutionary and antidemocratic romanticism. It approached a view which is rather old, as can be seen in the theories of the partisans of Philip the Fair or of Louis the Bavarian.[3]

---

[1] *Corruptio optimi pessima.* It has a profound significance that the third and greatest temptation of Christ was that of power. Cf. Matt. 4:8–10.

[2] Some of the dislike felt by Catholic philosophers for the ideology of excessive democratism in the nineteenth century is based on the belief that some of the reasons of that ideology are the consequences of a deistic theodicy.

[3] Cf. Richard Scholz, *Die Publizistik zur Zeit Philipps des Schönen und Bonifaz des VIII* (1903); *Unbekannte Streitschriften aus der Zeit Ludwigs des Bayern, 1327–1354* (Rome,

St. Chrysostom [4] in the early Christian period had already made the necessary distinction. "There is no power and authority that does not originate in God. What does the Apostle say? Ergo, every prince is appointed by God? I do not say that, because I am not speaking of a prince in particular but about the matter itself (authority in general). I say that the authority of the rulers is a work of divine wisdom and that it does not leave all things to the temerity of chance. Therefore the Apostle does not say, there is no ruler that does not come from God; but, speaking of the thing, he says, there is no power that is not from God."

The question with which we are here concerned is thus a parallel to that of the origin and birth of the state. There, too, we maintained that the origin of the state is, by way of the divinely instituted social nature of man and its perfection in political life, God Himself. The actual coming into existence, the actual founding of the order of legal justice, however, is regarded as happening not without the mediation of purely human and natural factors; and this is especially true when the question of right is considered. It is the morally necessary, but still free, decision of men uniting themselves to a *unitas ordinis* that is actually the immediate cause of the existence of the state; to explain that fact we use the legal figure of the social contract as a status contract. The problem here must be stated as follows: What is the reason (as distinguished from a mere factual cause) that this particular individual or group of individuals is the holder and dispenser of authority? Why did he or they become so? And why, therefore, must their commands be obeyed? It is true that a mere positivist standpoint is satisfied with the old adage, "Obedience makes the ruler." But a free moral being desires to know why he should obey. Human obedience to man must be a rational obedience. The adage just quoted would leave unanswered the objection that for the most part we do not obey on account of fear or intimidation (as is rather the rule under tyranny), but by a free submission to rules and commands as individual expressions of general rules, because we assent to the law and the commands as reasonable, because we assent to their objective purposes and ends. This makes possible the distinction between legitimate government and tyranny.

1911, 1914); also Jean Rivière, *Le problème de l'église et de l'état au temps de Philipp le Bel* (1910).

[4] Hom. 23, 1 and 3 (*Homilia de Epist. ad Rom,* 13); Migne, *PG,* LX, 615.

Thus our problem is not a historical one that could be answered: "Well, this ruling house has since early times held the *imperium* because it has some individual political skill or because the constitution says it should." Our question is that of the legal and moral reason of the institution itself. Who is the constitution-making authority? Nor is our problem a sociological or a psychological one, to explain the rise of this particular ruling house on account of the economic or social structure or the specific psychological mentality of this particular tribe, people, or nation. These are all interesting problems, but they are not our problem, which is of a moral and juridical nature. Mere facts beyond the order of law, natural and positive, do not constitute legitimacy.

The problem of the legitimacy of the power of an actual authority is not a question of fact, but a moral and juridical problem. Therefore our problem cannot be dismissed with, for instance, the cynical remark that wars, conquests, and successful usurpation, and the consequent power of facts such as the success in war or revolution, make our problem futile. Is not the end of the war a peace treaty that at least rationally presupposes the partly free moral consent of the loser? And is not that consent as a moral matter the real basis of all rights and duties? And again, do not all revolutionists, though among themselves they may joke about it, try to prove the legitimacy of their revolution even after their success? Napoleon thought an anointing and a consecration by the Pope was necessary. Our contemporary tyrants are inventive in proposing moral legitimations for their regimes: the salvation of the fatherland, the liberation of the suppressed world proletariat, the consent of the ruled in plebiscites, and even, blasphemously, an immediate mandate of the Lord God. So much are power and authority a moral affair, despite all the injustice of their acquisition and application, which history speaks of on pages filled with injustice, broken promises, bloodshed, and tears. Human life in community is impossible without the universal norm of morality.

II. Three Potential Answers to the Problem

There are three possible solutions to our problem of the moral and juridical legitimacy of power and authority in an actual order.

The first solution. Authority and power have been conferred upon a certain person by a special act of God, the supreme source of all authority and power. Consequently this person possesses authority by divine law. Such an authority cannot be abolished or transferred to somebody else by any human act or authority, but only by another specific divine intervention. The sovereign owns his authority as a property and he may dispose of it only by his own arbitrary action. This was early the thesis of the immediate divine right of the Byzantine emperors, as it later was the thesis of the imperial jurists in the medieval struggle between pope and emperor. It was renewed by the court theologians and jurists of princely absolutism, in the era of the Reformation, at the beginning of modern times, and later again by some political philosophers of the Restoration period, and in the monarchical theory of the nineteenth century in Central and Eastern Europe, particularly in Prussia and Russia. The special act of God was seen in various mysterious events; among the interpreters of these events was Lord Filmer, whose theory became famous on account of its absurdity.[5]

The second solution. At the time of the formation of the state one person was so distinguished by natural gifts and privileged esteem among his associates that he must be considered to have been marked thus by Providence as most able for the position of ruler. Though this person may not have a distinctive and original right to authority, there exists a duty of the members of the state to accept this person's authority as the best guaranty for the realization of the common good. The reason is that this person by his eminent gifts, his esteem, and his real authority, already exercises acts that are essentially of the kind exercised by a political authority. It must be kept in mind that this providential distinction and the guaranty of the common good would be the reason and cause that this person holds authority. The acceptance of this person as having authority and the consent of the members of the new political community would not be a cause but only a condition. Their consent would not transfer authority but only designate the person to hold authority. The extreme type of this theory may be represented by the Swiss convert, Von Haller.[6] He thinks that political authority arises from the influence and esteem of the most powerful patriarch in the prepolitical clan, and this by natural law.

[5] Thus Sir Robert Filmer contended in his Patriarcha, that Adam had all authority as father of the human race and that the royal houses inherited it from Adam.

[6] Karl Ludwig von Haller, Restoration der Staatswissenschaften (1820–25). He was of considerable influence on the antirevolutionary romantic school of political thought.

Another extreme type may be found in De Maistre's political theory of monarchy, in which history, that is, the providential direction of human affairs, designates the ruler valid in morality and law. History works here as a conservative demiurge.

The third solution. Authority, the necessary outgrowth of political union at the birth of the state, rested by natural law with the members of the body politic in the process of formation, with the citizens as a self-organizing political body. Nevertheless, on account of given circumstances, though these circumstances have no particular providential character, authority may be concentrated in and exercised by one individual citizen or a certain qualified group; for instance, the wealthiest or strongest or wisest. But their lawful possession of this new political authority as distinguished from a patriarchal authority is owing to a formal or informal consent and acceptance by the citizens originally forming the body politic. Thus the authority originally vested in the citizens (the fathers) as a whole can legally become the prerogative of an individual or a special group only by formal or informal transfer. Hence this transfer, irrespective of its kind and form, would represent the moral and juridical cause (*causa proxima*) of actual authority held by anybody but the community of citizens as a whole.

Some of the doctors are of the opinion that this kind of lasting transfer is for the citizens a moral necessity (Bellarmine [7]). Others teach that it is at the free judgment of the citizens as a whole to transfer or not to transfer, to transfer under specific conditions, or to keep the authority within themselves as a united body and delegate to individuals only the exercise of authority, not the right of authority itself (Suarezian school). The legal figure in which to express this thought would thus be a kind of pact of transfer, while the owner of authority by law of nature would be the citizens convening in a united whole. The divine origin of political authority is in no way impaired, though mediated through created secondary causes, the free moral decisions of men. Simultaneously with the birth of the *unitas ordinis,* the state, the *ordo justitiae legalis,* comes into existence and becomes valid. The point is, that it is a contract with which we are here concerned. The *ordo justitiae legalis* is therefore not a revocable transfer of individual rights to the authority so that this authority would be a mere bundle

[7] *De laicis,* chap. 6.

or sum of indivdual rights. On the contrary, the original human rights rooted in the dignity of the person as a likeness of God can never be thus transferred. Authority is in no way a sum or a quantity of rights transferred from the individuals. The individuals rather enter as members into a new status of social coexistence, a necessary one, given the idea of the perfection of human nature. And it is this new order as a necessary and lasting one, as a status order, that by its objective end now begets new duties and new rights without abolishing what we justly call inalienable rights.

III. The Place of the Problem in the System of Political Philosophy

The problem of the origin of political authority is important because it is always connected with, though not wholly dependent upon, the central problem of political ethics, the problem of legitimacy and justification of political authority. This problem has again and again attracted the attention of philosophers and nations. Especially since the beginning of modern times with the growing individualism and the withering away of the traditional religious background of political theory and practice, it has become the most pressing problem of all. The new individualist theory of natural law, developed since the eighteenth century, and modern constitutional theories are witnesses to this fact. The importance of this problem can thus be understood easily in the era of preponderant individualism and of various theories of legitimacy, whether those of the revolutionary rights of the peoples, or those of the divine right of kings advanced by the legitimists from William Barklay to Charles Maurras.

But we should note that this emphasis produces the danger that the shifting of accent to this special problem may result in a consequent neglect of equally important problems. The more the mutually exclusive answers to our problem lead away from a study of essentials to one of formalities, the more they reduce our discussion to mere oratory for political propaganda.

At the beginning of our discussion, therefore, we should not forget that the really central idea of Catholic political philosophy is that of the common good and its concrete realization. The foundation is the end of the state, which at the same time is the purpose of any power in the state. The common good is, by coincidence, normally the good of the individual citizens. Their original rights and their personal dignity are likewise of central importance. From no point of Catholic political philosophy can the body politic be considered the mere passive object of an absolute *imperium* and authority coming from outside. The *imperium*, the authority of government with its rights and duties corresponding to the rights and duties of the governed, center round the common good and the dignity of the human person with its spheres of life that are beyond state interference. But it was never considered to stand in omnipotent loftiness above the *ordo* that the state is. On the contrary, it was always considered to exist and operate, though not in every case under the positive legal order, in and under the order of natural law that bears all positive order of law. The wielding of authority is the act of an organ of the body politic; it is essentially of a service character to the common good and to persons. The Anglo-Saxon doctrine of the rule of law as superior to authority is an essential part of the Catholic tradition.[8] It contains the idea that both authority and subjects are bound by the order of political life, that law, the prerogative of authority, must be reason, and consequently that arbitrariness in the exercise of authority is a non-teleological exercise, not respecting the common good, and is void of moral obligation. The realization of the common good is not an exclusive result of the directive activity of authority, but the result of a cooperative effort of the directing authority and of the citizens with their moral and material social contributions.

Though the authority may here and there be called the formal cause of the body politic, that is not true in an exclusive sense. A necessary element of the formal cause is also the lasting will of the citizens to live in the more perfect order of the body politic and their readiness to obey freely the directive rules of authority, of which only a few are actually coercive. An equally necessary element is the readiness of the citizens to make sacrifices for their common end, the common good in the order of legal justice to which both, the persons in authority and

---

[8] To give some examples. Clement of Alexandria (*Stromata*, I, 24): "The king is he who rules according to the law." St. Ambrose (Ep. 21; *PL*, XVI, 1047): "The impartial enforcement of the law, once it is enacted, is not to be prevented by the caprices of the emperor." St. Ambrose says that, although the king may be *legibus solutus* juridically, he is in conscience bound by them. The Byzantine theory of the emperor as the living law himself and thus the lord of the law, was continuously rejected by the Fathers. Cf. St. Thomas, *Summa theol.*, Ia IIae, q.96, a.5 ad 3.

the citizens, are somehow servants. Thus this moral attitude and the coordinated virtues of the citizens belong just as much as authority and the virtues coordinated with it to the formal cause of the body politic and the *unitas ordinis*.[9] Political unity is the result of the continuous will to strive for the perfection of the idea of man in the good life and the ready acceptance of the directive power of authority. Even the absolute prince needs the *acclamatio populi,* and it is as if in reverence before this fact that the modern dictators cultivate the formalities of the Caesarian plebiscite.

IV. Theories of the Origin of Political Authority

The first theory, which was favored in the polemics of court theologians against demands for popular government, and which established a somewhat mystical divine right of kings, has had no influence in Catholic political philosophy. That theory, accurately stated, seems to be irreconcilable with the fundamental idea of a law of nature. It is significant that the few Catholic representatives of that theory either omit the rational, clear, traditional concept of natural law, as do some exponents of the philosophy of romantic restoration,[10] or indulge in a kind of irrational natural law, of a partly naturalistic origin, as does Von Haller. It is also significant that they usually exaggerate the malice in human nature and favor a conception of God in which omnipotence is made the main attribute of God revealing Himself in history. Frequently we find even an analogy between God's power of working miracles (God is *solutus legibus naturae*) and the power of the king *legibus solutus.* To God as the sovereign omnipotent lord over nature and its physical laws, corresponds the king as the supreme omnipotent lord over the laws of the body politic. In the fundamental problem, whether law is reason or is will, they all choose the second alternative (De Maistre, Donoso Cortes).[11]

[9] This is at least the ideal case and should be the normal case. St. Thomas does not exclude a rather despotic state when authority is the only *causa formalis,* but he concedes the participation of the governed as the ordinary form.

[10] These writers were fighting bitterly against the individualist natural law of the eighteenth-century rationalism. But it often happened that, indulging in the praise of history and positive law, they forgot the doctrine of the Catholic tradition.

[11] This criticism does not mean that these writers are wrong in all their theories. On the contrary, it is most fruitful to read and reread their books, which contain a wealth of fine observations and critical analyses of the secularist mind.

The second and third theories have been made the subject of controversies, especially since the development of princely absolutism in the seventeenth century and later, since the era of Restoration. Though they have had scarcely any influence in America, where the traditional scholastic idea of popular sovereignty never was the object of controversy, it may be worth while to give some time to a study of these theories, because they enable us to understand more completely some pages in the history of Catholic political philosophy.

The above-mentioned differences in theory cannot be fully explained as simply caused by historical environment, or by the continuous changes, in the historical scene, from a conservative attitude to a prevailing liberal attitude and then back to conservatism. Such explanations would not take into account the fact that Catholic political philosophy contains both conservative and liberal elements simultaneously; that it lives in a polar tension, though it is a unity. Thus it is neither monistic, as is Rousseau's theory, nor is it dualistic, as is Luther's theory. It would not agree with the antitheses: freedom or order, freedom or authority, the rights of the individuals or the rights of the state, nationalism or internationalism. It regards this monistic opposition of necessary human elements as a grave mistake. Freedom in order, the rights of the individuals corresponding to the duties of the state, and the rights of the state corresponding to the duties of the individual, the independence and sovereignty of the state in the community of nations, these are its problems.[12]

Nevertheless we may say that historical situations form a sort of principle of selection, so that in considering the opposing ideas. just enumerated as poles of tension but in an embracing unity, a shifting of the accent, if one may say so, may occur. Thus it may be explained that, under the impact of the French Revolution, there arose in Catholic political philosophy a school which in alliance with the political romantics turned against the dissolving and anarchical elements which, like the anti-Christian elements, not only slumbered, but were actually virulent, in the tenets of the Revolution. Anarchical individ-

---

[12] All perfectionists (and all pessimists as well) scold Catholic political philosophy for its inclusiveness. They decry it, as they do the Church, as a contradictory *complexio oppositorum*, forgetting that man lives in the tension of polar opposites. A fine definition of the "perfectionist" I find in Pope Leo XII's remarks about Lammenais. "He is an *esaltato*, a distinguished man of talents, knowledge, and good faith. But he is one of those lovers of perfection who, if one should leave them alone, would overthrow the whole world." Dudon, *Lammenais et le Saint-Siège* (Paris, 1911), p. 29.

ualism, the continuous revolution implied in the concept of popular sovereignty as propounded by the Revolution, and the overwhelming rationalism and frequent atheistic secularism that accompany the history of France and other European countries in the nineteenth century, were opposed by many writers of Catholic political philosophy. With some sacrifice of balance, these writers began to stress the traditional rights of the crown as the symbol of authority against uncontrolled, destructive popular ambition and avarice; to stress the providential direction of the nation in its historical development against an omnipotent majority without reverence before tradition and national history. They felt obliged to stress, against secularism and laicism, the traditional rights and the old order originating in the pre-revolutionary ideas of a connection and union of Church and state, a connection that was perhaps often too close.

In such circumstances it could happen that the very significant distinction between the new political institutions themselves and the philosophical and political arguments which the revolutionary forces advanced for them, would be forgotten. Not only was the erroneous and excessively individualist argument for universal franchise thus severely attacked by so eminent a philosopher as Tapparelli d'Azeglio,[18] but the institution itself was also attacked. Others, too, not content to fight the faulty arguments for popular sovereignty and democracy, or for the principle of freedom of conscience, assailed these political institutions themselves as found in modern constitutions. They forgot that technical political institutions may be indifferent, and may therefore be defended and upheld on the basis of Catholic political thought as long as they actually serve the common good.

By this proposition we mean that it is not so much the form or the existence of such institutions that makes them commendable, but their functioning in the realization of the common good in actual life. Their value is to be measured ultimately in this service to the common good and not in the ideologies that helped to introduce them into the constitutional order. To give an example: the constitutional protection of the freedom of conscience by the prohibition of a state religion or an established Church and by the separation of Church and state, may historically be proposed and introduced by a philosophically and

---

[18] The writer of the famous *Saggio theoretico del diritto naturale* published a strong attack upon universal franchise.

theologically wrong ideology. Such is an ideology that contends that there is no access to objective truth for man, that there are only subjective opinions equally true or false, and that God has never revealed Himself and Christ has never founded One Holy, Catholic, Apostolic Church. The organized religious groups, from the standpoint of an unknown truth, revealed or natural, are based only on subjective opinions and thus fulfill the irrepressible urge for religious sentiment of the citizens according to their various irrational tastes or are instruments of clerical attempts at control over the temporal power. As wrong as these arguments are, they do not wholly discredit the constitutional provisions of a separation of state and Church in their immediate legal meaning; these must be measured according to their service-value to the concrete common good.

The state has to do with such elements of the order as are truly common. If, therefore, masses of the citizen have practically given up the faith of their ancestors, nothing is left for the political order except to declare itself neutral; that is, to retreat from the sphere of religion as a legal, public, and direct part of the actual common good. If the state should compel an external acceptance of a national creed while prohibiting freedom of conscience, the consequent hypocrisy would be a grave danger to the unity of the nation and to the common good. We see at once that in this manner the political instituiton of freedom of conscience lives by its own practical merits and not by the philosophically and theologically wrong ideology that all subjective opinions are materially equal and that all creeds are equally true or false, as relativism contends.

Another example may be found in proportional representation. From an abstract and formal standpoint even a democracy is not ruled by the majority of the electorate. In some states women do not yet have the franchise. In others, the election districts controlled by one man may lead to the result that not the majority of the citizens but the better oiled party-machine of a minority actually controls the state. So people with strong feeling for formal justice have invented proportional representation in order that every citizen's vote may weigh in the election and that the numerically true majority may control the state. In an abstract sense of individualist justice, this seems to be right. Yet experience has shown that proportional representation was for the most part actually detrimental to the common good. It made the working of the democratic process of producing a consistent active unity in government very difficult since it gave extremists golden opportunity, as F. H. Hermens has proved in his learned criticism.[14]

By indifference we mean, further that these institutions individually are not philosophically necessary, but that they are born in the ceaseless flow of history, conditioned by the individual and particular circumstances of the state, of political development, of civilization, of education, or of the prevailing economic system, and that they are not in all circumstances equally ideal. Their value depends upon all these circumstances in their relation to the actual common good. Therefore it is inconsequential to impress them on each and every nation alike. In a unified Catholic nation, for instance, the principle of freedom of conscience, on the basis of the modern argument, is unfitting. In a low civilization with little or no popular education, representative government has not much chance of functioning for the common good, but is easily abused for the profit of a small ruling class. In such circumstances a monarch, independent of economically powerful interests, may be a better guaranty of the common good, of human dignity, and of working justice than a parliamentary democracy. In the nineteenth century there was a widespread unhistorical spirit, and we are still suffering from it today. A considerable part of the unrest after the First World War, for instance, in southeastern Europe, was caused by an uncritical rationalist transfer of the political institutions of Western civilization to nationalities which actually did not yet possess the social and educational framework that makes these political institutions work and function in the realization of the common good.

The Catholic thinkers of a strong conservative strain also exaggerated the dangers that every political institution presents when it is abused. In thus contending against the new revolution-born, political institutions, they were motivated by these abuses on the part of the revolutionists, so forgetting the above-mentioned indifference.[15] The revolutionists were perfectionists, and in a rather mechanical way presupposed that, given abstractly good political institutions, man would

14 F. A. Hermens, *Democracy or Anarchy* (1941).

15 That all political institutions contain the danger of abuse was strongly felt by the Fathers of the Constitution. Cf. the Bill of Rights against arbitrary use of majority rule. Compare further Newman's fear of the broadening of the franchise. W. Ward, *Life of Cardinal Newman* (1912), II, 118, 513.

become perfect, because, according to their philosophy, the people is always good, only institutions are bad. We may find, too, in Catholic political philosophy, an opposite accent. This is an identification of modern political institutions—the bill of rights, popular sovereignty, representative government, and democracy—with Catholicism. It is seen in the so-called Americanism of Father Hecker and in the French *Sillon* of Marc Sangnier, though any sincere student will agree that this occurs rather seldom. Leo XIII pointed out the right line of thought when he showed that these institutions themselves are historical, therefore philosophically indifferent, though the arguments for them and the spirit in which they are administered may well be far from indifferent. Hence wrong arguments and that anti-religious spirit may produce even a treacherous abuse of the institutions, as has been shown by the anticlerical legislation of the Third Republic in France and of the Popular Front regime in republican Spain.

V. The Designation Theory

In historical development we can thus distinguish two theories of the origin of political authority that have found adherents among Catholic political philosophers. The one is often called the designation theory, the other the translation theory. In the late Middle Ages the so-called concession theory found some acceptance among those political philosophers who wrote for the prerogatives of the emperor against the pope and were associated with the conciliar theory of Church authority. John of Janduno and Marsilius of Padua, the author of the *Defensor pacis,* are among the outstanding propagators of the concession theory. But this theory disappeared comparatively soon after the abandonment of the conciliar theory in canon law. The new princely absolutism did not like this theory either, because of its antimonarchical character. It made all forms of government mere magistratures, as later Rousseau did, and it had a strong laicist element, making the Church and the hierarchy a mere department of the state. Thus it could become of some influence only in the political theories of various Protestant sects and in modern laicism.

The designation theory, of hardly any influence on this side of the Atlantic, has had a considerable influence in Europe, especially after the romantic era. Why, we will explain later, but first let the theory itself be studied.

The problem is the same as in all other theories: How to explain why political authority with its conscience-binding power rests in this individual person, royal house, aristocratic senate, and the like. The Rousseauist "trick," as we said, is to declare that, by obeying the duly formed general will in the majority decision, we actually obey only our own will, though perhaps an improperly informed will, if we belong to the outvoted minority. But such reasoning cannot do away with the fact that, living in the *status civilis* of any form, we must obey. It cannot do away with the undeniable fact that in every political body there are rulers and ruled, that there is *imperium*, authority, and obedience of subjects; that there is—and this is the crucial problem—decisive, sovereign authority, against whose decision there is no appeal, except by a violent overthrow of the constitutional order. If we do not like an equally definitive decision of the president or board of trustees of our club or that of our employer, there is no natural and moral necessity for us to belong to this club or to work for that employer.[16] But since life under political authority is unavoidable for men and since there

---

[16] The root of the quest for freedom and for industrial democracy in the labor movement is precisely the fact that the worker today is not as free to select his own employer or to leave his employ as he is presumed to be. The labor contract is generally not a free purchasing contract (buying and selling of a commodity on the labor market). Moreover, it is largely a status contract by which the worker enters a set of rules instituted partly by the objective ends of production, partly by the more or less arbitrary decision of the individual employer, who is the only policy-making authority. The employer, before labor unionism and social legislation were introduced, was similar to the absolute prince. The contradiction of modern industrialism lies in the fact that it was necessary to transform the serf or bonded servant of old into a free worker in order to take away from the employer any responsibility for the person of the worker as distinguished from the seller of labor. Modern industrialism further needed the bill of rights for freedom of property and freedom of contract, in order to have a sphere of economic activity free from any arbitrary and incalculable intervention of the government. But that bill of rights, necessarily destroying all status privilege of the ancient regime, brought to labor the advantages of political liberty, of equality before the law, and of democracy. Nevertheless, as soon as the worker entered the factory—and he must do that in order to live—he entered a set of rules, a pattern of social control, that was not democratic, that gave no inalienable rights, and that often was arbitrary inasmuch as it was the individual profit motive of the employer which, in a conflict of capital and labor interests, was considered paramount. Catholic social philosophy has a strong preference for small business, the small shop, and a broad middle class. The reason for this preference is that, *ceteris paribus*, they offer the best opportunity for human relations in industrial life, as against large-scale production with its depersonalization and bureaucracy, its emptiness of or from human relations, and the consequent unavoidable class struggle.

is no appeal from this authority's decisions, the problem of obedience is truly crucial.

We have already seen that in obeying lawful authority we do not render servile but reasonable obedience, because by living in the order of the common good, realizing the idea of man, we ultimately obey neither one of our equals nor a majority of them—a mere change in quantity would not bind us more than before—but God Himself. Obeying some particular people merely because they form a majority is unworthy of a rational being. There is no difference in this sense between the tyranny of one and that of hundreds, as one of the fathers of American institutions aptly remarked. The basis of the majority rule in a free democracy is, first, that even the majority cannot make right what objectively is wrong, and that it cannot intrude arbitrarily into the sphere of the "inalienable" rights of the person, the family, the Church and the intermediary associations of individuals serving their own extra-state ends. Secondly, that there is, humanly speaking, the greatest probability that a majority decision reached by rational beings after due deliberation will be a reasonable decision and not an arbitrary one.

Thus it should be clear that in the *status civilis* we always have to obey men and not an abstract will of the state, or an abstract law, or anything else similarly abstract; nor do we by a mystical process obey only ourselves. Therefore the following problem remains. How do those authorities get their right from God to demand and to enforce obedience and loyalty; how can we be morally obliged to obey; and how does our moral and legal duty to obey originate? Obedience is morally possible only when the authority in the last resort is from God and when its demands are in conformity with the objective end of that necessary community, the body politic. This principle seems obvious as long as citizens believe in God.[17] So the question arises, of how that competence of political authority can be derived from God.

The designation theory now tells us that political authority is trans-

---

[17] The idea of God worked as a restraint even in the absolutism of the seventeenth and eighteenth centuries. This becomes clear if we compare that absolutism with the pagan tyrannies of our times, where no trace of freedom is left. Dostoevski sixty years ago warned the liberals of his time against the future pagan absolutism, compared with which the absolutism of the Czars would appear to be an embryo only. Indirectly this is proved by the relentless persecution which these pagan tyrannies use against, not so much the liberals, but the Christians. They know best who is their irreconcilable enemy.

ferred to its holder immediately by God. But this, it says, does not mean that authority was transferred to the ruler, whether he is a monarch or anyone else, by a special "mystical" act of God. What it says is: God works here, not by direct intervention, but indirectly through the secondary causes. Thus free human acts, the consent of the people or the election by electorate, is not excluded as it was excluded by the first-mentioned theory of the divine right of the ruler. But these human acts are not the cause of the transfer of authority; they are only the condition, the naturally necessary condition, of the transfer that proceeds immediately from God to the holder of authority. Therefore, when the fathers of families institute the state, authority does not in any way, even for a moment, rest with the people as a unity being organized into a body politic.

This theory instead declares that the people has the possibility only at the moment of the institution of the *status civilis* to designate one, or a collegium, as the political authority. Thus, according to this theory, authority and power are transferred immediately from God, the source of all authority and power, to this specific individual or these specific individuals. It should here be noted again that this theory in no way presupposes, like the early Protestant, the absolutist, or the romantic theory, a special mysterious act of transfer by God; that would make the designation superfluous.

What this theory means may be explained as follows. Historical development and the urge of man's social nature produce a status of social organization that requires a decisive political authority. Objective circumstances and the objective eminence and the natural gifts of leadership in some way mark a certain person as the most fit for holding authority. Then the community, being simultaneously transformed into a body politic, has a kind of moral duty, considering the common good, to designate this person or group of persons as the sovereign ruling authority. Therefore wholly in the natural order, that is, without the intervention of a special supernatural act of God, the transfer of authority is ascribed to providential direction, while to the citizens as a whole is ascribed only the designation of the person. Consequently there is in this theory little room for the contract theory concerning the birth of the state. This expressive human act is not necessary if the accent falls chiefly upon the natural historical circumstances providentially directed, rather than upon the free, though morally necessary, decision of the citizens uniting themselves in a body politic. The social contract thus disappears in the contract of subjection.

VI. The Translation Theory

The translation theory, as we called it, has a long tradition. Apart from the fact that the old Roman law of republican tradition favored it, it found some kind of formulation by the Church Fathers. As most authorities today agree, it was at the basis of the political theory of St. Thomas.[18] But shortly after St. Thomas and by such men as his famous disciple, Aegidius Romanus, the translation theory was distinctly formulated. Engelbert of Volkersdorf (1270–1327) distinguishes the *pactum subjectionis* by which the citizens, already united into a body politic, elect a king and so transfer to him the political authority that originally rested with them as a whole.[19] Nicholas of Cusa and his contemporary, Gerson, agree with this theory. Cusa uses again and again the technical expressions *concordantia subjectionalis, per viam voluntariae subjectionis et consensus.*[20] James Almainus (d. 1313) reports that it is the common opinion of the great doctors that the authority is transferred to the king by the political community itself. In what is usually called Late Scholasticism the theory was not only generally accepted but became broadly elaborated, and that in such a definite and convincing form that for centuries it became the only one taught. Only as a reaction to the Rousseauist ideas of the French Revolution and in consequence of the historical school as promoted by the romantic movement was the translation theory put more in the background, though it never was generally abandoned. In the European countries, it is true, theologians began to prefer the designation theory. But after the First World War the translation theory again returned to its old traditional place. It is, therefore, not an exaggeration when scholars conclude that the short-lived prevalence of the designation theory must be explained more by historical circumstances than by the exactness of its propositions, as we shall see later.

[18] This is commonly accepted by American philosophers and theologians and has found proponents in Joseph Mausbach and Peter Tischleder. The last, in his *Ursprung und Träger der Staatsgewalt*, has given the best arguments. Cf. also I. T. Delos, O. P., *La société internationale et les principes du droit publique.*

[19] *De ortu, progressu et fine Romani Imperii* (1307–1311; Basel, 1553), chap. 5.

[20] *De concordantia Catholica;* in Schard: *De jurisdictione imperatoris,* II, 12; III 4.

What, then, are the main propositions of the translation theory? Political authority, though of course originating in God, rests at the moment of the formation of the body politic in this body itself. No one of the members has, on account of individual wealth, gifts of leadership, or eminence, a right to the authority, because all men are born free and equal and remain free and equal before they unite into a body politic. Even at the moment of the formation of the latter they are still free and legally equal to the extent that the new *status civilis* and its objective end merely restrict that freedom in general and for the benefit of all. Hence, if we exclude an immediate supernatural and special act of God, there is no reason by natural law why a certain individual or group in the body politic should have any right to hold authority. And, strictly by force of natural law, there is no duty of the members of the body politic to transfer the political authority which is, of course, born simultaneously with the entry into the *status civilis* by the free consent of those who form the body politic. Thus it is the community itself organizing into the body politic that holds authority and continues to hold it as long as it is not transferred to an individual, to a family, or to a specific group. In order that a certain individual may become the holder of sovereign authority, the originally immediate (non-representative) democracy must by a free act of the people be transformed into another constitutional form. Consequently no ruler holds his authority by natural law, but by human law.

There is, then, only one constitution which, considered from the standpoint of the *quaestio juris,* exists by natural law, namely, immediate democracy, or the self-government of the people by the people without the intermediary of a representative body.[21] All other forms of government have their cause in a transfer of political authority from the people to an individual or a group. Or, to use another proposition, the constitution-making authority rests in the people, in the body politic itself, and this by natural law. Consequently all constitutions, all single organizations of political authority as we find them in history, exist by force of human positive law, not by divine or natural law. Thus it is the consent, the *pactum subjectionis,* the election, that

---

[21] Suarez, explicitly comparing the freedom of the individual with that of the body politic, says: "The body politic is originally free and *sui juris*. Freedom specifically includes the competence of self-government, and excludes subjection to a certain person, at least so far as natural law is concerned. *Def. fid.,* III, c.2, 11; cf. Rommen, *Suarez,* p. 343.

is really the cause of the transfer of political authority from the political community to an individual or a specified group.

It must not be forgotten that the state itself is a necessary social institution. Man is not free to live or not to live in the *status civilis*. The difference between this theory and the previously described designation theory is, consequently, that the free consent of those who become subjects of authority is the concrete historical cause of their being bound by the authority, though the inner reason for their obedience remains the moral necessity of perfecting the idea of man by living in a body politic, with all that this implies in a concrete situation. The designation theory, however, as to some extent it rejects the social contract, makes the consent (the election, or whatever form the human acts that institute a constitution may take) only a condition of immediate transfer of authority from God to the individual sovereign or other holder of political authority.

We should note that both theories proceed from the same basic concepts of Catholic social philosophy; namely, from the same ideas of the essence of human nature as social and political, of the secular and spiritual end of man, and of the nature, necessity, and purpose of the existence and validity of the natural law and the eternal law. The difference begins when this question is proposed: Generally and normally, how is the birth of the political order, the *ordo justitiae legalis*, to be explained; how can we establish the fact that someone, not identical with the people itself, holds political authority? We may easily see that the designation theory places the emphasis not upon the free will of man but upon the necessary natural development of man's social nature and upon providential direction. This is revealed in circumstances of historical development and conditions of eminence, wealth, or reputation of individual men, who have, so to speak, a divine vocation to become rulers. That is why some scholars said that there exists a moral duty of the people to designate such a person, who consequently acquires a kind of subjective right to be recognized as the ruler. From here the step to political legitimism is but a short one and has been made by some scholars in their fight against the revolutionary ideas of Rousseau and democraticism: in France since 1789, the date of the declaration of the principle of popular sovereignty; in Belgium since 1831; and in Germany and Austria since 1919.

There seems to be little doubt that the translation theory is the most time-honored and that the great majority of the eminent doctors followed it. Throughout the Middle Ages it prevailed in the universities. At the beginning of modern times it found its most perfect and most perfectly elaborated presentation in the voluminous writings of Francis Suarez; while practically all canonists and theologians, as well as philosophers, presented the theory in more or less elaborated form as a common doctrine. All names of some importance are counted among its adherents; Cajetan (d. 1534), Francis of Vittoria (d. 1577), De Soto (d. 1560), Diego Covarruviasy Leyva (d. 1577), Bartholomew Medina (d. 1581), St. Robert Bellarmine, Molina, Domingo Bañez (d. 1604), Luis de Montesinos (d. 1621), Johannes Wiggers (d. 1630?), Jean B. Gonet (d. 1684), Charles René Billuart (d. 1757), and also the famous school of the Salmanticenses: Andreas a Matre Dei (d. 1674) and Daniel Concina (d. 1756). Even since 1800, when the designation theory began to win ground, a galaxy of eminent scholars kept to the traditional theory. In America there is scarcely a writer of importance who would controvert the translation theory. And in Europe since the end of the First World War the translation theory regained much of the lost ground.

VII. The Suarezian Form of the Translation Theory

To get a clearer idea of the translation theory let us follow the arguments of Suarez, who is confessedly the best interpreter of it. After that we shall study some arguments that have been advanced by adherents of the designation theory. Suarez proceeds from the following propositions.

First proposition. Political authority is a necessary property of the body politic. Therefore a specific intervention of God is not necessary at the moment of the establishment of the body politic or afterward.[22] Political authority rests with the self-organizing political community as an essential property according to the nature of the political community. Or to use Suarez' arguments directly: as man, through the fact of creation and through obtaining the use of reason, has power over himself and is naturally free, that is, master of his acts, so the political community when first established has at once power over itself. As man is given natural freedom by the Author of human nature, al-

[22] *Qui dat formam dat consequentia ad formam.*

though not without the intervention of a proximate cause, the father who begets, so political authority is given to the political community although not without the intervention of the will and the consent of those who unite themselves in political life. As the will of the father and his intervention are necessary only for the procreation of the son, but a special act of the father is in no way necessary to give natural freedom to the son, so the will and consent of men is necessary only for the formation of the political body; that body's acquisition of its specific authority does not require a second act of men. The authority is rather a necessary consequence of the nature of the body politic, which is founded by God, the Author of that nature. In that sense political authority originates with God.[23] As soon as men by their free will and consent, though in consequence of the urge of their social nature and by force of the necessity of perfecting the good life, unite into a body politic, authority is simultaneously born and rests in the body politic. By natural law the body politic is the holder of political authority. The result is self-government in the form of immediate democracy.

Second proposition. All men are born free by the essence of their nature.[24] All the legal forms of servitude are created by man, not by God. The Aristotelian doctrine that some are born slaves and others free is completely wrong.[25] Furthermore, according to their nature men are equal because they are of the same species.[26] Consequently, by natural law, nobody can have a right to hold political authority over his equal and free compatriots. And there is no stringent reason why this particular individual and not another one should become the holder of authority.

Third proposition. Political authority consequently rests with the body politic itself in the form of direct self-government, and the body politic is originally democratic.[27]

Fourth proposition. This does not mean that, because of historical circumstances, social expediency, interest of the common good, and so on, the original immediate democracy cannot be given up. It means simply that if there is such a change it can legally occur only by the direct decision of the citizen or by other acts, but always human acts.

[23] Suarez, De leg., III, c.3, n.6.
[24] Ibid., c.2, n.3.
[25] To quote only one, Bellarmine, De officio principis, I, 21.
[26] Bellarmine, Comm. in Summam S. Thomae, ad IIam IIae, q.62, dub. 4.
[27] Suarez: "Si non mutaretur, democratica esset" (Def. fidei, III, c.2, n.9).

If we exclude such acts as the subjection of the original democracy by a neighboring kingdom on account of a just war, Suarez explains, there remains solely the consent of the citizen in various forms (election, acclamation, and so on) as the cause of any lawful change in the original democratic constitution. A transfer is the only natural title of authority in a person or a group of persons, if we exclude a quasi-supernatural act of God transferring the authority immediately. This last would have to be a revealed act, for natural knowledge does not show such an act of God. Therefore the conclusion is: If political authority is found in a holder different from the citizens of a body politic as a whole, there must have been a transfer by a free act and consent, formal or informal, of the citizens acting as a united people. The question whether there exist reasons for the people to transfer authority, is one of expediency, not one of absolute necessity.[28]

Conclusion. The constituent power rests with the people. Any holder of political authority different from the people acting in self-government, received authority by a free translation immediately, not by designation only.[29]

If we compare these arguments with those of the previously explained designation theory, we see at once that human free will is here more stressed. Human acts are not a mere condition for the transfer of authority from God immediately to a person or a group of persons; they are the immediate cause, because the people actually possessed political authority for a moment or for a longer time. As the will of those uniting for political life to perfect human social nature and to live the good life in the *ordo justitiae legalis,* is the cause of the state's coming into existence, the will of the people is the cause of the transfer of authority from itself to a king or anybody else. In other words, the constituent power is actually with the people and of the people.

When the translation theory speaks of cause, we should know that "cause" must be understood in the scholastic sense. It does not mean absolute, perfect, integral cause. The point is that it is a secondary and a proximate cause. For the Schoolmen there exists a hierarchy of causes, whose pinnacle is the will of God. And the free causes act in accordance with an objective end. The matter of the consent, therefore,

[28] In this problem there are differences of opinion: Suarez, though he thinks that a moderate monarchical government is preferable, does not speak of a necessity; Bellarmine seems to think that the transfer is of necessity. Cf. Arnold, *op. cit.,* p. 136.

[29] Suarez, *Def. fid.,* III, c. 2, n. 17; Rommen, *op. cit.,* p. 180.

can never be the objective, metaphysically necessary content of the order of legal justice. The state and its end and the nature of authority are coordinated and objective and thus far are beyond the will. Therefore the free consent does not concern the essential content, the objective validity of the principles of the order of legal justice, but only its accidental individual form *hic et nunc*. The political *ordo* is a status, and a necessary status, that has from its objective end (the perfection of the social nature of man and the good life) a natural content that is not at the mercy of the arbitrary will of the consenters. The social contract and the pact of subjection are status contracts. The status is ruled by its objective end, not by arbitrary subjective will. If we always bear in mind that metaphysics is the ever-present and controlling basis, then we will not fall so easily into mistakes. We shall avoid especially the mistake of drawing, from the use of outwardly identical words, formulas, or juridical figures (here, for instance, the figure of contract or pact or covenant) the conclusion that the thought or doctrine of adherents of different philosophies is the same or is similar.[80] What is important is not so much the verbal figure, here the contract, as the metaphysical thought which is intended by the use of the figure.

[80] This is the mistake of Gierke, Windelband, and other critics of this doctrine.

CHAPTER XX

The Controversy about the Two Theories

I. ABANDONMENT OF THE TRANSLATION THEORY

As HAS been already mentioned, the traditional translation theory was given up at the beginning of the nineteenth century by numerous theologians and political philosophers, after some oscillations between the philosophy of political Romanticism (Von Haller, De Maistre, A. Mueller) and what we called the designation theory. The latter won more and more adherents. Though the translation theory still preserved a proud company of defenders, the picture of a common opinion disappears at this period and we find the beginning of polemics against the traditional theory. This happens, of course, chiefly in those countries whose political and religious institutions have been changed, or at least endangered, by the ideas of 1789. In countries where traditional institutions were no longer present or were based on the new ideas of political liberty, as in the Anglo-Saxon world, this controversy was unimportant.

Joseph Mausbach, P. Tischleder, Costa Rosetti, S.J., and other scholars think that this change should be explained by reasons of historical developments in law and politics and by ethical and practical reasons. But they do not accept the contention that the polemic really has shattered the traditional theory. An indirect proof of the vitality of this theory is the fact that after World War I it again won adherents and wider acceptance as a result of more thorough research work. Thus the school that opposed the traditional theory, led by the Jesuits Taparelli, Meyer, and Cathrein, lost much influence even in Germany, where it had found its most perfect expression.

Nineteenth-century European history is to Catholicism the history of the fight against what the Syllabus of 1864, called "modern civilization," or the modern philosophy of law and the state, as it asserted itself more and more successfully after the French Revolution. The

Revolution, if one considers its intellectual, ethical, and economi
reasons as well as its political theories, is a class revolution: the revo
lution of the third estate. This estate, commonly called the bourgeoisie
had during the rise of capitalism already occupied the commandin
position in the economic world and, by the "philosophers," had a
sumed to a large degree control over the intellectual and cultural lif
of the nation; it then strove to become the nation, the whole in th
political sphere. The third estate, economically individualist an
liberalist, intellectually deistic or even agnostic, found in Rousseau
theory of popular sovereignty and political philosophy, which w
nothing but the same social principles it already cherished, a congenia
and helpful system of thought. It may be conceded that even withou
Rousseau's philosophy the political change from royal absolutism t
modern democratic forms of government would have come. Becaus
of the integrated unity that the intellectual, cultural, economic, an
juridical life of a nation represents, no deep change in one of thes
parts can go on without far-reaching changes in all other fields.

In the Europe of the eighteenth century quiet but forceful and pr
found revolutions were taking place in the social, the economic, an
the intellectual sphere. The nobility had lost its stamina after bein
transformed into the lazy servants of the *roi soleil*. Financiers and a
venturers had by marriage, adoption, and purchase of titles becom
intermixed with the nobility, which thus lost its *raison d'être*. Some o
the clergy were dissatisfied with an episcopate that was recruited a
most exclusively from the sons of noble families, while many of the
considered themselves spiritual gendarmes for the ruling system. Th
higher clergy, whose Gallican interests bound them to the absolu
king, were often civil servants of the crown rather than pastors of the
flocks; of the lower clergy quite a few adhered to the revolutiona
ideas; and a minority of both were "philosophers" rather than the
logians. The secularist, anticlerical theories of the intellectuals, th
skeptical unbelief of the popular philosophies, and the materiali
motive of unlimited profits for the rising capitalist class, began
permeate the national life. Thus this life was founded more and mo
on the excessively individualist concept of natural law as promulgate
by Enlightenment, the deistic theodicy, the anti-theological rationa
ism of the Encyclopedists.

Thus the traditional forms of social and political life were alread

ntellectually decomposed, as they were in practice abused by the po-
itical leaders: the king and his servile bureaucracy. The Revolution
)ecame the climax of a process that had been going on for a long time.
The contradiction of capitalism, rationalism, and liberalist tendencies
)n one side, and royal absolutism, privileged classes, and Gallicanism
)n the other, could not last long. Rousseau's political philosophy with
ull its ingredients then became the most important intellectual and
noral justification for the political revolution. There were, of course,
)ther justifications for that needed and unavoidable political up-
1eaval. Christian tradition itself afforded some justifications, and these
vere proffered in the first two years of the Revolution by clerical mem-
)ers of the National Assembly. But they did not have the power of the
rguments of Rousseau's disciples, the Jacobins. Thus the Revolution
:urned against the basic tenets that the Church held in theology, in
)hilosophy, and in social and political philosophy. From then on be-
;an a struggle between the concrete French and continental forms of
:he ideas of 1789, a struggle that with few interruptions lasted through
:he whole nineteenth century and has not ended today, although the
Third Republic is doomed in the deluge of ideas that are even more
1ostile than were those which caused so much trouble.

In other continental countries, such as Germany, Italy, and Austria,
:he contagion of the revolutionary ideas in their specific rationalist and
gnostic French form could not be prevented from spreading, not
:ven by the romantic reaction in the era of Restoration or by Metter-
1ich's repressive policy. The momentum was too great, especially in
:he intellectual and economic field. The field of politics could be
)etter protected, on account of the deeply embedded state administra-
:ions and the power of standing armies loyal to the crown. But step by
step the ideas of 1789, disguised as "Constitutionalism," progressed.
Thus a remarkable anachronism came into existence.

In the economic and intellectual world individualism and the
liberalist and agnostic expression of the idea of liberty and equality
:onquered quickly. But the political system was still ruled by the
ideas of the monarchical principle and the close unity of throne and
altar. Society economically and intellectually lived by the ethos of
1789, while the state lived by the ideas of the divine rights of kings.

Such an anachronism is, of course, in the long run unbearable. Thus
:he new classes, the liberal bourgeoisie and the socialist proletariat

which had just become conscious of itself and began to organize, eagerly embraced the Rousseauist doctrine. This they considered the best weapon of their ideologies, in their necessary fight for liberty and equality in the political field. It was this fact that led to the militant anticlericalism and the antiecclesiastical effects which we observe successively in Germany and Austria, in Italy, in Spain and Portugal. These new classes widely identified the Church with political reaction, as the defenders of the throne had done, who in Gallicanism, had too eagerly identified the absolute king's throne with the altar.

In almost all European countries the cry for liberty and democracy, first raised by the third estate (bourgeoisie) and then by the proletariat, was inspired by the Rousseauist theory. For this reason the adversaries of Rousseau were filled with suspicion of the kind of liberty, individual rights, and democracy that was thus justified. The new political institutions, in themselves indifferent, were stained by the theories which were advanced to justify them. Moreover, the drive for national unity could succeed only against the opposition of the presumed "divine right" of many small and large dynasties which were quick to seek help and defense from the Church. We must not forget that in some countries it was the secret societies nourished by the same Rousseauist ideas which were the most vociferous promoters of national unity; the Carbonari in Italy, for instance.

These developments explain the amazing fact that in the so-called Catholic countries like France, Spain, Italy, Portugal, and Austria the Church lost successively the greater part of the bourgeoisie, of the intellectuals, and of the proletariat, who became agnostic and often materialistic. In England and the United States we observe no similar result. There a large part of the bourgeoisie remained Christian, and the labor movement especially showed scarcely any signs of a militantly anti-Christian point of view. This fact can best be explained by the role the so-called Free Churches have played in these countries. The working classes, especially loathing the "alliance" of Established Church and capitalism as they saw it, did not, as their continental brothers did, drop away from the traditional religion into various substitutes for religion represented by Marxist socialism, syndicalism, and the like. The Free Churches offered the working classes an opportunity to fight against capitalism, to leave the Church presumably allied to it and still remain "Christians." As an English labor leader expressed it: "If one has been brought to our ranks by the study of Karl Marx's books, then a thousand have done so by reading the Gospel."

II. The Revolutionary Theory of Popular Sovereignty

What, then, were the tasks of Catholic moral and political philosophy in the above-mentioned milieu? Against the Rousseauist fiction that the will of the majority is necessarily always just and right, a point of view that must destroy the concept of natural law and natural rights as effectively as does Thomas Hobbes' theory, Catholic political philosophy had to stress the absolute, unchangeable character of natural law. Against the rationalist concept of the revolutionary natural law, which was essentially deistic and morally autonomous, the doctrine of the derivation of natural law from eternal law had to be expounded. Against the atomistic idea that the public authority is only a sum of the rights of the individuals freely transferred and thus revocable at whim, the proper value and objective function of public authority independent of the will of the individuals had to be established.

Against an outspokenly individualist and atomist interpretation of the social contract that made it the result of an absolutely free and arbitrary decision of autonomous and self-sufficient individuals, there had to be stressed the necessity of the social process in its development from the family to the state on the basis of the social nature of man. The legal figure of the social contract and that for which it stands, the positive will of the fathers uniting for political life, was therefore thrust more and more into the background. At the same time providentially prepared historical developments and the irresistible urge of the social nature to political life were brought to the foreground. Since the consequence of the radicalism of the revolutionary ideas appeared to be an arbitrary right of permanent revolution and since the idea of a general liberty seemed to do away with the solidity of any lasting order, it was thought necessary to stress the ideas of order, of duty, and of legitimate authority and its rights. Unfortunately the term "legitimate" could become identified with "traditional" and "time-honored," or the distinction between "legitimate" and "legal" could be too little considered; they could easily fuse into one as mere synonyms. When that occurred, not so much the realization of the common good, but the mere historical and inherited legal rights of the kings would finally be the measure of legitimacy. And it would become a moral duty to restore these rights which the Revolution had wantonly destroyed.

The radical idea of popular sovereignty was conceived from the new philosophy hostile to Christian faith and dogma and was borne by the militantly anti-Catholic Revolution. It became the basis of even more radical demands for freedom from and against the traditional institutions and values on the European continent. Against such revolutionary demands Catholic writers felt it necessary to stress the element of historical development, of tradition, in the theory of the origin of political authority. The more they could reduce the part played by men's free action as a cause of the origin of political authority in any person or group not identical with the body politic, the better—so they thought—they could oppose this idea of popular sovereignty so dangerous to their beloved traditional institutions. The more they could argue for a kind of immediate transfer of political authority upon this person or group directly, not so much of course by a supernatural act of God, as rather by the directing influence of Providence, the better—so they thought—they could defend those institutions and values.

It is well known how the romanticists of all Europe, in reaction against the unhistorical rationalism of the French Revolution [1] that rarely refers to historical rights and old customs, turned to history as the great teacher and became rather suspicious of reason, which had been accorded divine honors by the men of 1789. Catholic philosophers, too, already made suspicious of Revolutionary blessings by their Church's fate, turned to history. Thus the consensus which was, according to the traditional opinion, the cause of the transfer of political authority from the body politic, the original holder, became a mere condition. The transfer became actually a final designation of the person who is already to some extent designated by providence and recognizable by his extraordinary gifts. And even the duty of the people to designate this person alone may be argued for, so that for some of the nineteenth-century writers the consequence

---

[1] We do not find a similar unhistorical rationalism in the American Revolution. In that Revolution the old common-law tradition afforded an excellent connection with the past.

would be a right of such a person to the possession of political authority. These writers felt that they had first and above all to establish, against an arbitrary, radical, and absolute freedom and against the popular sovereignty of Rousseauist hybrid, the ideas of order and of the rights of the traditional authorities. Against a deistic voluntarism of free individuals and against abstract, rationalist schemes equally unhistorical, they presented the idea of the concrete and visible intervention of Providence in history.[2]

It must not be forgotten that many institutions to which the revolution, as it was called, gave birth, could rise only by fighting against old traditional institutions. It is true that these institutions, such as the guild system, the customary law, the now senseless feudal privileges, and the near relation between altar and throne, had been already much abused, or even made practically obsolescent by absolutism. Yet old, time-honored, and once efficient, they kept their lure for people who thought historically, who longed not so much for absolutism as for olden times when all these institutions flourished in their prime. The new institutions, stained with the faults of their origin and rising from a hostile philosophy, were not always carefully evaluated by their congruence with a new civilization. Their origin made them seem infected with a kind of original sin. So, instead of

[2] The grave suspicions which the romanticists entertained arose from sound feelings. Deism leads to a proud voluntarism. Though it accepts the world and the human mind as a rather unfree, mechanical apparatus ruled by scientific laws, it turns voluntarist inasmuch as it loses all respect for history and tradition, and consequently for the invisible hand of Providence, substituting for the last the invisible hand of human calculations and passions. The world then ceases to be the field of a free interaction between men and directing Providence. The world is but a field for the unlimited free play of human beings. We think that this attitude explains why the fervor for natural law, which we find so congenial to eighteenth-century deism, quickly gives way in the nineteenth century to Positivism, a general philosophy that makes the world an object of unlimited change for the unlimited will of man, a philosophy that is utterly irreverent and consequently "debunks" history. Deism cast God in the role of constitutional monarch, who reigns but does not govern. It removed Him far from the world and man. The next step is the denial of God. The idea of God is made the creature of human wishes and dreams or fears; or it is altogether abolished in materialism. In both atheistic ideologies, the world, the universe, becomes anarchic in its order and nature. Consequently either man or mysterious physical forces can do, or do, with the world whatever they like.

Some Christian sects fell into anarchism because they taught that by redemption the natural order was made superfluous. The atheists become anarchists because they have abolished with the idea of God the idea of a natural order. Consequently an atheist can do with the world, especially the social and moral world, whatever he likes, because he denies the transcendental, personal God only in order to become himself like God.

evaluating these institutions according to their working value in a
new civilization, as Leo XIII unsuccessfully tried to teach the French
episcopate to do,[3] their opponents centered all attacks upon the
arguments of the original, dubious promoters. This they did with
justice, but without reference to the fact that the institutions in themselves and in their working may be indifferent, and should be judged
objectively. The new secular civilization, as opposed to the older
Christian society of the faithful, was seen too much in the image of
Auguste Comte, Jeremy Bentham, and John Stuart Mill, who as
positivists believed in the gradual passing of the theological and
metaphysical periods of human evolution, apart from economics and
industrial technique, as lower periods of an endless process of immanent progress to human perfection without redemption, with the
abolition of sin by social economic progress and consequently without revealed religion.

The grave mistake was not so much the rise of the idea of the *civis*,
but the denial of the faithful; that is, the fact that religion was made
exclusively a private affair of the individual in his private life, but
was not tolerated as a public power. Here we have the root of militant
European agnosticism. The situation in England and America was
different; Manning was for the continuation of the established (High)
Church, and Washington stressed not religion in a vague sense, but
a Christian positivism as the basis for religion. Therefore these
democracies do not exhibit that frankly militant anticlericalism which
in a secular civilization is immutably anti-Church.[4] In most European
countries, however, this new civilization was openly antitraditional
and radically rationalist. Against this form of modern civilization as
it destructively spread its revolutionary propaganda in Italy, France,
Spain, and other European countries, against this philosophy and
their misinterpretation of modern political institutions, the popes of
the nineteenth century raised their protests, and Catholic thinkers like
Taparelli and Donoso Cortes contended. However they may have
exaggerated here and there, they often proved to be more far-sighted
than most of their bourgeois critics. They prophetically foresaw that
once this destructive philosophy of comfortable bourgeois agnosticism

---

[3] Compare, the invaluable memoires of Cardinal Ferrata (Apostolic nuncio in Paris)
Ma nonciature en France, 1921, and the failure of the policy of the "Ralliement."

[4] The "No-Popery" campaigns have a different flavor.

oozed down to the industrial masses, fallen out from their traditional religious framework, these masses would turn to destructive mass-revolutions of an atheistic and materialistic character. It was this foresight that drove these thinkers into a strong conservatism.

III. ALLEGED INFLUENCE OF HISTORICAL CIRCUMSTANCES

It was, therefore, not always seen that reasonable arguments exist, based on Christian philosophy, for these institutions, as for the rights of man, popular sovereignty, and general suffrage. So in the nineteenth century a dispute raged among Catholic philosophers over the concept of democracy and popular sovereignty, over the meaning of the rights of man, over liberalism, over the secular and the laicist state, and over the separation of Church and state. This dispute originated in France, led to heated controversies in Belgium in connection with the constitution of 1831, inflamed spirits in Italy, and occurred again in Germany and Austria in 1919 with the new constitutions based on the same modern political principles. If America was spared, that blessing may be attributed to the fact that in America there was no old order to be destroyed and that it was the common law and its Christian traditions rather than the ideas of 1789, Thomas Paine notwithstanding, that ruled men's minds. Today the controversy between the schools is practically dead. Today the new pagan Caesarism of the totalitarian state with its wholesale destruction of all traditions and of the Christian aura of Western civilization compels us to re-examine the true meaning of institutions, to elaborate the Christian aura in which alone they can continue to work. For institutions like freedom of speech, general suffrage, and popular sovereignty have in a mere formal yet distorted sense served the modern tyrannies as well as they have served modern democracy in their right form.

Nevertheless it is important to study the controversy in the nineteenth century between the translation theory and the designation theory, because this study may shed light on many hardly understood political controversies. Let us, then, weigh the arguments of the schools. The proponents of the designation theory first tried to prove that St. Thomas could not be considered an adherent of the translation theory. This proof has so far not wholly succeeded. There is still some disagreement, although we think that the arguments for St. Thomas' adherence are stronger than the arguments against it. One should, of course, not forget that St. Thomas could treat this subject only incidentally. In his time no such urge existed for a broad discussion as existed some decades after his death. But St. Thomas' disciples, who for centuries fostered the translation theory, would not have done so with that apparent confidence, if they were not sure that it was at least a conclusion from St. Thomas' principles.[5]

If St. Thomas, however, could at least be proved to follow the translation theory not unequivocally, then it could be construed that the main proponents of it in Late Scholasticism had left the tradition in some way and that what for centuries was believed to be a *consensus communis* really was only an innovation of the doctors of the sixteenth and seventeenth centuries. Thus the translation theory could be explained as the outcome of a particular historical situation. This could be argued in the following way. The times of Vittoria, Suarez, De Soto, Bannez, Bellarmine, Wiggers, and others were the times of a very spirited controversy about the nature, the field of action, and the relations of the ecclesiastical and the secular power. The Middle Ages, presenting a united *orbis christianus,* had seen the struggles between pope and emperor in this *orbis christianus.* In this struggle it was never denied that the Church universal was the real community. But meanwhile the first buds of the idea of the national state had sprung into blossom. Not only was the *imperium* in the process of dissolution, but the *orbis christianus,* the field of

---

[5] We may refer here to these principles, as follows. (1) It is the exclusive excellence of rational nature that it strives after its essential end in the way of self-leadership and self-direction *(quasi res agens vel ducens ad finem),* while the non-rational nature is directed by outside influence to its end *(Summa theol.,* Ia IIae, q.1, a.2). (2) To direct to the end is the task of him whose end it is *(ibid.,* q.90, a.3). (3) Human beings, uniting themselves in political life, are rational and free, and the end of their union is the common good. Then it would follow that to direct something to the common good is the task of the community, as St. Thomas asserts when asking: Whose task is it to direct to the common good? His answer is: It is the task of the community itself *(ibid.,* cf. *Contra Gentiles,* III, 110 f.). Thus St. Thomas' principles lead to the doctrine that originally the people in the act of uniting for the political life really became the holder, the self-directing subject, not the directed object, of political authority. The idea of the body politic as an independent, free, self-directing person is included in this reasoning. Consequently any other holder of political authority can legally hold it only by a free moral act of the community; whether the act is formal or informal is a subordinate question. We think that the exceptions against this argument and the interpretation of the Thomistic quotations advanced by Th. Meyer *(Institutiones juris naturalis,* II, 377) are not as compelling as the quotations themselves, mentioned above.

the Church universal, was threatened by the progress of Gallicanism in France and by the menacing growth of the idea of a national Church in Spain.

In the countries that adhered to the Reformation, the kings and princes actually made themselves the *summi episcopi,* the heads of their definitely national Churches, as in England and in the Germanic principalities. What Hobbes called the "Leviathan or the Matter, Form, and Power of a Commonwealth, Ecclesiastical and Civil," was in the process of birth. The royal civil power tried to unite and, in Protestant countries, actually did unite the ecclesiastical, spiritual power with itself. The new public-law doctrine of the absolute sovereignty of princes, profusely quoting the Bible, especially the immediate vocation of Saul and David to the Kingdom of Israel by God's command, veiled the power of the absolute king in a mystical theological vocation. The king's power must be equal to the pope's spiritual power, asserted the court theologians of the Protestant kings, and here and there the Gallican court preachers of France. That the pope's power now was immediately transferred by God and that the act of election was in no way a transfer of a power residing in the Church, was never doubted. Therefore, if the king got his power by an immediate act of God in the same way as did Saul or David, then the king's power was at least equal to that of the pope, and the king could rightly claim also the spiritual power in his realm, as the pope could do it in the States of the Church, but not beyond them.

It is clear that in the presence of such doctrines Late Scholasticism had the pressing task of reconsidering the nature of ecclesiastical and secular power, their fields of jurisdiction and their relations. So they first taught the eminence of the ecclesiastical power; then they taught that each power has its own independent end, although the two ends are connected, and that consequently each is supreme in its own order. But they strongly maintained that the papal power is of immediate divine institution by a supernatural act of God, whereas the king's sovereign power is and can be only of human origin, unless another origin is divinely revealed, as perhaps in the choice of Saul and David. Otherwise it is the act of transfer of power from the people to the king that is the cause of princely power; consequently his power is neither of positive divine law nor, like that of the people, of natural law, but is only of human law. Thus the translation theory served the apologetic purpose of defending the spiritual power against the destructive inroads of absolutism. The opponents of Suarez, Bellarmine, and Vittoria say that these doctors in their apologetic tendencies went too far in their ardor for their cause, even to the formulation of an extreme and unacceptable theory of the origin of political authority.[6] Against this criticism we have only to recur to what we have explained above, and we may again point out the fact that what is called the Suarezian doctrine was for centuries the common opinion and is now once more commonly accepted.

In this discussion one thing is certainly true: that after the rise of Late Scholasticism we find a fuller appreciation of individuality, of the personal and historical element in philosophy, an appreciation already prepared for by the Franciscan school of Scotus and by the mystics like Master Eckhart and the *devotio moderna* in the waning Middle Ages. The Late Scholasticism shows far more historical understanding than was ever seen in the Middle Ages. It felt obliged in theology to point out that human nature is not wholly corrupt, that man as a free rational being is not, as the Reformers contended, like a stone absolutely impotent before the grace of God, but that man by his free will cooperates with grace by helping to put himself into a disposition, into an openness to grace. The part of human free will in forming history was more carefully considered by them than by the too abstract treatises of decaying Scholasticism and its subtlety. Gustav Gundlach [7] points out this accentuation of individuality, of personal responsibility, of the role of personal decision in philosophy and theology, especially in the new religious societies like the Society of Jesus with its social philosophy. The ego and the will of the person arouse a stronger interest than before; a feeling for the colorful dynamism of historical evolution, of national differentiations, and of personal intervention in historical process steps alongside the more static element of medieval thinking.

No wonder, therefore, that in political philosophy, too, these elements, and especially the role of individuality, of the will, complete the rather strictly intellectual philosophy of the Thomists, already op-

[6] In this connection we may mention that Professor Hilling, the editor of the *Archiv für Katholisches Kirchenrecht*, fully approved all arguments against this contention, as they were set forth in my book *Die Staatslehre des Franz Suarez* (in his review in *Archiv für Katholisches Kirchenrecht*, 1927).

[7] *Soziologie der katholischen Ideenwelt und des Jesuitenordens* (1927).

posed during the Middle Ages by an outspoken voluntarism in the philosophy of the Scotist school. But this we consider something of a progress, not an abandonment of the tradition; it made the great Schoolmen of the sixteenth and seventeenth centuries fit to construct, in their treatises *De legibus, De justitia et jure,* the first examples of a more systematic political and legal philosophy, such as we hardly encounter in the Middle Ages, if we except the Commentaries on Aristotle's *Politics.* However, it is this individualism that induces men to explain the birth of the state as the union of the form (the idea) and the matter (the people), as the result of a conscious consent, caused by a conscious will to the status of political existence. It is thus the common will of the individuals motivated by the conception of the perfection of the idea of man and by the urge for sociality that produces the state and establishes its constitution. What produces the state is not the impersonal, external forces of history or the blind urge of nature or mere facts of war, subjection, or wealth.

The Late Scholastics had at their disposal far more objective material for their thinking than had the Middle Ages. The modern national states had since been born. The era of discovery had brought to them information about the states of the Indians, the Chinese, the Japanese. The dream of an *imperium,* a *civitas maxima,* was gone. The growing national states of absolutist rulers were each emulating the politics of the universal emperor. The absolute ruler longed for the same totality and sovereignty that was conceded to the *imperium;* he would be pope and emperor in a state homogeneous in religion, language, and civilization. (cf. the ideal of a racially and religiously unitarian state of Philip II in Spain.)

The centralism and the newly developed bureaucratic administration of the law courts and the economic system (mercantilism) found in the new ideal of absolute royal sovereignty based upon divine right a means of destroying the traditional social framework of self-governing towns, guilds, and juries. In the Machiavellian "reason of state," the ruler, already made the supreme and exclusive interpreter of divine law, was practically freed from the restrictions of both natural and divine law. The people with its liberties abolished was on the way to become mere matter of the prince's absolute will. The translation theory now made it possible to show that the common good of the people united for a more perfect life is the form of the state,

that consequently the prince does not own the state, but is an organ
of the body politic, a servant of the *respublica*. His constitutional
rights are of human, not divine, origin; to protect the personal rights
opposed to the totalitarian claims and quasi-divine pretensions of
the absolute king, his rights were subordinated to and measured by
his actual service to the common good. And the masters of Late
Scholasticism, on the same principle of limitations of sovereignty, discovered the constitution of the community of nations (international
law) before Hugo Grotius. These accomplishments were all made
easier by the translation theory. Thus the juridical and political
thought of Late Scholasticism is an integrated part of the body of
doctrine of the *philosophia perennis*. It is neither an abandonment
of the tradition nor simply a historically determined excursion. It is
far more a genuine development based on the traditional principles,
thus fulfilling the task which Petavius ascribed to these doctors: "the
explanation of all that the ancestors had taught implicitly, to develop
the germinal ideas of the predecessors." It is a historical truth that
from Francis de Vittoria on, the finest renaissance of the Thomistic
and Augustinian thought is born.

IV. Monarchy and the Contract Theory

Another argument against the translation theory is that it is unhistorical and contradicts the historical fact of the priority of the
monarchy and that there is no historical proof for a social contract and
a translation contract.[8] Such an important act, it is said, would not
have so completely been forgotten if the theory were more than an
abstract and rather arbitrary argument. Now, we are not discussing
a *quaestio facti*, but a *quaestio juris*. Therefore this argument is not
exactly relevant to our problem. Besides, recent research work in
ethnology has shown that the primitive cultures were essentially democratic and not monarchical. The chief is by no means a ruler of
absolute jurisdiction, but is rather a *primus inter pares*.[9]

The early history of Germanic culture likewise shows that in the
early stages of political life democratic institutions prevail. "The
holder and subject of political authority is the assembly of all free

[8] V. Cathrein, S.J., *Moralphilosophie*, II, 510.
[9] Koppers, *Anfänge des menschl. Gemeinschaftslebens*, pp. 104, 128.

men of the *civitas*. To it belong the decisions of peace and war. Its jurisdiction is concurrent with the jurisdiction of the ordinary court." [10] Historical ethnology, not the later developed myths offered in proof of the monarchic principles, is competent to decide this question, and it quite clearly gives evidence for the translation theory and popular sovereignty. If we go back to the primitive cultures as the school of Wilhelm Schmidt describes them, and not to the rather recent young cultures of Europe, we find that popular sovereignty and freedom precede the historical stage of popular subjection to the unlimited sovereignty of a monarch, which an adversary of the translation theory like Victor Cathrein erroneously considers the first and original form of government. Thus must be interpreted the old idea of a pact between king and people, according to which the king's rights are not original, but are derived from the people. The beginning of political evolution was not the subjection of the body politic to a prince who, so to speak, owned it, but, on the contrary, liberty and self-government in the form of popular sovereignty.[11]

Moreover, the common law and generally the Germanic law until the times of absolutism retained this idea of a pact in the form of a contract. By this pact something higher than the king's power appeared to be the decisive thing; specifically, the right of the body politic to the common good represented in the *ordo juris*, the rule of law, the law of the realm. This rule excelled all prerogatives of the king, whose power is not original but rests on the pact and is lost if he violates the pact. In the same way the generally accepted right of the people even to active resistance against the king who violates the "law," rests upon the idea of an original covenant as the cause of the king's authority.

It may be conceded that the legal figure of a formal contract deterred

---

[10] Dopsch: *Grundlagen der Europäischen Kulturentwicklung* (1923), I, 13. Heinrich Brunner, *Deutsche Rectsgeschichte* (2nd ed., 1906), Vol. I, §§ 16–18, where the meeting of the free citizens for legislation is said to have had the sovereign power in the original Germanic tribes which in no sense formed a monarchy as defined by the monarchic theories prevailing from the sixteenth to the nineteenth centuries.

[11] The Roman jurists also favored this idea. Ulpian (*Digest*, I, 4, 1): "*cum lege regia, quae de imperio ejus (principis) lata est, populus ei (principi) et in eum omne suam imperium et potestatem conferat*" ("*concessit*" in Justinian, *Instit.*, I, II, 3). The *princeps* (emperor) is bound by the laws as his own authority depends upon the authority of the law (*Cod. Justinian.*, I, 14, 4). Here the original sovereignty of the *populus Romanus* is clearly established as it is in the rescript of Theodosius II and Valentinian II. On the other hand, Justinian seems to favor the divine right of the emperor (*Cod. Justinian.*, I, 17, 2, 8): ". . . *imperium, quod nobis a coelesti majestate traditum est.*"

the thinkers of the nineteenth century, who saw before them the consequences of an extremely individualist political philosophy. They concluded that the idea of a contract is the genuine expression of that destructive individualism which threatened all political stability with its declamation of active resistance and established an anarchic right to permanent revolution. Yet these men did not see that what matters is a status contract, the essence of which is to give birth not only to individual rights, but first and foremost to a durable, peaceful status of common life, necessary for the common purpose of the good life, and so to the higher form of political existence which is the outgrowth of the idea of the perfection of human nature. The Christian idea of a right to resistance does not mean a right to permanent revolution; it means that the people has a right to the *status politicus* as it was agreed upon for perpetuity. That is the meaning of the old formula of all these political status contracts, that they are concluded forever, that they are beyond the arbitrary will of the parties. The idea is that the status and the objective end of necessary political life should control the subjective wills, and that the status is never at the mercy of the arbitrary will of individuals.[12] Of course, this is nothing strange. Lincoln in his first inaugural address expresses the same philosophy when he says that in the contemplation of universal law the Union of the States is perpetual and that this perpetuity is implied, if not expressed, in the fundamental law of all national governments.

This idea of a status contract may also serve to refute an argument that was made against the translation theory in the nineteenth cen-

---

12 We should always carefully distinguish this status contract from our usual contract in civil law; the content of the purchasing contract, for instance, is in the arbitrary will of the contracting parties, and the rules of commutative justice control the relations of the parties. In any kind of status contract there necessarily intervenes the distributive and legal justice. Here we find that the mutual rights are controlled by an objective teleology, not, as in the civil-law contract, predominantly by the arbitrary will of the parties. This explains the difficulties that arise in labor problems from the attempt to subordinate the labor contract absolutely to the rules of a purchasing contract, the content of which is labor power as a commodity.

Moreover, the limitation upon freedom of speech can be understood only when seen as subject to the objective ends of the *status civilis*. Even in our individualist society when a person becomes a member of a profession, he has to accept, even without his free decision, the duties that are objectively implied by the end of the profession and that are thus beyond any decision of individuals or majorities. The freedom to teach does not and cannot include such an abuse of this freedom as to teach treason against one's country. This freedom is teleologically controlled by the end of education, which is among other things, to educate young people to be good citizens.

tury; that the purposes, the duties, and the mutual rights of legal justice can not be made dependent upon a free contract. If they were so dependent, we could not explain the obligation of subsequent generations to execute a contract to which they personally were never partners. It is indubitable that such an argument would bear against Rousseau's theory, which can avoid its cogency only by some contradictory identification. But no adherent of the translation theory contends that the existence itself and the objective end, the mutual duties and the rights, of the *ordo justitiae legalis* are at the mercy of the arbitrary will of autonomous individuals or of a majority of these.

The social contract is a status contract. Thus it is man's nature and the teleology of the *status politicus* that as objective norms control the matter of the social contract; the purpose and necessary content of the social contract are in their very essence beyond the arbitrary will of the makers of the contract. The objective end is the basis of the objective mutual duties and rights of governed and governing in any form of government, whether monarchy or democracy, and this is the reason that the later generations are bound by a contract to which they were not parties. They are bound because the political life is an objective and necessary form of human life; if circumstances so demand, they may indeed change the actual form of government, but they cannot leave the *status civilis* in order to return to a *status naturalis*. Such a return would contradict the very nature of man and of the state which is "a more perfect union of men." [18] The juridical figure of "contract" contains only the following two factors:

First, the birth of the individual state cannot be thought to occur without the intervention of the will—however this will is informed and directed by the rational nature and end of men—of the fathers who agree to enter the *status civilis*. The states of men are different from the "states" of animals like ants and bees.

Secondly, the form of government (not of course the essential content of the *status civilis*, the *ordo justitiae legalis*) is not produced by a blind urge or a mere accident, but rests on the decision of the people; the people has the constituent power. The controlling idea is the common good, not an abstract freedom like Rousseau's. Rousseau's purpose was to guarantee in the political status the same freedom as

[18] Lincoln's address gives excellent expression to this theory of the Union. What he says would, of course, be valid a fortiori for any independent non-federated state.

individuals had in his idyllic natural status: an impossible achievement. The doctors, on the other hand, regard as primary the order of the common good, the more perfect life. Thus the exclusive object is not abstract freedom, but concrete freedom in the order of political existence. The Rousseauist idea, that to obey another man in authority is unworthy of the free individual, is in its bluntness utterly wrong, and consequently so is his contention that man obeys only himself when he agrees with the general will, practically the majority. In obeying the law we do not obey the abstract arbitrary will of another person, but the law as the order of reason, measured by objective ideas of justice and peace, of the idea of man, and of perfection. We thus obey ultimately the reason in the order of law. We do not obey blindly, but because of a more or less clear insight into the reasonableness of the law, the command, or the judgment. Precisely this fact renders it unnecessary to make actual compulsion a characteristic of law. It is by far more the reason in the law that motivates our obedience than the fear of compulsion and of a harmful reaction of the law. It is of course self-evident that the order of legal justice *in concreto* is just only so far as it preserves and protects what is meant by the concept of natural rights as an emanation of the dignity of the human person and its autonomous end. These rights, we repeat, are prior to the state and therefore in their essential substance independent of it. The order of political life may control their use under the rule of the common good, but only on the condition that their substance be guaranteed. A bill of rights in positive constitutional form does not grant these rights; its very end is to protect them as the original landmarks of personal freedom. A bill of rights has, therefore, only a declaratory character and not a constitutive creative character.

From a so-called realistic standpoint, one might object that this whole discussion seems unreal. History, it might be said, shows that most states came into existence by force, by wars and the naked power of arms. War, as it is the father of all, is especially the father of states. But this objection misses the point. It may be true that many states have been founded by war and by violence of reckless, powerful gangs. But even here it is never the *quaestio facti* of involuntary obedience to the oppressive group that matters, but the acceptance of such originally unjust rule by the ruled. Only by this moral acceptance is produced a state, a moral *unitas ordinis* with justice and peace; it is never produced by the mere fact of subjection. A legal and moral *sanatio in radice* of the usurper's originally unjust usurpation occurs only if the usurper is formally or informally accepted by the citizens as a ruler because he actually serves the common good and observes the *ordo justitiae legalis*. Consequently even in this case he acquires authority not by a mere fact, but by the consent of the community.

V. Leo XIII and the Translation Theory

It has been said that the traditional translation theory can no longer be followed because Leo XIII in various encyclicals, especially in *Diuturnum illud* [14] has expressly adopted the designation theory and rejected the principles that the people as a whole is the primary and original subject of political authority and able to transfer this power. It is true that Leo XIII says that those who are to be the holders of supreme power in a state may be elected freely and at the discretion of the people, but by such an election the *imperium,* the authority, is not transferred; only the subject of authority is designated, and it is decided by whom authority should be exercised. Is the traditional theory thus definitely rejected? Most scholars who have studied this problem do not think so. The traditional theory was, at the time of Leo XIII, still accepted by many authorities. Thus, to mention only one, Cardinal Manning in his *The Vatican Decrees* (1875), shows that he is an adherent of the traditional theory. Cardinal Billot in his *Tractatus de Ecclesia Christi* (Rome, 1921, p. 492) likewise follows the traditional school. This could not have happened if Leo XIII's intention had been to reject the translation theory.

How, then, may we now explain this difficulty? The Pope himself gives us an indication. Asked through a cardinal if he had intended to reject the translation theory, he answered that he did not mean to reject the opinions of Catholics, but only those doctrines which denied any dependence of political authority upon God and which taught that authority in no way originates in God but exclusively in the arbitrary will of men.[15] The same conclusion can be drawn, too, from

[14] Cf. Denzinger, *Enchiridion*, no. 1856.
[15] *Revue apologétique*, 1913, p. 161.

the Pope's encyclicals. What he attacked so sharply was the Rousseauist concept of popular sovereignty, or what he called the "modern law." The Pope criticizes it because it is so utterly individualistic. It presumes that political authority originates wholly in the free consent and makes this the exclusive and sufficient cause of political authority. It argues that political authority is nothing else than the sum of the conceded rights of the individuals, which consequently can be demanded back again at the arbitrary will of the individuals. Leo XIII says that a stable basis of political life would be impossible under such a theory, and the consequence would be permanent disorder. Furthermore—and this is its deistic or even atheistic basis—this theory denies that political authority has any relation, either as concerns origin or exercise, to God and God's will or to eternal and natural law; it practically and theoretically places a majority decision in the place of God. Therefore its basis is a rationalism that regards human reason as the autonomous source of all truth and morality. It is this kind of philosophical justification of popular sovereignty that Leo XIII again and again refutes, pointing out that it leads to the disease of communism, the gravedigger of state and civilization. Thus, as such authorities as Mausbach, Castelein, Costa Rosetti, Feret, and Tischleder hold, we may conclude that the Pope did not intend to reject the translation theory. Above all, the Pope does not condemn popular sovereignty as a political principle of constitutional law. On the contrary, he asserts that the constituent power—and that in the last resort means juridically the principle of popular sovereignty—rests with the nation, with the people.

In studying the utterances of the Pope in the nineteenth century, we must remember that they were not so much concerned with legal institutions in their positive form as with the philosophical justification of them. Leo XIII declares that the constitutions and the forms of government are human institutions: they change, and in emergencies must be changed, because in their positive form they are not eternal; they are not prescribed by natural law, but are accidental, historical, and transitory. Their positive value rests not so much in themselves as in the actual service they are able to afford to the common good. Thus, when Leo XIII seems to condemn the idea of majority decision, he does not condemn it as an institution, for we may well suppose that he knew legal and political history. But he does condemn the thesis that the majority decision is the exclusive source of all rights and all duties, an opinion that the fathers of the American Constitution feared so much that they felt it necessary to add the Bill of Rights to the Constitution.

VI. MERITS OF THE TRANSLATION THEORY

We think that the translation theory has the greater merits. It is more consistent and is better suited to explain the frequently occurring problem of revolutionary changes in constitutional law. Its tenets make it more evident that authority is more than a formal, abstract right of the persons in authority, that authority itself is materially measured by the fulfillment of its end. So the common good and its actual realization in the order of peace, justice and security, as the result of the united efforts of both authority and subjects, is clearly recognized as the principal idea and as the final cause of political life. We must, of course, not forget that the act of transfer as cause must be interpreted in such a sense as is appropriate to the underlying philosophical system: the act of transfer is a relative secondary cause, therefore not absolute but dependent upon the eternal and the natural law and so upon God. Critics of the translation theory point out that authority is thus weakened, since it is made too dependent upon the consent of the ruled, whereas the designation theory gives a better foundation for the authority of the ruler and makes the divine origin of political power clearer. It has been further said that the undeniable aura of dignity and majesty that surrounds authority and is visible in its symbols and in the oaths of allegiance, is better appreciated in the designation theory than in the logical coolness and juridical rationality of the translation theory. It is a fact that conservative thought will therefore have a frank predilection for the designation theory. The translation theory, however, does not despise these aspects of authority. It makes one thing clear: the state is *res publica*, the affair of both authority and citizen; the state is a moral organism, the soul of which is the order of the common good realized in mutual cooperation and allegiance by both authority and citizens. Political unity is as much the work of the citizens' loyalty as of the ordinating, directing authority. Especially is the service character of the state in relation to the person clearly established.

Whether the people uniting for a body politic merely designates the holder of authority, or transfers this authority, which it originally holds itself as immediate democracy, to the ruler, is the subject of controversy in which two trains of thought are manifest. The first stresses the endurance and stability of the order. It tries to lift authority beyond the changing, flowing life of the people; authority must be firmly established and be inaccessible to the irrational vacillating caprices of the masses. The lasting value of a solid order, imperturbable and tranquil in its firmness, seems to be the preferred idea. That there should be order seems to be more important than the disquieting question whether the existing order is appropriate to the historical circumstances and to the genuine idea of social progress. The state is *status* in a pronounced sense, the product of historical irrational forces, and of traditions much more independent of conscious, free intervention and determination by changing political fashions and popular moods. The translation theory does not, of course, neglect the value of order; but it is responsive to social dynamics, to the individuality of the states and their peoples, to historical development as a free decision of man. It accepts more fully the principle that man makes history and traditions rather than the opposite principle. It emphasizes the individual and the personal element in political philosophy, and consequently is more progressive than conservative, more liberal than traditional, more for social justice even at the price of changing the traditional order, than for solid stability. We should, of course, bear in mind that these differentiations are not absolute; they are styles or moods of thinking, not differentiations in basic principles.

The fact that we find these two schools in Catholic political philosophy is not surprising. Human life, especially social life, oscillates between opposing polar points: Individual—community; freedom and authority; constituted order with the tendency to form vested interests (expediency) and social justice; changing historical circumstances and unalterable general rules of natural law and morals. We find such a polarity also in other fields. In theology we may find it in the polemics between Thomists and Molinists, in philosophy between Thomists and Scotists. A person who from outside looks into the polemics of the schools may have the impression of a *complexio oppositorum;* he will at least find in historical development some changes in accentuation, as we found them in the history of Catholic political philosophy. But a person who sincerely studies these polemics will also find a ceaseless effort to bring into concord the poles that at first sight seem to exclude each other; a ceaseless effort to bind the world of opposing theories in the harmony of eternal ideas. It is the deep restlessness of all creatures for rest in God, which St. Augustine spoke of, that makes many people amazed. The conservative may be horrified to see Capuchin monks with the Irish rebels, and to hear the strong pleas for unionism and state intervention in social and economic problems. The liberalist believer in perpetual progress may become wrathful when he reads the Syllabus and encounters the pessimism that is so often uttered about a freedom in economic and marital life that such a believer considers the guaranty for the perfection of men.

But life and philosophy, even for the Christian, remain venturesome; we must live in the opposite poles and think between them. Only the final redemption, the lasting rest in God, will end the striving. For only God is perfect intellect and supreme will, charity and justice.

VII. Tyranny and the Popular Right to Resist

Political philosophy in Catholicism has developed and preserved a genuine concept of the tyrant. The epithet "tyrant" is a mark of the usurper or invader; that is, one who wantonly, without law or reason, displaces the legitimate and legal authority, whether by internal sedition or by invasion and conquest from without. But legally instituted authority, the so-called legitimate prince, may likewise become a tyrant, when he uses his authority against the common good. The measure of legitimacy is, therefore, not legal formalities and the mere legality of the acquisition of power, but the actual performance of the duties owed to the common good. The realization of the common good is not only the highest law, but also the reason and end of political authority as such. If, therefore, the legally instituted holder of political authority behaves toward his subjects as a master to slaves, an artisan to his tools, caring only for his personal profits and his lust to power, and not for the common good, then such a ruler is a robber of the people's freedom; his rule is the worst depravity of government.[16]

Active and passive resistance against the usurper is not only a right, but a duty for all citizens. For the usurper is an invader and his lawless power is violence, not authority; should he by terrorism and duress force the people to consent externally to his rule, such a legitimation is invalid.[17] His laws are not laws, but iniquities. The usurper is a foe of the *respublica,* and every one who acts against him acts in defense of the body politic.

But what about the *tyrannus secundum regimen tantum,* that is, the legal authority that becomes illegitimate through a grave violation of the common good? First of all, the people has a right to passive resistance. The tyrannical law that is a law against reason, a law not directed to a common good, is not true law, but a depravity of law.[18] Consequently it does not bind in conscience. This passive resistance becomes a duty when the tyrannical law demands something that is against the divine good (*bonum divinum*). A typical case would be a law to compel blasphemous adoration of the ruler as a quasi-divine being.[19]

But has the people a right also to active resistance against this kind of tyrant? St. Thomas and all the Schoolmen answer, Yes. Because popular uprising is then not sedition, but lawful defense of the body politic's inalienable right to the realization of the common good. As elsewhere, so here, it is the common good that focuses the whole discussion. And it does this to such an extent that the exercise of the right to active resistance is dependent upon one very concrete question: Is exercise of this right, under given circumstances, even more detrimental to the common good than the state of affairs as it now exists under tyrannical rule? Thus prudence must intervene in the individual case. But let it be noted that in principle a right of the people to active resistance exists, and that it rests not so much upon the translation theory, but upon the right of the body politic to its common good. Hence we must make a careful distinction. A revolu-

16 St. Thomas, *Summa theol.,* Ia IIae, q.95, a.4 c.
17 St. Thomas, *Sent.* II, Dist. 44, a.2 ad 5.
18 St. Thomas, *Summa theol.,* Ia IIae, q.92, a.1 ad 4.
19 *Ibid.,* q.96, a.4 c.

tion is sedition if it is a forcible attempt to overthrow not simply a
government, but a legal and continuously legitimate government,
one that takes care for the common good and observes the constitution in its service of the common good. But a revolution against a
tyrannical government is not sedition; it is a lawful use of the people's
right of resistance, for the tyrannical government itself is really the
rebel.

St. Thomas says that, because of the great power that the monarchical ruler has in his realm, this power easily turns into a tyranny.
Therefore he prefers the *regimen mixtum,* which contains all the
elements of monarchy, aristocracy, and democracy. Speaking of democracy, in which, according to him, all participate in government, he
says that by it the order and peace of the people is preserved and that
all love such an order and observe its rules,[20] because thus the people
is better protected against an abuse of that dangerous power, power
over men. The reason why the problem of tyranny has lost some of
its importance lies in the fact that restrictive institutions hindering
the concentration of power in the hands of one man have grown
stronger and more numerous since the overthrow of absolutism. Constitutional monarchy was the first form of limited rule, of a *regimen
mixtum.* In the Middle Ages restrictions existed in many forms.[21]
These restrictions have multiplied in our democratic republics in
the form of positive constitutional institutions like the bill of rights,
the taxation principle of ability to pay, representative government,
federalism and self-government, judicial control of administrative
acts, and independence of the courts, together with the principle of
division of power and responsibility of the government for wrongful
acts against the citizen. They have grown in international law, too,
in the principle of the responsibility of sovereign states before the
international court and in the rather unsuccessful attempts of the
League of Nations to mediate in international conflicts.

It was this growth of restrictive institutions that led Leo XIII to
the view that today the right of active resistance to tyranny is dormant.
In his encyclicals to the Irish episcopate (August 1, 1882, and June
24, 1888) and in various letters to the Archbishop of Dublin (January
3, 1881, and January 1, 1883), Leo, though not denying the miserable

[20] *Ibid.,* q. 105, a. 1 c.
[21] Cf. C. H. McIlwain, *Constitutionalism, Ancient and Modern* (1941).

condition of the Irish Catholics which had already lasted for centuries, warns against frivolous adventures and against secret societies that use violence and put their hopes in criminal acts. He does not deny Ireland's rights, but says that they can more easily and safely be realized by legal means.[22] Again and again he warns against the secret societies which, under pretense of defending the rights of Ireland, almost always in effect destroy the public order. Nothing is more harmful to a just cause than its defense by violence and injustice.[23] It is true that here, as the best critical study of Leo XIII's political philosophy contends,[24] practical considerations prevail. A revolution against England's suppressive power seemed futile to such an expert statesman as Leo proved himself to be. What order there was would only have disappeared in a bloody civil war, and a harsher suppression would have been the consequence. How far the old theory of the right of active resistance was accepted by Leo remains still disputable. It must not be forgotten that in the nineteenth century Catholic political philosophy was between the hammer and anvil, at least in the non-democratic countries. On the one hand, it had not much in common with the democratic and laicist ideas of continental liberalism; and on the other hand, it found itself hard pressed by conservative monarchism because its great masters had defended the right of active resistance. One has only to recall the much ado that was made about the so-called theory of the rightful murder of the tyrant advanced by Mariana. We may therefore conclude that the right to resistance in itself and *in abstracto* was not given up, but only that it was considered superfluous, according to the growth of constitutional restrictions of that dangerous absolute power so that the political functions of the right of active resistance were taken over by modern constitutionalism.[25]

[22] Letter to the Archbishop of Dublin (January 3, 1881): "*Multo tutius ac facilius fieri poterit ut ea, quae vult Hibernia consequatur, si modo via quam leges sinunt utatur, causasque offensionis evitet.*"

[23] Encyclical letter to the Irish bishops (August 1, 1882): "*Causae quantumvis justae nihil tam obest quam vi et injuriis esse defensam.*"

[24] Peter Tischleder, *Staatslehre Leos XIII*, p. 233.

[25] That the doctrine of resistance to tyranny has not been changed basically in modern times, especially when revolutionary parties abolish constitutionalism and proceed to wanton abuse of power, may be concluded from Pius XI's letter to the bishops of Mexico, *Firmissimam constantiam* (March 28, 1937); Denzinger, *Enchiridion*, no. 2278. Here the traditional doctrine is recapitulated and it is pointed out that the right to resistance belongs to the sphere of natural law and is not the task of Catholic Action.

CHAPTER XXI

Forms of Government

I. THE PHILOSOPHICAL INDIFFERENCE TO FORMS OF GOVERNMENT

IT IS the essential meaning of the translation theory that the constituent power rests by natural law with the people. This is acknowledged, too, by Leo XIII when he says that the nation has the right and the duty to form a new constitution, a new form of government, if the traditional form has broken down; or that the forms of government, i.e., monarchy, aristocracy, and democracy, are all neither definite and final nor inalterable. All of them are subject to changes and they are differentiated according to the history, the tradition, and the cultures of the different nations. Therefore the form of government is in itself morally and philosophically rather indifferent. No form has in itself an absolute validity. No one deserves a preference always and under all circumstances. Their value is functionally dependent on the actual service they afford in the actual circumstances to the realization of the common good. This alone is their last and most effective legitimation. Therefore neither hereditary monarchy, "sanctified through its old traditional continuity through centuries," nor representative democracy can claim an exclusive legitimacy on the basis of natural or divine law and in its name. The forms of government are changing patterns that the nation actually seeks through its history, influenced by its individual, cultural background and social ideals, in relation and continuous adaptation to its social life with the flourishing and withering social forms in class stratification, economic systems, international relations, and what is called its soul.

From this philosophical indifference to the forms of government, one may best understand that some excessive propositions of the founder of the Paulists, Father Hecker, were criticized by Leo XIII. The Pope praises the American Constitution and declares that the situation of the Catholic Church in the United States is very favorable. But to conclude, as Father Hecker did, that the specific form of democracy as represented in the American Constitution is everywhere and always an unsurpassable ideal for all nations and all times, was so unhistorical an assertion that Leo XIII protested. If it had been said that under prevailing circumstances the American form is the best, nobody would have protested. But the *philosophia politica perennis* cannot simply identify Catholicism and a historical political form, because the political form of government as such does not actually guarantee the best realization of the common good. Should that be the case, then Washington's demand for religion and morality as the essential conditions of the functioning of the democratic regime would be superfluous; then the Russian Constitution of 1936 would be a good thing and Hitler's contention would be justified, namely, that his rule is democratic because he always asks the nation in plebiscites for approval of his ways.

Democracy, as the term is used today, means not merely a definite set of technical rules of government, though it also means that, but rather what we call the spirit of the Constitution. This implies definite moral ideas of the dignity of the human person, not *in abstracto*, but *in concreto;* of the sanctity of the family realm and the home; of the equality of all citizens before the law; the equal protection of their freedom and their natural rights independent of political, racial, or religious affiliations. It means the active participation of the citizen in loyalty and in the spirit of sacrifice in the control of the administrative organs of government. It means the freedom of worship and the freedom for the parents to determine the education of their children. It means, too, the protection of those classes that, in an economy of wide and deep differences in wealth and social power, are in danger of being robbed of their rights or of having only ineffective rights. It means the protection by law against exploitation in any form. A country may have a democratic technique and still have grave economic and social injustices. But to call such a state "democracy" would be an abuse of the term. Therefore what rings as an undertone when we pronounce that much abused word "democracy," is almost more important than the technique. Lincoln's famous Gettysburg Address was a revelation of what is intended by the word "democracy: that this nation under God shall have a new birth of freedom and that government of the people, by the people, and for the people shall not perish from the earth." The perpetual, daily new birth of freedom, that is democracy.

Let us repeat that "freedom" means not some abstract thing, but these concrete freedoms that correspond to the dignity of the human person. Democracy is not the political form of religious and philosophical relativism. Freedom of conscience is based upon a reverence for the final unavoidable responsibility of the individual person for his salvation. Freedom of speech rests on the fact that man is a rational being, that therefore public discussion and deliberation should precede the legislative act. It is not a consequence of the belief that all opinions are equally true because there is no objective truth, but of man's having fundamentally access to truth. The freedom of association is not a guaranty of free propaganda and action for all associations without regard to the morality of their aims because there is no objective measure for any of them. This freedom flows from the principle of subsidiarity. Whatever, in the fields of economics, social welfare, culture, and education, the smaller associations of citizens can do, should be left to them and not be "confiscated" by a centralized state administration.

A person may "debunk" the freedom of property and of contract as a detestable device for capitalist exploitation and think he must do away with both, but that does not destroy the meaning of these freedoms, that they are the outgrowth and, as far as they are working principles, the guaranty of the dignity of the human person. The essential element of democracy, that is, government by open discussion, persuasion, and consent, rests on the moral idea of solidarity and loyalty to one another. Thus it is these essentially moral ideas that are meant with democracy. For these it is worth while to fight and die, yet not for a dead letter. Other forms of government in other nations with different traditions, with a different culture, may afford similar guaranties even under a monarch as was the case in the Middle Ages or as the case is in the Dutch monarchy. And we now know also that all forms of government can degenerate, as Aristotle taught us, and as we learn from the boss rule in some of our own cities.

The discussion of forms of government and of the best form of government constitutes philosophically a negligible part in Catholic political thought. This is easily explained. The problem of the best form of government is predominantly more a historical problem. It is to be answered by such concrete factors as national character, stage of civilization and education, congruency with traditional convictions and cultural climate, and many other factors. The philosophical problem concerns the realization of the common good under concrete circumstances, and the value of forms of government is determined concretely by this problem, not by an abstract idealizing of one or the other of the traditional forms of government.

It is true that at certain times lively discussions took place, when, for instance, after the French Revolution the problem of legitimism was brought up and the promoters of the Restoration tried to put Catholic political philosophy into its service. At that time the sincere defenders of the legitimacy of the old established monarchy sometimes made a mistake. They fought against the confessedly wrong foundations of the new democratic government, that is, rationalist and liberal bourgeois individualism, popular sovereignty in the anarchical Rousseauist form, deism, and so on. They fought also against the new political forms of democratic government, in themselves neutral and legitimate only by their service to the common good; they did not consider the fact that this last function alone is decisive. The historical foundation and justifications of the new institutions were identified with the forms themselves and therefore were condemned as against natural and divine law. They forgot a bit too quickly that often the foundation of monarchies was rather doubtful, too. They also forgot how often unjust conquest, successful treason, and breach of old established popular rights were used in forming a monarchical government. Likewise they ignored the fact that wrong theories, such as the immediate divine origin of monarchy, the quasi-divine *plenitudo potestatis* of the monarch, or a juridical formula from the pagan Roman law, were frequently used to legitimate monarchy. If Father Hecker and the French *Sillon* or Lammenais went too far, then surely De Maistre, the majority of the French episcopate during the efforts of Leo XIII's *ralliement* policy, and the adherents of Charles Maurras' *Action française,* also went too far.

II. Democracy and the French Revolution

In connection with the problem of forms of government we can now pick up and conclude an earlier discussion: the relation of the political philosophy in Catholicism to democracy. Historical study will show that, at the rise of modern democracy and its institutions in consequence of the bourgeois revolutions and the violent overthrow of the ancient regime, the great majority of Catholic writers in political philosophy were by no means friendly to democracy or liberal democracy. Furthermore, the famous encyclicals *Mirari vos arbitramur* of Gregory XVI (August 15, 1832) against De Lammenais and *Quanta cura* of Pius IX (December 8, 1864) together with the *Syllabus* published under the same date seemed to reject the new forms of government as a necessary outgrowth of the philosophical and theological errors so vehemently condemned in the encyclicals just mentioned. There were enough hotheads, such as Veuillot and his *Univers,* who propagated this theory. Actually the question of forms of government, of monarchy or democracy, are never mentioned in the encyclicals, which are neither antidemocratic nor pro-monarchical, as any careful reader can easily find out.

Furthermore, the same Pope Pius IX, who supposedly was antidemocratic in his official teaching, praised the position of the Catholic Church in the United States and lauded the American Constitution as almost every pope since then has done. When the majority of the French hierarchy, according to its traditional monarchism, resisted Leo XIII's policy of ralliement to reconcile French Catholicism with the Third Republic and its democratic institutions, at the same time we hear the Apostolic Delegate, Cardinal Satolli, express the following opinion: "The Magna Chartas of mankind are the Gospel of our Lord and the Constitution of the United States. . . . Forward on the way of progress: in one hand the book of Christian truth, the Gospels of our Lord; in the other hand the Constitution of the United States." [1]

In our time political commentaries of leftist or of liberal inclinations contend that "the Vatican" or "the Church" or "Catholicism" or "Catholic thought" in social and political philosophy is pro-Fascist, clerico-Fascist and consequently antidemocratic. There is no doubt that this is an unjustifiable exaggeration. On the other hand, it is evident that many or even the majority of the bishops in Spain and in Italy,[2] for instance, have sided with "authoritarian" or "Fascist" re-

[1] Cf. O'Connell, "Une idée nouvelle dans la vie du Père Hecker." *Compte rendu du 4ieme Congrès scientifique internationale des Catholiques* (Fribourg, IV, 1897, 78); and Archbishop Ireland, *The Church and Modern Society,* I, 127.

[2] For Italy, cf. D. A. Binchy's authoritative book, *Church and State in Fascist Italy*

gimes that pretended to be Catholic as against the anticlericalism of
their political democratic opponents. In books of some Catholic
writers in almost all countries we will find antidemocratic theories
which get a greater echo as soon as in these countries "authoritarian"
or Fascist or even clerico-Fascist regimes come to power. On the other
hand, *The Thomist* (1941–42) publishes a study by Mortimer Adler
and Walter Farrel, O.P., "The theory of democracy," which is decidedly pro-democratic; and Maritain writes his *Les droits de l'homme
et la loi naturelle* (New York, 1942), which also is pro-democratic
and anti-Fascist and argues against clericalism.

How are we to explain these facts, which can easily be augmented
and which have been observed since the French Revolution? Some
will say the whole proves the opportunism of the Catholic Church itself, or at least of the Vatican. Some will interpret the facts as an outgrowth of the Catholic *complexio oppositorum*, according to which
almost irreconcilable theses and antitheses are combined.

Cardinal Newman in his memorable preface to *The Via Media*
points out that "Christianity is at once a philosophy, a political power,
and a religious rite" (p. xl). The Church has three several departments
of duty: her government, her devotions, and her schools. "Truth is
the guiding principle of theology and theological inquiries; devotion
and edification, of worship; and of government, expedience. The
instrument of theology is reasoning; of worship, our emotional nature;
of rule, command and coercion. Further, in man as he is, reasoning
tends to rationalism; devotion to superstition and enthusiam; and
power to ambition and tyranny. . . . Each of the three has its separate
scope and direction; each has its own interests to promote and further;
each has to find room for the claims of the other two; and each will
find its own line of action influenced and modified by the others,
nay, sometimes in a particular case the necessity of the others converted into a rule of duty for itself" (*ibid.*, p. xli).

This passage in its masterly distinctions gives us the opportunity to
solve our problem.

(1942). In Spain, Cardinal Vidal, archbishop of Tarragona, refused to sign the pastoral
letter of the Spanish hierarchy declaring the justice of the Franco cause. See obituary in
New York Times, September 15, 1943.

III. Democracy in Christian Interpretation

Let us first make some distinctions concerning the meaning of "democracy." This word has a scientific meaning, but it is also surrounded by emotional connotations. Furthermore, many writers imply even a certain philosophy or a fundamental philosophical principle. There are thus many meanings involved and a man may be anti-democratic in the one meaning and yet accept the other meaning.

Democracy may mean a form of government as opposed to monarchy and aristocracy. It implies a republican form of government and, by intent, full equality before the law, equal protection of the law, equality of chance or the absence of juridical privileges based on birth, on membership in a group and so on. Sociologically it means, therefore, the absence of a hierarchical structure of society, though not of offices; it means free and equal access to all strata, to all offices and positions of power under equal conditions of competition. The quality of a citizen which as a rule accrues to everybody regardless of race, education, economic wealth, creed, or sex, is the exclusive basis for all political offices, for economic and social positions of power. Democracy thus involves a government of law in which in an egalitarian tendency the status of the individual and his associations and groups (e.g., family, cultural and economic associations) are all subject to a law that is common, to a law equal for all citizens.

Furthermore the law binds the governmental authorities, the magistrates or whoever rule in an office. Any order or command of an authority to an individual must be a reasonable, not an arbitrary, act which applies the general law. Sociologically there may exist and very likely there will exist a ruling class, but this class rules on account of social or economic power, not on account of juridical privilege as, for instance, the nobility did in earlier times or the clergy in the Papal States. A further implication, at least in intention, is that this rule of impersonal general law and the equality of practically all individuals before the law irrespective of their social or economic status should issue in a government that leaves in the sphere of communal life as much as possible to the free initiative of the citizens and their freely formed association, the only test being the accordance to the general law, the law common to all.

The basis for such a regime is the popular sovereignty of a republican constitution and consequently the people's control over the "magistrates," over its representatives. Election by majority vote is therefore the exclusive method of coming to the highest offices. Thus general suffrage and short terms in offices are consequences. The lifetime terms of justices of the highest courts or of technical administrators who do not formulate policy is not an exception. Those who belong to the judiciary should by life-terms become independent of changing party governments; by definition the judiciary is not a policy-making body; rather it is the guardian of the constitution and the law against arbitrary, unreasonable acts of the policy-making authority, the legislative and the executive.

Democracy's innate tendency to freedom is, in most instances, further characterized by a definite demarcation of a free sphere of personal and group initiative, a state-free sphere of human rights and rights of the citizen; the meaning of both is to protect the free citizen against arbitrary intervention of even the majority of the legislature, and these rights all together represent thus a constitutional protection of minorities.

Evidently a general trend to more freedom according to the principle—as much freedom as possible, as little coercion as necessary—is an essential feature and one of the paramount principles of interpretation for democratic institutions. A great, perhaps too optimistic, faith in freedom lies at the bottom of democratic thought. Freedom is the precondition and the formative element for the realization of a maximum of social justice and human happiness. Thus the rights of active citizenship, the control of the governmental authorities by the people, the independence of the courts, and the rule of the law receive their true proportion and their genuine interpretation from liberty, justice, happiness, words which are emphasized in the preamble of most democratic constitutions. In order to be workable, democracy needs a strong sense of unity in principles, balanced by a great tolerance in regard to all things that do not directly concern unity. Democracy thus supposes, instead of loyalties to persons, loyalties to moral ideas common to all. The collective moral will to live together in mutual solidarity must be so strong in all groups that their antagonistic interests, their dissatisfaction with the social and economic distribution of power, with apparent social injustices, will always be controlled by the stronger moral will to live together and thus use only the legal means of social and political reform and abstain from appeal to civil violence. Where the antagonism of groups or classes outbalances the will to live together, democracy becomes impossible, and its institutions are directly contributing factors to its destruction.

From the standpoint of Catholic political philosophy all these democratic institutions and political principles are unassailable. They are even founded in Christian ideas matured to their full meaning. It is the idea of the Christian personality, the Christian idea of "freedom of conscience as a personal prerogative of each individual" (Newman),[3] of individual reason—that endowment of the Creator to man, created as His image and not destroyed by the Fall—which is the foundation of all this, however much it may be obscured by wrong yet transitory philosophies.

Each man is the image of God; each man has a conscience which, as Cardinal Newman says, is "a messenger from Him who speaks to us behind a veil"; each man has a reason. Each individual soul is incomparably more precious than the whole world. There is no true humanity without these principles. Modern "humanity" as an abstract love for mankind forgets too often in its enthusiasm that each man is our neighbor. Each individual man is, therefore, not an indifferent technical "channel" for grand ideas; even the humblest are not merely "raw material" for superhuman leaders or intellectual aristocrats. Nor can one man become a mere instrument, a means, for the happiness of another man, of a nation, of mankind. We cannot agree to found the happiness of mankind upon the unjust suffering of a single innocent man. There is a majestic greatness about St. Babylas when he publicly and vehemently rebukes a Christian emperor, because the latter had a hostage murdered, a boy belonging to a barbarian tribe. This idea of the Christian person is illuminated by the doctrine that each for himself must stand before the divine Judge and is portrayed in those medieval pictures of the Last Judgment in

[3] The Catholic doctrine of conscience is well set forth in Cardinal Newman's *Letter to the Duke of Norfolk* (chapter 5). Newman therein quotes many theologians who affirm that even an erroneous conscience, whether in vincible or invincible error, binds strictly. This is general Catholic doctrine, not only a particularly stressed feature of the Augustinian tradition, which as a rule stresses conscience as the "light of God" (*videre in lumine Dei*) and is therefore less intellectualist and rational than Thomism. But in this doctrine there is no difference between Thomists and Augustinians.

which emperors and dukes, bishops and cardinals are among the condemned, thus showing the ultimate equality of all men.

IV. JUSTIFICATION OF DEMOCRATIC INSTITUTIONS

Undoubtedly many eminent ecclesiastics had and some still have a distrust of democracy, and there were always Catholic authors who gave such distrust literary expression. Whence comes this attitude? There are three principal answers.

First, the institutions of democracy, even its foundations, the rights of man, the tendency to freedom, the principle of popular sovereignty, have been derived from and championed by more than one philosophy. Several times we have already pointed out how the freedom of worship can be founded on a wrong religious indifferentism or on a right reverence toward consciences; how the natural rights can be founded on the dignity of the human person or on the wrong principle of subjective moral autonomy of the individual; how popular sovereignty can be upheld within the tenets of natural theology, of God as the supreme source of all human authority, and how popular sovereignty can be misinterpreted as the effect of a pantheistic immanentism. General suffrage could be based upon the metaphysical fact of individual reason with full awareness of its being wounded by the Fall; and it could be and has been based upon the Protestant religious principle of subjective individual judgment as the supreme authority in religious faith and in Rousseau's or Kant's moral autonomy of individual reason.

There is little doubt that historically the modern democratic movements, especially the revolutionary ones on the European continent, were born of the wrong philosophies. Thus they did not avoid the consequent extremes and wanton destruction of traditions that were irreconcilable with the new democracy. In the eyes of ecclesiastical rulers and of Catholic writers the latter was corrupted in its roots by these wrong philosophies; and the new democratic institutions were harmful to the traditions to which the common people still adhered, though the intellectual bourgeois elite, rationalist and deist as it was, had lost any feeling for these traditions.

In this connection we must not forget that the leading champions of democracy on the European continent were a small minority of intellectuals, blasé noblemen and members of the professions, steeped in deism or even atheistic materialism, while the common people, though partly at least neglected by their pastors, still lived securely in their religious and religiously inspired social traditions. These "champions of democracy" accused the Church, in its two offices of teacher and ruler, of refusing to understand the irresistible need of the new political forms. They castigated the Church for her alleged stubborn and selfish defense of her privileges all too much integrated with the political privileges of the ruling class in the ancient regime. They vehemently proclaimed that the Church suffered without strong protest an identification of ecclesiastical interests with political privilege of the old order. Yet the churchmen could easily point out in refutation that the new movements showed no sympathetic understanding of the difficulties of the Church as a body politic living still in a kind of symbiosis with the old order. Even more the Church and the writers defending her could without difficulty show that the "democrats" were definitely hostile, not so much to the transitory privileges but to her *raison d'être*, to her doctrine, to her perennial religious institutions and not only to the transitory forms of her symbiosis with the old order. It was the "democratic" philosophies which made a matter of policy and expediency and of contingent political technique a matter of principle, of philosophy, of erroneous absolute ethics. Thus the Church was compelled to defend her doctrine, her divine constitution, and her rights acquired through tradition against a new non-Christian or even anti-Christian philosophy. We have already pointed out that in this defense members of national hierarchies and Catholic authors did not always make the prudent distinctions which most of the great theologians and the popes so carefully made.

V. Propaganda for Democracy

Secondly, the progress of freedom and the democratic institutions were not altogether a blessing for all classes or for all nations. An exuberant secularism received such an advantage that the *unum necessarium*, the salvation of souls, was rendered much more difficult. The unchained spiritual and social energies that were poured into the world produced a high instability of social life, rendering the normal care of souls very difficult. The spirit of the "modern man" showed little understanding for the specific Christian virtues of contemplative life. A pursuit of material wealth with little regard for the consequent sacrifices in human happiness began to divert man's activity from the religious sphere. In fact, secular utopias of a democratic sort began to replace the genuine Christian eschatological hope. Democratic institutions often served to push the religious realm so much into the background, and to shove secular purposes into the foreground, that a silent and slow mass apostasy had to be feared. A democratic contest for equal public education for all could easily become a contest against the faith of a private religious group, a status to which the Church was demoted. "Opinion," in democracy, can mean something very good, namely, a judgment about a political action arrived at after rational discussion and reflective thinking by serious-minded men, fully aware of their responsibility to the moral law. It can also mean skeptical relativism, insincere propagandist abuse of the confidence of the common man in his political leaders. It was these potentialities, the wanton surrender of traditional and well-tested values which again made the conservatively minded Catholic writers doubtful and ecclesiastical authorities suspicious about what might result from the progress of freedom and of democracy.

Nobody will claim that they were themselves without faults. Frequently they were satisfied merely with condemning the wrong political philosophies and tolerated the grave social injustices from which these philosophies sprang. There is, to put it in a nutshell, little doubt that a Bishop Ketteler in Mexico or Spain would have saved the Church from many sufferings. This diffident attitude of churchmen and Catholic writers is occasioned also by an unjustified glorification of the Middle Ages as it occurred under the sway of romanticism. As an era of faith the Middle Ages will always be dear to Catholics. Yet in its social and economic life it left much to be desired. And we venture to say that many a glorifier of the Middle Ages would find it in reality impossible to live under the social and economic conditions and under the feudal state of birth-privileges so typical for that period. Objective historical research has meanwhile freed us from many romantic ideas about the medieval world, and has thus corrected in conservative Catholic minds both the picture of the Middle Ages and that of our democratic world. Today leading theological authorities admit that, in the early nineteenth century and all through this century of the rise of democracy, ecclesiastical authorities and conservative Catholic writers were often one-sided, more prone to condemn what was wrong than eager to praise what was good or could be righted.[4]

VI. Abuse of Democratic Institutions

Thirdly, the general enthusiasm of the revolution-born continental democracy together with the implied doctrine of national self-determination produced two difficult problems: a demand for the democratization of the Church and the abolition of the Papal States, and with it a grave danger to the independence of the Apostolic See on account of the demand of Italian democratic nationalism for all Italian territory.

The demand for democratization of the Church touched directly the constitution of the Church. It had little to do with democratic institution inside the Church and its religious orders and societies. For the latter are more democratically organized than the outsider knows. Election of superiors, decision by majority vote about constitutions and bylaws by a democratically elected general council of the religious order is quite common. Furthermore, access to the offices in Church and religious orders is democratic in so far as no test of wealth, station in life, or status of birth is required.[5] Popes and bishops, cardinals and general superiors (of religious orders) from the humblest origin are numerous. In the case of presidents of modern democracies similar origin is not so common.

Thus democratization of the Church meant something else: the election of the pastors by the people; the election of the pope in a way similar to that of a democratic president; the election of bishops by the people of the diocese. Under the decaying ancient regime the absolute prince, against the protest of the Church, wielded practically

---

[4] Cf. Tischleder, *Staatslehre Leos XIII*, pp. 10–12. Schmidlin, *Geschichte der Päpste* (Freiburg, 1933–38), in the chapters which appraise the pontificates; Cardinal Ferrata, *Ma nonciature en France* (popular edition; Paris, 1921).

[5] There were times when the ruling classes in the ancient regime reserved for their younger sons the best ecclesiastical benefices or when the cardinalate was in the hands of Italian noble families. Yet this is more the exception than the rule. Such "privileges" were felt at all times to be something irregular.

the decisive influence in the appointment of bishops and pastors to their benefices. When now the absolute prince's sovereignty returned to the people, where it belonged according to the democratic theory, then it seemed a legitimate claim of the people now to enter into the "rights" of the prince over the benefices, i.e., to elect their pastors and bishops by democratic vote. The propagandists even contended that such was the original procedure in the first Christian centuries.[6] But their case was theologically and canonically untenable.

Furthermore, the Church had fought the absolute prince's rights too hard to yield now freely what it had tolerated earlier only under duress. There is a further difference: in France and in Spain, in Austria and in Bavaria, the absolute king was a Catholic, but the election of bishops by the people would bring the Church in the various nations under the control of political groups that often were not even Catholic in name, but were adepts of deism or agnosticism. This would have meant the subjection of the Church, not under Catholic lay power, but under the power of unbelievers. A separation of state and Church was, under such conditions, a better guaranty of the freedom of the Church and the independence of her divinely founded constitution. While the monarchical constitution of the Church and the pope's authority of divine law could perhaps be declared a model for the constitution of the secular state, on the other hand the democratic constitution and the principle of popular sovereignty could not be declared a model for the constitution of the Church or for the ecclesiastical states. In his encyclical against Modernism, Pius X felt compelled to reject such demands for democratization of the Church. Modernism contends, so the Pope says, that the Church emanates from the collectivity of consciences and consequently her authority stems from the same source and is subject to that collectivity. As now, so Modernism argues, in political life public conscience has produced democracy, so the same conscience in man demands now democratic forms in the Church.[7] But such demands, originating in the democratic theory of popular sovereignty and in the principle that the constituent power belongs to the people, are in stark con-

---

[6] The election to the papacy has an involved history, as any history of the popes will show. But for a "democratic" election there is little room. The *acclamatio populi* was at times of some importance. Special literature by Johannes D. Sagmüller, *Lehrbuch des Kath. Kirchenrechts* (Freiburg, 1934), I, 480–90, notes.

[7] Denzinger, *Enchiridion*, no. 209.

tradiction to the Catholic doctrine of the nature of the Church. The constitution of the Church is of divine law and is not the result of a collective will of the members of the Church dependent on their constituent power. The pope, the bishops and the priests do not derive their authority from any corporate and sovereign will of the community of the faithful but from direct divine institution. Thus the hierarchical constitution of the Church is forever unchangeable and independent of the collective will of the faithful.

From the earliest times any democratic interpretation of the Church has been constantly rejected. The charismatic and democratic interpretation of early Christianity, the conciliar theory in the late Middle Ages according to which the ecumenical council was supreme, the episcopal theory in the eighteenth century (Febronianism), the acts of the Synod of Pistoia which stated that the ecclesiastical offices and their jurisdictional authority are derived from the community of the faithful: these various democratic theories about the constitution of the Church, were rejected again and again.[8] This does not exclude the fact that inside the Church in its religious communities democratic institutions exist. The constitutions of many religious orders and societies have many democratic features. Franciscanism undoubtedly contributed to the rise of a democratic attitude in the medieval towns. The principle of general suffrage, of representation, of the election of officers for short terms of office, all such institutions are familiar to the student of the charters or constitutions of religious orders and societies. It may well be that many a democratic institution took its origin from these constitutions.

Furthermore, liberalism and democracy had produced in capitalism a social and economic system which hardly agreed with the traditional Catholic attitude to economic life. All the antidemocratic writers are at the same time utterly anticapitalist. And they contend that it is democracy and liberalism which are at the source of the innate evils of capitalism and that consequently not by social legislation and by the progress of liberty can these evils be abolished, but only by a return to a political and social order modeled on the medieval order. And here we touch again a source of this diffidence and skeptical at-

---

[8] Cf. H. Dieckman, *Die Verfassung der Urkirche* (Berlin, 1923), pp. 14 ff., for early Christianity; Denzinger, *op. cit.*, no. 1500. Many Protestant sects which deny a hierarchical constitution adhere to the democratic corporate type of ecclesiastical constitution.

titude against democracy: a retrospective glorification of the Middle Ages as it was so characteristic also for the political theory of Romanticism.

Another reason deserves to be mentioned: the dangerous alliance between democracy and a nationalism upon an anti-Christian basis. Such an alliance became not only dangerous to the preservation of the temporal domain of the Papal States. What ecclesiastical authorities and many conservative writers feared was the destruction of the international ties which bound the European countries together as Christian states. Once democracy, the secularized state under laicist and anticlerical leadership, were carried away by nationalism as a substitute for religion, then the common bonds of a Christian civilization, international as it were, would be destroyed, too. The nationalist idea would become stronger than the Christian idea; a secularized nationalism of the democratic masses would thus not only endanger the universal Church, it would also destroy Europe as a Christian commonwealth. Furthermore, such a democratic nationalism would easily condemn Catholic minorities in the national states to a minor status; they would be considered nationally untrustworthy.[9]

These, then, are some reasons that explain why from some sides the reproach was made that Catholic political theory is fundamentally hostile to democracy. The same reasons or, better, the lack of such reasons in the country without any Middle Ages, that is, America, are sufficient to refute the reproach that the favorable position to democracy in America is based on opportunism. But any unbiased and comprehensive history of Catholic social and political thought in the nineteenth century would show that from the beginning of the rise of free and democratic institutions a great many authors of influence were critical enough of the old pre-revolutionary order and open-minded and confident enough of the new social and political institutions to understand that freedom and democracy must be valued

[9] This happened of course in practically all countries with the growth of nationalism; in France under the anticlerical and Masonic governments of the Third Republic from 1890 to World War I; in England even Gladstone was not free from such insinuations; Bismarck coined the expression "nationally untrustworthy." Although in the United States we have a native concept of "nation" and therefore a nationalism different from the European one, the Catholics here had to suffer from nationalist bigotry (A.P.A., Ku Klux Klan). To be sure, some of the antidemocratic forces which offered themselves as allies to the Church were nationalist, from the *Action française* to the newer Fascist groups. These were rather dubious "auxiliaries."

positively and can be valued so especially well from the principles ever present in Catholic thought. This applies also to the problem of Fascism and other authoritarian regimes. True, integralist writers and ecclesiastical authorities of the same mental structure as nineteenth-century conservatives, have shown a greater friendliness to these regimes than they were willing to show to democracy. But there are many more who, without any undue enthusiasm for liberal democracy, from the outset discovered the totalitarian and anti-Christian substance behind the propagandist and opportunist mask with which those regimes tried to recommend themselves to minds disturbed by the weakness of democracies against Bolshevism.[10]

VII. THE CONSERVATIVE MIND

But perhaps what is behind these two extreme ways of siding with monarchy or with democracy is nothing more than the already mentioned fact of polarity that appears in the history of political philosophy. Behind that criticism of modern democracy there probably lies the feeling that too much easygoing optimism prevails, too much reliance on the individual, weak in will and in reason, weak and endangered by passions that would now find none of the restrictions which had been built up in past centuries. In these conservative thinkers we find prevalent a kind of disbelief in progress and a delicate cultural pessimism. The optimistic belief in infinite progress, an exaggerated regard for the abilities of the free individual, the hypothesis that, if the individuals and their self-interests should only be left alone, then the order of the common good would automatically arise, all this was according to their feelings somewhat wrong. For these assumptions are a reckless misapprehension or even a contempt of the traditional way of life, of the historical culture of a particular nation built up in long, long centuries under unspeakable efforts of successive generations with all its restraints against uncontrolled popular passions and individual license.

Culture is not the mass civilization of a mass production era. Culture is the old families, the high standards of professions. Culture is the wisdom and the learning transmitted from generation to

[10] For Italy, cf. the authoritative work of Binchy; cf. also Sturzo's important book, *The Ethics of Political Collaboration* (London, 1938), chap. 5.

generation, something valuable in itself, not a tool for more profits. Culture is a continuous toilsome effort to build fences around the moral values against the threatening vandalism in men. Culture must be wrung from death and destructive forces in men. Culture demands the strenuous vigilance of the fathers and mothers in each generation; it can live only in a solid, stable order. It cannot be "made" like machines and "founded" like manufacturing corporations. It grows slowly. As a lasting order, culture is more than a sum of quickly made and quickly changed laws. Time, not as a mere addition of single years but as duration, that is the proof of institutions, not their quickly acquired and as quickly lost popularity. Time is, therefore, an honor for political institutions. There is wisdom in De Maistre's remark that time is the prime minister of Providence. It is time as duration that is a sign of the legitimacy of an institution because thus is shown approval by a long line of generations.

When these conservatives study politics, they study Aristotle and Thucydides, Tacitus and Plutarch, because they are convinced that all external technological and social progress and all the machines of mass education do not change human nature. They fear the mass civilization, the jungles of our modern cities. They do not trust in the sovereignty of the masses; in the majority decision of these, one cannot trust. The masses are not masters of themselves; therefore to hand the government over to them would be the dissolution of culture and order. The masses have no dignity and therefore no gift of distinction; they are an easy prey of faithless and selfish demagogues who lead them into anarchy. These conservative thinkers take Aristotle's definition of democracy literally; it is a degeneration of *politeia*.

This attitude loves the soil and the forests, the farms and the old small towns, the guilds of the Middle Ages. It is suspicious of the multimillionaires and the crowded industrial cities and the vast uniform masses of labor unions and the power of their bosses. It is distrustful of the many mass organizations before which the individual is not less impotent than he was earlier before the power of the absolute prince. It does not admire the machines and the machine-produced mass civilization, and its literature.

The conservative mind dislikes capitalism which denies that the absolute factory monarch has any social responsibility for the workers. To the conservative, capitalism has substituted for the master-servant relation, surrounded and permeated by mutual trust, loyalty, and responsibility, a cold labor contract supposedly regulating the sale of labor power between free individuals, but actually subjecting the laborer to a cruel and irresponsible rule of the profit motive of corporate money-power. The conservative mind spurns the egalitarian propositions of capitalism because it contends that capitalism, in spite of assumed democratic equality, produces by no means equality but a hideous economic hierarchy based on mere economic success without regard to moral values. It points out that democracy as the fertile soil of capitalism is only an illusory trapping for the inhuman tyranny of capital instead of the benevolent paternal rule of a monarch responsible to divine and natural law. Never has liberty existed more securely than under a pious king.[11]

This attitude may produce a gentle cynicism, but it will never produce an agnostic; for it believes that Church and religion form an essential part of time and so share its honor. The Church is to the conservative mind the greatest conservative power. The Church is the continuous admonition that there are higher values than profits and material pleasure. The Church's doctrine of original sin makes man aware of the precariousness of material progress, of the weakness of his nature; it shows the impossibility of the autonomy of the individual, and the futility of all attempts to surrender the public and moral order to the selfish free interests of free individuals. The Church, the protector of the family, stands high in the conservative mind because the latter values the family more than it does the liberty of the individual or the power of the state. If anyone tries to understand that this attitude is human and always partly justified, he will also better understand many antidemocratic and antiliberalist utterances of a Gregory XVI, a Pius IX, a Taparelli. Though perhaps extreme in their expression, they form strains of thought that are a part of Catholic political philosophy, which is as conservative as it is liberal.

[11] Cardinal Newman had many of these conservative features. Though he declined the theories of De Maistre, Veuillot, and William G. Ward concerning the theological doctrine of the sovereignty of the pope and the scope of his infallibility and stressed the rights and duties of individual conscience, he feared the rise of democracy in the sense of liberalism. (W. Ward, *Life of Cardinal Newman*, II, 118, 513.) In his famous *Letter to the Duke of Norfolk* (Works, 1896, II, 268) he confesses: "No one can dislike the democratic principle more than I do. . . . All I know is that Toryism, that is, loyalty to persons, springs immortal in the human breast." In the same letter may be found the most perfect theory of conscience which the liberal mind is so fond of (p. 246).

VIII. The Liberal Mind

But the edifice of political philosophy in Catholic thought contains also what is called the liberal mind. Since the early nineteenth century, the word "liberal" has received many connotations so that its meaning has become rather vague. But if we take it literally and free it from the polemic meanings which it received when opposed to terms like authority, monarchism, hierarchism, political privilege, or police-state, we may elucidate its true meaning. Then it means "liberty." Yet not an abstract liberty without any limitations and restrictions. On the contrary, it means liberties under the rule of law equal for all. When we ask "whose liberty?" it has further the meaning of individual personal liberty. But likewise it means liberty for the individuals to form, under the protection of law, associations for their freely chosen common purposes. "Liberal," therefore, implies denial of juridical status privileges. In a free state there cannot exist groups which have by law a privileged status from which other persons may be arbitrarily excluded on account of birth, wealth, or other accidental qualities. "Liberal" further means to be free from an overesteem of tradition and of the traditional order in state and society.

Whereas a conservative will be inclined to vote for tradition and order in a conflict between the latter and the demand for progressive justice, the liberal will vote for justice even if that means giving up beloved traditions and risking a threat to the public order. The liberal's mightiest urge is justice *hic et nunc,* not simply stability and static order, because he is convinced that liberty is the creator of justice. Therefore the liberal will eagerly suffer a danger to order if by that he has a good chance to realize a greater justice. He does not deny order, compulsion, authority. But he demands from order that it prove its value especially by being just and not merely long-existing; he demands from compulsion that it prove its unavoidable necessity (as much liberty as possible, as little compulsion as strictly necessary); he demands from authority that it show the rationality and justice of its commands. The liberal seeks to enlarge in social and political life the sphere of consent by persuasion and open discussion as an agreement freely enacted on account of the probability that free agreements offering free discussions of pros and cons have the greatest chance to be just and durable.

On the other hand, he tries to restrict the sphere of domination and compulsion. Agreement and compulsion are means to produce a unity of purpose and of order. The liberal is for as much coordination as possible and for as little subordination as strictly necessary. The famous dictum of the Duke of Lorraine, quoted by Rousseau (*Contrat social*, III, chap. 4 at the end), "I prefer dangerous liberty to quiet servitude," has a liberal ring and corresponds to the modern liberal's preference of liberty to comfortable security if the latter has to be acquired by the loss of liberty or even by a great limitation of liberty.

The liberal, less pessimistic in the concept of human nature than is the conservative, is deeply convinced of the dignity of the individual person, not as an abstract principle but as a fact. His is an unconditional reverence before that dignity in every man. He trusts the human reason, not only *in abstracto* but in every man, because every man's conscience is ordained to justice, and every man has the faculty of reason ordained to truth. That is the reason why he prefers discussion, persuasion, and consent as means for unity. Not that he thinks one opinion is as true as another. He only holds that fundamentally each man, because he is a rational being, has access to objective truth. The liberal does not accept the relativist theory that all opinions are equal because they are all equally right or wrong. Nor does he deny objective truth; he only contends that it is the reasonable soundness in the opinions that matters, and not who utters an opinion. The phrase, this is a government of law not of men, agrees with the liberal mind. For "law" means reason, and "men" means arbitrariness. The loyalty of the liberal is first to social and political ideals, and to persons only as servants or representatives of such ideals. From here issues his outspoken suspicion of those in power and his tendency to formalize the use of power, to supervise it, to subject it to checks and balances. Monarchy rests either on the mysticism of the better blood of the royal family or on a theory of divine right or on a patrimonial theory according to which the royal house, similar to a father, owns the state, or finally on tradition. But the liberal mind wishes his government to rest on reason and consent.

Consequently the liberal has a strong preference for the democratic form of government and is prone to social reform. When he uses the word "democracy" he means more than the techniques, the juridical constitutional forms. He means two things: republican government of and by the people, i.e., the immediate democracy of Swiss cantons, or representative democracy where the supreme power of legislative and executive power is delegated in free elections and where nobody has a formal right to political offices on account of legal privileges or birth or wealth and where perpetuity and heredity in the highest offices are legally excluded. Democracy, in opposition to monarchy and aristocracy, is thus a state without legally acknowledged privileges. But the liberal mind means more. The bill of rights, with its equality before the law, its equal opportunity, its freedom of religion, of speech, and of association, is even more important. What matters is this sphere of the individual person, of the family, and of the numerous free associations for cultural, educational, and economic purposes, just as much as the constitutional techniques. The reason is that the liberal mind expects so much from individual initiative and reason.

The liberal mind is the great champion of social reform. True, the conservative mind did not like the ravages of capitalism; but it longed for the precapitalist and predemocratic era. If it proposed and enacted social reform, it did so more in the sentiment of a benevolent paternal master who gives by magnanimity or charity or even with a view to getting the security of order by satisfying the most vociferous demands of the masses. To the liberal mind the rights of the socially underprivileged are what matters; justice demands social reform, not magnanimity or charity or prudence. The eternal quest for freedom and social justice does not halt until even the lowest of society has reached a status worthy of man.

The liberal mind thus sketched is quite different from that liberalism which was so severely condemned with its main tenets by the popes in the nineteenth century and after. This liberalism, for instance, in its application to economic life, was against social legislation. It based its demand for freedom of religion on the contention that the doctrine of the Church is superstition. Its demand for compulsory public education was based on the principles of secular rationalism. Its demand for freedom of conscience was based on the thesis that conscience is the individual's moral autonomy subject to none but itself and is not "the aboriginal Vicar of Christ . . . the messenger of Him, who, both in nature and grace, speaks to us behind a veil, and teaches and rules us by His representatives." [12] This liberalism, destroying in its autonomous ethics the universal moral law, denying in its principle of indifferentism religious truth and revelation, denying the rules of social justice in economic life with an appeal to supposedly immutable economic laws; this liberalism, which revels in the final secularization of our society and derides the old principle that the union of man with God is the union of man with man and that common brotherhood originates in the common father,[13] this is the liberalism with which the popes rightfully declined to be reconciled.

The liberal mind is subject to extremes as is the conservative mind. The latter might be induced to defend traditional forms even though they have become brittle prisons for live ideas yearning for a new, more timely external form. The liberal mind, in the quest for perfection, might be tempted to disparage the value of tradition. The conservative might be tempted to judge ecclesiastical policy and the Church in her being a body politic according to her protective assistance to the political and economic interests of the conservative groups; the liberal mind might fall into the modern temptation to judge the Church according to her readiness to serve an incessantly active political and socio-economic reform in the sense of a "social gospel" activism. The conservative mind, too fearful of immoderate growth of state activity by expanding social legislation, might forget the quest for social justice, while the liberal mind, in an unconditional quest for social justice and economic security, might underrate the growth of state activity and its intrinsic danger to the liberal ideals.[14]

[12] Cf. the immortal pages of Cardinal Newman in his *Letter to the Duke of Norfolk*, chap. 5.

[13] See, for instance, Harold Laski, *Reflections on the Revolutions of Our Time* (New York, 1943) pp. 196 f.

[14] The history of social and political thought since the French Revolution reveals those incessant discussions between the conservatives and the liberals under various names: from De Maistre and De Bonald versus Montalembert and Lacordaire to the *Action française* versus the *Sillon* in France, Lord Acton versus W. G. Ward in England; the Christian social reform movement (M. Gladbach, Center Party, Christian trade unions) versus Integralists (Berliner Richtung) in Germany; Don Sturzo versus Gemelli before the rise of Fascism in Italy and shortly thereafter. In our days both attitudes are revealed each in its position toward the Beveridge Report; the one critical, the other rather enthusiastic.

Political philosophy in Catholic thought with its constitutive polar system will, through all its eras, show a conservative and a liberal strain; it will depend upon the particular circumstances of an era which of them will be more outspoken. Furthermore, each of them keeps the other from falling into extremes. The continuous defense and attack that each needs and makes against the other prevents either from monopolizing political philosophy. But the student who by temperament and circumstances is inclined to the liberal pole, will do well to deepen his acquaintance with the ideas and arguments of the representatives of the conservative pole, like Taparelli, Donoso Cortes, and De Maistre. The student who is inclined to the conservative pole will avoid inflexibility, complacency with the existing imperfect order if he seeks counsel from the liberals. If such is not done, then we will experience the sorry spectacle of the conservatives, who, having lost the *distinctio christiana,* will uncritically accept any political doctrine and regime because it calls itself antidemocratic, antiliberal, authoritarian, as it has happened in our time with an uncritical praise for the different Fascist regimes. Or we may experience the equally sorry spectacle of liberals losing also the *distinctio christiana* and forgetting that social progress and secular happiness are not enough as the goal of life. We may see them, with uncritical enthusiasm for social reform, approve a strictly planned economy in which liberty becomes all too easily the price which has to be paid for full social and economic security. Theirs is the danger of Martha, of an excessive esteem for the active virtues, of being absorbed with the reform of conditions and losing sight of the one thing necessary.

IX. The Common Good as the Basis for the Legitimacy of Political Authority

According to our discussion, the people holds the constituent power, that authority and right to give itself a specific form of government, of political unity and existence. In the act of constituting itself a distinct, self-conscious political identity, the people simultaneously perfects its will to live together in a constitutional organization with or without a written document. But once this new constitutional order is founded in order to realize the concrete common good, once the citizens, by their formal or informal consensus to live together in a more perfect life, have established this new social order, then this order becomes an objective moral obligation by its very nature and legitimacy as an order to realize the common good. Thus "popular sovereignty" cannot mean absolute authority, arbitrary power, freedom from the obligations of natural and divine law. Even the majority will of a democracy is not by itself absolute authority. Neither to a pope nor to a king nor to a democratic majority does man as a rational being owe absolute obedience. The legitimacy of a constituted authority does not rest in itself. It is and must be based on something objective, independent of varying subjective and potentially faulty wills, free from the arbitrariness of one tyrant or five hundred tyrants. And in the last analysis this objective rule of legitimacy is the common good in its actual shape as a moral status of a more perfect life according to God's will revealed in man's nature and in natural and divine law.

The discussion about the best form of government is somewhat abstract if it does not refer to the relatively best form of government for the individual nation. Such discussion must concern itself with the realization of the common good of a particular nation with full appreciation of its geographic location, its economic basis of life, its national traditions, its particular cultural development, and all other such elements that establish the nation's individuality. A supposedly general discussion of the best form of government in the abstract sense means often not more than the disguised promotion of a particular theory of legitimacy. What matters is that each nation should find the constitutional form of government that fits its individuality and lets it thus realize *hic et nunc* the order of the common good, the objective and supreme standard of legitimacy.

In historic reality there will always exist a danger that the common good of all will not coincide with the particular interests of the ruling class, of the representative group that exists in every people on account of its social and economic organization. The moral nature of politics demands inexorably that whenever the common good and the particular interests of this ruling group do not coincide, these interests have to yield before the paramount common good. Political tranquillity is a sign of such a historical coincidence. Political unrest is the indisputable sign that for broad masses of the people such a coincidence is absent. Thus the common good is subordinated wrongly to the interests of the ruling or representative group as it naturally exists under whatever form of government, even under the most egalitarian socialist democratic form, however nicely it may be disguised as the vanguard of the proletariat.

In the face of a manifest and irreconcilable contradiction between objective common good and subjective interest of the ruling group, the common good must and will prevail. The consequent revolution is ultimately only the last stage in a process that began when that contradiction became irreconcilable on account of the selfish resistance of the "interests." And the legitimacy of the revolution and of the new groups which it brings to the fore is the more perfect realization of the common good and a new coincidence of the "interests" of the new ruling groups with the perennial objective common good. The new order thus finds its legitimacy, not in a "successful high treason," but in the consent of the people to the new form of realizing the common good. It is the people and its common good which live in durable identity under all the changes of constitutional law and social organization as the substance, as the body politic. The state, in this full sense as the *forma populi,* is more than its constitutional law and its administrative organs, which the jurist and the political scientist all too simply think to be the state. The state, as unity and order of and in the people, living through civil wars and revolutions, through defeats in battle, and the humiliations of conquest, is the indomitable will of the people to be itself, to live in security and independence. A nation is a political unity not only through its order of law but also through its consistent will to live together. It is this will, led by the paramount moral ideas, which logically is primary to positive law and constitutional form, though this will can realize itself only in the form of legal order.

Thus this will to the common good is perennial, but the actual forms of constitutional law, the forms of government, are variable. The state lives in the law, it never lives outside the law; but it is not merely the law nor does it live through the law. The state lives ultimately through the political virtues of its citizens, through justice and charity toward all, through the spirit of mutual help and sacrifice for the common good. "State" means not only a guaranty of rights, it means no less the eager acceptance of duties. The majesty and dignity which even a most democratic people gives its legislative, executive, and judiciary authorities, the symbols and solemnities with which it surrounds them, all point to political authority as the servant of the great moral ideas. We owe obedience, not because the authority commands, but because through the commands of authority shine the moral ideas, the will of God, through whom the kings rule. Only through the ultimate founding of authority and obedience on God Almighty, Creator and end of the moral universe, are the dignity of man and the moral nature of the state preserved.

PART III

CHURCH AND STATE

CHAPTER XXII

The Meaning of "Church"

I. *Libertas Ecclesiae*

IF IN any pair of words, then surely in this one are embraced the greatest and profoundest motifs of human community life. For many centuries these words formed the headlines over the most exciting chapters of political history, stirred generation after generation before which this same problem was put and is put anew today. The eras of political history are, indeed, distinguished according to their attempts, successes, and failures in finding their answers to this problem. For, what matters here is not a couple of abstract concepts. What matters here is not religion as a completely private affair of isolated individuals secluded from public life. What matters here is the *Una Sancta*, Christ living in and through a history that counts its periods of years before and after His birth. What matters here is the Church universal, the objective Christian religion as a living force, as the essential public form of Christian religion; Church is this one, Catholic, and Apostolic Church, having the promise that "He" will be with it till the end of time. An exciting word it is, the end of time, the death of history, the final emergence of the kingdom of God beyond the accidents of time and space. Church: that is additionally in a particular sense the Catholic Church, which lives beyond the narrow individualization of mankind in nations, races, and civilizations; the universal Church, the membership in which is based on human nature. Church means that hidden and public life of the saints and of the religious orders; it means the dogma and the sacramental life of the faithful in the form of the hierarchical order and of the rules of canon law that establish the Church as an independent perfect society, the visible community of the faithful.

The Church is the most powerful social form of history on earth, wise with a wisdom acquired in more than nineteen centuries, a wisdom accumulated in a continuous endeavor against those who out of sectarian individualism strove for new forms and norms of religious life, only to be secularized in the true sense or to hark back to her, the mother of the Churches, above all the thrones and the powers of the world. This Church is anything else but state, though it has always been imitated by the political powers. Again and again the states have tried to use for their finite political ideas the uniqueness and superiority of the Church, they have tried to copy the imperial power and the hierarchic majestic order, the absoluteness of its divinely instituted dogmas and morals. There were at all times and there are still in the world of states, those who aped Rome; they were and are always the mortal enemies of Rome.

Thus it is not religion in an abstract, generalized, and therefore empty sense that forms the problem. And it is not the many separated Christian communities that are the real problem. The real problem in universal history has been and still is the very old and ever present *libertas ecclesiae* of a Church which from her very beginning knew that she was universal, not a Church for the Jews, the Greeks, the citizens of Rome, but a Church where there is neither Jew nor barbarian, neither free nor slave (Gal. 3:28). A Church, therefore, that jealously watched against any kind of Erastianism, a Church that fought against emperors, kings, and democratic parliaments for her liberty and preferred this liberty to subservient establishment as a department of the omnipotent state.

II. The Catholic Church the Church *par excellence*

The Roman Church has been looked upon as the exemplary enemy by the states from the early Roman emperors, who showed so much tolerance for the innumerable mystery cults in their dissolving empire, down to modern totalitarians who with an amazing clairvoyance confess: Either Germany or Rome; Moscow or Rome. This anti-Catholic stand of nationalists, militant agnostics, and the Third International shows that the real foremost antagonist to the omnipotent state is the Catholic Church, and thus she is the first to be attacked however brutal the persecution of other Christian Churches may be.

This Church unites in history and reality the divine with the human. She lives apart in the world of the states, yet she enters into the new connections within their changing forms and has ever to fight for her liberty in opposition to them; still she remains the same. She is not a protean institution rambling through history in perpetually changing forms without unchangeable essence. This Church is the *Una Sancta,* the stumbling block of any state that makes itself the absolute. This Church is the *Mater Ecclesia* moving in calm majesty through centuries and over continents, now abused and again venerated, now glorified and again cursed, despised and exalted in turn by "the world" and even at times by her own.

There are not two Churches: A spiritual one, a Church of love, of freely breathing charisma, of pure divinity without the firm forms of dogma and a code of morals and, along with this, another, a mere external form of adaptation to the intrinsically "evil" world, an organized visible institution, a hierarchically ordered perfect society as a Church of legal forms that deals and struggles like a political changeable form with the states, herself becoming consequently a political form, a cultural secular way of life, indifferent to the hidden essence of religion. Had we such a division there would be no real problem in this pair of words. But the *Una Sancta* is both; charisma and dogma, sacramental mystery and hierarchical order and ecclesiastical law, spiritual community of the faithful and visible institution and a perfect society. She counts among her saints the militant statesman, Gregory VII, and the humble friend of men and animals, St. Francis; the great St. Thomas Aquinas, *Doctor ecclesiae* and teacher of the centuries, and the hidden Little Flower in a Carmelite convent, St. Theresa; St. Thomas More, scholarly author of *Utopia,* prudent jurist, stateman, and finally martyr for the *libertas ecclesiae,* together with solitary hermits of the desert, just as she counts among her saints common people from farms and shops, housewives and servants.

This same *Una Sancta,* emerging from the little dissolving Hebrew nation-state, living in the Ghettos and slums of the cities of antiquity as well as in the palaces of senatorial families and in the houses of philosophers, endures persecution in the catacombs till a shrewd emperor, partly to save the crumbling empire, makes her the Church of the realm. From then on, her vocation as Church universal is distinct. The *orbis mundi* becomes now the *orbis christianus.* And it is this Church with which the states and empires must arrange a *modus vivendi* or fight her, in the last resort without success. "The Church is the heiress."

And so this is the great theme of political history: this Church, in the identity of her essence and her mission, with or beside or against the ever-changing political forms of all the nations of the world. To repeat: what matters is not at all an abstract academic problem, that of religion as a natural abstract feature in man's character and its relation to the political sphere, to state, and to society *in abstracto.* What matters is not the logical delimitation of a formal abstract sphere of religion from a likewise formal and abstract sphere of the state. The problem is the endlessly new task for new forms of political life, to encounter the concrete fact of the universal, independent Church, older than any of the states, mightier than any coalition of them, in her end and organization transcendent to them: The Roman Catholic Church, from the beginning not directed to the *polis* but to the *cosmopolis;* she is not a community of worship of a nation or a tribe but of the people of God above nations and tribes though in the midst of them.

Therefore this chapter is confined to the Roman Catholic Church; it is centered round her relation to the diverse historical and national forms of political life. And this limitation implies no contempt for the other, separated Christian communities; because, as far as they contend for the freedom of the Church and for the freedom of conscience, they are exemplifications of the same problem. It would be folly to forget the valiant fight of the Free Churches against the intrusion of the state into the religious sphere just as it would be partial to forget that the Catholic Church had to fight in her own fold against mighty temptations to sacrifice the spiritual good for political power and influence. Gallicanism and such constitutional heresies as Febronianism show clearly enough that the temptations to yield to nationalism were not unknown to parts of the Roman Catholic Church. Yet today the separated Churches find in the Roman Catholic Church their mighty ally against the oppression of modern totalitarianism. And so far as the separated Churches have succumbed to the state, they cannot present an exemplification of this problem at all.

There is here neither room nor opportunity to give a full historical record of this perpetual process of arrangement between Church and state, the protocols and documents of which fill the archives of the states and of the Vatican, just as the scholarly treatments and the violent polemic pamphlets of it fill the libraries. Still the problem itself can best be shown, however sketchily delineated, by some historical phases of its development.

III. The Hierarchical Constitution of the Church

From the first epoch on, until she becomes the Church of the Empire under Constantine the Great, the Church develops her structure and elaborates her constitution on the basis of her divinely instituted sacramental and hierarchical order: a more internal life at the time of the slow process of dissolution of the Roman Empire and the ancient pagan civilization.

The early Church entered a world that comprised the political unity of the Empire welded by Augustus, his proconsuls, and his legions. Yet this Empire was not a unity of law and of religion. The conquered peoples, administered and exploited for tribute, retained their native laws as far as these did not clash with the right and the might of the conqueror. Not until A.D. 212 did the *Lex Antoniniana* under Emperor Caracalla give citizenship to the majority of the inhabitants of the Roman Empire and thus make the Roman law the common law of the Empire; the first time that Roman law conquered the world. Before that, the Jews, for instance, retained their own laws. Pontius Pilate surrendered Christ, in whom he himself could find no guilt, to the Jews who claimed the death penalty on account of their law.

The Roman law now was mostly not a written law; it was rather a judge-made law, created by the genius of the Roman jurists. Thus it early developed along with the strict formal law, the principles of equity that corresponded to legal reason and appeared as common to all men, as a *jus gentium*, a law innate in human reason. Even the sacred law of the gods that originally was the basis of the strict civil law had, at the time of the apostles, become more or less a ritual law for certain functions important for officials and soldiers. Thus Rome was very tolerant of the many cults and mysteries imported from the Orient and Egypt.

This was the legal world in which the early Church arose. But this new religious community was profoundly different from the other manifold cults and mysteries. These were more fashionable substitutes used by a snobbish decaying and skeptical society which long since had lost its traditional religious belief in the national gods. The cults did not embrace the whole of life but were an escape from the emptiness of a soulless urban civilization. But the Church, from the beginning, was no mere casual community of worship which released her members again into the secular sphere full of vices and empty of virtues. She was a total community of life, embracing the whole man in his very spiritual and moral existence. And the norms that were the sovereign rule of the Christian's life were divinely instituted and revealed laws, not transient man-made laws. The apostles, those to whom these laws were revealed, were God-sent. The living faith in redemption from guilt and sin, the blessed certainty of the truths revealed by God Himself concerning man's origin, fall, and salvation, were the basis of these norms; and man, through obedience to them, worked for his final salvation. This all-embracing community of love is to the converted a community of saints, the people of God. This people lives under its own divine order, led by ministers immediately called by God. Through the bishops as the successors of the apostles, under the primacy of the bishop of the Roman congregation and through the presbyters ordained and appointed by the bishops, God's will is revealed in the Church. The Father sent Christ; Christ sent the apostles; these sent the priests. It is not the congregation that transfers the office, nor can it deprive the priests of office.[1]

Such is the gist of Clement's *Letter to the Corinthians*. The Pope refers to the faithful as soldiers in God's army against the enemies of Christ. In the army there is authority, order, and subordination. The Christians are members of the mystical body of Christ; among members there is order and subordination. And this order, these authorities in hierarchical succession, are instituted by God. "He who follows the rules set up by the Lord remains without erring on the right path." [2] Thus this letter shows the constitution of the Church as already existing, and it likewise shows Rome as the center of the Church universal. Hence the Roman bishop settles a dispute that arises in the Corinthian community, when young men, under plea of a personal charismatic gift and applauded by some of the easily excited

[1] First letter of Pope Clement to the Corinthians, chap. 42.
[2] *Ibid.*, chap. 40.

members of the Corinthian congregation, removed the resident presbyters (priests) who had been invested with their office by the bishop.

Three decisive properties of the Church are thus already visible which later become more evident throughout the history of the Church. The Church is a visible community of divinely revealed faith with a constitution of divine law and therefore unalterable by the will of the congregations. The hierarchical order is established at the beginning of the Church's formation in the first, still enthusiastic period. The Church has never been, even initially, an anarchic sect of enthusiasts but rather a clearly organized community of worship with law and ministerial succession of offices. The "ministers" are not elected by the congregations even though an acclamation may have taken place. The spiritual authority is from Christ transferred directly to the apostles by ordination "from above," and the hierarchy of the ordained consists of the competent interpreters and bearers of the apostolic spirit; they are the inheritance of God. Equally distinctive, along with the rule of faith and the hierarchical constitution of the sacerdotal order, is the spiritual authority, the title of the Roman bishop to primacy. St. Ignatius of Antioch points this out when he writes: "Where the bishop is, there should be the congregation; just as where Christ is, there is the Catholic Church," in which the Church of Rome and its bishop hold the supreme authority.[3] "Catholic," "universal," Ignatius called the Church. The Church has thus even a greater amplitude than the Empire. The Church's congregations are in Italy and in Asia Minor, in Egypt and in the Iberian Peninsula, in North Africa, in Gaul, and at the banks of the Rhine.

But this was what prompted the pagan Roman Empire to persecute the Catholic Church more than any of the many religions in the realm. Under the emperors Decius and Valerian in the middle of the third century this persecution reached its height when the Emperors saw in the Church a state within the state, a state that did not consider the Emperor the Lord and God, that rejected the sacred law of the Roman Empire by refusing compliance with the pagan, sacramental forms of worship of the Emperor-God and instead declared its own

---

[3] St. Ignatius, *To the Smyrnaeans*, chap. 8. Cyprian (Ep., 48, 3): Rome is the *ecclesiae catholicae matrix et radix*. For the primacy of the Church of Rome and of the *cathedra Petri*, cf. P. Battifol, *L'église naissante et le Catholicisme* (9th ed., Paris, 1927); Karl Adam, "Die Ursprünge der Primatslehre" in *Tübinger theol. Quartalschrift*, 1928, pp. 161–265; H. Dieckmann, *De Ecclesia* (Friburgi, 1925).

spiritual law to be divine. This reproach has since then been repeated again and again, and it is unavoidable for the Church as a visible unity of divine law and spiritual independence. The reproach of a double and therefore doubtful allegiance is and will be reiterated wherever the state invades the proper sphere of the Church or where the state makes itself total and absolute. Only a visible Church, as a perfect society, can be open to this kind of blame. An invisible Church, a mere spiritual unity without visible legal constitution, is not a problem at all once the right of the individual person to follow his own conscience in the sphere of private life is conceded.

In these first centuries the Church turned to the practice of every-day work. She rejected the disintegrating doctrines of the Gnosis, which the ancient philosophy had tried in many ways to smuggle into the body of doctrine. By this very struggle against the first heresies she had defined and clarified her teaching in dogma and morals. The world had now ceased to be an indifferent matter for the Christian, as compared to earlier times. The world, the professions and vocations, the family and the state, become the fields in which, by obedience to God's laws, the Christian works for his salvation; the practical pastoral task has to devise more and particular rules for the spiritual and social life of the Christian in the world. Before St. Augustine thus is born the idea of the Church as the City of God, living, though itself of divine law, among the many cities of men, which are of mere human law. The Church arms herself for the sanctification of the secular framework of man's life in this world as the providentially arranged way to eternal happiness.

IV. The Rise of the Problem of Church and State

Constantine was converted to Christianity to no small degree because he thought it possible and even necessary to prop the tottering framework of the decrepit Empire, which was drained of all vital power by pagan skepticism and hopeless melancholy by calling on the new powers that radiated from the Church into the world and society. Thus the Church finally emerges from the catacombs, whether from the real ones or from the figurative catacombs of a merely tolerated, private existence, and steps beside the state or even into it as the recognized honored Church of the realm. Here begins the

struggle for the liberty and independence of the Church, a struggle
that never since has ceased.

Over the wreckage of the ancient world civilization, over the
Church that, through the mischance of opportunist mass conversions,
threatens to become a means to the political ends of the emperors and
their imperial ambitions, over the Church torn by great heresies that
are in some measure but masks for political ambitions, of which
Arianism is a striking example, hovers the spirit of the great African
Bishop of Hippo, St. Augustine. Rich himself with the treasures of
ancient culture, he looks sadly into the present; for the picture he
sees is wretched. And when he looks forward there is little promise
and much despair. So he unburdens his mind in his *Civitas Dei,* one
of the few books that have shaped history. This, the first Christian
philosophy of history contains, too, the first expression of Christian
political philosophy. There is only one way of salvation for the state:
to become truly Christian. As a purely secular state it will lapse from
bad to worse, driven by unbridled ambitions and lust for power. It
is itself in want of a supporting, hallowing order, of the *Civitas Dei.*
Only if the new realm rests upon Christianity as the successor to the
Old Testament theocracy, only if the state sees its aim to be the realization of justice in the service of God, only then can a new life flourish.

If the state should serve only secular ends, it would succumb to
the temptations of selfish glory and wanton lust for power and thus
become nothing but a big organized band of gangsters (*magnum
latrocinium*). Then only is the Emperor the best preserver of the
Realm when he is the first servant of the Church. Peace, order, and
justice have no separate natural existence; they can truly be realized
only by the knowledge of God and in His service, as the Church
teaches. Not by the power of nature, so terribly wounded by original
sin, can the Realm be built, but only by reliance on God's revealed
truth, dispensed by this Church.

There is undeniably a theocratic strain in St. Augustine's political
philosophy resting on his pessimism about human nature. With respect to the naturally good character of social and political life, his
philosophy led to an undervaluation that had to be corrected by the
less pessimistic outlook of St. Thomas. St. Augustine's theocratism
could easily lead and has led to the idea that the state's mission is
wholly subordinated to the Church, even that it is a function of the

Church. No wonder that out of the *Civitas Dei* grew the political ideal of the Middle Ages: Christianity, the *mundus Christianus,* as an all-embracing unity. Thence arose the political problems of the Middle Ages, those of the new Roman Empire with the Church. One of the consequences of this conception was the struggle between the emperor, who even as a faithful Christian was yet tempted to become Caesar and pope, and the pope, who must not become a mere court chaplain of the Emperor. The pope must thus fight for the *libertas ecclesiae;* on the other hand, in the structure of the medieval Christian world, he lived in the temptation of trying to become emperor and thus reduce the emperor to a dependent secular arm without true sovereignty and independence.

The perpetual struggle between emperor and pope—"emperor" here is only a symbol for secular order or law, state, and lay power— now begins. Again and again jurists and philosophers develop systems of a peaceful and well ordered symbiosis or of a clean separation of Church and state without any political interdependence. But in actual life there remains always a sphere of matters that are common to both, however much they may devote themselves to their own fields as delimited by their specific objective ends. If both recognize their specific fields, the real problem is this field where civil life coincides with religious life, as in education, in matrimony, i.e., where man as a citizen has duties to the state, and as a believer to the Church, in matters that are claimed and actually regulated by both. Here conflicts of duties and loyalties may arise for the Christian citizen.

The problem is: Who decides how far a matter is common? And how is this question to be settled? The answer to that question, however philosophical or theological the foundation may be, is in actuality a political problem because it is concerned with the living order in social life. If both parties are of good will and of mutual understanding, ready to cooperate for the good of men who are citizens of both, then concord will find a solution or at least a peaceful *modus vivendi.* If one of the parties refuses,—and it is mostly the state that does so— the question becomes one of power: the state uses its material power and secularist philosophies, perhaps disguised as a pseudo-religious ideology; the Church, relying on the Lord's promise to be with her, defends her rights, not always successfully, not always prudently, until a new *modus vivendi* or a new concord can be agreed upon. Thus the theoretical problem is accompanied by the practical political problem of realizing the perennial ideal in changing forms of living together. Even the clear separation of state and Church, though it simplifies the practical problem, raises the new problem: What happens to the secular state if the Christian inheritance of its citizen is definitely pushed into the sphere of private life, and public life is thus completely dechristianized, with no longer a Christian atmosphere?

Even under the rule of separation the problem becomes complicated when the liberal state, with the principle of the least possible intervention, is by the development of social integration compelled to intervene more and more in the field of the supposedly free society. A point may easily be reached where that intervention touches the recognized sphere of the Church. Thus even the most friendly policy of separation may again face the old problem: Who decides what is essentially a spiritual matter, and how shall the common matters be regulated? As long as the Church believes in her public mission and feels that she is a visible witness and a spiritual yet perfect community, she cannot leave this answer simply to the state, nor can she leave the answer to the final decision of an outside arbiter. She must decide in conjunction with the state. The *libertas ecclesiae,* the independence of the order of the canon law, the true sovereignty of the pope, representing the Church, these cannot be given up without surrendering the mission of the Church. Between Church and state or whatever may be the combination of names, there exists a system of relations that from time to time needs a concordat, an agreement regulating the matters common to both with respect of their mutual independent competence in the order specific to each. If such a concordat or *modus vivendi* is not possible, the result will be a struggle for the *libertas ecclesiae* against the state, which changes from being a partner or a neutral into being a persecutor.

On the facts just mentioned is based the contention that, in the last analysis, it is the Catholic Church that is usually meant in the expression "Church and state." She has taken up the fight for the *libertas Ecclesiae* after each defeat and restored that *libertas.* The Eastern Church and so many separated Churches have succumbed to the subjugation of the Church to supposedly Christian rulers in more or less open Erastianism. However much and often the papal Church may have fallen into the temptation of acquiescence to control by the state, her history is richer in victories over this temptation and the tempters than in defeats and momentary surrenders. This fact gives to the Roman Church that power to attract to reunion, for she tries to unite the separated Churches though none of them tries seriously to win over the Roman Church.

V. Types of Relationship of Church and State

Without exaggerating the dynamic course of history, we may distinguish, in the perpetual quest for the due arrangement between Church and state since the decline of antiquity, six main eras with many mixed forms. First period: the struggle of the Church for her liberty against the attempts at identification of Empire and Church on the part of the rulers of the Western and the Eastern Roman Empire after Constantine. This identification finally succeeded in Byzantium after the schism and from there found its Erastian form in the Orthodox Church of Russia till the downfall of Czarism. In the Western part of the Empire the great popes, such as Innocent I, Leo the Great, Gelasius I, and Gregory the Great, successfully defended the liberty and independence of the Church from the Empire and of the pope from the emperor, with the galaxy of such divines as St. Ambrose, Hosius of Cordoba, and St. Augustine, assisted by the faithful doctors of the East, such as St. Athanasius and St. John Chrysostom. The Ambrosian principle, that even the most Christian emperor is *in* the Church but not *over* the Church (*Sermo contra Auxentium*, 36; Migne, *PL*, XVI, 1061) was upheld successfully during this struggle lasting three centuries against Byzantine Caesaropapism, which puts the emperor of divine right over the Church as the *autocrator* in both the spiritual and the secular field of the one Christian Empire and the imperial Church.

Second period: the Church, almost succumbing to the Empire's sovereignty, with the pope almost becoming a dependent court bishop, is finally liberated by the successful contest of Gregory VII for the liberty of the Church. Third period: an era in which the Christian world, for a short time at least, is ruled by the *plenitudo potestatis* of the pope as the lord of that *orbis Christianus* supported by the canonists, only to lose rather suddenly that exalted position and fall under the power of France, the first national state in the Middle

Ages, in the so-called Babylonian captivity at Avignon. This period is marked by Innocent III and Boniface VIII and the transfer of the Apostolic See to Avignon; it ends with the double dissolution of the *mundus Christianus:* politically with the emergence of sovereign nation-states and sovereign territorial states of absolute princes; and religiously with the Reformation and the final establishment of separated Churches often becoming national Churches. These are the marks of the fourth period.

The fifth period begins with the bourgeois revolutions, with the rise of the secularist civilization of the new ruling classes, when the state has ceased to be Christian and has become, in relation to religion, indifferent, militantly laic, or simply neutral. After World War I, the first period of a world revolution the outcome of which is still undecided, the sixth period starts with the rise of modern racial, nationalist, or proletarian totalitarianism. In the Middle Ages the state was Christian, Catholic; after the Reformation the state was at first strictly denominational under absolutism, following the political principle: *Cujus regio ejus religio,* a token that homogeniety in religion of the subjects was still considered the basis of civic loyalty and of political existence. With the ideas of personal liberty, freedom of conscience and of worship, so old but yet newly and differently founded, first the tolerant state emerges. It is still Christian so far as it recognizes the different Christian churches as public institutions of equal rights or at least tolerates those that are not expressly state Churches (established Churches).

Later, with the progress of secularization and after the futile attempts at a united state Church and under pressure of the dissenting sects or Churches, the neutral state emerges. Religion is no longer of importance as a basis for political homogeneity. The neutral state introduces the separation of Church and state either resulting in a peaceful *modus vivendi* safeguarding the liberty of the Church as, for instance, in the United States, or turning anti-Church under the disguise of anticlericalism. Thus it transforms the political expediency of separation into a philosophy of indifferentism, and introduces a third denomination, a new political and civic pseudo-religion in the form of agnostic secularism, in public life as it occurred in the Third Republic in France, or of religious and philosophical Liberalism in Italy since late in the nineteenth century and in Spain from

1931 to 1938. In these countries Latin freemasonry was the leader in the fight. However, at the same time there evolved a process of general secularization more and more transforming modern society, traditionally still living on its Christian inheritance, into a less Christian and a more and more non-Christian status. There are still Christians in this case, but there is no Christian society. The result is modern civilization, positivist, antitheological, purely secular, given utterly to material progress and a thousand diverse philosophies. But the human soul and the soul of a people have a true *horror vacui* in regard to the religious sphere. Thus the new totalitarian beliefs, sham substitutes for religion which has ceased to animate the framework of human society, find the stage prepared. The perpetual problem of Church and state enters its last and most decisive era, the outcome of which in the individual states is either a rebirth of Christianity and with it of all things that dignify man and make human life worth-while, or the emergence of the godless mass state of human robots and slaves working for empty ideals of a millennial earthly paradise under the senseless domination of limitless dictatorship.

The great theologians and philosophers, in their voluminous works and profound theories, delineate the history of this development, but not as partisans like the legists or the curialists who pleaded for political issues. The theologians and philosophers try rather by cool reasoning and hard thinking to state the problem and to find the solution from theology and natural law, from political philosophy. Bright examples are St. Thomas Aquinas, Suarez, Bellarmine, Leo XIII, Pope, philosopher and statesman in one, and Pius XI the Pope of the interregnum bridging the bloody phases of the world revolution, the two world wars.

CHAPTER XXIII

Church and State in the Era of Faith

I. THE FIGHT AGAINST CAESAROPAPISM

AFTER the establishment of Christianity as the public religion in the Empire of Constantine (311), the first struggle for the *libertas ecclesiae* begins with the Caesaropapist efforts of the new Christian emperors in both halves of the Empire: in the Western part (Rome) and in the Eastern part (Byzantium). In the latter Caesaropapism finally wins after the great schism and so concerns us no further in our discussions, however interesting may be its history from the standpoint of the perennial problem of Church and state. The great bishops and patriarchs of Byzantium (St. Athanasius, St. John Chrysostom, St. John Damascene), who fought as valiantly as did the great Western doctors against this Erastian identification of *sacerdotium* and *imperium,* of the temporal and the spiritual power, could not avert this Caesaropapism that eventually died in the bloody throes of the Bolshevist revolution. From here Eastern Christianity may arise again with its valuable theological wisdom, its colorful rites, and its profound mystical tradition.

But in the West the fight was successful against these Caesaropapist efforts of Christian emperors who were still too much subject to the idea of a certain divinity claimed by their pagan predecessors. Here that atrophying of life, spiritual and political, so characteristic of Byzantium, never occurred. Here, under the leadership of the See of Rome and, at times of weaknesses and defeats in this See, under the leadership of great theologians and bishops, the fight against the encroachments of Caesaropapism was repeatedly resumed. Here the theoretical weapons for mastering this eternal problem of the mutual relation between Church and state were forged and improved, not without the help of Eastern ecclesiastics, like St. Athanasius.

Only the peaks of this development can be treated here, without pretense of completeness or just distribution of accent in the importance of the peaks here brought before the reader. As we said in a previous chapter, the history of this problem is so extensive and intricate because, since the coming of Christ, all history is permeated by the history of the Church, the most gripping part of universal history; not without reason do we measure historical time in years before and after Christ.

Without doing injustice to any of the Church Fathers, we may say that the most important formulation of the problem of Church and state was made by St. Ambrose. A scion of old senatorial nobility and a consul for the Italian provinces of Liguria and Aemilia, Ambrose by the acclamation of the electorate was made Bishop of Milan as successor of the Arian Auxentius, before he was even baptized, though he had received a Christian education. During his episcopate the Western Roman emperors resided mostly in his diocese. Thus he had the opportunity as well as the duty of maintaining the freedom of the Church universal whenever imperial ambitions endangered it. In spiritual matters, Ambrose explains, a layman, even the emperor, has no authority or competence. In that realm authority belongs to the bishops even over the Christian emperors.[1] To the emperor belong the palaces, to the priest the Church. The Church is thus independent in her creed, in her sacred law, and in her properties devoted to worship. Ambrose rejects vehemently the theory that the emperor is the living law (*lex animata*), that the emperor has by divine right an absolute political power over all matters spiritual and temporal. The pagan philosopher Themistius had propounded the thesis that the Deity had sent down from heaven the imperial authority upon earth, in order that men might appeal from the immovable rigid law to a law that breathes and lives.[2] Thus the emperor's will would be law upon earth in the Church as well as in the state, as Emperor Constantine actually contended when he said: "Whatever I will, that is to be considered a canon" (ecclesiastical law).[3] He considered himself the law, spiritual and secular.

Ambrose refutes this theory of Caesaropapism and says that the emperor is in the Church, not over the Church, and that, even when he

[1] *Ep.* 21; Migne, *PL*, XVI, 1046.

[2] Cf. E. R. Goodenough, "The Political Philosophy of Hellenistic Kingship," *Yale Classical Studies*, I (1928), 94 ff.

[3] St. Athanasius, *Histor. Arian*, chap. 33; Migne, *PG*, XXV, 732.

legislates in his temporal field, he is not entirely *legibus solutus;* he is subject not only to the divine laws but also to his own conscience which tells him to keep the laws; for the objective application of the law, once the law is made, must not be prevented by the caprices and arbitrariness of the emperor.[4] The great Ambrose addresses Theodosius thus: "It is not worthy of the emperor to deny the freedom of speech, or of a bishop not to say what he thinks. Nothing makes you emperors so beloved as your regard for the freedom even of those who owe you military obedience. For this is the difference between the good and the bad princes, that the good love liberty while the bad love servitude. Nothing is to the priest so dangerous before God and so ignominious before men as not to say freely what he thinks." [5] The *libertas christiana* and the proud consciousness of the spiritual power, of ecclesiastical independence, are combined in these words.

The next peak in the theoretical development of this problem occurs with Pope Gelasius I (492–496). In his famous treatises about the two powers, Gelasius had already, when deacon and secretary of Pope Felix III, in the great letter of 488 pointed out that the emperor is not the lord of the Church but the son of the Church. He continued that the emperor cannot intervene in the spiritual order, for here the priests, not the secular power are competent. When he was Pope, in his famous letter to Emperor Anastasius, he developed the theory of the two powers as it is commonly known. The famous sentences of that letter have been quoted and interpreted in every discussion of the problem of Church and state, from the early Middle Ages down to the Gallican disputes and modern scientific discussions.[6]

"Two things there are by which the world is ruled, the sacred authority of the pope and the royal power. Christ has ordered different dignities and duties to the offices of each power . . . so that the Christian emperors need the pontiffs for the things that pertain to everlasting life, while these need the imperial dispositions for the course of things temporal." Here the independence and the liberty of the Church as a *potestas* [7] at least equal to that of the state is clearly

---

[4] *Ep.* 21; Migne, *PL*, XVI, 1047: *Apol. Proph. David*, I, 77.

[5] *Ep.* 40 (Ad Theodosium); Migne, *PL*, XVI, 1148.

[6] A wealth of literature on this subject is given by Erich Caspar, *Geschichte des Papsttums* (1933), II, 749 ff. For the text of the letters, see Migne, *PL*, LIX, 42.

[7] There has been an attempt to ascribe a specific meaning to the distinction between "sacred authority" and "royal power." However much *auctoritas* and *potestas* may be

established, and so is the conclusion that to each is assigned a specific sphere, the spiritual religious sphere to the Church, the temporal secular sphere to the state. The whole problem from now on is the distinction between these spheres, the subordination of their specific matters under each of them; and then the problem of the mixed matters, matters that by their very nature may belong to both powers, for instance, education or matrimony. It may be noted that, after the victory of religious individualism and the principle of separation of Church and state, the problem remains, but it is now the right of freedom of worship as an inalienable right of the person which in the constitutional law of the religiously neutral state is the basis for the distinction. Freedom of worship implies an obligation of the secular power to abstain strictly from any interference in the religious sphere, this abstention being thus the formal presupposition of that inalienable right. For the Church, of course, this right is not one against the spiritual authority, its constitution and its law, but a protective limitation against the state, although this principle also forbids the state to offer the use of the secular power in the interest of the spiritual power and for the protection of the dogmas and discipline against apostates and heretics who are citizens or residents of the state. Thus in the neutral state this right serves as a basis for the liberty of the Church against state intervention. This right, in the form of freedom of the faithful from the state, offers the freedom of the Church from the state.

---

distinguished in ancient Roman constitutional law (cf. R. Heinze in *Hermes*, LX, 348), the distinction disappears early in the Christian era. Cyprian uses *potestas* and *auctoritas* without distinction. Cf. H. Koch, *Cathedra Petri* (1930), p. 55, note 1. And Gelasius speaks of *utraque potestas* and during the Middle Ages it was always *duo potestates*. For the power of the pope, of the Church, and of the king, St. Thomas consistently uses the word *potestas* and not *auctoritas*. Boniface VIII in *Unam Sanctam* (Denz., nos. 468 ff.) uses *spiritualis potestas* and *terrena potestas*, and says: *Oportet autem . . . et temporalem auctoritatem spirituali subjici potestati*. In Late Scholasticism only *potestas* is used. Cf. Bellarmine, *De potestate Summi Pontificis;* Carerius Alexander Petavinus, *De potestate Romani Pontificis*. An exception is Cajetan, *Commentarii de comparatione auctoritatis papae et concilii*. However, Gerson, Herveus Natalis, Quidort, Joh. Parisiensis, and most authors from the fifteenth century on use *potestas*. Leo XIII also consistently uses *potestas ecclesiae* and *potestas civilis*, as a perusal of his encyclicals will show. In the canon law (Codex, can. 218) it is said that the pope has sovereign and full power (*supremam et plenam potestatem jurisdictionis*) as concerns faith and morals, discipline and government. This *potestas* is independent *a quavis humana auctoritate*. The alleged distinction between *auctoritas* (of the Church) and *potestas* (of the state) seems thus without specific meaning.

II. Conversion of the Germanic Tribes

While the Eastern patriarchate, from the Caesaropapism of Justinian on, gradually lost its freedom and, after its separation from Rome, definitely became a dependency of the state, the Roman pontiffs succeeded in preserving the necessary independence of the religious sphere in the organized papal Church. Just before the shaky political structure of the Empire bordering the Mediterranean collapsed before the tribes of the barbarian invasions, Gregory the Great sent his missioners to England. From there the conversion of the Germanic tribes beyond the Roman frontiers could be initiated. So a new Christian Europe was prepared in the homelands of those Germanic tribes that, first as mercenary soldiers and generals and then as masters, had come to the world of Roman civilization. At the cradle of this new Europe, of these new political formations of feudal states, stood the popes, minded to preserve the *libertas ecclesiae*. Gregory the Great, in the epitaph upon his tombstone, was called *Consul Dei*. Not a consul of the Roman Republic but the Consul of the new rising *Civitas Dei* in the Middle Ages.[8]

Yet from the Christianized Germanic peoples and their legal thinking arose the greatest danger to the liberty and independence of the Church, namely, the intrusion of their national law of family and consanguineous relations and their particular, somewhat materialist, legal concepts of landed property. These secular laws threatened to overcome the spiritual law and thus to split up the Church universal into national Churches dependent on the state. If victorious in a new empire, they would make the pope the court chaplain of the Emperor, and the Church a servant of the imperial power. From the conversion of Clovis, the King of the Franks (465–511), this process of a "germanization" of the canon law quickened its step under Charlemagne and led finally to the formidable clash between Gregory VII and Henry IV.

St. Boniface, the English missioner of the Saxons, and his helpers in the conversion of other German tribes, like St. Ludger and St. Adalbert, had implanted the gospel. The prudent Greek, Pope Zacharias, had recognized Pepin, the mayor of the palace of the

---

[8] The epitaph is given in Gregorovius, *Die Grabdenkmaeler der Päpste*, ed. Schillmann, 1911, p. 11.

Merovingian dynasty, contrary to the law of succession of the Merovingian royal house. "To him is owed the name king, who has the power of the king." Charlemagne had then united the Imperium and the Church in the new Holy Roman Empire. He began to consider the bishops somewhat as imperial officials for the administration of the Empire, and the hierarchical system with its learned clerics as a useful organization for the same purpose. This is easily conceivable because the unity of the Empire as a body politic needed a staff of skilled administrators of whom there were none to be found other than in the ecclesiastical organization. The danger which here loomed up was perceived by such an eminent Pope as Nicholas I. What had happened to the Eastern Church under the Caesaropapism of Byzantine emperors threatened now to engulf the Roman Church. Yet this Church had until now successfully upheld the principle that the Church of Christ must remain free and independent. But before Nicholas I could perform his task, he died.

About this time the Empire of Charlemagne had been divided into the Gallic Roman part and the Frankish German part. Though remaining parts of the medieval world, these two parts developed independently and produced the opposition of Romanism (Latinism) versus Germanism. Meanwhile the papacy had fallen into the darkness of the tenth century. The papal throne had become the spoil in the political struggle of Roman noble families. Yet in Germany ecclesiastical life flourished. Great emperors, filled with the theocratic dreams of Charlemagne, became reformers of the Church in the Holy Roman Empire which was definitely established by Otto the Great. But this reforming intent constituted, on the basis of the Germanic feudal law, a grave danger for both the Empire and the Church. Otto the Great perceived that the increasing hereditary character of the fiefs, which were the foundation of the Empire's administrative system because the income from them supported the administrators, must menace the unity of the Empire. So he began to prefer bishops as holders of imperial fiefs and consequently of administrative offices, because the fiefs would return to the emperor at the death of the bishops as these could not have legitimate offspring. He furthered this practice by making the bearers of his policy clerics, and he invested them with ring and crosier, looking more for administrative ability in these men than for ecclesiastical and priestly fitness. His successors,

filled likewise with the dream of the new Empire, continued his practice. *Bona fide* as they were, they tried mostly to follow the line of
reform as it emanated from the religious earnestness and spiritual
enthusiasm of the Cluniac reform. But they could not avoid the intrinsic contradiction of their policy: the spirit of Cluniac reform and
of independence of the Church as against their political expediency of
using the hierarchy for the secular purposes of the Empire. The
greatest spirit of the Cluniac reform, Gregory VII, when as the monk
Hildebrand he served in the Roman Curia, had to oppose this contradiction in the struggle for the *libertas ecclesiae* from imperial
power, and for the independence of spiritual sacramental law from
the secular consanguinity and family law of Germanic origin.

Simony and marriage of clerics had long been the external signs
of decay. Emperors, like St. Henry II, filled by the spirit of Cluny,
had to intervene against these ecclesiastical malpractices. But there
was, too, a practical cause for intervention; for, if clerical celibacy disappeared, then the hereditary character of the ecclesiastical offices
followed. This very feature would weaken the unity of the Empire by
the growing might of feudal families as hereditary holders of the
imperial fiefs. But with what justification could the emperor proceed
against simony and the traffickers in eccesiastical offices if he himself,
though not wielding spiritual authority, arbitrarily appointed to
spiritual offices?

At the bottom of this dilemma, as the very basis of the whole question we find the Germanic law of fiefs and of the family, and the institution of the "private church" (*Eigenkirche*).[9] It was a particular
feature of Germanic law, especially in its earlier and cruder form,
to have the rights of persons rooted in landed property. This view of
an economic civilization that rested almost wholly on agricultural
property and on income from it, mostly in kind, makes the ownership
of real property and its inheritance in the family the center of the
legal system. Real property thus becomes the foundation of almost
all other rights, private and public. And this was especially so since
the cruder Germanic law, unlike the Roman law, did not carefully

---

[9] The literature about the *Eigenkirche* (*ecclesia propria*) is extensive. Ulrich Stutz
and his disciples have clarified the nature and history of this institution in numerous
books. Opposition to the theories of Stutz has been voiced by A. Dopsch, *Wirtschaftliche
und soziale Grundlagen der europäischen Kulturentwicklung von Caesar bis auf Karl d.
Gr.*, 2d ed., II (1924), 230 ff.

distinguish between private and public law. Consequently the owner of real property, the family under the father, had a right to all other rights in any way connected with the landed property. Jurisdiction in civil and criminal law was accordingly rooted in the ownership of big estates; and this jurisdiction, like other rights, was salable. Consequently the nobleman who built a church or a chapel on his estate, the king who founded a monastery or built a cathedral for a bishop, both considered themselves the owners of the church and holders of such rights in the church as patronal care for divine service, direction and use of the income from the church, and the appointment and deposition of the priest or bishop. Thus the ordination and episcopal consecration as legal institutions of the spiritual law, of the sacramental order, became more and more to them a mere external condition and not the basis and very essence of the ecclesiastic office. This office was thus in a certain way secularized and laicized. Not the ecclesiastic law but the secular law became decisive.

The king consequently regarded all churches, especially episcopal churches, as under his jurisdiction; his sovereignty on the basis of secular law encroached upon the sphere of the Church and threatened to supersede the canon law. Instead of the free spiritual succession by sacramental law, supranational and supernatural in ordination and in the laying-on of hands by the spiritual authority, the mere secular law of blood and family succession began to prevail. When the episcopal churches were considered thus the king's own churches, the bishops who were at the same time imperial administrators must become servants of the king. Henry III seems to have regarded even the episcopal church of the pope as his own imperial church, when he pronounced Gregory VI guilty of simony and deposed him by his own authority, in spite of the accepted and time-honored rule which declared: *Prima sedes a nemine judicatur.*[10] The Emperor considered himself the *rector ecclesiae.*

The bishops meanwhile had thus become the vassals of the king. Yet this identity of sacerdotal dignity and administrative office seemed in the eyes of the emperors, animated by the will to reform, to be a right thing; and it might appear so as long as the emperors gave the sec-

---

[10] Originally from the Symmachian falsifications. Cf. L. Duchesne, *Liber pontificalis*, Vol. I (1886), pp. cxxxiii ff.; and E. Caspar, *Geschichte des Papsttums*, Vol. II (1933), pp. 107 ff.

ular office that was at the same time an ecclesiastical office to a worthy, spiritual ecclesiastic. But it is clear that all independence of the Church was thus lost. The supernatural, spiritual office and the sacramental law have become a mere annex to the law of family succession and real property; they are suffocated in this embrace. Simony and an abominable spoils system of ecclesiastical offices are the consequence, though never so intended by the emperors. The identification of *Imperium and Ecclesia,* of secular office and ecclesiastical dignity, of real property rights and canon law, was the fundamental, vicious cause. The struggle for the liberty of the Church, for the independence of the spiritual authority and the canon law in all its branches, from the secular power and the secular family law was inevitable. And this struggle had to become a struggle for leadership in the *mundus Christianus,* for in this light both emperor and pope alike conceived the medieval society. This struggle, so often misrepresented, took place between Gregory VII and Henry IV.

III. GREGORY VII AND HENRY IV

In promoting the Cluniac reform the German emperors contributed much to the growth of a Christian civilization and actually freed the papacy from the jealous strife of the Roman nobility. But this fact has nothing to do with this struggle. It is quite clear that the imperial attempts to reform the Church rested upon legal conceptions which neither the papacy nor the *Ecclesia universalis* could accept. It is true that Henry II and Henry III fought against the marriage of clerics the same contest as that of Gregory VII. Yet their legal reasons and motives were very different. The emperors would have free fiefs, not heritable in a family. The celibate holder of an imperial fief, the spiritual and secular officeholder, unable to bequeath the fief and office to his own progeny, increased the imperial power and the unity of the realm against the centrifugal tendencies of a feudalism with its heritable fiefs. But what mattered to Gregory was the continuity and independence of the spiritual law, of the ecclesiastical office and thus the liberty of the Church. The institution of private churches and the marriage of clerics threatened to bind the sacramental succession of ecclesiastical offices, freely transferred by spiritual authority in the hierarchical order of the Church, to the secular law of blood

and family. They threatened thus to make them mere legal de
pendencies of the sovereign national laws of the German peoples. The
marriage of priests with the consequent hereditary character of the
ecclesiastical office and spiritual authority in the officeholder's family
according to secular, national law would destroy the sacramental law
and the unity of the Church just as much as would the investiture of
bishops with ring and crosier by the king. In place of the ordination
and consecration according to spiritual law, there would be investiture
according to national law. The national secular law would thus en
compass the spiritual law and destroy the supranational unity of the
Church. No longer would the spiritual order, effected through
spiritual succession and free sacramental transfer, rule in the Church
universal, but rather the secular law of blood, of the family, of the
clan.

Every law based on blood and family is bound by tribal, national
homogeneity. Consequently, if ruled by this law, the unity of the
Church universal and the supranational character of the canon law
would decay, and national Churches would replace the Catholic
Church. The danger was not so much to any secular claims of the
papacy, any petty ambitions of the hierarchy, but to the spiritual life
of God's people, the very liberty of the divinely instituted Church.
That liberty was the essential object of the fierce struggle which was
fought so bitterly because on both sides there existed a consciousness
of well-grounded rights. To Henry IV, Gregory's demands were
secular innovations. What he put forth against such innovations was
in his eyes a good right and a just competence inherited from pious
ancestors who had used such rights in order to reform the Church and
to improve ecclesiastical discipline. Yet in the eyes of Gregory, what
Henry IV asserts is sin and offense against the time-honored un
changeable law of the divine order through which alone man can
receive divine grace and salvation. So for Gregory the liberty of the
Church becomes the dominating idea. The imperial secular power
has no right to bestow spiritual offices, bishoprics and abbeys. Lay
men have no competences in the realm of ecclesiastical law. The mar
riage of priests is proscribed. Nobody is permitted to attend the Masses
of a married priest. Gregory is aware that his restoration of ecclesi
astical law to its due place means suffering and tears, war and persecu
tion for many, especially for himself. He is convinced, however, that

e is not fighting for his personal rights but for the imperishable right
f the Church, of the sacramental order.

The King is not perturbed by Gregory's new and yet so old decrees.
[e continues to appoint bishops and to invest them with the symbols
f their spiritual authority. Then Gregory thus addresses the King:
Thou, Henry, promisest much, but thou actest against the rules of
1e Church, and that means of St. Peter. We merely restore the right
f old, of the holy fathers, in our decrees, to which all princes and
eoples must bow as to verities necessary for salvation." [11] If the King
ersists in his practice, the Pope will not only excommunicate the
uilty one but threatens also to release all subjects of the King from
1eir oath of allegiance. That would mean the destruction of the
gal and moral structure of the feudal system at the top of which
eigns the imperial majesty legitimated by these oaths. Henry answers
1eeringly in addressing his letter to Hildebrand, not Pope, but the
false monk" and calls out to him: "In virtue of my office as *Patricius
Romanus* given to me by God and the Roman people, I revoke from
1ee all papal authority and order thee: Descend." [12] This is the
ssence of the struggle: the Emperor as *Patricius Romanus* claims to
e the owner of the Roman Church as his private church and conequently claims supreme authority over the spiritual order and the
cclesiastical hierarchy. The Church as an institution would become
 mere administrative instrument of secular authority, which would
ot become spiritual by the contention that the emperor's office also
 of divine origin and has a sacred character as the protector of the
hurch of Christ.

To Gregory VII nothing is left but to make real his threat and to
ronounce the canonical excommunication. He does this in the form
f a prayer to St. Peter: "By virtue of thy grace, not for the sake of my
eeds, it hath pleased thee that thy Christian people obey me. . . .
'o the honor and for the protection of thy Church . . . in virtue of
1y authority I forbid King Henry, Emperor Henry's son, who has
sen against thy Church with unheard of arrogance, the government
f the Empire and of Italy. And I release all Christians from the oath
1ey have sworn to him. . . . In thy stead I bind him with the tie of

[11] *Registr. Gregorii VII*, III, 10; ed. E. Caspar, pp. 263 ff.
[12] The original by E. Bernheim, *Quellen zur Geschichte des Investiturstreites*, II, 70;
 p. 77.

curse, in order that the people recognize that thou art Peter and
that upon thee, the rock, the Son of the living God has built His
Church which the gates of hell shall not overcome." [18] Excommunica
tion struck the heir of the emperors when he was at the height of his
worldly power. For the emperors had indeed established that identity
of Church and Empire which consequently bound to the spiritual
excommunication the secular ban and logically led to the legal de
struction of Henry's political authority. When Henry saw that his
vassals, the princes of the realm, preferred to follow the Pope's spiritual
authority, the King went to Canossa. After the struggle had lasted
longer than the lifetime of Gregory and Henry, the immediate cause
was settled in the Concordat of Worms (1122). In this the Pope re
ceived what he needed, the spiritual free transfer of the hierarchical
offices. The successful fight against clerical marriage had meanwhile
frustrated the inheritance of spiritual offices and of ecclesiastical
property by the offspring of the clergy according to secular, national
law. The independence of the canon law and the free spiritual suc
cession of ecclesiastical offices and thus the liberty of the Church had
been established, until the struggle flared up anew at the time of
princely absolutism and the victory of its nationalist states.

IV. CURIALISTS AND LEGISTS

What distinguished this medieval era from the later era of
pluralism of sovereign nation-states was the consciousness of its people
that Church and Empire do not live in separate spheres and that they
are not two societies. The dominating consciousness was rather that
one Christianity reigned in the universal *mundus Christianus* and
that the Christian had a double citizenship: in the Empire and in the
Church. The contemporary writers, therefore, did not speak so much
of the relations between Church and state as of the relations of the
two powers, the imperial and the papal power, the secular and the
spiritual sword. The medieval struggle between the two powers was
therefore, also a struggle for the superiority of the one over the other
in the leadership of this universal Christianity united in faith and
morals. With this problem are concerned the propositions of the
Dictatus Papae Gregorii. The right to this leadership filled the mind

[18] *Registr. Greg. VII*, III, 10; ed. E. Caspar, pp. 270 ff.

of Innocent III. It found its last and proudest expression in Boniface VIII's bull *Unam Sanctam* at a time when the realization of this claim was already an impossibility, shortly before the outrage of Anagni (1303). Yet the claim of the medieval papacy was directed not only against the assertion of the emperor's superiority. This claim struck also at the tendencies toward national independence in spiritual matters among powerful bishops who in one and the same person were princes of the Church and the Empire's highest princes as the Emperor's vassals. Many of these mighty men had looked with suspicion upon the efforts of Nicholas I (858–67), who worked hard for the freedom of the Church from the encroachments of the imperial power. These bishops had reproachfully contended that the Pope was trying to make himself the supreme lord and the emperor of the world.

In a peculiar way, contrasting lines of thought are thus entangled in the idea of the *mundus Christianus*. On the basis of the unity of the Church, the pope claims the primacy over national synods and over bishops who, as officials and vassals of the emperor, are bound to the latter by their oath of feudal allegiance. The struggle for the unity of the Church becomes a struggle for the liberty of the Church. In the light of the ideological unity of the *mundus Christianus*, this easily becomes a claim to superiority over the emperor. However much the national tendencies have outlasted the papal and imperial idea of the unity of the Empire, in the minds of the contemporary theologians, canonists, and legists, the idea of the unity between *Imperium* and *Ecclesia* was dominant, on the basis of the common Christian faith which formed the element of political homogeneity.

This unity was so strong that whoever revolted against the secular order sinned also against the spiritual order according to the common opinion; and whoever, by spreading heretical opinions, endangered the unity of the Church violated also the secular public order. Thus excommunication by the spiritual power was followed by the ban, outlawry on the side of the secular power,[14] which became thus the secular arm of the spiritual power. The Christian faith, membership in the Church, was in the laws of the Empire the foundation of man's earthly citizenship. This explains the legal status of the Jews who lived, so to speak, as alien residents, under a kind of *jus peregrinorum*. And this explains, too, why this whole struggle was so bitterly con-

14 Cf. Eduard Eichmann, *Acht und Bann im Reichsrecht des Mittelalters*, 1909.

tested. Moreover, it helps us to grasp why the partisans of both fac
tions, the curialists and the legists, did not shrink from falsification
like the Donation of Constantine and why the legists used the Roman
law of the pagan emperors for their arguments.[15]

The curialists contended that the two swords (Luke 22:38) had
been given by Christ, the Priest and King, to the pope and that the
secular sword had been only lent to the emperor by the pope. The
legists asserted that the emperor's power was derived from the old
Roman emperors. They also claimed that the emperor had received
the secular sword in the same way as the pope had received the spiritual
sword, namely, by divine right. Innocent III once claimed that, in
the medieval feudal structure, the emperor is the highest vassal of
the pope.[16] It is true that Pope Innocent declares that the King of
France does not recognize a superior in temporal matters and is there
fore in the secular field free and independent, i.e., sovereign. It is
true that the popes usually claimed jurisdiction over the secular
princes only on account of moral sins because the princes, as mem
bers of the Church, were subject to the canon law and the moral
rules of divine and natural law, of which the Church is the supreme
judge and the interpreting authority.

While thus theoretically clear lines of distinction could be drawn
between the field of secular competence and independence and the
field of the spiritual supreme authority and the canon law, we must
not forget that, for the medieval mind with its strong consciousness of
unity, these lines were in practice rather indistinct. In the juridical
field we find a competition between the ecclesiastical courts and the
civil courts without such clear definition of their mutual competence
in practice as could be determined upon theoretical reasoning. The
pope can depose the emperor and other princes whenever they
violate their duties to the Church or to their subjects, that is, when
ever they commit a sin against their political duties. The bond between
the ruler and the ruled was the feudal pact of mutual loyalty. If the
ruler broke this pact, he broke a secular contract indifferent in re
lation to the spiritual law, but he also broke the moral law and in some

[15] Bartolus says (Ad L. Hostes and L 24 De capt. et postlim. 49. 15 n 7): "Whoever denies
that the emperor is the lord and monarch of the whole world is truly a heretic." Cf
Suarez, De leg., III, chap. 7.
[16] Cf. Eichmann, op. cit., p. 50.

way the spiritual law, as the mutual oath of loyalty had been sworn in solemn form surrounded by the rites of the Church.

The emperor's power and the pope's power are related like moon and sun. As the moon receives its power from the sun, so the emperor receives his power from the pope. Thus the curialists asserted the superiority of the spiritual power over the secular power. When the legists asserted the equality of the secular power, Boniface VIII answered: "The Church has only one head, not two heads like a monster." [17] The original coordination and equality shows thus a strong tendency to a superiority of one power over the other. Innocent IV stresses this oneness against the earlier dualism when he says that the successors of St. Peter with the pontifical power received simultaneously the secular power. That could be directed against those legists who asserted that whatever secular power the pope held in his Patrimony of Peter, he had received it from the predecessors of the emperor, whether Constantine the Great or Charlemagne. Yet the curialists meant the empire, not the small papal states. These polemics of the partisans must seem strange to the student of history when he recalls that at their very height, in the late thirteenth century, the kings of the growing states of France and England had already dissolved the idea of the universal empire in favor of one of a pluralism of sovereign states; likewise that the national tendencies in these countries began to show up again in the national hierarchies, for instance, in the form of Gallicanism in France and similar tendencies in the English hierarchy. All this made Henry VIII's breach with Rome easy because the majority of the bishops with their clergy sided promptly with the national kingdom.

The papal and the imperial doctrine of oneness thus carried the germs of decay in themselves. Imperial superiority would mean the Erastian subservience of the Church, the loss of the freedom of the Church, the end of the independence of the spiritual order; therefore of the main presupposition of the *orbis Christianus*, its intact faith. Papal superiority, according to the claims of the curialists, took away from the emperor his highest divine legitimation confronted by the powerful feudal lords and national kings and their

---

[17] In *Ausculta fili*. In the famous bull *Unam Sanctam*, Boniface used a similar expression.

ceaseless struggle for sovereignty. Yet any weakening of the Empire struck back against the papacy since the rising national princes, when they had destroyed the Empire, found a favorable opportunity, at the time of the Reformation, to establish national Churches in the Protestant countries, and state churches in Catholic countries according to the Gallican pattern.

The student of history knows that the dominating unitarian idea was the Augustinian concept of the *Civitas Dei,* mixed, in contradiction to St. Augustine's ideas, with theories that the Empire or the papacy was the legal successor of the old Roman Empire, which had become "Holy" through Christianity.[18]

V. RELATION OF CHURCH AND STATE IN MEDIEVAL THOUGHT

Yet with the rise of Aristotelianism in the medieval universities, far away from the noise of political polemics between the papal curialists and the imperial legists, a new political philosophy, a new concept of the state, had developed. In a scarcely perceptible process there evolved an interpretation of Augustinian ideas in the sense of Thomist Aristotelianism. The new concept of the state is based upon the theory of natural law independent of ecclesiastical ways of thinking. *Imperium* and *sacerdotium* are no longer one and the same. The state is conceived as a natural intrinsically good form of political, self-sufficient life. It is a perfect society with a proper specific end, the secular common good, and in its proper field it is independent of the spiritual power. The mutual duties and rights of the citizens and of the temporal power are independent of the status of the citizens as Christians. Even the pagan state is no longer, like the Augustinian *civitas terrena,* morally bad. So the concept of the state is freed from the ideological cloaks of the curialist thinking. On the other hand, the Church is also recognized as a perfect society with its spiritual end, sovereign in the spiritual order, free in the world of the states. The Church steps into the place of the *respublica Christiana,* but as a spiritual society. The Empire is recognized for what it is, an unrealizable political dream; a pluralism of states, forming a genuine

[18] For a criticism of this medieval misinterpretation of St. Augustine's ideas, cf. Delos, O.P., *op. cit.,* p. 195.

community of nations on the basis of natural law, is willingly accepted.

St. Thomas acknowledges in principle the political rule of infidels over Christians. The divine law originating in grace does not abolish human law. Most certainly it does not abolish any already existing political authority of an infidel, because political authority rests upon natural law. The infidelity of the ruler does not exclude the obedience of the Christian citizen. Of course, when the ruler of a homogeneously Christian people apostatized or used his authority against the religion of his people, then the ruler deserved to be deposed. In the eyes of St. Thomas it was therefore not a deposition in the legal sense when the pope declared that the apostate ruler had lost his rights and that the subjects were freed from their duties of allegiance. The spiritual power that had consecrated the pact between king and people at the solemn coronation made a declaratory statement about the *de facto* breach already existing. And such a declaratory (not constitutive) statement was at that time deemed necessary because the pact was sealed by solemn religious oath. The declaration that the oaths were annulled was necessary in the interest of the certainty of law and order. In other words, the competence of the spiritual power to declare secular rulers deposed and to release their subjects from allegiance depends on positive law and on historical circumstances. After such laws and circumstances ceased to exist, the declaration of the Church would be in the field of the secular order without legal consequences. The foundation of this doctrine rests upon a distinction of the two powers and the assignment of different spheres of human life to each of them, the distinction of two orders, of two spheres: one of them coordinated to the spiritual power, and the other to the secular power.

Besides, the singleness of the Empire was given up and the pluralism of independent states was recognized. Therefore the problem of superiority of one power over the other changed. No longer was the problem the actual superiority in the one and universal *orbis Christianus*. With the plurality of states the question became this: What spheres of human life belong to the Church, and what spheres belong to the state? The state was now based on natural law, not upon a Christianized form of the positive law of the old Roman Empire, the universal monarchy which Eusebius had spoken of, as well as so many of the early Fathers. Thus was cleared up one line of thought which Augustine had first touched upon in his *Civitas Dei* but which had been obscured by the early medieval idea of the Christian Empire as the *Civitas Dei;* namely, that the dream of a universal empire coinciding with the universal Church with the abolition of the pluralism of states has never been realized and will hardly be realized. The Augustinian skepticism about the Roman Empire, which under the pagan emperors was for St. Augustine the *Civitas terrena,* anything but an ideal, appeared anew in the foreground. With it arose the idea of a pluralism of independent states living naturally in a peaceful community.[19]

"Both powers originate in God. Therefore the secular power is subordinated to the spiritual power in matters that concern the salvation of souls. In matters that concern more the civil common good, a person is obliged to obey the secular power rather than the spiritual power; . . . unless with the spiritual power is connected the secular power as in the Church states where the pope holds the acme of both powers, the spiritual and the secular." [20] This last sentence must not be taken in an absolute sense; it means only the recognition of a legal positive fact, namely, that where the pope has the secular power by positive law, the distinction is not applicable. It cannot mean that in virtue of his spiritual power and on account of the fact that the spiritual power is superior, the pope holds *ipso jure* by divine dispensation also all secular power directly and necessarily. The decisive fact remains the clear distinction of two orders, of two different spheres, one belonging to the state, the other to the Church. What matters is the recognition that the secular common good and its order of law is independent and original and is not a positive legal concession from the Church.

[19] St. Augustine was skeptical about the much praised Caesar Augustus; for Augustus extorted from the Romans their already weakened liberty (*De Civ. Dei,* III, 21). The vaunted *pax romana* under Augustus actually never existed: St. Augustine objects vehemently: "It is not yet accomplished, as we see. There are still wars going on among nations for rule, and between sects there is war" (Migne, *PL*, XXXVI, 522). The Church is not limited to the Empire. The Church finds beyond the Empire nations that she has to Christianize. The Church is not the Empire. The Church is *inter gentes,* among and above nations. This is a line of thinking that was now revived. It is certain that the first travels of Marco Polo discovering the Empire of the Chinese, and the missionary journeys of Franciscan friars beyond the frontiers of the Empire and to countries that never had belonged to the Empire, conjured up this new thought of a plurality of states.

[20] *Sent. II,* Dist. 44, q. 2, a. 3 ad 4.

Of course, a sphere and a form of coordination exist between Church and state. This proposition depends naturally upon the fact that the Church is supranational. Wherever the Church is nationalized, she will live in freedom only at the pleasure of the state. Yet as little as the Church exists at the mercy of the state, just so little does the state exist at the mercy of the Church. The state owes its being, which is morally good, not to a consecration by the Church nor to the supernatural order of grace. It is good by its nature. Its legitimation is ultimately the common good, not its service and subordination to the Church. The state of the natural order, even the non-Christian state, is not a product of the devil or a consequence of sin.

St. Thomas recognizes the problem not as a legal problem based on Roman law or on legal documents of which some were forged by the partisans of the Emperor or of the Pope, but as a philosophical one: Church and state in general, not as a practical problem of a historical situation as the curialists and the legists saw it, namely, superiority of the papal spiritual power or the imperial temporal power, one over the other in the unitarian Empire of the *mundus Christianus*. The validity of the constitutional law of this *mundus Christianus* in its historical form at some moment during the Middle Ages was not the subject of discussion. What arose as the eternal problem was the relation between the Christian state or the state by virtue of natural law on the one hand and the Church, supranational, established by positive divine law, on the other.

Some scholars thought they discovered in this new idea of the state, introduced by the Thomistic adoption of the Aristotelian polity, a kind of dynamite, with which the medieval universalism in its theocratic structure was blown up.[21] This is doubtful. There is no reason to suppose that St. Thomas knew about such consequences or expected them. He was indifferent to the political life of his time, though his era was shaken by the heated disputes between the Guelphs and the Ghibellines, between the Pope and the Emperor. His works reflect no part of this moving struggle. Nevertheless the new and yet very old political philosophy was used against the medieval world by the political propagandists of the rising national states. Their propagandists exaggerated one idea of the new doctrine, the sovereignty and the

[21] For instance, Otto von Gierke and Wilhelm Windelband, the latter more for the political theory of Late Scholasticism. Cf. Rommen, *Suarez*, pp. 148 ff. and *passim*.

independence of the state, by removing the idea from the totality of the doctrinal cosmos and making this independence absolute. Yet against such abuses there is no protection. When Luther or Jansenius took from St. Augustine's doctrine of grace one idea and made it absolute and thus falsified it, they, too, arrived at wrong and mutually contradictory theological consequences.

It was not the theologians and scholars who used the new idea of the state based upon natural law as a destructive criticism of the medieval political ideals. The political and literary enemies of the papacy (Marsilius of Padua, Occam, and other partisans of Louis the Bavarian or partisans of Philip the Fair) are the ones who deserve such a reproach. The nominalist school of Occam is on the whole the representative force in the decomposition of the medieval world of thought. The unity of tension, the harmony so typical for the Thomistic philosophy and theology, is slowly dissolved by exaggerating one side of the polar unity of tension, by one-sided consideration of an idea in the cosmos of ideas. Through this, the order in the tension, the unity that arches over and embraces the opposing poles, is destroyed. Thus it is that the Occamist doctrine of the precedence of will and omnipotence over the intellect in God makes the idea of a natural law impossible; the strong individualist trend makes the community recede, as it puts the will into the foreground and neglects the order in the universe. This individualism develops, as it does in religion so also in the sphere of political and international life. This, then, is the autumn of the Middle Ages when the winter seed of the modern era is sown.

Such theologians as Marsilius of Padua draw the picture of a secular power which is the representation of God ruling sovereignly over the state and the Church. The perfect life that man is destined to accomplish in the state is the temporal and the spiritual life. Consequently the priesthood is only an office in the state along with other offices and vocations. The people is the true sovereign, and the monarch holds his power and office only through concession from a general council consisting of priests and laymen. Neither the power of emperor or prince nor the power of the pope is of divine right. The pope is not the vicar of Christ, but the vicar of the General Council. The pope has no sovereign power because the priesthood is merely an office in the state. Religious education and instruction in the Gospel is the task of the pope and the priest; but they have no power to discipline and punish. Such a power belongs only to the community and to the General Council; the state may lend its secular arm only where the transgression of the canon law was at the same time a transgression of the secular law. This is the complete inversion of the extreme curialist theory of Augustinus Triumphus,[22] who ascribed to the pope the *plenitudo potestatis* over the whole Christian empire by virtue of positive divine law. Now in the thought of Marsilius the secular power takes the place of the pope, or better the sovereign imperial people rules the empire in which there is no place for the Church as an independent perfect society with its own spiritual law and its own hierarchical order of offices. Marsilius did not accept the hierarchy; for him there is no difference of jurisdiction between pope, bishop, priest, or layman.

Thus of the potential forms of the relation between Church and state which modern history will produce, some forms are already anticipated in medieval political life and theory. There is, of course, this difference: in the Middle Ages the political framework is the universal *mundus Christianus,* in modern history it is the pluralism of sovereign states. The Caesaropapism of Frederic II and of Marsilius of Padua is followed by the Erastian national Churches under the rule of the "enlightened despot." Then in Thomism comes the coordination of Church and state in the concordat in which each is considered supreme *in suo ordine,* and this concordat as a public treaty regulates the matters which as *res mixtae* concern both. The form of a complete separation of Church and the religiously neutral state was an impossibility for the Middle Ages with its unquestioned fact of a united Christianity.

[22] *Summa de potestate Ecclesiae* (ed. by Richard Scholz, 1929), a controversial book against Occam's *Somnium viridarii.* The Franciscan William of Ockham or simply Occam, the prince of the nominalists and inaugurator of the *via moderna* in Scholasticism, was a fertile author of treatises in political philosophy. Most of them are printed (though not faultlessly) in Goldhast, *Monarchia Romani Imperii* (1613), 313 ff. Cf. further, Philotheus Boehmer, O.F.M., "Ockham's Political Ideas," *Review of Politics,* V, 462 ff. For a short biography of this interesting friar, see R. L. Poole in *Dictionary of National Biography,* XLI, 351 ff. Marsilius of Padua developed his theory in the famous *Defensor pacis* (latest edition by Richard Scholz, 1933), which he wrote together with John of Janduno, who had connections with the school of Joachim de Fiori and their theory of the *ecclesia spiritualis* without power, canon law, or hierarchy.

CHAPTER XXIV

The Era of the Reformation

I. LATE SCHOLASTIC THEORY OF CHURCH AND STATE

THE so-called Babylonian captivity of the popes in Avignon (1309–76) is, after the last and exaggerated claims of Boniface VIII and of Louis of Bavaria, not only the end of the medieval opposition of papal and imperial power in the unity of the Empire. It is also the beginning of a new era. For the kings of France were as hostile to the Empire as they were hostile to the papal claims of superiority. The *mundus Christianus* dissolves definitely into the pluralism of national states, and the rest of the Empire under the Hapsburg monarchy is equally subjected to a process of dissolution in the growing might of the princes in their territories. Although these territories continue to be nominally parts of the Empire, the actual power and the juridical independence of the princes is mightily fostered through the Reformation and the acquisition of the title *Summepiscopus* on the part of the Protestant princes, imitated by their Catholic colleagues in the *Staatskirchentum*. This was a policy to make the national hierarchy subject to the prince, to make the Church organization a department of the state, and to diminish the spiritual supreme jurisdiction of the pope in favor of national synods or of the national hierarchy dependent on the absolute prince.

Now the modern problem of Church and state arises. In the idea of state we must make some distinctions: the Catholic state, as, for instance, France under the ancient regime with the outspoken nationalist features of Gallicanism and practically no tolerance for heretics, which later, after the revolutionary movements, was given up in favor of the principle of tolerance; the Protestant state, like England, the Scandinavian countries, and Saxony, with an established Church of national and Erastian character which shows originally no tolerance for Catholics or dissidents but later accepts the principle of tolerance as distinguished from the principle of equality; Christian states with a strong Catholic minority under recognition of the principle of parity or equality of the various Christian denominations (Prussia, the German Reich of Bismarck); the denominationally neutral state like the United States, then the anticlerical or laic state as it emerged in the Third Republic of France since 1904, and finally the non-Christian states of pagan countries as the era of discovery brings them forth. In our times we have to add the anti-Christian totalitarian states like Nazi Germany and Soviet Russia. In each of these there will arise specific answers to the problem of Church and state.

It is upon the Thomistic political philosophy and not upon the exaggerated theories of some medieval popes and their curial partisans like Augustinus Triumphus that the doctors of Late Scholasticism, such as Vittoria, Suarez, Bellarmine, attempt a new solution for the perennial problem, just as later Leo XIII, pope and political philosopher, answered the problem for the modern political era upon the same basis. Between them lie the attempts to nationalize the Church in Catholic countries (Gallicanism) and the more or less successful attempts of princely absolutism to establish state Churches, that is, to make the Church a mere administrative department of the absolutist state in order to control the whole life of its citizens.

Two new points of view about the relation between Church and state emerge in the sixteenth century. First, the full unification of the plenitude of spiritual and of temporal power in the hands of the absolute monarch through the Reformation as, for instance, under Henry VIII and James I in England. Secondly, the non-Christian (pagan) state in the newly discovered continents, for instance, in China, in Japan, and in Mexico. These afforded an excellent example for the natural-law concept of the state. Both these events serve the doctors of Late Scholasticism as an opportunity for a more profound study of the relation between Church and state. In the following part we shall refer to Suarez and Bellarmine, though it would be easy to quote numerous other scholars of the time.

It is true that both doctors, Suarez and Bellarmine, laid down their theory at least partly in controversial works. But this must not divert our attention from the fact that in their non-controversial and usually more profound books the tenets of their theory are fully developed, so that we need not depend on the merely polemic literature. On the other hand, the controversial books give a vivid presentation of the actual problems because they answer the attacks of the opponents.[1]

What were the assertions of these opponents? As Marsilius already had done, they denied any jurisdiction, spiritual or temporal, of the pope and the Church under him. For James I, to use this royal controversialist as an example, there is no distinction between the spiritual and the temporal power. Both belong to the king. The royal power is of divine right just as much as the pope's authority. Even more so, because the pope's authority is derived from the original authority resting in the ecumenical council. The divine right of the king can be restricted only through an act of grace by the sovereign, but not by a pact between king and people. Even less can the king's divine right be restricted by the pope's spiritual or temporal power, direct or indirect; for already before there was a pope the divine right of the kings was established, as the Bible proves. James suffered himself to be called a vicar of Christ. The power of the king is compared to the power of God to work miracles.[2]

Because the royal authority is immediately of divine origin, it cannot be restricted by the human decrees of Parliament or by the spiritual authority of the pope. This lay theologian, James I, who props up his theologically founded absolutism with strange theories taken from the Old Testament, places the royal power over the papal power. The royal power, being of divine right, is unrestricted and truly absolute. As soon as the Church is nationalized, the king unites in his power the plenitude of power in the spiritual and in the temporal realm. Consequently he has full jurisdiction in matters spiritual. We see that the arguments which Marsilius of Padua, for instance, proffered are repeated here. But now, instead of popular sovereignty, we have the king's divine right, and instead of the Empire we have the state. The arguments are still clothed in medieval language and figures as they are even in Hobbes' books.[3] They abound with quotations from the Bible and theological authors.

1 Suarez wrote: *Defensio fidei catholicae adversus anglicanae sectae errores.* Numerous editions; the latest, 1859. Bellarmine's controversial books against Barclay, James I, and others are to be found in *Opera omnia* (Paris, 1870–74). Cf. Rommen, *op. cit.,* pp. 235–69.

2 Francis Bacon, *De augm. scient.,* VII, 2; cf. also the instructive thesis of Marc Bloch, *Les rois thaumaturges* (Publications of the Faculté des lettres of the University of Strasbourg, 1924).

3 Hobbes' *Leviathan,* Part III, offers a strange mixture of rationalism and biblical belief (cf. chaps. 32 ff.). In the most interesting chapter (42), he asserts that the civil

Suarez and Bellarmine assert against this argumentation that the Church is an institution established by a direct and immediate divine act of Christ; that the Church is a perfect society and has her own entirely independent and specific end, the salvation of the souls for which Christ sacrificed Himself upon the Cross. The constitution of the Church, her hierarchical order culminating in the supreme and prime authority of the pope as the successor of St. Peter, is likewise instituted by direct divine dispensation even as her unity and universality throughout the whole world is beyond national, racial, and other distinctions. And further, the pope's authority is not derived from a concession by the Church either as the community of the faithful or as represented in the ecumenical councils. The papal authority is truly of divine right. The so-called conciliar theory as it was propounded by the conciliar movement at the time of the councils at Basle (1431–37) and Constance (1415–18) by men like John Gerson,[4] is fully refuted. In the elective act to the papacy the cardinals do not transfer an authority that somehow after the pope's death and before the legitimate election of a new pope rests with the Church as an organized body or with the College of Cardinals. The elective act of the latter merely designates the new bearer of the monarchical papal power of divine right.[5]

Very different are the facts concerning political authority and the king's power. It is true, this power originates ultimately also from God. But this authority in its concrete form as monarchy, aristocracy, democracy, or as any sort of mixture of those, is not instituted by a divine act. This concrete form is, on the contrary, of human right. When, therefore, anybody not identical with the people itself is vested with it, this is owing to an act of transfer from the people, at least if we consider the *quaestio juris.* Any historical constitutional organization of political authority is consequently *juris humani,* not *juris divini.* There exists no divine right of the king as asserted by the partisans of the kings.

---

sovereign, if a Christian, is head of the Church in his own realm. In the following paragraphs he presents a refutation of Bellarmine's *De Summo Pontifice.* The arguments of all controversialists are similar on each side. Therefore we can content ourselves with the arguments of representative authors like James I or Hobbes, and Suarez or Bellarmine.

[4] Cf. Bishop Hefele's *Conciliengeschichte* (2d ed.), Vol. III, chap. 4.

[5] For Suarez, see Rommen, *op. cit.,* pp. 247 ff.

Similarly while the Church's end is supernatural, the state's end is a natural one: the good status and the perfect order of the common good in the sphere of secular life. Hence political power is called secular and temporal. Furthermore, whereas the Church is necessarily universal and unique, i.e., catholic, the pluralism of the states is quite natural according to the nature of the secular end. Yet even if the rather utopian dream of a world state could be accepted, this would not change the fact that the end of this *civitas maxima* is still secular and temporal.[6]

From these differences in origin, end, and constitution, follows a superiority of the Church over the state. But what does this statement mean? It means first a sublimity of the Church over the state, a primacy of the spiritual. As the eternal salvation of the immortal soul is more sublime than the secular welfare and the temporal order, so is the Church more sublime than the state. As the spiritual power, being spiritual and immediately instituted by God, has a higher degree of participation in God's omnipotence than the secular power engaged in the ordering of the secular sphere, so the spiritual authority is more sublime than the temporal power. As in the hierarchical order of the ends of creation the sacred and the spiritual end is higher than earthly happiness, as the soul is higher than the body, so is the communion of the saints, the Church, higher than the secular state. The end of the state, the values it is called on to produce, are essentially intermediary in the order of human ends and in relation to higher ends. The last and supreme end, at least as long as men believe in the immortality of the soul and in the holiness of Almighty God, is the salvation of souls and the glory of God.

II. The Theory of Indirect Power of the Church

The Church is the mediator of salvation and the communion of the faithful united in holy sacrifice for the glory of God. The state, in which man lives in the order of peace, justice, and tranquillity as

---

[6] Suarez is decidedly against a unified world state. Bellarmine is more friendly to a *civitas maxima;* but at the end of his discussion of this problem he says that it may not be possible to construct such a world state and that consequently a pluralism of smaller states under the rule of international law may be preferable (Suarez, *De leg.*, III, chap. 2, n.5; *Opus de triplici virtute theologica*, Disp. 9, sect. 6, n.17; Bellarmine, *De Summo Pontifice*, I, 9; *Opera*, I, 488).

in the *status viae,* in which man has to work for his salvation, the state is only an intermediary end. According to the order of the ends there is an order of the communities serving these ends. The higher the end, the higher the community devoted to the realization of this end. In Christianity there is no standpoint from which the salvation of the soul is not higher than all secular happiness, no standpoint from which heaven is not higher than the world; there is, therefore, no standpoint from which this subordination of the secular happiness to eternal salvation can be doubted. Hence the superiority of the religious sphere over the secular and consequently of the visible Church over the secular communities, the spiritual over the secular power. The modern neutral or even agnostic state recognizes·this fact principally by abstaining from any intereference in the religious sphere, through recognition of the freedom of worship as a fundamental right of man, not only of the citizen.

Yet with the establishment, generally and abstractly, of the greater sublimity and superiority of the Church and of the spiritual power, the concrete problem of the interrelation of both powers and of the competency of the spiritual power in the field of the temporal power is not solved. The doctors of Late Scholasticism, in accordance with St. Thomas' political philosophy, had distinctly elaborated the thesis of the true sovereignty and independence of the secular power *in suo ordine.* This *"in suo ordine"* meant, besides other things, especially a demarcation of the order of the spiritual power. Bellarmine and Suarez refute the medieval curialist theory of the unrestricted power of the pope *in temporalibus.* Such a thesis could not be upheld after St. Thomas founded the state upon the basis of natural law, however understandable it was against the background of a feudal system and the idea of the universal Empire of the *mundus Christianus.* The curialist theory of the so-called *potestas directa in temporalibus* was not taken seriously by Suarez or Bellarmine.[7]

[7] The books of Bellarmine and Vittoria, asserting that the pope has no temporal jurisdiction by divine law, were put on the Index under the conservative rule of Sixtus V. After the death of this Pope the prohibition was quickly revoked. Cf. Le Bachelet, S.J., *Bellarmine avant son cardinalat* (Paris, 1911), pp. 259 ff. A good report of Vittoria's theory may be found in *Zeitschrift für kath. Theol.,* LI (1927), 548. Suarez was denounced but not put on the Index. This shows that at that time there were still powerful circles that upheld the long since vanished medieval views. These views were not held by all the popes. Even Innocent III, as we have seen, agreed that the King of France *in temporalibus superiorem minime recognoscat* (Decretal, *Per venerabilem;* Migne, *PL,* CCIV, 1132).

These doctors develop instead the so-called theory of the indirect power in matters temporal. The presupposition of such a theory is the proposition that the state is principally sovereign *in suo ordine*, that there exists a sphere of full independence for the temporal power ordinarily and as a rule, because the state has a relatively independent end and is truly a perfect society. Yet we have to point out again an important distinction. Much depends on what the state is in the combination, Church and state. Is it a Christian state? Is the king or whoever wields supreme authority a Christian, and is the people, whose political *forma* is the state, a Christian people? Or are the ruler and a greater part of the people non-Christian? We must further remark that for none of the doctors did there exist separated Christian Churches or different Christian denominations. There exists only one Catholic Church and those Christians who had left the Catholic Church were, in the eyes of these doctors, heretics. The doctors, indeed, refused to acknowledge the destruction of the unity of the faith as a definite fact and therefore were more inclined to consider the Protestant faithful as personally guilty of heresy in the meaning of the canon law.[8] Therefore whenever these doctors speak of the Christian state or the Christian ruler they mean a Catholic ruler and a Catholic people, though in the eyes of the canon law they may be heretics.

Since the Christian ruler and a Christian people are, as Catholics, members of the Church and thus subject to the spiritual power and the canon law, there is no legitimate doubt that to such extent a clearly definable *potestas indirecta* exists in all such political matters as concern the spiritual sphere. In such cases the pope has the authority to bind morally and in conscience the sovereign and the citizen; he has the right to void secular laws that are against religion, against the faith, and against Catholic morals; he has the right to free Catholic citizens from their allegiance to a Catholic but heretical king, if the king abuses his power against the Church and the faith or if

[8] In a strict sense a heretic is anyone who, though by valid baptism a member of the Catholic Church and retaining the name of a Christian, pertinaciously denies or brings into doubt any of the truths to be believed by divine and Catholic faith (C.J.C., can. 1325 § 2). For a person to be guilty of heresy, he must obstinately maintain false doctrine. Leo XIII acknowledges that *Alieni a Jesu Christo plerique sunt ignoratione magis quam voluntate improba* (*Tametsi futura*, November 1, 1900). Such *alieni* are not heretics in the strict sense, though their opinions are heretical, and their Churches are heretical Churches in an objective sense.

he gravely endangers the common good. But a canonical proceeding, a legal sentence concerning the unjust act or law, is strictly necessary; in other words, the strict and formal application of the rules of procedure of the canon law is the presupposition of the papal judgment. And we should not forget that at this time the canon law was considered valid in the Christian states concurrently with the secular law and even above the latter in spiritual matters.[9]

If in the relation of Church and state the latter means the non-Christian state, that is, a state in which the citizens are neither Catholics nor heretics in the strict sense, and the rulers of which are not subject to the spiritual authority, because they are not baptized and thus are not validly members of the Church, then the picture changes. The doctors had a good example to illustrate their theory after the discoveries of the pagan states in Asia and America. In these non-Christian states the citizens of which, as non-baptized pagans, are not subject to the canon law, the independence of the state on the basis of natural law becomes evident. The pope has no right to transfer the sovereignty of such states to Christian princes. Not even under appeal to the divine commission of converting the heathen has the pope any right to infringe the sovereignty of these states, however much international law acknowledges the freedom of the missioners to enter the territory of these states in order to preach the gospel. These non-Christian sovereigns of non-Christian citizens cannot be deposed or punished by the pope, even if the crimes committed should be against natural reason.[10] Over the infidels the pope has no competence or jurisdiction, generally and normally. Only when the non-Christian sovereign uses his power to hinder the free preaching of the gospel, or when he persecutes wantonly those of his citizens who have received the faith, or when the pagan sovereign indulges in human sacrifice, then may the pope summon Christian princes to enter the country of the non-Christian prince in order to hinder these crimes. Yet, as Suarez points out, not so much on account of a specific spiritual power as on account of international law that guarantees

[9] The strict application of the canon law, even when the "crime" of the ruler is notorious, is strongly upheld by both Suarez and Bellarmine, against some minor writers of their time. Cf. Rommen, *op. cit.*, p. 261.

[10] Suarez, *Op. de tripl. virt. theol.*, Disp. 18, sect. 4, n.3. Bellarmine, *de Summo Pontifice*, XV, 6. This argument is against Wyclif, who contends that Christians must not obey a king who sins.

the freedom of the mission and gives to the members of the international community the right to protect the innocent against the crime of human sacrifice.

We see here that the doctors of Late Scholasticism would not allow any abuse of the faith or of the Church to excuse the colonial imperialism of the era of discovery. The basis for this theory is the principle that the state, founded upon natural law, has a true and genuine sovereignty and has an independent end upon earth. Grace does not abolish nature; so too, the Church does not make the natural community of the state superfluous. From this principle follows the practice of tolerance. Subjects of a Christian prince who have never been baptized (the opposite are the heretics in the sense of canon law) can under no circumstances be compelled to become Christians. Bellarmine is even opposed to the practice of inciting non-Christians to baptism by offering them certain privileges and advantages, for, as he says, to believe is an act of the free will.[11]

The famous theory of the indirect power of the pope in the temporal field means only this: By divine institution the pope has no temporal power nor any direct power in the field of secular political life. His authority is in the formal sense spiritual, not temporal, power. This does not deny that the pope may rightly acquire temporal power in a territory, the Church state, nor does it exclude the pope's political sovereignty in such a territory as a political necessity for the true and effective independence of the spiritual power.

On account of the subordination of the end of the state, the secular happiness, to the end of the Church, the salvation of the souls, a subordination of the temporal power to the spiritual power is a necessary consequence in the interest of the superior end and only so far as this end is concerned. The spiritual power has the right to intervene in the field of the temporal power if acts of the latter injure or actually endanger the superior end. Evidently such an act of intervention is extraordinary and cannot be considered arbitrary as the burden of proof, so to speak, lies with the intervening spiritual authority. This theory of the indirect power of the spiritual authority in the sphere of the temporal authority is, therefore, by no means simply the opposite to Hobbes' theory. Thomas Hobbes actually gives to the secular ruler the full spiritual and secular power, just as Rous-

11 Franz X. Arnold, *Staatslehre des Cardinal Bellarmin*, p. 341.

seau, in his demand for a *religion civile*, gives such a power to the government. Yet the doctors of Late Scholasticism utterly refuted the equivalent but reversed theory of the curialists (hierocratic theory), namely, that the pope wields the full spiritual and temporal power in the Christian world. They contend that the pope's power is one, the spiritual power; and it is this power that intervenes indirectly in the temporal sphere, which is in itself subject to an independent, truly sovereign, temporal power.[12]

III. The Situation in the Sixteenth Century

The relations between Church and state, though philosophically they may be determined with comparative clarity, demand in practical policy and in the individual historical situation a concrete determination by positive law. Therefore the history of the theory of the relations between Church and state is accompanied by the history of the political struggle between the spiritual and the temporal law, between the policy of the popes and the Curia vis-à-vis the policy of the temporal rulers and vice versa. As long as the Christian world existed as a unity and even later, as long as the national states considered themselves Christian because the people were still consciously and practically Christian, in other words before the rise of a mere secular civilization and before the state became religiously neutral, during all this time any change in the field of one of the parties, Church or state, caused a change in the other.

The time when Bellarmine and Suarez wrote was a period in which the widening of the rent in the garment of the Church together with the rise of the national state produced a favorable environment for the rise of established national Churches and thus gravely endangered the existence of the supranational Church universal. The king assumed a new form of the older concept of sovereignty more as a personal property, less as a property pertaining to the state or to political authority *in abstracto*. The sovereign *legibus solutus*, freed from the older conception of the law as a pact between the king and the estates of the realm and therefore unchangeable by the one-sided

---

12 Only in the Church-state the pope has both powers, yet *casualiter* (by chance). Cf. Innocent III, Decretal, *Per venerabilem:* "In certain countries we exercise by chance also the temporal power."

act of the king, this sovereign insisted also that he should be freed
from the restriction imposed by the spiritual law. And so the sovereigns become now the opponents of the pope, whose sovereignty in
the Church is established after the rejection of the conciliar theory
and the successful Counter Reformation through the decrees of the
Council of Trent.

It was feudal legal institutions and the ideas of the Roman law
with which the medieval curialist, the promoter of a papal theocracy
in the *orbis Christianus,* had cloaked his theory of the all-embracing
plenitude of the papal power. Now the sovereigns of the rising states
and their helpers, the legists, made use of the same Roman law against
the curialist and against the imperial theory. They apply the ideas
of the Roman law used by Augustus Caesar and his successors, the
emperors of the world, and later by the curialist, to their own national
sovereignty. Thus the secular sovereigns gain a formidable increase
in centralized power that gives them the legitimation to destroy the
feudal centrifugal institutions and the liberties and the self-government of the cities and towns and the rights of the estates; all inhabitants become unrestrictedly subjects of the sovereign.

At the same time the spiritual law of the Middle Ages, a potent
regulator of a great part of political and economic life, was either
transformed into national law in the Protestant states or brought,
partly at least, under the control of the sovereign by Gallicanism.
The philosophical theory had been propounded by men like Marsilius
of Padua whose *Defensor pacis* was after 1500 frequently printed.
Though the phraseology continued to be redolent of medieval forms,
the ideas themselves were modern. The national kings found further
powerful allies in the ideas of the Renaissance and in the spirit of
humanism. The former turned minds away from the asceticism and
supernaturalism of the Middle Ages toward an optimistic *joie de
vivre,* toward an accentuating of worldly arts and secular sciences.
Machiavelli wrote his new textbook of politics and put the "reason
of state" upon the throne. Thus he weakened the influence of morals
in politics and produced an art of politics beyond the rules of
morality. The humanists considered themselves courtiers and ad-
visers to the sovereigns as they were the successors of the clerics and,
feeling the urge of freedom together with the burghers in the town,
helped to inaugurate a new secular culture, by no means pagan or

unchristian but with a strong consciousness of independence from clerical leadership and from theology.

On the other hand the claims of the curialists and the actual political influence of the papacy did not agree. The Babylonian captivity in Avignon, the schism of the antipopes (1378–1417), and the rise of the conciliar theory had weakened the papal authority. Under the doubtful political practice of playing one king against another, the power of the papacy grew weaker and weaker. The people's faith and their regard for the coercive means of the canon law and for the justice and holiness of the Roman Curia had suffered grievously during this period. Once, in the era of faith, the canon law had influence in many fields in the social and economic spheres of medieval life either because the temporal law was imperfect and unfit or because the canon law courts, using the more flexible rules of equity and natural law, were better dispensers of justice than the rigid and formal native law.

But meanwhile the canon law had lost much of its reputation because it was too often used as a mere instrument in the political struggle of worldly-minded princes of the Church for power and enrichment and because its certainty and moral power had immensely suffered when pope and antipope used it against each other's followers. So in the minds of the people, who were influenced by the mockeries of many humanists comparing the ideals and the dark reality of clerical life, the spiritual law and the clergy lost much of their power. After 1450 louder and louder rose the call for secularization of Church property and of ecclesiastical law, which were still spiritual and sacred only in name. Pious souls retired from the world and found the way to modern devotion (*devotia moderna*) in the communities of the Brethren of the Common Life and in other congregations, whose spirit found its best expression in *The Imitation of Christ* by Thomas à Kempis. The more active Christian elements longing for a reform in head and members, such as John Gerson and Cardinal Nicholas of Cusa, favored the conciliar theory (Council at Constance, 1414–18, and Council of Basle, 1431–37) because they had grave doubts about a reform of the Church coming from Rome and therefore turned to a council as the highest authority able to inaugurate the longed-for reform of the desolate condition of the Church. Yet this conciliar theory actually became a weapon in the hands of the absolute secular sovereign for the establishment of state Churchdom in the sense of Gallicanism. On the other hand some princes, animated by the fervor of reform, began on their own authority to reform the ecclesiastical conditions in their realms. Thus they helped to prepare the way for national Churches in establishing the right to control the external organization of the Church. Other princes not so pious used these developments to enrich themselves or to aggrandize their power.

IV. Influence of the Reformation

Shaken out of its complacency by the tempests of the Reformation, the papacy began its own reform helped by new religious orders, especially the Jesuits. What it had lost of its medieval glory and power the papacy and the Church partly recovered through its growing spiritual and moral power. Yet it could not prevent the development of the Gallican ideas and of national Churches in which a great part of the spiritual law, bereft of its independence, was transformed into a law controlled by the secular authority of the absolute king.

The adversaries against whom the doctors of Late Scholasticism had to fight were the partisans of the rising absolute sovereignty of the national kings, who claimed not only the plenitude of temporal power but also full sovereignty in the spiritual sphere and over the canon law. The Erastian subordination of the national Church is the consequence of the new concept of absolute sovereignty. This concept meant also freedom from the rules of the spiritual law, either by exemption from this law on account of the divine right of the king, or by claiming the full spiritual power and uniting it with the temporal power. This, then, is the new rival of the Church and the pope: the absolute king of divine right. This theory of the divine right should serve to make the king in all ways at least an equal of the pope; it should serve also to make the king the sovereign over vast fields of spiritual law, if not its full master as was demanded by the Protestant princes who became the *summi episcopi* of their state Churches. The absolute prince calls himself "king by the grace of God." This very old formula was now directed against the formula "by the grace of the people" and also against "by the grace of God and the favor of the Apostolic See."

The English *Book of Canons* (by Laud, 1640) declares in canon

1: "The most high and sacred order of Kings is of divine right, being the ordinance of God himself, founded in the laws of nature and clearly established by express texts both of the Old and of the New Testament." Each of these princes of divine right considers himself a sort of god. So Grassaille, a partisan of the French monarchists, wrote in 1538: "The king of France is in his kingdom like a bodily god (*corporalis deus*)."

We have already pointed out that the king was considered to have a miracle-working, sacred power. The old religious custom of the anointing of the king when he was crowned was now interpreted as a kind of sacral act conferring immediate divine powers upon the king. In corroboration, such oratorical phrases as that of Peter Damian were used: "The kings are also priests of God and of Christ and they deserve to be called so because they have received the sacrament of their office" (*Lib. grat.*, chap. 10). The king, so Chateaubriand centuries later still held, thus becomes the head of the Gallican Church.[18] Any such "sanctification" of the king's majesty in the dispute between spiritual and secular power had manifestly the aim of repressing the spiritual power or of subjecting it in most of its competences to the divine right of the king.

This exalting of the king's sovereignty, of the temporal power, to a mystical height, to a quasi-divine majesty conferred on the sovereign directly by God, is found everywhere: in Spain and England, in France and the many smaller principalities in Germany, when at this time the latter began to thrust off the overlordship of the Emperor in Vienna. This general trend is common to the princes irrespective of their being Catholics or Protestants.

Without doubt the Reformation powerfully helped this trend since Luther especially had to ally himself and his separated Churches with the Protestant princes revolting against the Emperor, who remained Catholic. No wonder that, in spite of Luther's originally spiritual concept of the Church, the Lutheran Church with the secular prince as the supreme head and in England the Established Church became the classical type of national Church. Calvinism, with its strong feeling for the visibility of the Church, in its whole outlook more activist and independent, felt little inclination to the idea of national Churches, and in its fold we find the school of those who

[18] *Œuvres complètes*, VII, 170; cf. Bloch, *op. cit.*, pp. 186 ff.

contend against the absolute monarchs and their divine right or spiritual supremacy, a contest incomprehensible to the Lutherans or the Erastians of the Established Church. In Catholic political philosophy the divine-right theory was always opposed, as is shown by the much discussed theory of the tyrant and the right of the people to depose and execute the tyrant. This theory, totally irreconcilable with the doctrine of the divine right, presupposes a merely human right of the king and a distinction between the spiritual papal power and the secular royal power.

V. Gallicanism and Nationalism

So the era of national Churches begins. It lasts until the ideas of liberty in the modern revolutions become victorious; out of these ideas arises step by step the modern, religiously neutral state. Yet these ideas of civil liberty proceed partly also from the famous freedom of the individual conscience, an idea that slowly develops from the earlier idea of religious tolerance. Puritanism and sectarianism are the roots of this freedom. Both, as minorities, deny the right of the state and of the king, a heretical ruler in their eyes, to intervene in questions of religion. Thus under Cromwell the English Parliament declares: "As for the truth and power of religion it being a thing intrinsical between God and the soul, we conceive, there is no human power of coercion thereunto." Upon this right of religious freedom of conscience were founded later the rights of man and of the citizen. After the great secularization by the philosophers, these rights became the magna charta of the modern democratic and neutral state. Here begins a new phase in the relation of state and Church, marked by the tendency to establish the various types of separation of state and Church.

Let us return to the idea of national Churches. Its more or less distinct presupposition is that, as in the Middle Ages, the religious faith of the people is still considered the necessary basis of political homogeneity. The religious minority is politically disfranchised or persecuted, like the Catholics in England and in the Scandinavian countries, or the Protestants in Spain; or it is compelled to emigrate as long as the abominable principle prevailed: *Cujus regio ejus religio.* This principle was later replaced by the principle of civil tolerance after the wars of religion had failed to restore in the various states a uniform and compulsory state religion. Yet tolerance is a wide and ambiguous concept. There are many degrees and kinds of tolerance.

In its historical development, it means first the right of religious dissenters to be free from compulsory conformity. This does not exclude the state Church as the Established Church nor does it imply civil equality before the law of the land; it means only that the dissenters may privately, though not publicly, worship God without hindrance from the government. The next form of tolerance may be that the dissenters acquire the right of public worship and are politically emancipated, though the state Church continues to be the Established Church with all that is implied thereby, for instance, that the taxes paid by the dissenters are used for the state contributions to the state Church. Finally there appears religious equality. No Established Church exists. But the Christian Churches, the Lutheran, the Reformist and the Catholic Church, all three are recognized as privileged Churches, as "corporations of public law"; they are financially supported by the state that considers itself a genuine Christian state on account of this public and constitutional recognition of the Christian denominations. Typical for such a relation between state and Churches were Prussia, Switzerland, the Netherlands in the nineteenth century; in these states there exists tolerance for all who do not belong to the privileged Churches. So we see that the concept of tolerance presupposes one or more privileged Churches that legally have a union with the state and whose members enjoy, at least practically if not legally, certain political privileges, such as easier admission to public offices, grants to the Churches, to the seminaries and schools from the general public funds.

The religiously uniform state of the absolute prince, whether that of the Reformation or that of the Counter Reformation especially in connection with the rise of nationalism, must come into conflict with the universal spiritual power of the Church. The reason is that the absolute king, if he is a Protestant, claims as *summus episcopus* the full spiritual power in Protestant states; if he is a Catholic, he claims in his domain a wide control of the exercise of the spiritual power of the universal Church and of her head, the pope. The classical type of this for Catholic countries is Gallicanism.[14]

Gallicanism, which has been called rather a political practice than an elaborated system, reaches back in some of its elements to the times of Charlemagne. Yet only under Philip the Fair did it receive its national form. It grew until, under the convert Henry IV, it reached its first formulation in the book, *The Liberties of the Gallican Church*, written in 1594 by Pithou, a convert from Calvinism.

Common to all types of national Churches is the denial of the pope's jurisdictional primacy, as distinguished from the teaching primacy, from which follows the thesis of the supremacy of the general council, or, under special circumstances, even of the national council. Another common principle is that no indirect power is acknowledged in the temporal sphere. It is the king who rules, though not in the dogmatic and sacramental order, yet in the external organizational and legal order, of the Church: he has the right to appoint and depose bishops. All ecclesiastical decrees of bishops and of the pope need his approval (his placet). The king has the right to convoke a national and a general council. He may forbid appeals from national ecclesiastical courts to the court of appeal at the Apostolic See. Anybody, especially members of the clergy, can appeal to the king's court against alleged

14 Though Gallicanism is a product of France, it has found imitations in other Catholic monarchies, for instance, in Austria-Hungary, under the name of Josephinism. This Josephinism, named after Joseph II, prospered also in the Italian small states in the eighteenth century. Under the name of Febronianism we find a similar ecclesiastical policy in the smaller principalities of western and southern Germany. But that the root of both is Gallicanism is beyond question. Febronius, the pseudonym for Johann Nikolaus von Hontheim, auxiliary bishop of Trier, became acquainted with Gallicanism during his study at the University of Louvain. His theory is a conciliar-episcopal one. He denies the monarchical power of the pope. The supreme ecclesiastical power rests with the general council as the representative of the universal Catholic Church. The bishops are exempt from the jurisdictional primacy of the pope. They are therefore sovereign in their dioceses, just as the prince is sovereign in his state. Yet the princes have the right of the external rule over the Church in their states though they have no sacramental power. Hence they nominate the bishops and parish priests, they have control over the education and instruction of the candidates for the priesthood; all the bulls and other pronouncements of the pope need the approval of the prince; that is, they are subject to the censorship of the prince (the so-called placet). Lastly, anybody, priest or layman, has the right to appeal from any decision of a spiritual superior or canon-law court to the king through the *recursus ab abusu*, appeal to the secular power on account of alleged abuse of the spiritual power. Here the superiority of the secular power and the denial of a true sovereignty of the Church and the spiritual power of the pope *in suo ordine* become evident; for it is the secular power that definitely and without any further appeal judges the competence of the spiritual power.

abuses by the spiritual power. The pope cannot levy taxes or other contributions from the faithful in the king's realm without the permission of the king; nor can the pope excommunicate and depose any royal official, especially the king himself, on account of any official act which is allegedly unjust or against faith and morals but is in conformity with the secular law. These liberties of the Gallican Church, —it is contended—are original rights, not derived from revocable concessions on the part of the pope. They are not graciously conceded privileges, but inalienable rights.

The absolute prince, as we pointed out, had denied any kind of original right of the estates or of the people, independent of the power of the sovereign. Any alleged rights of the estates or of the people to participation in government were interpreted as freely conceded, therefore arbitrarily revocable, privileges on the part of the king. All so-called liberties of the subjects are merely revocable privileges freely granted by the absolute king. But the liberties of the Gallican Church under the king are in no way privileges granted by the monarchical head of the Church, the pope; no, they are rather original rights against the pope. The king now makes the pope a monarch by the grace of the general council, or of a national council, as representing the body of the faithful, after having, by his theory of divine right, abolished in his realm all vestiges of popular sovereignty. Truly in Gallicanism there does not exist a state religion, but the religion is the state, and the state is the religion. The complete unity of state and nationalized Church is the effect. The canon law and the hierarchical order of the Church work under the rule and at the whim of the king, who, of course, must be formally a Catholic, as in the Protestant countries the prince as *summus episcopus* must be a member of the established or state Church.

This Gallican theory, if we may so name a thing that was largely a polity and practice of the king and of the national episcopate concerning the relations between national state and the Church, found its formulation in the Declaration of the French Clergy in 1682 under Louis XIV, in the four Gallican articles, written by Bossuet, the court theologian of princely absolutism. These articles say: First: The Pope and the Church have only spiritual power. The king is in all things temporal not subject to any direct or indirect spiritual power. The king cannot be deposed by the pope, nor can the latter absolve the citizens from the oath of allegiance or from obedience to the king.[15] Second: Though the spiritual power belongs fully to the pope, he has no absolute power but a limited one, as he is always subordinated to the general council, not merely at the time of a papal schism. Third: The spiritual power is limited by the generally accepted canon rules of the whole Church and by the rights, customs, and institutions of the Gallican Church. Fourth: Though, in matters of the faith, the pope is primary authority, he is not infallible unless the whole Church agrees to his pronounced dogmatic decisions.

It seems as if the tables are turned. All that the pope claimed for the liberty of the Church is now claimed by the absolute king; all that the absolute king rejected (popular sovereignty, limitation of the royal power by popular rights, traditional customs), these, transferred into Gallican "law," are now used against the alleged absolutism of the pope. No wonder that the reflective Fénelon called those liberties of the Gallican Church "servitudes." The king, says Fénelon, is practically more the head of the Church than is the pope. Liberties from the pope, servitudes to the king. The laity rules over the bishops.[16] Especially the intrusion of the highest royal courts, the parliaments, helped to transform the alleged liberties into servitudes as they used the appeals from abuse of spiritual power as the means to control the canon law and the spiritual authorities.

One may concede that the worst could be avoided as long as the king, the courts, and the public officials were faithful members of the Church. But when the agnostic philosophers of the Enlightenment gave up the traditional religion and indulged in rationalism without a positive Christian faith, what would remain? The Church, religion, is now degraded to a mere instrument of secular politics. Its truth is denied by the ruling class. But its utility for the control of the still faithful people, politically and economically oppressed, is undeniable. Catholicism especially is firm in its principles and does not leave much room for revolutionary private opinions of individuals. Therefore, as a popular state religion, Catholicism is eminently useful, however ridiculous may be its dogma to the enlightened classes. The

---

15 Frayssinous, a moderate Gallican, interpreted this to mean that under no circumstances may a king be deposed by the pope, the Church, or a council, even though he should be a tyrant, a heretic, a persecutor, or an atheist. Cf. W. Gurian, *op. cit.*, p. 6.

16 Cf. Joseph de Maistre, *De l'église gallicane* (p. 312 of the 1874 edition), which is a continuation of his famous *Du pape*.

priest is an excellent teacher of obedience to the authorities, and he works for less than do the gendarmes; he will take care that the belief in the divine right will endure all oppressive polity. Thus eventually the Church becomes a mere instrument of politics in the hands of the absolute king. But the monarch will now regard her only for her usefulness to this end, without respect of her truth, her independence, and her own sovereignty. This is the last consequence of Gallicanism when the political authorities have become religiously indifferent.[17] This position of the Church in the state explains, partly at least, the fury against the Church, which fills the revolutionary mind. Since the Church has become too much a political institution, the revolutionary zeal turns, as it does against the throne, so against the latter's political instrument, the Church and the clergy. This explains, though it does not justify, the militant, anti-ecclesiastical passion of the revolutionists in the old Catholic countries and the fact that their systems of the separation of state and Church actually became systems of a militant oppression of the Church and its educational and religious institutions.

We have presented Gallicanism as the typical form of the relations of Church and state under absolutism. By Church is meant of course the Catholic Church. Princely absolutism is convinced that the full and undivided allegiance to the crown depends on religious homogeneity of the people. Absolutism is further convinced that, for the attainment of this full allegiance, the Church must be wholly subject to the control of the crown in all matters that are not purely sacramental and strictly dogmatic. Thus the external order of the Church, the hierarchy and the clergy, her property and the institutions of education and charity, all must be subjected to a minute petty control of the state.

Thus a union between state and Church or, as the slogan went, between throne and altar, was established. Yet in this union there were not two free and equal partners established in a *modus vivendi* in those fields of human social life in which both had an interest, while outside of these both enjoyed the liberty and independence of perfect societies, each sovereign in its order. On the contrary, the union was

---

[17] A careful observer will notice that Mussolini has uttered opinions which look suspiciously like Gallicanism, as do opinions expressed by some adherents of Franco in Spain. This is not astonishing. Fascism in a Catholic country will follow Gallican lines because of its secularized nationalism and its inherent totalitarianism.

established by the servitude of the Church and the domination of the absolute state. So it is no wonder that the enemies of the absolutism, the philosophers of the era of Enlightenment and the rising bourgeois classes together with the religious nonconformists in the Protestant countries, fought, as they did against the throne, so against the altar, the state Church. The least these groups demanded was that the political rights of the citizen should be dissociated from membership in the Church: the freedom of the individual to religious dissent without any consequences for his standing as a citizen. Full tolerance in religious matters was demanded even though an established Church or a union between Church and state should continue because the majority of the people in fact belonged to the established Church, the Church privileged by the state. The most that these groups demanded was a full and definite separation of state and organized Church. This separation could mean a simple and pure neutrality of the secular power or a militant secularism that intended to produce a political pseudo-religion, a civil religion, which was claimed by Rousseau and his disciples, the freemasons of the French Third Republic, as in our times it is thus claimed by Nazism and communism. The principle of freedom of conscience used against the organized Church would then become a powerful weapon of persecution of the Churches.

CHAPTER XXV

The Modern Secularized State

I. The Rise of Unbelief

Out of the turbulent revolutions of the eighteenth and nineteenth centuries emerges the modern state. It is built upon the rights of man and of the citizen. It adheres to the principle of popular sovereignty. It produces a new ruling class. The clergy of the ancient regime is succeeded by the intellectual man of secular education who in the European continental countries is most often an agnostic or even a militant anticlerical. The nobility is succeeded by the entrepreneurs and capitalist proprietors. Often these latter are interested in a sustained influence of the Church only as long as that influence serves their interest.

The new political principles and the new economic system are in themselves not opposed to the doctrine of the Church. But the theoretical point of view from which they are demanded and the materialist interpretation which they receive may well be irreconcilable with the teaching of the Church, as we have pointed out again and again.

The new state is not a state founded on unity of faith. Moreover, some of its elements were already astir in the ancient regime. The words "tolerance" and "freedom of conscience" were already used in the articles of the Peace Treaty of 1648 that ended the Thirty Years' War. Whereas on the European continent spiritual "personalism" of the individual conscience in religion could not prevail, if we except the small groups of pietists, this "personalism" developed more successfully in the Anglo-Saxon world. Its roots were the doctrines of the Nonconformists and the spiritual enthusiasm of the many sectarian movements; most of these adhered to the doctrine of predestination. Yet, if the individual is predestined, all external attempts of the state or organized Church to influence the internal relation between individual soul and God must be futile. Consequently freedom of conscience is the first religious principle, a natural right, as Oliver Cromwell said. (cf. Cromwell, *Speeches*, ed. by Carlyle, III, 68.)

The overemphasis on the inner life of the soul, the invisibility of the Church, the rejection of a hierarchically organized Church as the mediator between individual soul and God, the enthusiastic prophecy and the evangelical revival in the religious community with the denial of sacred offices instituted by divine law, all this leads to an outspoken religious individualism and to egalitarian democratism in the religious community. This is simply the individualist form of common priesthood and the rejection of all hierarchical elements. "We are not over one another, but with one another"; "consociation not subordination": these are the new principles. Full tolerance, full political rights for Jews, Turks, and pagans are the consequence.[1]

Only against Catholics was tolerance not much exercised either in England or in the New England colonies. For these "national" democrats, the pope was a foreign sovereign; the Catholic who recognized the pope's spiritual authority was considered a political enemy incapable of civil rights. This is understandable only if by this word "tolerance" was meant, not a genuine freedom of conscience, but rather a practical principle in politics. Tolerance meant, therefore, adherence to religious individualism and implied theologically the rejection of the Catholic Church, so that a Catholic adhering to an "intolerant" dogmatic faith could himself not claim "tolerance."

From this strongly individualist freedom of conscience is derived as something new the freedom of the person, of property, and of speech, just as the ecclesiastical egalitarianism in the congregation leads to popular sovereignty in polity. The remarkable thing is that, whenever possible, a peaceful separation of state and Church is introduced, but without that anti-Christian militancy that later is so evident in the countries of the European continent. On the contrary, a sort of Christian aura permeates the new democratism. Yet the liberties that were considered new were not so new in political constitutional prac-

1 Cf. the Baptist Tracts on liberty of conscience (1614–61), 1846 edition, where Busher says (p. 33): "The King and parliament may please to permit all sorts of Christians, yea: Jews, Turks, and pagans. so long as they are peaceable." The import of the predestination theory upon the Established Church in England is understood by the latter when it is said in the declaration of the Thirty-nine Articles of 1628: "Predestination is the root of all Puritanism, and Puritanism is the root of all rebellion."

tice. But these liberties of old tradition, naturally somewhat changed in the new social environment, received a different interpretation and a new foundation.

These liberties in their new interpretation became at once the subject of discussion between state and Church. And the more so as in the continental countries the new interpretations had a militant and outspoken antitraditional and anti-Catholic bias. This is the result of modern naturalism, which sprang from the spirit of the Renaissance. Nikolai Berdyaev rightly points out (*The End of Our Time*, chapter 1) that the humanism of the Renaissance, in spite of its incorporation of antiquity, was not anti-Christian. On the contrary, it was a great daring attempt to fuse classical antiquity with Christian humanism that issued from medieval Christianity. Yet the era of Renaissance humanism contained the germs of decay.

It was through the absorption of Christianity with the theological controversies between Reformation and Counter Reformation that the other half of Renaissance humanism (natural man, free individual personality as distinguished from the *anima Christiana*) was set free and shed its Christian theological tradition. Yet this meant that then human energies went wholly into the field of secular philosophy and art, into the natural sciences, into politics freed from the restriction of Christian ethics, into economics separated likewise from Christian ethics. Reason and will, not faith and ascetical virtue, earthly happiness and freedom of the individual with a naturalist connotation, not the salvation of the soul and the consoling membership in the mystical body of Christ, these became the prevailing values. So it happened that modern civilization which is natural and is without an understanding for the supernatural faith, which is secular and is without consideration of the life beyond, which is consequently concerned mostly with the production of hedonistic material values, denied the real values of revealed religion by measuring it according to its contribution to material progress. The outcome of this process of dechristianization is then indifferentism, the final belief that it is neither truth nor God's revealed word nor virtue that matters, but utility for material progress and success.

So modern secularist civilization was produced. Life circles around man as the secular citizen and his economic, political, and scientific interests. Undeniably there is a strong tendency to put the religious

life into the private sphere, to regard man as the believer, the faithful
Christian who makes civilization a Christian one, as a somewhat
strange figure in public life. Religion becomes a private affair or even
perhaps the pardonable oddity of the private citizen. The Church
becomes an association, a private organization of people, legally not
different from clubs and associations of men with hobbies. The accent
in this secularist civilization is on material values and consequently
produces the utilitarian and hedonistic ethics of the nineteenth
century with their premiums upon material success and material
pleasure. Hence the social institutions, as, for example, marriage,
change their meaning. Marriage becomes wholly dependent on the
ability of the partners to find subjective satisfaction without much
regard for the objective end of marriage, transcendent to individual
interests. The state, too, loses its dignity as a means to the perfect life;
it becomes a night-watchman of safes and stands for the promotion of
trade, of profits. Education here means less a strengthening of the
moral character; ever more and more it means technical preparation
for a lucrative job. This new secular civilization is predominantly
materialistic. It can last only because it lives on the inherited values of
Christianity, and it can last only so long as this inheritance is not
squandered. But the process of dechristianizing society is undeniable,
and it is indirectly shown by the attempt of the Church to rechristianize
society.

Under these circumstances the modern state became neutral in
relation to the Church, however much in some countries an aura of
Christian culture survived. This neutrality as a practical polity was
the recognition of the fact that the people living in the state were
religiously split up into numerous groups, none of which was even a
considerable minority, not to speak of a majority. The peaceful separation of state and Church was thus the consequence; for it is the unified
religion of the great majority of its citizens that makes the state a
Catholic or a Protestant state. Therefore the modern constitutions
established the principle of the free Church in the free state. When
the ruling class in the modern state is violently anti-Christian, then of
course the separation of state and Church becomes, under the name of
laicism, a persecution of at least the Catholic Church, as has happened
in Latin.countries. A third type of the modern state, usually possible
only when the traditional monarchical element has not been over-

thrown, is the Christian state, that is, a state which gives civil tolerance to all religious groups, but privileges in public law to the Christian Churches (and the Synagogues) under the rule of equality. This Christian state practices a legal and political cooperation with the Church by concordat, thus maintaining a qualified union between Church and state.

German states like Prussia and Bavaria until 1918, Belgium, Switzerland, and the Netherlands are typical for this kind of Christian state, while the outstanding example of a peaceful and friendly separation is the United States. On the other hand, France under the Third Republic since 1903 and the late Spanish Republic of 1931 are examples of the militant laicist type of separation.

II. The Answer of the Church

The Church answers the new civilization and the new philosophy of law and of state in condemning the principle of indifferentism as the basis of tolerance, in repudiating the principle of the separation of Church and state as an ideal of political progress. The Church rejects the new positivist doctrine that makes the sovereign will of the state the source of all law and thus denies both the validity of natural law and divine law and the independence of the sacred order of canon law. The Church exposes the materialist philosophy and the naturalist ethics that underlie this positivist philosophy, whether a capitalist or a Marxist sort, which pretends to represent the heir of the bygone theological and metaphysical era, leading mankind now in an infinite immanent progress to an earthly paradise. The Church also rejects the essentials of Gallicanism, the appeal from the spiritual courts to the secular courts on account of an alleged abuse of spiritual power and because of a miscarriage of justice by the ecclesiastical courts or administrative offices. She condemns the principle that always and everywhere the secular law should prevail over the canon law, as she rejects the doctrine that concordats may be arbitrarily revoked by the state according to the state's interests and according to political expediency, and she rejects the modern thesis that the Church has no rights in education and instruction of the faithful and their children.[2]

---

[2] Cf. Denzinger (1937), no. 1613. Encyclical *Mirari vos* (no. 1677); encyclical *Quanta cura* (no. 1688); and the Syllabus of 1864 (nos. 1701 ff.). As Denzinger's footnote says, the true

The most decisive act to strengthen the Church in her encounter with the new civilization was the declaration of the Vatican Council that the pope is infallible when he pronounces *ex cathedra* definitions of faith and morals for the whole Church. At the same time this Council did away with the remnants of the conciliar theory, of the Febronian and Gallican theories. Thus was the Church now prepared to challenge the new secular civilization marked by optimistic faith

---

sense of the Syllabus may be found only by relating the propositions to the context of the various documents (mostly encyclicals and allocutions) from which the condemnations are taken. If this advice were followed by all who pretend to know the Syllabus, much hard feeling and misunderstanding would be avoided. The context is decisive, showing the light in which the propositions are condemned. And it is the task of theology to elaborate the sense of the positive proposition that follows from the form of the condemned proposition.

The condemned proposition no. 63 may serve as an example. "It is allowed to withdraw obedience from legitimate princes and to rebel against them." The right thesis is then: It is not allowed, etc. But this proposition must be read and understood in the light of the tradition of Catholic theology and political philosophy. If this is done, it appears that "legitimate," as we have seen, must be understood not in the sense of a legitimist theory of De Maistre or other romanticists, nor in the light of the theory of the divine right of princes, but in the sense of St. Thomas, Suarez, Bellarmine, and the Schools. Or would it not be preposterous to demand obedience to the prince who is formally and juridically legitimate, if he should demand obedience to a law that is evidently against natural or divine law? Some of the propositions have to be interpreted within the historical background of a militant anti-Christian liberalism in countries where only a small ruling class indulged in this antireligious liberalism while the majority of the people were faithful adherents to the Catholic faith. This liberalism has, therefore, little to do with the social and political ideals of Lacordaire, Ozanam, and Montalembert, the liberal Catholics in France, or with what is today called a liberal, that is, a person who fights for the liberation of the proletariat, who prefers democracy, who is in favor of social legislation. These "liberal Catholics" were never condemned, as Bishop Dupanloup explained in his pamphlet about the Syllabus and the Encyclicals. This pamphlet was approved by Rome. Cf. W. Gurian, *op. cit.*, p. 233; art. "Liberalisme catholique" in *Dict. de theol. cath.*

In regard to tolerance, we must distinguish between theoretical dogmatic tolerance, civil tolerance, and political tolerance. The first is impossible. Either the Church has the truth or it has not the truth. If the latter were true, all religions would be on a par, as indifferentism holds. But no genuine religion, no Church, can tolerate in its fold contradictory dogmas. What about civil tolerance? Pius IX (Denz., no. 1678) condemns any enmity toward non-Catholics and admonishes that the law of charity demands that we do good to them. What is political tolerance? It is equal treatment in political matters of all religions. Of course, this is conditioned by historical circumstances. When in 1906 the Center Party in Germany demanded, in its Tolerance Bill, equality of treatment for all religions, this bill was never disapproved by any ecclesiastical authority. Here the concrete interests of the common good have to be considered. The religious freedom which the Catholics of the United States enjoy by the constitutional provision of the separation of Church and state has been praised by Pius IX and Leo XIII and their successors. From these remarks it follows that we should devote as much time to the study of ecclesiastical documents and their true meaning as we are accustomed to give to studying legal texts or philosophical propositions.

in infinite progress and despair of faith and religion, by thousands of isms in religion, in ethics, and in philosophy, by blatant agnostic secularism, by relativism, by nationalism in international life, by positivism and materialism in social science, by the worship of might.

On September 20, 1870, the white flag of military surrender was hoisted over the Vatican. The secular dominion of the pope, the Church-state, was swallowed up by the new national state of Italy. Yet this flag was not so much a token of capitulation and decline, as the adversaries all too optimistically predicted and the unbelieving intellectuals with a condescending sentiment of pity presumed. The event was rather a symbol that the Church looked confidently with all her spiritual weapons to a new conquest of modern civilization. We find this optimism in Bishop Ketteler, Ozanam, and Cardinal Gibbons, and in the numerous Catholic movements in theology and philosophy, in the revival of Catholic literature, in the imposing movements for social legislation. There awakens something like the spirit of Gregory the Great, who left the declining Roman culture and began the mission among the barbarians, as the effete and snobbish Romans called the Anglo-Saxon and the Germanic tribes.

All these currents unite in the venerable personality of Leo XIII, pope, philosopher, and statesman. He inaugurates a new meeting between the Church and modern civilization. He did not speak the austere and pessimistic language of Pius IX who, disappointed after his early friendliness toward the liberal tendencies before 1848, condemned in angry sentences the materialist and agnostic foundations of modern civilization. Leo XIII spoke a language which the modern world could understand and, while in principles he remained as firm as Pius IX, he showed much understanding for the new institutions in the social, economic, and political world. So the modern world began again not only to understand the language of the pope, but it also felt the spiritual and moral power of a Church that had been declared antiquated and outmoded by the intellectual leaders of secularist civilization in the nineteenth century. Leo XIII made Thomistic philosophy the norm of Catholic studies. He inaugurated the *Ralliement* policy in France, in order to reconcile the democratic Republic and French Catholicism. He ended the Kulturkampf in Prussia and so prepared for the rise of Catholicism as a social and intellectual power for the re-Christianizing of society in the exemplary

social movement of German Catholicism. Cardinal Gibbons found in
Leo XIII profound understanding for the specific situation of the
Church in the United States and for the liberty of the Church under a
constitution that had established separation between Church and state
as a principle of polity.

In numerous encyclicals and allocations this Pope, who became a
social and political philosopher of world-wide reputation, enunciated
the same principles as had stood for centuries in the shelter of Catholic
political philosophy. Yet he set them forth in a language that was
classical and modern at the same time. And the principles were not
pronounced in an abstract manner but were used to show the way
to the solutions of the concrete problems that had been produced by
the new democratic and republican constitutions of the modern state,
by the social problems that capitalism had produced, by the philosophical problems that the development of the sciences and historical
research had evoked.

Thus there arises a new form of the doctrine concerning the relation
between Church and state. It is a new state that produces the problem,
not a changed Church. Scholars not conversant with the history of
Catholic political philosophy even went so far as to say that only
since Leo XIII has there existed a Catholic political philosophy which
is adapted to the modern times and enables the Catholic people to
have its own polity.[3] Only the last part of this statement is correct, and
eminently so. It is, therefore, necessary to give a report of this Leonine
theory in which the problem of the relation between Church and
modern state is presented in masterly fashion and which is for the
time being the pattern for political philosophy as well as for ecclesiastical polity.

III. LEO XIII ON THE *Libertas Ecclesiae*

The form of the Christian religion was from the beginning and by
divine institution a hierarchically constituted community with a
distinct constitution and a definite internal order. The Christian
religion is a visible, organized Church, not a sect in the sociological
sense. At none of its historical stages of development was Christianity
merely a spiritual, invisible community of subjective religious rapture,

[3] Thus the Protestant scholar Bredt in *Geist der deutschen Verfassung* (1924), p. 56.

merely an unorganized group of religious people with the same religious personal experiences and emotions. The Christian Church participates in the two natures of its divine founder.

Leo XIII points out that in Christ, the head of the Church and the example for it, there are united the human and the divine nature, a visible and an invisible nature. In the same way the Church as the mystical body of Christ is the true Church because its visible members draw their life and their vigor from the supernatural gifts and the other roots whence their proper nature and life emanate. Therefore we can see the Church as a social body, the animating principle of which is Christ. For Christ would not merely have disciples of His doctrine; He wished that His disciples should unite in a society, in one social body, that is, in a Church. Thus the Church has not merely developed into a perfect society, but this nature of a perfect society was established by its Founder so that the Church for the good of mankind may fight like a well-organized army. This constitution of the visible Church is unchangeable and perennial. The Church is a perfect society because it has an internal principle of life and a visible constitution that do not come from without; on the contrary, these are intrinsic and essential to the Church by divine dispensation. Therefore the Church, by its very nature, has its own and original legislative authority. It is a demand of true order that the Church's legislative authority should be independent; the Church must be free in its organizational and juridical life.[4]

Yet, in spite of many similarities, there is a great difference between the Church and the state according to their different origins, ends, and intrinsic natures. The origin of the Church is the direct divine act of founding; the Church is of divine right. The state originates in human nature and exists by natural law. The end of the Church is the salvation of souls. The end of the state is secular order and earthly happiness. The constitution and the offices of the Church are divine law, unchangeable, perennial. The constitutions and governments of the states are of mere human law to be changed whenever the common good of the people requires it. The people as citizens and as Christian members of the Church are embraced by both, the spiritual and the secular society. Yet each of these societies has certain limita-

---

[4] The original text may be found in *Alloc.*, IV, 14; V, 269; VI, 158. Tischleder gives the texts, *op. cit.*, pp. 489 ff.

tions indicated by their proximate ends and their different natures. Each of them is circumscribed as by a circle, to use Leo XIII's own words, inside of which each acts in accordance with its own independent rule of law.[5]

Consequently the subjection of the Church to the sovereignty of the state as Gallicanism and Erastianism practice it, is to Leo a grave misunderstanding of the end and the nature of the Church as a true perfect society. The Church must be free and independent in her sphere. In her hierarchical order and in her canon law and in her freedom to teach, the spiritual authority must be the independent master and the sovereign judge of her own affairs, undisturbed on the part of the secular power by any considerations of expediency and usefulness for the secular field. Whatever in human affairs in any way belongs to the sacred sphere or to the salvation of souls or to divine worship, all that is wholly under the authority and the independent judgment of the Church.[6]

To this sphere of the Church belong the sacraments and their unhindered administration by those whom the spiritual authority has called and ordained. To it belong also the free preaching of the gospel and of the doctrine of the Church, the freedom of missionary activity, the freedom of worshiping in accordance with the teaching and the spiritual law of the Church; to it belongs the freedom of the spiritual authorities to direct the clergy in upholding the ecclesiastical discipline free from any intervention by the secular power on account of an alleged secular sovereignty or of social expediency. The Church, therefore, cannot be compared to a private association of citizens which receives its charter from the secular power, is subject to the control of the secular power, and obtains its power to legislate by the grace of the state.

What is the content of this liberty of the Church? Some essential elements may illustrate this: the hierarchical order, the election of the pope, the transfer of the episcopal office, the education and ordination of the clergy and its subordination under the hierarchical authorities and under the canon law in doctrine, in ecclesiastical administration, and in discipline. The election of the pope must be free; and no secular authority has any right of direct or indirect,

---

[5] *Alloc.*, II, 152 ff. (Encyclical *Immortale Dei*).
[6] *Ibid.*, p. 153.

positive or negative, intervention. Since Pius X's Constitution *Vacante Sede Apostolica* (December 25, 1914), the veto of the Austrian Emperor as the successor of the medieval emperors has been abolished. This veto (or "exclusive") constituted the emperor's competency to give notice to the electing cardinals that the probable candidate for the papacy was not *persona grata* to the emperor, His Apostolic Majesty. It was last used against Cardinal Rampolla in 1903. Today any such "exclusive," even the simple expressed desire of any secular power for the election of a certain candidate, is absolutely prohibited.

The appointment to the episcopal dignity likewise must be free. No secular power has any right to appoint a cleric to the episcopal office. By virtue of concordats the secular authorities may have a certain influence upon the appointment of bishops. Thus most concordats provide that the future bishop must be a citizen of the state in which his diocese is situated. Often the pope agreed to communicate to the secular government the name of the candidate for the bishopric in order to learn if the candidate was, for reasons of a general political nature, not *persona grata* to the government. If after a certain time the government has made no statement, the pope is entitled to make the appointment. In most concordats it is confirmed that the holders of such ecclesiastical benefices as are fully or partly supported by the state, must hold citizenship in the state and must have a general education such as prescribed by the government. Other stipulations regulate the opening of establishments of religious orders and societies and the administration of their properties, or they may determine that in this regard the canon law exclusively should rule without any intervention of the government. In some of the last concordats (e.g., Germany, Italy) the clergy has been barred from political activity on behalf of any political party. This is nothing extraordinary nor does it mean any sacrifice of the political rights of the individual priest in favor of Fascism. The canon law as a rule states that members of the clergy must not be candidates for the office of deputy in the representative chambers, and that they must not accept such office without the permission of their own bishop and of the bishop in whose diocese the election takes place (can. 138 §4).

The education of the clergy must be free from state interference. Leo XIII compares the right of the Church to educate her clergy to the claim of the state to educate its army officers. Just as here the state claims full and exclusive rights of education by loyal and expert officers, so the Church has the right to require that the candidates for the priesthood be chosen and educated according to canon law. This right is of the utmost importance for a true freedom of the Church. The absolute princes have always tried to get control over the education of the clergy. Thus they would have a kind of spiritual gendarmery that could be used in the interest of the state; and the clergy, imbued with Erastian ideas, could be used against Rome and the papacy, as a suitable tool for the repression of the freedom of the Church.

The freedom of the gospel and of doctrine means the denial of any competence of the secular power to censure or suppress papal or episcopal encyclicals and letters. It means the freedom of the teaching Church to impart her doctrine to her members and to pronounce it openly before the public. The freedom of the sacramental dispensation means that no secular power has the right to disqualify a man on account of race, language, or color from his right as a Christian to have access to the sacraments and the houses of worship.

IV. The Field of Cooperation

What has been dealt with so far is clearly of the spiritual sphere, where the true sovereignty of the Church and of her spiritual order is beyond question. Yet we find social institutions that concern both the Church and the state. Thus marriage between Catholics may be subject to both laws, the canon law and the civil law. The Church considers matrimony a supernatural covenant. Its essential properties are unity and indissolubility, and these obtain in Christian matrimony a special fixity on account of the sacramental character of matrimony (C.J.C., can. 1013 §2). Consequently the marriage of all those who by valid baptism are members of the Church is subject not only to divine law but also to the canon law, while the secular power has the competence to regulate the civil effects of matrimony.

In modern times the earlier identity of canon and civil law concerning the essentials of matrimony, the full recognition of canon law for matrimony by the secular power for its Christian citizens, has ceased to exist. It is an undeniable trend of modern civilization to secularize social life, to loosen social institutions and the political order from religion in its objective divine form, from the Church.

Thus the foundation of matrimony has become a civil-law contract which, subject to the general rules of the law of contract, is dissoluble under civil law at the will of the contracting partners in certain conditions determined by civil law. So the modern civil law denies such an essential property of matrimony as its indissolubility, in contradiction to divine and natural law. The Church, therefore, cannot acknowledge the civil law concerning the bond of matrimony, especially for those who are validly baptized and are consequently members of the Church, subject in matrimonial law to the divine and canon law. Marriage between Christians is in its concept and essence something intrinsically sacred. Therefore it is just and equitable that it is ordered, not by the ordinances of the state, but by the authority of the Church, which alone has power over the sacred.[7]

The sacrament in marriage is by no means a mere adornment, a superfluous religious ceremony that is added to the essential civil-law contract of matrimony, so that juridically this civil-law contract, subject alone to the secular authority, is the main point and the sacrament unessential. On the contrary, in all matters that concern the bond of matrimony and its essentials, only the Church and her spiritual law is competent. Therefore the Church can under no circumstances acknowledge the secular jurisdiction in matters concerning the bond of matrimony. Divorce pronounced by the secular judge for members of the Church duly married in accordance with canon law is in flagrant contradiction to the divine and canon law and to the sacramental character of matrimony. Especially in countries where the great majority of the people are Catholics, such a contradiction between civil law and canon law is out of place. Things may be different in countries where the majority of the citizens are not members of the Church, as we shall see later.

This claim of the Church over the bond of matrimony does not mean that the Church claims an exclusive jurisdiction in matrimonial law. It means only the precedence of the sacramental law over the civil law in matters that concern the sacramental character of matrimony for members of the Church. Yet the Church does not deny that matrimony, as it serves for the preservation and propagation of human society, is closely connected with human relations that immediately follow from matrimony but belong to the sphere of secular life, such

[7] *Ibid.,* VI, 29; VII, 179; VIII, 175.

as the property relations between husband and wife, the legal liabilities of the husband for the wife and vice versa, the mutual duties of support and also all those matters that are connected with matrimony as a social and economic union. To regulate these relations between husband and wife and between the married couple and third parties is clearly in the competence of the secular authority, to which is entrusted the care for the common good and whose duty it is to direct the social community of matrimony and of the family to the common good.[8] Yet the state, the civil law, has no authority to void the sacramental union between members of the Church. It has no jurisdiction over the bond of matrimony. Therefore divorce according to the civil law has not the power to void the matrimonial contract validly concluded by members of the Church. It is thus impossible for the Church to acknowledge a right of the state to void the matrimonial bond between validly baptized persons on account of racial discriminations, as the Nürnberg anti-Semitic laws provided.

The sacramental character of matrimony, and the identity of matrimonial contract and sacrament for Christians have, furthermore, the effect that the Church cannot acknowledge the mere civil-law marriage as matrimony between Christians. The Syllabus of 1864 declares that a mere civil-law marriage cannot constitute a valid marriage between Christians, i.e., between members of the Church. Leo XIII confirms that the union between Christians without the sacramental form is not Christian matrimony at all. If Christians conclude a marriage only before the civil authorities, they fulfill a "custom" of the secular society but, according to canon law, they live in illicit concubinage and incur the appropriate censures of the canon law. The validity of matrimony between Christians is thus determined by spiritual law.

This does not exclude the Church's tolerance of laws which prescribe a civil marriage ceremony for Christian citizens as a requisite condition for the legal effects of marriage in civil life. To fulfill the demands of the civil law concerning marriage may even be a duty for Christians in order to secure to the married and to the children those legal rights and that legal status which the civil law affords. Of course, in states where the great majority of the people are still members of the Church in law and in fact, the ideal is that the civil law simply

[8] *Ibid.*, I, 133 (Encyclical *Arcanum divinae sapientiae*).

acknowledge the norms of the canon law concerning the bond of marriage and the matrimonial contract. Consequently in such states the civil law should not allow divorce for citizens who as Christians have contracted a marriage according to canon law. In the concordat with Austria (1934) it is agreed that the Republic of Austria acknowledges all marriages contracted in accordance with the canon law and grants them the full legal status of the civil law; Austria acknowledges further the competence of the ecclesiastical courts concerning the bond of matrimony; i.e., the validity of a marriage is exclusively ruled by canon law with full effect in civil law.

Evidently such a rule of the canon law presupposes the unity in faith and Church membership of the people. Wherever the people are not in great majority members of the Church, there the state and the civil law must legislate about the form of marriage, about the matrimonial contract and all the legal effects of the latter. And it may even be tolerated that a state, in which only a minority of the citizens are members of the Church in law and in fact, does not acknowledge the norms of the canon law concerning marriage even for its Catholic citizens, at least as long as the civil law does not command something that is in contradiction to the canon law. This status is indeed not an ideal one, because the civil law may acknowledge between members of the Church a matrimonial contract that according to canon law is void and forbidden. For example, the state gives full legal status to the second marriage of divorced Catholics, whereas the canon law regards such a marriage as bigamy. By such a discrepancy between the civil law and the ecclesiastical matrimonial law the latter becomes a mere accessory to the decisive and exclusively enforcible civil law.

The least tolerable status exists where the canon law is expressly invalidated and has no influence at all recognized by civil law. Here the civil law seems to consider Christian matrimony merely as a private affair or a tolerated custom of pious people. Yet matrimony between Christians can never be a worldy affair. It is not a contract like any other contract concerning worldly affairs. As a true status contract and a sacrament, matrimony is beyond the whim and selfish interests of husband and wife. Most especially has the modern trend to facilitate divorce, in connection with the materialist philosophy of birth control, undermined the pillars upon which rests the wealth of nations, the family. Yet the Church, presupposing the state and the family as the secular forms of the social life of the people of God, cannot leave these forms to the vagaries of quickly changing popular philosophies. It will always be the purpose of the Church to reach a status where the same person may live as a Christian under the norms of the spiritual law and as a citizen under the rules of the civil law, both acknowledging Christian matrimony as a sacrament and as the spring of life for the people of God and the people of the state.

The foundations of this ideal of cooperation between Church and state are first, the proposition that no real contradiction can exist between the rights and duties of a Christian and those of the citizen. This follows from the order of ends of the human communities. This order, derived from the idea of man's metaphysical nature and end, directs the various communities (the family, the state, the community of nations) to their corresponding ends. The Church, issuing from the same divine origin though in a supernatural revelation, has her own end. This end is autonomous, and the Church is a self-sufficient, perfect society. She is not a mere religious society beside the secular societies; she is not subject to the sovereignty of other societies, such as that of the national state or of the majority of the members of the Church in the sense of popular sovereignty, or of a Utopian world state.

Furthermore, the whole body of the ends of the various communities does not constitute a mere agglomeration but an order in which one end is above another or under another in spite of its relative independence. Thus the family, although its objective end is essentially independent of arbitrary interference by the state, is subject to the regulative power of the state. And the state on its part, although it is sovereign, is yet as a member of the community of nations subject to the demands of the international common good and the rules that logically follow from this mode of existence. From this we conclude that on the order of ends follows an order of the corresponding communities. And in this sense we say that the Church, whose spiritual end is superior to the ends of other communities, is superior to the other communities so far as the realization of her end is concerned. Hence the spiritual power is in the same way superior to the power of the state. Yet to conclude that therefore the secular power is in all matters and in every regard subject to the spiritual power is, as we have seen, very wrong, because political authority is truly sovereign *in suo ordine,* in its realm.

However clear and distinct this proposition may be *in abstracto,* the concrete life may, on account of its ever-changing circumstances, of abnormal individual situations, produce a conflict. When both powers contend that in a specific matter they are sovereign, when the secular law demands an exclusive right and absolute loyalty where the Church cannot grant it, what then? In this case the superiority becomes evident. The Church, conscious of her vocation and of her divinely instituted authority as teacher and interpreter of the revealed word of God, will assert her superiority. For the Church is then in the same position in which the individual Christian conscience is when met by a demand of the state that is against conscience. Just as the Christian conscience then affirms that it must obey God rather than men, so the Church must say that she must obey God and not men. And she will do so because, though the individual conscience may be erroneous, the Church and her supreme authority do not err, however inadequate, in individual cases, the polity and practical means of asserting this superiority may have been. Only to an era dominated by materialism or agnosticism, does this principle seem strange. Yet, whenever the spiritual end of man is acknowledged and God's revealed word recognized, this superiority is the necessary consequence, if the Church and not the isolated individual conscience is recognized as the divinely instituted spiritual authority.

It is now this order of human ends that forbids the Church to be indifferent to the sphere of political life. The Church, says Leo XIII, cannot be indifferent to the laws that are valid in the various states, not so far as they are secular laws, but so far as they transgress the competency of the state and trespass upon the field of the exclusive competency of the Church. In such a case the Church has the God-given duty to resist, when a law of the state violates religion. The Church must then do all in her power that the Spirit of the Gospels rule in the laws and institutions of the state.[9] If ever the Church should abandon this fundamental position, she would abandon herself. The Church would then be degraded to a mere private association for the furtherance of private religious or ethical ends of private

[9] *Ibid.,* IV, 19 (Encyclical *Sapientiae Christianae*).

individuals under the sovereign domination of the state; or the Church would become a department of state administration for the furtherance of secular ends of the secular, cultural polity of an absolute state. Yet even the religious liberty of the individual is directed against the state, against its abuse of compulsory power to religious conformity on account of political reasons. For the members of the Church there cannot exist an unlimited right to religious freedom, because this would contradict the nature of the Church as a perfect society gifted with spiritual authority. The right to religious freedom means ultimately the freedom of the Church, not a freedom of the individual against the Church. So even the modern secular or religiously neutral state recognizes in its right of religious freedom the spiritual sphere in which the Church is supreme.

In trying to visualize this relation between state and Church, we may suppose two intersecting circles. The segment common to both circles would represent the mixed matters, where both communities have an interest, while the rest of the circles would fall strictly under the supreme rule of either Church or state. How great that segment of the mixed matters may be, depends largely on historical circumstances. Thus it may be greater in predominantly Catholic countries, while it may be very small when the state, on account of the number of denominations among its citizens, is religiously neutral and confines itself to purely secular fields under the regime of the separation of Church and state. Yet any total absorption of the state by the Church or the vice versa would be disastrous to both. The Church absorbing the state's power and end would be in danger of using spiritual power for the political ends of the state it has absorbed. The state absorbing the Church would be easily tempted to abuse political power in the realm of religion and faith, which again is vicious because, as St. Augustine says, man can believe only with his free will.[10] Political compulsion in matters of faith is a contradiction in itself. Caesaropapism is just as wrong as papocaesarism.

The indirect power of the Church in matters temporal must be distinguished from the concordatory rule over the mixed matters. This indirect power originates in the qualitative superiority of the Church's end and consequently of the ecclesiastical authority. It is the power of teaching and of judging. It means that the Church has

[10] *Tract. XXVI in Joann.*, no. 2.

the right and the duty to teach the state in matters of polity in so far as they concern the ultimate end of man, the salvation of souls, and the glory of God. It means that to the Church belongs the power to judge the sins of the political power and to proclaim what is morally right or wrong in politics upon the basis of natural law or positive divine law. The pope, says Leo XIII, must be able to confirm authoritatively what is contained in divine revelation, to declare which political doctrines are in agreement with it and which are in contradiction to it. In the same way the pope must be able to confirm what is intrinsically good or bad in the realm of morals, what has to be done or omitted for the salvation of souls. Otherwise he could be neither a secure interpreter of God's word nor a secure leader for man to eternal life.[11]

V. The Independence of Political Authority

Too easily modern writers draw from this statement the conclusion that this claim of the ecclesiastical authority to interpret the word of God and to judge over the whole field of morality necessarily contracts the independence and liberty of the political authority in its secular order, which has been confirmed and acknowledged before. Thus, it is said, through this claim the spiritual authority, infallible in these matters of faith and morals, actually subordinates the totality of the social and political life to its supreme and final control. Papal theocracy, with its absolute rule over the state and the social and economic life, would be the consequence.[12] But this is certainly absurd. For it would presuppose that neither a natural law nor a divine revelation

11 *Alloc.*, IV, 17 (Encyclical *Sapientiae Christianae*).

12 Especially after the Vatican Council's declaration of the dogma of papal infallibility were such fears or suspicions aroused. Gladstone's aggressive pamphlet against the Vatican Council and the replies of Manning and Newman are famous. Actually the dogma was not a new doctrine, but as old as the institution of the papacy. Certainly this infallibility does not refer to juridical matters as, for instance, the deposition of princes. Pius IX so expressly declared in his allocution of 1871; cf. Fessler (Secretary of the Council), *La vraie et la fausse infallibilité des papes;* translated from the German, 1872). It does not reach into the field of mere political and economic problems. When the cardinal legate, Serafino Vanutelli, in his address at the Catholic Meeting in Essen (1906), demanded strict obedience to the papal authority in political and social matters, this was later qualified with the words "in so far as religion is concerned." This qualification was stressed by Pius X in his brief of October 30, 1906, to Cardinal Fischer of Cologne, proclaiming freedom of Catholics in matters non-religious; cf. Joseph Schmidlin, *op. cit.*, III, 98, 158.

exists, and it would further presuppose that the political authorities are eager to issue laws and decrees that are flagrantly in contradiction to natural and divine law. But it is preposterous to suppose such a thing with the exception, of course, of the new pagan tyrannies. Yet it is amazing to observe that the world, earlier so jealous of its freedom from papal criticism and so sensitive to any exercise of this papal prerogative, now complains so loudly that the pope does not vigorously enough condemn political practices of the tyrants.

It must not be forgotten that, on account of the long influence of Christianity, political authorities rarely issue laws or follow a policy which is directly in contradiction with divine and natural law. Church history shows us very few interventions of the highest ecclesiastical authority in politics and even fewer which were not, at once or later, acclaimed by the majority of impartial persons as sound and justified. Besides, to declare a state law ineffective because it openly contradicts natural or divine law, adds no new obligation to the citizen's duties to hold such a law ineffective, nor does a declaration of this sort make such a law invalid. Such a law is intrinsically void by its own merits. We must note further that this claim of indirect power does not imply a positive direction of the political authority in ways and means to the furtherance of the common good. The positive task of political authority is its very own and is under its own jurisdiction and sovereign competence.

The competence of the Church in matters of morality does not imply any competence of the Church to teach or judge about what is economically sound or useful in economic policy, about what has to be done concretely by social legislation to fulfill the demands of social justice, about which are the best means to avoid wars or to guarantee peace, about which are the best methods in education, which illegal acts must be punished and how. All this is left to the free decision of political authority. Thus this indirect power is not a distinct power in itself in addition to the spiritual power. It is the same spiritual power turning its face to the world of politics, to the secular realm. This indirect power does not mean a power over political and secular matters inasmuch as they are of a political nature, but inasmuch as they are subject to the rule of natural and divine law, of which the Church is the teacher and authoritative interpreter. Whoever denies such a power, asserts implicitly that political authority is intrinsically infallible or that the spiritual power has no competence to declare a sin to be a sin, an injustice to be an injustice.

There is still rampant a political modernism that thinks itself free from the teaching and judging authority of the Church and claims the entire secular world for its own sovereign and absolute rule. This modernism [18] considers itself free to disregard the authoritative decisions and teachings of the Church in moral, legal, and social matters. It holds that the principle of a living wage, not merely the practical ways and means for attaining it, is morally without obligation or that the principles of social justice, however clearly taught by Leo XIII, are of no importance for the shaping of the social and economic order. From the standpoint of Catholicism there is no doubt that such a modernism is inadmissible. For it would surrender the objective rules of universal natural and supernatural morality to the sovereign judgment of individuals or to the subjective and often unstable opinions of interested groups. So this modernism is not so much a defender of liberty from supposedly arbitrary acts of the spiritual authority, but rather the denial of authority itself and of spiritual authority even in its own field.

Pope Leo XIII, who asserted the independence and liberty of the Church as a true perfect society, who urged the superiority of the Church and her end in the hierarchy of ends, this same Pope does not tire of stressing the true sovereignty of the state *in suo ordine* and its nature as a perfect society. Seldom has a political philosopher so earnestly emphasized the dignity and the majesty of the secular authority. For Leo XIII the state is a dispensation of God's will revealing Himself in the law of nature. Hence it stands of itself and does not need a consecration by the spiritual authority. Obedience is due by the Christian to political authority for the sake of the common good irrespective of the denomination to which the person in authority belongs, even though he is an agnostic or a pagan. The state has its own independent sphere, its own end in which it lives and rules without the fear of an arbitrary intervention by ecclesiastic authority. All that concerns the political and civic field is of full right subject to the sovereign decision of the political authority. The reason is, as Leo XIII asserts again and again, that both authorities are sovereign

---

[18] So termed by Pius XI in his encyclical *Ubi arcano* (December 23, 1922). Cf. James A. Ryan, *Encyclicals of Pius XI* (1927), pp. 40 f.

in their respective spheres and that both should be mutually independent and unhindered in the realization of their specific ends, in accordance with divine dispensation in the form of positive divine law for the Church, in the form of natural law equally of divine origin for the state. This sovereignty which Leo XIII and the whole tradition attributes to each perfect society, to state and to Church, is not absolute and unlimited power embracing all spheres of the individual and social existence of man.

On the contrary, this concept of sovereignty, besides being subject to the clearly defined divine and natural law, means that in the totality of human life certain distinct spheres are assigned to each of these sovereign authorities. The objection that the Church claims the supreme decision in the problem of what has to be regarded as divine and natural law in application to concrete cases, does not carry weight. For if we accept the fact that God has revealed His will in the Scriptures and in natural law, it is obvious that in the fundamental principles there can be no disagreement. For in this case both authorities acknowledge that they are subject alike to the clearly revealed will of God. As long as both authorities are conscious of being subject to objective supreme rules which necessarily are clear and unequivocal, a conflict can arise only about the application to a concrete situation of conclusions remote from the first principles, or the conflict will be one about the concrete elements of a factual situation. In such cases the appropriate method is that of peaceful negotiation until an agreement about the remote conclusions or the elements of the concrete situation is reached. This will be easy if on both sides there exist mutual confidence and good will.

The great difficulties arise when in the mind of one of the authorities —since the rise of princely absolutism this has been in the mind of the political authority—the idea of divine and especially of natural law fades away and its will, the will of the state endowed with compulsory power, is declared to be everywhere and without any limitation the supreme law. Then of course any common basis for a peaceful cooperation is lacking. To the Church nothing is left but to resist and to fight for her liberty. This must especially occur where the totalitarian state goes so far as to abridge even the religious freedom of the individual citizen, that is, when the state makes its political ideology a religion and demands from the citizen an absolute and exclusive loyalty such as is owed only to God. Then the Church would be driven again into the catacombs because the Christians could not continue to live as Christian people upon the basis of the fundamental right of the religious freedom of the individual.

Against the accusations of nineteenth-century liberalism it can be said that the liberty of the Church was at the same time the best guaranty of the freedom of conscience. For history shows that it was far more the state that threatened the freedom of conscience than did the Church. And whenever it seemed that the ecclesiastical authority oppressed the consciences, we will find that it was not this authority that oppressed but the secular authority which by chance was united with an ecclesiastical dignity and abused the ecclesiastical authority. Today we see that no secular government was so outspoken against totalitarianism as were the pope and, for instance, German bishops.

CHAPTER XXVI

Cooperation and Separation

I. THE CONCORDAT

THE difference of the spheres in which each perfect society is sovereign does not exclude their mutual cooperation in the formation of man's life as a citizen and as a faithful member of the Church. We have already pointed out that there exists a sphere of mixed matters where the same institutions (e.g., matrimony) are governed by canon law and by civil law. Further, the state, though excluded from any influence in the sphere of hierarchical order, may have an interest in the political loyalty of the clergy and of those clerics who will be made bishops. National minorities in a multinational state may rightfully demand priests who are able to fulfill their ecclesiastical duties by mastering the language and culture of these minorities. The central government in such a state is interested to see that this right is not abused for disruptive propaganda by the state to which this minority by its language and culture is kindred.[1]

Especially where by custom and tradition institutional remnants of the earlier strong union between Church and state are still existing or where the people are in an overwhelming majority still members of the Church, there actually the same men are embraced by two spheres of duties as members of the *Corpus Christi mysticum* and as members of the *Corpus politicum mysticum*. Thus the Church is called to serve the welfare of the same men and the same society whom the state serves; in such a case an intimate cooperation between Church and state is most fitting. Yet even where Catholics are a minority in a state, a concordatory cooperation between Church and state and not a separation may be useful.

[1] The problems of minorities have found consideration in many concordats of recent decades. Cf. concordat with Poland (February 10, 1925), with Lithuania (April 4, 1924), with Rumania (May 10, 1927).

Fundamentally such a cooperation between Church and state is the best polity, though in concrete situations the separation of state and Church may be more fruitful. This cooperation in the form of a concordat does not presuppose that the Catholic Church is privileged by public law or is the only recognized religion in a state because the people are Catholic.[2] Nor is the concordatory cooperation hindered when the constitution asserts the fullest freedom of religion and declares that no established Church exists. In some European states the Lutheran, the Reformist, and the Catholic Church have the privileges of corporations of public law with the right to public exercise of their cult, to autonomy, and to collection of taxes with the help of the state for their subsistence. But this condition does not exclude the fact that principally the separation of the Church from the state exists. The relations between the two are in the various countries so conditioned by tradition and the development of constitutional law that it is impossible to bring the whole problem under the simple alternative of established Church or Gallican state Church on the one hand, and separation of Church and state on the other hand. Nor is separation a single and unequivocal type since, as we shall see, there are several types of separation.

The reason for concordatory agreements is stated by Leo XIII. It is true that the proximate end of the political authority is different from the end of the spiritual authority and that it realizes its end in different ways from those of the latter. Yet inevitably the two authorities in their activities will come into contact. Each of them rules over the same men; sometimes it happens that both authorities have to regulate the same matters though from different points of view. A clash between them would be contrary to good sense and to God's wise ordinance. Consequently, whenever both authorities meet in the

[2] The concordat with Spain (1851) states, for instance, that the "Catholic Apostolic Roman religion" is the only religion of the Spanish nation. The concordat with Ecuador (1862) states that the Catholic Apostolic Roman religion "is the religion of the Republic of Ecuador and will be forever preserved in all its rights and prerogatives." About Church and state in Latin America, see J. Lloyd Mecham's book of that title (1934). The concordat with Italy (February 11, 1929) likewise says in Art. 1 that the Catholic Apostolic Roman religion is the sole religion of the state, yet without excluding the exercise of other religious cults or the freedom of conscience. All this is simply a declaratory statement of facts. The Austrian concordat of June 5, 1934, states only that "the Austrian Republic grants and secures to the Holy Roman Catholic Church the free exercise of its spiritual power and the free and public exercise of its cult." The right of religious freedom is guaranteed in Art. 28 of the Constitution of May 1, 1934.

regulation of the same matter, it is just that an order and a rule should exist by which their mutual interests and rights are established, and the causes of clashes are removed in order that a collaboration in concord may be made possible.[8]

Such a mutual agreement concerning the relations between Church and state and their rights and duties in matters where both have a vital interest, since early times has been called a concordat. Such a solemn juridical treaty presupposes that the Church is considered an independent and sovereign perfect society which lives and negotiates by its own right, not by any concession of the state.

It deserves mention that concordats seldom demand sacrifices from the sovereign state, though nineteenth-century liberalism often contended otherwise. Most often the Church shows greater understanding for the needs of the state than the latter shows for the spiritual interests of the Church. The offenders against the spirit and letter of the concordats have been the states and their rulers. The old saying, that the history of the concordats is the history of the griefs of the Church, is quite true. Often the political rulers approached the Church with friendly gestures in order to make a concordat and thus appear as parties worthy of international confidence; or they tried to kill in the bud the suspicions of their Catholic subjects by coming to an understanding with the Holy See. As soon as this "scrap of paper" was signed and the useful political purpose thus had been achieved, then "smart" interpretation or incompatible legislation on the part of the political ruler began to void the rights and competencies of the Church so solemnly agreed upon. Hitler is the latest example of this practice.[4] Another way for the state to rid itself of its obligations is the one-sided annulment of the concordat by appeal to high sounding phrases, such as "freedom of conscience" or "liberation from clericalism."

II. The Legal Nature of the Concordat

The legal nature of the concordat has long been a matter of dispute. The curialist partisans of the medieval theocratic theory con-

[8] This is the main thought in various utterances of Leo XIII; cf. *Alloc.*, I, 133; II, 48; III, 108 (Encyclical *Arcanum divinae sapientiae*).

[4] Cf. Nathaniel Micklem, *National Socialism and the Roman Catholic Church* (1938), pp. 62 ff.

tended that the concordat has the legal nature of a privilege granted freely by the pope to the state. As it was a privilege, though vested in the form of a treaty, the grantor was considered to have the power to annul the privilege at any time and unilaterally, whenever its continuation would be of advantage only to the state. Yet from the side of the state the concordat would be irrevocable as long as it was favorable for the Church. The reason is that as a privilege the concordat is actually an ecclesiastical law and therefore wholly subject to ecclesiastical authority. The partisans of the rising absolute state, with its ideal of a state-controlled Church, answered with the so-called legal theory. The Church being only a community in the state, not a sovereign community beside the state, is in her external and legal organization subject to the state. A coordination of state and Church, both sovereign and free, would then be absurd. Consequently the concordat is not a genuine treaty; for that would mean that the sovereign absolute state concludes a treaty with its own subjects; evidently an absurdity. Therefore the concordat is, so far as its contents are concerned, a free concession of the state in the legally insignificant form of a contract or treaty. Actually the concordat legally exists only as a state law. Consequently the state can annul the concordat whenever it pleases, since it is not legally bound by its own law; for the state is absolute.

The extremist nature of both theories is obvious. The commonly accepted theory among Catholic authorities in canon law and political philosophy is that the concordat is a true legal treaty in the sense of the general theory of contracts and specifically in the sense of international law. The concordat is a bilateral, legally binding treaty under the rules of international law, which recognizes both parties, the state and the Church, as having moral personality, with rights and duties, as subjects sovereign and independent, therefore competent to contract treaties. The Holy See, the pope, is recognized as a sovereign authority by the practice of the majority of the states which entertain diplomatic relations with the Holy See by plenipotentiary ambassadors or ministers and which recognize an Apostolic nuncio as the representative of the Holy See to their governments in accordance with international law. Even states that do not entertain international relations with the pope recognize his sovereignty in the sense of international law.

That the concordat participates in the nature of international treaties becomes evident when we scrutinize the papal views. A treaty is an agreement of two parties about the same object. This definition is given by Leo XIII when he states that the concordat is concluded when rulers of states and the Roman Pontiff come to an agreement of minds on a special matter.[5] The French concordat is called a solemn bilateral pact by Leo XIII, and Pius X calls it a bilateral agreement obliging both parties, like all treaties of this kind; the concordat, according to Pius X, is to be judged by the same rules as all international treaties, that is, according to international law.[6]

This nature of the concordat as a legal treaty implies the following difficulty. Both parties of the treaty are sovereign. They are consequently not subordinated to any higher authority competent to arbitrate or to judge, when a dispute between the parties arises over the interpretation or the application of the treaty in a concrete case, or over the important problem which arises when one party contends that the treaty has become inapplicable on account of a substantial change in the circumstances which gave rise to it. This is the general problem of the *clausula rebus sic stantibus*. It means that, when a notable change has occurred in the circumstances and matters with which the treaty deals, the literal application of the treaty to the unforeseen changes would be against equity and justice, especially so if the application of the treaty provisions should endanger the substance of the independence and existence of one of the parties. If such a notable change and a danger to the existence and independence actually exists, this cannot be decided by a superior authority in a final decision because no earthly authority exists over the Church by definition, even if the utopian dream of a world state should become true, because even then the Church would be a potential partner to the world state and never its subject.

This seems to be theoretically a dilemma on account of the immanent limits of the juridical form. Yet it does not prevent the establishing of a new agreement by mutual consent. At least the popes

---

[5] *Alloc.*, II, 153 (*Immortale Dei*). For other quotations from Leo XIII's writings as evidence of the treaty character of the concordat, cf. P. Tischleder, *op. cit.*, p. 293. Victor Cathrein, *Lehrbuch der Moralphilosophie*, II, 602, gives quotations from other popes that corroborate the legal nature of the concordat as a true bilateral treaty legally and equally obliging both parties.

[6] Encyclical *Vehementer nos*, to the clergy and people of France, February 11, 1906.

have shown much readiness to oblige in such cases. Those who usually appealed to the *clausula* were the states which, under the influence of liberalist agnosticism, tried to get rid of treaties that were reproaches to their materialist polity. With full confidence we can say that, in such disputes, the Church has always shown a full understanding and complaisance. This fact is evident in the history of such events; for instance the Prussian Kulturkampf or the dispute with the Third Republic in France. Therefore it is wrong to characterize the concordat as a mere armistice in the unceasing struggle between the spiritual and the temporal power. The Church's point of view is that a peace is possible and that she is ready to make all sacrifices necessary in the interest of a peaceful *modus vivendi,* one compatible with her essence and divine task. We must not forget that the stronger an authority is morally, the easier it is for such an authority to yield to the justified demands of someone else; the quick appeal to a sensitive prestige is a mask of moral weakness and uncertainty.

It must be kept in mind that the Church can do without concordats. The fully satisfactory situation of the Catholic Church in the United States seems to be a proof of this. A shrewd observer remarked that, since Leo XIII, the Church has ceased to address herself to the rulers and the princes, and addresses herself more and more directly to the Christian people. Apparently, with the progress of popular governments and the principle of a free Church in the free state, the spiritual authority can rely more upon the faithful people and their increasing efforts to re-Christianize modern society than upon the political exigencies of an authoritarian government. The same trend becomes apparent in the new papal policy to keep the Church and the clergy out of the arena of politics, as provided for in some of the latest concordats. As a more proficient method to accomplish the same purpose, the ultimate task of the Church, the salvation of souls and the formation of a social and economic environment from which a new Christian society may once more arise, Catholic Action may be more important than reliance on the legal letters of concordatory treaties, however little we should depreciate their value. The solution of the so-called Roman question, namely, the Lateran Treaty with Italy and the recognition of Vatican City as the sovereign patrimony of St. Peter, minutely small when compared with the expropriated Papal States, points in the same direction.

The Lateran Treaty has not "restored" the political independence of the pope by his control over a territory that would enable him to defend his independence and the liberty of the Church with armies, as was a historical necessity in the Middle Ages and in the era of absolutism. Pius XI openly declared that he would not rely on international legal guaranties but on the moral guaranties which, of course, rest in the souls of the faithful and in the minds of all who again, after the ravages of an agnostic faith in reason, science, economics, or political power, believe in the spiritual power of religion and understand that man is more a *homo religiosus* than a *homo politicus* or *economicus* and even less a *res cogitans* or a *homo proletarius*.

III. A Wrong Idea of Union between Church and State

The concordat is not necessarily a token that no separation of Church and state exists, though its foundation is a mutual acknowledgement that the Church and the state should collaborate. This is without doubt the ideal situation. We do not use here the term "union of Church and state." We wish to avoid any mistaken notion of an identity between Church and secular society or state in the form of national Churches. State and Church are two societies different in end and power and organization, two distinct perfect societies. St. Robert Bellarmine explicitly denies that even the Christian state (i.e., the body politic of a Catholic people) and the Church are united as matter and form, body and soul.[7] So we have to distinguish the Catholic type of a friendly cooperation between Church and Christian state in a legal form from the full union between Church and state as it has existed in England since the break with Rome, in the

---

[7] Cf. Arnold, *op. cit.*, p. 100 note 64. Is this a criticism of St. Thomas (*Summa theol.*, IIa IIae, q.60, a.6 ad 3) who, quoting St. Gregory Nazianzen, says that the temporal power is subordinated to the spiritual power as is the body to the soul? We think this analogy should not be exaggerated, however much it may have been used in earlier times. Bellarmine will under all circumstances have the independence of both the state and the Church preserved in their own order. The Christian world contains two perfect societies, each of which has its own form and its own matter; they do not constitute a moral organism in the strict sense. Yet they have to cooperate in concord and unity for the good of the people who are both citizen and faithful. For this cooperation the order of charity is not sufficient. The order of justice, a legal order of friendly cooperation, is necessary. We should again point out that Bellarmine's "state" is a Christian state, the citizens of which are all together members of the universal Church.

Established Church, and as it existed in the various forms of national Churches in other predominantly Protestant countries. But this Catholic type must be distinguished also from Gallicanism and other attempts to nationalize the Catholic Church as we found them in the eighteenth century. An example of these attempts is proposition 85 of the Synod of Pistoia (September, 1786), which proclaimed that a national council could decide without appeal to Rome in controversies concerning faith and morals, so that such a national council would be declared as quasi-infallible in questions of faith and morals (Denzinger, nos. 1593 ff.)

The union of Church and state in England as declared in Article 37 of the Thirty-nine Articles is also different. While the Gallican Church acknowledged the doctrinal authority of the pope and his spiritual power beside that of the general councils and the rules, customs, and institutions preserved by the French Kingdom and the Gallican Church, the English Church denies any doctrinal authority and any spiritual power, especially any canonical jurisdiction, of the pope. Consequently the king and his courts, though they do not assume doctrinal authority, have jurisdiction over the Church at least to the extent that the spiritual law of the Church and the order and discipline in the Church, the Prayerbook included, are subject to the approval of the king (today the Parliament and the Judicial Committee of the Privy Council), so that the essential act of ecclesiastical legislation, the sanction, is in the hands of the supposedly still Christian yet temporal authority.

Such a union is not acceptable from the standpoint of Catholic doctrine. A union between Church and state, or better a cooperation in concord and unity of both, would mean mutual respect for the independence of each in *suo ordine*. It would mean the acknowledgment of the canon law in matters that are admittedly of spiritual nature (e.g., matrimony, hierarchy, clerical education, and legal exemption of the clergy from the secular jurisdiction in certain matters); the recognition of the Catholic religion as the religion of the people with these consequences: privilege of exclusive public cult, recognition of Church holydays, Catholic public schools, protection of the Church, her institutions, sacraments, and doctrine against libel, contempt, etc., in the penal law, membership of higher state officials in the Church, and financial support by the state for the ecclesiastical institutions so far as they cannot fulfill their functions on their own resources.

It needs no proof that such a union is possible as a practical policy only where the people of the state are in great majority Catholics. Yet under this condition the union is actually no problem at all, but simply a truism. Therefore it would be wrong to say that such a union between state and Church is a necessity or should always take place. The condemned thesis 55 of the Syllabus of 1864 (the Church should be separated from the state, and the state from the Church) does not imply this. The true thesis would demand that the circumstances be considered. St. Robert Bellarmine expressly states that state and Church may live in union or in separation, because fundamentally each can exist without the other.[8] Yet this fact does not nullify the principle that the ideal status is the union between Church and state whenever the circumstances allow it, and that the separation is never *in abstracto* an ideal status. From this it follows that the circumstances make the actual separation of state and Church a tolerable or even a salutary status in the concrete interest of the common good as well as in the interest of the Church.

IV. Religious Tolerance and Separation

We must now distinguish between tolerance and separation. Tolerance implies that the state, however much it acknowledges a state religion or gives public privileges to the religion of the majority of its people, does allow dissidents certain minority rights and refuses to use political pressure and juridical compulsion to force them into the privileged religion. Various types of tolerance are possible. First a simple absence of legal compulsion (persecution) without giving the religious minority any rights as citizens, though the state may give them protection as aliens. They are allowed to practice their worship privately in their homes or in meeting-houses by special concession from the state. They may even be allowed to have their private schools. Such was the tolerance given to the Jews and to the infidels in the medieval cities. In the second type the dissidents are admitted to full

[8] *De potest. pont.*, c.5, c.17. *In auct. bell.*, p. 255. Bellarmine even declares that it would be the ideal if the pontiffs had to deal only with spiritual affairs, the prince only with secular or temporal affairs.

ights as private citizens but are unable to hold offices in the state, to vote, etc., as was the rule in England before the Emancipation Act for Catholics, and in Spain for Protestants in the early nineteenth century. The third type would be full tolerance for organized Churches under the principle of parity as it slowly developed after the wars of religion on the European continent and as it was applied in the Germanic states in the nineteenth century. In these states the members of the Christian Churches (i.e., the Lutheran, the Reformist, the Calvinist, and the Catholic Church) enjoy the same rights, civil and political, as publicly recognized religions. In addition, on account of the bill of rights, each citizen has the right to religious freedom. This means—to mention only one constitution, that of Bavaria of 1818—that the simple worship in the private home is allowed to everybody irrespective of the religion which he professes. It means further that in the choice of his religion every adult citizen is free or that a change of religion has no juridical or political effects. In such a state of parity of the Christian Churches, these latter enjoy nevertheless certain privileges over other religions: they enjoy public worship, their holydays are recognized as public holidays, all instruction in public elementary schools is given on a denominational basis, they enjoy protection of their institutions and worship from public libel, derision, and public contempt. In such a state of parity, as we have pointed out, the Catholic Church usually entertains concordatory relations. This implies that the Church accepts these parity states and their policy of full tolerance as necessitated by the actual requirements of the common good.

Yet the Church cannot approve the philosophical principle of religious indifferentism distinguished from the practice of tolerance as a political principle of constitutional law in the interest of the common good. The philosophically untenable and theologically heretical principle of indifferentism implies that all Churches are equal because none of them has the whole truth, and that the individual person's opinion determines what is true, what is good, and what is God's word. Therefore it denies divine revelation and the Church as the institution created by Christ for the salvation of souls. Indifferentism, together with the principle of religious freedom or freedom of conscience based upon indifferentism, means the denial of objective truth in religion, of the revelation of God, and philosophically the denial of the ability of the human reason to reach objective truth. Indifferentism is thus nothing but religious and philosophical agnosticism. It is obvious that these philosophical and theological theories of indifferentism exclude the nature, end, and claims of the Church, and vice versa. Thus the Church can never reconcile herself to indifferentism as a philosophical and theological principle, however much she shows understanding for what the state on account of religious divisions among its citizens can do and cannot do in the interest of interdenominational peace and the furtherance of the common good.

The student of the history of the nineteenth century will know that the circumstances under which the Church was constrained to accept religious freedom and equal tolerance in wholly Catholic countries have been wantonly and artificially produced by small cliques of anticlerical radicals as they called themselves, though they actually were zealous enemies of the Church. These comparatively small groups of bourgeois intelligentsia in the Latin countries were mostly associated with or united in the freemason lodges.[9]

Through control over public opinion and over the new universities and through their political influence in the representative bodies of the new constitutions which were introduced after the French Revolution in all monarchies, these members of the liberalist bourgeois intelligentsia won an influence far beyond their numerical strength, especially since their political aims were favorable to the *laissez-faire* economic ideals of the bourgeois entrepreneurs. So they thrust their antireligious policy upon nations that were not only nominally but in their greatest part, though perhaps not sufficiently vocal, still profoundly Catholic. In the possession of political power, of the means to form public opinion, they inaugurated against the Catholic Church a policy of religious oppression in the name of religious freedom but with the actual denial to Catholic religious orders and to the Catholic

---

[9] The lodges in Italy, Spain, and France were the rendezvous and the hotbed of an utterly militant anti-Catholicism; they were the spearheads of the attacks not only against the clergy but against anything that is Catholic or even Christian. They were filled with the spirit of Rousseauist Jacobinism. The masonic lodges in the Germanic and Scandinavian countries (with the exception of Austria) and in Anglo-Saxon countries (e.g., England and the United States) appear rather to be fraternal and social organizations for humanitarian purposes or for business connections and do not show the abovementioned militant anti-Catholic spirit, though they may be tainted with the rationalist spirit of the Enlightenment from which the lodges originated.

people of the same principle of freedom for which they pretended to fight, as any fair history of the Church under the Third Republic in France will show.

It cannot be denied, on the other hand, that this influence is partly owing to the reluctance of not a few members of the clergy and the episcopate in these Latin countries to separate from the ancient regime and accept the new constitutional principles of popular sovereignty or more democratic restrictions of the monarchical power. This reluctance was only too good an opportunity for the ultraconservative or even reactionary powers to take the Church as a kind of auxiliary force into its service. It must furthermore be mentioned that in these countries the workers in the rapidly growing industrial centers were qiuckly lost to the Church. The pastoral care and the education of the clergy in pastoral theology were not developed in the direction of counteracting the successful propaganda of Marxist socialism, which contained philosophic tenets closely related to those of the agnostic intellectuals. Often a deep cleavage thus appeared between a rural Catholic population and an urban agnostic population. This cleavage weakened the influence of the Church in the most populous sections of modern civilization, in the urban industrial masses.

We think that Lacordaire, Ozanam, and Montalembert, who acknowledged the inevitable trend of modern civilization toward more freedom, were more right than their Catholic adversaries like Veuillot. Historical honesty demands also that we concede that certain popes (e.g., Gregory XVI and Pius IX, in the latter part of his pontificate) did not always show an appreciation of this trend. According to Schmidlin, a great drawback in Pius IX's pontificate was that his methods and maxims were often mistaken and ill-advised; that his political views and ecclesiastical policy, after the terrible disappointment of the revolution of 1848, turned from excessive enthusiasm for liberty to the opposite pole of rigid conservatism, so that, however fruitful his pontificate was for the spiritual well-being of the Church, he almost failed in all that had to do with material culture.[10]

---

[10] Joseph Schmidlin, *op. cit.*, II, 109. In his memoires, Cardinal Ferrata notes that Pius was aware of these shortcomings: "My system and my policy have had their time; but I am too old to change. My successor will have to do it" (Ferrata, *Memoires*, 1920, I, 32). Whoever studies the pontificate of Leo XIII will see how excellently and successfully the successor changed that course.

The *Memoires* of Cardinal Ferrata show also how a part of the French episcopate reacted against the conciliatory policy of Leo XIII and thus contributed to the victory of the principles of continental liberalism against which they had fought so bitterly.

The separation of Church and state is the final stage of development in most of these Latin countries, though in Italy and Portugal a new concordatory regime exists and one is in preparation in Spain. How much this regime depends on the admittedly transitory political regimes, at least in Spain and Italy, only the future will tell. In the United States we find, from the beginning of its formation, the separation of state and Church in the constitutional provision that there shall not be an established Church.

V. THE NATURE OF SEPARATION

Before we discuss the two principal types of the separation of Church and state, we shall give a clearer description of this rather vague and ambiguous phrase. The separation of Church and state is a recent affair. In history, the idea occurs perhaps first in the spiritualist concept of the Church as Luther in his earlier years favored it when he burned the *Corpus juris canonici*. In this symbolic act he struck at the visible Church with her hierarchy, her distinction between clergy as the teaching and jurisdictional part and the laity as the taught and governed part of the Church. He struck at the visible Church of the sacramental and hierarchical order and of the canon law, which claimed to be the divinely instituted mediator between the Christian soul and God. Surprisingly soon, Luther gave up this idea, and Lutheranism surrendered readily to an Erastian subjection under the prince as *summus episcopus*, i.e., to the strictest union of Church and state with the Christian ruler as the head of the organized Church and with membership of all subjects in this Church as a form of political homogeneity. Many sects tried a separation in the time after Luther. Yet here, too, the sects showed a remarkable tendency to let the whole realm of civil and political life be controlled by their religious dogmas whenever they could do so, as, for instance, the early Puritans in colonial New England showed in their theocracy, which is a union between Church as an organized religious group and the political community. Only after the principle of tolerance had given the religious minorities a guaranty of non-interference by the government and after the acknowledgment of the freedom of conscience as a human right in states without a unified religious majority, could the idea of a separation of state and Church arise. For from now on, the state not only retires from any intervention in the spiritual sphere, but declares full indifference to and disinterestedness in the religious opinions of its citizens and the organized religious groups in the state, thus separating man as a church-member from man as citizen. Politically the sphere of religion is wholly and strictly neutralized, and the state becomes a secular institution with a Christian atmosphere as long as the majority of the citizens hold some essential tenets of Christian doctrine and morals. The state may become a wholly secularized non-Christian state when, in its external and internal policy, even these Christian tenets are surrendered. Then even the Christian religious faith of a group of its citizens is as indifferent to the state as is membership in a club for the promotion of spiritism or of vegetarianism.

The constitutional principle of separation implies the following. First, no religious group or Church enjoys any juridical or political privileges, none receives any direct or indirect financial support from the state, however much differentiation may exist socially between Churches for the wealthy, for the poor, for fundamentalists, or for liberals. Secondly, the Churches and the religious associations, the parishes and the dioceses, are legally organized upon the basis of the civil law, the law of the land. They are not corporations of public law, that is, with privileges and prerogatives acknowledged by the state, such as the right to make laws, to levy taxes, to be exempt from certain rules of civil law. In the United States, cities and towns are corporations of public law. Thirdly, from the standpoint of the secular law the organization of the Churches is left to the will of the members. This led to the difficulties of trusteeism in the United States, a situation that was remedied by internal ecclesiastical means, not by any assistance from the civil law and the secular authority. Fourthly, the legal relations between Church and state are reduced to a minimum. The state may regard the Church as a social and spiritual influence able to affect certain internal and external policy favorably or unfavorably. But legally the Church and the state have no official relations with each other. The separation presupposes full religious freedom and at least a kind of government in which man as a believer is separate from man as a citizen. This seems to be Leo XIII's view of separation, which he declared to be the result of the separation of human legislation from the Christian and divine legislation.[11]

Such a separation is never the ideal in theory. Under certain historical circumstances it may be the best form of the relation between Church and state in a secularized civilization. This is so especially when the majority of the citizens no longer belong to the established Church or when the continuation of the union between the Church and the state would lead to compulsion in faith and to hypocrisy, because the majority of the people have actually given up allegiance to the Christian Church. Then religious freedom and the legal neutrality of the state is the honest consequence in order to give to the missionary power of the Church that freedom which may once again produce a state of affairs where a re-Christianized people will find a form of political existence, a state, that deserves by its reverence for the Church, her law, and her end, the adjective Christian or Catholic.

VI. The Hostile Type of Separation

When we now study the separation of Church and state we should, with Leo XIII, distinguish the radical or militantly hostile type from the peaceful, friendly type. The first we find in the so-called Catholic countries affected by the above mentioned anti-Catholic intellectual and social groups. The second type has found its best expression in the United States.

The radical type, militantly hostile to the Church, has been developed mostly in the so-called Catholic countries. The basis for the separation was not solicitude for the common good, it was not the desire for peace among a plurality of Churches and sects, but rather an adherence to the philosophical tenets of rationalist liberalism as a kind of civil religion in Rousseau's meaning. Supernatural faith is here simply denied. The Christian rules of morality and the divine law are publicly declared either a myth, irreconcilable with modern science or with the proletarian revolution, or they are said to be only a propaganda instrument of clerical arrogance and of political anti-democratic reaction. Social and political life consequently are to be

[11] Encyclical *Au milieu.*

ruled without consideration of absolute Christian and divinely re-vealed law, but exclusively by the immanent rules of political or social or even proletarian science.

It can easily be seen that such a "religion" of indifferentism, even of anti-Christian rationalist scientism, in the new laic religion of the state, when imposed upon the citizens in public universities and schools, in the laws and administrative practices, makes of the state an instrument of the rationalist unbelievers of the intellectual ruling class to destroy the traditional religion of the still Christian people. This new religion becomes the public religion of the state while the Catholic religion is declared to be exclusively and wholly a private affair of the citizen.

To pursue this anti-Catholic policy in a state where the people still have a strong Catholic tradition, the Church and her institutions are made the subject of exceptional laws standing in contradiction to the bill of rights and to the democratic, liberal tenets of the political constitution. So the state claims absolute control over all education outside the family. The state destroys the Catholic schools, the in-dependent universities under the Church. It forbids the religious teaching-orders to continue their schools though their members have qualified as teachers in examinations ordered by the general laws of the state. The property of the Church is confiscated and, in violation of the will of the donors, it is used for the promotion of the godless instruction of a non-religious civic morality in public schools. The cathedrals and other churches are declared national property and given to the Catholic people for use only. Tax privileges in accord-ance with general laws given to institutions of charitable, educational, and religious character, granted without any restrictions to associa-tions conformed to the new "religion" of neutrality, are denied to Catholic institutions. The priest is even denied entrance into publicly owned hospitals to administer the last rites to a patient, however much the patient or his relatives may demand it.[12]

[12] These astonishing practices and laws can be found in the statute books of the French Republic; cf. Lecanuet, *L'église de la France sous la troisième république*, Vol. III. For exceptional legislation, cf. Constitution of the Spanish Republic, Art. 26. In all countries where democratic forms of government were propagated in an alliance between a Marxist labor movement and an agnostic bourgeoisie under the leadership of Latin freemasonry, the rights of the common general law and of the bill of rights have been denied to Catholics and especially to Catholic religious orders and their members.

The principle of religious neutrality of the public schools, according to the separation

The basis of such a type of separation is that fervent philosophical liberalism in the traditionally Catholic countries of the European continent which, in its militant agnosticism and optimistic progressivism, is as much a foe of revealed religion as Marxism is. The separation is, therefore, not simply a demand of practical policy on account of the fact that modern society and civilization is factually non-Christian and religiously indifferent so that the state as the secular form of such a society has indeed no relations with the Church. On the contrary, the separation is a political weapon against all revealed religion on the ground that religion is the foe of freedom or opium for the masses, because religion and the Church are regarded as the reactionary foes of the secular ideals of this kind of liberalism. The political purpose of the separation is thus the destruction of revealed religion and of the Church as its preserver. From this standpoint we must understand the violent reaction of Church authorities and of the Catholic laity against this sort of liberalism and this type of separation, both very much different from liberalism and separation in the Anglo-Saxon countries.

---

of Church and state, was not accepted *bona fide* by the anticlerical government of the Third Republic. Aristide Briand's assertion that the grand purpose of the non-religious public schools was the suppression of all religious faith, shows that in the mind of the anticlerical enemies of the Church "neutrality" was only a crafty slogan to deceive well-meaning Catholics, as pointed out by George Sorel (*Réflexions sur la violence*, 6th ed., p. 423, note).

As an example to show how far blind bigotry can go, let us cite the following from France. A law of 1885 confiscated in the form of a tax the sum accruing to a religious order through the death of a member of that order, because the order inherited the "dowry" (*dos* in the meaning of the C.J.C., can 547 ff.) of the deceased member. During the outbreak of yellow fever in the French Sudan, the government demanded about 20,000 francs as a dowry tax from the motherhouse for nuns who, upon the request of the government, had hastened to the stricken districts and died there nursing the sick. Cf. Lecanuet, *op. cit.*, III, 23. This is not an exceptional case.

As we have already pointed out, the attitude of the episcopate and the clergy in these Catholic countries was not always politically faultless. The struggle between the religious and the antireligious powers was sometimes allowed to become identified with the struggle between monarchism or reactionary conservatism or antiliberal enmity to the new political institutions on the one hand, and republicanism, democratic government, or more liberal forms of political and social life on the other hand. Thus the fundamental dispute between opposing religious and philosophical principles was easily overshadowed by a strife over less fundamental issues, over the modern political, economic, and social institutions which, against all logic, became the symbols of the conflict over the fundamental issues. Thus we do not deny that, for instance, the French episcopate would have offered less material for reproach from the antireligious promoters of the new political forms which were certain to develop, than if all the bishops had accepted the wise *Ralliement* policy of Leo XIII. The study of the memoirs of Cardinal Ferrata and of other pertinent works (e.g., of Lecanuet, Gurian, Schmidlin) will bear witness to the correctness of this conclusion.

That the Church in the person of the popes from Pius IX to Pius X vehemently protested against such a hostile separation of Church and state, cannot be surprising. Leo XIII was quite right when he said that such a type of separation denies to Catholic citizens the minimum of fundamental rights and all the rights of the common general laws of the land, subjecting them to an exceptional legislation inimical to the principles of democracy in the name of which this legislation was hypocritically inaugurated. Leo XIII was right when he stated that such a type of separation can only be called a persecution of the Church in order to substitute a new paganism for the Christian faith. Consequently this type of separation is solemnly condemned as irreconcilable with the faith, the divine and natural law, and as intolerable under all circumstances. For this hostile separation robs the Church of her rights, the Catholics of their religious freedom, and God of the public honor due to Him; it also undermines the state itself and its authority. For no state can live without the beneficent forces of divine religion. The new pagan political religion of agnostic scientism must lead to general skepticism and cynical ridicule of the fiber of moral and civil virtues through which alone, in the last analysis, the body politic thrives. No state can live, no laws and rights can preserve their vigor, no civil loyalty can survive, when the government in the name of religious freedom persecutes the Church and tries to establish the transitory and barren philosophy of relativist agnosticism as a civil religion. The state may be neutral with regard to the religious beliefs of its citizens; but this neutrality must not be made a civil religion.

VII. The Acceptable Type of Separation

For the discussion of the milder type of separation, the United States offers the best example. This type, in common with the hostile type, has as its principle that the Church is not recognized by the laws as a perfect society with her own laws. The canon law regulating matrimony, for instance, is considered legally not existent. The Church in her organizational parts, diocese and parish, is organized under the civil law of the state like any other incorporated association. The existence of the Church is thus not endangered, yet her character as a perfect society with original authority of legislation and jurisdiction, with disciplinary and penal law, is disregarded. Thus the

Church may simply admonish, advise, and influence the faithful, and this only so far as these latter voluntarily accept it. Theoretically this practice of the state denies the nature of this divine society and treats it like any other of the free associations of the citizens in the state, as Leo XIII points out.[18]

Yet this state of affairs is inevitable when the majority of the citizens belong neither actually nor juridically to one religion or Church, when the people are divided among many Churches, none of them representing the majority. Since a specific form of religion is not common to the people, the state as the promoter of the common good cannot afford special privileges to any of them, because this would be contrary to the constitutional principle of equality before the law. Under such circumstances the positive furtherance of the true Church of Christ through privileged legislation may be considered beyond the scope of the state because such a furtherance is not considered a part of the common good. The protection of the religious conscience, of the religious convictions of the individual citizen, becomes a task of the common good. Yet it seems evident that this form of religious freedom, protected from political interference, has not that militant and antireligious character which the same constitutional principle of religious freedom can receive when the totalitarian state demands an exclusive and absolute loyalty from its citizens in all human matters; for here the principle is manifestly used to persecute and destroy the Church as a foe of the only admissible forms of a pseudo-religion, that of communism or of racialism or of nationalism.

It is true that, according to theology, there is only one true, Apostolic and Catholic Church, and this Church, as a divinely instituted perfect society, deserves a privileged position since truth has always privileges over anything that is not truth. Yet, under the above-mentioned conditions, the state does better to become religiously neutral; i.e., the state gives full religious freedom, retires from any positive or negative intervention into the religious life of its citizen. And it does so simply as a matter of political prudence and as the protector of the common good. It abstains from any judgment about religious truth; it abstains from intervention, not because it adheres to the theory that all religions are equally true or false. Its practice of religious freedom and separation is a mere policy exercised in the

[18] *Alloc.*, III, 118.

interest of the common good without any philosophical pretense of indifferentism as a philosophical or theological principle which, applied to politics, leads by intrinsic consequence to the separation of Church and state.

Thus it must be clearly understood that the separation as a constitutional practical principle of policy must not be the consequence of the philosophy or theology of liberalism or indifferentism that has been so strongly condemned by all popes from the encyclical *Mirari vos arbitramur* (1832) of Gregory XVI to Pius XI. Consequently the same constitutional article ordering the separation of Church and state may be harshly criticized and condemned if the people living under that constitution are in great majority faithful members of the Catholic Church. The same article, in the constitution of a people widely divided in its religious creeds, may be not only tolerated but actually welcomed as, *rebus sic stantibus,* the only suitable plan and, for the Church, the best regulation of this matter. The encyclicals just mentioned, with their stern protests against the introduction of the separation of Church and state in countries having a majority of Catholic citizens, does not contradict the favorable attitude of the Catholic hierarchy in the United States toward the separation in practice here.

Pius IX, the Pope of the Syllabus of 1864, praised the status of the Catholic Church in the United States because it enjoyed "unrestricted freedom" (cf. Schmidlin *op. cit.,* II, 211). Leo XIII praised the just laws and the good constitution of the United States, which enable the Church to live and work in full security and without any prejudice under the protection of the law of the land and of just courts.[14]

This acknowledgment of the fine status of the Church in the United States must not lead to the conclusion that consequently the separation of Church and state is always and intrinsically good and should be the example for all states. Leo XIII expressly denies this opinion. He says it is a false opinion to hold that this status of the Church is intrinsically the best and exemplary.

[14] *Longinqua oceani* (January 16, 1895); *Alloc.,* VI, 14 ff. In the letter to the American Catholics (April 15, 1902; *Alloc.,* VIII, 101 ff.), Leo XIII acknowledges that, although the Catholics do not enjoy any privileges, the government deserves praise because the Catholics are in no way hindered in the enjoyment of their just freedom.

CHAPTER XXVII

Social and Political Catholicism

I. The "Neutral" Democratic State

WE HAVE said that in many countries today the neutral state, with its various types of separation of state and Church or only loose collaboration between them, is characteristic of modern times. The earlier presuppositions for a strong union between them had vanished. The monarchy with its quasi-divine right, founded on tradition and religious sentiments independent of popular views, could not be maintained in the face of growing unbelief among the ruling classes of the modern national states. This fact diminished the possibility of publicly showing the Christian character of the common people; the modern national and democratic state became their form of political existence. Thus the neutral state is the concomitant development of the process of a secularization of the citizen, who in his private life may remain a Christian, but in his political life becomes a citizen in the strict sense, namely, abstracting from his Christianity. The unity in faith and religion is no longer considered a necessary element of homogeneity for political unity. The national consciousness, the national culture or civilization, steps into the place of religion. To be sure, the people still live on the Christian inheritance; there exists still a Christian aura represented in the customs and mores, in the religious folklore, and in the spiritual life of the religious communities. But it is undeniable that the Christian substance is either progressively dissolved by agnosticism in the ruling educated classes and by its cruder form (popular Marxist socialism) or is diluted by doctrinal indifference to a mere social morality helpful for respectability and necessary in its disciplinary power of tradition for the protection of that minimum of public morality and private honesty without which no ordered polity can exist.

Being a Christian becomes politically more and more irrelevant.

It occurs in some states that the politically ruling classes become even militantly anticlerical, and glorify a secular humanism as a "civil religion" in the deistic sense of Rousseau. Consequently the various fields of public life are slowly dechristianized as, for instance, education and the universities. Thus many of the institutional channels through which the Christian tradition of a people were handed down from earlier generations are secularized. Furthermore, the impetuous industrialization drives millions from the rural districts, where Christian environment is still strong, into industrial cities, where the masses often starve religiously and turn then to religious substitutes like proletarian socialism or to popular unbelief, or to the many superstitious pseudo-religions, such as astrology, or political radicalism of a communist or Fascist sort. On the other hand, the neutral state as a democratic polity with representative government and freedom of association gave to that part of the people who remained Christian the possibility of organizing popular movements for the defense of their Church and for the re-Christianizing of society and of the nation in its cultural and economic life.

So it comes that the age of the neutral state, the era of progressive secularization, becomes the age of the great, popular Catholic movements of political and social Catholicism. These movements use the modern political liberties for the protection of their religious life and its institutions against parliamentary groups that, like the liberalist anticlerical parties, try to oppress the Church, to monopolize education for their unchristian philosophy, and to abolish the religious orders and congregations. Furthermore, they are convinced that the economic conditions of the proletarian urban masses form the fertile soil for proletarian socialism. And they recognize the justice of many demands of the modern labor movement, and the necessity of preserving the rural form of life for a large class of farmers and, by such means as cooperatives, of preserving a broad middle class in business life. The existence of this class rests on property and not on contracts, but is threatened by the development of big business. For these reasons, Catholics organize their movements to promote social legislation for the free development of Christian trade-unionism, for the cooperatives in protection of farmers, small businessmen, and artisans, against the overpowering competition and monopolist tendency of capitalist "big business."

"Political Catholicism" was necessary wherever the political groups that controlled the "neutral" state showed an outspoken enmity against the Church, as in France. The political organization of Catholics became inevitable wherever a nationalist political doctrine regarded the Catholic Church as a state within the state thus endangering the national unity, as Bismarck did in imperial Germany when he initiated the Kulturkampf. Social Catholicism became a necessity wherever the industrial masses, loosened from their religious tradition, were an easy prey to antireligious Marxist socialism. For Marxism, in spite of the theoretical dullness of Karl Marx' writings, found in the eyes of the proletarians a spectacular justification when extremely conservative churchmen, misunderstanding the changed social and economic conditions, sided with the capitalist class against even the just demands of the industrial workers. In countries with a traditional and constitutional union of Church and state, this estrangement of the industrial masses, following a similar estrangement of the educated classes, from the established Church, Protestant or Catholic, led easily to the theory that the Church, united with the state, unfriendly to the proletarian masses, is simply a means of oppression of these masses. Thus we witness in such countries the great apostasy of the urban masses from the established Churches. The reason was that the latter, out of inertia, aloofness, or misunderstanding of the radicalism of the workers' movement, did not early enough develop social movements which acknowledged the just demands of the industrial masses. The bourgeois state, the capitalist class, and the nobility tried to control and to use the Church for the protection of their political and economic privileges, not always without success on account of the shortsightedness of churchmen. When, therefore, Church authorities did not appreciate the just demands of the proletarian classes but were satisfied with a mere condemnation of proletarian socialism, the Church appeared to be an auxiliary of the ruling classes. Consequently the hatred against the ruling classes and the bourgeois state in union with the Church was transferred to the Church, whose separation from the state and even active suppression became a demand of radical proletarian socialism. This is indirectly confirmed by the very different development in the Anglo-Saxon countries. However much of this difference we may ascribe to particular historical development, to national character, and other such influences, it is

undeniable that the long established existence of Free Churches alongside the state-Church, and the social reforming zeal of the first made
it possible for the labor movement in these countries not to be associated in the same degree with a mass apostasy mixed with enmity
against religion as we find it to be in other countries. It is obvious
that a merely negative condemnation of proletarian Marxism without a full recognition of the quest for social justice in the industrial
proletariat is of little influence and that the positive task, the realization of the demands for social justice by social Catholicism, was the
right answer to these questions.

These movements had been developed with the assistance of an
understanding clergy and the sympathy of a far-sighted hierarchy.
Above all, they had been developed by an enthusiastic laity which
recognized the signs of the times. Thus their object was not merely
defensive, preservative. These movements would do more than simply
protect those who were still Catholic and preserve their faith. A
missionary spirit animated them. They saw as their task the re-
Christianizing of industrial society and of modern secularized culture.
They knew that a "sanctuary Catholicism" or a "Sunday Catholicism"
is not enough. Aware of the intimate relations between an economic
system and morality, between a good order in state and society and
the good life and the salvation of souls, they considered it their
task to rebuild a Christian society and a Christian culture. Thus these
movements embraced the Catholic not only as citizen but as a member of the economic society and of the nation, and inspired him with
the will to re-christianize these orders of human social life. A flourishing organizational life developed thus in countries where the missionary spirit fostered these movements. In Germany we find the
Volksverein, founded by Windhorst the statesman, by Hitze the priest,
by Brandts the entrepreneur; the Christian trade unions; the Christian farmers' cooperative; the Catholic youth organizations of workers
and students; the Görres Society for the advancement of sciences, the
teachers' association, and the Borromeo Libraries Association. In Belgium and the Netherlands we find similar organizations of which
the *Jocists* is one of the most effective. The richness of this organizational life is ably depicted in numerous scholarly books.

In the parliaments, Catholics, sometimes together with Christians
of other denominations, formed political parties such as the Center

Party in Germany, the Catholic Party in Belgium and the Netherlands, the Christian Social Party in Austria-Hungary and, in later times, the Popular Party in Italy under Don Sturzo, and the Catholic party under Gil Robles in Spain.

II. DESTRUCTION OF POLITICAL AND SOCIAL CATHOLICISM BY THE TOTALITARIAN STATES

Some people have spoken disparagingly about these movements, particularly about "political Catholicism." These criticisms have been made especially since in Italy, Germany, and Spain these Catholic parties were unable to prevent the rise of dictatorial totalitarian regimes. It has been said that such parties proved a burden for the Church because their existence led to an identification of party politics with the Church. Foes of the Church condemned these parties as a modern secular arm of the Church and ridiculed them as clerical parties.[1] Both views are wrong. These parties were not a secular arm of the Vatican serving its policies nor did they identify themselves with the Church as a hierarchically organized religious institution. They were simply political associations of Catholic citizens, using the democratic political liberties for the good of the whole people, working for the preservation of Christianity, of Christian morals, and of natural law in political and international life as well as in the national and economic life of their own states.

They were and still are the answer to the problems of their times by Catholic people, living in the framework of a neutral state, threatened by other parliamentary parties hostile to their faith and their Christian way of life, eager to defend themselves but eager also to serve the common good on the basis of natural law and political justice. By defending their constitutional rights they held the field open for the work of the numerous organizations of the so-called social Catholicism. This is indirectly proved by the fact that the totalitarian states not

[1] It should be noted here that the Center Party in Germany, according to its Constitution, was a "Christian constitutional party" open to non-Catholic Christians. Although its members and deputies were mostly Catholics, the Center Party was not a denominational party. On the other hand, the frequent reproach of interdenominationalism is unjustified. This fact gave rise to a heated dispute in the first decade of the twentieth century in connection with the discussion about the Christian (not "Catholic") trade unions. Cf. J. Bachem, *Geschichte der Zentrumspartei*, Vol. III; Nell-Breuning, *op. cit.*, pp. 62 ff.; *Staatslexikon der Görres-Gesellschaft*, art. "Gewerkschaftsstreit."

only destroyed the "Catholic" parties, a logical move since such parties presuppose representative government and a party system, but also began to destroy the organization of social Catholicism with the greatest ruthlessness as if they knew that here was the real enemy of totalitarianism. The Church tried to preserve certain organizations, contending that their main purpose was a religious one and consequently belonged to the protected field of Catholic Action. Even a superficial study of the fate of these organizations in Nazi Germany or Fascist Italy shows how ineffectual this protest was.[2] It is of course true that the one-party governments, for reasons of propaganda, tried to distinguish between "political" Catholicism and, as they called it, "religious" Catholicism. They professed themselves the defenders of "religious," that is, genuine, Catholicism, in suppressing "political" Catholicism, which they accused as a degeneration and betrayal of religious Catholicism. Thus they made use of the time-worn propaganda of agnostic liberalism. It is further true that the Church concluded concordats with Fascist Italy and Nazi Germany and that in both cases the Church's concept of "religious Catholicism" embraced the activities of most of the organizations of social Catholicism. But the inner logic of totalitarianism made the protective articles of the concordats a dead letter in both cases.

The professed antiliberalism of the totalitarian regimes and their much advertised love for the Christian national traditions led to oppressions of Catholic life compared with which the anticlerical liberalism of the Third Republic is preferable. These organizations stand, so to speak, between "Church" and "world." Through them accordingly the religious forces radiate into the public life in order to re-Christianize it; by destroying or restricting them and thus limiting the Church to the "sacristy," totalitarianism tries to establish its world outlook, its philosophy of racism or nationalism as a civil religion in place of the traditional religion of the people. It does the very thing that Rousseau proclaimed necessary for national unity and that Cambon tried to do in his laicist legislation of the Third Republic. The terrible difference is, of course, that the totalitarian regimes use more ruthless, more perfidious, and more cruel means than ever anticlerical liberalism could afford to use.

No shortsighted criticism should blind us to the fact that an active

[2] Cf. Micklem, *op. cit.*, pp. 53 ff., 84 ff.

work for the re-Christianizing of modern society in all its spheres, in philosophy and ethics, in literature and education, in economics and politics, national and international, demands not only faith but also the good works. It demands that ideals become embodied in institutions, in laws, in the practice of economic life, in the artistic standards of literature, in the common convictions of the people; the realization of the ideals in such good works comes not by orders and commands of ecclesiastical authorities alone. It will be the work of the faithful as citizens, as members of their vocations and professions, as scholars, scientists, authors, and artists. All too often a contempt of social Catholicism and, where it existed, of political Catholicism comes from a sort of supernaturalism which escapes from a materialist post-Christian civilization in despair and without hope to re-Christianize it, and expects divine intervention or indulges in eschatological prophecies. It leaves thus the natural world, the secular realm, to the forces of evil.

We are aware that the activities in social and political Catholicism can lead to an exaggeration of the active life which loses sight of the *unum necessarium*. Such misplaced emphasis can lead to a routine of organizational technique which so encloses the supernatural motive and the religious center that the latter are in danger of being stifled by externals. External activity can thus submerge the sacramental life. But there exists a right medium between the extremes. The Christian is a citizen of two worlds, of the City of God and of the City of men. He is destined for the former, but he must live and work for his salvation in the latter. Only a choice few can leave the world and devote themselves wholly to the contemplative life. The others must live and work in the world though they must not become of the world.[8]

[8] The influence of Social Catholicism in preserving from mass apostasy especially the industrial workers is indirectly proved if we contemplate the religious fervor and the respect the Church commands in various countries, which is directly proportionate to the size of Social Catholicism and other Catholic mass organization. Any comparison of the respective figures will show this. Compare, for instance, the very few organizations of Social Catholicism in Mexico or Spain, and the undeniable fact that the industrial workers in these "Catholic" countries are almost wholly anti-Church, and the many organizations of Social Catholicism in Belgium, Germany, or Holland, and the equally undeniable fact that in these countries the industrial workers are only partly estranged from the Church.

CHAPTER XXVIII

The Nature and Scope of International Law

I. THE PLURALITY OF STATES

THE state is the completion of man's social nature. The process of social evolution finds in the forms of political life its terminus, its essential fulfillment. But in time and space the individuality of the single state does not rest solely upon its being a social and technical apparatus, a juridical framework of mere formal norms for qualityless "individuals." On the contrary, the actual state is a historical form that receives its individuality in time and space from the people, the nation, of which it is the form of political existence. The state is the "form" of the people, so that the individualization of the state is established by the people and the geographical space where they are settled.

"Nation," derived from *"nasci,"* means that the individual man is not only a rational animal in the abstract sense of the philosophers, but also a being who receives his individuality by being born in a specific environment and into a specific family that is itself, in its biological, spiritual, and cultural existence, a part of a greater pre-political unity, the nation. The nation is individualized by its historical self-consciousness and its traditions in manners and morals, and by the educational influences of its traditional religion and its intellectual life, i.e., by its culture. De Maistre and Montesquieu both describe this historical individuality of the nation, which tends to find its independent form of political existence in the state. De Maistre, criticizing the rationalist abstractions of the men of 1789, says that they tried to make laws for "man." But no "man" in this abstract sense lives upon this earth. "I have seen Frenchmen, Italians, Russians, but as concerns man, I declare that never in my life have I encountered him." [1] Similarly the subtitle of Montesquieu's famous

---

[1] De Maistre, *Considérations sur la France,* chap. 4.

book, *Esprit des Lois,* points out the relations that laws have with the constitution of each government, with the mores, the climate, the religion, and the commerce of the people. De Maistre's criticism, which is common to the members of the romanticist movement, was directed against the rabid rationalism of the men of the Revolution, the sons of the rationalist Enlightenment. It stressed or perhaps exaggerated the fact that in time and space these irreducible individualities of peoples or nations are what form the individualizing material element of the state. Consequently there exists in history a plurality of states. And upon this plurality rests the fact that the states among themselves have a disposition toward a community of states, a family of nations. The principle, "wherever there is society there is law," is as valid for it as ever; and this law is the law of the family of nations.

Thus the idea of the autarchy, of the independence, of the liberty and sovereignty of the state, the thesis that the social process of man's nature perfects itself in his political existence as a citizen, does not deny that the state is some way open to its equals. It does not deny that beyond the individual state there exists a broader, more comprehensive community, mankind. The philosophical basis for this community is the fact that all Frenchmen, Italians, and Russians are beings of the same metaphysical essence; they are all national animals. Gifted with an immortal soul, the individual person as an "image of God" receives an incomparable dignity irrespective of his nationality. This dignity arises from man's being ordered to God, who is, as personal Goodness, the absolute end of man, transcendent to national determinations.

II. The Brotherhood of All Men

Man's social nature is based as much on his personality as on his individuality; men as men, not only as Frenchmen or Russians, participate in the great *Benedicite* of all creatures to the Creator. This philosophical idea of a brotherhood of all men in the international community in a realistic sense not unknown to Stoic philosophy received in Christian political philosophy a powerful support from the idea of the universal Church, the Church beyond nations and races, where there are neither Greeks nor barbarians.

The Church, as we said, is ordered not to the *polis,* but to the *cosmopolis;* it has as its counterpart mankind organized in a community of nations. Christian political philosophy, starting with these ideas, could therefore uphold the plurality of the states, the idea of the particular state as a perfect society, and still exclude the nationalist philosophy of power politics, according to which the states necessarily live in a kind of natural status like wild beasts, as the pessimism of Thomas Hobbes pictured it. The states by their very pluralism are destined to coexist as members of an international community of nations with its coordinated constitution and system of legal norms, just as the citizens of the states all have human nature in common and upon this basis form the highest and broadest community, mankind. This is why Catholic political philosophy never indulged in the unreal dream of a world-state without force and power, as did humanitarian pacifism. This, too, is why it did not content itself with the pessimistic statement that a perpetual state of war, interrupted by short truces, is unavoidable simply because there really exist only nations living without a real communion among themselves. On the contrary, the pluralism of the states finds its existential perfection in the order of the community of nations, in the teleological ordination of the individual states to the common good of mankind in which political life finds its ultimate form of perfection. Christian political philosophy, convinced of the proper value of the state and the uniqueness of the one Church coordinated to all mankind, cannot be satisfied with the individualism of states. The states form a community and are not isolated, absolutely independent forms, but are called to live in mutual solidarity in the order of justice and of peace, realizing in interdependent action the common good of the community of nations. This is a perpetual indestructible form, issuing from the actual pluralism of the states on the one hand and from the fact of mankind as a real community on the other.

That this idea of the community of mankind found its home especially in Catholic political philosophy is no wonder, for all the fundamental principles of this philosophy favor it. The idea of God, for example: there is only one God, not a pluralism of national deities; the worship of God is therefore in its essence human, not national. Or the idea of man as a person with original dignity, an immortal soul, a transcendent end beyond the world of mortal states and transitory national cultures; there will be at the end of time a redeemed mankind when the world of states has vanished. Or its idea of natural law resting upon the metaphysical order of being, and its teleological ordination turning into the moral normative order for the free will informed by the intellect of man, irrespective of birth. From this standpoint the states, themselves collective persons, are subject to the order of natural law and are directed to the last end of the creation, to imitate the divine order of justice and peace revealed in the creation.

So strong is the natural idea of a community of nations that it is more or less clearly conceived in history as soon as the tribes awake from the materialism of animalist blood relations and catch a glimpse of their equality in human nature. The exchange of goods and native products by commerce and travel is carried on for a more perfect life of the participants, however much the proximate purpose may be individual gain. As the moral and legal basis of such exchanges is recognized, apart from the internal norms, it presupposes that commonly acknowledged norms are recognized for the participants. Without reliance upon such norms, no intercourse would be possible. Even war as an act of one people against another people is recognized early in history as an affair that partly emerges into the external form of law or that is at least a matter capable of the legal form and able to settle normatively relations between peoples, to beget a new status of mutual interdependence and of reliance upon the newly established, firm, and durable treaties as the foundation of continued intercourse. We know how strictly and formally the Romans adhered to the legal ritual in the declaration of war and the negotiations for peace.

Yet a clear and distinctly circumscribed international law and a scientific understanding and clarification of these customary norms arise very late. Ancient Greece was not well equipped for such understanding because the deeply-rooted distinction between Greeks and barbarians permitted only a law common to the Greek city-states and their colonies. Consequently the basic homogeneity of that law was not human nature or mankind, but Greek culture. The Roman jurist, his mind inspired, in spite of imperialist expansion, by the Stoic vision of a world-state, was the first who aproached in a scientific manner the idea of an international legal order under the name of *jus gentium*. For Stoic philosophy, all men, whether slaves or free men, are brethren, equal members of the great community of mankind.[2] Thus Marcus Aurelius, the emperor-philosopher, said: "In so far as I am Antonine, Rome is my fatherland; in so far as I am man, the world is my homeland." During the Middle Ages, many, at least the most important, rules of a cooperation of nations lay hidden in the common feudal law system, at the pinnacle of which the canonists put the pope. The legists assigned that eminence to the emperor. Still it is the religious cultural homogeneity of the *orbis christianus* that is the foundation of intercourse between members of different nations and between the nations themselves. A genuine international law, however, based principally on the law of nature and ordered to mankind as distinct from Christendom, was valid in the sphere of nature and independent of the order of grace or supernature. Such an international law could be conceived only on the basis of Thomistic philosophy. This philosophy put the state on a strictly human and natural basis. It distinguished between theology, the order of grace and faith, on the one hand, and rational philosophy, the order of nature, experience and human nature, on the other hand.

Thus St. Thomas laid down the theoretical basis. After the emergence of the nation-state from the feudal embrace and the discovery of non-Christian states in the Orient and the Americas, the doctors of Late Scholasticism could build upon the Thomistic basis their concept of the community of nations and its order of law. And this was possible because, on the basis of the Thomistic political philosophy, the Christian nation-states and the newly discovered states were both apprehended as truly independent states, regardless of their belonging to Christendom. Thus the great doctors of Late Scholasticism developed first, before Hugo Grotius, a complete scientific system of international law as the constitution of the community of nations and of mankind. They did not, of course, invent or introduce this law. Some such law, as a customary rule to which men consider themselves bound, is present as soon as a regular intercourse between tribes, and between city-states or peoples arises out of the ever-present idea of natural law and common legal reason, however clouded and overshadowed by national prejudices and tribal exclusiveness. The origin of international law is the intercourse of the nations among themselves and even a slight grasp of their common

[2] Seneca, *Epistulae*, no. 95, 32.

interests and their common nature. What the great doctors did was first of all to make these customs the subject matter of a systematic scientific study. They found the principles, the nature, and the meaning of these customs and with these the rational order in the community of nations; they initiated the philosophy and the juridical theory of international law. They could do so because the feudal jurisprudence was proven unable to grasp the reality of the nation-states and of the newly discovered states in the East and the West Indies while Thomistic political philosophy gave them the scientific instruments for a full comprehension of the new facts. A strong contributory factor was the attempt of Iberian colonial imperialism to justify its conquests and wanton destruction of pagan states in "India" with the contention that it did so to spread the gospel and expand Christendom. In strongly criticizing this unjust and aggressive imperialism, Vittoria, Suarez, and their companions had to elaborate the concept of international law as to form and content.

III. DEVELOPMENT OF A LAW OF NATIONS

We said above that the behavior of tribes and nations obeying acknowledged rules and customs of their intercourse preceded the scientific understanding of these sociological facts and working rules. Now the Hellenistic community of city-states practiced such rules and customs. Though the Greek philosophers but seldom made these norms and rules the subject of studies, they at least arrived at the distinction between the particular laws of the different individual city-states and other rules which were common to all of them and even to some adjacent nations. These laws were therefore able to govern relations among themselves and their citizens in intercourse with one another on the basis of these commonly accepted rules and customs. Aristotle, who received this distinction from Heraclitus, noticed that this common law was widely identical with what he called natural law, so that it appeared as a determination of natural law.

The outspokenly normative mind of the Romans under Stoic influences incorporated in its own thought this idea of an international law dimly appearing in the thought of Aristotle; although, of course, on account of similar historical circumstances the legal mind of Rome could have developed this idea. As long as Rome was a small agricultural community it lived according to its *jus proprium*, its rigid civil law erected on the personal basis of citizenship and unable to deal legally with a non-citizen. But with the development of intercourse and of commercial exchange with neighboring states and with seafaring trader nations, customs and rules for contractual dealings with the alien traders were developed by a special judicial magistrate, the *praetor peregrinus* (242 B.C.).[3] The practice of this praetor in his decisions and opinions now developed certain rules for economic intercourse that contained immediately evident legal principles of the juridical reason, principles of natural law and equity and conclusions therefrom.[4] This early law of aliens, the cradle of the *jus gentium*, is international commercial law, equitable and flexible, the informal result of legal reason. Later these rules were applied, precisely because of their propriety, among citizens themselves. To the legal reason, then, the free human person appeared as the subject of these rules irrespective of personal civil, i.e., national law. Thus there was perceived as the unwritten product of natural reason, a law common to all free men and valid for all, a law of all peoples (*jus gentium*). It contains three essential elements: it is common to all men; it is observed by all men; it is not the product of a national lawmaker but of natural reason.[5] Thus the Roman jurists were inclined to identify *jus gentium* and natural law and in addition to place under the label *jus gentium* what today is differentiated as international private and international public law, at least so far as it is unwritten law.[6] In this definition, the idea of an international law enters scholastic political philosophy through Isidore of Seville's *Etymologiae*.[7]

St. Thomas uses the word *"jus"* in two ways. First, it means "law"

---

[3] Before that time the foreigners or aliens could have the use of some norms of the civil law by the privilege of the *jus commercii*. Cf. Voight, *Die Lehre vom jus naturale, aequum et bonum und jus gentium der Römer* (1856), I, 258 ff.; Coleman Philipson, *The International Law and Customs of Ancient Greece and Rome*, I, 94.

[4] Cf. Sir Henry Maine, *Ancient law* (Everyman's Library), pp. 196 f.

[5] Cajus, *Institutiones*, I, 1: "All nations that are ruled by laws and customs use partly their own laws, partly such as are common to all men. For whatever each nation establishes for itself is its national law and is called civil law as the particular law of this *civitas*. But what natural reason has established among all men, is observed by all nations everywhere and is called *jus gentium*, as the law that all nations (*gentes*) observe."

[6] The narrower definition is given by Ulpian: "Quod natura omnia animalia docet," confining it to family law and considering nature as opposed to mind (Cajus, *loc. cit.*).

[7] V, c.4, n, 6.

as legal norm; secondly, it means the matter of the norm, the "justum" as the juridical good. Therefore the *jus gentium* can mean general juridical norms usually found in almost all national law systems, as a law common to all peoples.[8] On the other hand, St. Thomas says that one must distinguish a twofold *justum naturale:* one that is common to all animals [9] and one that belongs to man, the rational being, as a rule of his social life. Whenever St. Thomas speaks of the *justum naturale* in this sense, as the content of *jus gentium*, he means those necessary conclusions from the principles of natural law that by force of inference are themselves natural law, though the form of these norms of the *jus gentium* may be positive inasmuch as they form integral parts of the proper laws of all nations.[10] We should note that by "conclusion" is meant what is accepted generally and equally by all nations as a true moral and legal norm, recognized with certainty as obligating and commonly observed, in this way sanctioned and acquiring the form of positive law. But we still see that a clear distinction between an international private law and an international public law ruling the community of nations is not urged. The reason is the medieval idea that the *orbus christianus,* headed by the emperor or the pope, was actually a continuation of the ancient Roman Empire and its constitutional law.[11] Under this presumption, of course, the *jus gentium* would be conclusions from the principles of natural law as to content, and as to form and sanction it would be international civil law instituted in all nations alike as the integral basis of social life.[12]

8 St. Thomas, *Summa theol.,* Ia IIae, q.94, a.4: "dividitur jus positivum in jus gentium et jus civile."

9 St. Thomas means here Ulpian's definition of *jus naturale:* "quod natura omnia animalia docet."

10 Cf. Cicero, *De offic.,* III, 5, 23; Cathrein, *Grundlage des Völkerrechts* (1918), p. 57; Mausbach, *Naturrecht u. Völkerrecht* (1918), p. 67.

11 The jurists of the Middle Ages favored one *quaestio* especially: Has the emperor the power to oblige the whole world by his laws? Most of them (e.g., Bartolus) answered in the affirmative.

12 Because this natural-law content of the concept of *jus gentium* in St. Thomas' writings has not been clearly distinguished from the later content of *jus gentium*, namely, that it contained positive rules agreed upon by treaty-making nations (voluntarist interpretation), grave misunderstandings may occur. St. Thomas says that private property is an institute of *jus gentium*, while Leo XIII defends the institute of private property against socialism as based upon natural law. Some saw in this alleged difference a contradiction. Actually, there is no such contradiction if the *jus gentium* in the mind of St. Thomas contains conclusions from the principles of natural law, that is, natural law itself. The critics have overlooked the difference between the Thomistic *jus gentium*, which contains natural law, and the modern *jus gentium* since Vattel, which upon its

The change could come only when, first, the state was recognized as a self-sufficient sovereign body politic with supreme ultimate power of decision in its sphere, as an autonomous moral person not subject to a superior, whether emperor or pope, as supreme lord of the *orbis christianus*. Then the Empire is not the only body politic, a *civitas maxima*, for there exists a plurality of independent states. And secondly, it had to be acknowledged that in spite of the independence of these states and of their sovereignty they form genuine parts of this universal community, mankind, organized into a true community of nations with a specific order of law, as a counterpart of the Church universal. These presuppositions become more and more distinct as the medieval idea of the *orbis christianus*, organized into one great *civitas* (the *imperium* with its feudal interpretations), fades away with the rise of the national states in France, in England, and in the Iberian peninsula. At the same time the discoveries of new states in the Far East and in the West Indies ascertain the fact that there exist beyond the Empire independent states which no legal interpretation can subordinate to the emperor.

Now the time is ripe for a scientific concept and a systematic presentation of international law as the public order of the community of nations. And it is thus the great masters of Late Scholasticism and of the Thomistic revival in Spain become the fathers of international law: Vittoria and Suarez. They are more than mere forerunners of Hugo Grotius. Hugo himself in the Preface to his famous work, *De jure pacis et belli*, acknowledges how much he owes to these men. Hugo, of course, was to find a new situation. The wars of religion had stabilized the dissolution of the Church universal. The new state Churches let accrue to the national state a formidable increase in power, transforming them into absolute sovereign states without any supereminent authority. Thus Hugo had actually to begin anew, while for Vittoria and Suarez the Church universal was still an important element of the idea of the community of nations.

IV. NATURAL LAW AND INTERNATIONAL LAW

What, then, is the basis and what are the principles of international law as a public order of the community of nations? We have to put

---

voluntarist basis contains in contractual form freely produced positive laws that are valid only because the wills of the contractual partners have so decided.

this question first to distinguish the order of and for the community of nations from the norms that rule the system of international private law as emphasized by the Romans in their *jus gentium* in opposition to what may be called *jus inter gentes*. We may, therefore, use the figure of a stratification in the rules that order human social life in its entirety. There exists, so to speak, a sphere of rights of the human person anterior to the political forms of existence. This sphere is that which is today made concrete in the bills of rights that are part of the modern constitutional law of civilized nations. They are a genuine limit to state interference. These rights are not national but human, and are consequently international human rights.[13] Their substance, however different may be the positive formulation, is life, liberty, property.

Their recognition, their protection in due process of law in the legal system of a state, is the *conditio sine qua non* of the recognition of any state as a member of the community of nations. Vittoria meant this when he said that the right to international commerce is a natural right which is, of course, feasible only if the above-mentioned rights are recognized. Thus we have a sphere of rules that are valid not because states recognized them, but because they arise immediately from man's social nature and personal dignity; a sphere of rights that are human and therefore international, and thus beyond the sovereignty and the arbitrary will of the state. That these rights and the objective rules following from them are based in natural law is certain. Consequently they are ordinances of natural law to the states and thus are part of the order of international law inasmuch as they produce obligations of the states. Their positive formulation appears in the treatment of aliens, in the protection aliens receive from their home state; this protective right, this duty of the home state, results in restricting the power of the state where the alien lives. It is consequently against international law to deprive aliens of life or property without due process of law, to arrest them in an illegal or arbitrary manner without cause, or to deny them access to the courts. Even if the respective state's own national laws are below this international standard, this is not an excuse for the violation of these international

[13] Cf. The Declaration of the International Rights of Man by the Institut de Droit International, October 12, 1929 (Briarcliff Lodge, New York).

human rights and the necessary conclusions therefrom. They represent a genuine objective limitation of sovereignty; their consistent and wanton violation may become a just cause of war. An appeal against them to the national common good is impossible because this common good itself is essentially a concrete order to preserve and to protect the fundamental rights of the citizens of the particular state not as citizens, but as human persons.[14]

On the basis of natural law thus arise for man as individual person certain rules establishing the international rights of man that consequently become obligations for the states. The reason is man's social nature, beyond his equally natural situation as a citizen of a specific nation; and these rights as human rights penetrate the borders of the states, making them cooperative members of humanity. This is acknowledged by all doctrines that recognize natural law. Natural law, however conceived, is a law that rules human relations regardless of citizenship, i.e., membership in a body politic united by a positive legal order. The *jus gentium* of the Roman jurist and of St. Thomas rules human relations in the absence of the positive law of a state. And it may be conceived as the law of the natural status as opposed theoretically to the civil status. Hence issues at once the great difference between the Thomistic *jus naturale* and, for instance, the Hobbesian-Spinozistic *jus naturale*. For the Roman jurists and for St. Thomas the *jus naturale* referring to man, not to the citizen, is reason; for Hobbes *jus naturale* is nature as opposed to reason, and is consequently might; the ability of self-preservation by physical force is the basic right from which issues the war of all against all.[15] The civil status then assumes to itself all natural law and natural rights, transforming them by the social contract in the form of the *Pactum subjectionis* into internal positive law. The states in their absolute sovereignty then live for themselves in a status of natural law which is identical with that under which the individuals lived. Internationally right is might, as it was before the individuals formed their states. The way out of this dilemma would be a world-state, which, then, is the only logical solution for pacifist positivism.

---

[14] This is Vittoria's and Suarez' idea when they declare that the human sacrifice of pagan nations is a true cause for a just war of intervention.

[15] Hobbes, *Leviathan*, I, chap. 13; Spinoza, *Tractatus politicus*, II, §§ 4, 9, 12, 18.

V. Municipal Law and International Law

Beside this *jus naturale gentium* as distinguished from a *jus inter gentes* exists the internal (municipal) law of the individual states. Man as a human person has, rooted in his very nature and his end, rights transcendent to the state, forming a barrier against intrusion of the state in internal national law. But man as a citizen, in his social and economic life and in his cultural life, is surrounded and ruled by this internal law. Still, as a human being, man again emerges beyond the confines of national law into that ultimate community, mankind. This community, however loosely knitted, compared with the relative density of the state, still is a true community and has its own constitution, fundamentally the natural law, as had been remarked by the Roman jurists when they found this natural law to be the content of their *jus gentium*. This view of man as essentially living in various communities and belonging to different legal systems is the only reliable basis for a true concept of the international order. For once the national law-system is made the only valid and active one, then, on account of the implied absolute sovereignty of the state in relation to the individual person internally and to mankind and other states externally, either an international order as an objective fact with its moral and legal implications must be denied or, if it is accepted, it must be considered to be totally at the will and pleasure of the individual states. Such an order, of course, endangered by any whim of any state, would lack an essential of the order idea, namely, duration and objective validity. It would thus represent nothing but an empty, powerless legal camouflage of an irrational and never-ceasing struggle for power.

If mankind is established as a real community based in human nature and in the image of God of this nature, it follows that this human community must be an organized order, moral and legal, of the states which are, as we have seen, the outcome of that same social nature of man. The idea of the self-sufficiency and autonomy of the state, of its being a perfect society, does not exclude the membership of the state in that community of nations. For an individual state, for reasons of efficiency and expediency, for reasons of history, geography, biology, climate, and culture, is necessarily restricted to a part of mankind, to nations or other social groups, as its matter, and is confined to a specific part of the surface of the earth, as experience and history tell us. Thus, in addition to the specific metaphysical unity of all who are men, it follows from the fact of the coexistence of states that these states form a true political organization of mankind.

A social nature and a receptiveness to social forms of life that we find in man, we find also in the state, whose self-sufficiency is not an absolute one. The state is a member of the *universum* that in some way is itself *una respublica*.[16] From this social fact, and because the states are moral persons, there arises the necessity of establishing an order of law by which the relations of the members of the community are ruled and directed. This order as a positive one receives its principles and its end from the objective ideal, from the universal community of nations destined to live in peace and secure coordination and to realize concrete justice and mutual help in furthering the welfare of all and in perfecting the social nature of man. This quality, as we have seen, is not a privilege of any specific state but goes beyond the reach of the state. Thus this social philosophy starts with the dignity and end of the individual human person and his fundamental rights as directive to any kind of community and communal authority as the forms of social life in which man accomplishes his end. The social forms serve ultimately the individual person's spiritual and material interests. The idea of man that is the origin of all social forms, from family to mankind, is also the ultimate end of all social forms, for their end is the perfection of the idea of man in the individual persons.

This, then, is the basis of a coordination of the international order among the states and of the internal order in the states: they are coordinated as their specific objects and their common goods are coordinated and directed to the ultimate end, the perfection and happiness of man.

VI. Monism in International Law

Catholic political philosophy can accept neither the monistic nor the dualistic interpretation of international law. Certainly not the monistic one, for it would establish either the international legal

---

[16] "Totus orbis qui in aliquo modo est una respublica." Vittoria, *De pot. civ.* (Lyons edition), p. 120; about Suarez, cf. Rommen, *loc. cit.,* p. 278.

order or the national legal order as the supreme order. In the first case the internal national order would be nothing but a derivation, an authorization and delegation from the international order. There would be only one true state, the *civitas maxima* of the community of nations, by the grace of which the individual states would live. Thus even the internal sovereignty of the state would disappear; the internal order would, irrespective of its autonomous interests and its common good, form merely a dependent part of the soveriegn international order. The states would then not even have that independence which, for instance, the autonomous dominions in the British Commonwealth of Nations have, or that independence which the League of Nations presupposed. They would be administrative bodies, not "ruling themselves freely"; their "territorial integrity and political independence" [17] would not be a presupposition of the international order, but a mere grant revocable as the interest of the *civitas maxima* demanded. All national affairs would be decided by the exigencies of international interests. Thus would be born a super-state, which must be carefully distinguished from a federation.

A federation is a status of symbiosis of free states, in which only interests and competencies are divided between the central government and the member states, while the liberty and the autonomy of internal competencies is guaranteed by the status, the *pactum foederis*, not by the central government; the free states, therefore, remain independent in their competencies. A conflict can arise between a state law and the federal constitution; yet the conflict between a state law and a federal law is always a conflict concerning competencies divided by the *pactum foederis*, not by the will of the central government. We may further say that even the federal states presuppose for their actual *vis vivendi* a minimum of cultural and historical homogeneity surpassing by far the homogeneity of mankind. So the international order presupposes the independent and free states; for they are as such the addressees of its laws, and the order itself can achieve its actual positive form only through the states, whose internal working order and sovereignty is a *conditio sine qua non* of the international order.

A second monistic scheme proceeds from the supposition of the absolute sovereignty of the individual state. In its extreme form it

17 League of Nations Pact, Arts. 1 and 10.

denies absolutely and with much intrinsic logic that the international order is an obligating one. There is, then, no legal order between states. What controls so-called international life is power and selfish national interests. All that rules among the nations is a natural status such as Hobbes supposed to exist before fear of violent death and need for security compelled the individuals to put an end to the war of all against all. And this war is interrupted only by short-lived truces made for merely opportunist reasons. A true legal order is considered impossible among sovereign states.

There exists only one source of law, the will of the sovereign state, and that will is exclusively devoted to the furtherance of the national interests. A more considered view does not deny the possibility and historical existence of a legal order among sovereign states even though they may be the exclusive sources of law. So international law is said to originate in a temporary self-limitation of the sovereign states for opportunist reasons or out of a suitable utilitarianism. It is thus the positive will of the states that creates the international law *in toto,* and any state may arbitrarily revoke it if its interest changes. Supposedly there exists no true community of nations with such specific common good as the organic unity of the common interests, of justice, peace, and security. Consequently what is called international law is such as an external law of the states yet dependent only upon the actual will of the states.

Feeling that this is a rather shaky basis for the international order, some maintain that, though the whole of the international law is created only by positive will and depends only upon it, nevertheless the duration of the law is guaranteed by the general legal principle common to and, so to speak, axiomatic for all law. *Pacta sunt servanda.* This is, of course, no real help. First, one of the practical reasons of the self-limitation theory was exactly to void treaties that had lost their meaning or had turned against the national interest, the supreme master of self-limitation. Thus the principle of *pacta sunt servanda* became relative by the demand of the state to decide by itself and for itself under what conditions the general rule should be actually discarded. International law so becomes merely contractual law. All international relations, like human relations, according to this way of thinking, have their exclusive basis in subjective interests and find their exclusive form in contractual consent that produces by the union

of subjective wills for the time being an order resting merely on those
subjective wills. The status, the fact that to live together is more
than contractual relations, is just as completely disregarded as the
fact that even contractual consent receives its objective meaning not
so much from the arbitrary wills of the contractual partners as from
the objective idea and objective end for whose realization the contract
is initiated; the communion of men in the objective ideas, peace,
justice, and the perfection of man's nature, disappears here. What remains is a mere formality of contractual relations.

We may understand why the monistic foundation of international
law is unsatisfactory by considering the following points. First, it is
an attempt to avoid natural law by recognizing only positivism, i.e.,
the theory that the will of the state alone is not only the producer,
but also the source of obligation, of law. Law is will, actual will and
nothing else. Thus is denied the metaphysical basis of any legal and
moral norms in the intrinsic essence of man, of the state, of mankind,
norms which for the practical reason and the free will become ideas
and ends to be realized and are thus directive and regulative norms
for human acts in realizing their ends. No longer does objective being,
the idea, control the autonomous will; utility, opportunist purposes,
lust for power, fear for self-preservation or the power of circumstances
may control it, but not the eternal norms that the Creator revealed
in His creation. This resignation rests upon the agnostic theory that
our mind cannot penetrate into the essences of things, that what we
experience are only the external phenomena which give us no knowledge of the thing in itself, of the idea of man and of state and of
mankind.

Consequently it is impossible to discover the *universum* of human
social and political life as an intrinsic order of being, in which corresponding ends or goods exist for the individual person, for the
state, and for the international community of states as an organization
of mankind; the earthly end and good of the person, the common
good of the state, and the common good of the international community that as directive and regulative ideas represent the absolute
norms independent of our concrete will in its production of the
forms of our social and political life. This agnosticism by implication
makes one blind to finality (teleology), to the end of an institution or
a social form, to its *causa finalis*, its nature and idea.

A further consequence is that the moral law and the ethical ideals are declared to be worthless and needless for the legal order, so that law in the positivist sense becomes order by compulsion. Then, of course, there is only one choice: either there is an international legal order, necessarily an order of compulsion with a sovereign ultimate power in the community of nations, reducing the states to mere executive, administrative servants of that truly total and imperial *civitas maxima,* the present God; or what we call international order is something that lives only by the grace and the subjective wills of the states, strictly and absolutely dependent upon their changing dynamic interests. The phrase "international community" corresponds to no reality; it is only a convenient expression without any *fundamentum in re.* So the reason of state of each state, the *ragione del stato* of Machiavelli, becomes the supreme lord of this freak international law. Peace, justice, and security are not international objective goods, but subjective opinions or propaganda slogans, while the only reality is the self-interest and the self-aggrandizement of the individual state.

VII. Insufficiency of Positivism

There is little doubt that these monistic theories are unsatisfactory. They are so much the consequences of a scientific ideal devoid of experience, however much they appeal only to factual study and experience as against metaphysics, that they have created between science and common sense a cleavage so deep that political and social sciences have become by far more a secret science than ever was scholastic philosophy, which rightfully has been called the educated sister of common sense. And so irreconcilable with the facts are these theories that their propounders, not only when they turn practical political leaders but even while they propound their theories, appeal to ideas and profess very concrete ideals. This very professing is as good evidence against their theories as Karl Marx's repeated appeals to justice and morals are evidence against his professed historical materialism.

Let me give an example that speaks for itself. In his *Lehrbuch des Völkerrects,* translated into most modern languages, Friedrich von Liszt tries to remain a positivist while attempting to recognize the legal character of the international order. That the law obliges even against the will is for him the decisive distinction of legal norms. The norms of religion or morals on the contrary, he says, are autonomous; they do not oblige the person against his will. But to oblige against subjective will is characteristic of any norm, technical, religious, legal, or ethical. Liszt says that the state must remain a member of the international community of nations, because the state is so bound by the strong ties of international traffic that it cannot leave this community even though it should will to do so. The power of circumstances ties it to the community and that is, he says, proof of the legal nature of international (public) law.[18]

But he forgets that moral law and legal law oblige equally. The difference is that in legal law there exists a procedural way of enforcement. Besides its internal obligation, presumably just, it has an external necessitation. It is a discipline of compulsion. But is it not true that such an enforcibility is in international law scarcely developed? Is only that part of international law obligating which can be physically enforced, or the enforcement of which by others must be feared by the single state? Thus the question of what internal obligation is, becomes a question of application of power; that is, no obligation at all. The so-called international order would become an order of power relations, the opposite of its true meaning, and opposed to what almost every international agreement professes as its purpose: namely, to develop international cooperation and to guarantee peace and security on the basis of justice and honor, as, for instance, we find stated in the preamble of the Covenant of the League of Nations.

The will of the states, whether in the form of a mutual contract or in the form of a multilateral covenant, is not enough to oblige these autonomous wills. The obligation must be an objective one. And this is so obvious that Liszt himself, against his own positivist theory, acknowledges it. He says that the community of nations rests on the idea of a coordination of the various states with their individually defined circles of rule and mutually acknowledged realms of power. From this fundamental idea follows directly a whole series of legal norms by which rights and duties of states are determined between themselves. These norms need no special contractual acknowledgment to have obliging force. They form the solid substance of the

18 *Das Völkerrecht* (12th ed.), p. 11.

unwritten international law, its oldest, most important, most sacred content.

These rights (fundamental rights of the states), he continues, are not imaginary natural-law concepts, but legal norms that, according to the thesis of non-contradiction, follow from the concept of the community of nations and do not need the form of positive law, because without them an international law is unthinkable. As the rights that follow from this basic idea are immediately due to each state as a member of the international community, they may be called international fundamental rights of the states. They are implied in the concept of the state as a subject of rights in the international community and as a member of this community. So far as these fundamental rights are objects of positive agreements between states, such agreements have a mere declaratory character, or what matters, are specific applications of a self-evident principle.[19]

What is interesting in these sentences is the fact that here an a priori of the positive law is openly admitted: that from the assumed essence of the states and the nature of the international community as objective realities follow legal consequences, legal rules that are legal without the intervention of the positive will of the states; that have the criteria of natural law. The difference between Liszt, who professes himself a positivist, and Vittoria or Suarez is not the thing itself. The difference is that Suarez and Vittoria openly call these a prioris natural law, which they evidently are, and that Liszt is ashamed to use that abhorred word. These criteria are not legally irrelevant moral ideas, but legal norms that oblige independently of any will other than that of the Creator of man, of states, and of the universe. They are the juridical principles for the positive international law and the directive principles for its formulation.

VIII. NATURAL LAW AS THE COMMON BASIS

On the basis of natural law, then, we may also find the solution of the relation between the internal order of the national laws and the external order of international law. They have a common source, human sociality and the nature of man which finds its realizations in the state as well as in the community of nations, inasmuch as both

[19] *Ibid.*, pp. 116 f.

are forms of perfection of the idea of man in his rational, spiritual, and material existence. They have a common end, the perfection and happiness of man in his social and political existence. They have a common principle, the natural law; and they have different positive elements, though these are coordinated to one another.[20] Rules of international law are appropriated by the internal order of municipal law; or the international order commands or forbids something to the municipal law; it superimposes itself upon the municipal law, demanding that the latter fulfill certain standards of civilization, which the community of nations considers the minima for all its free and independent members.[21]

On the basis of natural law, certain fields of human life and certain institutions are coordinated either to the individual, to the state, or to the community of nations as fields of autonomous proper affairs, as spheres of fundamental liberties and of self-initiative. For the individual these liberties are embodied in the constitutional bill of rights. As liberties of the free and independent states they have found their formulations in the above-mentioned fundamental rights of the states as members of the international community, as the a priori of the latter's very existence and functioning. Such, for instance, are the rights of each nation freely to determine its form of government, provided that the standards of international ethics and civilization are met; of each nation in independence to realize the order of the common good in its economic, legal, and social institutions; of each nation to protect its citizens at home and abroad.

Such a right in relation to fellow members is the right to be undisturbed by foreign intervention in its own affairs, a right that imposes a duty upon other states not to disturb the internal order of any fellow state by furthering fifth-column activity or by aiding seditious groups or conspiracy against the established government, provided again that the general standards of internationally recognized political ethics and civilization are not offended by the established government

---

[20] Modern constitutions express this truth by explicitly or implicitly stating that the commonly acknowledged principles of international law are part of the national law. Cf. Constitution of the United States, Art. III, 2; German Constitution of the Weimar Republic, 1919–1933, Art. 4; Austrian Constitution of 1919–1934, Art. 9, and the new Constitution (Dollfuss), Art. 8; Constitution of the Spanish Republic, 1931; 1938, Arts. 6 and 7.

[21] For particulars, cf. the excellent treatise of E. Kaufmann, *Règles générales du droit de la paix* (Paris, 1936), pp. 128 ff.

in question. This qualification must be made because any grave violation of the fundamental natural law by a tyrannical government necessarily becomes an international affair. For such an open violation of the very basis of the international order is an immediate danger to the international order itself. The principle of non-intervention does not justify the toleration of such an outrage against the essence of the international order.

These rights are largely internal, protecting the sphere of the state; other rights are external. The very existence of the community of nations implies the right of external commerce, the access to the wealth of the earth.[22] This is a consequence of the interdependence of the members of the community of nations and would therefore make illegal a total economic autarchy with absolute separation from the world economy. Hence a certain degree of free access to the world's raw materials is a genuine right of the members of the international community. To this right corresponds a duty of the individual state to take into consideration the welfare of other states, whenever, in the interest of its own common good, it thinks itself to be compelled to protect its internal industry and agriculture by high tariff walls.

The international community has its own common good, in which each state as a member of this community participates. The national common good is not an absolute and egotistic value that justifies any and all measures of seclusion from international economic life. Consequently peace and international justice demand that each state in adjusting its economic policy under the guidance of the idea of the national common good should take care that such a policy does not gravely violate the international common good. The right to freedom and independence in any community is always controlled by a responsibility of its members to the end, to the common good which is the *raison d'être* of this community. Economic nationalism can never be justified by appeal to the national common good, because it leads to the dissolution of the material basis of the international community and so eventually, out of fear and jealousy, to a Hobbesian natural status of international life.

While these rights refer to the status of peace, there are other rights that emerge in the status of war. From the principle of territorial

<hr>

[22] Pius XII, Peace program (December 24, 1941). Cf. Harry C. Koenig, *Principles of Peace*, no. 1760.

integrity and protection of its internal order of the common good, the individual state has not only the right of self-defense but the duty of self-defense. And further, as long as the international community has not developed a procedure of arbitration and forcible protection of its members, even a right to offensive war by an individual state may be acknowledged, when directed against an unjust international status quo. As we will devote a special section to the ethics of war, we do not enter into further discussions here.

What, then, is the meaning of these rights?

Rights are never abstract legal entities, but are always related to the objective norms of a social order of duration, to an order of functional integration in solidarist group life. Whenever we say "rights" we mean rights that are founded in a social order of solidarist common existence. Therefore in actual life we cannot separate rights from duties. The rights and duties are thus the complement of the social order as the law of the group or community and of its constitution and of its institutional productions. But this presupposes not a simple indifferent fact, like the order in the beehive, but a common end of the group as the reason of its constitution and institutions. For the difference between the beehive and the human society, whatever its name (family, labor union, state, or community of nations), is that the human society has its end in itself and that this objective end is sought in freedom by the free acts of the rational members. The order of the group, its actual functional organization, is therefore regulated and measured by this idea. The idea as the final cause is the principle for judging the communities as the realizations of the idea in history. For in human societies we have always a moral, internal "ought" beside the physical "must," while in beehives there is only a physical "must" and no "ought" at all. Therefore the rights, though abstractly implied in the existence of the subject, are the counterpart of the functional integration of the subject into the actual order. The rights become actual in the social function performed by the subject of the right as a participant in the solidarist life of the whole of the group or community. Yet the rights are not mere reflexes of the concrete functioning; they are the consequence of the substantial dignity of the human personal subject as a self-value; and they are also the consequences of the social nature of the subject and his natural end that can be reached only by life in society. Therefore it is the objective end of the communal life as a service to the objective natural end of the member that forms the basis and the regulative norm of these rights and duties.

Hence we cannot say that these rights are bestowed exclusively by the will of the community or its will-endowed authority. Nor can we say that the order and the authority of the community is a simple concession or transfer of original rights from the members to the directing organ or authority. The nature and the end of the community directly and the nature and end of man ultimately are what form the basis of the order of law. The concrete acts of will of the constituents by which the community is produced and holders of authority are determined, produce the historical community as a realization of the idea and of the end. The plurality of independent states and of mankind as a true community, therefore represents a being that exists, not as a free production that could be or could not be, but as the natural outgrowth of human social nature. The end is peace and justice, that is, the justice, order, and security of mankind, that whole which is divided into a pluralism of states; the object of each of them is the same: justice, order, and security internally. Of course this order itself is again related to man's last aim: to achieve the salvation of the soul and perpetual happiness. And it is also a way to perform the last end of all creation, the glorifying of God. As man is the image of God, and as God reveals Himself in the ideal order of being as a result of the analogy of being, this order becomes the end of all human social cooperation and of community life in all its variety of forms.

It is this objective basis of the positive law of nations that is the most important contribution of Catholic political philosophy to the theory of international law.

IX. Sovereignty

Leo XIII criticizes the nineteenth-century theory of international law for excluding the Christian moral norms from the general law of nations.[23] These norms had the wonderful power of uniting the nations into one family. But the nations, rejecting them, began a reckless pursuit of their selfish interests and power politics and poisoned

[23] *Annum ingressi sumus* (March 19, 1902).

their common life by an envious imperialism. The general rules of morality and justice were discarded; the security and freedom of the small nations from the arrogance of the more powerful states were forgotten. The exclusive aim of a non-moral foreign policy became the increase of one's own power and one's own national wealth; and that international policy was ruled by momentary utility and material advantage to such an extent that the success of an act, even of the most immoral act, was thought to be the true measure of international procedure. Thus, Leo XIII says, material power is made the highest norm of human relations. This is the reason for the enormous armament race. The dubious peace which is preserved at that price inflicts damage that measures up to the damage of a devastating war.

Again and again, from the earliest time on, Catholic political philosophy, proceeding from the idea of man's dignity and man's prerogative of ruling the earth, has declared the fact that mankind is a true community, *quasi una respublica,* a family of nations, bound by brotherly love. And this fact, distinct and fundamental enough so that even tyrants and conquerors desecrate it by using it as a sort of propaganda for their wanton aggression, is the intrinsic measure of all positive parts of international law, not the absolute sovereign will of the state or the success of power politics. The international common good, the order of justice, peace, and security for the individual man's sake, is the purpose of international cooperation. All nations are, intentionally from their subjective existence and teleologically from their very objective nature, as parts ordered to the whole, to mankind, and they form a genuine community of objective character. The will of the state finds the norms of natural social justice as given. What the will can do is to make concrete in the historical circumstances this ideal objective end; but the will of the state does not create it.

There is, therefore, no place for unlimited absolute sovereignty in the international order. Liberty and independence, yes. Liberty to rule internally as the individuality of the nation, born out of history, tradition, culture, and climate, wills it, in the ever-valid framework of natural law that refers to man and not to national individuality. Independence, that is, to live for itself, to decide for itself the forms of government, the economic order, and the social order without disturbance from other states as long as its decisions are not against the universal law of mankind, against natural law. The authority and power of the individual state in its competence and exercise is thus coordinated to the fundamental fact that each state is a member of the family of nations, subject therefore to the eternal laws of the end and life of this international body. Thus the fundamental order of international law is *realiter* given with the pluralism of states and *idealiter* with the nature of man and the end of mankind. This order is objective and, in its essence and end, is not created either by the will of the sovereign states or by a self-limitation of the absolute sovereignty of the states.

There is, consequently, no place in this philosophy of international law for the principle of strict nonintervention. The realization of the international order is the task of the cooperative effort of the individual states, and the continuous existence of the positive order is their responsibility, individually and solidarily. The right of liberty and independence of the individual state receives its measure also from the *international* common good, from the undeniable fact that each state can fulfill its humane mission as well as its national destiny only as a member of the community of nations. Therefore the continuous existence and the preservation and the defense of the rights of each member is not only the duty of each member but is also a matter of solidary responsibility of all the member states, as this solidary responsibility is the guarantee and makes possible the efficiency of the international order itself. If by wanton disregard of the basis of these rights the liberty and independence of one member state is endangered by unjust aggression, that aggression is an affair of all member states. To say "I am not my brother's keeper" is simply a denial of the objective order itself. The offer of one's good services in a quarrel between nations was never considered an intervention, even when the principle of nonintervention on the basis of absolute sovereignty prevailed. Thus we have a silent proof of the validity of the supereminence of the international order. The richer a nation is in population and in natural resources, the less it can retire from the duty of upholding the international order even by intervention, provided that the ways and means of actual intervention are sound policy under given circumstances. Strict adherence to the principle of nonintervention puts the principle of might makes right first in international life because it puts a material premium on the violation of the international order. This is the reason why the principle of nonintervention has been condemned by Pius IX.[24]

International law especially is in need of natural law because it lives not by an administrative system of enforcement, as does internal state law, but is in its influence and regulative power dependent upon the cooperative, coordinated acceptance of its obligation by the states, because it lives by mutual good will and moral consent far more than by enforcement. It thus lives, and it must live, by natural law rather than by positive law. So powerful and unavoidable is this truth that even those who do not believe in peace and justice, the aggressors and conquerors, appeal to the emotional power of natural law in defense of their violations of the international order. This they do by propounding a new and apparently juster order. Thus even in their crime they bow before the might of the moral natural law as it lives in the eternal laws of the coexistence of free nations within the international community; a law that "ought" to rule impressing itself as God's will upon the conscience; an order of peace and justice whose rules are not silenced, even if the voice of all other laws is drowned out by the inhuman noise of arms.

[24] It is utterly wrong to attribute this condemnation of the principle of nonintervention to the political situation of the Papal States, whose existence was threatened by the Italian movement for national unity. It is sometimes said that Pius condemned nonintervention only because in this case it was urged by the House of Savoy against the protection afforded to the Papal States by Napoleon III and against pleas of the Papal States for intervention to the Austro-Hungarian monarchy. It should not be forgotten that the principle of nonintervention is condemned together with the following: That might makes right; that the success of an unjust act cures the injustice; and that the motive of patriotism excuses any crime. The title of section 7 calls these doctrines *Errores de ethica naturali et christiana.*

CHAPTER XXIX

The Catholic Doctrine about War

I. WAR AND PEACE

THE common good of the international community is justice, peace, and security for its members. An international order is fundamentally the consequence of the pluralism of states and nations. Moreover, this order lives by the actual consent and acceptance of the member states. But for the time being, as an order of coordination, it lacks an undisputed sovereign legislative power other than the members themselves, and lacks also an executive apparatus of enforcement. Once these truths are conceded, we are confronted with the problem of peace, justice, and security as the object to be realized wherever it arises, or the problem of what means there are to enforce the continuous validity of the international order. This is the problem of peace and war.

This problem can be solved only on the basis of natural law. During the times when the nations had surrendered to the power idea and to economic imperialism, Catholic political philosophy raised its solitary voice in praise of peace, of natural justice, of mutual understanding, and of conscience in international life. Furthermore, it worked for the introduction of new legal institutions able to reconcile the opposing interests produced by the changing life of the international community, which knows nothing of an eternal, static *status quo*. It is not enough to abhor war and to shout: "No more wars!" A certain kind of pacifism is so quietist and passive in its belief in progress as to think that merely to will "no war" is enough. We know that international life, like all human efforts, lives under the law of imperfection; that therefore the will for peace must realize itself in elastic but strong new institutions, in which and through which the abstract demand for justice produces what is concretely just. Thus from the beginning Catholic political philosophy rejected the emotionalism that calls the soldier "murderer," that depreciates the ethical virtues connected with war, such as patriotism, fortitude, and the solidarist spirit of comradeship in arms. It did not despise the soldier, however sternly it condemned the merely instrumental militarism which is never concerned with the moral problem in war but only with tactics and strategy, with mere technique. This militarism, once it is set free from moral obligation, makes war a craft to be practiced by human hordes of robots unable to rebuild, able only to destroy.

Whenever the lovers of peace indulge in a merely emotional and negative attitude, whenever they try to "buy" peace instead of building it, then instrumental militarism will win the day. It is not enough to long for peace: we must build institutions that are fit not only to produce peace, which is the mere absence of war, but also to produce justice and the just order among nations. And even more important is that rational, strong, ethical will to realize, in a historical situation, peace through justice, an ethical will that looks beyond patriotism, beyond historical legalities, to the international common good as the paramount principle of legitimacy in international law. It is this ethical will that gives to the positive legal institutions their strength, their efficiency, and their dignity. Peace means originally well-established order; peace, therefore, is just order among nations. That this can be established without appeal to arms is the fundamental conviction of Catholic political philosophy.

War is not the effect of a mystical, biological force called "life"; it is not a natural effect, unavoidable and irrepressible, as natural as birth and death. That war is such an effect has been asserted again and again and not disproved by centuries of experience alone. Yet its true basis is a materialist concept of international life. According to this concept the states will live forever in a natural status of one state being wolf to the other. The states are in themselves irrational and irresponsible creatures of that unfathomable, unconscious force called "life," the cruel goddess. They are born in and by a struggle beyond reason and law, grow so, and die in struggles with younger, more powerful states that will follow their predecessors in mortal struggle, in an unending cycle.

Whether the ultimate reason is the struggle of races, as Gumplowicz saw it, or of classes, as Marx interpreted it, or of mysterious souls of nations, as modern nationalism saw it, is indifferent. That mysterious force, life, is primary and uncontrollable, it is said; we can but execute its hidden drive or surrender in suicidal defenselessness. Any attempt to see in history more than this funereal procession of nations and states, senseless, incomprehensible, enigmatic, is futile. However great the variance in particulars, such is the fundamental assumption of those who, because they have despaired of sense in history or of reason in man and thus of God as the Lord of history and of nations and of men, think that peace is a chimera and war the most natural effect of life.

It should be noted that on this assumption not human imperfection, not insufficient reason, not a low degree of international morality, is the reason and cause of war; life or nature, itself irrational and sense-less, is the cause of war, and peace is therefore a pause, a recess forced by exhaustion or taken for preparation of new wars. And the state? The state is then a body politic that by destiny conducts war. Law is then a blind natural law like gravity, and human belief that law is a moral rule for free human acts is an unreal reflex in human conscious-ness which itself is unreal reflex, a dream of the only reality, life. Right is then the conscious reflex of the *status quo* of power. Might makes right. From the enthusiasts of the philosophy of life to the technicians of militarism, from the believers in perpetual return to the cynical skeptics who despair of a sense in history and of reason in man, all are of the same opinion: war is a natural, unavoidable event.

II. Pacifism, Economic and Humanitarian

Against this radical prowar philosophy there has stood, ever since the rise of modern bourgeois society, an antiwar philosophy as radical as the first. We may reduce this philosophy to three main forms, how-ever often fusions of these forms may occur. What is common to all these forms is an idea of evolutionary progress that in the end will produce a stateless society, a *civitas maxima* of all mankind, where wars are superfluous because the true source of wars, the plurality of states, has been removed and where a millennial realm of peace and of perfect, secure life will be achieved.

We may characterize the first of these forms as economic pacifism. Its basis is the belief of classical economy that with the development of an international division of labor the world economy will ultimately make states superfluous. Instead of competitive national economics, with the consequence of wars in protection of the national economies, their market, and their raw-material sources, there will arise a pacified world economy in which economic individuals, but not national economies, compete. The general dislike of state and polity as an uneconomic, irrational element in their rationalist world-view made most of these thinkers cosmopolitans, to whom patriotism is the remnant of a cruder stage of social progress. As economic liberty and self-interest, like an invisible hand internally and without state intervention, produce social harmony, so will the same principles, once the plurality of the states is fading away, produce a world harmony. Holders of this theory pointed out that wars are economically unsound and never pay, that modern technique is international, and that progress points to an economically founded *civitas maxima.*

Another form of pacifism may be characterized as humanitarian. Its adherents originate in two groups that form international strata through our national communities. The specific ends and interests of these groups are, or at least seem to be, not directed to national states but to mankind. One of these groups comprises the scholars, literary men, and artists so far as in their artistic creation they are related to mankind. Thus mankind and the cosmopolitan ideal of an international fraternity of the servants of the True, of the Good, and of the Beautiful are the unifying forces of a humanity that is broad instead of nationally narrow. On the secularized basis these men try to emulate the medieval idea of a unified *orbis christianus.* Perhaps they too easily equate mankind with modern bourgeois society in its international features. They usually show the same disdain for the idea of nation, of state, and of polity as do some of the economic pacifists; and they show, too, a certain pleasure in "debunking" what they call the myths of national histories, heros, and governments. This brings them close to the pacifism that found its home in the modern proletarian movement of international socialism. That socialism, too, believes in the final deliverance of mankind in a *civitas maxima* without states. They maintain that states are only instruments of exploitation by the capitalist classes, and all wars are therefore rooted in the existence of these exploiting instruments. Once the proletariat, whose very existence directs it to mankind, and not to states and nations, rises in a world revolution, it will, after the short epoch of proletarian dictatorship, give birth to a *civitas maxima* without classes, states, or nations, and consequently without wars. The *Communist Manifesto* is the best expression of this prophetic expectance. What is common to the international of the mind and of the proletariat is that both see in the nation and in the state only transitory forms of social development, which are already losing their function and need only be revealed as the base instruments of reaction or oppression. These men do their best to vilify the soldier as the military servant of the state, the soldier who for the Christians fulfills a true vocation; wherefore we speak of Christian soldiers. These men debase patriotism and other virtues like fortitude when these are related to war. They ridicule military discipline and national history. Hence they deny implicitly the ethical problem of war. But some of them may at the same time glorify the solidarity of the class warriors, the wild violence of the proletarian masses rising in revolution against their oppressors.

According to the view of this humanitarian and proletarian pacifism, the course of historical development will produce the republic of world citizens, either as enlightened minds freed from dangerous emotions and tribal allegiances or as economic producers freed from all class distinctions and war producing class struggles. Consequently this development, so it is said, will bring about the perfection of mankind, which, without national tensions and class conflicts, produces eternal peace in the complete satisfaction of all man's desires, spiritual and material. This pacifist belief in perpetual progress is anthropocentric and immanent since it supposes an immanent general law of progress and an immanent historical teleology of this progress that ends in an earthly paradise. Its secularism is distinct.

III. RADICAL FORMS OF RELIGIOUS PACIFISM

The strongest expression of modern pacifism is founded on religious beliefs. This religiously founded pacifism, like religiously founded nationalism, the source of "holy" wars, ranges from Mahatma Ghandi and his followers in the doctrine of non-resistance through many Christian sects (e.g., the Friends and the Mennonites) to groups in the Catholic Church. These last are found especially among social reformers and youth groups who strive for total or radical Christianity.

Any genuine religion is by definition not immanent but transcendental. Any genuine religion refers beyond the visible nation to the invisible brotherhood of mankind. Any genuine religion strives to let the peace of the soul in the divine life, under whatever masks it may be hidden, radiate into the world; for the mind is stronger than weapons; love, not war, is the ultimate producer of peace. Any religion not content with merely determining the life of the individual, always intends the reform of social groups, too. The adage, *unus christianus, mullus christianus*, is a general criterion of all transcendental religions. Furthermore, however quietistic a religion may be, its implication is always that the world has to conform to the transcendental religion's ideal, absolute and exemplary as it is. Therefore all higher religions are apocalyptic and have their specific eschatology: an ideal status of the world at the end of time, for which all adherents must work. Of course this is not the immanent natural progress of nineteenth-century liberal secularism, nor that of historical materialism. It is the outcome of man's moral conformity to the religious ideal with the aid of divine intervention and leadership.

The ideal of Buddhism is flight from the noisy world into the quietist contemplation of the world beyond, even though that is the complete passivity of nirvana. But this very ideal reflects into the world an abhorrence of war and declares peace to be the proper status of the world on the basis of common brotherhood. The doctrines of Confucius and the religion of Tao oppose all the emotional passions that produce war. Similarly the records of wars in ancient Jewish history must not make us forget that the religious leaders, the prophets, proclaim a reign of peace as the end of Juda, as Isaias said: "they shall turn their swords into plowshares, and their spears into sickles" (Isa. 2:4).

The ideal of peace as the result of religion has found its most perfect expression in Christianity. The Christian gospel is a sermon in behalf of peace. Love even for the enemy [1] is a command, not simply

---

[1] Nationalist thinkers have maintained that, in Matt. 5:43 f. and Luke 6:27, the word "enemy" should be understood as meaning private adversary, not political enemy or foreign enemy. But this view is preposterous. For the Jews, the non-Jew might be a

a counsel. Christ is the Prince of peace; He brings peace to men of good will. True, this peace that Christ gives, the world cannot itself give. Thus Christ's peace means not only and not even primarily a community of nations without wars. The peace of Christ means first of all that by redemption the original, true order between God and men has been restored; it means reconciliation with God, an internal resting in the peace of the soul that is again received into the order of God and the communion with God. That is the peace that the world cannot give. As little as this peace can be made a humanitarian ideal of "this world," so little can it be a secluded affair perpetually alien to the world. The peace of Christ radiates as a formative power into the world.

In the world, too, there ought to be peace; the order of justice glorified by the fundamental law of neighborly love ought to rule. For man works out his salvation in this world. Man needs the peace and security of this life. The Church prays every day for "peace in our days," that we may be "secure from all disturbance" (*Canon Missae: "Libera nos"*). We lead the virtuous life best in peace and security. And that means in a well-established social, political, and spiritual order. Security must not be understood as only economic security. It means in the first place spiritual security of the conscience found in a working ethical order with undoubted, commonly accepted moral ideals. We should bear in mind how much this security is threatened by the passions of license, of hatred, of lust, of vanity, and by the diabolical lust for destruction of material and spiritual values. We should know how unordered sexual passions and unordered acquisitiveness and profit-seeking endanger the peace of our social and economic life. Man's life is generally possible only in an order of peace. The Christian, however much he reverences the heroic virtues of the soldier in defense of the order, does not believe in the intrinsic wholesomeness of war. The Christian, however much he venerates the citizen who in war sacrifices his life and possessions for the common good of

_____

national enemy. But this attitude was changed by Christ. He said that every man is our neighbor, even the Samaritan whom the orthodox Jews despised as a heretic. Christ's friendliness to the publicans, those hated tax-collectors of the Romans, His miraculous favor to an officer of the occupation army, and many other incidents in the Gospels show that the command, "Love your enemy," must not be restricted to the private sphere, but extends to the political sphere also. The Christian citizen may have a political foe whom he fights, but he must not hate him.

the body politic, does not believe in war as the creator of new values. For war is only protection or restoration of the order of peace and, in itself, is not productive. This is the commonly accepted and, from Christian premises, the necessary doctrinal basis of the ethics of peace and war.

If, then, Christian groups have a specific pacifism of their own, they go beyond this common standpoint; they imply that they draw more far-reaching conclusions than are generally drawn by the common doctrine. Some Christian sects (e.g., the Manichaeans, the Wycliffites in the late Middle Ages, and the Friends and the Witnesses of Jehovah in our own time) believe Christianity and peace to be so identical that war of any kind is forbidden to the disciples of Christ. In the Catholic Church, especially since the end of World War I, certain youth groups and authors, laymen as well as priests, without any intention of abandoning the traditional doctrine, began, not indeed to erect a new doctrine, but rather to propound the theory that, because of the modern technological development of our time, a just war must be considered impossible. They hold that one of the requirements of a just war, the suitableness of the means of war to the purpose of war, cannot be met today. Some of these men, too, declared that since about 1600 a certain feebleness and compliance with nationalism had appeared in the ethics of war, together with a weakening in principles. There had become apparent a diversion from full religious Christianity to a social and cultural Christianity that was inclined to yield to the demands of the world (the capitalist world, they frequently emphasized). Casuistical moral theology and the tendency to accommodate oneself in some way to the new, at least non-Christian, secular civilization had produced a kind of diluted Christianity as compared to the full Christianity of the Gospels. The representative saint of these groups is St. Francis of Assisi. Consequently the spirit of brotherly love is accentuated to the utmost. The strict rationality, the necessarily separative and unemotional properties of law, of order, and of justice remain in the background. The sacrificial spirit of community is extolled at the expense of the rights of the individual.

Let me quote a typical statement: "War is unchristian, if by Christianity we mean, not a measure of duty and a minimum, but a complete surrender to the spirit of Christ and a full realization of His example. According to the standards of a final, full, and perfect Christianity, war is unjust for the Christian. There remains only passive resistance, but not active warfare." [2] An apocalyptic strain is evident; the realm of God is near. "The victory of pacifism stands before the blood-stained doorsteps of mankind." The pacifism of these Christian groups, especially that of Catholic groups just described, must not be confused with the pacifism of leftist-communist or skeptical groups. The pacifism of communist groups is too instrumental. For any kind of pacifism in a bourgeois state that is a potential aggressor against the fatherland of the proletariat is a protection for the latter. The pacifism of a disillusioned, skeptical youth, nourished by intellectuals who lost the national and traditional ideals of progress and culture in doubt and despair, is a weary, overmature pacifism without idealistic ends. It is self-irony caused by the loss of nationalist ideals and an awakening to the dreary emptiness of a life where a person works that he may not despair.

Radical pacifism, whether on a merely humanitarian or on a religious basis, is characterized by a frank neglect of the problems of political philosophy, of state, of government, of sovereignty, of international law, and of power. Therefore the real problem of war is scarcely grasped. Furthermore, we must not forget that several of these groups neglect the important distinction between the spiritual sphere and the secular sphere; small religious groups living in the framework of an ordered state can easily regulate their affairs by an identification of the spiritual and secular spheres. The historical record of such groups may show that the spiritual leader tends to become the lawmaker, the judge, and the economic director of these communities in the secular sphere of their existence. Hence they can do without government, state, or the like, because they are a religious and secular political community in one. But the guaranty of their existence is exactly the existence of the political order that surrounds their communities.

[2] Such statements as this, from *Der Sieg des Pacifismus* (Berlin, Verlag der Scholle), could be found everywhere in Germany after 1919, and in France, England, and Austria, and also in the United States and in the Netherlands; a token of how deeply the postwar generation was moved by the love of peace, and how much it felt betrayed by governments that continued power politics, business as usual, and petty politics.

IV. The Ideal of a World State

The true problems of war and peace arise from the premise that mankind is organized into a plurality of independent, free states that live in an order of coordination and not of subordination of one to the other. And this order, upheld by the consent and active support of the member states must guarantee to its members independence, freedom, and integrity, even though for the time being it lacks compulsory instruments and organs to enforce its functioning and to prevent the disturbance of these rights. Even if we supposed that such an organization existed, there still would remain the problem of a defensive war. If even in the best organized state the police cannot be omnipresent, we are still less entitled to expect complete protection from a more cumbersome international organization. The problem of war and peace, along with the distinction between just and unjust war, presupposes the independence, the territorial and juridical independence, and the freedom of states. For once the *civitas maxima* is realized in its full meaning, any war would be civil war or would be a punitive police action of the world sovereign against subordinate law-breaking social groups.

Thus the first question is either a plurality of states or a *civitas maxima* with paramount world sovereignty. Such a world sovereignty is not implied in the idea of the unity of the human conscience, of the natural and moral law; nor does it follow from the designation of God as the supreme and universal ruler. For sovereignty includes the power to decide, without appeal, an actual juridical problem, to effect a decision by application of the general rule or norm. The sovereign power acts by deciding, not *in abstracto* about general rules, but *in concreto* about the validity of the rule *hic et nunc*, of its application *hic et nunc*. The sovereign makes the positive law; he embodies the abstract rules of natural law in the positive law. In the international community, therefore, the only possible sovereign would be an assembly of the nations. It alone could set up rules. It could institute organs to enforce these rules in matters that are the affair of the community by consent or by the very nature of the community, with due respect to the equally natural prerogatives of the members. A community so constituted would be nearer to a federation with divided sovereignty than to a unified *civitas maxima* with unlimited sovereignty or competence.

It is a fact that Catholic political philosophy in general does not propound such a universal world monarchy or empire of a *civitas maxima*. But the temptation to do so was strong, especially during the time of the medieval *orbis christianus*. The legists, the court jurists of the emperor, tried to prove that the emperor is the universal monarch, while the curialists, as late as 1595, declared that the pope is the sovereign of the *orbis christianus* with absolute and unlimited power in temporalia.[3] Dante in his *Monarchia* dreamt of such a universal monarchy under a Christian emperor. But the great philosophers thought otherwise. Although St. Augustine, for instance, believes that such a world state would be of advantage for peace and order, he maintains that a plurality of small states living in peace is preferable. St. Thomas, too, presupposes such a plurality of states, independent and free. Of the Late Scholastics who very broadly discussed problems of political philosophy, Suarez expressly repudiates the idea of a world monarchy [4] or world republic. Moreover, he did so while fully aware that, as the secular partner of a universal Church, a universal world state would powerfully recommend itself to the thinker. The nationalization of the Protestant Churches and the consequent intensification of nationalism was, at that time, not yet accepted as an established fact.

Bellarmine, although more friendly to such an idea, declares at once that he is thinking chiefly about a federation of sovereign princes under the emperor, in the sense of the Roman law. As he believes that such a federation cannot be realized without grave wars and violence, he comes to the conclusion that precisely because of national and geographic differentiation a plurality of individual independent states is justified.[5] This statement is very important. The concrete state is individualized as the political form of existence by its "matter" (*materia secunda*); that is, its people settled in its geographical situation.

---

[3] Cf. *Auctuarium Bellarminum* (10th ed., Le Bachelet, 1913), p. 426; cf. James Brodrick, *The Life and Work of Blessed Robert Francis Cardinal Bellarmine* (London, 1928), I, 216.
[4] Cf. Rommen, *Staatslehre des Franz Suarez*, pp. 138 f.
[5] *De Summo Pontifice* (*Opera omnia*, I, 488); cf. V. Cathrein, S.J., *Moralphilosophie*, II, 619; cf. further the conspicuous reserve of the popes on this question: Tischleder, *Staatslehre Leo XIII*, pp. 400 ff.

The common good can be realized only by adaptation of political and legal institutions to the prepolitical individuality of the people who form the state and to the exigencies of that geographical and climatic part of the globe in which the people live. The greater a state becomes, the less political coherence it has and the more bureaucratic centralization may be needed to guarantee the necessary unity and the minimum of a working order. The international community is therefore *una respublica* only in a limited sense, in so far as it has natural law for its constitutional rule. But it is not a true *respublica* because it has not by its very nature a sovereign universal power of decisions beyond appeal and of lawmaking. Hence in the event of a grave violation of the objective order or of the rights of one state by another, there is no international sovereign power to restore the order and punish the violator, or to restore and protect the infringed rights. For the state there remains only self-action by force: war.

V. The Just War

Obviously the aim of war is peace; that is, the solidarist order of coexistence and cooperation, an order that implies the integrity and independence of the partners in the order which realizes the common good of the community of nations. Order and the rights of the states imply each other; they coexist and are valueless in themselves and apart from each other. If we speak of external sovereignty, we can mean only such a sovereignty as is compatible with the solidarist order. Hence what limits the sovereignty is the fact of the order that limits the sovereignty. It is not self-limitation of the absolute, unlimited sovereign will that produces directly or indirectly the basic principles of the order, however much the competence of international organs may be increased by a retreat of state sovereignty from specific political fields of action.

Thus arises the problem of war as a restoration of the violated order or as a protection of infringed rights. And from both these elements must be drawn the criteria of the just or unjust war.

The distinction between just and unjust war implies that war is not intrinsically unjust, either from the standpoint of natural law or from the standpoint of Christian ethics.

The state has two aspects. Internally it is a self-sufficient entity, a closed institutional system essentially sovereign so that it may fulfill its end, the common good, which coincides with the good of the people considered individually as persons and groups and associations of persons. Externally the state is quite open to cooperation in the realization of the international order that is peace, justice, and security for all nations. The actual fulfillment of its internal end, the temporal common good, is the presupposition of its international cooperation, or, as we put it above, sovereignty has as its counterpart international responsibility. To be a responsible member of the international community presupposes independence and self-sufficiency in the internal order. The duty of the state in international cooperation for the realization of the international common good is the complement of its undisturbed right of existence as an independent, sovereign national order. To fulfill its common good is therefore the *conditio sine qua non* of the state's international duties.

The state is temporal and, as Thomas Hobbes rightly said, mortal. So is its end. A surrender of its right to defend the order of the finite common good would be for the state a self-contradiction. There is no parallel with the right of the individual person to non-resistance and to abandonment of self-defense because of Christian love. The individual person may act so because his end is spiritual and because he is immortal. The *ordo caritatis* may induce an individual to non-resistance, to voluntary sacrifice of his life for the life of another person. (But even here we must qualify. Theologians maintain that, for example, a father should not sacrifice his life for that of an individual without dependents; for the *ordo caritatis* does not abolish the *ordo justitiae*.) [6] But this individual right of non-resistance is not for the state. The state is mortal; its end is finite and temporal. Should the realization of this end be gravely endangered by foreign "unprovoked aggression," [7] then the mortal state has in fact no choice. It has not only the right to defend itself in war, but it has the duty to resist; a duty to itself and to the people, the political form of whose existence it is, as well as a duty to the international order that can function only as long as the individual states uphold their independence in realizing the order of the national common good. But the

<hr>

[6] Cf. Suarez, *Opus de triplici virtute theologica*, Tract., III, Disp. 9.

[7] The formula of modern treaties of arbitration and conciliation; e.g., the Treaty of Locarno (Art. 2), which implied, of course, that a provoked aggression was considered possible.

state as represented by the government cannot sacrifice the majority of its people. Moreover, apparent aggression may really be a
prudent and timely act of defensive warfare. A nation need not wait
until the armed forces of another country have actually invaded its
frontiers.

But has not Christianity made wars superfluous? Must what may
be a right and a duty for natural man, remain a right and a duty for
a Christian? We have already pointed out that war has generally been
considered unjust, and therefore forbidden to Christians by various
Christian sects since the early centuries. Against this opinion it must
be stated that, as long as there does not exist a practical instrument of
international arbitration and conciliation which would make wars
superfluous, Christian ethics has never considered war intrinsically
unjust, however much it hoped that Christian brotherly love would
do away with the causes of war. From the early Church Fathers on, the
great doctors have declined to condemn war absolutely. St. Ambrose
condemns wars of looting, but not military service; he even praises
military fortitude in war as a Christian virtue.[8] St. Augustine, who
was a lover of peace, writes: "Do not believe that he who serves in
war cannot please God." [9] St. Bernard says to the soldiers that Christians who kill their enemies do not sin, nor do they lose their souls
when slain in action.[10] This is a permanent doctrine of Christian
ethics. When authors like Father Stratmann or Vanderpool or Father
O'Toole profess that war today is always unjust, they imply that, on
account of contemporary circumstances such as the total character of
war, the intrinsic viciousness of this kind of warfare and the development of international law have made modern war an inefficient, senseless, and superfluous means for the vindication of international justice.
But they cannot say that war was at all times and under all circumstances against Christian ethics.

War is not a natural, irrational event like a thunderstorm or an
earthquake. War is intrinsically the servant of justice and peace. It is
a means to defend rights or to restore the international order of peace.
The aim of war is peace with justice. Therefore war can be directed
against an unjust peace, an unjust *status quo*. But it is never an end

---

8 *Sermo* 7; *De officiis*, I, 1. chap. 40.
9 *Epistolae* 205 and 207, *ad Bonifacium.*
10 *Sermo ad milites*, chap. 3.

in itself, nor is it the irrational instrument of blind natural forces that supposedly rule human destiny. War is thus principally a problem of political ethics and of justice; the art of warfare is merely a servant controlled by moral and juridical categories. When war and the art of war are made ends in themselves, then we have cruel, immoral militarism and the subordination of all values to the technicalities of strategy and tactics raging with destructive power through the world and trampling down peace, justice, and civil order. Not the peaceful tractor but the destructive tank and the bomber are the gods of such a new order.

War is a problem of ethics and law. It is either just or unjust. The other distinction of aggressive and defensive war is not at all so decisive that any aggressive war attempting to change the *status quo* as it happens to exist must be always and under all circumstances unjust. Such a presumption would suppose that the *status quo* is necessarily just, or that there exist means other than war to rectify an unjust *status quo*. But a *status quo* with a mere absence of war can be, as St. Augustine said, a false peace. Therefore the distinction between a just and an unjust war is not identical with the distinction between aggressive and defensive war.[11] There is, of course, a strong presumption that a defensive war is in general just. But it does not follow that any aggressive war is always unjust. We should not forget that, like the modern concept of nonintervention and of neutrality, the identification of aggressive war with unjust war is rather new.

The principle of nonintervention was formulated as late as the time of the Holy Alliance. It was directed against the claim of the Holy Alliance of a right to intervene in internal affairs of other states in protection of its principle of legitimacy. The principle of nonintervention had, therefore, two elements. First, it proclaimed the right of self-determination of nations in an antilegitimist, prodemo-

---

[11] A good illustration is offered by the second Finno-Russian war in 1941. Finland declared war to recover territory that it had ceded to Russia by a peace treaty in March 1940 after military defeat. Thus a new *status quo*, technically peaceful, existed. In July, 1941, Finland attacked Russia after Hitler had made an aggression upon the latter on June 22, 1941. The most peaceful nations approved of the Finnish aggressive war as long as its aim was the restoration of the *status quo* of 1939 as it had been established by various treaties from 1919 on. Only when the Finnish state continued the war beyond the lines of the *status quo* of 1939 and began to claim new territory, did allies of Russia declare war against Finland. Secretary of State Hull declared that Finland now was indulging in unjust aggression: this implies that before the *status quo* of 1939 was reached, Finland could be considered a just aggressor.

cratic sense. Secondly, it claimed that any intervention for the protection of the monarchical internal *status quo* of a nation represented an unjust aggression.

Apart from this, the principle of nonintervention can mean, and has meant, that the sovereignty of a state goes so far that even help to an aggressively invaded nation is considered unjust and a violation of the principle itself. Apart from help based on alliances, therefore, neutrality was considered an obligation for all states not immediately concerned. It does not require much reflection to understand that the foundation of such a concept is the modern idea of unrestricted sovereignty on the one hand and a voluntarist concept of the international order on the other; that consequently war is a morally indifferent affair between states, and therefore not subject to qualifications of just or unjust before the forum of natural morality. On the basis of such reasoning, war is a technical means of national policy; devoid of morality, its conduct may be standardized by the international rules of warfare on land and on sea. For purposes of propaganda, moral grounds will be professed to justify a war. But for the positivist idea of international law the actual morality of the cause of the war is irrelevant. Only rights and duties created by treaties and now in dispute among sovereign states are at issue and are to be protected or enforced by arms. Consequently what is violated by war is not the objective order of the international community, for which all members are responsible. Rather it is only these particular rights and duties. If that is granted, there must exist as a counterpart to the right of war a right of nonintervention and a duty of neutrality for the states that are not parties to the treaty. But if we put the international objective order first, to be realized by coordinated responsibility of the members, if we proceed from the idea of a community of nations, the existence of which is not the result of the changeable will of states with unlimited sovereignty, then the problem of nonintervention is very different. For now evidently the validity and working of the international order, in peace and in war, depends on the solidarity of all states to the international common good. And it becomes clear that all states are collectively and individually responsible for the continuous realization and protection of the order. Hence a breach of that order becomes an affair for all members and may give them a just cause and even a duty of positive intervention under certain conditions.

It should not be forgotten that the justice of the *status quo* is as important for the justice of a war as is the violation of contractual rights. On the other hand, we should keep in mind that the policy as distinguished from the principle of nonintervention had a salutary effect, too, during the era of imperialism. This policy made it possible to localize wars by hindering any dispute between neighboring states from developing into a war of allied groups taking active sides in a quarrel which in itself was usually limited and did not basically change the existing *status quo* and balance of power. The constitution of the League of Nations understood the nature of an unjust *status quo* when in Article 19 it stated that treaties should be revised if their maintenance presents a danger to world peace. The international community lacks for the time being a sovereign authority that, like the state authority internally, can rightfully change a *status quo* which has become unjust. Therefore if peaceful means are of no avail to change an unjust *status quo,* there may arise the actual oppression of a state by this *status quo.* Let us not identify the just war with the defensive war generally and absolutely.

VI. CRITERIA OF A JUST WAR

What, then, are the criteria of a just war, always provided that no obligatory arbitration is established and that peaceful instruments for settling international disputes are not available?

The just war requires several conditions. First, that it should be declared and conducted by legitimate sovereign authority. "Sovereign" in this sense means, as Vittoria, Suarez, and Bellarmine say, that the contestants have no possibility of appeal to a court of arbitration for settlement of their dispute or for the reparation of an injury suffered.[12] Warfare is the prerogative of sovereign states; their constitutional authorities exclusively are allowed to resort to war. War is protection or restoration of law and of a legal order between sovereign states. As long as no instruments for these specific purposes are created by

---

[12] Cf. Rommen, *op. cit.,* p. 297; Bellarmine, *De laicis,* chap. 15; Vittoria, *Relectio* 3 and *De jure belli.*

the community of nations, the only instrument to establish and protect the international order by compulsion is war. War is realization of law and justice. There is no enduring legal order possible without the certainty of its enforcement; a violation of the basic rights of one participant in the order is intrinsically a violation of the order itself. Only where the participants in a legal order protecting their very coexistence have a certainty that all members will conduct themselves according to the order, binding on all, is there peace and security. But this certainty depends upon the actual chance that any violator of the legal order will be punished and that the order will be restored by actual compulsory intervention. In any system of subordination the sovereign authority has the right and duty to compel.

In the international order of coordination such an authority, protecting by force and sovereignly deciding rights, violations, punishments, and reparations or restitutions, is not innate. The application of force necessary in this legal order is, therefore, an affair of the injured party or of other members of the order of coordination, at least as long as the participants in the order have not by mutual agreement set up international bodies for the protection of the order and for the settlement of disputes among themselves. Even if these bodies were introduced, the execution of their decisions would still be left to the members of the order, so that the order is as strong as is the willingness of the members to enforce it by arms. The collapse of the League of Nations was caused by the unwillingness of its most powerful and therefore most responsible members to fulfill their obligations of forcibly protecting the order. "Appeasement" was a wrong policy because it did not protect the order but considered only the individual interests of the appeasing nations. It thus introduced a premium on unjust aggression in places where the individual interests of the appeasing nations were thought, although wrongly, not to be involved. For this appeasement policy clearly showed that the exclusive argument in international life was power and armaments. The controlling idea in the problem of war is therefore the existence and validity of the international order, not only the individual interest and security, and the rights of the individual state, as if these states lived in a Hobbesian natural status of a war of all against all. That is why, for instance, Vittoria says that the rulers have the duty to protect and restore the international order since they themselves are, as we may say in modern terms, the organs of the international community.[13]

The second criterion is a just and sufficient cause. Here again we have to start from the idea of the international order and from the fact of the community of nations. The justice of a cause for war is dependent upon that. There is not possible a cause at once just and opposed to the common good of the community of nations. National glory, aggrandizement of the individual nation, and selfish lust for wealth cannot be just causes, however nicely they may be disguised in slogans as a right to living space, a right to raw materials, or a right to prosperity.

The duty of all nations to promote international trade and the corresponding interests of all nations in international commerce, the cooperation in international exchange, and free access to the so-called world market show by contrast the vagueness of the above-mentioned slogans. The slogans are actually an inversion of cause and effect. For the same nations that first proclaimed them proclaimed perfect economic autarchy as their political purpose, and then complained that they were suffocated in their poor countries without raw materials, the access to which was forbidden them supposedly by the "have" nations. The sophistry of this argument appears at once if we are aware that their political aim is complete autarchy, which is an impossibility for most nations and would destroy that international community which is a community of mutual exchange and commerce for material wealth, as well as for civilizing accomplishments in scientific, cultural, and intellectual life. The idea of complete economic and national autarchy would actually reject the community of nations. It would not remove frictions; it would immensely increase them, as recent events prove. If autarchy is once conceived as pauperization, and international exchange as prosperity, it follows that the development of an international exchange of goods and services in peaceful cooperation is the best guaranty of the independent existence of the nations and that seclusion in autarchy, economic and national, on the contrary, is the breeding ground of ceaseless wars.

[13] Vittoria, *loc. cit.* (Ingolst. ed., p. 65).

VII. The Doctrine of *Causa Justa*

The justice of the *causa belli* presupposes the international order and the existential security of its members. Thence it follows that as a just cause for war, irrespective of the distinction between aggressive or defensive war, there can be considered only a violation of the international order and an injury to one of its members. And, we must add at once, a grave violation of order and rights. For war is itself such a calamity, it brings forth so much unhappiness, destruction, and sorrow, that the rule of proportion must be applied. War must be the servant of a higher purpose, which can be only the preservation of the international order and the protection of the members' right of existence, i.e., of their solidarist and individual existence and liberty. A war is just when it protects the internal common good and is correlated to the common good of the nations, to their peaceful and secure coexistence, and to their mutually guaranteed liberty and integrity of life and honor. Consequently only a grave violation of the order and a grave injury to a member makes war just as a punishment and a restoration or restitution.

Materialiter, a just cause is, first, a violation of the territorial integrity of a state by force of arms and a refusal to restore the *status quo* and to pay indemnity. Secondly, a grave violation of the fundamental rules of the community of nations. Thirdly, a grave injury to the honor of a nation. The first point is obvious. An international order has as its main function peace and security, i.e., integrity of existence and of territory, as well as independence of the members and reliance upon loyal fulfillment of the international obligations, whether they arise from the order itself implicitly or from particular treaties. All great documents of international law prove that. The League of Nations Covenant formulates these principles in its preamble as the very purpose of its existence. The so-called Protocol of Geneva of October 2, 1924, likewise sets up as its purpose the preservation of the peace and security of nations whose existence, independence, and territory may be endangered. The Locarno Treaty similarly declares the nations' desire for security. These documents speak, too, about the solidarity that unites the members of the international community, of the necessity to observe scrupulously the obligations of treaties.

The second point needs more discussion, especially as it has been neglected since the eighteenth cntury under the domination of the idea of absolute sovereignty, and of a voluntarist concept of international law and the so-called principle of nonintervention. We say that it has been neglected, inasmuch as it was applied only to nations considered inferior or uncivilized. France, England, Germany, Italy, and Russia each preserved a right of intervention in certain spheres of interest in various parts of the world, and they all considered it their right to intervene when Christian citizens or residents in Turkey or China were ill-treated in violation of the fundamental rules of international law. There existed, of course, a tendency to call such interventions punitive expeditions and not wars, although St. Thomas would have called some of these expeditions just wars and very likely would, on the other hand, have refused to give the title of just war to many struggles among civilized nations that were claimed to be just wars in the last centuries. The idea of civilization to a certain extent includes the assumption that a code of generally accepted fundamental principles of international law exists and that to observe this code is the presupposition of being considered a member of civilization and of the community of nations.

How far, then, is a grave violation of international law a just cause of war if the violation at the same time is not a direct, grave injury against a member state? The founders of the theory of international law, Vittoria, Suarez, and other philosophers of Late Scholasticism, had an immediate occasion to discuss this point, an occasion furnished by the Spanish and Portuguese conquistadors and their colonial conquests in the newly discovered Indies. The conquistadors tried to justify their imperialist wars by saying that they were mainly interested in the destruction of idolatry and other crimes against natural morality and were fighting for the propagation of Christianity. Thus also the conquistadors of our day pretend to fight for a new and therefore supposedly better order, for the spread of Aryan civilization, or for communist justice. What is the answer of Vittoria, Suarez, Soto, Bellarmine? They utterly deny that such claims are just causes for war. Suarez, as he denies any right to dispossess the infidels of the Holy Land simply because they are infidels, so he denies any right of a Christian state to make war upon a pagan state simply because the latter indulges in idolatry. He denies further the presumed right of armed protection for missioners.

But what if Christian subjects of a pagan state are persecuted by the state authorities? Then the Christians should first make use of their right of emigration. Only as a last resort will Suarez allow war, armed intervention, for the protection of persecuted Christians. But this intervention is permissible in the first place not as the prerogative of a Christian ruler, but as the result of the pope's appeal to the Christian ruler, who is thus clearly an instrument of the papal competence; the Christian ruler as Christian ruler has no such competence [14] to begin with. It is the defense of innocents that could in this case afford a just cause of war. St. Robert Bellarmine makes at this point a good distinction between violations of natural morality and violations of natural justice. Only the latter are subject to punishment by human authorities as violations of social duties. Violations of the rights of God (idolatry) and sins directly against oneself (e.g., intoxication) are not the affair of human authority first and directly. Thus, only if there occurs a grave violation of the *jus humanae societatis* or a serious offense against innocents, can an intervention by war be justified. Even then the intervention must be suited to reach its purpose without still graver damages to peace and order. Thus the injury of innocents is the typical case of a grave violation of the international order and represents a just cause of war, always supposing that the intervention is capable of attaining its purpose and that the damages caused by intervention are not greater than the damage to the common good, national and international, caused by the violation.

A further restriction is that the right and duty of intervention depend upon the duty to the state's own common good. If by intervention the common good of the intervening state is gravely imperiled, this state has no duty to intervene. For the restoration of peace and restitution for the injury are the purpose of war. If the material means are insufficient, even a just cause does not afford either right or duty of intervention. Thence it follows that the preservation of the international order and its vindication in the face of violators are especially the task of the wealthy and mighty states, not of the small and weak nations. Wealth and its social effect, power, bring with them in any kind of human community a higher responsibility for the preservation of the just order in this community. In fact, the inequality in

[14] Cf. Rommen, *op. cit.*, pp. 265, 298; Vittoria, *op. cit.*, 2; Cajetan on St. Thomas, *Summa theol.*, IIa IIae, q.66, a.8; Soto, *De justitia et de jure*, I, 5, q.e, a.5.

wealth and the consequent increase in power of the richer nations is justifiable only by assuming higher and more comprehensive responsibilities. The League of Nations was progressively suffocated as the more powerful nations ignored their higher responsibilities and left the smaller nations without protection.

The philosophers of Late Scholasticism regarded as a just cause of war a state's continued and unreasonable refusal to afford freedom of commerce and of traffic, that is, a complete refusal to participate in the international order, because such a strict and unconditional refusal is against the very essence of humanity as a true community and would repudiate the international common good, apart from the fact that it would be a grave violation of charity. The basis of this contention is the general law of natural sociality, the conviction that human society and its law, natural justice, are prior to the state and that the states themselves have a duty to cooperate for the realization of the ideal universal community of nations as a natural tendency of humanity which is transcendent to the individual state. Hence the tendencies to economic autarchy and seclusion achieved by the exaggerated protection of high tariffs may easily be considered breeding grounds for war, whereas the development of international economic cooperation and trade may establish such an interdependence that, under certain circumstances, war becomes a thing that does not pay.

The third element is a grave injury to the reputation and honor of a nation by another nation or by subjects of another nation for whom this nation, according to its internal constitution and international law and usages, is responsible. At a time of nationalist vanity and of exaggerated sensitiveness in questions of national prestige, this element needs a careful discussion. We must again proceed from the existence of the international order itself. Wherever there is society there is law, and wherever there is law there are persons. Personality implies dignity as the ontological consequence, and honor as the social consequence. Mutual honor is a requisite of any human community. It is the reflex of liberty, independence, and the intrinsic value of the member as a person. A community that does not protect the honor as well as the existence and liberty of its members cannot endure, for, as St. Thomas says, honor is the highest of external goods.[15] In its ultimate cause, the destruction of honor is the destruction of the

---

[15] *Summa theol.*, IIa IIae, q.103, a.1; q.129, a.1.

dignity of the person and renders him incapable of full membership in the community. Honor means, so to speak, moral existence, and is a genuine object of the inalienable right of self-preservation. An unjust and grave attack upon the honor of one nation by another nation is, therefore, as serious an injury as a grave violation of its territorial integrity would be.[16]

Honor is indeed one of the fundamental rights of the members of the international community, the relations of which are founded, as the covenant of the League of Nations declares, upon "justice and honor." If, then, a grave injury to honor cannot be repaired except by warlike acts, war is in principle, as *ultima ratio,* justified. Appeasement by France and England in 1938 was a serious dereliction of the duty of solidarist defense of the honor of the international community's small members, to the extent that it condoned Hitler's abominable vituperations upon the Austrian and Czechoslovakian governments and nations. Too late France and England understood that this vituperation could not be justified by "peace in our time." All these things—liberty, independence, self-preservation, solidarity of the community of nations, and honor—are integral parts of a whole that cannot exist with any one of them lacking. The fact that, for moral reasons, individuals may suffer vilification voluntarily and refuse to defend their honor, is not a sound reason for demanding by an appeal to charity a similar attitude from the state. The state that has lost its honor is no longer a state. Its moral existence is destroyed. A state that is unwilling to defend its honor would actually help to weaken the international order, for that order morally exists by and through mutual honor. Furthermore, any human community for human and earthly purposes has first to accomplish justice and then charity. What is owed by justice (and honor is so owed) cannot be replaced by charity. Justice and honor are the foundation, charity the crown, of all human communities.

We must now add a last criterion: the justice of the cause must be certain. The authority that declares war must be certain of its right and of the objective justice of its cause. The sovereign authority is here implicitly judge in its own cause; although in conducting war the sovereign authority acts as an organ of the community of nations, its

---

[16] This is commonly accepted doctrine; cf. Liszt-Fleischmann, *op. cit.,* p. 123; Kaufmann, *op. cit.,* p. 276.

own rights are also the question at issue. It is largely party and judge, so that impartiality is a most difficult moral task. And this difficulty increases if, instead of full certainty, only a probability about the justness of the *casus belli* can be reached. Although in such a case the general principle of courts, that the degree of probability fixes the right in litigation, is applicable, the better course is arbitration by an impartial authority. Only if this is not accepted by the opponent, then may the claimant proceed to war. But what if the claims of both states are equally probable? If it is a claim for territory, the general rule, *melior est conditio possidentis,* prevails, on the assumption that the possessor is in good faith. Apart from this, there would not be a just cause for either party. They would be bound by duty not to proceed to war but to submit the problem to arbitration.

It need not be especially stressed that the right intention is a necessary part of the just cause, that the justice of the cause and the justice of the actual conduct of war are controlled by the purpose of the war, and that the restoration of peace is determined by reparation for the injury that itself was a violation of the international order. A war that goes beyond these limits, a war that is one of revenge, that is malicious destruction or has as its object conquest beyond restoration, war in which the just cause and the right intention are superseded by militarist, immoral pleasure in military adventure, such a war becomes unjust, however just it may have been in the beginning. War is strictly just only as a means for the protection and restoration of order and peace; it is the *ultima ratio* and is a just means only if no other way is possible for the achievement of peace.[17]

VIII. The Just Conduct of War

The third condition of a just war which was especially noted by Late Scholasticism is the requirement of the *debitus modus.* This condition means that, before a state proceeds to an aggressive war to rectify an injury inflicted upon it by another state or by citizens under the responsibility of that state, the injured state has a strict duty to try all peaceful means of diplomatic negotiation, offer of arbitration, and so forth, before it may justly proceed to war, that is, forcibly establish its right. As the object of war is the restoration of a broken

---

[17] Augustine, *De civitate Dei,* XIX, 18.

order of peace, the protection of rights and the reparation of injuries in the order of peace, the just cause disappears as soon as the offending state offers satisfaction—restoration of the right and indemnification for the damages.

War as an act of international justice remains essentially under the rules of international law, which, therefore, governs the whole conduct of war. War and its acts are not beyond law and order. The Christian philosophers and theologians have striven for humanization of warfare, as it has been called since the nineteenth century. Many rules that the Hague Conferences enacted as international law in 1899 and in 1907 had been anticipated by the Church and the first students of international law in Late Scholasticism. The *Treuga Dei* (end of the eleventh century) protected the civilian population and their homesteads as inviolable. War is conducted between armies and states, not between civilians and peoples. The killing of civilians, people who do not bear arms, is unjust if it is intentionally or negligently done and not by mere and unavoidable accident.[18] Leo XIII's furtherance of all steps taken toward humanizing warfare is common knowledge, although Italy succeeded in its protest against the participation of a papal representative in the negogiations at The Hague. The work of Benedict XV and later of Pius XII to promote further humanization is too well known to need a detailed account.[19]

In connection with the *debitus modus* of warfare there arises a particular modern problem. Has not the mode of warfare become so indiscriminate and inhuman because of total and mechanized war with airplanes, submarines, and tanks, that a *debitus modus* is today impossible? Is not a reasonable balance practically excluded between the purpose of war and the destruction which modern instruments of war inflict on armies, nations, and national fortunes, not only on those immediately concerned but on all members of the international community? Some Catholic writers[20] contend that such a balance is impossible. We must bear in mind that most of the above-mentioned

---

[18] Cf. Suarez, *De bello rect.*, c.6, n.8–11; c.7, n.3–14. Bellarmine, *Comm.*, IIa IIae, q.40: see Father X. Arnold, *Staatslehre des Card. Bell.*, p. 289. Late Scholasticism represents a great progress beyond the Thomistic theory of war. St. Thomas did not especially mention the *debitus modus* as an element of a just war. He remains in many matters too dependent upon Roman law in its application to warfare: cf. O. Schilling, *Staats-und Sociallehre des hl. Thomas v. Aquin*, 2nd ed., 1930, pp. 203 ff.

[19] Cf. *Principles of Peace*, ed. by Harry C. Koenig, Washington, 1943.

[20] E.g., Father Stratmann, O.P., *Weltkirche u. Weltfriede*, 1924.

rules concern not so much defensive war as they do aggressive war and its justice. A state may be free not to resort to aggressive war to restore a certain right or to repair an injury inflicted upon itself, an injury that is not itself war but still an international *delictum*. Yet it is not free to refuse defense against an unjust aggression. For defense against unjust aggression is not only a duty of the state to its own citizens in the protection of the internal common good; it is also a duty to the international community. The international order is preserved not by a superior authority with sovereign compulsory power, but by the free and independent members of the community in their own solidarist and individual responsibility. Therefore non-resistance to the unjust aggressor would be an unjustified invalidation of the international order by the non-resisting state. The undoubted right of self-preservation is in an order of coordination logically balanced by a duty of self-preservation.

IX. The Duties of Public Authorities

We have stated the doctrine of just war chiefly from an objective point of view. Let us now discuss it from the subjective point of view, and consider the questions which arise. What are the rights and duties of the public authority, of the soldier, and of the citizen?

The real problem is this: Under what conditions is an aggressive war justified as punishment for a violation of the international order or as a redress for an injury suffered? Defensive war offers fewer problems. We have already pointed out that the justice of the cause of war must be certain for the public authority. Hence the other party in the dispute is *formaliter* and *materialiter* in the wrong; its grave violation of a right or rule of the international order makes it guilty; legally and morally the offense is an international *delictum*. Consequently the war as *ultima ratio* of the enforcement of law then falls under the rules of vindictive justice. Precisely because of this fact the state proceeding to war as vindicator must be certain about all the elements of guilt: evil intention or grave negligence, notorious illegality of the act that is declared to be a violation, and absence of any doubt about the material facts and about the legal rule that governs the case. The soldier who participates in such a war can generally rely upon the rightfulness of the decision by the public authority, as can the citizens.

The complication arises in territoral disputes or in such disputes as are usually enumerated in treaties of arbitration and mediation. These disputes may arise about existence, interpretation, and application of treaties between the parties to the dispute; about the existence and application of a rule of international law concerning the dispute; about the elements of a fact or about an act of one of the parties that, if proved to exist, would be a violation of an international obligation.[21] It is implied in cases where there is no certainty about the justice and the legality of the object of the dispute or about *prima facie* guilt of one of the parties. To say that this is a good case for arbitration or mediation is no great help; for the real problem of war arises after one of the parties has declined any sort of legal settlement under the treaty or under positive international law, because it contends that the question in dispute falls neither under the treaty nor under any commonly accepted positive rule of international law. Then only arises the crucial question, whether the party that proposed all peaceful means has now the right to enforce its contention by war. Of course we must suppose that the whole matter is of such importance as to be proportionate to the unavoidable damages that any war causes. The difficulty seems to be that the dispute is originally similar to disputes of the civil law and of distributive or commutative justice, and not parallel to those of penal law and therefore of vindictive justice; and further, that in such disputes the certitude of the just cause is implicitly not complete and beyond any doubt, so that war would become the arbiter between parties which have no unquestionable and full right, although the right of one party may be better and more probable than that of the other and, in addition, both parties may be in good faith.

The decision would be that the state declining prosposals of arbitration and mediation thus violates the international order, because the very essence of peace and order presupposes the willingness to have disputes arbitrated or otherwise peacefully settled in justice and equity. The state that wantonly declines an arbitration or other peaceful settlement of the dispute commits an injury against the international order, an injury that, if grave enough, would give the other party in the dispute the right of resort to war as the only available way of settlement, because in the international order as yet no superior

[21] Cf. Covenant of the League of Nations, Art. 13 § 2.

power enforces the law. The just cause is, then, not so much the presumed or altogether certain justice of the claim of the one party, but the wanton refusal of the other party to settle the dispute peacefully. In this case the soldier and the citizen may rely upon the public authority, because it has rightfully fulfilled all international obligations of law and morality.[22]

A crucial case would be one in which both parties refuse to resort, or fail to resort, to arbitration or mediation at all. If in such a dispute the right of one party is more probable than that of the other party, has the former party the right to proceed to war? Here the authorities disagree. Suarez decides that the state with the better right may proceed to war, if after careful scrutiny a judge would have decided a similar dispute in favor of that state. Vasquez and Layman disagree. St. Alphonsus, though not rejecting Suarez' opinion, concludes that in practice no just war ever occurred which rested on only probable and not certain rights.[23] There is unanimity when the rights in the dispute are equally probable. Here there exists no cause for a just war without the intervention of arbitration and mediation. For the outcome would be a just war on both sides, which is monstrous.[24]

[22] The League of Nations Covenant is in aggreement with this scholastic doctrine (Art. 12, 13, 15, 16).

[23] Suarez: *De bello*, sect. 6, n.2. Alphonsus Liguori, *Theol. mor.*, Bk. III, tract. 4, cap. 1, n.404, with quotations from Vasquez and Layman. Cf. J. B. Schuster, "Bemerkungen zur Kriegslehre des Fr. Suarez," *Scholastik*, XV (1930), 387.

[24] Concerning these last discussions, some disputes have arisen since A. Vanderpol (in *La guerre devant le Christianisme*, 1911, and especially in *La doctrine scolastique du droit de guerre*, 1919) asserted that since the era of Late Scholasticism, especially since Suarez and Molina, a weakening of the theory of the just war occurred, to the great damage of human society. To St. Augustine and St. Thomas war is exclusively an instrument of vindictive justice, and therefore a punishment for a certain and grave moral and legal guilt. Suarez and Molina, Vanderpol says, subordinated war to the rules of distributive justice by assuming that one party in an international dispute may, on account of a *jus melius*, resort to war; Molina even introduced commutative justice and the opinion that material wrong (without guilt) would be a cause for a just (aggressive) war; consequently a state that possesses a part of another state's territory in good faith, though without right, and the state that legally owns the right could resort to a war which for both parties would be just, because the possessor in good faith would have a cause for a just defensive war while the legal owner would have a cause for a just aggressive war by his objective title of ownership. Vanderpol has found a supporter in Father Stratmann, *Weltfriede und Weltkirche* ("Lockerung der alten, strengen Kriegsmoral," p. 86), although apparently the majority of authorities do not follow suit. (Cf. Rommen, *Staatslehre des Fr. Suarez*, p. 301; Schuster, *loc. cit.*; F. X. Arnold, *Staatslehre Bellarmins*, pp. 284 f.).

Vanderpol and Stratmann, both ardent pacifists, have not sufficiently considered the fact that, while St. Augustine and St. Thomas remain rather general in their remarks, the

What about the individual citizen's conscience? First let us repeat that the question concerns the justice of the war, not aggressive or defensive war. The problem would be simplified if it concerned only defensive war; for there is a strong presumption that a defensive war is just. But defensive war is presumably just not only because the general rule applies, that *melior est conditio possidentis,* or because it may be said that the *status quo* of peace has always the presumption of justice, or that in defensive war undoubted rights under the given *status quo* are always defended against unjust aggression. A just defensive war is also a realization of the international order of peace and justice; the attacked state not only defends itself and its rights but it likewise defends the international order, international justice and morality, on which the defended rights legally and morally rest. But defense of the international order is, in addition to the redress for an injury or the readjustment of an obviously unjust *status quo,* the function of an aggressive just war, too. The moral and legal justice of an aggressive war is far more complicated. Here the difficulties for the individual conscience may arise. It is easy to say simply that nobody must participate in an unquestionably unjust aggressive war. But in reality there are practically almost never such unequivocal cases. If, then, most cases are so complicated, how can the individual conscience come to its decision? To say that it may in all wars not openly and clearly unjust rely upon the decision of the public authority is obviously not a fully satisfactory solution.

Perhaps we may come nearer to the heart of the problem by the

---

late scholastic philosophers, more historically minded and concerned with the actual concrete problems of international law, by no means "weakened" the strict principles, but tried to apply the general principles and conclusions in the more complicated world of sovereign states that they saw around them. The "cases" of St. Thomas are far less complicated and intricate than those that the late Scholastics had to consider. And most international disputes are not so simple and open as Vanderpol and Stratmann suppose. It would be better to stress how strongly the late Scholastics urged arbitration and mediation as the presupposition of resort to war in these cases. All too often well-meaning friends of world peace simplify too much the intricacies of international life and order. By narrowing down the just war either to defensive war, which is a sanctification of a possibly very wrong *status quo,* or to an aggressive war only as an instrument of vindictive justice, the real causes of war, precisely the complicated disputes, are not solved. The nearer we come to the complicated facts the more we will be impressed by the necessity of working out peaceful instruments for the settlement of international disputes. This forced simplification so common among pacifists of the more emotional kind makes their power of persuasion often impotent. Furthermore, the idea of vindictive justice is rather difficult in an order of coordination. Some authors, like Leclerque, reject it because it is, they say, without merit.

following reasoning. The best opportunities for the individual exist where there are freedom of the press and freedom of speech. They afford a chance for the issue to be presented broadly and objectively and for both sides to be heard. A good opportunity exists also where the representatives of the people have some control over the foreign policy of the government. Another favorable factor would be a constitutional provision that the most concentrated competence of sovereignty—the declaration of war—be exercised "by plebiscite or at least by resolution of representatives of the people." [25] And lastly, that "diplomacy shall proceed always frankly and in the public view." [26]

Only where these factors in some way operate, has the individual citizen an access to the elements of fact and of law that make the justice of the case. Where no freedom of speech and no freedom of the press exist, where the public authority is uncontrolled and the citizen is merely the subject of tendentious propaganda, he has hardly any access to the objective facts which constitute the truth and to the justice of the case, and must *nolens volens* rely upon authority. The more that international frictions may arise through the growth of international interdependence, the more should the opportunities for judgment of the individual citizen be increased by the general acceptance of the constitutional rights just mentioned. The more, too, should intellectual cooperation of nations, of international understanding between economic and cultural and religious communities, be promoted. And let us not forget that it is the acceptance by rulers and ruled of the universal rule of an equally universal morality that will afford the best chance for the individual conscience to decide upon justice and injustice. For we believe that dictators and dishonest cliques or ruthless pressure groups in more democratic states, can drive John Doe and Richard Roe into wars only because, by insincere "patriotic" propaganda, they are able to make them believe in the justice of their cause.

[25] This proposal was made by Cardinal Gasparri in an authorized interpretation of Pope Benedict XV's peace action of August, 1917 (*A.A.S.*, IX, 417) in the letter of the Cardinal to Archbishop Chesnelong of Sens (France), October 7, 1917.

[26] First of President Wilson's famous Fourteen Points in his message to Congress (January 8, 1918).

CHAPTER XXX

Means of Avoiding War

I. THE MORAL WILL FOR JUSTICE

EVIDENTLY only a few wars can be considered just wars if measured by these strict standards. Yet wars seem to spring up suddenly from nowhere and to erupt irrationally like earthquakes. Any war, just or unjust, is the father of many evils; a disruption of the internal social order, of families, of industrial production, of intellectual and moral progress, and of the educational process. Thus it is not so much the legalization of war, the attempt to subject even war and warfare to legal and moral rules inspired by humanity and Christian morality, that is the main goal of Catholic political philosophy. That goal is rather the law of peace. War is at best a doubtful means of restoring the order of peace. Therefore other, peaceful, means of avoiding war and of preserving peace have to be found. Such a task may be reasonably propounded only if we are convinced that war is not a natural necessity in international life. And it involves a clear understanding of the causes of war. Peace at any price may be even more wrong than war, however imperfect a means war may be of deciding just and unjust; and how imperfect a war is may be illustrated by the cynical remark that God, the Lord of justice, is always with the stronger battalions. Thus arises the demand to substitute the moral power of right for the material power of weapons; to set up the power of right in opposition to the right of power.[1]

Of course this demand is something other than a demand to avoid war by simple passivity on the principle of non-resistance. It means an active and strenuous striving for the rule of law, and the continuous adaptation of treaties that represent the positive international order to the ever-changing economic interests and political relations

---

[1] Benedict XV, *A.A.S.*, IX (1917), 417. Leo XIII, Letter to the Russian Czar, September 15, 1898.

of the members of the community of nations. The "rule of law" may be an empty phrase and, worse, a propagandist weapon of power politics for the preservation of the positive international *status quo* among nations, no matter how "unjust" that positive *status quo* may have become because of changing population trends, economic conditions, and national "interests," and because of aggressive political ideologies. A democracy may thus be considered an excellent political form because it is flexible, because it is not a narrow, rigid form of the simply existing social *status quo*, but affords unrevolutionary ways and means of changing the social order according to the life, the interests, and the progress of the whole, as well as of the persons and their associations which form the whole. Thus internal political frictions need not result in external nationalist aggression as a diversion from internal revolt.

What matters is the inner spirit of the peaceful equalization of opposing group-interests, of unselfish cooperation in the service of the country, of government by consent, and of free creation of new public and private agencies to promote the common good. What matters is the willingness of each group to acknowledge the freedom and the interests of the other groups and the willingness of each group to avoid identifying its particular good and interest with the common good, and therefore itself with the nation. All these make possible a peaceful, unrevolutionary, but necessary and just change in the internal social *status quo* without an external explosion into war. And let us not forget that government by consent does not mean the passive "yes" of the majority, but does actually mean the willing cooperation and active participation of all, numerical majority as well as minority, in the furtherance of the common good that belongs to all and never to a single group. Thus a democracy lives in the order of law, but by the social and political virtues of patriotism, honesty, incorruptibility, cooperation, and mutual fraternal love.

In the international order it is fundamentally the same. With profound meaning Benedict XV spoke of the moral force of right. In that is included, apart from positive law, the spirit of natural equity, the willingness for cooperative charity, and the mutual moral consent to protect one's own rights only by service to the rights of others and not by their denial. The mere positive form of law in its rigidity is not enough to guarantee peace as a living order for active realization of the common good. The idea of the League of Nations has suffered much because there arose among several states the suspicion that the League had become a political device for some of the great powers to legitimate the *status quo* set up by the peace treaties; and by the suspicion of smaller states that some members of the Council interpreted the Covenant so as to avoid international responsibilities for collective security under the Covenant. The ill-famed Hoare-Laval agreement upon Ethopia, a member of the League, is a good example of such evasion. That public opinion assailed this deal as treason against the spirit of the Covenant, corroborates the view that it is the spirit and not the legal letter that vivifies.

However much we may praise the positive form of law, law itself is the servant of order, of the international common good that lives by the power of moral virtues. Diplomats steeped in legalistic thinking and narrow nationalism are not always lovers of peace. There is an erroneous jurisprudence that distorts the moral content of law by callous interpretation of the letter. Such interpretation may make right wrong and wrong right without an evident change in the letter. Thus there must be developed and fostered in a deeper sphere of the mind the virtues of justice and of charity. *Juris praecepta sunt haec: honeste vivere, neminem laedere, suum cuique tribuere.* The *honeste vivere* is the first precept and the basis of the two other precepts. The rigid order of formal law is never sufficient. It must be completed by the order of natural equity and ultimately by the order of fraternal charity, by a final unity of moral standards common to humanity and perfected by Christianity. The early idealism of the League of Nations was slowly stifled partly by the passive spirit of "splendid isolation" exhibited by the most powerful democracy, and partly by the rise in the successor-states of the Austrian monarchy, of new nationalisms that were fundamentally a denial of the common good on which the structure of Geneva had to be built.

Positive law is always somewhat imperfect. There is something tragic in positive formal law, in the sense that such law is necessarily rational, rigid, and productive of vested interests which may become diametrically opposed to justice and charity. Law is always in danger of becoming a dishonored servant of power-politics instead of being the directive power of social life. Formal law has inherent limitations. Therefore, to fulfill its mission, it requires a higher moral order as its perennial mitigating corrective. That order will always be the order of natural equity and justice and, as the last and sovereign order, the order of charity, the order of solidarist responsibility of all participants to all and to each.

Law separates; charity and fraternal solidarity unite. Only on the basis of this natural equality and this fraternity can the order of positive international law be constructed. Only then will the law be truly a directive moral power, the supreme guaranty of peace, and not merely a new instrument of power-politics. For solely by this sanctification of positive law may its enforcement in international life be justified. Not the letter of the law by itself but the spirit of justice makes the enforcement of the letter legitimate. In the international order these principles are far more important than in the internal order. The international order, less dense and less comprehensive than the national order, its members less homogeneous than those of the nation, is an order of consent and coordination rather than of subordination and of that sentimental emotional coherence so typical of the national community. Therefore it rests to a greater extent than the national order upon natural equity and solidarist fraternity. In the internal order we appeal to our national traditions, to patriotism, to common economic and cultural interests, to the law of the land, and to the spirit of our people as concrete historical entities. In the international order the appeal is necessarily to more general ideas: to humanity, to Christianity, and to natural equity. This does not mean that the appeal is morally weaker; it means only that greater obstacles are to be overcome before these ideas can exercise their actual influence.

But let there be no mistake: the more loosely knit an order legally is and the more obscure the actual interdependence in a community is, the more must that order be built on the principle of coordination and the more must the freedom and integrity of its members be stressed. In short, the order in such a community depends more upon the rule of moral ideas, on mutual fraternal love, and on an agreement upon the *honeste vivere*. Failure to comprehend this truth is what Pius XI rebuked in the years after World War I: "Peace was only written into treaties. It was not received into the hearts of men. . . . Unfortunately, the law of violence held sway so long that it has weakened and almost obliterated all traces of those natural feelings of love and mercy which the law of Christian charity has done so much to encourage." [2]

But just as formal law without the ideas of equity and charity is without force to produce a real peace, so, on the other hand, do these ideas, in order to be working forces in society, need the positive form of law and enforceable rules. *Ubi societas, ibi jus.* International law is the reflex of the actually existing community of nations; and this community is made a community by common interests, by a common end, by allegiance to common values. It is the prelegal end that calls for the legal forms. But the legal forms have to follow the society's specific nature and mode of existence. A society of coordinated free and independent members can be organized only on the basis of a true common good, whose furtherance is conceived as common interest; a common good, whose realization coincides with the particular good of each member. There is no place for superior claims and superior rights because of race superiority, of cultural superiority, or of economic imperialism in such a society, since such claims would deny the fundamental equality of the members before the law. Thus the legal institutions for avoidance of war and promotion of peace need the continuous daily consent of the member states. That fact is the specific, unavoidable difficulty of an order of coordination. It requires, for the creation of institutions for arbitration and mediation with decisive authority, "unanimity and general consent," as Leo XIII rightly said. [3]

We must not forget that the old *debellatio,* the political annihilation of a state, even if it gravely violates the international order, is today obsolete. The single nation consents to an international league, a federation, or whatever we may call it, *salvis istis juribus,* with the rights of independence, territorial integrity, etc., preserved, the right of self-preservation first of all. In other words, no international tribunal may issue the death sentence of a member state any more than in a true federation the central authority by its own competence may dissolve a member state. The sense of all legal order is granting the demarcation and coordination of spheres of liberty of discretionary competence and individual action, to the constituents. Thus a growth of international law means the assignment of fields of social life to

[2] Encyclical *Ubi arcano.*
[3] Wehberg, *Papsttum und Weltfriede,* 1915, p. 99.

international regulations; but if the transfer were total, there would not be states any more, but only the *civitas maxima*.

II. Liability for Acts of Government

Here arises one of the most complicated problems in international law and international ethics: the liability, moral and legal, of a people, a nation, politically organized into an independent state, for the illegal and criminal acts of its government, which constitutionally represents the organized nation in international life. That these acts, such as an unjust aggressive war, cannot be executed by the government, i.e., the few persons in authority, alone, but must be executed by armies, navies, and airforces, i.e., by millions of citizens, makes the difficulty. The punishment of those constitutionally responsible for the criminal act is a simpler proposition. But what about those millions which are the nation? If the nation is declared guilty, can then the state, as the political form of existence of the nation, be dissolved or dismembered as a sort of political death penalty?

The difficulties are many. First, the state is not a substance, a hypostasis, in reality separable from the people or the nation. To dissolve or dismember the state must mean, therefore, the destruction of the nation, of that "matter" of which the state is merely the political and legal, but not the exclusive, form of social existence. What is important is the self-consciousness of the nation under the abstraction of its "state" (political status). As long as this self-consciousness lives, the dismemberment can be enforced only by actual and continuous force, as the example of Poland amply proves (from 1795 to 1919). The dismemberment of a historically established nation can be effected only by its dispersion through the world, as the Romans dispersed the Jewish nation.

Secondly, in modern criminal law it is accepted that a non-individual criminal guilt, a collective guilt (e.g., of a lynching mob), cannot be accepted (with a few rather artificial exceptions). The canon law still acknowledges, in the interdictum, for instance, collective punishment, because it accepts collective crimes of communities such as parishes, dioceses, towns, and states. But the canon law treats such communities as minors (cf. can. 100 §3 with can. 2204) and thus

diminishes the imputability. It states further that those not personally guilty are exempt from the main punishment, prohibition of
the reception of the sacraments (can. 2276).[4] But never is the dismemberment of the community a legal punishment.

Thirdly, the individual citizen in the compulsory framework of
even a democratic state, not to mention a totalitarian state of Caesar-
ean dictatorship or of an absolute monarchy, does not actually have
that freedom of individual decision and of individual active and open
resistance against the dubious or apparently evil acts of this government that any theory of collective "guilt" presupposes. The individual, with his whole existence, is so immersed in his national culture,
in the political entity of which he is a member, that only exile can
free him from this immersion. This fact makes it almost impossible
for him to have full knowledge and to freely accept or tolerate the
"criminal act" of his government. Thus the individual guilt of his
acquiescence in face of coercion by his government is scarcely evident.

Fourthly, the tacit presupposition of such a theory of collective
guilt is the following fallacy: Each nation or people has that government which it likes or deserves, and consequently the government
in power can stay in power only because the people approve of it, or
at least morally support it, and silently condone the criminal acts,
although, according to the fallacy, they need not do so. This contention is fallacious when applied to non-traditional governments,
i.e., when applied to dictatorial regimes that stay in power by terror,
by denying any sort of bill of rights or any kind of impartial and
independent judiciary. Hence the citizens are unable to register disapproval openly and collectively. The dictatorial government controls
all associations of the citizen in such a state with the help of the
privileged class, the party; it thus dissolves any other association. The
denial of freedom of speech and of association and the control of permissible associations by the one party means that the disapproving
citizens are isolated and cannot collectively organize their disapproval actively. They cannot do so even passively, since the dictatorial
regime compels the isolated citizen to be a member of the controlled
organizations, professional, economic, cultural, and, if possible, religious. In a country with a bill of rights and free elections, a government cannot stay in power against the will of the majority. But in a

---

[4] Cf. Eduard Eichmann, *Strafrecht des Codex Juris Canonici*, 1920, pp. 99 ff.

dictatorship such a condition is not only possible; it is of dictatorship's very essence. By monopolizing all economic, social, and political power through the controlled associations and by compelling the individual citizen to belong to them or to be economically destroyed, such a government can, with a strictly organized and conspiratory party, control absolutely the large disapproving majority, which is not an organized majority but merely the arithmetic sum of millions of isolated dissenting individuals.

These considerations make it very difficult to construe a "collective guilt" in the sense of penal law and retributive justice. It must not, however, be assumed that those whose rights are violated by the aggressive dictatorship have no just claims for reparation and restitution for damages. The people under dictatorial government, though not criminally guilty as a collective whole, may still be liable for the sufferings of the unjustly attacked neighbors. This liability arises from the illegality of the collective acts and the consequent imputability of the effects of the acts to the collectivity. In municipal civil and penal law we have a similar situation. A city government is liable for damages suffered by persons on the icy sidewalks of that city, though it may be considered impossible for the government to rectify the situation. A railroad is liable for all damages, even if it has done everything that may be reasonably expected of it to prevent accidents. A corporation—not only its managers—may be fined for violation of anti-trust laws, though the corporation as an impersonal association of capital cannot commit a crime.

Of primary importance at this point is the following consideration. The legal order exists to protect all members, to forbid and to concede acts to members. When, through the illegal act of a collectivity, though without "guilt" of the latter, the rights of other members are violated, justice then demands first of all that these rights be restored and damages paid, because security in one's rights is the first *raison d'être* of a legal order. So the duty of reparation is imposed upon those who caused the violation, irrespective of actual personal "guilt." Furthermore, it seems to be a right of the members of the international order to impose upon the state which "caused" the illegal acts certain individual obligations and restrictions in rights in order to achieve security, if the danger of illegal acts exists and even if the people or nation as such is not unequivocally "guilty" of that danger. The only admissible criterion is the security of the international order, and not the pre-established "moral guilt" of the nation for the criminal acts of its "government," against which this nation would have to be "protected" if erroneous ideas—such as nonintervention or absolute sovereignty—or even collusion of interested groups in other states did not prohibit such "protection."

III. ARBITRATION

We may distinguish between instruments for the avoidance of war and instruments for positively securing peace and increasing the chances for the continuation of the *tranquillitas ordinis*. To increase these chances would mean especially to hinder the development of potential causes of war and the development of situations in international affairs which, by their injustice, may potentially be remote causes of wars and may by carelessness or complacency quickly become so dangerous that the merely negative instruments for avoiding war will be an insufficient dam for accumulated emotional forces.

As means of avoiding war there early appear conciliation, mediation, and arbitration. The first two are by their nature political. It is not so much a legal problem that is to be solved, but a problem for which there exists no clear and commonly accepted or positive rule or treaty. The third, arbitration, is rather a formal judiciary proceeding used for the solution of legal problems like the interpretation of an international treaty or of any point of international law, the existence of a fact that, if proven, would represent a violation of an international treaty, the nature and scope of the reparation due on account of the violation of an international obligation.[5] A court of arbitration may be set up from time to time for the settlement of individual cases or, like the international court of arbitration organized by the Hague Conventions in 1899 and 1907, it may be set up as an institutional, permanent court of arbitration. Some powers had proposed to make this court a court of obligatory arbitration; yet this proposal did not find approval. The court remained one of facultative arbitration and thus lost much of its influence. The sentence of a court of arbitration is a true legal decision (Art. 81 of the Hague

[5] Cf. the numerous treaties of arbitration and mediation in any textbook of international law.

Convention of 1907). This of course presupposes a legal matter as subject of the sentence. Yet there are many cases where the disputes are not of a legal nature but concern political or economic interests, as, for instance, the demarcation of spheres of influence in undeveloped countries. Often the parties except from treaties of arbitration such disputes as concern "vital interests," "national honor," or the "integrity of their territory." Then the procedure of conciliation should follow that drawn up in the peace plan of Secretary of State William Jennings Bryan. According to the provisions of this plan the states should oblige themselves through a system of bilateral treaties to submit to an investigating commission such disputes as are not suitable for judicial arbitration. The treaty parties bind themselves not to proceed to war before the report of the commission has been published.

A noteworthy development of the idea of arbitration is to be found in the Treaty of Arbitration and Conciliation between the German Republic and Switzerland (1921) [6] because this treaty makes the formal procedure of conciliation obligatory if one of the litigants claims that the case is not a legally arbitrable matter, but concerns its political independence, territorial integrity, or most vital interests. Then the court of arbitration decides upon this exception and authoritatively rejects it or refers it to the permanent council of conciliation. The report of this council is, of course, not a decision that binds the litigants.

A step further, at least so far as legal problems are concerned, is the Permanent Court of International Justice established at the Hague in 1920 according to Article 14 of the Covenant of the League of Nations. Its decisions in legal disputes as well as its opinions on legal matters sought by the Council of the League of Nations, have contributed greatly to the development of international law. Nevertheless, even the Covenant of the League of Nations does not establish a strict, obligatory arbitration. The 1924 Protocol of Geneva, which would make arbitration or acceptance of the jurisdiction of the international court obligatory (Art. 3, 4), was never ratified by a sufficient majority of the member nations.

Mediation and conciliation are specific political means for the

---

[6] Similarly, Locarno Treaty, Art. III, and in connection with the various Western treaties, Appendixes B, C, D, E (Belgium, France, Poland, Czechoslovakia).

solution of international disputes of a political, non-legal character. The Hague Conventions of 1907 declare in the Second Title that any member of the international community has the right to offer its good services of mediation to disputing states and that such an offer of mediation may never be considered an unfriendly act. In the Covenant of the League of Nations an elaborate apparatus of conciliation and mediation was worked out. It contains first the quasi-coercive conciliatory intervention of Article 12, by which the members are obliged to submit to arbitration or judiciary decision, or to an examination by the Council, any differences that might lead to a rupture; they must in no case proceed to war before the expiration of a three-month delay after the decision of the arbitrators, or of the court, or the report of the Council has been rendered. Although under the Covenant conciliation or arbitration (submitting the dispute to the international court) seems obligatory, actually Article 15 presupposes that this is not so, because it obliges the member states to submit any international dispute to the Council for complete examination. If the Council's report is accepted unanimously by the members of the Council (the litigants not counted) then the member states oblige themselves not to proceed to war against the litigant accepting and abiding by the recommendations or decisions of the report. If no unanimity is reached, though all rules of conciliation are observed, the members are free to decide about the necessary means, including even war, of maintenance of right and justice (Article 15). Any member, or even non-member, of the League that does not abide by the rules of conciliation and proceeds to war without regard to the rules, is considered to have declared war against all the other members. Consequently economic, financial, and military sanctions may be used against the law-breaking state. But how and when the sanctions should be used is a decision left to the members; the Covenant did not envisage an international military police force and did not introduce federal execution.

All these various means of avoiding war were embodied in the Covenant of the League of Nations, the purpose of which, according to the preamble, is "to guarantee security and the rule of international law on the basis of justice and honor." Thus the League Covenant codifies a quasi-coercive conciliation procedure, as we have seen. It shows further a strong tendency to make arbitration obligatory where the dispute is arbitrable. It introduces a regime of facultative military sanctions (not an international police force) and of obligatory economic and financial sanctions against a state that proceeds to war in violation of the League Covenant. It endorses the reduction of armaments to the lowest point consistent with "national" security (not "domestic," as in Wilson's fourth point).[7]

This hopeful development in international law has been applauded and assisted by Catholic political philosophy. Pius IX heartily welcomed the disarmament proposal of Napoleon III. Leo XIII was a studious proponent of the ideas of the Hague Conferences, especially of the proposal for arbitration of international disputes, which, he thought, should be by its nature obligatory and compulsory.[8] In the *consortium* of the nations, says Leo XIII, there is lacking a system of legal and moral means to ensure the right of every nation. Therefore nothing is left but to resort immediately to the use of force and thence arises the competition of states in the development of their military power. In these circumstances the institute of mediation and arbitration is most opportune, and corresponds in every regard to the aspirations of the Holy See. That attitude is a confirmation of the traditional theory of international law in Catholic thought. We have earlier described the scholastic doctrine and shown that Vittoria, Suarez, and the others think that in the *orbis christianus*, because of the moral authority of the pope, it is a moral obligation for Catholic rulers to appeal to the pope as mediator and arbitrator before going to war. The same scholars regularly hold it a duty that, before proceeding to war (defense against unjust aggression excluded), the states must submit their dispute to mediation and arbitration. Moreover, as we have seen, it is the refusal to submit the dispute to such a procedure that represents a just cause for war; at least, as just as the rights in dispute. According to Catholic political philosophy, war is not an unavoidable event, but an imperfect, very imperfect institution of positive international law, to be abolished by better, more perfect means of establishing justice among free nations. Military victory is not always proof of the better right, but is often only the proof of better armaments and more ruthless violence. (Cf. St. Thomas, in *Pol.*, I, 6, lectio 4.)

[7] The term "National" was substituted upon the demand of Japan.
[8] Tischleder, pp. 400 f.

Leo XIII himself acted as mediator in international disputes. In 1885 he acted with success as mediator between Germany and Spain in the disputes about sovereignty over the Carolines Archipelago in the South Pacific. In the first decade of the twentieth century Pius X arbitrated the dispute between Brazil, on the one side, and Peru and Bolivia, on the other side, concerning the territory of Acre in the Amazon region.[9] During the First World War, Benedict XV, whose highest honor was the generally attributed title "Pope of Peace," never desisted from attempts at mediation. On August 17, 1917, he demonstrated in his peace message that the fundamental point is to substitute the power of law for material force by the introduction of obligatory arbitration and consequently of sanctions against a state refusing to submit its international disputes to arbitration or refusing to accept the decisions of arbitration.[10] Numerous Catholic associations for international peace have been the promoters of obligatory arbitration and welcomed the corresponding articles of the League of Nations, just as they were the most disappointed when the League began to show that institutions without strong moral ideas all too easily succumb.

IV. DISARMAMENT

Perhaps the most important contribution to a durable peace would have been disarmament. Since the standing army first appeared under the rule of the absolute princes and in the service of their policy of aggrandizement, the friends of peace have always insisted upon disarmament as an integral element in the preservation of peace. Disarmament became even more important when, during the French Revolution, general conscription was introduced. This was made possible, of course, by the industrial revolution. Modern technique made it possible to equip peoples in arms with all the appurtenances of modern warfare. Now there has been added the privately owned and capitalistically managed armament industry. Under the law of capitalist production, the profits from arms manufacture produce, together with rising nationalism and imperialist expansion, an unstable

---

[9] Cf. Ives de la Brière, *L'organisation internationale et la papauté souveraine*, Paris, 1924, I, 38 ff.
[10] *A.A.S.*, IX (1917), 417 ff.

balance between peace and war. However much capitalism or free
trade may in theory prefer peace, historically the alliance between
capitalist technology, nationalism, and economic imperialism produced, together with conscription, a political atmosphere charged
indeed with dangers of explosion. Industrialism thus produced a high
potential of war and a trend away from limited warfare and limited
war aims to more or less unlimited war aims and total warfare. No
wonder that the demand for disarmament grew in intensity in the
same ratio, from Czar Alexander I's proposal in 1816 to the proposals
of the Hague Peace Conferences in 1899 and 1907. These attempts
met with little success, because of the spirit of nationalism and the
materialist belief in the power of armies as the best means of economic imperialism. The conflagration of 1914–1918 again proved the
need of disarmament as an integral part of a durable peace. So it
was, then, that disarmament was made one of the main tasks of the
League of Nations.

No greater help to disarmament has been given than by Catholic
political philosophy as enunciated by the popes of the nineteenth
and twentieth centuries. Especially Leo XIII never tired of pointing
out the necessity of disarmament. "For many years past," Leo says,
"peace has been rather an appearance than a reality. Possessed by
mutual suspicions, almost all nations are competing with one another
in equipping themselves with military armaments. . . . This armed
peace cannot last much longer." [11] Against the widely quoted adage,
"*Si vis pacem para bellum,*" Leo declared that the enormous armaments may perhaps put off for a certain time the outbreak of war,
but that they are unable to afford a solid and durable peace. These
armament races produce distrust and jealousy rather than abate them.
They let men look sorrowfully into the future and put burdens on
the nations that may be even more unbearable than war itself.[12]
Conscription is bitterly criticized: "Inexperienced youth is given to
the dangers of military life far away from the counsels and education
of parents; in the flower of youth young men are taken away from the
farms and the colleges, from trade and factories, to the camps. The
expenditures for armaments exhaust the treasury, the wealth of nations melts away and the wealth of the citizens is crippled; this armed

[11] *Ibid.*, XXVI (1894), 714.
[12] *Ibid.*, XXI (1889), 387.

peace is intolerable." [18] The solution of this problem is a contractual limitation of armament for all nations on the basis of equality. This equal renunciation of an exaggerated militarism would liberate valuable powers and means for peaceful work that are now bound.[14] Benedict XV in his peace appeal proposed a just agreement upon a mutual and simultaneous disarmament, following common rules and guaranties within the necessary and sufficient limits of the preservation of the public order in each state.[15] Similarly, obligatory military service should be abolished by general agreement; and, as a sanction against violations of the latter agreement, a general world boycott should be proclaimed against the nation that reintroduces universal military service.

[18] *Ibid.*, XXVI (1894), 714.
[14] Hans Wehberg, *Papsttum und Weltfriede*, 1915, p. 50.
[15] *A.A.S.*, IV (1917), 417.

CHAPTER XXXI

Abolishing the Causes of War

I. NATIONALISM AS A CAUSE OF WAR

THE measures just discussed are mostly concerned with the avoidance of war as a means of restoring justice or of defending it. From them we must distinguish measures whose first purpose is the avoidance of any state of affairs that would produce conditions that may lead to war as the only solution for correcting an unjust *status quo*. We must be aware that a strict legal *status quo* in the international community is as impossible as is a consitutional *status quo* within a nation. The better the means which a constitution provides for adapting the political framework and the law to changes in the social and economic world, the less such a nation is threatened with civil war. Peace does not imply the rigid security of a *status quo,* but the community's ability to change the *status quo* by peaceful means whenever its continuance becomes a grave injustice. Thus other means of securing peace in a changing world are as important as the means of merely avoiding war. In other words, we must strive to do away with the potential causes of war. Such causes may be of economic origin. A national population, for example, so increases that it cannot live upon its own country's fertility, at least not with such a standard of living as its history and civilization make suitable. The macabre device of artificial birth control is unacceptable because it is against natural law. There remains emigration or development of export industries, the products of which can then serve as payment for the importation of food and raw materials. Now it is clear that actually the life of such a nation depends upon the sure expectation that the basic principles of international law implied in the existence of a true community of nations will be generally observed. Such principles include freedom of the seas, the unhindered access to raw materials, and the adoption of a prudent tariff policy by the other members of the community of nations in which the interests of all, as parts of the international common good, receive due consideration apart from any single national interest; a selfish and reckless nationalist tariff policy is just as disruptive of the international order as wars are. The defense of a nationalist tariff policy by the urging of the sovereign common good overlooks the fact that the national common good is in some way dependent upon the international common good, the order among nations. Consequently economic collaboration and a just compromise between free trade and protection of home industries, free access to raw materials, and freedom of the sea are as necessary for peace and security as are disarmament and the machinery of mediation and arbitration.

Modern nationalism has produced other potent causes of war in cultural autarchy and nationalist vanity, in the claim of being a chosen people, a master race, or the vanguard of liberation of the proletariat. All these arrogant presumptions have one thing in common: they live upon the destruction of the very basis of the community of nations (its common values, its universal rules which unite the members), and they introduce instead political principles of organization which keep the members apart and set them one against the other. Any community, especially the international community, which as an order of coordination lacks that intensity of social coherence so typical of the nation, lives by what is consciously and intentionally common to all members. To reduce or to extirpate what is common (common economic interests, commonly accepted basic values, common ethical rules, formed into law, or common philosophical and religious convictions) means of course to destroy the community and to return to the lawless "natural" status of the war of all against all.

No doubt, the more the nations turned to nationalism, the more they destroyed their common heritage of Christian culture, and the fewer were the restraints encountered by that arrogant nationalism which, being materialist, is simply blind to the transcendental immaterial values that are by nature international. So it becomes an imperative necessity to develop cultural and intellectual collaboration to revitalize, to preserve, and to increase the common heritage, to redeem the nations from the narrowness of their nationalist greeds.

In education, in our intellectual life, we must turn increasingly to an understanding of other nations, we must cultivate what is *com-*

munis. Here the role of Christianity has been far too neglected. The agnostic mind of the nineteenth century, the proud positivist followers of Comte who substituted Humanity for Christianity, the modern secularist turning quickly into the materialist, the admirers of a non-Christian idea of a laicist humanity, considering religion a private affair of individuals in seclusion from public life, they and their ideologies have proven themselves impotent. Thus cultural and intellectual collaboration must reflect Christianity as the common heritage, reviving what so long has been buried under the vain proclamations of an agnostic philosophy and relativist ethics. One cannot build an enduring community (i.e., unity founded on a common end) upon a negative unity that denies common values and ends.

II. National Minorities

In connection with this point it may be remarked that nationalism produced the awkward problem of national minorities,[1] making minorities conscious of themselves by attempts at denationalization and delivering to them the weapons for their struggle for liberation. The growth of nationalism increased state interference in education, in religious life, and in folk traditions with a view to complete assimilation and thus, at a progressive ratio, sought to suppress national minorities at the very time they were becoming progressively conscious of themselves by that very growth of nationalism. So nationalism left to the world after 1918 a problem that has not yet found a satisfactory solution. The continuation of this war-breeding state of affairs was owing to several causes: first, the "overcompensated" nationalism of the new states in Eastern and Southeastern Europe; secondly, the increase of state activity in the lives of the citizens arising from this new cultural nationalism and a narrow-minded economic nationalism; thirdly, the jealousy of the controlling national majorities in the new states, one against the other;[2] fourthly, the

---

[1] There exists an enormous literature about minorities and especially about national minorities. Cf. *National States and National Minorities* (Royal Institute of International Affairs, London, 1934); Robert Redslob, *Le principe des nationalités,* Paris, 1930; Ignaz Seipel, *Die geistigen Grundlagen der Minderheitenfrage,* 1928. An excellent critical discussion is that of Erich Hula, "National Self-determination Reconsidered" in *Social Research,* X (1943), 1 ff.

[2] Best illustrated by the participation of Poland and Hungary in the dismemberment of the Czechoslovakian state in the aftermath of the Munich Conference of September, 1938.

contradiction between an abstract concept of the principle of national self-determination and the economic and political reality. There was besides, the partial application of the principle, a fact that was consequently considered a diminution of their sovereignty by the nations upon whom treaties for the protection of minorities were enforced by international law and the League of Nations: Poland, Czechoslovakia, Hungary, Rumania, and others, as compared, for instance, with Italy (Tyrol) or Belgium (Eupen-Malmedy). Furthermore, some minorities were border minorities and looked therefore for protection not to the League, but to the fatherland. Thus the new states felt dubious about the loyalties of their minorities and became suspicious and jealous of the "protector" states. A condition developed that was far more influenced by power politics than by law and order. When the League of Nations was broken in its prestige and power by the independent great powers seeking only their own interests, it was no wonder that with the conquest of Austria the whole framework of the peace treaties was destroyed under the impact of Nazism, then tolerated by the Western statesmen as a presumptive *cordon sanitaire* against Bolshevism.

Before the national revolutions of the third estate there scarcely existed a problem of national minorities. Medieval civilization was not even aware of this problem. The peoples of the various lords and free towns, the inhabitants of geographically circumscribed provinces, lived under the slenderly developed state of a king, and their loyalty to him united them but loosely. The more comprehensive unity of existence of all these people living according to their traditional particular laws and customs and economically self-sufficient was the Church, was Christendom with pope and emperor. These two were the bonds of unity. The Church and the canon law ruled many human affairs and developed and administered many secular functions, such as social welfare, protection of the poor, and education, which only in modern times were taken over by the state. The Church as Christendom was the integrating element of political unity.

The nations—the Germanic nation, the Gallic nation, and so on—felt themselves to be the daughters of the Church. Then the absolute prince, in the same historical process in which the medieval universe fell to pieces (namely, the rising of nation states), united in his sovereignty all the political power that during feudalism and city-freedom had been distributed, sold, or granted to the lower communities. His new sovereignty was a polemical concept directed first against the Holy Roman Empire, the *orbis christianus,* and against the representatives of this empire, the emperor and the pope singly or together, and against the political freedoms of the cities and against the immediate power wielded by the feudal lords over their territories. Thus the absolute prince became the exclusive representative of the "people" in his realm, while the medieval forms of popular representation, the estates, either disappeared or became powerless. Thus the modern nation-state is established from above by the sovereign prince, not from below by the people as a united, self-conscious nation striving by its own decision and power for the political form of life, the state. The "nation" in the modern sense, then, is not an entity determined in its historical identity by itself biologically or racially, or by its metaphysical collective spirit. On the contrary, the "nations" are the product of the political will of kings and statesmen like Richelieu and Cromwell, Cavour and Bismarck, the Romanoffs and the Hapsburgs (in Spain), at least as much as of the collective will of that entity, the nation. There does not exist one exclusively determinant factor which produces a "nation," either race, geography, biological characteristics or the fabulous pre-existing national spirit. Historically the nations are the result of a variety of fostering and retarding factors, but never of one or two distinct factors alone.

But even under the cover of absolute sovereignty the regions, the old tribal unities, and the provinces preserved to a certain degree their individuality and traditional way of life, and continued to live their own lives in comparative tranquillity beyond the line fixed by the administrative and judicial centralism of the absolute princes. It was the French Revolution that pitted against the exclusive representation of the country by the sovereign king the sovereignty of the people and the national assembly as the representative of the nation, one and indivisible. The legal basis of this new order is the self-determination of the nation as opposed to the rule of the absolute king. The political ideal is the unity of the nation in the political form of representative democracy. Each nation, awakened to self-conscious life, is thus considered to have a natural right to political independence, not only from the princely ruler (result: democracy) but also from the historical political frame in which the now self-conscious national unit lives. "No nation has a right to exist save as a state" (Wyspianski) The principle of self-determination, therefore, means internally popular sovereignty and democratic rule. Externally it means the right of secession from the older non-national state created by conquest, marriage, or inheritance by the royal house and kept together by a traditional loyalty and "the sweet and paternal symbols of legitimacy." Of this last the Austro-Hungarian monarchy is the outstanding example, though not the only one.

After the First World War the historical framework of the non-national state of the Hapsburgs was destroyed by appeal to the rather abstract principle of national self-determination, i.e., national sovereignty. But in its abstractness this principle is in such stark contradiction of the facts that the result of the destruction of the Hapsburg monarchy was the rise, not of nationally unified states, but of multinational states, such as Poland, Czechoslovakia, Rumania, and Yugoslavia. The democratic element of self-determination, representative government, was not of much avail. Most of the new states turned rather quickly away from representative government to various dictatorial forms or at least to a clear and sovereign control of the multinational state by the nationally strongest group.

Thus they brought into doubt the principle of the equality of the national groups; i.e., one of the national groups took over the role of preferential representative of the multinational state. Most of them gave up full democracy partly to establish a working political unity through the control of the ruling national group and partly to counteract the centrifugal tendency of the new minorities which the democratic form of government encouraged more than had the discarded so-called autocratic monarchic form. Moreover, the successor states feared that the principle of national self-determination itself would be a continuous danger to the political existence of their new states containing national minorities akin to neighboring powerful nations. This principle gave rise to divided loyalties by its very nature: loyalty to the nation-state to which the minorities were *nationally* akin; loyalty to the residence state of which they were politically citizens. This weakness was, of course, recognized by the framers of postwar Europe, and they attempted to draw up a set of rules for the protection of the rights of national, religious, and racial minorities under the guaranty of the League of Nations. Such an enforced protection was considered especially necessary since on some occasions the boundaries of the new states were determined principally by strategical considerations.

III. TREATIES PROTECTING MINORITIES

These treaties for the protection of national, religious, and racial [3] minorities impose upon the successor-state an international duty to bestow equal constitutional, political, and civil rights upon the members of the minorities. These rights included the following: franchise; protection of life, liberty, and property; equality before the law; equal access to administrative positions; freedom of religion. In their positive part, these treaties also guarantee to the minorities the right of free use of their language in private life, in commerce, in church, in books, in the press, in public meetings, and before the courts; and the right to establish and maintain at their own expense charitable, social, religious, and educational institutions. Furthermore, where a minority represents a considerable part of the district population, public instruction has to be given in its language in the public schools that must be financed proportionally out of the public treasury. For the benefit of Jews it is especially stated that they may not be compelled to actions that violate their religious rules concerning the Sabbath and that no public election shall take place on that day.[4] All these obligations of the residence-state are by agreement parts of the constitution of that state, so that the rights of the minorities are fundamental rights which must not be contravened by any laws or decrees. It is agreed, furthermore, that the obligations are of international interest and are under the guaranty of the League of Nations. Any dispute between the residence-state and another member of the League concerning such treaties is a dispute of international character, open to the procedure of quasi-coercive conciliation of the

[3] Protection of religious minorities came up under the Turkish rule in the Balkans in the interest of Christian peoples. These minorities are important today in some states where, de facto at least, a positive religion forms the uniting political link; for instance, in Serbia. The term "racial minority" refers mostly to the Eastern Jews. Their emancipation was for the most part merely inscribed in the statutes; actually they were not considered citizens with full rights, as the successful anti-Semitic propaganda of Nazism in these countries proves only too well.

[4] Treaty between the Allied and Associated Powers and Poland (Versailles, June 28, 1919); cf. Strupp, *Documents pour servir à l'histoire du droit des gens*, IV, 596. See also similar treaties with Czechoslovakia, Yugoslavia, and Rumania.

Council of the League, or, on demand, is brought before the international court, the decision of which is binding. The preamble of the treaty declares the intention of the residence-state to conform its institutions to the principle of freedom and justice and to give a sure guaranty to all inhabitants of the territory over which it has assumed sovereignty.

The history of the troubled period between 1919 and 1938 (e.g., the dismemberment of the Czechoslovakian state by appeal to the principle of self-determination) has shown that even with such well-intentioned treaties the problem of national minorities is not solved. In an unexpected and revolutionary way Hitler used the principle of self-determination and thus disguised his urge for expansion. At the same time he robbed the western democracies of any valid reason to protect the attacked state, since they had to accept the *Anschluss* and the return of the Sudeten to the fatherland. Only too late did they discover the international dynamite which lay hidden in an uncritical acceptance of the principle of national self-determination.

The reason for this failure is partly owing to the fact that in real life the enforcement of the rights of minorities is dependent upon diplomatic and political considerations of the individual members of the League of Nations rather than upon any abstract principles. Consequently it is generally the "fatherland" of the supposedly persecuted minority that brings the matter before the public forum. Since there is then lacking an impartial protector of the minorities, this action already constitutes a potential cause of increasing tension: the violation of the rights of the national minority is too quickly considered a violation of the honor of the fatherland. Then, too, if a minority has no such "born" protector, its appeal against the violation of its rights will not be like an appeal to an impartial court, it will not be a nonpolitical affair, but will be an affair of political expediency. The state to which the minority appeals may find it inconvenient to follow the call of the minority because it needs the political help of the state against which the minority is complaining. We must not forget that new states usually are jealous for their new sovereignty and feel insecure because neither history nor tradition has fixed the loyalty of its citizens. To be subject to an impartial procedure before a world court—by far the best way of enforcing these treaties—is felt as an infringement of their sovereignty, especially if they see that other states with national minorities, like Italy and Belgium, are free from positive international obligations and from the threat of international interference.

In the last resort it is the spirit of modern nationalism in connection with exaggerated sovereignty that lies at the basis of the difficulty. Modern nationalism makes the nation the exclusive legitimation of the state. The ideal state is the nation-state, the identification of nation and state. National homogeneity is considered the only reliable basis for political loyalty. Consequently resident citizens who do not belong to the nation are subjected to enforced assimilation or are degraded, in fact though perhaps not in law, to a minor status in all fields where the state has influence. But is the nation-state actually an ideal simply and in all circumstances? Seipel, the eminent scholar and statesman, says: "The nation is not a legally constituted community like the state or the Church, not an institution which is distinguishable from the individuals that form it and to which the individual owes legal obligations." [5]

The nation has no formal authority as such, has no external legal means of enforcement. "Nation," as the term itself makes clear, has to do with family (generation, *nasci*) and with culture, language, folklore, sagas, literature. Nation is a cultural and educational milieu, forming and determining the individual in his actuality as a member born into the nation. In that sense of "nation" I cannot as easily change my nation as I can change my citizenship. I feel *pietas* to my nation, but loyalty to my state. Nation is, therefore, different from state. I do not love my state as such. I honor it, I am loyal to it, I obey its laws.[6] But I love the nation into which I was born; I love the language in which my mother first taught me to pray, to sing the old songs, to know the sagas of my nation, not of my state as such. That is what Seipel meant when he said that *natio* and *respublica* are not the same, as is shown by many states like Switzerland, the late Austro-Hungarian monarchy and all its successor states, the Union of the Socialist Soviet Republics, Belgium, and, by the way, Spain with its Basques and Catalans.

[5] *Nation und Staat*, 1915, p. 2.

[6] Concerning the treaties for the protection of national, racial, and religious minorities, the League of Nations has constantly maintained that a minority's right to national autonomy and international protection against oppression implies its moral and legal duty to cooperate with the government as loyal citizens.

If *natio* and *respublica* ought to be always the same, then the inevitable consequence would be political nationalism which may easily produce a totalitarian state, while true free democracy, that is, restriction of state power, freedom of religion, freedom of education, and freedom of language, would be the only solution of the problem. But the state is not the one and all. There is no sovereignty that actually must control human life in every smallest detail. There exist not only the rights of the individual. There exist also the rights of the family, of the religious community, and of the national groups in contrast to the state. It is wrong to contend that political unity is possible only on the basis of exclusive uniformity in religion, race, and national culture, just as it is not necessary to build political unity upon economic and social equality. What a state needs is justice in a concrete order of law, and that presupposes only moral unity in the zeal for the common good; it does not presuppose either economic, religious, or "national" uniformity. Where history and the circumstances of geography and providence have cooperated to produce a nation-state, it is well; where history, geography, or historical settlement or migration has not produced a framework for a nation-state, the non-national state, with political liberty and justice and moral unity though without national uniformity, is the better thing. A confederation of nationalities, a federation of free self-governing groups with a common foreign policy, a common army, and an economic unity, is enough for the free existence of the different nationalities.[7] In those parts of the world (India is a new problem) where national groups live intermingled, where the national state is impossible, the non-national state on the principle of federalism and cultural freedom or autonomy is the only guaranty of peace.

IV. NATIONAL SELF-DETERMINATION

If the principle of national self-determination should mean the right to political sovereignty by any group that feels itself to be or claims to be a distinctive national unit, such self-determination would

[7] That is the organization which the Polish and Czechoslovakian governments have in mind in their agreement of January 23, 1942. *Department of State Bulletin*, February 15, 1942.

become disruptive and revolutionary in the event that it is inter-preted by a wrong theory of "personification" of the nation or the nationality as an absolute and inalienable right. There are other factors like geographical conditions, economic development and eco-nomic supplementary completion, common historical destiny, affinity in religion, and common danger from a covetous, expansive, power-ful state. All these influences counterbalance the right to national self-determination, if it means that inalienable right to political sovereignty. This is, indeed, the *opinio communis* of international jurists. The international commission of jurists considering the ques-tion of the Aland Islands pronounced that the principle of national self-determination does not apply to definitely constituted multi-national states, that further, even in the transformation and dismem-berment of states, it does not apply exclusively because, in spite of its predominant role in the formation of new states, considerations of geography and economics and other similar considerations may stand in the way of its integral realization.

Thus, for instance, in southeastern Europe there are interspersed settlements in "language islands" or there exist nations of small popu-lation unable to establish an independent state strong enough to with-stand the political pressure of powerful neighbors. In such cases, in the interest of peace it is better that such a small or dispersed group should live in comparative cultural autonomy in a non-national or multinational powerful state able to afford protection, rather than that a vacuum of power be created by the existence of small nation-states, jealous of one another and therefore an easy prey for an ex-pansive neighboring power with its natural attraction of small states into its power orbit. Even a perfect system of collective security will be unable actively and forcibly to protect splinter-states against eco-nomic or cultural "peaceful invasion" and consequent disguised con-trol. The preferable solution of this dilemma is more internal liberty, less administrative centralization, less imitation of the internal policy of the centralized nation-state as an absolute or superior ideal. Earlier ages regarded religious homogeneity as the necessary basis of political loyalty. We have learned that this is not true. Why should national homogeneity be so? Seipel thought that the nineteenth-century nation-state is an inferior kind of state, and that the federated state represents

a higher and older political idea and form: a state in which many nations live in mutual understanding and esteem, educating one another
to higher ideas than the mere national ones.

Thus the redemption from the spirit of nationalism is a *conditio
sine qua non* for securing peace. This in turn is intrinsically connected
with the revival of those common ideas that materialism as well as
nationalism has obscured. The isolation of the virtue of patriotism
from the universal law of morality produced unlimited nationalist
egoism. The spirit of secularism drove Christianity from being an
active public power back into private life, thus freeing that egoism
from the many restrictions imposed by a vivid consciousness of the
more comprehensive unity of Christendom.

It also produced a new ethics of utilitarianism. What is useful to the
individual nation and its aggrandizement is right. The "rights" of the
nation are almost alone stressed; the communal duties, the reflex of
the rights, of the nation as a member of a genuine community of
nations, are forgotten. Hence arises an excessive sensibility, so typical
of the egocentric concept of rights, and national prestige supersedes
the moral and social phenomenon of honor. The progress of power
politics is the consequence. Thus the separation of international
politics as a question of individual usefulness and potential material
power from universal morality as the basis and pre-condition of a
working comunity of nations is only one element in a general modern
trend. This trend is the separation of public and private life from the
universal spirit of Christianity; the liberalist separation of politics
from ethics, of national ethics from universal religion, of positive law
from natural law, of civic education from religion, of economic private
profit from service to the common good.

This trend is the primary cause of the discord among the nations, of
the impotence of international law, of the rule of brute power in international politics. Wherever the universal values and ideas, intrinsically
immaterial, spiritual and thus communicable, are repressed, the
powers of egoism, of force, and of selfishness inevitably invade the
vacuum so created. But these attitudes are unable to produce order in
international life from which there have been obliterated the ideas
creative of order. Peace is tranquillity of order, the order of justice and
charity. St. Thomas says that peace belongs more to charity than to
justice. Whereas justice removes the obstacles to peace and inequities,

peace itself is properly the result of charity's overcoming the diverse separating interests and opinions and thus is the truly uniting power.[8]

Pius XI declared again and again that strict justice alone cannot produce peace unless it is mitigated by charity. After the end of the First World War, he urged that the question of reparations to be paid by the conquered nations should be ruled by a spirit that unites the feelings of justice with those of social charity. Justice, human justice *in concreto*, is not by itself able to produce always and everywhere the order of peace. Justice, as we have seen, cries for the positive law, the rational form, and the definite security of social and national interests in social and international life. But interests, like the groups from which they issue, change. Thus the concrete order of law must be adapted to the changes. This can be done only by the intervention of a power that is greater than strict law, by natural equity and charity.

Like any community, the state does not live by the law alone, however much the law as the product of justice is the *conditio sine qua non* of its existence. In the final analysis any community lives by the internal will for charity, for concord, for loyalty, for honesty, for the host of social virtues. They are the direct principle of life, the order of law is the framework, absolutely necessary, but not itself the life; especially does the international community need these social virtues, and charity first of all. Justice and the law guarantee the independent existence, the liberty, of the members of the international community; but charity and its issue, peace, unite the community and make it a living, cooperative unity of mutual help and cultural development.

We speak of the reconciliation of the nations; this presupposes the recognition that hatred must be overcome by charity. Now charity is intentionally directed to every man, as a man, not to individuals of nations, of races, or of cultures. Thus charity intends mankind as its *terminus ad quem;* every man is thy neighbor. This charity is not, of course, understood in the abstract sense of nineteenth-century agnosticism, which substituted humanity for God. For such an agnostic charity forgets the essential basis of charity: the image of God is the end of charity, it is not the mere fact of likeness. Charity toward mankind draws life from religion, from the faith in the common Father, who is the source of common brotherhood. The sin of materialism,

[8] St. Thomas, *Summa theol.*, IIa IIae, q.29, a.3.

racial, class, or national, is this, that it destroys the one potential
basis of the community of nations because it has destroyed the faith,
the Christian faith in God the Father and supreme Lawgiver. Peace,
the *ordo rerum humanarum,* calls for the consciousness of a common
brotherhood in sonship of the common divine Father.[9] The city of
men cannot endure in peace without the city of God. Religious truth,
as Ranke once said, must remind the state continuously of its origin
and of the end of all earthly life, of the rights of its neighbors and of
the kinship of all nations; otherwise the state becomes a tyrant, and
the nation degenerates into hatred of all other nations. In the era of
materialism the nations have tried to build the city of men upon the
so-called solidarity of economic interests, upon the secular fraternity
of man, upon the socialism of the international proletariat, all this
to little avail. Evidently these partial bases for peace in that city of
men were lacking in solidity. Moreover, precisely on account of their
materialistic elements, they contributed to the promotion of hostile
nationalisms. Let us, then, return to an attempt to build the city of
men in the likeness of the city of God; let us try Christianity.

V. THE LEAGUE OF NATIONS

We may now enter upon a brief sketch of the shortcomings in the
efforts to establish a lasting peace after 1918 and of institutions for the
preservation of peace after the war. The only human result of the First
World War could have been world peace. But it was not a durable
peace that resulted; instead, a new and greater world conflagration
broke out in the short period of twenty years. What was wrong with
the institutions created by the peace treaties for the preservation of
international peace? In particular, what was wrong with the League
of Nations?

---

9 Even wars are conducted less cruelly as long as this feeling of brotherhood unconsciously connects what political strife and war put asunder and against one another.
The adversary is then not a subhuman being, a "beast," or a "mad dog," whose extermi-
nation is a meritorious act. This feeling, even in war, keeps the soldier from personally
hating his foe; it makes him esteem in the foe something that is common to himself and
the enemy. This esteem and its basis are what distinguishes from a murderer the soldier
who is conscious of serving a greater thing than personal hatred or personal profit. A
murderer's purpose is hatred or material profit; his intention is to exterminate, to destroy
the foe simply, for he destroys the most precious good, personal life, for material goods.
The soldier is free from both these intentions.

The first fault was the lack of a new spirit, less materialist and less nationalist than the spirit that had produced the hidden causes of the war. The peoples and their leaders soon preferred to return to what they called normalcy, which was nothing but the old spirit as it prevailed before the war. The postwar period did not solve the moral crisis of which the war was the cataclysmic outcome. There did not occur among the nations and their leaders that repentant change of heart for which so many on both sides of no man's land had prayed, sacrificed, and hoped. The short period of idealistic internationalism, whatever its philosophical basis, was quickly overcome by the resurgence of a new nationalism and by the exaggerated optimism, that the new institutions (the League, the International Court, and the attendant treaties) would, together with the "new capialism" and social progress, automatically free man from the need of a laborious quest for peace. Monarchs and generals had muddled the affairs of international life. Now the businessmen, the engineers, the economic leaders, with or without social legislation, would produce the conditions of enduring peace. The most astounding fact of this postwar period is the conviction that institutions and economic conditions make men good and peaceful because men, or the people, are intrinsically good; if they seem to be not good, what makes them evil is evil institutions and evil economic conditions.

This social determinism was satisfied with the construction of new, "good" institutions, but it never considered seriously the need of a spiritual conversion of the peoples. So it overlooked simply that great danger even to good institutions; namely, that they can be abused by "bad" men. It is the weakness, especially of legal institutions, that they themselves may become simply means for a primary struggle for power. Such institutions are in themselves not a substitute for power politics. Abstractly speaking, law is not a substitute for power. To solemnly outlaw war as a means of national politics does not mean much if there is lacking the innermost moral will in all participants to honor their promise, even when not forced to do so by overwhelming power or by material advantages. There is much human wisdom in the old definition of justice as the "constant and perpetual will" to give to each what is his due (Gajus, *Instit.*, Bk. I, introd.), or that justice is a virtue, a habit of the will. Hence it is the right spirit that makes the legal institutions work. And this right spirit was lacking in 1918.

For the more profound thinker the decade after the Treaty of Versailles was one of disillusion and cynicism. For the future historians it will be an enigma that the institution of the great powers on the principle of the balance of power and the old capitalism, so despised because of attendant power politics, produced fewer deadly conflicts in the nineteenth century than did the short time after the First World War with all the new international institutions.

A second fault, especially of the League, was lack of universality. The United States, the greatest world power on account of its economic wealth, on account of the influence of its political institutions, so often imitated, and on account of its power as the creditor of all nations, absented itself from the League. The President of the United States had been the promoter of the League. Victors and conquered alike looked upon him as the bearer of peace. The new upsurge of democratic ideals in the defeated nations and in the new successor-states in Southern and Eastern Europe was nourished by the slogan: Make the world safe for democracy. Especially did the defeated nations in the travail of their democratic rebirth hope to get a fair deal in the postwar settlement under the impartial, idealistic leadership of that great nation with which all of them, by immigration of their nationals, had a stronger sentimental connection than the European states had among themselves. But the United States surrendered all strict responsibility: politically it returned to isolationism, and economically it only augmented its creditor status by high protective tariffs. On the other hand, the League accepted to membership certain states with antagonistic interests, states that were too far away for an effective forcible intervention by the League. Thus the failure of the League undermined its authority as much as did the absence of the United States.

A third weakness was manifested in the rift that appeared early in the League of Nations between the so-called revisionist group and the *status quo* group. This rift was not identical with that between the victors and the vanquished, since Fascist Italy and political groups as well as powerful private individuals and groups in England and the United States became allied to the revisionist party. The League of Nations seemed to the revisionist a mere instrument of those interested in the *status quo,* as a machinery to perpetuate a questionable or even unjust *status quo* and to cover it with the high-sounding ideal of the League. On the other hand, the revisionists appeared to those nations which stressed the *status quo* as men faithlessly abusing the League for purposes of secession and power politics. This rift partly paralyzed any progressive action of the League and made it a mere "atmosphere," a kind of perpetual council of the old concert of the great European powers augmented by some non-European countries.

No wonder that the League too often shirked its responsibility in serious cases and (for instance, in the dispute between Italy and Greece) permitted a non-League authority, the Council of Ambassadors of the Allied and Associated Powers, actually to decide the dispute according to political expediency and not according to justice. A second rift also appeared and helped to transform the League into a mere collectivist instrument of revived power politics: the rift between the capitalist nations and the Union of the Socialist Soviet Republics. The Soviet Union was admitted to the League when the political interests of France and England required the admission as a counterbalance to the menace of Hitlerism. How little even the leaders of the *status quo* party put their trust in the League may be seen from the numerous military alliances that paralyzed the activity of the League. These rifts then caused the numerous disarmament conferences to collapse and brought the demand of all nations for security back to these nations individually and separately. Instead of making the League strong, the powers made themselves strong, each concerned too much only with itself.

We should bear in mind that the above-mentioned rifts were also internal rifts in the member states themselves. Moreover, there arose *status quo* parties and revisionist parties, procapitalist groups and pro-Soviet groups, prodisarmament and antidisarmament groups. As these groups changed in the governments of their countries (for instance, MacDonald's Labor cabinet and Baldwin's Tory cabinet), the political balance in the League changed, too. This condition created an instability in the League that again weakened its authority and induced member states to look to their own interests which were supposedly or really not protected by the League. They turned to special alliances irrespective of the League's authority and influence, however much it was insisted that these alliances existed within the framework of the League. They existed within the framework by considerably weakening it.

VI. Political Internationalism and Economic Nationalism

The trend to economic nationalism and to a neomercantilist trade policy progressively weakened the economic interdependence of nations, one of the most important bases of international cooperation. At the same time tendencies toward economic autarchy were promoted by states of a Fascist or semi-Fascist nature. Thus not only was an increase in economic interdependence restrained, but the existing interdependence was lessened: in this way the national economies could be prepared for war by the promoters of economic autarchy as a political instrument of power politics. Now it is evident that the League as a going concern presupposes in reality a continually increasing economic interdependence among the member states, for its obligatory sanctions against a lawbreaking state were economic and financial sanctions, while military sanctions were optional. Consequently any decrease of economic interdependence undermined the power potential of the League, and the new political and military alliances just mentioned practically excluded military sanctions as coercive actions of the League as such. And so the international scenery offered the strange picture of contradictory tendencies in reality and in ideologies. On one hand was a development of international institutions by the power of ideologies which presuppose economic and cultural interdependence and exchange. On the other hand was a reduction of this economic and cultural interdependence in favor of nationalist ideologies antagonistic to the ethical and philosophical foundations of the desired growth of the new international institutions. Here was an ideological contest against sovereignty and nationalism and an increase of economic nationalism and of internal sovereignty by a steady enlargement of state intervention in the economic and cultural life of the individual nation, as economic and cultural nationalism demands it.

As internal and external sovereignty means but two fields of action for the one power of decision beyond appeal, this increase in internal sovereignty of course resulted also in an increase of external sovereignty, in stark contradiction to the international ideology. The League became more and more a mere concert of Great Powers, but a concert that lacked, in opposition to that of the nineteenth century, a common basis in outlook and culture. Hitlerism, Fascism, Bolshevism, and Western Democracy had far less in common than did the members of the European Concert in the last century. Nay, they had practically nothing in common; they had only deadly conflicting interests and contradictory political ideologies. Thus peace again ceased to be a collective affair, the *raison d'être* of the League. Peace became armed truce, dependent on power politics, on industrial potential of war, and on the military risks of the individual powers. A kind of *status naturalis* among the nations returned. The Covenant of the League became an empty legal hulk. The material force of arms triumphed again over the moral power of right.

The League's promoters had fostered, partly in sincerity, partly to counteract the appeal of Soviet Russia to the "international proletariat," the development of international standards for social legislation among member states.[10] They hoped that the various national labor movements, with their frankly international outlook, would afford the League a powerful support. But this plan received a first, though not decisive, setback from the economic reparations of the peace treaties, which burdened the workers of the defeated nations. The second and final stroke came with the growth of Fascism and the subsequent destruction of the labor movement in the Fascistic and semi-Fascistic countries and in those countries that abandoned social democracy and introduced semidictatorial regimes with the subsequent curtailment of labor movements. An additional loss of prestige for the League was caused by its inability to deal with long-term unemployment before and after the crisis year of 1929.

All these factors contributed to the qualitative change in the character of the League. Instead of being a universal, though open, confederation with authority and competencies, equipped with agencies and formal procedures to deal with international problems, the League became no more than an "atmosphere," a sort of international congress permanently in session but without appropriate power to execute its decisions. Thus often the members were able to transfer their individual responsibility, which they had on account of their real power, to the international community, to the collective organ. But as this "congress" lacked the real power corresponding to the responsibility which had been ideologically transferred to it, power and responsibility were separated. The power still rested with the individual

[10] Art. 23 of the Covenant, and Part XIII, art. 387-427 of the Versailles Treaty.

sovereign great powers. The responsibility was heaped upon the League and its organs without primary or derivative real power. Thus the League was in reality not endowed with that power demanded by its responsibility and the tasks it had to fulfill. The League lacked the specific authority and legitimacy that springs from the union of moral responsibility and power.

The Protestant denominations and the Catholic Church were known to be very friendly to the idea of a League of Nations. From the ecumenical movement under Archbishop Söderblum the League got every help. Not less friendly were the Catholics in the various countries and Pope Benedict XV and Pope Pius XI. It is true that in the beginning a few Catholic groups, because of a misunderstanding, resented the exclusion of the Holy See from the League.[11] But this difficulty was of no importance for the great majority of Catholics, who felt that the League's aims agreed with their doctrines about the international community and with their sacred tradition: the unity

[11] Italy had protested against the admission of the Holy See to the peace conferences at the Hague in 1899 and 1907, and had hurt the feelings of Leo XIII considerably. The French representative Renault later opened a way for the admission of the Holy See by his successful proposal to substitute in the Hague treaties dealing with the admission of states that had not been originally invited, instead of the word "states" the word "puissances" (powers). As nobody could deny that the Holy See was a power, though from 1870 till 1929 it was not a state with territorial sovereignty, the way was open for the representatives of the Holy See to a participation in the Hague conferences and in the court of arbitration. But the change of "state" to "power" was of little avail, because Italy succeeded in making the admission of new participants to the Hague Conference dependent upon a preceding agreement between the original contracting parties, as Lord Paunceforte proposed. Thus Italy succeeded in excluding the Holy See from the Hague. In the secret treaty of 1915 between Italy, Great Britain, and France about the ultimate peace treaties at the end of the war, Italy succeeded again in excluding the Holy See from all conferences. When, therefore, the Covenant of the League named as members not the "puissances" (powers), but states, dominions, and self-governing colonies, some Catholic groups, remembering the earlier protest of Italy, saw in this wording a deliberate offense to the Holy See and were inclined to consider the League only as the ideological product of freemasonry and as having an anticlerical character. But only a few groups made support of the League dependent upon the admission of the Holy See. The great majority followed the policy of the English Catholic Council for International Relations in giving full-hearted support to the League, a policy that was approved by the popes, who directly cooperated with the League during the Russian famine of 1921 and in the Palestine affair of the Christian minorities and of the Christian holy places in the proposed Jewish national home. Catholics became fervent sponsors of the League in France and England, as well as in the defeated countries, especially in Germany, where the Center Party and numerous Catholic associations (e.g., Internationaler Gesellentag, Cologne, 1928) earnestly worked for the League against many nationalist groups. Cf. Yves de la Brière, *La papauté souveraine*, 2 vols., and *Politisches Jahrbuch der Zentrumspartei*, 1925, 1926, 1927.

of mankind, the peaceful cooperation of all nations for the international common good, and the settlement of international disputes by peaceful procedures on the basis of justice, honor, and charity. But this full agreement and active support by the Churches did not hinder the decline of the League. One may, of course, try to explain that by the undeniable decline of the influence of Christianity in most modern states during the era of nineteenth-century secularism, by the undeniable fact that the renaissance of Christianity as manifested in the Catholic revival in various countries was but a slow and weary process in a world that fell more and more into skepticism, in a world that wished too eagerly to forget the war and to return to the comfortable privileges, profits, and ease that the era of materialism had afforded.

I think that here we have a clue. In the last resort the League, and with it the peace, failed because the nations, and the ruling classes in the nations, insisted upon returning to their cherished fetishes of profits, of privileges, of rugged individualism and secular license without obligations, and of national sovereignty as a curtain behind which ruled the invisible sovereigns of profit, of relativism, and of complacency without sacrifices. The moral basis for the League as it ought to be was far too narrow.

VII. Need of a Spiritual Basis

It is true that no one of these developments, nor all of them together, give a sufficient explanation of the vanishing of mankind's hope in 1919. Something deeper, more decisive, must be the cause. And that is the return to the nineteenth-century spirit of nationalism. The World War seemed to many people a mere interruption of an era of continuous economic progress, of a happy secular prosperity with ever longer week ends, a prosperity undisturbed by spiritual doubts, attenuated by such social work as was deemed necessary to avoid social revolution. But the old ideologies, the way of thinking and the conduct of life to which one wished to return, were incompatible with the postwar world. That world needed a new enthusiasm, a new social spirit of devotion. In a few men and groups this new ethos showed itself: in the popes, in the various youth groups that moved beyond nationalism and beyond the amenities of bourgeois security in mind and life, in a few statesmen. But the majority continued to think in the old ways of national self-interest, of rugged individualism, and of greed for material wealth. Therefore Pius XI rightly charged that "the peace is only signed in public documents, but is not written in the hearts of men."

The Pope then criticizes especially the revived nationalism, the economic and national egoism that is unable to see in the neighbor a brother according to Christ's command, but sees in him merely a potential robber of accumulated and hoarded wealth. This national egoism destroys the community, which becomes to its members a mere instrument for their own selfish purposes, to be discarded as soon as its services are not needed. "Patriotism is not enough," said Edith Cavell. Pius XI repeats it. And how often patriotism itself is only a cloak for nationalist egoism! How often are crimes that everyone abhors easily committed and excused, or even praised, if they serve the nation! But justice and charity draw life only from religion. Thus Pius XI concludes that the final cause of the unpeaceful condition of the world is the general and practical emancipation of politics, of economics, and of international life from the law of God. "Where God and Christ are banned from the laws and from political life . . . where the laws of Christian morality are despised, we must not wonder . . . that this war has not destroyed hatred, force, or revenge, but has actually increased it."

A definite conversion from an exaggerated esteem of economic, secular, material goods to a true esteem of spiritual goods is a *conditio sine qua non* for a lasting peace: for the restoration of the right balance between the material goods by which we live bodily and the spiritual goods by which we live humanly, for a revival of the right hierarchy of values in which the material goods are subservient as means to the spiritual goods as ends. Deliverance from the tyranny of money and of material success as the only measure of human value or of moral value, and the direction of our lives toward the virtues of justice, honesty, and charity, in short, the moral and intellectual perfection of man as the image of God, are the only things that can form the homogeneity of a new state of peace in which all is justly and perfectly ordered.

But this effort presupposes that, in the hierarchy of human values, religion, so long excluded from public life, so long made a private affair of the inner man without much bearing on public life, on economics, on education, on politics, or on international life, shall be restored to its supreme place. Too often religion, the eternal truth and the nursery of the social virtues, has been judged purely from a utilitarian standpoint. Religion, it has been said, is of good service for success in life, for social respectability, for tranquillity in society; religion is a good servant in the preservation of the economic order as it is, irrespective of its justice; religion, mistakenly understood, gives those in political and economic power an additional security for the maintenance of the social *status quo*. And it is a therapeutical means of recreation at week ends from the hard work of the materialist struggle for success on workdays.

Of course, this is the basest conception of religion, valuing it by its service for material goods. The restoration of religion requires its liberation from this position of handmaid and then its restoration to supreme rank by the subordination of material happiness, of family life, of political and international life, under the eternal law of justice and charity that are nourished by the spirit of religion for its own sake. Our era must go through the same development as many converts from materialism to religion have gone through. They first thought of religion as the enemy of civilization; then they reflected that perhaps religion might be useful as a subordinate aid to civilization; eventually they came to the conviction that religion is the very soul and end of civilization.

According to Pius XI, the right and competence of the Church as the mightiest force for international peace arises from the fact that the Church alone has never floundered in its doctrine that all human activity in private life and in economic and political life is subject to the rules of the universal law of justice and charity. He further notes that the Church alone has never indulged in that unwholesome separation of private morality from political morality, of ethics from politics. The universal law applies to everyone as man, whether private individual or public authority, economic man or diplomat. Only if the states accept the doctrines of Christ as the inviolable rule for their internal and external affairs, can they enjoy peace and meet one another in such mutual trust that a peaceful settlement of their differences is possible.

However the citizens may be separated in their religious affiliations, however strong or weak may be their longings for a final reconciliation in faith, for their return to the Church universal, they may agree with St. Augustine's words addressed to the Church: "Thou art it that befriendeth the citizen to the citizen, the nation to the nation, and that uniteth in the memory of their common origin all men, not only into one society, but into one fraternal community." [12] Furthermore, they can agree that these demands are actually the standards and measures for all actual attempts at a lasting peace; that these demands form the unconditional framework in which alone in concrete form we will find a positive working peace order.

VIII. ECONOMIC INTERDEPENDENCE

Nobody will deny that much of the content of international life deals with economic intercourse. Nobody will reject the truth that, through modern means of transportation, the growth of economic interdependence and the shrinking of distances bring nations nearer together than ever before. Nor will there be any objection to the statement that hence arises a moral obligation for men and nations to promote economic international cooperation as the best means of affording a better, broader, and more secure material basis for the spiritual life.

Yet we must guard against a fallacy which may be hidden in the argument that the growth of economic interdependence and the shrinking of space are sufficient to produce a greater spiritual coherence and a profounder moral unity; or that technological progress in the production of more and destructive armaments makes war less and less a paying proposition.

Yet, after all, wars are conducted in a certain social, economic, and political system with the means which such a system offers. Some generals, such as Von Seekt and De Gaulle, from the fact of technological progress derived the idea of a small professional attacking army made up of highly specialized military mechanics. This technological progress might even give rise to the idea that a small air force, loyal to a general with dictatorial ambitions, could easily subject a peaceful democracy. Furthermore, in many nations the officer corps, if sociologically well established and able to unite with some other minority

[12] Quoted by Yves de la Brière, *op. cit.*, I, p. 48.

groups which have considerable economic power, may easily over-throw popular and representative government. By thus conquering the extended state apparatus—extended because of a high degree of social and economic integration in modern society—such a small group could easily indulge in aggressive militarism by harnessing the economic life to war industry and thus approximate self-sufficiency. Such attempts of militarist control of the extended modern state apparatus have occurred, as is well known, in many countries and were successful in some of them. Very often democratic and peace-loving nations, influenced by business interests dealing with such militarist controlled nations, helped to solidify the rule of the officer corps by continuing economic intercourse with these nations. And thus they indirectly financed the militarist program and helped to establish a war economy in spite of the growth of world-wide economic integration. Neither this growth of economic integration nor technological progress nor the terrible increase of destructiveness in weapons is thus itself a protection against war.

The growth of economic interdependence is not by itself a protection against war nor does it represent prohibitive costs for war-minded people. When we look at our modern economic society we find there, on account of a high degree of division of labor, an equally high functional integration. For a simple railroad journey, a multitude of individuals must be minutely integrated in their services in order that the passenger may expect to arrive on time and without accident. For our diversified demands for a myriad of goods and services, we must rely on the coordinated efforts of farmers, miners, transport workers, producers, wholesalers and retailers. Thus the economic interdependence in our industrial society is greater than at any other time. Yet in almost no other society were there so many social tensions, so many deep political cleavages as in our society.[18]

18 Leo XIII, Pius XI, and Pius XII have spoken of these facts again and again. Cf. Pius XII, *Christmas Eve Allocution*, 1943. There are those "who placed all their faith in a world expansion of economic life, thinking that this alone would suffice to draw the people together in a spirit of brotherhood. . . . With what complacency and pride did they not contemplate a world growth of commerce, the interchange between continents of all goods and inventions and products, the triumphal march of widely diffused modern technical perfection, overcoming all limits of time and space! What is the reality that they behold today? They see now that this economic life with all its gigantic contracts and wide ramifications, with its superabundance, division, and multiplication of labor, has contributed in a thousand ways to generalize and accentuate the crisis of mankind;

Considering this fact, we are almost tempted to say that the danger to moral and political unity increases with the growth of social and economic interdependence. If thus in the internal life of states the economic integration by itself is unable to produce a morally and politically strong spirit of unity but must concede that this spirit of unity is the product of additional moral, national, and traditional factors of political integration, then with even greater probability we must expect the same for the international community. The growth of economic interdependence may thus imply a moral obligation for more intimate political cooperation and may even represent a strong material motive for it. But that is all it can do.

The reason for this modern reliance on merely economic interdependence and for shrinking of distances as motives potent enough to produce a general preference for peace and a revulsion against war as economically disruptive, is the rationalism of the *homo economicus* and the contention that economic reasons carry an outspokenly strong rational element. Against this rationalism all appeals to politics, to the national mysticism, to the irrationalities of tradition or of Messianic dreams of the proletariat, are considered invalid. Yet history, until now at least, is full of records that peoples or groups dominating peoples have acted so irrationally; they have voluntarily or under the pressure of the power apparatus of the modern state together with nationalist propaganda preferred guns to butter, the socialist future to a present rise of the living standard, national autarchy and consequently a free hand in power politics to a greater satisfaction of economic wants by dependence on a world economy. However strong this rationalism of the economic factors, however strong the motives of economic interdependence may be in international life, it remains doubtful if these factors and motives are by themselves decisive enough. Evidently the unifying moral and religious ideals, the ideas of justice and charity, of liberality and fraternity (and their opposites) are even more important.

The arguments of Benjamin Constant or of Herbert Spencer and their philosophy of history as infinite progress are fallacious as we may see from any comparison of Constant's treatise, *The Spirit of*

---

while, not having the corrective of any moral control or any guiding light from beyond this world, it could not but end in the unworthy and humiliating exploitation of the nature and personality of man."

Conquest (1814), with history since that year. Constant's thesis—
and Spencer's is the same—is that the era of commerce and industry
following the era of wars and political conquest in a feudalist society
prone to political exploitation of the subjected peoples or classes,
makes war superfluous. The economic era obtains a better and more
complete satisfaction of wants through peaceful industrial production
and economic exchange than could be obtained by war, i.e., by political robbery of the vanquished. Consequently war no longer pays.
Furthermore, the technological progress, especially the artillery (as
a modern weapon introduced by Napoleon), has robbed warfare of all
those motives which made it attractive in earlier times, such as personal
heroism, chivalry, adventure. Constant argues that, on account of the
economic uselessness of war and the disenchantment of warfare, any
inclination for war will disappear, and economic intercourse, along
with economic civilized and rational calculation, will inexorably
produce an era of international peace. Yet the irrational powers of
nationalist aggrandizement and the notion of a chosen people's imperialist destiny have proved stronger than that civilized economic
rationalism.

The growth of economic interdependence, the progress of the technological destructiveness of armaments, and the reduction of distances through modern means of transportation, are not automatically
factors for peace, as the aging Spencer felt so vividly. The history of
the last century shows that the moral and religious ideas and the
political virtues are still the primary factors in establishing peace. It
shows also that the economic interdependence, as means for a more
perfect life, can and ought to be the factual basis and a strong motive
for the moral obligations of nations to use this economic interdependence for restrictions of national sovereignty. There should follow
a development of international political and juridical institutions to
preserve peace and establish justice in a changing world, institutions
that would be more powerful for this purpose than was the era of
commerce and industry with its appeal to economic rationalist calculation.[14]

[14] Cf. Pius XI, *Ubi Arcano.*

CHAPTER XXXII

The Basis of International Peace

I. LEGALITY AND LEGITIMACY

IN THE preceding pages, we did not lay stress on juridical institutions, such as a world court. Rather we discussed the universal law of morality, of justice and charity.

We did this in order to give a basis for the discussion of some problems connected with an overconfident faith in the efficiency of certain new or old international institutions deemed able to preserve peace in international life without hallowing the current international *status quo*. For we must be clear about this: the real peace problem is to change the juridical *status quo* embodied in international treaties without appeal to war. In the internal life of the state we have a similar problem.

The constitutional order, as does any juridical order, distributes competencies, liberties, and wealth, distributes competencies of individual and group initiative in the social and economic field and thus distributes social and economic power and, indirectly, political power among the citizenry. The *status quo* distribution now may become unjust though it still remains legal in the framework of the constitution. The dissatisfied citizen begins to speak about unjustified privileges, abuses of power, and arbitrariness as opposed to reason, the injustices of vested interests, and contends that the common good is raided for private interests. If such a criticism reaches large masses, then a juridical dilemma appears: the contradiction between the formal legality of the criticized privileges in the concrete order and the legitimacy and moral justice of the concrete order as a systematic whole, the contradiction between the idea, the ideals of the constitution, and the social reality.

The first stage of this struggle may be a still peaceful struggle with the available legal instruments that range in difference, of course, from a monarchical constitution with a bill of rights to a change in party control in a democratic constitution. A democratic constitution affords the greatest chance for a peaceful and gradual change of the constitutional order of power distribution; the revolutions consequently take place peacefully, since the political homogeneity, the national unity, in a democracy are usually strong enough to avoid an active class struggle or party strife, i.e., a civil war that destroys the political unity of the citizens, and in a sanguinary revolution establishes a new order.

But the peaceful change implies that this unity, which is the moral agreement about the basic idea and the common ideals, is paramount and that the allegiance to the political unity is supreme and subjects to itself the allegiance to the party or class. If that is not the case, then the necessary or desired change of the internal order will be attempted by active revolution with the threat of civil war. The defensive party stresses the legality of the *status quo* and calls the opponents rebels. The aggressive party stresses the natural justice of its demands and rejects, not the formal legality of the attacked *status quo*, but its legitimacy, on the basis of the idea or the meaning of the constitution.

The reason for this split between legality and legitimacy, positive law and natural justice, lies in social life itself. The continuous changes in economic life, in social mores, the rise of new classes and new collective interests never foreseen by the framers of the *status quo*, the rise of new social ideals or ideologies with powerful mass-appeal, the demoralization of the ruling classes by loss of confidence in the righteousness of their legal position, all such manifold factors continually change the material presuppositions of the legal *status quo*. For law, in the sense of positive legal order, is in its true meaning a form of that matter which we may, for simplicity's sake, call the economic and spiritual life of a people; a form contingent and concrete, without the presumption of being perennially just though intended as durable.

It is, of course, true that the order itself, especially in a democracy, contains legal institutions like the amending power by majority of the representatives of the people or by the people itself in plebiscite, or even by the slow process of juridical adaptation of the order to the new demands by a highly esteemed judiciary or by a change in party control of the legislature. But even in a democracy the groups, the one defending the *status quo*, the other demanding a radical change, may resort to the use of arms, i.e., to civil war. It is the particular political prudence of the statesman or of the ruling class to anticipate such revolutionary situations by peaceful reform of the social order. It is the merit of democracy that, through freedom of speech, of the press, and of association, it has an opportunity to detect early these discrepancies between the legal form and the social matter before so much political distrust, mass anger, and economic despair have accumulated that an armed conflict is inevitable, since the moral will to live together has already been relinquished in favor of the attempt to subjugate the opposition.

It is not much different in the international order as concretely fixed in positive treaties, agreements, and covenants. It, too, is an order for the distribution of economic and political power, of the liberties and competencies of the individual member state. One fine distinction, however, exists. The material presupposition, the communal life of the legal order as the form, contains far fewer unifying elements than the nation-state contains, and, in addition, these elements are less intense. The difference between a Yankee and a Southerner is much less than that between a Mexican and an inhabitant of India. Of course the latter need less homogeneity, because their living together is less intense. But the point is that the stark difference of their ways of life, their mores and traditions, their religions, narrows down so greatly the basis for communal action that in few matters will they be able to agree. Their first interest will remain self-preservation and self-determination.

This presents the first difficulty in the paramount task of the preservation of peace, i.e., a peaceful change of the *status quo*, which is no less necessary than in the internal order, since nations and states are subject to changes just as much as are classes and groups inside the nation. Old and powerful nations, having set up in treaties an international legal *status quo* corresponding to their actual power, may lose that power by their inability to follow new economic trends, by a declining birthrate, by a lack of a high industrial potential for war, or by the discovery of new ways of international traffic which may raise to power younger nations with antagonistic interests. To try to preserve the *status quo* or the security legally embodied in the treaties and covenants, means to provoke war, not to avoid it. Yet in the case of nations once powerful but now proud and ambitious beyond their actual power, the surrender of their legal position in the *status quo* is harder than it is for the ruling groups within the nations. The reason for this is that a superior allegiance to a more comprehensive body of which the nation is a member is not strong enough to counterbalance the hallowed allegiance to the country. This is to say that patriotism is likely to be stronger than the love for mankind. And this is merely the complement of the fact that beyond the national sphere the international homogeneity as a formative factor is indubitably weaker. Even the common Christian faith, even Christendom in the Middle Ages, though far more powerful than its weak substitute of today, the humanitarian world brotherhood of secular origin, did not constitute a moral homogeneity intense enough to avoid all warfare.

II. Legal International Institutions

The first requirement for a durable peace is thus a greater moral homogeneity, a common acceptance of the living principles of natural law strengthened by the consciousness of common brotherhood through a common sonship of one God and Father. Patriotism is not enough unless it is completed and balanced by such a moral bond of homogeneity. For only then will the nations interested in the preservation of the *status quo* and the nations with a just demand for its change and reform both be able to reach a genuine compromise, a new and just *status quo*, without recourse to armed power. The compromise will be effected by a degree of sacrifice of legal rights on the one hand, and a scaling down of impetuous and ambitious demands on the other. An inevitable precondition is, of course, the preservation of the objective vital interests and honor of the participants because the meaning of law as a *unitas ordinis* is itself destroyed if one of the constituents of the community should, through the establishment of the new *status quo*, be compelled to sacrifice vital interests or honor. A nation cannot sacrifice itself, it cannot be asked to give up its existence for the benefit of another nation or even the majority of nations. A nation may voluntarily give up its independent political existence to join another nation in a new federated political existence for a more perfect life. But then it does so in its own interest, not exclusively in the interest of world peace.

These considerations afford a critical basis from which to judge realistically many theories and proposals which pretend to establish collective security without perpetuating the presently existing international *status quo* and which try to institute legal machinery for the peaceful settlement of international disputes.

Such theories and proposals concern ideas about the abolition of national sovereignty and the formation of a world state or at least world government, of a new federation of comprehensive or only regional character, of a world court vested with supreme power to settle all disputes and having at its disposal as an enforcing power an international police force. Practically all of the many proposals contain utopian elements and are based, at least partly, on an illusory concept of law and society. If not divested of these utopian elements, they are a danger to world peace. They arouse people in times of war to great hopes in their intrinsic yet abstract perfection and lead to an optimistic belief that, once such legal machinery is instituted, it will work automatically, without the catalyst of personal or communal authority and moral responsibility, so that each nation can then return to its internal policy without bothering about a foreign policy, i.e., power politics, and individual responsibility for peace.

The underlying illusion is that legal institutions are a full substitute for power. Or, what means the same thing, the thesis that power itself is evil, and the Rousseauist assertion that if there exist perfect institutions then all will be well since the people are good and any form of evil must spring simply from imperfect or corrupt institutions. Thus it is enough to set up such perfect institutions and then automatically a good and just order will continuously produce itself. Neglected is the problem that perfect institutions may not work because the persons who administer them neglect their duties and abuse their authority in contradiction to the very essence and meaning of the institutions. Forgotten is the fact that legal institutions themselves can be made the object of the non-legal power struggle. Who does not know that in a nation the courts or the judges themselves are subject to the power strife, showing itself in the public propaganda of contradictory social ideals? We must acknowledge that often their authoritative decisions are influenced by such propaganda. Then they "interpret" the law or even bend it in the interest of one of the struggling power groups, led by expediency or by their solidarist interest with one of the groups.

Impartial justice often is not the decisive factor, as any history of the judiciary struggle against the labor movement will show.

The legal institutions do not carry in themselves such a power monopoly as this theory ascribes to them. What gives these institutions power is the moral confidence of the people, the vivid moral responsibility, the common moral convictions, and the specific impartial service for the common good; in other words, that strong moral homogeneity which is more the presupposition of the success of these institutions than their product. This, then, is a new proof that peace depends on inner moral will more than on external institutional organization. Furthermore, power (the ability to compel others to at least external obedience or conformity to one's demands by being able to inflict major disadvantages for nonconformity) is not in itself evil. What is wrong is the arbitrary and unreasonable, the unjust and immoral use of power for objectively wrong ends or for purposes contradictory to the self-interest and the dignity of those subject to the use of power. Conformity by obedience to power without the more laborious process of conformity by persuasion and free consent is in political, social, and economic life more often necessary than not; power is as original a social fact as is law itself. Nay, law is direction and sanction of power but not its substitute.

It may well be that all this diffidence about power, power politics, and so on, stems from a particular animosity against political power as distinguished from social and economic power. Classic liberalism depreciated political power and tried hard to abolish it in the political sphere. This it attempted by reducing the idea of the state to a mere system of legal norms, by stressing the judiciary supremacy in constitutional law by its anti-authoritarian demand for government only by free consent, by its identification of rulers and ruled in contradiction to Disraeli's saying, that a people is governed either by tradition or by compulsion. Yet economic and non-moral power in the politically free economic sphere of society and thence in the political sphere, was never so shamelessly used as in the era of *laissez faire* capitalism; the workers significantly called themselves, not without a grain of truth, wage-slaves. The competitive struggle of finance, industry, and agriculture, of big business against small business: all that is power struggle and internal power politics.

Who is blind to the fact that, behind the visible legal institutions and government, there raged and still rages a reckless power struggle of collective interests before which the individual is almost powerless? Who can fail to sense the unequal struggle heavily weighted in favor of economic corporate power, political party bosses, and labor czars? The large modern economic and social groups (giant industrial mergers, big labor unions, manufacturers' associations, big agricultural organizations) and the vested interests of their managerial bureaucracies, have tremendous social and economic power, and consequently indirect political power. In fact, today this power is so enormous that the individual needs the protection of the state against these powers. Thus in countries where industrial cartels have come to power, it became necessary to introduce legislation against the abuse of the economic power of cartels or against the formation of trusts. Officers of labor unions can, under special conditions, rise to such heights of power over the jobs, the only basis of existence for the propertyless worker, that the union member and the small businessman are wholly unprotected against the abuse of such power. Therefore they appeal to the state's intervention for protection of their individual rights. Herbert Spencer's formula, "Man versus the State," thus becomes, Member versus the power of the managers of the great groups. The state is called in for protection and for the establishment of a bill of rights against such power. The power element, it seems, cannot be eliminated; it cannot be replaced by law if the latter is not itself made a superior power to bend and direct social and economic private powers.

That such power politics, this foreign policy of groups inside the state and for the control of its institutions, does not lead to open civil and class war, is owing to the fact that all the groups are still interested in national unity; that they do not follow the pluralist theory but shrink from the rupture of national unity, which is considered supreme. And this it is that makes the legal institutions work more or less efficiently, this will, durable and supreme, to live together in national solidarity. This will is decisive for the function of the legal institutions, which do not establish national unity, but testify to it, support it, and make it endure.

III. Utopian Elements in Foreign Policy

Thus law and legal institutions in internal national life are not a substitute for power, in itself supposedly evil, but are directive of power struggles, tamed by the common will to unity. In the less intense, less solidary international community, we cannot expect law and legal institutions to become a substitute for power and power politics. A solidarity similar to the national solidarity cannot be expected to arise easily. Not only national interests but regional interests differ far more than the interests of labor and capital inside a nation. Consequently the basis for a world state, or even for a working supreme world government, in the legal cloak of a world federation abolishing the sovereignty of the member states, seems too narrow. Apart from the difficult conciliation between the supreme power of such a world government and the principles of liberty, independence, and self-determination of the federated states, the idea of a world federation suffers from another shortcoming. That is the Rousseauist theory that, if we discard all particular and group-interests in a community and establish liberty and equality for each member, then the will of all transforms itself without the intervention of a concrete authority into the general will of the new community, a general will that cannot err. This theory supposes further that the public opinion of the world, or at least of the majority of the states, is always right.

None of these assertions is realistic. First, there does not exist at the foundation that solidarity of interests. Moreover, we cannot do away with *de facto* or *de jure* alliances in international life, or with particular interests (e.g., the Monroe Doctrine or the British Commonwealth of Nations). Nor is it possible to disregard the fact that there exist great powers and small powers, nation-states with a population of 100,000,000, with immense natural resources, practically self-sufficient, and with a formidable potential of war, and nations with a million inhabitants and economic dependence upon other nations. With or without a world government, there is little danger that war will break out between small nations if the great powers or a group of them (the others being disinterested) do not so wish. On the other hand, with or without world government, if a grave clash of interests should arise between the great powers directly or between smaller states where one or more of the great powers think their vital interests are affected and no compromise proves acceptable, there will be war though it may be called differently. If the world federation exists, such a conflict may be called secession or civil war. With the rupture of solidary interests among the great powers, the organization that rests upon the reality of solidarity breaks up, too.

As long as the great powers, fully aware of their indivisible responsibility for peace and justice even against some secondary selfish interests of their own, act together in solidarity, the law can be enforced. But let us note that in the international community there does not exist, as distinguished from the great powers themselves, a *potestas* that can enforce the law as it is enforced by the police within the nation-state. The impartial enforcement of the law in the internal national order is made possible by setting apart an organization, the police force, whose only function under the law is the enforcement of the law. The international community could, of course, entrust one power or a group of powers with the enforcement of law. But such a power or group of powers would lack that functional impartiality of an internal police power. Especially in the crucial cases, it would be in a real or imaginary collision of duties between self-interest and sacrifice of material wealth and blood for the international order. Thus it would preserve for itself the discretionary right to decide when to enforce the law; that is, it would become the real sovereign and it would be quickly accused of imperialism. Thus only a real concert of great powers could guarantee the enforcement of law.

But will not an international police force avoid such a situation? That can scarcely be expected. An international police force is nothing more than an organization of national contingents, the greatest of which will derive from the great powers, because equality of contingents is too unbearable a burden for small nations. These contingents would owe allegiance to the world government—and to their native states. In a grave conflict between the great powers, which are the actual rulers and leaders in the federated world government, the federation itself would break up, the conflict of allegiance would rend asunder the leaders and men of the international police force and transform a police action into a war of secession or a civil war.

IV. Power and Moral Responsibility

There is no possible evasion of the general principle that power and wealth are the measure of public responsibility for the common weal. As long as the great powers, in accordance with the moral will to justice and in accordance with the acceptance of the duties of liberality and natural equity, take over the responsibility to preserve peace and to compromise in conflicts of interest, a responsibility which Providence has laid on their shoulders, just so long shall we have peace. As long as the great powers accept the moral duty of changing an unjust *status quo* even if it means sacrifice to them, just so long will there be peace. A formulation of these moral duties in legal machinery, in international institutions of conciliation and arbitration, will indeed facilitate the exercise of these responsibilites and moral dutes, will promote common uniting interests against dissolving particular interests, will be able to crystallize an international public opinion that makes the individual citizen aware of his double allegiance to the national and international common good.

Yes, legal institutions may well do all this, if the first and basic presuppositions are realized. If they are not realized, the legal institutions which have in themselves no supreme authority and which work only by the intervention of the moral will of persons or groups of persons, will collapse just as surely as did the League of Nations as soon as the great states became divided into *status quo* powers and revisionist powers and when one of the latter, Italy, defied the League. That is, the *status quo* group which, disunited as it was, did not fully apply the economic sanctions of the Covenant (Italy declaring an oil embargo a *casus belli*), would not risk military sanctions in order to save something of the League. The League could not be saved after the unpunished conquest of one of its small members (Ethopia) and the disunity of the great powers.

There are no automatic legal institutions which by their formal perfection realize justice. Through each such institution it is the moral will of the persons that transforms, as moral authority, an abstract demand of justice into concrete realization here and now. In each decision regarding a concrete case of law, two elements are comprised: one is the rule of law, technical and formal, and the evaluation of the concrete facts of the case under the general rule, a rather logical procedure. The other is the moral acceptance by the people or the society which lives under that rule and by the functionaries of the legal institutions of the moral ideas and the moral order which have been vested in the legal forms. Where there exists a great moral and cultural unity and homogeneity, naturally the intrinsic justice of the order as a whole is seldom consciously taken into consideration; it is simply implied.

But it happens also that not so much the mere legality of a decision and of the law applied is in doubt as the legitimacy of the concrete legal order. In other words, the positive law and the demand for intrinsic justice are no longer considered identical; the legal order is condemned as unjust. This may happen on account of the rise of a new class internally or on account of the decay of one great power and the rise of a smaller nation to the standards of a great power; or a colony, a backward country, rises to the standards of a "civilized" nation; or a new idea like national self-determination spreads over a whole continent still organized according to the principle of historical monarchic legitimacy; or new economic developments make the retention of full sovereignty of smaller nations over their economic life a disservice to their own and to the international common good. In all these cases the existing legal order itself is attacked with the demand for a new order. A kind of tragic dilemma develops easily: the one party claiming the principle, *pacta sunt servanda;* the other asking for a change of these very pacts which constitute the concrete legal order because they have become unjust, because the vital circumstances have fundamentally changed. It is quite clear that now the problem is one of natural justice and of equity, and that the only admissible solution is a genuine moral compromise by mutual consent, or a case for arbitration by a commonly acknowledged higher moral authority. This authority, weighing all circumstances, may propose a compromise and not a perfectly just decision, because it has to take into consideration the relative power, the relatively just demands, and the chances of acceptance of the arbitration decision.

Since the French Revolution two political principles have been in dispute: the principle of democratic national self-determination and the principle of historical monarchic legitimacy. In Italy these principles clashed in the Papal States. Italian national unity, democratic and secular, could be fully attained only by the destruction of the

historical rights of the papacy to its states. Under the Catholic Risorgi-
mento a genuine compromise would perhaps have been possible;
under the ideology of Mazzini and Cavour, on the other hand, a
compromise was impossible; the consequence was war. When, as in
the past, international communism as a principle of international
organization is opposed to national capitalisms of bourgeoisies, we
have again an antagonism of principle which may admit of political
compromise but not of a legal decision according to some abstract
rule, because such a commonly accepted rule is absent in the face of
such a mutually exclusive antagonism of principles. It follows that
law can supersede power only in so far as the litigants have accepted
a universal law binding upon both and upon their dispute. Therefore the unconditional presupposition of international peace is not
legal institutions, but rather the acceptance of a universal moral law
and mutual charity, as the popes have again and again repeated. If
that presuposition exists, then and only then are the legal institutions
of any value. Otherwise they themselves become mere instruments of
power politics.

Cardinal Newman, in his *Letter to the Duke of Norfolk* (p. 220),
relates Pius IX's declaration about the pope's power to release subjects from the obligation of loyalty and to depose sovereigns. Pius IX
asserted that such a right had undoubtedly been exercised in special
circumstances. But this right was exercised in the ages of faith when
the pope was considered the supreme judge of a united Christendom
and when the advantages of this office were recognized by the peoples
and the sovereigns; when, further, this right of the pope was acknowledged by public law and by the common consent as a duty to be
exercised in the most important interest of states and their rulers.
Newman points out the limits of the exercise of this right: the ages
of faith (the moral unity and homogeneity of the *orbis christianus*)
and the consequent ability of this community to enforce the right
by the common consent of a united Christian people, one in faith.

This common consent, this concert, is usually taken for granted.
But it becomes a problem if the moral homogeneity and unity of the
people concerning the moral ideas, and the self-consciousness of its
distinct existence through which it is integrated to a political unity,
are questioned, and a contradiction is felt between the eternal idea
of justice and its imperfect unjust realization in the concrete condi-

tions of existence. So we come to the conclusion that the consciences of persons, moral ideas and natural law comprehended by persons, are the transformer which realizes the abstract legal rule and gives vigor and validity to the legal institutions. And moral ideas, the consciences of persons, are the more important the less in a given society unity and homogeneity are definite, strong, and ordinarily unquestioned.

Since armed conflict is not a regular, normal, social institution and since its causes are often irrational and complex (really abnormal), legal institutions to avoid war must rest even more than others on moral ideas, with appeal to conscience. "State and Church in their demand of positive acceptance of their authority have no more profound and more original power to which they can appeal than that moral conscience innate in human nature." [1] Politics, concerned predominantly with the preservation of the moral will to live together peacefully and to produce *and change* the legal institutions through which normally the minima of rights and duties of the individual members of a society are protected and enforced, is thus so much a matter of ethics, that it cannot be simply replaced by positive law.

Positive law is rather the external visible element which rests upon the invisible moral ideas—foundations are always invisible—and upon the steady common will of a people to produce a more perfect life in living together. In this sense all forms of government, except tyranny, rest in fact upon a consent of the people. This consent is a moral and legal duty of the people in the interest of the common good. And this consent is an explicit or implied acceptance of moral values to be realized by the state in the order of law and, if compulsion against dissent is deemed necessary in the interest of the common good, to be enforced by legitimate power.

From this it follows that, as long as a plurality of states lives in an order of coordination on the basis of independence, self-determination, and integrity of the members, foreign policy cannot be abolished in favor of abstractly perfect legal institutions through which, so to speak, automatically the will of all is transformed mysteriously into the general will, implicitly just and infallibly true in the concrete case. "In reality the international life continues to rest on the good

1 Cf. Joseph Mausbach, *System der christlich katholischen Ethik,* 1913, p. 91. Cf. St. Robert Bellarmine: *De Rom. Pont.* IV, 20.

will of the nations to cooperate, to arrange themselves, to settle disputes through a willing understanding of the interests and mentality of the other party, assisted, if necessary, by the mediative and conciliatory efforts of third powers. The peace depends on moral factors, not on strictly formulated legal rules and on sanctions provided in advance." Thus Erich Kaufmann concludes a comprehensive and penetrating study of collective security under the League of Nations.

Collective security embodied in the network of international treaties between two or more states on account of their common interests can work only as long as these treaties correspond to the vital interests and to the moral ideas and rules under which the states actually agree to live. If the vital interests change, if a dispute arises about the application of a moral idea to a concrete case implying evidently the contention that the treaties have become oppressive or, as the Covenant said, "inapplicable" (Art. 19), then a moral conflict will ensue. Collective security itself becomes the object of dispute, the revisionist powers asserting that only a change of the treaties can establish security, and the *status quo* powers complaining that the demand for revision is aggression against the *beati possidentes*.

Thus the problem of preserving peace amounts to this: to change peacefully the positive order of treaties, the *status quo*. And it is here that the acceptance of the moral ideas of justice, liberality, and charity must prevail and that the legal institutions like a court of arbitration or a world court or a Council of a League of Nations with strictly formulated competencies, are of minor importance, because they cannot work if the real presupposition of their efficiency (the unity in moral ideas and the consciousness of a common good) is actually questioned. In other words, when the question at issue is not the legality of actions and situations under the concrete order of treaties, but the legitimacy and the justice of that concrete order and its actual distribution of power, wealth, influence, competency of leadership. For example, the international system of the Holy Alliance rested on the historical, traditional rights of the princes and the integrity of their territories, not upon the assent of various national groups of their peoples. The defenders of the principle of democratic national self-determination implicitly attacked the actual international system of the Holy Alliance since their principle of legitimacy had to lead to the dissolution of monarchies ruling over different nationalities.

Such a dispute about principles of legitimacy is internally solved by revolutions, more or less sanguinary but still by violence, and in the international scene by wars, unless through mutual understanding and a generous and genuine compromise the doctrinaire rigidity of opposing principles is bent and the *status quo* is changed. But legal institutions like a supreme court for constitutional law cannot decide about the legitimacy of the Constitution of which it is itself a creation, but only about the legality of an act of the legislature under the Constitution. Consequently when the latter as the legal order, instituted by the political decision of the nation and expressing its perpetual will to live under this constitutional order, is itself at stake, then a supreme court is eliminated, as the experience of the United States before the outbreak of the Civil War proves. Positive law and legal institutions have their intrinsic limitations.

V. A WORLD STATE

We have now a basis for a reserved judgment about so many proffered proposals to preserve peace by the introduction of a world state or a world government after the abolition of national sovereignty, or by the introduction of an international court with the competency to decide on all international disputes and, because of its control over an international police force, with the power to enforce its decisions.

Many people think that the abolition of national sovereignty and the transfer of the competencies which it contains to an international authority, whether that is world state, world government or world court, would result in perpetual peace. These people do not mean sovereignty with all its implications, for at the same time they staunchly uphold national self-determination, liberty, and independence of nations. What they mean is this one competency of sovereignty, namely, to decide what *in concreto* is a case of just war; in other words, the right of sovereign nations to decide about the right to make war. And it is this right, according to this opinion, which the independent nations ought to transfer to an international authority. Little doubt exists that in all international disputes of minor importance such a transfer of this part of sovereignty would be possible. But should the dispute involve what a nation deems its vital interests, its existential security, its independence and liberty, and should an alert nation be aware of it, we may well doubt that it will let any authority but itself decide. If that nation should be a great power, it would secede from the legal international unity, the supreme organ of which is that international authority. It would risk sanctions, economic and financial and eventually military sanctions, i.e., war. A small nation (e.g., Czechoslovakia) may of course have to yield in such a case. But if, as is likely in such cases, some other nations are unconvinced of the justice of such a decision and are not impressed merely by its political expediency for peace in our time, then the international institution loses its moral authority and thus its *raison d'être.*

So we come to the conclusion that, however much we may be able to limit the right to wage war, to subject the appeal to it to the various processes of conciliation, mediation, and arbitration, or to the final judgment of a world court, there remains a residue of sovereignty coincident with the meaning of national liberty and independence and self-determination where at least a great power preserves this right of war for itself. The framers of the League of Nations, less utopian than those of the Kellog Pact, knew about this and consequently did not exclude war, as we have pointed out. Therefore, when such a situation arises where great nations are honestly convinced that their vital interests are involved, they may come to a peaceful political compromise through political prudence and moral motives. Yet they will never subject the decision over what they think to be their vital interests to an international tribunal, the decision of which would in such a case not be a mere legal decision.

On the contrary, the court would have to form its decision under considerations of political prudence and expediency, i.e., extra-legal considerations of power relations, of what may reasonably be expected to be acceptable to both parties, implying of course that ultimately the decision rests with the sovereign parties involved. As soon as we lay the concept of sovereignty aside and enter practical questions, we see that the attacks against sovereignty are often futile. The attackers of sovereignty accept, for instance, the principle of national self-determination, of liberty and independence. By these terms they mean what may be called internal sovereignty, and they attack only external sovereignty. But in reality these two sovereignties are one.

Many acts of internal sovereignty have direct repercussions in international life. A change in government from democratic to autocratic, Fascist, or communist form is not without effects upon neighboring nations. Changes in immigration and naturalization policy, in social legislation or trade policy, all of which may be considered domestic affairs, influence international life. Would the United States allow an international authority to decide what kind of immigrants it must accept? Would not the nation insist on deciding this problem upon its own opinion about the immigrants being readily assimilated? If a change in monetary policy is considered in the interest of the national common good, would any great power—small powers have usually no independent monetary policy—submit the question to the final decision of an international authority? In such cases the methods of political negotiation and of political compromise by attempts at reconciling national interest and international common good through mutual understanding, through acceptance of moral duties that defy strict legal formulation, will be the appropriate form. A world court may act as legal adviser, but not as deciding sovereign.

What can be meant by some form of world government? Obviously a representative legislative body and a senate representing the states, an executive power and a supreme court according to a federal constitution uniting sovereign states and dividing competencies between states and world government. On paper such a world government has a fine appearance. In reality its difficulties and the likelihood of its collapse are greater than those of the much maligned Concert of Great Powers in nineteenth-century Europe. As soon as an issue which some states consider of vital interest for themselves should be decided against them by even a qualified majority, they would secede. And any legislation would be the result of power politics by pressure groups of states highly organized and efficient. Since power is a fact of life resisting nice legalities, such a world government can function only so long as the great powers are willing to cooperate; if they refuse to do so, then the world government collapses just as the League did. In other words, these schemes will not work at that crucial moment when they should prove their right to existence. They can work in all minor problems for all common interests agreed upon. But so could the League and many other standing international associations like the Universal Telegraphic Union, the General Postal Union, the numerous regulations for railroads, for shipping, for the protection of industrial property, for judicial assistance, the conventions against piracy, against contagious diseases, against the slave trade, against the abuse of opium and alcohol, for international social legislation: in all of these the League worked very satisfactorily.

A world government that would perform what its promoters expect it to perform would have to become a superstate with the right of continuous intervention in the domestic affairs of the member states. But such interventions would be tolerated only if the loyalty of all men to the world government superseded the loyalty to their nations in all decisive cases. And further, such interventions would presuppose that there are no great and small powers in the true sense, a distinction that does not depend on mere numbers. India's teeming 340,000,000 would not be and could not be, even after reaching full independence, a great power equal in influence, leadership, and prestige to France, for instance. We cannot escape the fact that nations exist with their own historical momentum, their particular way of life, their traditions and individuality. It cannot be helped that the individual person, immersed in his nation, bound by innumerable spiritual and material bonds to the political community to which he belongs, is determined more by being a member of a nation and of a particular state than by being a world citizen. As a rule, therefore, the loyalty to the nation and to the state will, in contradiction to pluralist theories, prevail over the loyalty to a world state or government whenever a genuine choice between them has to be made. And this fact will enervate the power of a world government precisely when it needs its power most.

VI. A World Court

Another proposal to preserve peace is the institution of a world court having exclusive competency to decide about international disputes, and endowed with the power to enforce its definitive decisions through an international police force. No doubt many international disputes are of a legal nature and are consequently justiciable. That is, the dispute arises about the existence, interpretation, and application of a rule of international law or of an international treaty, about a fact or act that, if evidenced, would be a violation of an international obligation, about an act of internal sovereignty conflicting with the rights of other states or with international duty. All this presupposes that the legal rule and the rights and duties are legally clear and generally unquestioned. In all such cases a legal procedure is possible. The dispute is justiciable; it is a genuine legal affair open to a court of law and equity. Usually such disputes are not of a kind to endanger peace and security.

But there are certain disputes between nations, and there may arise certain international situations dangerous to world peace, which have not been foreseen by positive law or treaty and consequently are not open to legal procedure. In many arbitration and conciliation treaties, disputes about territorial integrity, political independence, or other vital interests are exempted from the judicial procedure. We have already pointed out that the *clausula rebus sic stantibus* may be appealed to because the letter of the treaty has become obsolete, and its application *hic et nunc* would violate the spirit of the treaty. That is, the treaty has become inapplicable. Such an exception makes the dispute a non-legal issue, a political one. The parties competent to make treaties, i.e., the states, must by mutual agreement come to a new treaty. A court of law could only declare the treaty, or parts of it, either still valid or void, but the court could not make a new treaty that would bind the partners. Therefore a world court could be of value only if the dispute were justiciable. If the court should be empowered to decide the so-called political disputes, the court would itself become the supreme political authority of the world by this extension of its powers to that of supreme legislator. And since by presupposition the dispute is not a legal one, considerations of expediency and political prudence, and the weighing of power relations (instead of the clear, circumscribed rights and duties) would determine the decision, thus stripping it of its juridical character.

Let us suppose that the parties to the dispute accept this decision of the Court. It is still their decision, however conformable to their intrinsic duties as members of the international community, as it was their sovereign decision to submit the dispute to the Court. That is, in such cases the Court has no original jurisdiction but only a delegated one, the competency of which rests upon the decision of the parties to the dispute or upon the decision of all members to submit their disputes to the decision of the Court. But let us suppose that one party does not accept the decision of the Court, of course with the contention that the decision is against "legality," inasmuch as the Court's decision changed certain rights and duties established in solemnly sworn treaties. Here we have the fundamental conflict, already mentioned, between the two legal principles upon which the international order rests: *pacta sunt servanda,* and the *clausula rebus sic stantibus.* One party appeals to the first principle, the other to the second. The one claims an identity of legality and justice in the case, the other a contradiction between legality and justice, demanding of course that the latter prevail. On account of the contingency of human existence, it is possible that both are *bona fide* subjectively. But in the case of the one that refuses to accept the decision, would it not be its duty, in the interest of peace and the legal security of the international order, to accept the decision, which it considers unjust? This would be validly countered by the question: For what purpose does the international order exist? For justice or for the security of the *beati possidentes?*

The problem of *quis judicabit* may still be considered solvable. But what about the thorny problem of who is to enforce the decision against the will of one party? It is easy to say the international police force. Such a force is very likely not a neutral, impartial force headed by a general subject and owing allegiance only to the world court; this force will actually consist of national contingents; consequently the great powers will predominate. In the event that one of the great powers does not accept the decision of the Court, the force will fall apart, and either the decision is not enforced or war results. If the Court, foreseeing this, should formulate its decision according to expediency and prudence, it would lose its authority as a court of law. This difficulty of enforcement is inherent in an order of coordination, which the international order is as long as we desire the liberty, independence, and self-determination of the separate member nations. Therefore the decisions of international authorities, of a world court, of a court of arbitration, of the conciliatory procedure of the Council of a League, must either be voluntarily accepted and executed by the disputing parties or they must be enforced by the members of the international community itself, by the states. Thus we are again in the midst of our problem, namely, that the enforced execution depends upon the acknowledgment of the moral ideas, of the moral duty to the international common good.[2] This moral responsibility, especially of the great powers, is the ultimate basis of world peace, because on it rests the realization of actual justice and of peaceful changes in the international order demanded by justice, tempered by liberality and charity.

VII. WORLD PEACE

There is no evasion of this moral responsibility of all the nations and especially of the most powerful nations for that peace and justice which, together with the security of one's own nation, is the object of foreign policy. Too many people who eagerly draw up perfect blueprints for world organization are secretly influenced by the expectation that after the establishment of such legal institutions they will get rid of the continuous responsibility of a burdensome foreign policy. They have fallen into the same fallacy as the classical liberal economists, namely, that if a certain set of legal institutions should be introduced, then out of the individuals' efforts to pursue their unrestricted self-interest the social harmony would automatically ensue. The result was, of course, not social harmony but the power struggle of collective interests, class struggles, and the like. If in the national order the merely legalistic concept of the state according to the liberal pattern is impossible, a complete juridification of the international order will be even less possible.

Too many of the planners, moreover, have an optimistic though mechanistic psychology according to which man is the creature of his institutional environment, that is, he is a bundle of causal reactions to the primary acting environmental and objective institutional factors. But this psychology of determinism forgets that man is conditioned and motivated, but not causally determined, by these institutional factors. There remains a residual sphere beyond all causal determinations, where man is morally free and can become truly culpable, not innocently guilty as in the ancient tragedy. Sometimes this over-all juridification is caused by a tacit rejection of man's moral nature. And contradictions appear, such as this, that Hitler is wholly explained causally as the effect of causes that are sociological, insti-

---

[2] Cf. *Review of Politics*, Vol. VI, 1944: articles by Waldemar Gurian, "Perpetual Peace"; by Stefan Possonz, "No Peace without Arms."

tutional, and so on, and yet considered personally and morally guilty.

Politics is an integral part of ethics, as is law. Arbitrary power must be controlled by positive law. But, that law may be enabled to do so, it must itself be backed by power responsible to the moral ideas, to the national common good. The strife among nations can be best settled if the universal law of morality, the principles of natural law as the unwritten constitution of the international community, are commonly accepted. For then power is put in the service of the fundamental moral ideas. And there is no evasion of the principle that the greater the power, influence, and prestige of a nation, the greater is its responsibility for peace and justice. Moreover, the less can this responsibility be shifted to any legal institution, however abstractly perfect, and the nation still hope to return securely to a splendid isolation and to the sole pursuit of its own national happiness. On the other hand, only after the powerful nations are ready to accept in mutual understanding their direct and inseparable responsibility for peace, only then will the legal institutions work. But just as important is the perpetual will to establish justice, that is, to work for changes of the actual *status quo* when it has become an obviously unjust status, the continuation of which would endanger the peace of the world. Peace is the work of justice. Hence it will always be this moral will to justice that gives the legal institutions power. Without this moral will and concordant responsibility, the institutions will be empty hulks, a derision of the idea of law. Though peace, the tranquillity of the order, is the work of justice, justice itself ought to be vivified by charity, based on the common brotherhood of men and on the common fatherhood of God. These three—charity vivifying justice, justice working peace, and peace being tranquillity of the order—by permeating and inspiring the legal institutions, are the real guaranty for the peace of the world.

Index

Absolutism, 544 ff.
  Barklay, 420
  the Church and, 561
  development of, 690
  Gallicanism, 561
  Hobbes, 420
  influence of the Reformation, 554
  seventeenth century, 334
  subordination of the spiritual power, 392, 554
Aegidius Romanus, 444
Agnosticism and democracy, 117
Alainus, James, 444
Alkidamos, 158
Alphonsus Liguori, St.: on just war, 669
Ambrose, St.: on emperor and Church, 518; on *legibus solutus*, 434 note; on *lex animata*, 522
Americanism, 20, 417, 478
Analogia entis, 106, 164, 166
Anarchism of Christian sects, 116 note, 373
Antigone by Sophocles, 159
Apostasy of industrial masses, 608
Arbitration of international disputes, 638
Arianism and political theology, 98
Aristotle
  end of the state, 224
  form and matter, 134 ff.
  monarchy, 98
  natural law, 158
  philia, 46
  political philosophy of, 24-27
  societas perfecta, 250
  on sympathetic acts, 222
  and Thomism, 21 ff.
Atheism: and anarchism, 103; and totalitarian collectivism, 129
Auctoritas: and *potestas*, 380, 523 note; in Roman law, 382, 523 note
Augustine, St.
  Church and state, 515
  community, 39 note
  eternal law, 173, 426
  faith and free will, 368
  justice and state, 54
  misinterpretation by Reformers, 229 note
  natural law, 164

Augustine, St. (*continued*)
  Roman Empire, 538 note
  the state and original sin, 76
  status naturalis, 229 note
  world-state, 651
Augustus (emperor), 383
Authority, 77, 422, 434; *see also* Political authority
Autonomy of lower communities, 354 ff.

Babylas, St.: on murder of hostage, 485
Bäumker, Clemens, 22
Bannez on translation theory, 447, 460
Barth on the emperor's power, 485
Bellarmine, St. Robert
  Church and state, 543 ff., 594
  Consensus, 242 note
  and his times, 460 ff.
  law, 244
  sovereignty, 398, 651
  transfer of sovereignty, 432
  translation theory, 447 ff.
  union of Church and state, 543 ff., 594
  world state, 403 note, 651
Benedict XIV (pope) on status of Jews, 190 note
Benedict XV (pope): on disarmament, 686; on moral power of right, 673; peace efforts of, 684
Bentham, F., 458
Berdyaev, 565
Bergbohm, 214
Bernhart, J., 104
Billot (cardinal), 467
Billuart, 447
Biological theories, 40, 131 ff., 140, 180
Bismarck, 166 note, 111
Bodinus, Jean, 390 ff.
Bolshevism, 386
Boniface VIII (pope) on Church and state, 535
Bossuet, 8
Briand, Aristide, 602 note
Bryan, W. J., 681

Caesaropapism, 521 ff.
Cajetan (cardinal), 447